THE
BUILDING REGUI

EXPLAINED & ILLUSTRATED

THE
BUILDING
REGULATIONS

EXPLAINED & ILLUSTRATED

EIGHTH EDITION

Vincent Powell-Smith

LLM, DLitt, FCIArb, MBAE

and

M. J. Billington

BSc, ARICS

OXFORD

BSP PROFESSIONAL BOOKS

LONDON EDINBURGH BOSTON

MELBOURNE PARIS BERLIN VIENNA

Copyright © 1967, 1968, 1970, 1973, 1981,
1982 by Walter S. Whyte
and Vincent Powell-Smith
Seventh Edition copyright © Ingramlight
Properties Ltd and Walter S. Whyte 1986
New material copyright © Ingramlight
Properties Ltd and M. J. Billington 1986
Eighth edition copyright © Ingramlight
Properties Ltd and M. J. Billington 1990

BSP Professional Books
A division of Blackwell Scientific
  Publications Ltd
Editorial offices:
Osney Mead, Oxford OX2 0EL
25 John Street, London WC1N 2BL
23 Ainslie Place, Edinburgh EH3 6AJ
3 Cambridge Center, Cambridge,
  MA 02142, USA
54 University Street, Carlton,
  Victoria 3053, Australia

First published in Great Britain 1967
by Crosby Lockwood & Son Ltd
Second edition 1968
Third edition with metric supplement 1970
Reprinted 1972
Fourth edition 1973
Second impression 1974
Third impression (with supplement) 1976
Reprinted 1979
Fifth edition (amended) 1981
Sixth edition 1982
Reprinted with amendments 1983
Reprinted with minor revisions by
Collins Professional Books 1984
Reprinted with amendments 1985
Seventh edition 1986
Reprinted 1986, 1987
Reprinted by BSP Professional Books 1987
Reprinted with amendments 1988, 1989
(three times)
Eighth edition published by
BSP Professional Books 1990
Reprinted with updates 1991

Printed and bound in Great Britain by
Billing & Sons, Worcester

DISTRIBUTORS

Marston Book Services Ltd
PO Box 87
Oxford OX2 0DT
(*Orders*: Tel: 0865 791155
    Fax: 0865 791927
    Telex: 837515)

USA
  Blackwell Scientific Publications, Inc.
  3 Cambridge Center
  Cambridge, MA 02142
  (*Orders*: Tel: (800) 759-6102)

Canada
  Oxford University Press
  70 Wynford Drive
  Don Mills
  Ontario M3C IJ9
  (*Orders*: Tel: (416) 441-2941)

Australia
  Blackwell Scientific Publications
  (Australia) Pty Ltd
  54 University Street
  Carlton, Victoria 3053
  (*Orders*: Tel: (03) 347-0300)

British Library
Cataloguing in Publication Data
Powell-Smith, Vincent
  The building regulations: explained &
  illustrated. – 8th ed., *Vincent Powell-
  Smith and M. J. Billington.*
  1. England. Buildings. Construction.
  Law: Building Regulations 1985
  I. Title   II. Billington, M. J.
  (Michael J.).
  344.2037869

  ISBN 0–632–02869–6 hardback
  ISBN 0–632–02401–1 paperback

Contents

Contents

III Appendices

Preface

The last edition of this book was published in 1986 and has since gone through many reprintings, during which we have had the opportunity of making minor amendments. This, the eighth edition, incorporates a new chapter on Access for the Disabled and revised chapters on ventilation, hygiene, drainage, heating appliances and conservation of fuel and power to incorporate the 1989 revisions to the Regulations and Approved Documents in these areas. These revisions introduced important changes with regard to the higher levels of thermal insulation which are now required by Approved Document L and the associated increased risk of problems from interstitial condensation. Other new material has been added, including more on the NHBC building control service, and selected sections on The Fire Precautions Act 1971, as amended.

The call for a reprint of this edition has enabled us to update Chapter 5 (Legal Liabilities) so as to take account of two important decisions of the House of Lords [(*Murphy* v. *Brentwood District Council* (1990) and *Department of the Environment* v. *Thomas Bates & Son Ltd* (1990)] which have narrowed the legal liabilities of both building control authorities and building contractors for negligence. The reprint has also given us the opportunity of making other textual amendments so as to update the book to the end of December 1990.

The continual changes are the bane of the industry and commentators alike but the thrust of the latest changes in the building control documents is to provide us with more flexible, realistic and sensible guidance in all the vital areas. It is a matter of regret that there should still be so many local enactments to contend with, despite s. 262 of the Local Government Act 1972 which attempted to shake out un-needed local Acts, much of the content of which is similar.

The aim of this book remains to provide a straightforward guide and reference to a complex and constantly evolving subject. It is a guide to the regulations and approved and other documents and is not a substitute for them. We hope that all those concerned with building control – architects, building control officers, building surveyors and approved inspectors – will find the book of help and interest. In our revision we have also borne in mind the needs of both teachers and students in the relevant disciplines.

We are grateful to Richard Hatfield for providing the illustrations as well as to Julia Burden of the publishers who, once again, saw the book through with her usual courtesy and efficiency.

Those provisions of the Building Act 1984 which are not yet in force are indicated by an asterisk (*) in the margin.

Vincent Powell-Smith
Michael Billington

January 1991

ACKNOWLEDGEMENTS

The tables reproduced from the Approved Documents are Crown copyright and are reproduced with the permission of the Controller of HMSO.

I
Legal and Administrative

Chapter 1

Building control: an overview

Introduction

The building control system in England and Wales was radically revised in 1985. After a long period of gestation, the Building Regulations 1985 were laid before Parliament and came into general operation on 11 November 1985. They have applied to Inner London from 6 January 1986. Subject to specified exemptions, all building work (as defined in the regulations) in England and Wales is governed by them. A separate system of building control applies in Scotland and in Northern Ireland.

The power to make building regulations is vested in the Secretary of State for the Environment by section 1 of the Building Act 1984 which sets out the basic framework. Building regulations may be made for the following broad purposes:

(a) Securing the health, safety, welfare and convenience of people in or about buildings and of others who may be affected by buildings or matters connected with buildings.
(b) Furthering the conservation of fuel and power.
(c) Preventing waste, undue consumption, misuse or contamination of water.

The Building Regulations 1985 are much shorter and simpler than their predecessors, and contain no technical detail. That is found in a series of thirteen Approved Documents and certain other non-statutory guidance, all of which refer to other non-statutory documents such as British Standards and Codes of Practice, with the objective of making the system more flexible and easier to use. The process of revision is still continuing, as the content of the Approved Documents is under review. The 1985 regulations eliminated controls over the erection of certain small buildings and extensions and some alterations and changes of use.

A significant feature of the system is that there are alternative systems of building control – one by local authorities, and the other a private system of certification which relies on 'approved inspectors' operating under a separate set of regulations called The Building (Approved Inspectors, etc.) Regulations 1985. These set out the detailed procedures for operating the system of private certification and came into effect at the same time as the main regulations, although to date the only approved inspector is NHBC Building Control Services Ltd.

The Building Act 1984

The Building Act 1984 received the Royal Assent on 31 October 1984 and the majority of its provisions came into force on 1 December 1984. It consolidates most, but not all, of the primary legislation relating to building which was formerly scattered in numerous other Acts of Parliament.

Part I of the Building Act 1984 is concerned with building regulations and related matters, while Part II deals with the system of private certification discussed in Chapter 4. Other provisions about buildings are contained in Part III which, amongst other things, covers drainage, the provision of sanitary conveniences, and so on, as well as the local authority's powers in relation to dangerous buildings, defective premises, etc.

The provisions of the 1984 Act are of the greatest importance in practice, and many of them are referred to in this and subsequent chapters. Some of the more important sections of the Act are set out in Appendix 1.

1984 Act, sec. 121   'Building' is defined in the 1984 Act in very wide terms. A building is 'any permanent or temporary building and, unless the context otherwise requires, it includes any other structure or erection of whatever kind or nature (whether permanent or temporary)'. 'Structure or erection' includes a vehicle, vessel, hovercraft, aircraft or other movable object of any kind in such circumstances as may be prescribed by the Secretary of State. The Secretary of State's opinion is, however, qualified. The circumstances must be those which 'in [his] opinion . . . justify treating it . . . as a building'.

The result of this definition is that many things which would not otherwise be thought of as a building may fall under the Act – fences, radio towers, silos, air-supported structures and the like. Happily, as will be seen, there is a more restrictive definition of 'building' for the purposes of the Building Regulations 1985, but a comprehensive definition is essential for general purposes, e.g. in connection with the local authority's powers to deal with dangerous structures. Hence the statutory definition is necessarily couched in the widest possible terms. In general usage (and at common law) the word 'building' ordinarily means 'a structure of considerable size intended to be permanent or at least to last for a considerable time' (*Stevens* v. *Gourely* (1859)) and considerable practical difficulties arose as to the scope of earlier building regulations which the 1984 definition has removed. Thus, in *Seabrink Residents Association* v. *Robert Walpole Campion and*

Partners (1988), the High Court held that walls and bridges on a residential development were not subject to the then Building Regulations 1972 because they were not part of 'a building'. The development was not to be considered as a homogenous whole. The then regulations, said Judge Esyr Lewis, QC, were 'concerned with structures which have walls and roofs into which people can go and in which goods can be stored'. Each structure in the development must be looked at separately to see whether the regulations applied. 'Obviously a wall may be part of a building and so, in my view, may be a bridge'.

The linked powers

Local authorities exercise a number of statutory public health functions in conjunction with the process of building control – for example, controls on construction over drains and sewers. These provisions are commonly called 'the linked powers' because their operation is linked with the local authority's building control functions, both in checking deposited plans or considering a building notice, and under the private certification scheme. Many of the former linked powers have been brought under the Building Regulations 1985, but local authorities are responsible for certain functions now found in the 1984 Act. In those cases, the local authority must reject the plans (or building notice) or the approved inspector's initial notice if relevant compliance is not achieved or else must impose suitable safeguards. The relevant provisions are:

(a) Construction over drains and sewers. Section 18 controls new building on top of drains and sewers. The local authority must reject plans submitted if they propose building over a sewer or drain shown on the relevant public maps, unless they are satisfied that they can properly give consent either unconditionally or subject to conditions. The most usual condition is that the building owner enters into an access agreement for maintenance purposes. The local authority notify the water authority of the proposal and the water authority may give directions to the local authority as to how their section 18 functions are to be exercised. Disputes under the section are determined by a magistrates' court. *1984 Act, sec. 18*

(b) Provision of drainage. The local authority must similarly reject plans submitted for a new building or extension unless they show that the provision for drainage is satisfactory. They can insist that the drainage connects to a nearby public sewer. Disputes under section 21 are also dealt with by a magistrates' court. *1984 Act, sec. 24*

A related provision is section 16 of the Water Act 1983 under which owners or occupiers of premises can require the water authority to provide a public sewer for domestic purposes in their area, subject to various conditions which can include in an appropriate case the making of a financial contribution. *Water Act 1973, sec. 16*

(c) Provision of access and exit in public buildings. Section 24 requires *1984 Act, sec. 24* the local authority to reject plans submitted unless they show adequate means of ingress and egress in prescribed cases of places of public resort. Disputes as to whether the exits, etc., are satisfactory are determined by the magistrates' court.

1984 Act,
sec. 25

(d) Provision of water supply. Section 25 requires the local authority to reject plans of a house submitted under the Building Regulations unless they are satisfied with the proposals for providing the occupants with a sufficient supply of wholesome water for domestic purposes, by pipes or otherwise. Usually, of course, this will be by means of a mains supply provided by the water authority under the Water Acts 1945 and 1973. Disputes are determined by the magistrates' court.

Water Act
1945, sec.
37

A related provision is section 37 of the Water Act 1945 which enables a landowner who proposes to erect buildings to require the water authority to lay necessary mains for the supply of water for domestic purposes to a point which will enable the buildings to be connected to the mains at a reasonable cost, a provision which is of considerable use to developers. The water authority can require an initial deposit as well as an annual contribution towards the cost of laying the necessary mains. This provision was considered by the House of Lords in *Royco Homes Ltd* v. *Southern Water Authority* (1979) where the distribution mains nearest to the site of the proposed housing estate were fully committed. The water authority proposed to lay a main from some 3 km away and the developer disputed their requirement of a deposit and annual contribution. The House of Lords held that the starting point for the new main had to be determined in accordance with good engineering practice. The proposed main was in the circumstances a 'necessary main' for which a deposit and annual contribution could be required.

Building regulations

1984 Act,
sec. 1

The Secretary of State is given power to make comprehensive regulations about the provision of services, fittings and equipment in or in connection with buildings as well as about the design and construction of buildings. A very comprehensive list of the subject matter of building regulations is contained in Schedule 1. The regulations are supported by approved documents, giving 'practical guidance': see below, p. 2.3 ff.

1984 Act,
secs 6 & 7

Building regulations may include provision as to the deposit of plans of executed, as well as proposed work; for example where work has been done without the deposit of plans or there has been a departure from the approved plans. Broad powers are given to make building regulations about the inspection and testing of work, and the taking of samples.

Prescribed classes of buildings, services, etc. may be wholly or partially exempted from regulation requirements. Similarly, the

Secretary of State may, by direction, exempt any particular building or buildings at a particular location.

Schedule 1 of the 1984 Act is a flexible provision and covers the application of the regulations to existing buildings. It enables regulations to be made regarding not only alterations and extensions, but also the provision, alteration or extension of services, fittings and equipment in or in connection with existing buildings. It also enables the regulations to be applied on a *material change of use* as defined in the regulations and, very importantly, makes it possible for the regulations to apply where re-construction is taking place, so that the regulations can deal with the whole of the building concerned and not merely with the new work.

Building regulations apply to maintained schools and colleges as well as to the buildings of statutory undertakers. Special arrangements may be made for the approval of the plans of educational institutions.

The 1984 Act contains enabling powers for the making of regulations on a number of procedural matters.

1984 Act, Sch. 1

1984 Act, secs 3 & 4

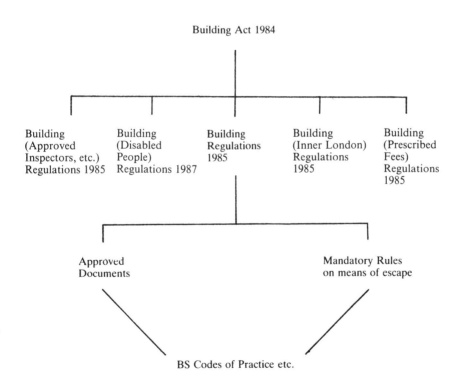

Fig. 1.1 Building control: the legislative scheme.

The regulations made and currently in force are:

- The Building Regulations 1985
- The Building (Approved Inspectors, etc.) Regulations 1985
- The Building (Prescribed Fees) Regulations 1985
- The Building (Inner London) Regulations 1985
- The Building (Disabled People) Regulations 1987

Miscellaneous

There is power to approve the plans of a proposed building by stages. Usually, the initiative will rest with the applicant as to whether to seek approval by stages – subject to the local authority's agreement. However, local authorities may – of their own initiative – give approval by stages; they might, for example, await further information. In giving stage approval, local authorities will be able to impose a condition that certain work will not start until the relevant information has been produced.

Plans may also be approved subject to agreed modifications, e.g. where there is a minor defect in the plans.

1984 Act,
sec. 20 Section 20 of the Building Act 1984 deals with materials unsuitable for use in permanent buildings. The provision applies where plans, although conforming with the regulations, include the use of items listed in the regulations for the purpose of section 20. In such circumstances the local authority has a discretion:

(i) to pass the plans;
(ii) to reject the plans; *or*
(iii) to pass them subject to the imposition of a time limit, whether conditionally or otherwise.

Section 19 is a temporary provision dealing in similar terms with short-lived materials.

As will be seen, regulation 7 of the Building Regulations 1985 requires that 'any building work shall be carried out with proper materials . . .' and the supporting approved document deals with the use of short-lived materials.

It should be noted that these powers can be applied to prescribed types of materials and components used in the construction of particular parts of a building and to prescribed types of services, fittings and equipment. The local authority may impose a time limit either on the whole of a building or on particular work. Additionally, they may impose conditions as to the use of a building or the particular items concerned. Appeal against the local authority's decision lies to the Secretary of State.

The powers may be applied to work which is subject to building regulations but in respect of which plans are not required to be submitted. This might be needed, for example, for water or electrical installations if details of those installations are not required to be shown on plans.

Building regulations may impose continuing requirements on the owners and occupiers of buildings, including buildings which were not, at the time of their erection, subject to building regulations. These requirements are of two kinds. Continuing requirements may be imposed *first*, in respect of designated provisions of the regulations to ensure that their purpose is not frustrated, e.g. the keeping clear of fire escapes; and *second*, in respect of services, fittings and equipment, e.g. a requirement for the periodical maintenance and inspection of lifts in flats. *(1984 Act, sec. 2)*

Type relaxations may be granted by the Secretary of State; he may dispense with or relax some regulation requirement generally. A type relaxation can be made subject to conditions or for a limited period only. It should be noted that before granting a type relaxation the Secretary of State must consult such bodies as appear to him to be representative of the interests concerned and he has to publish notice of any relaxations issued. *(1984 Act, sec. 11)*

The Secretary of State may issue a certificate of approval of a type of building matter as complying with the regulations, e.g. in the case of some new product. This will not be available as a substitute for any requirement to deposit plans, but will be in support of the submission of plans. This power to issue certificates of type approval may be delegated. *(1984 Act, * sec. 12)*

Section 33 of the 1984 Act empowers local authorities to require or carry out tests to ascertain conformity with the regulations. Any person by whom (or on whose behalf) work is proposed to be carried out or has been done may be required to carry out the relevant tests, or the local authority may carry out the tests themselves. *(1984 Act, sec. 13 1984 Act, * sec. 33)*

The principal appeals to the Secretary of State are:

(a) Appeals against rejection of plans by a local authority. *(1984 act, * sec. 16)*

(b) Appeals against a local authority's refusal to give a direction dispensing with or relaxing a requirement of the regulations or against a condition attached by them to such a direction. *(1984 Act, sec. 39)*

The Building Act 1984, sections 39 to 43, contain the appeal provisions. *(1984 Act, secs 39 to 43)*

Breach of duty imposed by the regulations is actionable at civil law, where damage is caused, except where the regulations otherwise provide. 'Damage' is defined as including the death of, or injury to, any person (including any disease or any impairment of a person's physical or mental condition). The regulations themselves may provide for defences to such a civil action. This provision has not yet been activated. The liabilities which may arise under the general law are discussed in Chapter 5. Section 38 will not, when operative, prejudice any right which exists at common law. *(1984 Act, * sec. 38)*

1984 Act,
* sec. 44
* sec. 45

Section 44 applies the *substantive* provisions of the building regulations to Crown buildings, but the procedural arrangements do not apply. It affects defence establishments, NHS hospitals and various Government offices. Similar provision is made (section 45) for the buildings of the United Kingdom Atomic Energy Authority.

Dangerous Structures, etc.

1984 Act,
sec. 77

Local authorities have power to deal with a building or structure which is in a dangerous condition or is overloaded. The procedure is for the local authority to apply to the magistrates' court for an order requiring the owner to carry out remedial works or, at his option, to demolish the building or structure and remove the resultant rubbish. The court may restrict the use of the building if the danger arises from overloading. If the owner fails to comply with the order within the time limit specified by the court, the local authority may execute the works themselves and recover the expenses incurred from the owner, who is also liable to a fine.

1984 Act,
sec. 78

The local authority may take immediate action in an emergency so as to remove the danger, e.g., if a wall is in danger of imminent collapse. Where it is practicable to do so, they must give notice of the proposed action to the owner and occupier. The local authority may recover expenses which they have reasonably incurred in taking emergency action, unless the magistrates' court considers that they might reasonably have proceeded under section 77. An owner or occupier who suffers damage as a result of action taken under section 78 may in some circumstances be entitled to recover compensation from the local authority.

1984 Act,
sec. 79

Section 79 of the 1984 Act empowers local authorities to deal with ruinous and dilapidated buildings or structures and neglected sites 'in the interests of amenity', which is a term of wider significance than 'health and safety': *Re Ellis and Ruislip and Northwood UDC* [1920] 1 KB 343. (Section 76 of the Act enables them to deal with defective premises which are 'prejudicial to health or a nuisance'.)

1984 Act,
sec. 76

Under section 79, where a building or structure is in such a ruinous or dilapidated condition as to be seriously detrimental to the amenities of the neighbourhood, the local authority may serve notice on the owner requiring him to repair or restore it or, at his option, demolish the building or structure and clear the site.

1984 Act,
sec. 80

Demolition is itself subject to control. Section 80 requires a person who intends to demolish the whole or part of a building to notify the local authority, the occupier of any adjacent building and the gas and electricity authorities of his intention to demolish. He must also comply with any requirements which the local authority may impose by notice under section 82.

The demolition notice procedure does not apply to the demolition of:

- An internal part of an occupied building where it is intended that the building should continue to be occupied.
- A building with a cubic content (ascertained by external measurement) of not more than 1750 cubic feet or a greenhouse, conservatory, shed or prefabricated garage which forms part of a larger building.
- An agricultural building unless it is contiguous to a non-agricultural building or falls within the preceding paragraph.

The local authority may by notice require a person undertaking demolition to carry out certain works:

1984 Act, secs 81 & 82

- To shore up any adjacent building.
- To weatherproof any surfaces of an adjacent building exposed by the demolition.
- To repair and make good any damage to any adjacent building caused by the demolition.
- To remove material and rubbish resulting from the demolition and clearance of the site.
- To disconnect and seal and/or remove any sewers or drains in or under the building.
- To make good the ground surface.
- To make arrangements with the gas, electricity and water authorities for the disconnection of supplies.
- To make suitable arrangements with the fire authority (and Health and Safety Executive, if appropriate) with regard to burning of structures or materials on site.
- To take such steps in connection with the demolition as are necessary for the protection of the public and the preservation of public amenity.

Local legislation

Although the Building Act 1984 attempted to rationalise the main controls over buildings, there are in fact a great many pieces of local legislation with the result that many local authorities have special powers relevant to building control. Where a local Act is in force, its provisions must also be complied with, and the regulations make it clear that local enactments must be taken into account.

Table 1.1 summarises the more important of the local Acts relevant to local government counties in England and Wales. The most common local provisions relating to building control are:

- *Special fire precautions for basement garages or for large garages.*
The usual provision is that if a basement garage for more than three vehicles or a garage for more than twenty vehicles is to be erected, the local authority can impose access, ventilation and safety requirements.

Table 1.1 Local Acts with building control provisions.

There is a large body of local legislation including provisions relating to building control and developers must always check what local legislation is in force in a particular area. Such Acts are referred to as, e.g. the East Sussex Act 1981. They are listed alphabetically in this table, with a note of the year in which the Act received the Royal Assent.*

Local Government Area	Year
Avon	1981
Berkshire	1986
Bournemouth	1985
Cheshire	1980
Cleveland	1987
Clywyd	1985
Cumbria	1982
Derbyshire	1981
Dyfed	1987
East Sussex	1981
Essex	1987
Greater Manchester	1981
Hampshire	1983
Humberside	1982
Isle of Wight	1980
Kent	1981
Lancashire	1984
Leicestershire	1985
Merseyside	1980
Mid Glamorgan	1987
Poole	1985
South Glamorgan	1976
South Yorkshire	1980
Staffordshire	1983
Surrey	1985
Tyne and Wear	1980
West Glamorgan	1987
West Midlands	1980
West Yorkshire	1980
York City Council	1987

*The unrepealed provisions of London Building Acts 1930–1982 apply to Inner London.

● *Access for the fire brigade.*
There must be adequate access for the fire brigade.

● *Fire precautions for high buildings.*
A high building is one in excess of 18.3 metres and the local authority must be satisfied with the fire precautions and may impose conditions, e.g. fire alarm systems, fire brigade access, etc.

● *Extension of means of escape provisions.*
The Building Act 1984, section 72, is a provision under which the local authority can insist on the provision of means of escape where there is a storey which is more than twenty feet above ground level in certain types of building, e.g. hotels, boarding houses, hospitals, etc. Local enactments replace the twenty feet height by 4.5 metres and make certain other amendments to the national provisions.

● *Drainage systems.*
In some cases, local legislation requires that every building must have a separate system of drainage.

● *Retaining walls.*
In some areas, local Acts impose control over retaining walls.

Inner London

Originally, the Building Regulations did not apply to Inner London which continued to be dealt with by the Greater London Council under the London Building Acts 1930 to 1982 and the building byelaws made under them.

This was altered on 6 January 1986 when the Building (Inner London) Regulations came into operation. Following the abolition of the Greater London Council on 1 April 1986, its building control functions and those of district surveyors under the London Building Acts were transferred to the Common Council of the City of London and the twelve Inner London borough councils: Camden, Greenwich, Hackney, Hammersmith and Fulham, Islington, Kensington and Chelsea, Lambeth, Lewisham, Southwark, Tower Hamlets, Wandsworth and Westminster.

The regulations brought in force in Inner London:

● The Building Act 1984:
  section 8 – relaxation of building regulations
  section 9 – application for relaxation
  section 10 – advertisement of proposal for relaxation of building regulations
  section 16 – passing or rejection of plans
  section 32 – lapse of deposit of plans
  section 36 – removal or alteration of offending work
  section 37 – obtaining report where section 36 notice given
  section 39 – appeal against refusal etc. to relax building regulations
  section 40 – appeal against section 36 notice
● The Building Regulations 1985
● The Building (Approved Inspectors, etc.) Regulations 1985
● The Building (Prescribed Fees, etc.) Regulations 1985

Certain transitional provisions were made, but as a result of the new regulations, Inner London building control procedures became essentially the same as elsewhere in England and Wales, since all the London building byelaws and many sections of the London Building Acts were repealed, and other sections were amended.

Building control in Inner London is more complex than in other areas (even where local legislation applies) because of the retention of additional requirements. The most important of these are:

- Buildings in excess height and excess cubical extent.

Section 20 of the London Building Acts (Amendment) Act 1939 applies special fire precautions in high buildings, i.e., a building which has a storey at greater height than 30 m (or 25 m if the area of the building exceeds 930 m²) or is a large trade building (over 7100 m³).

Trade buildings can be divided up by division walls and there are special requirements for their construction since division walls are not covered by regs B2–B4 or AD B2/3/4. A wide range of fire protection can be required, and there are extra requirements for areas of 'special fire risks' such as boiler rooms.

Plans must be deposited before any alterations are made to buildings of excess height or excess cubical extent, and the borough council must consult with the London Fire Authority before issuing consent.

- Uniting of buildings: 1939 Act, section 21.
- Special and temporary structures: 1939 Act, sections 29–31.
- Means of escape in case of fire: 1939 Act, sections 33–34. Certain new buildings not covered by B1 of the Building Regulations 1985 are subject to control. A wide range of buildings is covered and more stringent conditions can be attached than those in CP3 CL.IV or BS 5588, discussed in Chapter 7.
- Rights of building and adjoining owners: 1939 Act, sections 44–59.

These sections contain useful provisions and procedures for party walls.

- Dangerous and neglected structures: 1939 Act, sections 60–70.

This includes service of a dangerous structure notice and is far more efficacious than the procedure in sections 77 and 78 of the Building Act 1984.

There are many other special provisions and detailed discussion of the position in Inner London is found in *Building Control in Inner London* by P. H. Pitt.

To some extent the position in Inner London is analogous to that in certain other areas (mostly large conurbations) where local legislation is applicable, as discussed in the preceding section, but is of greater complexity and with different enforcement methods. Logic dictates that these local provisions – which are obviously necessary – should be rationalised and made applicable to all major urban areas. If this were done, it should follow that Codes of Practice similar to those excellent documents published by the former GLC on means of escape, temporary structures and other matters (all of which continue in force in Inner London) should be issued so as to ensure uniformity of interpretation and practice.

The Building (Prescribed Fees, etc.) Regulations 1985

These regulations authorise local authorities to charge the following fees:

- A plan fee for the passing or rejection of plans of proposed work deposited with them.
- An inspection fee for inspection of the work.
- A building notice fee where the building notice procedure applies.
- A reversion fee where the private certification is used and the initial notice is cancelled so that control reverts to the local authority: see p. 4.8.

There is a flat rate fee for small domestic buildings, small detached garages and carports with a floor area up to 40 m², domestic extensions and alterations up to 40 m² floor area and loft conversions and associated work.

All other types of work are subject to variable fees which are related to the value of the work.

Fees are also payable where application is made to the Secretary of State or determination of questions under sections 16 and 50 of the Building Act 1984.

The original fee levels have been raised in line with inflation on a number of occasions. Table 1.2 sets out the current prescribed fees in accordance with The Building (Amendment of Prescribed Fees) Regulations 1989.

Table 1.2 Prescribed fees 1989.

The Building (Amendment of Prescribed Fees) Regulations 1989
All Fees are Inclusive of VAT at 15%
Schedule 1 – Small Domestic Buildings

Plan Fee		Inspection Fee	
No of dwellings	Fee (£)	£101.20 × number of dwellings where floor area of dwelling exceeds 64 m² an additional fee as table below	
1	60.95		
2	121.90	Dwelling per building with 64 m² floor area	Additional Fee (£)
3	182.85		
4	243.80		
5	304.75		
6	345.00		
7	385.25	1	60.95
8	425.50	2	121.90
9	465.75	3	182.85
10	506.00	4	243.80
11	527.85	5	304.75
12	547.40	6	325.45
13	568.10	7	345.00
14	587.65	8	365.70
15	608.35	9	385.25
16	629.05	10 or more	405.95
17	648.60		
18	669.30		
19	690.00		
20 or more	709.55		

Schedule 2 – Domestic Alterations and Extensions

Type of Work	Plan Fee (£)	Inspection Fee (£)
1. An alteration or extension consisting of the provision of one or more rooms in roof space, including means of escape	32.20	98.90
2. Any extension (not falling within paragraph 1 above) the total floor area of which does not exceed 20 m²	16.10	49.45
3. Any extension (not falling within paragraph 1 above) the total floor area of which exceeds 20 m² but not exceeding 40 m²	32.20	98.90
4. A detached garage or carport with a floor area not exceeding 40 m² and used in common with an existing building and which is not an exempt building	16.10	49.45

Table 1.2 *(contd)*

Schedule 3 – Other Work

70% of estimated cost	Plan fee (£)	Inspection fee (£)
Under £1,000	6.90	20.70
1,000 and under 2,000	11.50	34.50
2,000 and under 3,000	13.80	41.40
3,000 and under 4,000	18.40	55.20
4,000 and under 5,000	23.00	69.00
5,000 and under 6,000	27.60	82.80
6,000 and under 7,000	32.20	96.60
7,000 and under 8,000	36.80	110.40
8,000 and under 9,000	39.10	117.30
9,000 and under 10,000	41.40	124.20
10,000 and under 12,000	46.00	138.00
12,000 and under 14,000	52.90	158.70
14,000 and under 16,000	59.80	179.40
16,000 and under 18,000	66.70	200.10
18,000 and under 20,000	73.60	220.80
20,000 and under 25,000	86.25	258.75
25,000 and under 30,000	97.75	293.25
30,000 and under 35,000	109.25	327.75
35,000 and under 40,000	126.50	379.50
40,000 and under 45,000	138.00	414.00
45,000 and under 50,000	149.50	448.50
50,000 and under 60,000	166.75	500.25
60,000 and under 70,000	195.50	586.50
70,000 and under 80,000	224.25	672.75
80,000 and under 90,000	241.50	724.50
90,000 and under 100,000	264.50	793.50
100,000 and under 140,000	293.25	879.75
140,000 and under 180,000	379.50	1138.50
180,000 and under 240,000	471.50	1414.50
240,000 and under 300,000	586.50	1759.50
300,000 and under 400,000	701.50	2104.50
400,000 and under 500,000	891.25	2673.75
500,000 and under 700,000	1046.50	3139.50
700,000 up to and including 1,000,000	1352.75	4088.25
Thereafter for each additional 100,000 and part thereof	230.00	690.00

Chapter 2

The Building Regulations and Approved Documents

Introduction

Although the statutory framework of building control is found in the Building Act 1984, the Building Regulations 1985 contain the detailed rules and procedures. They are much shorter than previous building regulations because the technical requirements have mostly been recast in a functional form.

Each technical requirement is supported by a document approved by the Secretary of State intended to give practical guidance on how to comply with the requirements. The Approved Documents refer to British Standards, and are intended to give designers and builders a greater degree of flexibility than was available under the old and very detailed regulations. There are mandatory rules for means of escape in case of fire which describe the only ways in which the requirements may be met.

There is also a *Manual to the Building Regulations* giving informal guidance and reprinting the actual text of the regulations with very brief comment. The set of Approved Documents and the *Manual* may be purchased together (price £35) from Her Majesty's Stationery Office.

The 1985 regulations became effective on 11 November 1985.

Division of the regulations

There are twenty regulations, arranged logically in five parts. The division is as follows:

PART I: GENERAL

Reg. 1.   Title, commencement and application.
Reg. 2.   Interpretation.

PART II: CONTROL OF BUILDING WORK

Reg. 3.   Meaning of building work.
Reg. 4.   Requirements relating to building work.
Reg. 5.   Meaning of material change of use.
Reg. 6.   Requirements relating to material change of use.
Reg. 7.   Materials and workmanship.
Reg. 8.   Limitation on requirements.
Reg. 9.   Exempt buildings and work.

PART III: RELAXATION OF REQUIREMENTS

Reg. 10.   Power to dispense with or relax requirements.

PART IV: NOTICES AND PLANS

Reg. 11.   Giving of a building notice or deposit of plans.
Reg. 12.   Particulars and plans where a building notice is given.
Reg. 13.   Full plans.
Reg. 14.   Notice of commencement and completion of certain stages of work.

PART V: MISCELLANEOUS

Reg. 15.   Testing of drains and private sewers.
Reg. 16.   Sampling of material.
Reg. 17.   Supervision of building work otherwise than by local authorities.
Reg. 18.   Repeals.
Reg. 19.   Revocations.
Reg. 20.   Transitional provisions.

There are also three schedules:

SCHEDULE 1 – REQUIREMENTS

This contains thirty-six technical requirements which are almost all expressed in functional terms and grouped in eleven parts set out in tabular form:

PART A: STRUCTURE – covers loading, ground movement and disproportionate collapse.

PART B: FIRE – covers means of escape, and internal and external fire spread.

PART C: SITE PREPARATION AND RESISTANCE TO MOISTURE – covers preparation of site, dangerous and offensive substances, subsoil drainage, and resistance to weather and ground moisture.

PART D: TOXIC SUBSTANCES – deals with cavity insulation.

PART E: RESISTANCE TO THE PASSAGE OF SOUND – covers airborne and impact sound.

PART F: VENTILATION – covers means of ventilation and condensation.

PART G: HYGIENE – deals with bathrooms, hot water storage and sanitary conveniences.

PART H: DRAINAGE AND WASTE DISPOSAL – deals with sanitary pipework and drainage, cesspools, septic tanks and settlement tanks, rainwater drainage and solid waste storage.

PART J: HEAT PRODUCING APPLIANCES – covers air supply, discharge of combustion products and protection of the building.

PART K: STAIRWAYS, RAMPS AND GUARDS – covers stairways and ramps, protection from falling and vehicle barriers.

PART L: CONSERVATION OF FUEL AND POWER – deals with resistance to the passage of heat in buildings, heating system controls and the insulation of heating services.

PART M: FACILITIES FOR DISABLED PEOPLE – deals with the provision of facilities for the disabled. Part M was added by the Building (Disabled People) Regulations 1987 and requires reasonable provision to be made for the disabled. It replaced the original Schedule 2 which provided a 'deemed-to-satisfy' solution.

SCHEDULE 3 – EXEMPT BUILDINGS AND WORK

This lists exempt buildings and work in seven classes, and one of its effects is significantly to reduce the extent of control by giving complete exemptions for certain buildings and extensions.

SCHEDULE 4 – REVOCATIONS

Reg. 19   This lists the former regulations which are now revoked, i.e. the Building Regulations 1976 and the four sets of amending regulations. The former regulations continue to govern plans deposited before 11 November 1985 and work carried out in accordance with them.

Approved Documents

There are thirteen Approved Documents intended to give practical guidance on how the technical requirements of Schedule 1 may be complied with. They are written in straightforward technical terms with accompanying diagrams and the intention is that they will be quickly updated as necessary.

The status and use of Approved Documents is prescribed in sections 6 and 7 of the Building Act 1984. Section 6 provides for documents giving 'practical guidance with respect to the requirements of any provision of building regulations' to be approved by the Secretary of State or some body designated by him. The documents so far issued have been approved by the Secretary of State, although they refer to other non-statutory material. **Building Act, 1984, secs 6 & 7**

The legal effect of 'approved documents' is specified in section 7. Their use is not mandatory, and failure to comply with their recommendations does not involve any civil or criminal liability, but they can be relied upon by either party in any proceedings about an alleged contravention of the requirements of the regulations. If the designer or contractor proves that he has complied with the requirements of an approved document, in any proceedings which are brought against him he can rely upon this 'as tending to negative liability'. Conversely, failure to comply with an approved document may be relied on by the local authority 'as tending to establish liability'. In other words, the onus will be upon the designer or contractor to establish that he has met the functional requirements in some other way. **1984 Act, sec. 7**

The position is illustrated by *Rickards* v. *Kerrier District Council* (1987), where it was held that if the local authority proved that the works did not comply with the approved document, it was then for the appellant to show compliance with the regulations. If the designer fails to follow an approved document, it is for him to prove (if prosecuted) that he used an equally effective method or practice.

All the Approved Documents are in a common format, and their provisions are considered in subsequent chapters. They may be summarised as follows:

● A: STRUCTURE – This supports Schedule 1, A1/A2 and A3. Section 1, which deals with houses and other small buildings, contains tables for timber sizes, wall thicknesses, etc., and a lot of technical guidance. Section 2 deals with disproportionate collapse and is relevant to all types of building. It lists Codes and Standards for structural design and construction for all building types and emphasises certain basic principles which must be taken into account if other approaches are adopted.

● B: FIRE – This supports Schedule 1, B2/B3/B4, and has separate sections dealing with each building type. This treatment leads to a certain amount of repetition.

● C: SITE PREPARATION AND RESISTANCE TO MOISTURE – Read in conjunction with Schedule 1, Part C, it deals with the necessary basic requirements. Section 1 covers site preparation and site drainage and Section 2 deals with contaminants. It covers any substances in the ground which might cause a danger to health, and its provisions effectively replace those of the repealed section 29 of the Building Act 1984. An Appendix contains an 'introduction to remedial measures' in respect of contaminants, which is phrased in the most general terms. C 4 describes the measures necessary in order to prevent the passage of moisture to the inside of the building.

- D: TOXIC SUBSTANCES – This supports Schedule 1, Part D and it is very short. It gives advice on guarding against fumes from urea formaldehyde foam.

- E: SOUND – This supports Schedule 1, Part E.

- F: VENTILATION – Supporting Part F of Schedule 1 it covers means of ventilation including the precautions to be taken to prevent excessive condensation in the roof voids of dwellings.

- G: HYGIENE – Supporting Part G of Schedule 1 it includes the requirements of certain repealed sections (sections 26 to 28) of the Building Act 1984 dealing with water closets, bathrooms and food storage, as well as covering unvented hot water systems.

- H: DRAINAGE AND WASTE DISPOSAL – This supports Part H of Schedule 1 and covers above and below ground drainage, cesspools and tanks, rainwater drainage and solid waste storage and takes the place of the repealed sub-sections of section 23 of the Building Act 1984.

- J: HEAT PRODUCING APPLIANCES – Supporting Part J of Schedule 1, it deals with gas appliances up to 60 kW and solid and oil fuel appliances up to 45 kW.

- K: STAIRWAYS, RAMPS AND GUARDS – This supports Part K of Schedule 1.

- L: CONSERVATION OF FUEL AND POWER – Supporting Part L.

- M: ACCESS FOR DISABLED PEOPLE – Supporting Part M of Schedule 1 this gives practical guidance on means of access, sanitary conveniences and audience or spectator seating.

There is a further Approved Document – MATERIALS AND WORKMANSHIP – to support regulation 7 – and it is phrased in very general terms.

Mandatory document

There is one mandatory document – MANDATORY RULES FOR MEANS OF ESCAPE IN CASE OF FIRE – and the only way of complying with Schedule 1, paragraph B1 is by following the rules it lays down. The relevant types of building are dealt with by references to clauses in British Standards and Codes of Practice and the document gives no guidance on how to comply. Appendix A contains definitions, while Appendix B gives advice on loft conversions.

Relaxations of the mandatory requirements may be given only by local authorities in appropriate cases, with the possibility of an appeal against refusal to the Secretary of State. An approved inspector cannot grant a relaxation.   **Reg. 10**

Definitions in the regulations

One of the criticisms of the previous regulations was that definitions were scattered throughout the text wherever their use was first required. An attempt has been made to meet this criticism by providing twenty-seven general definitions in regulation 2, but not all the definitions are equally important or helpful. Indeed, the regulations have adopted the common practice of defining something by reference to another provision. For example, 'building notice' is defined as having 'the meaning given in regulation 11(1)(a)'. In this section full definitions are given for purposes of ease of reference, although the various special definitions will be referred to again in later chapters. The definitions are:

THE ACT – This means the Building Act 1984.   **Reg. 2(1)**

AREA – In relation to a building, this means the area calculated by reference to its finished internal faces: see Fig. 2.1.

BASEMENT – This means a storey of which the floor at any point is more than 1.2. metres below the finished surface of the adjacent ground: see Fig. 2.2.

BUILDING – The regulations apply only to buildings as defined. There is a narrow definition of 'building' for the purposes of the regulations:

'A building is any permanent or temporary building but not any kind of structure or erection'. When 'a building' is referred to in the regulations this includes a part of a building.

The effect of this definition is to exclude from control under the regulations such things as garden walls, fences, silos, air-supported structures and so forth.

BUILDING NOTICE – A notice in prescribed form given to the local authority under regulation 12 informing the authority of proposed works.

BUILDING WORK – The regulations apply only to building work as defined in regulation 3(1); any work not coming within the definition is not controlled. Building work means:

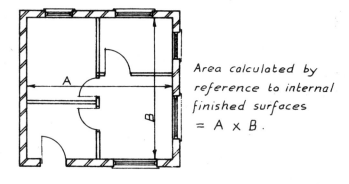

Area calculated by
reference to internal
finished surfaces
$= A \times B$.

Area

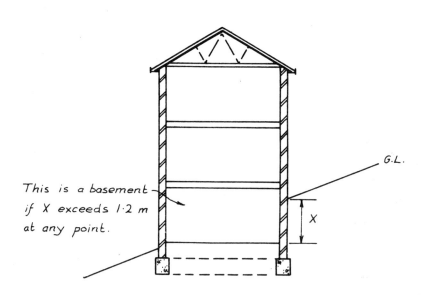

This is a basement
if X exceeds 1·2 m
at any point.

G.L.

Basement

Fig. 2.1 Area and basement – Regulation 2.

All external walls apart from AB
are exposed.

This section of
wall is exposed
element

AB is semi-exposed
element

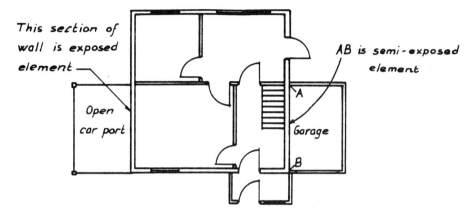

Dwelling

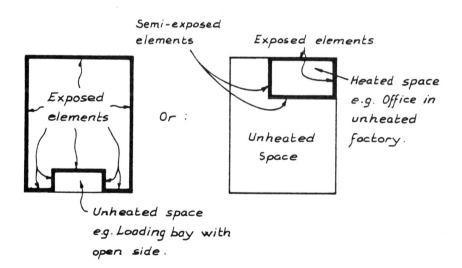

Other Building

Fig. 2.2 Exposed elements.

- The erection or extension of a building;
- The material alteration of a building;
- The provision of services or fittings required by Schedule 1, Parts G, H, J and L (and called 'controlled services or fittings'); or,
- Work required by regulation 6 – which sets out the requirements relating to 'material change of use' (see below).

CONTROLLED SERVICE OR FITTING – This means services or fittings required by paragraphs G2, G3, G4, Parts H or J or sections 2 and 3 of paragraph L1, i.e. bathrooms, hot water supply systems, sanitary conveniences, drainage and waste disposal, certain fixed heat producing appliances and certain heating systems.

DWELLING – This includes a dwelling-house and a flat.

DWELLING-HOUSE excludes a flat or building containing a flat.

ELEMENT – A wall, floor or roof, although this definition no longer appears in Approved Document L.

EXPOSED – Approved Document L defines this as meaning exposed to the outside air.

FLAT – Separate and self-contained premises (including a maisonnette) constructed or adapted for residential purposes and forming part of a building divided horizontally from some other part: see Fig. 2.3.

FLOOR AREA – This means the aggregate area of every floor in a building or extension. The area is to be calculated by reference to the finished internal faces of the enclosing walls or, where there is no enclosing wall, to the outermost edge of the floor: see Fig. 2.4.

FULL PLANS – Defined in regulation 13(2). The Building Act 1984, section 126, gives a definition of 'plans' as including drawings of any description and specifications or other information in any form.

HEIGHT – This means the height of a building measured from the mean level of the ground adjoining the outside external walls to a level of half the vertical height of the roof, or to the top of any walls or parapet, whichever is the higher: see Fig. 2.4.

INDUSTRIAL BUILDING – Although no longer specifically defined in Paragraph L1 of Schedule 1, this is taken to mean a factory as in turn defined by section 175 of the Factories Act 1961, with certain exclusions. The restricted definition of factory is 'any premises in which, or within the close or curtilage of which, people are employed in manual labour in any process for or incidental to (a) the making of any article or part of an article; (b) the altering, repairing, ornamenting, finishing, cleaning or washing, or the breaking up of any article or

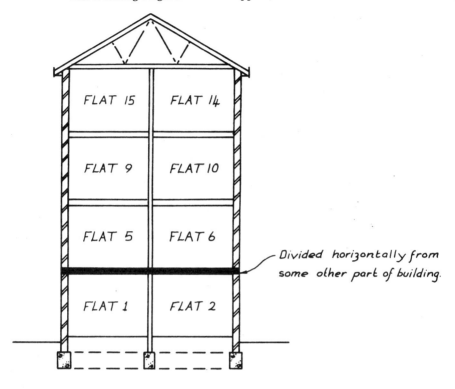

Divided horizontally from some other part of building.

Section X-X

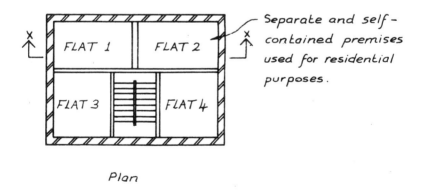

Separate and self-contained premises used for residential purposes.

Plan

Fig. 2.3 Flat – Regulation 2.

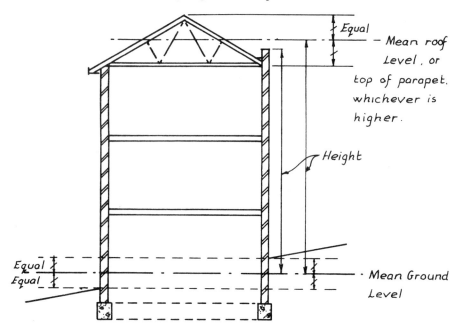

Equal

Mean roof Level, or top of parapet, whichever is higher.

Height

Equal
Equal

Mean Ground Level

Height

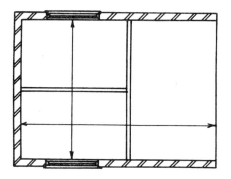

Floor area = aggregate area if every floor in building.

Measure to internal finished surfaces or outside of floor edge if no wall.

Floor Area

Fig. 2.4 Floor area and height – Regulation 2.

adapting any article for sale'. If non-lawyers find this confusing, they should not be surprised; the judges have also found it so!

INSTITUTION – This means a hospital, home, school, etc. used as living accommodation for, or for the treatment, care, etc., of people suffering from disabilities due to illness or old age or other physical or mental disability or who are under five years old. Those concerned must sleep on the premises and so day care centres, etc., are not included.

MATERIAL ALTERATION – This means (regulation 3(2)) an alteration for which the regulations make requirements and which consists of: **Reg. 3(2)**

- Work which would adversely affect the compliance of the existing building with the requirements for structural stability, means of escape or internal and external fire spread; or,
- Cavity wall insulating; or,
- Underpinning a building; or,
- Work which would adversely affect an existing building as respects access and facilities for disabled people.

It is best to consider the meaning of 'adversely affect' at this stage. In simple terms it means that the work itself must comply with the regulation requirements, and that the existing building must not be made worse than it was as regards those requirements: see regulation 2 (4).   **Reg. 2(4)**

MATERIAL CHANGE OF USE – This is defined by reference to regulation 5 and there are five cases: **Reg. 2(1)**

- Where a building becomes a dwelling when it was not one before.
- Where a building will contain a flat for the first time.
- Where a building becomes a hotel or institution, where it previously was not.
- Where a building becomes a public building and it was not before.
- Where a building was previously exempt from control (see Schedule 3, below), but is no longer so exempt.

OFFICE – This is defined as premises where a whole range of secretarial and administrative activity is carried on: administration, clerical work (including writing, book-keeping, sorting papers, filing, typing, duplicating, machine calculating, drawing and the editorial preparation of matter for publication), handling money or telephone and telegraph operating.

PUBLIC BUILDING – This means a building which consists of or contains: **Reg. 2(2)**

- A theatre, hall or other place of public resort;
- A school or other educational establishment which is not exempt under the 1984 Act, section 4 (1)(a);
- A place of public worship.

The definition is restrictive because occasional visits by the public to restaurants, shops, stores, warehouses or private houses do not make the building a public building.

Reg. 2(1)   SHOP – This bears an extended meaning. It means premises used for a retail trade or business (including sales to the public of food or drink for immediate consumption, retail sales by auction, the business of lending books or periodicals for the purposes of gain and a barber's or hairdresser's business), and also premises to which the public are invited to deliver goods for repair or treatment or for themselves to carry out such repairs or treatment.

Reg. 2(3)   STOREY – This is not defined in regulation 2 but is used in other parts of the regulation. A basement is not regarded as a storey in the regulations except in regulation 2 (i.e. the definition of 'basement'), in Paragraph A3 of Schedule 1, which deals with disproportionate collapse and in Part M.

Reg. 2(1)
AD L   U VALUE – This term is again defined in AD L. It is the thermal transmittance coefficient in watts per square metre of fabric per kelvin.

Exempt buildings and work

Certain buildings and extensions are granted complete exemption from control. The exempt buildings and work fall into seven classes listed in Schedule 3:

CLASS I – BUILDINGS CONTROLLED UNDER OTHER LEGISLATION
- Buildings subject to the Explosives Acts 1875 and 1923.
- Buildings (other than dwellings, offices or canteens) on a site licensed under the Nuclear Installations Act 1965.
- Buildings scheduled under section 1 of the Ancient Monuments and Archaeological Areas Act 1979.

CLASS II – BUILDINGS NOT FREQUENTED BY PEOPLE
- Detached buildings into which people cannot or do not normally go.
- Detached buildings housing fixed plant or machinery, normally visited only intermittently for the purpose of inspecting or maintaining the plant, etc.

CLASS III – GREENHOUSES AND AGRICULTURAL BUILDINGS

- A building used as a greenhouse.

A greenhouse is not exempted if the main purpose for which it is used is retailing, packing or exhibiting, e.g. one at a garden centre.

- A building used for agriculture which is:
  Sited at a distance not less than one and a half times its own height from any building containing sleeping accommodation; *and*;
  is provided with a fire exit not more than 30 metres from any point within the building.

There is an extended definition of 'agriculture'. It includes horticulture, fruit growing, seed growing, dairy farming, fish farming and the breeding and keeping of livestock (including any creature kept for the production of food, wool, skins or fur or for the purpose of its use in the farming of land).

CLASS IV – TEMPORARY BUILDINGS AND MOBILE HOMES

- A building intended to remain where it is erected for less than 28 days, e.g. exhibition stands.
- Mobile homes covered by the Mobile Homes Act 1983.

CLASS V – ANCILLARY BUILDINGS

- Buildings on an estate used only in connection with the letting or sale of buildings or building plots on that estate.
- Buildings used only in connection with and during the construction, alteration, extension or repair of a building during the course of the work, e.g. large site huts.
- Buildings erected in connection with a mine or quarry.

The exemption does not apply to buildings containing a dwelling or used as an office or showroom.

CLASS VI – SMALL DETACHED BUILDINGS

- Detached buildings of less than 30 m^2 floor area, with no sleeping accommodation.

For the exemption to apply, such buildings must be either:
Situated more than one metre from the boundary of its curtilage; *or*;
Single storey buildings wholly constructed of non-combustible material.

- Detached buildings of less than 30 m^2 intended to shelter people from the effects of nuclear, chemical or conventional weapons and not used for any other purpose. The excavation for the building must be no closer to any exposed part of another building or structure than a distance equal to the depth of the excavation plus one metre.

CLASS VII – EXTENSIONS
- Ground level extensions of less than 30 m² floor area which are greenhouses, conservatories, porches, covered yards or ways or a carport open on at least two sides.

The regulations do not apply to the erection of any building set out in Classes I to VI or to extension work in Class VII. Furthermore, they have no application at all to *any* work done to or in connection with buildings in Classes I to VI provided, of course, that the work does not involve a change of use which takes the building out of exemption, e.g. a barn conversion.

Application of the regulations

The Building Regulations 1985 apply only to 'building work' or to a 'material change of use', i.e. use for a different purpose. Work or a change of use not coming under these headings is not controlled.

Meaning of 'building work'
The definition of 'building work' means that the regulations apply in four cases:

ERECTION OR EXTENSION OF A BUILDING

Subject to the exemptions set out in the preceding section, the regulations apply to the erection or extension of all buildings. Unlike the old regulations, no attempt is made to define what is meant by 'erection of a building', nor is any definition really necessary. There is a good deal of obscure case law under other legislation as to what amounts to 'erection of a building', but none of it is particularly helpful in the light of section 123 of the Building Act 1984.

1984 Act, sec. 123

This gives a relevant statutory definition. For the purposes of Part II of the Act and for building regulation purposes, erection will include related operations 'whether for the reconstruction of a building, [and] the roofing over of an open space between walls or buildings'.

For the purposes of Part III of the 1984 Act (other provisions about buildings) which is also relevant to building control, *certain* building operations are 'deemed to be the erection of a building'. These are:

(a) Re-erection of any building or part of a building when an outer wall has been pulled or burnt down to within ten feet of the surface of the ground adjoining the lowest storey of the building.
    It follows that the outer wall must have been demolished throughout its length to within ten feet of ground level to constitute re-erection.
(b) The re-erection of any frame building when it has been so far pulled or burnt down that only the framework of the lowest storey remains.

(c) Roofing over any space between walls or buildings. Clearly other operations could be 'the erection of a building'.

MATERIAL ALTERATION OF A BUILDING

The material alteration of an existing building falls within the definition of building work, and is subject to the regulation requirements. Other alterations are not controlled. There are three cases where an alteration is material:

1985 Regs, Reg. 3(2)

- An alteration to a building, or part of the work involved, which would *adversely affect* the existing building as regards the requirements of Schedule 1, Part A (structure), Parts B1 (means of escape), B3 and B4 (fire spread) and Part M (Disabled People). In simple terms, alterations are not controlled unless they could adversely affect structural stability, means of escape, the spread of fire, or access for the disabled.

  The work done must itself comply with all the requirements of Schedule 1 and the existing building must not be adversely affected, i.e. made worse when judged against the Schedule 1 standards. In general it is not necessary to bring the existing building up to regulation standards, but in certain cases this will be necessary.
- The insertion of cavity fill in an existing wall. The work done must then comply with certain specific regulation requirements, namely, C4 (resistance of walls to the passage of moisture) and D1 (toxic substances).
- The underpinning of any existing building.

CONTROLLED SERVICES AND FITTINGS

Controlled services and fittings are those required by specified parts of Schedule 1:

Reg. 3(3)

- G2 – Bathrooms in dwellings.
- G3 – Hot water supply systems, except space heating systems, industrial systems, or those with a storage capacity of 15 litres or less.
- G4 – Sanitary conveniences.
- H – Drainage and waste disposal.
- J – Fixed heat producing appliances burning solid or oil fuel or gas or incinerators.
- L1, Section 1 – Certain space heating or hot water systems.

Controlled services and fittings do *not* include those heating or storing water for an industrial process.

- L1, Section 2 – Insulation of heating services other than industrial process systems.

WORK IN CONSEQUENCE OF A MATERIAL CHANGE OF USE

Reg. 6

When there is a material change of use, as defined in regulation 5 (above, p. 2.12), work must be done to make the building comply with some of the regulations, as explained below. Such work is, of course, then subject to control, just as the material change of use is itself controlled. In practical terms, change of use is only subject to control if the change involves the provision of sleeping accommodation or use as a public building or where the building was previously exempt.

'Material change of use' requirements
Material change of use has already been defined (above, p. 2.12), and in the five cases falling within that definition, specific technical requirements from Schedule 1 are made to apply in the interests of health and safety, which is the philosophy behind building control. Interestingly, there is no requirement applicable in respect of such things as sound resistance, foul or surface water drainage, stairs or thermal insulation, nor is there any definition of 'part' of a building.

The parts of the regulations applicable in the five cases are set out in Table 2.1:

Table 2.1. Requirements applicable according to material change of use.

Case	*Schedule 1 requirements*
[A] All cases (dwellings, flats, hotels and institutions, public buildings, no longer exempt)	B1 (means of escape) B2 and B3 (internal fire spread) B4(2) (external fire spread – roofs) F1 and F2 (ventilation) G2 (bathrooms) G4 (sanitary conveniences) H4 (solid waste storage) J1 to J3 (heat producing appliances)
[B] Exempt building to non-exempt	As in [A] plus A1 to A3 (structure)
[C] Building more than 15 metres in height	As in [A] plus B4(1) (external fire spread – walls)
[D] Change of use of part only of a building	The part itself must comply with the relevant requirements as [A] and [B]. In case [C] the whole building must comply with B4(1)

Regulation requirements

The regulations impose broad general requirements on the builder. Breach of these requirements does not, of itself, involve the builder in any civil liability although such liability may arise, quite independently, at common law as explained in Chapter 5.

Compliance with Schedule 1 is mandatory. All building work must be carried out so that it complies with the requirements set out in that Schedule. The method adopted for compliance must not result in the contravention of another requirement. The work is also to be carried out so that, after completion, an existing building, controlled service or fitting, to which work has been done is not 'adversely affected' as regards compliance with Schedule 1 requirements.

1985 Regs Reg. 4(1)

Regulation 2(4) defines 'adversely affected' (see above), and regulation 2(5) sets out certain assumptions which apply in considering whether work adversely affects an existing building, etc. These are that both the altered or extended and the existing building, etc., are being provided in their proposed form. Regard should be taken of the intended use that the building is to be put to after completion of the work, etc., in considering whether the requirements will be adversely affected.

Schedule 1 – Technical Requirements

Schedule 1 contains the technical requirements, which are discussed in Chapters 6 to 17 and which are almost all expressed functionally, e.g. C1 dealing with site preparation states that 'the ground to be covered by the building shall be reasonably free from vegetable matter'. These requirements cannot be subject to relaxation.

Which requirements apply depends on the type of building being constructed, but the majority of them is of universal application.

Materials and workmanship

Regulation 7 provides: 'Any building work shall be carried out with proper materials and in a good and workmanlike manner'. This is a general statutory obligation imposed on the builder. Guidance on how the obligation may be met is contained in Approved Document 7 'Materials and workmanship', although that guidance is of a very general nature.

Reg. 7

This statutory obligation is, in fact, the same as a building contractor's obligation at common law when, in the absence of a contrary term in the contract, the builder's duty is to do the work in a good and workmanlike manner, to supply good and proper materials and to provide a building reasonably fit for its intended purpose: *Hancock* v. *B.W. Brazier (Anerley) Ltd* (1966). This threefold obligation would normally be implied in any case where a contractor was employed to both design and build, but the third limb of the duty would not arise, for example, where the client employs his own architect (*Lynch* v. *Thorne* (1956)) although the other two limbs remain. This matter is explored further in Chapter 5.

The principal object of the regulations is to ensure that buildings meet reasonable standards of health and safety, and this is spelled out in regulation 8:

Reg. 8

'No obligation imposed by these regulations to comply with any requirements in Parts A to K of Schedule 1 or by regulation 7 shall require anything to be done beyond what is reasonably necessary to secure *reasonable standards of health and safety* for persons in or about the building and others who may be affected by any failure to comply with that requirement'.

The obligations imposed by the regulations are not therefore absolute obligations, but rather a duty to use reasonable skill and care to secure reasonable standards of health and safety of people using the building and others who may be affected by failure to comply with the requirements of the regulations. This has important legal consequences, as discussed in Chapter 5.

Relaxation of regulation requirements

1984 Act, sec. 8

Section 8 of the Building Act 1984 enables the Secretary of State to dispense with or relax any requirement of the regulations 'if he considers that the operation of [that] requirement would be unreasonable in relation to the particular case'. This power has been delegated to the local authority which may grant a relaxation if, because of special circumstances, the terms of a requirement cannot be fully met.

1985 Regs Reg. 10(1)

However, the majority of regulation requirements cannot be relaxed because they require something to be provided at an 'adequate' or 'satisfactory' level, and to grant a relaxation would mean acceptance of something that was 'inadequate' or 'unsatisfactory'.

There is only one case in which the regulations are relaxable:

● Schedule 1, B1 – Means of escape in case of fire. This is supported by a mandatory document, and its specific requirements may be relaxed in an appropriate case.

The application procedure is laid down in sections 9 and 10 of the 1984 Act. There is no prescribed form. Only the local authority (or the Secretary of State on appeal) can grant a relaxation; approved inspectors have no power to do so.

At least 21 days before giving a decision on an application for dispensation or relaxation of any requirement, the local authority must advertise the application in a local newspaper unless the application relates only to internal work. The notice must indicate the situation and nature of the work, and the requirement which it is sought to relax or dispense with. Objections may then be made on grounds of public health or safety. No notice need be published if the effect of the proposal is confined to adjoining premises only, but notice must then be given to the owner and occupier of those premises.

1984 Act, sec. 10

Where a local authority refuse an application they must notify the applicant of his right of appeal to the Secretary of State. This must be exercised within one month of the date of refusal. The grounds of the appeal must be set out in writing, and a copy must be sent to the local authority, who must send it to the Secretary of State with a copy of all relevant documents, and any representations they wish to make. The applicant must be informed of the local authority's representations. There is no time limit prescribed for the Secretary of State's decision on the the appeal.

1985 Regs, Reg. 10(2)

1984 Act, sec. 39

Where a local authority fail to give a decision on an application within two months, it is deemed to be refused and the applicant may appeal forthwith.

Neither the Secretary of State nor the local authority may give a direction for any relaxation of the regulations where, before the application is made, the local authority has become statutorily entitled to demolish, remove or alter any work to which the application relates, i.e. as a result of service of a notice under section 36 of the 1984 Act. The same prohibition applies where a court has issued an injunction requiring the work to be demolished, altered or removed.

1984 Act, sec. 36

The procedure may be summarised in tabular form:

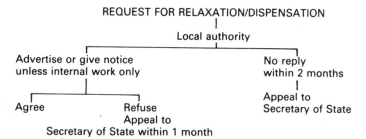

Type relaxations

The local authority's power of dispensation and relaxation must be distinguished from that of the Secretary of State to grant a type relaxation, i.e. to dispense with a requirement of the regulations generally. A type relaxation can be made subject to conditions and can be for a limited period only. It can be issued on application to the Secretary of State, e.g. from a manufacturer, in which case a fee may be charged. The Secretary of State may also make a type relaxation of his own accord. Before granting a relaxation the Secretary of State must consult such bodies as appear to him to be representative of the interests concerned and must publish notice of any relaxation issued. No such type applications have been granted, under the current legislation.

1984 Act, sec. 11

Approval of types of buildings

1984 Act,
sec. 12 *

The Secretary of State may issue a certificate of approval of a type of building matter complying with the regulations, either of his own volition or as a result of an application made to him. In the latter case, there is provision for fees to be charged. The power could be used, for example, to enable a new system of construction intended for general use to be formally assessed for regulation purposes. In appropriate cases a type relaxation (above) could be issued in conjunction

1984 Act,
sec. 13 *

with the type approval. The approval can be general or limited to particular cases, and can be for a limited period only. These powers may be delegated to an appropriate body, e.g. the Agrément Board.

Continuing requirements

1984 Act,
sec. 2

Building regulations can impose continuing requirements on owners and occupiers of buildings. These requirements are of two kinds:

- Continuing requirements in respect of designated provisions of the building regulations, to ensure that the purpose of the provision is not frustrated.

For example, where an item is required to be provided, there could be a requirement that it should continue to be provided or kept in working order. Examples of the possible use of the power are the operation of mechanical ventilation which is necessary for health reasons or the operation of any lifts required to be provided in blocks of flats.

- Requirements with regard to services, fittings and equipment. This enables requirements to be imposed on buildings whenever they were erected and independently of the normal application of building regulations to a building.

This makes it possible for regulations to supersede the continuing requirements of the water byelaws at present made under section 17 of the Water Act 1945. Another possible use of this power would be to require the maintenance and periodic inspection of lifts in flats if they are to be kept in use.

Testing and sampling

1985 Regs,
Regs 15 &
16

Two regulations empower the local authority to test drains and sewers to ensure compliance with the requirements of Part H of Schedule 1 and to take samples of materials *to be used* in the carrying out of building work. The wording does not appear to cover materials which are already incorporated in the building, but this is probably of no

1984 Act,
* sec. 33

importance in light of the provisions of section 33 of the Building Act 1984, when it is activated.

Under that section the local authority may test for compliance with the regulations. They may also require a builder or developer to carry out reasonable tests or may carry out such tests themselves and also take samples for the purpose. Section 33 (3) sets out the following matters with respect to which tests may be made:

(a) Test of the soil or subsoil of the site of any building.
(b) Tests of any material or component or combination of components.
(c) Tests of any service, fitting or equipment.

This is not an exhaustive description of the matters which may be subjected to tests.

The cost of testing is to be borne by the builder or developer, and there is a right to apply to a magistrates' court regarding the reasonableness of any test required or of any decision of the local authority on meeting the cost of the test. It should be noted that the local authority have a discretionary power to bear the whole or part of the costs themselves.

In fact the power of testing is given to 'a duly authorised officer of the local authority'. 'Authorised officer' is defined in section 126 of the Building Act 1984 as:

'. . . an officer of the local authority authorised by them in writing, either generally or specially, to act in matters of any special kind, or in any specified matter; or . . . by virtue of his appointment and for the purpose of matters within his province, a proper officer of the local authority . . .'

Section 95 of the 1984 Act confers upon an authorised officer appropriate powers of entry, and penalties for obstructing any person acting in the execution of the regulations are provided by section 112.

A duly authorised officer of the local authority must also be permitted to take samples of the materials used in works or fittings, to see whether they comply with the requirements of the regulations. In practice the authorised officer may ask the builder to have the tests carried out and to submit a report to the local authority. In any event, the builder should be notified of the result of the tests.

It should be noted, however, that regulations 15 and 16 do not apply where the work is privately certified or is done under a public body's notice. 1985 Regs, Reg. 17

Contravening works

Where a building is erected, or work is done contrary to the regulations, the local authority may require its removal or alteration by serving notice on the owner of the building. Where work is required to be removed or altered, and the owner fails to comply with the local Building Act 1984, sec. 36

authority's notice within a period of 28 days, the local authority may remove the contravening work or execute the necessary work themselves so as to ensure compliance with the regulations, recovering their expenses in so doing so from the defaulter.

sec. 36(5)   A section 36 notice may not be given after the expiration of twelve months from the date on which the work was completed. A notice cannot be served where the local authority have passed the plans and the work has been carried out in accordance with the deposited plans.

The recipient of a section 36 notice has a right of appeal to the magistrates court. The burden of proving non-compliance with the Regulations lies on the authority, but if they show that the works do not comply with an approved document (under section 6) then the burden shifts. The appellant against the notice must then prove compliance with the Regulations: *Rickards* v. *Kerrier District Council* (1987).

1984 Act, sec. 37   Section 37 provides an alternative to the ordinary appeal procedure. Under that section, the owner may notify the local authority of his intention to obtain from 'a suitably qualified person' a written report about the matter to which the section 36 notice relates. Such notices are served where the local authority considers that the technical requirements of the regulations have been infringed.

The expert's report is then submitted to the local authority. In light of it the local authority may withdraw the section 36 notice and *may* pay the owner the expenses which he has reasonably incurred in consequence of the service of the notice, including his expenses in obtaining the report. Adopting this procedure has the effect of extending the time for compliance with the notice or appeal against it from 28 to 70 days.

If the local authority rejects the report, it can then be used as evidence in any appeal under section 40 and section 40 (6) provides that

> 'if, on appeal . . . there is produced to the court a report that has been submitted to the local authority . . . the court, in making an order as to costs, may treat the expenses incurred in obtaining the report as expenses for the purposes of the appeal'.

Thus, in the normal course of events, if the appeal was successful, the owner would recover the cost of obtaining the report as well as his other costs.

The local authority – or anyone else – may also apply to the civil courts for an injunction requiring the removal or alteration of any contravening works. This power is exercisable even in respect of work which has been carried out in accordance with deposited plans, e.g. oversight or mistake on the part of the local authority. In such a case the court might well order the local authority to pay compensation to the owner. The twelve months' time limit does not apply to this procedure which is, however, unusual and rarely invoked in practice. The Attorney-General, as guardian of public rights, may seek an

injunction in similar circumstances, and in practice proceedings for an
injunction must be taken in his name and with his consent.   sec. 36(6)

Where a person contravenes any provision in the building regulations,
he renders himself liable to prosecution by the local authority. The
case is dealt with in the magistrates' court. The maximum fine on
conviction is £2000, with a continuing penalty of £50 a day.   sec. 35

Chapter 3

Local authority control

Introduction

Local authorities have exercised control over buildings in England and Wales since 1189, but it was not until 1965 that uniform national building regulations were made applicable throughout the country generally. Inner London retained its own system of control based on the London Building Acts 1930 to 1978 and byelaws made thereunder until 6 January 1986. Building regulations now apply to Inner London, although many provisions of the London Building Acts continue to apply in modified form.

1985 Regs, Regs. 11 to 14 Part IV of the Building Regulations 1985 contains the procedural requirements which must be observed where a person proposes to undertake building work covered by the regulations and opts for local authority control. Most building work will continue to be under local authority control and supervision because the alternative – private control and supervision by an approved inspector, as explained in Chapter 4 – may well be confined to registered house-builders under the National House Building Council (NHBC) scheme. The NHBC employs qualified field staff to exercise approved inspector functions on its behalf. Details of the NHBC scheme are given in Appendix 3.

Two main procedural options are available under the local authority system of control:

- Control based on service of a building notice.
- Control based on the deposit of full plans.

There is also a case – where the work consists only of the installation of certain gas heating appliances by, or under the supervision of, a Gas Board – where neither notice nor deposit of plans is required. It is also possible to have an intermediate situation where plans may be passed in stages.

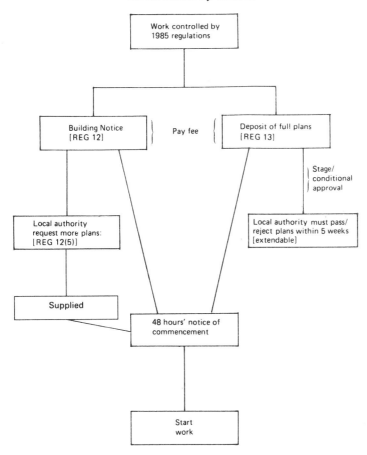

Fig. 3.1 Local authority supervision.

The local authority

The local authority for the purposes of the regulations is the district council, a London borough council, the Common Council of the City of London, the Sub-Treasurer of the Inner Temple, the Under Treasurer of the Inner Temple, and the Council of the Isles of Scilly.

1984 Act, sec. 126(1) and Sch. 3

Building notice procedure

A major procedural innovation introduced by the 1985 regulations is based on service of a building notice. There is no approval of plans. Interestingly, this is copied from the former Inner London system.

1985 Regs,
Reg. 11
A person intending to carry out building work may give a building notice to the local authority unless the building concerned is one for which a means of escape is required *and* which is designated under the Fire Precautions Act 1971. The following buildings are designated under the Act:

● *Hotels and boarding houses*
Where there is sleeping accommodation for six or more guests or staff or any number of guests or staff above the first floor or below the ground floor.

● *Factories, offices, shops and railway premises*
Where more than twenty people are employed or more than ten people are employed other than on the ground floor or in factories only where explosive or highly flammable materials are stored or used.

Reg. 11(2)   The building concerned must also fall into the cases specified in B1 of Schedule 1 (see Table 3.1). If these conditions are satisfied, then full plans must be deposited.

Table 3.1. Means of escape – regulation B1.

B1 only applies to erection of the following buildings:
 ● Dwellinghouses of three or more storeys*
 ● Buildings of more than three storeys containing a flat
 ● Buildings consisting of offices or containing an office
 ● Shops

---

* The rules also apply where a dwellinghouse is extended or altered so that it will have three or more storeys *and* where the use of any building of three or more storeys is materially changed to use as a dwellinghouse.

Offices and shops are therefore excluded from the building notice procedure, but hotels and boarding houses are not.

There is no prescribed form of building notice. The notice must be
Reg. 12(1)   signed by the person intending to carry out the work or on his behalf, and must contain or be accompanied by the following information:

● The name and address of the person intending to carry out the work.
● A statement that it is given in accordance with regulation 11 (1)(a).
● A description of the location of the building to which the proposal relates and the use or intended use of that building.
Reg. 12(2)   ● If it relates to the erection or extension of a building it must be supported by a plan to a scale of not less than 1:1250, showing size and position in relation to streets and adjoining buildings on the same site, the number of storeys, and details of the drainage. Where any local legislation applies, the notice must state how it will be complied with.

- If it relates to erecting a new building or extending an existing one covered by section 24 of the Building Act 1984, details of entrances, exits, etc., must be given. Section 24 applies to theatres, halls used by the public, restaurants, shops or warehouses used by the public and in which more than twenty people are employed, clubs, educational buildings and places of public worship.
- Where the building notice involves cavity wall insulation, information must be given about the insulating material to be used and whether or not it has an Agrément Certificate or conforms to British Standards, and whether or not the installer has a BSI Certificate of Registration or has been approved by an Agrément Board.   **Reg. 12(3)**
- If the work includes the provision of a hot water storage system covered by Schedule 1, G3 [e.g. a system with a storage capacity of 16 litres or more] details of the system and whether or not the system and its installer are approved.   **Reg. 12(4)**

The local authority are not required to approve or reject the building notice and, indeed, have no power to do so. However, they are entitled to ask for any plans they think are necessary to enable them to discharge their building control functions and may specify a time limit for their provision. They may also require the person giving the notice for information in connection with their linked powers under sections 18 to 21 of the Building Act 1984 (see pp. 1.3–1.4), and if the work involves building over a sewer, they can require an access agreement.

The regulations make plain that the building notice and plans shall not be 'treated as having been *deposited* in accordance with the building regulations'. In some ways this is an odd provision because the relevant building control sections of many of the local Acts of Parliament mentioned in Chapter 1 – and which provide for special local requirements – are triggered off by the 'deposit' of plans. At first sight, therefore, this would render such requirements inoperative, but presumably it is thought that compliance will be ensured through the requirement that the building notice must contain a statement of the steps to be taken to comply with any local enactment.   **Reg. 12(6)**

Once a building notice has been given, work can be commenced, although there is a requirement (see below) that the local authority be notified at least 48 hours before work commences.

Installation of heat-producing gas appliances

No building notice (or deposit of plans) is required where the building work consists *only* of the installation of a heat-producing gas appliance which is to be installed by, or under the supervision of, the British Gas Corporation. This exemption covers gas-fired heaters of various sorts, and does not apply if other building work is involved. No definition of the word 'supervision' is given. In its ordinary English meaning, 'to supervise' means to direct or oversee the performance of something or to watch over it. Presumably it is to be interpreted sensibly so as to   **Reg. 11(3)** cover installations by installers who have been approved by the Gas Boards.

Deposit of plans

Reg. 11(1)
(6)

This is the traditional system of building control by which full plans are deposited with the appropriate local authority in accordance with section 16 of the Building Act 1984, as supplemented by regulation 13. Section 16 imposes a duty on the building control authority itself to either pass or reject plans deposited for the proposed work. In *Murphy* v. *Brentwood District Council* (1988) the High Court held that the duty is non-delegable and the local authority does not discharge its duty by delegating its performance to a third party. If, as in that case, the local authority leaves it to outside consultant engineers to decide whether or not plans are to be passed or rejected, the authority is liable for any negligence on the part of the outside engineers. The authority has a duty to take reasonable care to see that the regulations are complied with and that the plans are not otherwise defective. If the plans submitted are not defective the authority has no alternative but to approve them unless, of course, they contravene the linked powers discussed in Chapter 1.

1984 Act,
sec. 16(6)

Where the proposed works are subject to the regulations, and it is proposed to deposit full plans, the provisions of section 16 and regulation 13 must be observed. The local authority must give notice of approval or rejection of plans within five weeks unless the period is extended by written agreement. The extended period cannot be later than two months from the deposit of plans, and any extension must be agreed before the five week period expires. However, the five week period does not begin to run unless the applicant submits a 'reasonable estimate' of the cost of the works and pays the prescribed fees at the same time as the plans are deposited.

1984 Act,
sec. 32

The approval lapses if the work is not commenced within a period of three years from the date of the deposit of the plans, provided the local authority gives formal notice to this effect. The local authority must pass the plans of any proposed work deposited with them in accordance with the regulations unless the plans are defective, or show that the proposed work would contravene the regulations. The notice of rejection must specify the defects or non-conformity, and the applicant may then ask the Secretary of State to determine the issue. His decision is then final. The Secretary of State may refer questions of law to the High Court and must do so if the High Court so directs.

1984 Act,
sec. 16

The local authority may pass plans by stages and, where they do, they must impose conditions as to the deposit of further plans. They may also impose conditions to ensure that the work does not proceed beyond the authorised stage. They have power to approve plans subject to agreed modifications, e.g. where the plans are defective in a minor respect or show a minor contravention. However, it should be noted that local authorities are not obliged to pass plans conditionally or in stages, and the applicant must agree in writing to these procedures.

The 'full plans' required under the deposit method are the same as those required under the building notice procedure, together with such other plans as are necessary to show that the work will comply with the building regulations except sections 2 and 3 of Paragraph L1 of Schedule 1, i.e. heating system controls and insulation of pipes, etc. **1985 Regs, Reg. 13**

Regulation 13 specifies that the plans must be deposited in duplicate; the local authority retains one set of plans and returns the other set to the applicant. They must be accompanied by a statement that they are deposited in accordance with regulation 11 (1) (b) of the Building Regulations 1985.

Work may be commenced as soon as plans have been deposited – although the local authority must be given notice of commencement at least 48 hours before work commences – but it is an unwise practice to commence work before notice of approval is received.

The advantage of the full deposit of plans method of control is that if the work is carried out exactly in conformity with the plans as passed by the local authority, they cannot take any action in respect of an alleged contravention under section 36 of the Building Act 1964. Moreover, the work involved is supervised by the local authority's building control officer, which many applicants believe to be an additional protection.

The deposit of full plans procedure and the possible alternative solutions are shown diagramatically in Fig. 3.2.

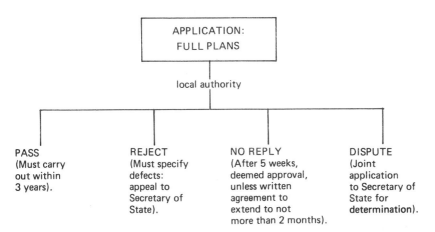

Fig. 3.2.

Notice requirements

Wherever the work is to be supervised by the local authority, in addition to the building notice or deposit of plans, the person **1985 Regs, Reg. 14** undertaking the work must give certain notices to the local authority. The notices must be in writing 'or by such other means as [the local authority] may agree', e.g. by telephone, but most building control authorities provide applicants who deposit plans with pre-printed postcards.

Failure to give the required notices is a criminal offence, punishable on summary conviction by a substantial fine. Under the previous regulations, the Court of Appeal has ruled that failure to deposit plans and give notices under the building regulations is not a continuing offence, with the result that magistrates have no power to try informations laid more than six months after the relevant period for compliance. The regulations require the notices to be given by a specified deadline, and once that deadline has passed, the offence has been committed: *Hertsmere Borough Council* v. *Alan Dunn Building Contractors Ltd* (1985).

In practice the majority of local authorities do not seek to enforce the penalty but rely on their powers to serve written notice requiring the person concerned within a reasonable time to cut into, lay open or pull down so much of the work as is necessary to enable them to check whether it complies with the regulations.

Where the person carrying out the work is advised in writing by the local authority of contravening works, and has rectified these as required by the local authority, he must give the authority written notice within a reasonable time after the completion of the further work.

'Reasonable time' is not defined in either situation; it is a question of fact in each case. The phrase has been judicially defined as being 'reasonable under ordinary circumstances': *Wright* v. *New Zealand Shipping Co.* (1878).

Regulation 14 requires the giving of the following notices to the local authority:

- At least 48 hours' notice of commencement before commencing the work.
- At least 24 hours' notice of:
    the covering up of any foundation excavation, foundation, damp-proof course, concrete or other material laid over a site;
    the haunching or covering up of any drain or private sewer subject to the regulations.

The local authority must be given notice by the person undertaking the work not more than seven days after the completion of:

- The laying of any drain or private sewer, including any haunching, surrounding or trench backfilling.
- The erection of a building.
- The completion of any other work.

Where a building or part of a building is occupied before completion, the local authority must be given notice at least seven days before occupation. This notice is additional to the required notice after completion.

There is a special definition which applies to Reg. 14 (1):

In calculating the period of *hours* for notice purposes, the time period does not include a Saturday, Sunday, Christmas Day, Good Friday, Bank Holiday or day appointed for public thanksgiving or mourning.

There is no definition of *day*, and it is suggested that an ordinary calendar day is meant.

Chapter 4

Private certification

Introduction

One of the Government's aims in reforming the previous system of building control was to provide an opportunity for self-regulation by the construction industry through a scheme of private certification. This is not a complete substitute for local authority control, because local authorities remain responsible for taking any enforcement action which may be necessary. Indeed, in certain closely-defined circumstances they may resume their control functions. The local authority also remain responsible for inspecting any connection to, or building over, an existing sewer as well as for work which is covered by local legislation.

The developer is given the option of having the work supervised privately, rather than relying on the local authority control system described in the previous chapter. Essentially, the private certification scheme is based on the proposals set out in a Government White Paper – 'The Future of Building Control in England and Wales' – published by HMSO in February 1981.

1984 Act, secs 47–53 The statutory framework of the alternative system is contained in Part II of the Building Act 1984. In broad terms, this provides that the responsibility for ensuring compliance with building regulations may, at the option of the person intending to carry out the work, be given to an approved inspector instead of to the local authority. It also enables **1984 Act, sec. 54** approved public bodies to supervise their own work. Various supplementary provisions deal with appeals, offences, and the registration of **1984 Act, secs 55–58** certain information.

The detailed rules and procedures relating to private certification are to be found in the Building (Approved Inspectors, etc.) Regulations 1985, which also contain prescribed forms which must be used. However, the full operation of private certification depends to a large extent upon the availability of adequate insurance cover, and agreement on the qualifications of individual approved inspectors. These are matters which are to some extent currently under discussion. The National House Building Council (NHBC) has been designated as an approved inspector. The NHBC is a non-profit making insurance company recognised by Statute, and its Chairman is appointed by the Secretary of State for the Environment. The NHBC is an approved inspector for dwellings, and its insurance scheme is an improved form of the well-known ten year warranty (which is a no fault insurance scheme), plus fifteen year cover where there is negligence. Appendix 3 gives details of the NHBC Scheme.

The Royal Institution of Chartered Surveyors has also begun the process of approving certain of its members as approved inspectors, initially adopting a process of interviewing to establish that applicants are duly qualified. In the longer term it is expected that examinations will be prescribed, probably in conjunction with some of the other professional bodies.

Approval of inspectors

Section 49 of the Building Act 1984 defines an 'approved inspector' as being a person approved by the Secretary of State or a body designated by him for that purpose. Part II of the Building (Approved Inspectors, etc.) Regulations 1985 sets out the detailed arrangements and procedures for the grant and withdrawal of approval. **1984 Act, sec. 49**
AI Regs, 3–7

There are two types of approved inspector:

- Corporate bodies, such as the NHBC.
- Individuals, not firms, who must be approved by a designated body.

Approval may limit the description of work in relation to which the person concerned is an approved inspector.

The bodies so far designated are:

- The Chartered Institute of Building
- The Faculty of Architects and Surveyors
- The Incorporated Association of Architects and Surveyors
- The Institution of Building Control Officers
- The Institution of Civil Engineers
- The Institution of Structural Engineers
- The Royal Institute of British Architects
- The Royal Institution of Chartered Surveyors

The same eight bodies, together with the Chartered Institution of Building Services Engineers, have been designated to approve private individuals who wish to be approved persons who can certify plans to be deposited with the local authority as complying with the energy conservation requirements. **1984 Act, sec. 16(9)**

The Institution of Civil Engineers and the Institution of Structural Engineers have been designated to approve persons to certify plans as complying with the structural requirements. **1984 Act, sec. 16(9)**

Approval of an inspector is not automatic. Someone wishing to be an approved inspector must apply to a designated body, giving details **AI Regs, Reg. 3** of his qualifications and experience, and answer any inquiries which may be made about those matters. Individuals will be approved for a period of five years. A designated body can withdraw its approval – for example, if the inspector has contravened any relevant rules of conduct or shown that he is unfitted for the work.

AI Regs,
Reg. 6

More seriously, where an individual approved inspector is convicted of an offence under section 57 of the 1984 Act (which deals with false or misleading notices and certificates, etc.), the designated body which approved him must immediately withdraw their approval. The convicted person's name will be removed from the list for a period of five years. There is no provision for appeals or reinstatement.

AI Regs,
Reg. 6(3)

The Secretary of State may himself withdraw his approval of any designated body, thus ensuring that the designated bodies act responsibly in giving approvals.

AI Regs,
Reg. 7

Provision is made for the Department of the Environment to keep lists of designated bodies and any inspectors approved by the Secretary of State, and for their supply to local authorities and the designated bodies themselves.

Designated bodies must also maintain a list of inspectors whom they have approved. There is no express provision for these lists to be open to public inspection, although the designated body is bound to inform the appropriate local authority if it withdraws its approval from any inspector.

1984 Act,
sec. 49(2)

In approving any inspector, either the Secretary of State or a designated body may limit the description of work in relation to which the person concerned is approved. Any limitations will be noted in the official lists, as will any date of expiry of approval.

From the outset of the discussions about private certification, the Secretary of State has made it clear that it is for the designated bodies to decide on questions of competency. It appears that there are four criteria for approval:

- Professional qualifications
- Practical experience
- Indemnity insurance
- Knowledge of the building regulations

Discussions are currently taking place between the professional bodies involved about examinations and other criteria for approval. The approval arrangements are expected to be self-financing.

Independence of approved inspectors

AI Regs,
Reg. 9

An approved inspector cannot supervise work in which he has a professional or financial interest, unless it is 'minor work'. In this context, 'minor work' means:

(a) The material alteration or extension of a dwelling-house (not including a flat or a building including a flat) which has two storeys or less before the work is carried out and which afterwards has no more than three storeys. A basement is not regarded as a storey.

(b) The provision, extension or material alteration of controlled services or fittings, i.e. bathrooms, hot water supply systems, sanitary conveniences, drainage and waste disposal, heat producing appliances, heating system controls or insulation of heating services.

Independence is not required of an inspector supervising minor work but the limitation on the number of storeys should be noted. It is, perhaps, surprising that the exemption is not more limited.

There is a broad definition of what is meant by having a professional or financial interest in the work, the effect of which is to debar the following:

- Anyone who is or has been responsible for the design or construction of the work in any capacity.
- Anyone who or whose nominee is a member, officer or employee of a company or other body which has a professional or financial interest in the work, e.g. a shareholder in a building company.
- Anyone who is a partner or employee of someone who has a professional or financial interest in the work.

However, involvement in the work as an approved inspector on a fee basis is not a debarring interest!

Approval of public bodies

Public bodies, such as nationalised industries, are able to supervise their own building work by following a special procedure, which is detailed in the regulations.

1984 Act, sec. 54

Regulation 19 empowers the Secretary of State to approve public bodies for this purpose although, curiously, no criteria have been laid down as to the qualification and experience of the personnel involved. The regulation confers wide discretionary powers on the Secretary of State, but clearly approval will be limited to those bodies which may reasonably be expected to operate responsibly without detailed supervision. Many of the bodies, originally proposed in 1981 have been 'privatised'. Table 4.1. sets out the original list.

AI Regs, Reg. 19

Private certification procedure

Initial notice

If the developer decides to employ an approved inspector, whether an

1984 Act, secs 47 & 48

Table 4.1. Public bodies.

British Aerospace
British Airports Authority
British Airways
British Gas Corporation
British Leyland
British National Oil Corporation
British Nuclear Fuels Ltd
British Railways Board
British Shipbuilders
British Steel Corporation
British Waterways Board
Central Electricity Generating Board
Area Electricity Boards
Civil Aviation Authority
National Bus Company
National Coal Board
Ports Authorities
Post Office Corporation
Rolls-Royce
Trinity House

** From paragraph 6, Annex A, of 'The Future of Building Control in England and Wales' (1981).

individual or the NHBC, the first stage in the process is for the applicant and the approved inspector jointly to give to the local authority an *initial notice* in a prescribed form. This must be accompanied by plans and other supporting documents and, very importantly, by a declaration that an approved insurance scheme applies to the work. This declaration must be signed by the insurer. The initial notice must contain:

- A description of the work.
- In the case of a new building or extension, a site plan on a scale of not less than 1:1250 showing the boundaries and location of the site, together with relevant documents showing the approximate location of any proposed connection to be made to a sewer or other drainage proposals or the reasons why no drainage is necessary. If it is proposed to build over an existing sewer, the information given must indicate what precautions will be taken to protect it. The local authority need this information in connection with their powers under sections 18 to 21 of the Building Act 1984. If local legislation is applicable in the area, the necessary information must be provided. For example, some local Acts of Parliament require separate drainage for foul water and rainwater, and others require access for the fire brigade.

It is essential that the initial notice should contain full information, because otherwise it may be rejected. The initial notice must also state whether or not the work is 'minor work'. This is defined in regulation 9 (5) (see p. 4.3, above) and is basically work which consists of alteration or extension to a one or two storey house provided that not more than three storeys result. AI Regs, Reg. 8(3) & Sch. 3

An undertaking to consult the fire authority must also be included, if appropriate, as well as a statement of awareness of the applicable statutory obligations.

An initial notice submitted by an individual approved inspector must be supported by a copy of the notice of his approval by a designated body.

The initial notice must be on the prescribed form, and it is a contravention of the regulations to start work before the notice has been accepted. Figure 4.1 shows a completed form of initial notice.

The local authority must accept or reject the initial notice within ten working days, which run from the date of its receipt. When sent by post, the presumption is that the notice is received in normal course of post, i.e. assuming first class postage is paid, the notice will be delivered on the working day following posting. AI Regs, Reg. 8(4)

Once accepted, the local authority's powers to enforce the Building Regulations 1985 are suspended so long as the initial notice remains in force.

There are only twelve grounds on which the notice may be rejected by the local authority. These are: AI Regs, Sch. 3

- The notice is not in the prescribed form.
- The notice has been served on the wrong local authority.
- The person who signed the notice as an approved inspector is not an approved inspector.
- The information supplied is deficient because neither the notice nor plans show the location and description of the work (including the use of any building to which the work relates) or it contains insufficient information about drainage, etc.
- The initial notice is not accompanied by an individual approved inspector's notice of approval.
- Evidence of approved insurance is not supplied.
- The notice does not contain an undertaking to consult the fire authority if this is appropriate.
- The inspector is not independent, i.e. he has a professional or financial interest in the work. (Independence is not required in the case of minor work: see p. 4.3.)
- The local authority is not satisfied about the drainage proposals.
- The work includes the erection or extension of a building over an existing sewer and the local authority is not satisfied that it may properly consent, either conditionally or unconditionally.
- Local legislative requirements will not be complied with.
- There is an overlap with an earlier initial notice which is still effective.

The Building Act 1984, section 47, and the Building (Approved Inspectors, etc.) Regulations 1985.

INITIAL NOTICE

To: The Cawsand District Council, Probity House, Cawsand

1. This notice relates to the following work:
   Alteration and extension to dwelling house known as Tragedy House, Cawsand

2. The approved inspector in relation to the work is:
   John Jorrocks, Esq., RIBA, 3 Redcoat Place, Cawsand
   Tel: Cawsand 123

3. The person intending to carry out the work is:
   Facey Romford, Esq., Tragedy House, Cawsand.
   Tel: Cawsand 456

4. With this notice are the following documents, which are those relevant to the work described in this notice:
   [a] A copy of the approved inspector's notice of approval.
   [b] A declaration of insurance duly signed on behalf of Structural Failures Insurance Co. PLC.
   [c] A plan (1:1250 scale) showing the boundaries and location of the site and details of the proposed sewer connection.

5. The work is not minor work.

6. I, John Jorrocks, declare that I do not, and will not while this notice is in force, have any financial or professional interest in the work described.

7. The approved inspector will be obliged to consult the fire authority

8. I, John Jorrocks, undertake to consult the fire authority before giving a plans certificate in accordance with section 50 of the Act or a final certificate in accordance with section 51 of the Act in respect of any of the work described above.

9. I, John Jorrocks, am aware of the obligations laid upon me by Part II of the Act and by regulation 10 of the 1985 regulations.

Signed   Signed

John Jorrocks   *Facey Romford*

Approved Inspector   Person intending to carry
                                           out the work

7 January 1990   7 January 1990

Fig. 4.1 Completed form of initial notice.

If the local authority do not reject the initial notice within ten working days, it is deemed to have been accepted.

The local authority may impose conditions when accepting an initial notice. For example, under section 18 of the Building Act 1984, if the building will be over a sewer, they will usually require the building owner to enter into an access agreement so as to enable the sewer to be properly maintained, while under section 21 of the 1984 Act they can insist that the drainage system is connected to an existing public sewer in defined circumstances. 1984 Act, secs 18–25

Once the initial notice is accepted, the local authority's powers to enforce the building regulations are suspended, and supervision of the works is the responsibility of the approved inspector.

The initial notice generally remains in force during the currency of the works, although as explained below it may be cancelled in certain circumstances. Moreover, after the lapse of certain defined periods of time it will cease to have effect. The time periods depend on the circumstances, but the position may be summarised as follows: 1984 Act, secs 48, 52 & 53

AI Regs, Reg. 16

[1] Where a final certificate is rejected – one week from the date of rejection.

[2] Occupied buildings and extensions – if no final certificate is issued, six weeks from the date of occupation, but in the case of a designated building (Fire Precautions Act 1971), the period is one day.

[3] Changes of use which have commenced – six weeks from the date of occupation if no final certificate is issued.

[4] All other work – six weeks from the date on which the work is 'substantially completed' if no final certificate is issued.

The local authority is given power to extend these time periods.

Cancellation of initial notice

In a number of cases, the approved inspector must cancel the initial notice by issuing to the local authority a cancellation notice in a prescribed form. 1984 Act, sec. 52; AI Regs, Reg. 17

The grounds on which the initial notice must be cancelled are:

- The approved inspector becomes or expects to become unable to carry out (or to continue to carry out) his functions.
- He is of the opinion that because of the way in which the work is being carried out he cannot adequately perform his functions.
- He believes that the requirements of the Building Regulations 1985 are being contravened and has given notice of contravention to the person carrying out the work and that person has not complied with the notice.

The detailed provisions about contravention are specified in regulation 17. The notice of contravention must inform the person carrying out the work that unless he rectifies the contravention within a period of three months the approved inspector will cancel the initial notice.

If the approved inspector is no longer willing or able to carry out his functions (for example, an individual inspector has died) then the building owner must issue a cancellation notice in the prescribed form and serve it on the local authority and, if practicable, on the approved inspector. Failure by the building owner to issue a cancellation notice is a criminal offence, punishable on conviction by a maximum fine of £2000.

1984 Act,
sec. 52(4)

AI Regs,
Reg. 18

In both cases, the local authority resume their building control functions and take over the supervision of the work unless a new initial notice is given and accepted. Regulation 18 provides that where the local authority take over they may give a notice to the owner requiring (i) plans of work not covered by a plans certificate to show compliance with the regulations and (ii) where a plans certificate was given and accepted, a copy of the plans as certified. The local authority may also require opening up, etc., of work (not covered by a final certificate) if this is necessary for them to ensure compliance with the regulations.

If the building owner intends to carry out any further work which will be supervised by the local authority, he must deposit plans with the local authority showing that the intended work will comply with the Building Regulations 1985. This obligation extends to depositing plans of work already carried out so far as this is necessary to show that future work will comply.

1984 Act,
sec. 32

Where the work covered by the initial notice has not been begun within three years, the local authority may (not must) cancel the initial notice.

Functions of approved inspectors

. AI Regs,
Reg. 10

The fees payable to an approved inspector are a matter for negotiation; there is no prescribed scale. The functions which an approved inspector must carry out are specified and detailed in the regulations, and his obligation is to 'take such steps as are reasonable to enable him to be satisfied within the limits of professional care and skill that' specified requirements are complied with. An approved inspector is liable for negligence and it is suggested that he *must* inspect the work to ensure compliance, in contrast to local authorities who have a discretion as to whether or not to inspect, as explained in Chapter 5.

1984 Act,
sec. 49(8)

The approved inspector may arrange for plans or work to be inspected on his behalf by someone else (although only the approved inspector can give plans or final certificates), but delegation does not affect any civil or criminal liability. In particular, the 1984 Act states that:

'an approved inspector is liable for negligence on the part of a person carrying out an inspection on his behalf in like manner as if it were negligence by a servant of his acting in the course of his employment'.

The approved inspector must be satisfied that:

AI Regs,
Reg. 10(1)

- The requirements relating to building work and material change of use specified in regulations 4 and 6 of the Building Regulations 1985 are complied with.
- Satisfactory provision is made for drainage.
- Adequate exits, etc., are provided in cases where section 24 of the 1984 Act applies, e.g. public buildings generally.

Where cavity wall insulation is inserted, the approved inspector need not supervise the insulation work, but is required to state in his final certificate whether or not the work has been carried out.

AI Regs,
Reg. 10(2)

As the works progress, if the approved inspector finds that the work is being carried out over a public sewer, he must notify the local authority 'as soon as practicable' of the location of the work unless, of course, the local authority are already aware of the fact from the information provided with the initial notice.

AI Regs,
Reg. 10(3)

Consultation with the fire authority

Where the building will be put to a use designated under section 1 of the Fire Precautions Act 1971 and must be provided with means of escape in case of fire, the approved inspector must consult the fire authority and give them 'sufficient' plans to show that the means of escape comply with the Building Regulations 1985, Schedule 1, Paragraph B1. He must do this at least fifteen working days before issuing a plans certificate or a final certificate. Thus, the fire authority is given an effective period of three weeks in which to make comment. Silence by the fire authority will imply approval. The approved inspector must 'have regard to any views' expressed by the fire authority.

AI Regs,
Reg. 11

Some local Acts of Parliament impose more extensive consultation requirements than the national legislation. The approved inspector must undertake any consultation required by the local legislation.

Plans certificates

A plans certificate is a certificate issued by an approved inspector certifying that the design has been checked and that the plans comply with the Building Regulation 1985. Its issue is entirely at the option of the person carrying out the work, and is issued by the approved inspector to the local authority and the building owner.

1984 Act,
sec. 50

If the approved inspector is asked to issue a plans certificate and declines to do so on the grounds that the plans do not comply with the building regulations, the building owner can refer the dispute to the

Secretary of State for a determination. A plans certificate can be issued at the same time as the initial notice or at a later stage, provided the work has not been carried out. There are two prescribed forms of plans certificate.

There are three preconditions to its issue:

- The approved inspector must have inspected the plans specified in the initial notice.
- He must be satisfied that the plans are neither defective nor show any contravention of the regulation requirements.
- He must have complied with any requirements about consultation, etc.

If a plans certificate is issued and accepted and, at a later stage, the initial notice ceases to be effective, the local authority cannot take enforcement action in respect of any work described in the plans certificate if it has been done in accordance with those plans.

The local authority have ten working days in which to reject the plans certificate, but may only do so on certain specified grounds:

- The plans certificate is not in the prescribed form.
- It does not describe the work to which it relates.
- It does not specify the plans to which it relates.
- Unless it is combined with an initial notice, that no initial notice is in force.
- The certificate is not signed by the approved inspector who gave the initial notice or that he is no longer an approved inspector.
- The required declaration of insurance is not given.
- There is no declaration that the fire authority has been consulted (if appropriate).
- There is no declaration of independence (except for minor work).

When combined with an initial notice, the grounds for rejecting an initial notice specified in Schedule 3 (above, p. 4.6) also apply.

Final certificates

The final certificate should be issued by the approved inspector when the work is completed, but curiously there are no sanctions against an approved inspector who fails to issue a final certificate. The final certificate need not relate to all the work covered by the initial notice; it can, for example, be given in respect of part of a building which complies with the Building Regulations 1985, or one or more of the houses on a development covered by an initial notice. Once given and accepted the initial notice ceases to apply.

It is to be issued, in a prescribed form, where an approved inspector is satisfied that any work specified in an initial notice given by him has been completed and certifies that 'the work described . . . has been completed' and that the inspector has performed the functions assigned to him by the regulations. If the local authority do not reject the final certificate within ten working days they are deemed to have accepted it. A final certificate can only be rejected on limited grounds. These are:

AI Regs,
Reg. 15;
Sch. 5

- The certificate is not in the prescribed form.
- It does not describe the work to which it relates.
- No initial notice relating to the work is in force.
- The certificate is not signed by the approved inspector who gave the notice or he is no longer an approved inspector.
- The required declaration of insurance is not provided.
- There is no declaration that the fire authority has been consulted (if appropriate).
- There is no declaration of independence (except for minor works)
The flow chart in Fig. 4.2 shows private certification procedure.

Public body's notices and certificates

Part VII of the Building (Approved Inspectors, etc.) Regulations 1985 is concerned with public bodies and, read in conjunction with section 54 of the Building Act 1984, its effect is to enable designated public bodies to self-certify their own work.

1984 Act,
sec. 54;
AI Regs,
Regs. 19 to
26

Public bodies are approved by the Secretary of State, and the regulations relating to notices, consultation with the fire authority, plans certificates and final certificates mirror those of Part III dealing with approved inspectors. The grounds on which the local authority may reject a public body's notice, etc., mirror those applicable to private certification, except that:

- There is no provision for cancellation of a public body's notice.
- There is no requirement that there should be an approved insurance scheme in force.

Certificates of compliance

Section 16 (9) of the Building Act 1984 provides for *approved persons* to give certificates that the plans show compliance with certain requirements of the Building Regulations 1985, namely:

1984 Act,
sec. 16(9);
AI Regs,
Reg. 27

- Schedule 1, Part A – Structural Stability
- Schedule 1, Part L – Energy requirements

This procedure is applicable under the local authority system of building control described in Chapter 3, where full plans are deposited with the local authority.

Certificates of compliance can only be given by persons approved for

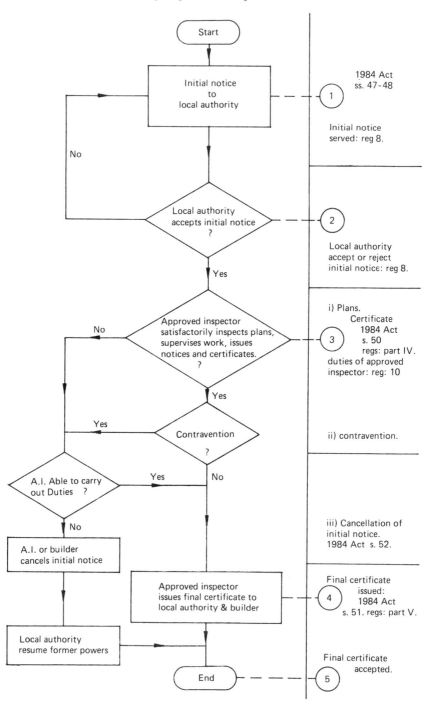

Fig. 4.2 Private certification procedure.

the purposes of section 16 (9), and must be accompanied by a declaration that an approved insurance scheme applies.

It is important to note that limited self-certification is possible because a declaration of independence is only required in a certificate of compliance with Part A where the building has five or more storeys (including basement storeys) or is a public building with a span of over 9 metres between supports. Thus, members of the Institutions of Civil and Structural Engineers who are approved persons may give certificates of compliance in respect of work in which they have an interest. Both of the specified categories of buildings are restricted, and self-certification is possible for other buildings which could have a high occupancy.

Similarly, self-certification by an approved person with an interest in the work is possible in the case of energy conservation calculations (see p. 16.29), by a person approved by the appropriate bodies, without any limitation. At present there are no approved persons.

Prescribed forms

Eleven prescribed forms are set out in Schedule 2 of the Building (Approved Inspectors, etc.) Regulations 1985. These are reproduced in Appendix 2. Regulation 2 (1) provides that where the regulations require the use of one of the numbered forms set out in Schedule 2, 'a form substantially to the like effect may be used'. Approved inspectors, public bodies, and local authorities, etc., may therefore have their own forms printed, provided they follow the precedents laid down in Schedule 2.

AI Regs, Sch. 2

Chapter 5

Legal liabilities

Introduction

The Building Regulations 1985 impose specific statutory duties on those intending to carry out buildings work and on those actually carrying it out. Similarly, the Building (Approved Inspectors, etc.) Regulations 1985 place obligations on approved inspectors. Breach of the provisions of the regulations is a criminal offence punishable on conviction by a fine. This is provided for by section 35 of the Building Act 1984 which says:

> 'If a person contravenes any provision contained in building regulations, other than a provision designated in the regulations as one to which this section does not apply, he is liable on summary conviction to a fine not exceeding level 5 on the standard scale and to a further fine not exceeding £50 for each day on which the default continues after he is convicted'.

Similar penal provisions are made in respect of specific offences in relation to private certification, e.g. section 52(1) of the 1984 Act, as regards the duty to cancel an initial notice in specified circumstances.

Local authorities are under statutory duties in relation to building control, principally under the Building Act 1984, and the regulations made thereunder. For example, section 16 of the 1984 Act states that where plans of any proposed work are deposited with them under the regulations, it is their duty to pass the plans unless they are defective or show a contravention of the regulations, subject to their other powers to reject the plans. More generally, section 91(1) of the 1984 Act prescribes that 'it is the duty of local authorities to carry this Act into execution in their areas'.

Breach of statutory duty

The Building Act 1984 imposes duties of various kinds on several groups of people: local authorities, builders, approved inspectors, and those intending to carry out building work, amongst others.

Breach of duty imposed by building control legislation, and the regulations, may result in civil liability giving rise to a claim for damages by someone who suffers loss or damage as a result, the liability being for the tort of breach of statutory duty. Section 38 of the 1984 Act deals with civil liability so far as breach of regulation requirements is concerned. It provides that, except where the regulations otherwise, 'breach of a duty imposed by building regulations, so far as it causes damage is actionable'.

'Damage' is defined as including the death of, or injury to, any person (including any disease or any impairment of a person's physical or mental condition).

Significantly, the section goes on to provide that it does not affect the extent (if any) to which breach of a duty imposed by or arising under Part I of the Act or other relevant legislation or of duties imposed by the regulations generally is actionable at civil law, nor does it 'prejudice a right of action that exists apart from the enactments relating to building regulations'.

Section 38 has not yet been brought into force, and until it is activated the position appears to be that breach of the building regulations as such does not of itself give rise to liability in damages for breach of statutory duty. There is a good deal of relevant case law.

For example, in *Eames London Estates Ltd* v. *North Hertfordshire District Council* (1980), Judge Edgar Fay QC held that builders were liable for breach of building by-laws irrespective of negligence. In so doing he applied a dictum of Lord Wilberforce in the now discredited case of *Anns* v. *London Borough of Merton* (1977) where he said

> since it is the duty of the builder (owner or not) to comply with by-laws I would be of opinion that an action could be brought against him, in effect, for breach of statutory duty by any person for whose benefit or protection the byelaw was made'.

However, later cases suggest that this cannot be so. In *Worlock* v. *SAWS and Rushmoor Borough Council* (1981), Mr Justice Woolf was satisfied that it was wrong to regard the building regulations (which took the place of building by-laws in 1966) as giving rise to a statutory duty creating an absolute liability, irrespective of negligence, and a similar view was expressed in the Court of appeal by Lord Justice Waller in *Taylor Woodrow Construction (Midlands) Ltd* v. *Charcon Structures Ltd* (1982). He said:

> 'Whether or not a breach of a (building regulation) would by itself give rise to an action for damages without proof of negligence is to say the least doubtful ... I say that the question of proof of negligence is doubtful because the only expression of view which gives any support to any other view was contained in the speech of Lord Wilberforce in *Anns* v. *London Borough of Merton* ... Mr Justice Woolf, in *Worlock* v. *SAWS and Rushmoor Borough Council* came to

the conclusion that it was not an absolute statutory duty but a duty which was a duty of care, and without expressing a concluded opinion about it, it seems to me . .. that a regulation of this kind is very difficult to construe as a regulation imposing an absolute duty in an action for damages'.

The law was fully reviewed and the relevant authorities were considered in *Perry* v. *Tendring District Council* (1985), where Judge John Newey QC held that breach of the former building by-laws did not give rise to liability in damages. The liability imposed on the local authority was not an absolute one. His Honour's reasoning was applied by the late Judge David Smout QC in *Kimbell* v. *Hart District Council* (1987), who held that a breach of statutory duty, as set out in section 64 of the Public Health Act 1936, such as a failure to reject plans, did not of itself give rise to a claim in damages. The statutory duty was not an absolute one, and the plaintiff could only succeed on proof of negligence. *Perry* v. *Tendring District Council* was also followed in *Kijowksi* v. *New Capital Properties Ltd* (1988), where Judge Esyr Lewis QC expressly held that breach of the Building Regulations 1965 did not of itself give rise to liability in damages.

In light of these decisions, it is suggested that this is also the position under the current regulations. Accordingly, unless and until section 38 of the 1984 Act is brought into effect, any breach of the regulations without proof of negligence does not of itself give rise to a claim for damages.

Liability in negligence

The question of whether or not local authorities are liable for negligence in the exercise of their statutory powers in relation to building control has been the subject of a great deal of recent case law development, culminating in the landmark decision of the House of Lords in *Murphy* v. *London Borough of Brentwood* (1990) which halted 13 years of expansionist development.

Recent cases have also restated the builder's liability in tort and continue the trend towards restricting liability in negligence. The latest case – *Department of the Environment* v. *Thomas Bates & Son Ltd* (1990) – signals a return to the classic position expressed by Lord Atkin in *Donoghue* v. *Stevenson* (1932) which is the foundation of the modern law of negligence.

In *Donoghue* v. *Stevenson* Lord Atkin formulated the famous 'neighbour principle' in the following terms:

'You must take reasonable care to avoid acts or omissions which you can reasonably foresee would be likely to injure your neighbour. Who then in law is my neighbour? The answer seems to be – persons who are so closely and directly affected by my act or omission that I ought reasonably to have them in contemplation as being so affected when I am directing my mind to the facts or omissions which are called in question'.

Position of the local authority

The local authorities are under various public duties in the exercise of their building control functions. They are public bodies discharging duties under statute and their powers and duties are defined in terms of public law. This has important consequences as regards the scope of their duty and liabilities.

What is now clear is that a local authority exercising its building control functions owes no duty to protect property owners from purely economic or financial loss and the unsatisfactory case of *Anns* v. *London Borough of Merton* (1977) has been held to have been wrongly decided

'as regards the scope of any private law duty of care resting on local authorities in relation to their function of taking steps to secure compliance with building . . . regulations'.

Because of this,

'it follows that *Dutton* v. *Bognor Regis Urban District Council* (1971) should be overruled, as should all cases subsequent to *Anns* which were decided in reliance on it'.
[Lord Keith in *Murphy* v. *Brentwood District Council* (1990)].

In *Murphy* v. *Brentwood District Council* the plaintiff's semi-detached house was built in 1969. It was one of a number of houses on an estate, and the Council had given building regulation approval for its construction. It was realized that the nature of the site might give rise to the risk of differential settlement and a special raft foundation was designed, the plans for which were considered and approved by an independent firm of consultant engineers on the Council's behalf.

The trial judge found that the design of the raft foundation was defective and that the consultant engineers had been negligent in approving the design.

The plaintiff purchased the house in February 1970 and first discovered serious cracks (which he repaired) in 1977. In 1981, the plaintiff's insurers commissioned consulting engineers to investigate further serious cracks which appeared in the internal walls.

Their investigations disclosed that the raft foundation had subsided differentially and caused cracking and distortion. In 1985 a gas leak occurred which was probably caused by the pipe fracturing because of distortion of the floor slab. The soil pipe leading to the main drain had also cracked and was leaking into the foundations.

The plaintiff's neighbour also suffered damage to his house through settlement, but was not able to afford any contribution to the cost of remedial work to the joint structure of the two houses. Repairs to the plaintiff's house alone were not practicable and so he sold it to a builder who was aware of the structural defects.

The insurers settled his claim for subsidence damage for £35,000, which was the loss of value sustained on the sale of the house, and this was the sum at issue.

Both the trial judge and the Court of Appeal found for the plaintiff, holding that the defendants were liable in negligence under the principle of *Anns* v. *London Borough of Merton* (1977), and that the diminution in value of the house by reason of the state of its foundations was recoverable as damages. The Council appealed to the House of Lords against this ruling.

In *Anns*, the House of Lords held that a local authority, in exercising its statutory functions of building control, could be liable in tort to occupiers of a building for the cost of remedying defects in it which amounted to a present or imminent danger to health or safety, if the defects resulted from the negligent failure of the council or its building inspector to ensure that the building was erected in conformity with building regulations.

The effect of *Anns* – where the loss was in truth pure economic loss, even though it was characterized as physical damage by Lord Wilberforce – was generally to hold building control authorities and, indeed, builders liable, not only where personal injury or damage to other property resulted from defective construction, but also where the damage was to the actual building itself.

However, since 1978, the courts had begun to limit the operation of the so-called *Anns* doctrine, particularly by limiting the class of people to whom the duty was owed.

The appeal in *Murphy* v. *Brentwood District Council* gave the House of Lords the opportunity of reconsidering *Anns* and held that it was wrongly decided. A local authority exercising its building control functions is not under a duty to protect property owners from pure economic loss.

However, it is not clear whether local authorities have *no* liability at all to future owners or merely no liability for financial loss.

The uncertainty arises principally from a passage in the speech of Lord Keith where he said:

'[The council] did not seek to argue that a local authority owes no duty at all to persons who might suffer injury through a failure to take reasonable care to secure compliance with building [regulations]. [They were] content to accept that such a duty existed but maintained that its scope did not extend beyond injury to person or health and (possibly) damage to property other than the defective building itself. ... I prefer to reserve my opinion on the question whether any duty at all exists. So far as I am aware, there has not yet been any case of claims against a local authority based on injury to person or health through a failure to secure compliance with building [regulations]. If and when such a case arises, that question may require further consideration'.

The possibility remains, therefore, that a building control authority might be held liable if its failure to take reasonable care to ensure compliance with the building regulations resulted in personal injury or death or injury to health or damage to other property. All that can be said with certainty is that a building control authority when exercising its statutory functions owes no duty of care to owners or occupiers of houses to safeguard them against purely economic loss.

Position of approved inspector

The approved inspector is a new creature in law, and his liabilities are not necessarily the same as those of a local authority because they are governed by private law.

There is one obvious difference between the liabiility of a local authority and that of an approved inspector. The approved inspector is in a contractual relationship with the builder or other person who employs him; the local authority is not. The ordinary rules of the law of contract apply to contracts made with an approved inspector, just as they apply to those made with an architect, engineer or surveyor or other professional man. The sensible approved inspector will ensure that his contract sets out clearly that his liabilities are limited to matters of health and safety and to the specific functions set out in the Building (Approved Inspector, etc.) Regulations 1985, regulation 10. It is thought that an exclusion clause which limited the approved inspector's liabilities to matters of health and safety would not fall foul of the Unfair Contract Terms Act 1977. Under regulation 10(1) the approved inspector's functions are to 'take such steps as are reasonable to enable him to be satisfied within the limits of professional skill and care that' the building regulations are complied with so as to secure reasonable standards of health and safety for persons in or about the building and others who may be affected by any failure to comply with the regulations. The standard of care to be exercised whilst discharging his duties is that which is ordinarily expected of any professional man.

The classic statement of the law is to be found in the judgement of Mr Justice McNair in *Bolam* v. *Friern Hospital Management Committee* (1957):

'Where you get a situation which involves the use of some special skill or competence, then the test as to whether there has been negligence or not is not the test of the man on the top of the Clapham omnibus, because he has not got that special skill. The test is the standard of the ordinary skilled man exercising and professing to have that special skill. A man need not possess the highest expert skill; it is well established law that it is sufficient that he exercises the ordinary skill of an ordinary competent man exercising that particular art'.

This test has been applied time and again to the analogous cases of architects, engineers and surveyors. In carrying out the functions allotted to him, the approved inspector must use reasonable professional care and skill, and in particular ensure that the relevant regulations are complied with. This duty is a continuing one: *Brickfield Properties Ltd* v. *Newton* (1971).

Whether or not the approved inspector is negligent is to be judged by the standards prevailing at the time of the alleged negligent act or omission. This is illustrated by a number of decided cases involving architects and others. For example, in *Kimbell* v. *Hart District Council* (1986), a decision of the late Judge David Smout QC, given at a time when building control authorities might be held liable, it was held that the council were not negligent in failing to reject plans which showed that the proposed work contravened the regulations because the relevant technical publications available at the time would not have alerted them to the danger.

His duty is to supervise the work to ensure that it complies with the requirements of the regulations, and it is suggested that this involves his making the necessary inspections if he is properly to carry out his functions. It is improbable that the approved inspector has the same discretion as a local authority as to whether or not to inspect, and most certainly the approved inspector must inspect at the stages set out in the building regulations when the builder must notify the local authority: see regulation 14.

Position of the builder

When carrying out building work, a building contractor is under obligations deriving from a variety of sources. Firstly, he is liable to his client under the terms of the contract between them. The obligations imposed by the contract may have been expressly agreed between the parties or they may be implied or written in by the general law. The terms of the contract may also be affected by relevant statutory provisions, such as the Defective Premises Act 1972 and the Supply of Goods and Services Act 1982. The builder's liability to his client will be determined solely by the terms of the contract between them: *Greater Nottingham Co-operative Society* v. *Cementation Piling and Foundation Ltd* (1988).

The builder may also be liable in tort at common law to third parties who suffer physical damage to person or property although recent developments have confined this liability.

A third type of liability arises as a result of statutory obligation. As we have seen, the Building Regulations 1985 impose specific duties on the person undertaking work controlled by the regulations. Regulation

1985 Regs,
Reg. 7

7 requires that 'any building work shall be carried out with proper materials and in a workmanlike manner', while work which is subject to the regulations must also be carried out so that it complies with the

Reg. 4

specific requirements of the regulations: Regulation 4. Breach of these regulation requirements does not at present give rise to liability in damages, but may result in a criminal prosecution and/or the taking of enforcement action by the local authority. Oddly, the 1985 regulations nowhere refer to 'the builder'; in some instances they refer to 'a person who intends to carry out building work' (as in regulation 11(1)) and in others to 'a person carrying out building work'. Reg. 11

The Building Act 1984 does not itself state in terms who is to comply with the regulations, but section 36 dealing with removal or alteration of offending work refers to notices to be served on 'the owner', while section 30 provides for the determination of disputes between the local authority and 'a person who has executed, or proposes to execute, any work'. This means 'the builder' and it is the builder who personally or by his own employees carries out works of construction who has to comply with the regulations, although enforcement notices must necessarily be served on the owner since only he can alter or destroy his property: *Perry* v. *Tendring District Council* (1984). It is therefore the builder who is primarily responsible for complying with the building regulations, and it has been held at first instance (in *Anglia Commercial Properties Ltd* v. *South Bedfordshire District Council* (1984)) that a building owner is not itself under an absolute non-delegable duty to comply with the building regulations in contrast with an owner-builder as such unless he or the architect or anyone else deliberately intervenes to cause a non-compliance with the regulations, and this was not doubted when the case went on appeal as *Investors in Industry Commercial Properties Ltd* v. *South Bedfordshire District Council* (1986). Building
Act 1984,
sec. 36

sec. 30

The trial judge based his decision on the views expressed by Lord Justice Stephenson in the Court of Appeal in *Acrecrest Ltd* v. *W.S. Hattrell & Partners* (1983), which was overruled by the House of Lords in *Peabody Donation Fund* v. *Sir Lindsay Parkinson & Co. Ltd* (1984) on the basis that the Court of Appeal had 'failed to appreciate correctly the course of Lord Wilberforce's reasoning and consequently misapplied the decision in *Anns* v. *London Borough of Merton* (1977)'.

However, those parts of the Court of Appeal's decision which dealt with position of the building owner as regards liability under building regulations were not expressly disapproved or overruled. It is therefore suggested that the position as stated in *Acrecrest Ltd* v. *W.S. Hattrell & Partners* is still good law and, at the very least, even if the building owner is under a statutory duty to comply with the building regulations, that duty is not of an absolute and non-delegable type such as to render him liable for the negligence of his independent contractors, such as the builder or the architect.

It must be emphasised that it is wrong to regard the building regulations as giving rise to a statutory duty creating an absolute liability, for reasons already explained above. So far as the builder is concerned, most of the commonly used standard form building contracts contain an express provision requiring the contractor to comply with all relevant statutory obligations – including the building regulations. It is in any event an implied term of all building contracts that the builder will comply with the regulations and this was so held in *Street* v. *Sibbabridge* (1980), where the judge said:

'The term that the building would be constructed in accordance with the building regulations must flow from the fact that the builder is the person upon whom the regulations are binding. It is he who commits a criminal offence if the regulations are breached'.

Interestingly, it was also held that the obligation to comply with the regulations 'must override any matter in the plans incorporated into the contract which it conflicts with'. In that case, the drawings showed a foundation 2 feet 9 inches deep and that is what the builder put in. The regulations required another type of foundation, either different or deeper in character. The builder's duty was to do what the regulations required.

Common law liabilities

Although the majority of building contracts are entered into in a standard form – such as one of the several sets of conditions produced by the Joint Contracts Tribunal – which contain very detailed terms, in some circumstances terms will be implied into the contract under the general law. In some cases, they will be implied as a result of statute. For example, the Supply of Goods and Services Act introduces statutory implied terms into contracts of various kinds, including 'contracts for work and materials', which include building contracts.

Statute apart, in some cases the courts will write implied terms into a contract in order to give it business efficacy and/or to make it work. However, where there is a contract of a very detailed nature, there is little if any room for the implication of terms. In *Lynch* v. *Thorne* (1956), for example, there was an express contract as to the way in which a house was to be constructed and the builder had complied with those express terms, it was held that there was no room for an implied term that the walls would be waterproof. Lord Evershed MR stated the general position thus:

'Where there is a written contract expressly setting forth the bargain between the parties it is, as a general rule, also well established that you only imply terms under the necessity of some compulsion'.

The voluminous case law and the minutiae of the subject are adequately discussed in the books on building contracts. For the purposes of this book, the position at common law is straightforward:

- In a building contract, unless the parties have agreed otherwise, there are implied terms that the builder will do his work in a good and workmanlike manner, using good and proper materials and provide a building reasonably fit for human habitation (in the case of a dwelling) or otherwise reasonably fit for its intended purpose: *Hancock* v. *B.W. Brazier (Anerley) Ltd* (1966); *Independent Broad-*

casting Authority v. *EMI Electronics Ltd and BICC Construction Ltd* (1980).

In *Test Valley Borough Council* v. *Greater London Council* (1979), Mr Justice Phillips explained the position in this way:

'Where a house proves defective, the defects may be of materials, of workmanship or of design. The duty of the [builder] will depend on all the circumstances, and, in particular, upon whether he is responsible for the design. Where he is, the duty is said to be to do the work in a good and workmanlike manner, to supply good and proper materials and to provide a building reasonably fit for human habitation ... Of course, the circumstances may be such that the third limb of the duty does not arise: for example, where the client employs his own architect: see *Lynch* v. *Thorne* (1956). Similar duties arise in the case of a "package deal" or a "design and build" contract: see *Greaves & Co. (Contractors) Ltd* v. *Baynham Meikle & Partners* (1975).'

The important point which emerges from the decision of the House of Lords in *IBA* v. *EMI and BICC* (1980) is that if the contractor undertakes design in whole or in part, the third limb of liability will be based on reasonable fitness for purpose of the finished structure, irrespective of negligence or fault and irrespective of whether the unfitness for purpose derives from the quality of work or materials or defects of design.

● Under the regulations and in contract generally, i.e. where the third limb is inapplicable, the standard of care to be exercised by the builder is that of a reasonably competent and experienced building contractor.

In *Worlock* v. *SAWS and Rushmoor Borough Council* (1982), the builder had tendered on a labour-only basis and was in a small way of business. This was held to make no difference to the situation. He was to be judged by the standards of the reasonably competent building contractor.

'The fact that the builder had ... contracted to provide labour only did not ... detract from the duty imposed upon him under the contract ... he must in law have been required to exercise the ordinary standard of care in so doing. He was not a navvy employed to dig foundations; he was a building contractor engaged to build a house, albeit with materials to a large extent supplied by his employer'.

● Apart from his contractual liability to the building owner, the builder may be liable if his negligence in the construction process causes physical injury to people or damage to property other than the building itself.

It has long been settled law that a builder is liable to third parties if his negligent construction causes physical harm to either people or property. This liability arises under the principle of *Donoghue* v. *Stevenson* (1932).

For example, in *Sharpe* v. *E.T. Sweeting & Son Ltd* (1963), the defendant contractors built council houses for the local authority to the local authority's design. They negligently constructed a concrete canopy over the front door of one of the houses, which Mr and Mrs Sharpe occupied as tenants of the council. The canopy collapsed and fell on Mrs Sharpe's foot. The plaintiff was successful in her claim for damages against the builders who were held to owe her a duty of care under the principle of *Donoghue* v. *Stevenson*.

In a series of cases in the last two decades the tort of negligence developed rapidly with the result that builders were held liable not only where personal injury or damage to other property resulted from negligent construction, but also where the damage was to the very property which the builder has constructed, largely as a result of the development of the doctrine given impetus by *Anns* v. *London Borough of Merton* (1977).

In *D & F Estates Ltd* v. *Church Commissioners for England* (1988), the House of Lords first questioned the basis of the *Anns* doctrine and signalled the end of the expansionist era of negligence liability.

In *D & F Estates*, plastering sub-contractors applied plaster to the ceilings of a flat negligently so that some 15 years later it fell off. The tenant of the flat sued the main contractors alleging that they had negligently supervised the work of the sub-contractors and claiming that they were responsible personally for the whole of the works, and claiming, amongst other things, the cost of repairing the ceiling. The House of Lords rejected the claim. There was no damage to the person or other property of the tenant and the cost of repairing the ceiling was pure economic loss which was held to be irrecoverable.

The House held in effect:

- A builder owes no duty of care in tort towards subsequent owners or occupiers of a building which he has erected in respect of purely economic loss.

To make the builder liable in this way would be to impose upon him for the benefit of those with whom he has no contractual relationship the obligation of someone who gives a transmissible warranty of fitness for purpose.

- A main contractor owes no duty of care to future occupiers of a building which he is erecting to supervise the work of his sub-contractors so as to ensure that the sub-contracted work is not negligently performed so as to give rise to latent defects. The main contractor is not vicariously liable for the negligence of his sub-contractors.

- A builder owes no duty of care to future occupiers of buildings which he erects to take care that the buildings contain no hidden defects except those of a kind which may cause injury to people or property other than the building itself. He is only liable to future occupiers of the building – within the period of limitation – so far as the negligently caused defects cause personal injury or damage to *other* property.

D & F Estates soon gave rise to further litigation in order to determine its meaning and scope on the vital question of whether a remote purchaser could recover from the negligent builder or designer the cost of averting *imminent* danger to persons or other property.

Moreover, in an attempt to rationalise the previous case law, two members of the House of Lords expressed the view that in the case of a complex structure, like a building, it was arguable that damage to one part of the building caused by negligent construction, e.g., the foundations, which in turn caused damage to another part, such as cracking of the walls, might be the subject of a claim in negligence because the walls would be 'other property' and that in those circumstances damages might be recoverable not only to repair the cracks in the walls but also to repair the foundations which caused the damage.

The uncertainty has now been ended by the House of Lords' decisions in *Murphy* v. *Brentwood District Council* (1990) and *Department of Environment* v. *Thomas Bates & Son Ltd* (1990), which involved claims for pure economic loss against a building control authority and a builder respectively and the 'complex structure' theory has effectively been abandoned.

In *Department of the Environment* v. *Thomas Bates & Son Ltd* the short facts were that the DoE, as long-lessees of part of a building complex, sought to recover from the builders, with whom they had no contract, the cost of strengthening defective concrete pillars. The strengthening had been carried out, not with a view to avoiding any imminent danger to persons or property, but in order to make the building fit for its design load.

The House of Lords held that the claim must fail.

Lord Keith said:

'It has been held by this House in *Murphy* v. *Brentwood District Council* that *Anns* was wrongly decided and should be departed from, by reason of the erroneous views there expressed as to the scope of any duty of care owed to purchasers of houses by local authorities when exercising the powers conferred upon them for the purpose of securing compliance with building regulations. The process of reasoning by which the House reached its conclusion necessarily included close examination of the position of the builder who was primarily responsible, through lack of care in the construction process, for the presence of defects in the building. It was the unanimous view that, while the builder would be liable under the principle of *Donoghue* v. *Stevenson* (1932) in the event of the defect, before it had been discovered, causing physical injury to persons or damage to property other than the building itself, there was no sound basis in principle for holding him liable for the pure economic loss suffered by a purchaser who discovered the defect, however such discovery might come about, and required to expend money in order to make the building safe and suitable for its intended purpose.

In the present case it is clear that the loss suffered by the plaintiffs is pure economic loss. At the time the plaintiffs carried out the remedial work on the concrete pillars the building was not unsafe by reason of the defective construction of these pillars. It did, however, suffer from a defect of quality which made the plaintiffs' lease less valuable than it would otherwise have been, in respect that the building could not be loaded up to its design capacity unless any occupier who wished so to load it had incurred the expenditure necessary for the strengthening of the pillars. It was wholly uncertain whether during the currency of their lease the plaintiffs themselves would ever be likely to require to load the building up to its design capacity, but a purchaser from them might well have wanted to do so. Such a purchaser, faced with the need to strengthen the pillars, would obviously have paid less for the lease than if they had been sound. This underlines the purely economic character of the plaintiffs' loss. To hold in favour of the plaintiffs would involve a very significant extension of the doctrine of *Anns* as to cover the situation where there existed no damage to the building and no imminent danger to personal safety or health. If *Anns* were correctly decided, such an extension could reasonably be regarded as entirely logical. The undesirability of such an extension, for the reasons stated in *Murphy* v. *Brentwood District Council*, formed an important part of the grounds which led to the conclusion that *Anns* was not correctly decided. That conclusion must lead inevitably to the result that the plaintiffs' claim fails.'

It is now clear, therefore, that mere defects in the quality of a building do not enable those who are not in a direct contractual relationship with the builder, such as subsequent purchasers, tenants and occupiers, to recover pure economic loss against the builder in tort. Only if a latent defect in the building causes actual physical injury to people or damage to property other than the building itself before the defect is discovered, will the negligent builder be liable.

The 'complex structure' has also been effectively abandoned. In *Murphy* v. *Brentwood District Council* Lord Keith was quite emphatic. He said that it would be unrealistic to regard 'a building the whole of which had been erected and equipped by the same contractor' as a 'complex structure' so as to make the contractor liable if damage to one part of the building from negligent construction caused damage to another part of the building and to regard that other part as 'other property'.

In that situation, he remarked,

> 'the whole package provided by the contractor would . . . fall to be regarded as one unit rendered unsound by such a defect in the particular part'.

Lord Bridge also concluded that a building is *not* a complex structure in this sense.

He said:

> 'The reality is that the structural elements of any building form a single indivisible unit of which the different parts are essentially interdependent. To the extent that there is any defect in one part of the structure it must to a greater or lesser degree necessarily affect all other parts of the structure. Therefore any defect in the structure is a defect in the quality of the whole and it is quite artificial . . . to treat a defect in an integral structure, so far as it weakens the structure, as a dangerous defect liable to cause damage to "other property"'.

It may be different, however, in respect of fittings and services negligently installed by sub-contractors and in practice much of the actual work of construction is carried out by sub-contractors. Where this is so,

> 'for example, the electric wiring had been installed by a sub-contractor and due to a defect caused by lack of care a fire occurred which destroyed the building it might not be stretching ordinary principles too far to hold the electrical sub-contractor liable for the damage',

Lord Keith remarked.

Lord Bridge also conceded that the position would be different if, for example, a defective central heating boiler explodes and damages the house or a defective electrical installation malfunctions and sets the house on fire. In those circumstances, subject to proof of negligence, the sub-contractor would be liable on *Donoghue* v. *Stevenson* principles.

Thus, while both *Murphy* and *Bates* confirm the limits on a builder's liability in negligence, a sub-contractor may be exposed to the risk of a negligence action if his work or installation is done negligently and causes damage to the rest of the building.

- Where appropriate, he owes duties under the Defective Premises Act 1972.

The construction of dwellings is subject to the provisions of the Defective Premises Act 1972, and the duty imposed by the Act is in addition to any duty which a builder or developer may owe apart from the Act.

Defective Premises Act 1972, sec. 1(1)

Section 1(1) provides:

'Any person taking on work for or in connection with the provision of a dwelling . . . owes a duty to see that the work that he takes on is done in a workmanlike manner, with proper materials . . . and so as to be fit for the purpose required . . .'

The Act excludes dwellings sold with National House Building Council guarantees because, under the NHBC scheme, express warranties are given in the same terms as the ones implied by the Act.

The NHBC scheme was altered with effect from 1 April 1988 and is now called 'The Buildmark'. Coverage was extended to include disputes relating to the general warranty given by the builder in relation to workmanship, materials and fitness for habitation. The arbitration clause covers all disputes, whether between builders or purchasers, or between purchasers and the NHBC, arising under The Buildmark.

However, when it is brought into force, the effect of the Consumer Arbitration Agreements Act 1988 must be borne in mind. This Act applies to consumer contracts and will apply to properties covered by The Buildmark where the acceptance form for the scheme is returned by the purchaser after the date of the Act's introduction. The effect of the Act is that the arbitration clause cannot be enforced against a purchaser where the proceedings are within the jurisdiction of the County Court (currently £5,000, but subject to review) or in other circumstances yet to be specified by the Government. The arbitration clause will then only be enforceable against the purchaser where he agrees to arbitration after the dispute has arisen or where the court so orders. In practical terms, for claims under the county court limit the purchaser will have the alternative of referring the dispute to court.

Civil Liability (Contribution) Act 1978

The Civil Liability (Contribution) Act 1978 deals with contribution between wrongdoers liable in respect of any damage, whether in tort, breach of contract or otherwise: 1978 Act, section 6(1). It covers damage which occurred on or after 1 January 1979 and applies to contracts made on or after that date.

Section 1(1) of the 1978 Act enables

'any person liable in respect of damage suffered by another person [to] recover contribution from any other person liable in respect of the same damages (whether jointly with him or otherwise)'.

So, for example, a building owner may sue the architect for negligence in design and supervision. Under the Act, the architect may bring into the proceedings the contractor, sub-contractors and the approved inspector or the local authority.

A contribution can also be recovered by someone who has made a sec. 1(4) payment in *bona fide* settlement of a claim 'without regard to whether or not he himself is or ever was liable in respect of the damage'.

In all cases, the amount of the contribution is a matter for the discretion of the court. The amount is to be 'just and equitable' having regard to the person's liability for the damage in question, and the best analogy about apportionment of liability is with the liability of local authorities for the negligence of their building control officers, where the courts adopt a broad brush approach.

In *Eames* v. *North Hertfordshire District Council* (1980), Judge Edgar Fay QC put the position simply:

> [The] blameworthiness of the policeman who fails to detect the crime is less than that of the criminal himself, and I have in a typical case arising out of negligent passing of defective foundations held a local authority to be 25 per cent to blame and the builder [or architect] 75 per cent'.

In general, for reasons explained in Chapter 4, the approved inspector cannot be an employee of the person undertaking the work, because of the requirement of independence. But he can be an employee when the work which he supervises is 'minor work' as defined. In that event, it is suggested that by analogy with the position of an employed clerk of works, the employer would be vicariously liable for his negligence, and the practical effect of that would be to reduce by the appropriate percentage the damages recoverable by the employer in an action for negligence against the architect. This was the ruling of Judge David Smout QC in *Kensington and Chelsea and Westminster Area Health Authority* v. *Wettern Composites and Others* (1984), where the responsibility of the clerk of works was assessed at 20 per cent and that of the architects at 80 per cent.

The result of the 1978 Act – as has been well said – is to increase the readiness of building owners to sue everybody in sight when things go wrong, leaving it to the court to assess the contribution on the basis of what is 'just and equitable'.

Limitation of actions

The law imposes time limits within which legal actions must be brought. The Limitations Act 1980 specifies a general limitation period of six years for actions based on simple contract or tort. Other periods are laid down in other cases, e.g., two years for a claim to recover contribution under the Civil Liability (Contribution) Act 1978 and three years in the case of personal injuries. 'Limitation' is the term used by lawyers for prescribing the periods within which actions must be started. An action which is commenced outside the prescribed period of limitation is said to be 'statute-barred'. The right of action is not itself extinguished but, provided the defendant pleads that the action is statute-barred, the claim is unenforceable. In litigation in the High Court, the writ must be issued within the specified limitation period.

Section 2 of the 1980 Act sets the time limit for claims in tort, including negligence. It says:

'An action founded on tort shall not be brought after the expiration of six years from *the date on which the cause of action accrued*' (emphasis supplied).

In *Pirelli General Cable Works Ltd* v. *Oscar Faber & Partners* (1982) the House of Lords laid down that 'the date on which the cause of action acrues' in the case of negligent design and construction of a building is the date when the physical damage which gives rise to it occurs, even though that damage was not reasonably discoverable until a later date. In consequence of the *Pirelli* case, Parliament enacted the Latent Damage Act 1986 to cover the case of latent damage not involving personal injuries as discussed below, but the Act does not alter the test laid down in *Pirelli* that the plaintiff's cause of action will not accrue until *damage* occurs and did not come into force until 18 September 1986.

In the context of claims against local authorities the material date is when the state of the building is such that there is present or imminent danger to the health or safety of the persons occupying it. Determining the date of proven or imminent danger to health or safety in any given circumstances has given rise to great difficulty. It is for the plaintiff to show, on the balance of probabilities, that his cause of action came into existence within the limitation period: *London Congregational Union Inc* v. *Harriss and Harriss* (1986).

The *Pirelli* case related to a tall factory chimney built with unsuitable lining material in 1969 as a result of which cracks developed in April 1970, but which were not reasonably discoverable before October 1972 and were not in fact discovered until November 1977. Lord Fraser stated the legal position as follows:

'The plaintiff's cause of action will not accrue until damage occurs, which will commonly consist of cracks coming into existence as a result of the defect even though the cracks or the defects may be undiscovered or undiscoverable. There may perhaps be cases where the defect is so gross that the building is doomed from the start, and where the owner's cause of action will accrue as soon as it is built, but it seems unlikely that such a defect would not be discovered within the limitation period. Such cases, if they exist, would be exceptional'.

The *Pirelli* case dealt with engineers and by analogy with architects and builders, and the position of local authorities exercising building control functions was expressly referred to by Lord Fraser. He quoted with approval the views of Lord Wilberforce in *Anns* v. *London Borough of Merton* (1977), to the effect that in such a case the material date is when there is 'present or imminent danger . . . to the health or safety of the owners or occupiers' as stated by the Court of Appeal in *Sparham-*

Souter v. *Town & Country Developments (Essex) Ltd* (1976), which was related to the particular duty resting upon the local authority, which is different from that resting on builders, architects and the like.

There is also a restriction on the *damages* recoverable against the local authority for breach of duty. That limitation was originally laid down by Lord Wilberforce in the *Anns* case:

'The damages recoverable include all those which foreseeably arise from the breach of the duty of ... reasonable care to secure compliance with the [regulations]. Subject always to adequate proof of causation, these damages may include damages for personal injury and damage to property ... [They] may also include damage to the dwelling house itself ... [The] relevant damage is ... material, physical damage, and what is recoverable is the amount of expenditure necessary to restore the dwelling to a condition in which it is no longer a danger to the health or safety of persons occupying and possibly (depending on the circumstances) expenses arising from the necessary displacement'.

The limitation is on the area or items of damage in respect of which recovery is possible: *Billam* v. *Cheltenham Borough Council* (1985).

For all practical purposes, Lord Fraser's reference in *Pirelli* to buildings 'doomed from the start' can be ignored, as Lord Keith made clear in *Ketteman* v. *Hansel Properties Ltd* (1987), where it was argued that

'a distinction fell to be drawn between the cases where the defect in a building was such that damage must inevitably eventuate at some time and the case of a defect such that damage might or might not eventuate.'

The former case was said to be that of a building 'doomed from the start'. Lord Keith gave that argument short shrift. He said:

'My Lords, whatever Lord Fraser may have had in mind in uttering the *dicta* in question, it cannot, in my opinion, have been a building with a latent defect which must inevitably result in damage at some stage. That is precisely the kind of building that *Pirelli* was concerned with, and in relation to which it was held that the cause of action accrued when the damage occurred. This case is undistinguishable from *Pirelli* and must be decided similarly.'

The start of the limitation period may be postponed by ineffective remedial work which delays the moment at which the building becomes a danger to health or safety. This was so held by an official referee in *Billam and Billam* v. *Cheltenham Borough Council* (1985) since the plaintiffs' cause of action against the negligent local authority only arose when there was 'present or imminent danger to the health or safety of the' occupiers. The effect of the remedial work, although ultimately unsuccessful, was to postpone the moment at which the relevant danger arose and therefore to postpone the start of the limitation period.

The start of the limitation period will also be postponed where there is fraud, deliberate concealment or mistake. This is provided for by section 32 of the Limitation Act 1980. 'Fraud' is not limited to criminal fraud but includes deliberate concealment of a breach of duty (including negligence and breach of statutory duty) and, by section 32(2) deliberate concealment includes circumstances where there has been a deliberate breach of duty which is unlikely to be discovered for some time. 'Deliberate concealment' was considered by Sir William Stabb QC, sitting as a deputy official referee, in *Gray and Others (Special Trustees of the London Hospital)* v. *T.P. Bennett & Son* (1987), where a hospital had been built in 1962 and 1963. In November 1979 a bulge was noticed in the brickwork panel. It was then discovered that inaccuracies made when setting out concrete panels had resulted in lack of fit in brick cladding, and that during construction concrete nibs had been severely hacked back to attempt to accommodate the brickwork. Judgement was given for the employer against the contractor, the judge finding that this wrongful and destructive action was deliberately concealed from the plaintiffs' supervisors. As a result, section 32 of the 1980 Act meant that the limitation period did not begin to run until the plaintiffs had, or could with reasonable diligence have, discovered the concealment. That was in November 1979 when the bulge in the brickwork was discovered. Interestingly, the judge also held that since the contractor's employees had deliberately concealed the bad work from the plaintiffs' supervisers, that amounted to fraudulent concealment which prevented the contractors from relying on the final certificate under the building contract that the works had been properly carried out. 'The final certificate was rendered invalid on the principle that fraud unravels all', he said.

The Latent Damage Act 1986

On 29 November 1984, the Law Reform Committee published a report on latent damage (Cmnd 9390) which concluded that the then law of limitation gave rise to uncertainty and might cause injustice to both plaintiffs and defendants. Latent damage is damage which may lie hidden for many years after the negligence which caused it – defective foundations are a typical example – and by the time the damage is discovered or becomes discoverable, the plaintiff's claim might be statute-barred under the ruling in *Pirelli*.

The Law Reform Committee also found that the rules were unfair to defendants in such cases. In particular, the difficulty of establishing satisfactorily the date when damage actually occurred meant that potentially liability might be open-ended. Accordingly, the Committee recommended changes in the law, and this recommendation resulted in the enactment of the Latent Damage Act 1986. It came into force on 18 September 1986, and does not apply to any action commenced before that date, nor does it enable actions to be brought in respect of damage which occurred before 18 September 1986.

The Act is extremely complex, and its main provisions are:

- In the case of latent damage not involving personal injuries, the action can be brought *either* six years from the date on which the cause of action accrued *or* three years from the 'starting date' if that is later.

The 'starting date' is the earliest date on which the plaintiff (or any person in whom the cause of action was vested before him) had knowledge of the material facts about the damage and a right to bring such an action: 1986 Act, section 1. The three years can be extended where the plaintiff is under a disability.

This is a new section 14A of the Limitation Act 1980. Curiously, 'latent damage' is not defined. Section 14A applies to 'any action for damages for negligence' for latent damage not involving personal injuries. 'Negligence' is not defined in the Act, but it is thought to cover not only actions for the tort of negligence but also the negligent breach by local authorities of their building control powers.

- There is an overall 15 year long stop from the date of the breach of duty to which the damage is attributable: 1980 Act, section 14B. This protects defendants from stale claims. The 15 year long stop runs from the date of the *breach of duty*. This is not necessarily the date of the completion of the building. 'Breach of duty' is defined as the date (or last date) on which there occurred 'any act or omission which is alleged to constitute negligence and to which the damage is attributable'. In the case of fraud, concealment or mistake, time does not begin to run out until the plaintiff had discovered the fraud, etc., or could with reasonable diligence have discovered it. In all other cases, however, once the 15 years has expired, no action can be brought. This applies whether or not the relevant facts were known and even if the damage has not yet occurred.

Illustration

The longstop would apply and any action would be time-barred:

January 1971	Breach of duty
January 1981	Damage occurs
January 1985	Damage discoverable
January 1986	Act in force
March 1987	Writ issued

This is a straightforward example and there are many variations on the theme. Because of the practice of joining as many defendants as possible, the limitation period operates in different ways. A claim against a negligent local authority in respect of a building regulations inspection in January 1968 would be barred where the danger to health and safety occurred in March 1981 and the writ was not issued until February 1987. On the same facts, the action against the builder would not be barred where he had unsuccessfully tried to repair the damage in November 1980, the final certificate under the building contract having been issued in December 1972.

● Section 3 of the Latent Damage Act 1986 stands on its own and provides a cause of action in respect of latent damage for successive owners. It applies, for example, where someone purchases a house which has a latent defect and then sells it to someone else 'before the material facts about the damage have become known to any person who, at the time when he first has knowledge of those facts, has any interest in the property'. In those circumstances, the second purchaser acquires a fresh cause of action on the date on which he acquires his interest in the property. In fact, how this provision is intended to operate in practice is the subject of debate amongst legal commentators, but effectively the purchaser gets a 3 year extension, subject to the overall long stop of 15 years.

A comprehensive treatment of the Act and its impact on the construction industry will be found in *The Latent Damage Act 1986* (1987) by Phillip Capper, where the many problems are fully discussed.

II
Technical

Chapter 6

Structural stability

Introduction

Part A of Schedule 1 to the Building Regulations 1985 is concerned with the strength, stability and resistance to deformation of the building and its parts. The loads to be allowed for in the design calculations are specified, and recommendations as to construction are given.

In line with the Government's intention to remove from the regulations those matters which are not directly concerned with public health and safety or the conservation of fuel and power, the previous requirements regarding the ability of a building structure or foundation to resist *damage* due to settlement etc., have been omitted.

Additionally, control of deflection or deformation of the building structure is only relevant if it would impair the stability of *another* building.

It is conceivable, therefore, that a building, constructed under the regulations, could be safe and stable but could settle and deflect to such an extent that it would be ususable. In that event, of course, the owner would probably have redress against the designer and/or builder under the general law by way of an action for damages.

The section of the regulations dealing with disproportionate collapse has been extended to include public buildings with clear spans in excess of 9 m in addition to the previous requirements for buildings of five storeys or more.

Loading

Buildings must be constructed so that all dead, imposed and wind loads are sustained and transmitted to the ground: Regs Sch. 1 A1

(a) safely, and,
(b) without causing such settlement of the ground, or such deflection or deformation of the building, as will impair the stability of any other building.

The imposed and wind loads referred to above are those to which the building is likely to be subjected in the normal course of its use and for the purpose for which it is intended.

Structural safety depends on the successful interrelationship between design and construction, particularly with regard to:

- Degree of loading.
- The properties of the materials chosen.
- The design analysis used.
- Constructional details.
- Safety factors.
- Standards of workmanship on site.

Approved Document A1/2 sets out three alternative approaches which may be adopted, if relevant, at the discretion of the designer. Where precise guidance is not given regard should be given to the factors listed above.

- Section 1 allows the sizes of certain structural members to be assessed in small buildings of traditional masonry construction.
- Section 2 lists various codes and standards for structural design and construction and is relevant to all types of buildings.
- Other approaches may be adopted but it is clear that no guidance can be given for novel or unusual building structures – these must be judged on their own merits. Allowance should be made, however, for possible dynamic, concentrated or peak load effects
that may occur in a building.

Design of structural members in houses and other small buildings

Definitions

The following definitions apply throughout section 1 of AD A1/2.

BUTTRESSING WALL – a wall which provides lateral support, from base to top, to another wall perpendicular to it.

CAVITY WIDTH – the horizontal distance between the leaves in a cavity wall.

COMPARTMENT WALL – see Chapter 7, Fire.

DEAD LOAD – the load due to the weight of all roofs, floors, walls and partitions i.e. all the permanent construction.

IMPOSED LOAD – the load assumed to be produced by the intended occupancy or use, including distributed, concentrated, impact, inertia and snow loads, but *excluding* wind loads.

PIER – an integral part of a wall which consists of a thickened section occurring at intervals along a wall to which it is bonded or securely tied so as to afford lateral support.

SEPARATING WALL – a wall which is common to two adjoining buildings (see Chapter 7, Fire, p. 7.1).

SPACING – the centre to centre distance between two adjacent timbers measured in a plane parallel to the plane of the structure of which they form part.

SPAN – the distance measured along the centre line of a member between centres of adjacent bearings. (However, it should be noted that the spans given in the tables for floor joists, rafters, purlins, ceiling joists, binders and roof joists are *clear spans* i.e. measured between the faces of supports.)

SUPPORTED WALL – a wall which is supported by buttressing walls, piers or chimneys, or floor or roof lateral support arrangements.

WIND LOADS – all loads due to the effect of wind pressure or suction.

AD A1/2
sec. 1
1.3.

Structural stability

The basic stability of a small house of traditional masonry construction is largely dependent on the provision of a braced roof structure which is adequately anchored to walls restrained laterally by buttressing walls, piers or chimneys. If this can be achieved then it should not be necessary to take additional precautions against wind loading.

A traditional fully boarded or hipped roof provides in-built resistance to instability however, where this is not provided then extra wind bracing may be required.

Trussed rafter roofs have, in the past, been susceptible to collapse during high winds. If this form of construction is used it should be braced in accordance with BS 5268: *Code of practice for the structural use of timber;* Part 3: 1985 *Code of practice for trussed rafter roofs.* The recommendations of this code may also be used for traditional roofs where bracing is inadequate.

Small buildings of masonry construction having walls designed in accordance with Part C of section 1 of AD A1/2 and roofs and floors designed in accordance with Part B of section 1 of AD A1/2 will be satisfactory with regard to structural stability if the roof is braced as mentioned above.

AD A1/2
sec. 1
Part A
A1 to A3

Structural work of timber in single family houses

Part B of section 1 of AD A1/2 provides that if the work concerned is in a floor, ceiling or roof of a single occupancy house of not more than three storeys, that work will be satisfactory if the grades and dimensions of the timbers used are at least equal to those given in Tables B3 to B28 of AD A1/2 and if the work complies in other respects with BS 5268 *Code of practice for the structural use of timber; Part 2: 1984 Code of practice for permissible stress design, materials and workmanship.*

In effect this means that for a house of this type it is not necessary to calculate the size of joists, rafters, purlins, etc.; one merely selects the appropriate sizes from the tables in AD A1/2. Unusual load or support conditions might necessitate a check calculation by the recommendations in BS 5268: Part 2: 1984.

Tables B3 to B28 apply to all floor, ceiling and roof timbers in a single occupancy house of three storeys or less.

The timber used for any binder, beam, joist, purlin or rafter must be of a species, origin and grade specified in Table B1 to AD A1/2 (see below) or as given in the more comprehensive tables of BS 5268: Part 2: 1984.

When using Tables B3 to B28 the following points should also be taken into account:

● The imposed load to be sustained by the floor, ceiling or roof of which the member forms part should not exceed:

(a) In the case of a floor, 1.5 kN/m^2 (Tables B3 and B4).
(b) In the case of a ceiling, 0.25 kN/m^2 and a concentrated load of 0.9 kN acting with the imposed load (Tables B5 to B8).
(c) In the case of a flat roof with access not limited to the purposes of maintenance or repair, 1.5 kN/m^2 or a concentrated load of 1.8 kN (Tables B23 and B24).
(d) In the case of a roof (flat or pitched up to 30°) with access only for maintenance, 0.75 kN/m^2 or a concentrated load of 0.9 kN (Tables B9 to B16 inclusive, B21 and B22).
(e) In the case of a roof pitched at more than 30°, with maintenance and repair access only, 0.75 kN/m^2, less 50 N/m^2 for every 3° by which the pitch exceeds 30° (Tables B17 to B20 inclusive).
(f) In the case of a roof supporting sheeting or decking pitched at between 10° and 35°, 0.75 kN/m^2 measured on slope, less 50 N/m^2 for every 3° by which the pitch exceeds 30° (Tables B25 to B28 inclusive).

● Floorboarding is assumed to comply with BS 1297: 1970 *Grading and sizing of softwood flooring* and Table 6.1. (See below).
● Unless otherwise stated, cross-sectional dimensions given in the tables are basic sawn sizes from BS 4471 *Specification for dimensions for softwood,* Part 1: 1978 *Sizes of sawn and planed timber.*
● Notches and holes in floor and roof joists should comply with Fig. 6.1.

AD A1/2

Table **B1**   **Common species/grade combinations** which satisfy the requirements for the strength classes to which Tables B2 to B28 relate[1]

Species	Origin	Grading rules[2]	Grades to satisfy strength class	
			SC3	SC4
Redwood	imported	BS 4978	GS, M50	SS, M75†
Whitewood	imported	BS 4978	GS, M50	SS, M75†
Douglas Fir-Larch	Canada Canada	BS 4978 joist and plank structural light framing	GS No. 1, No. 2 No. 1, No. 2	SS select select
Hem-Fir	Canada	BS 4978 joist and plank structural light framing	GS, M50 No. 1, No. 2 No. 1, No. 2	SS, M75 select select
Spruce-Pine-Fir	Canada	BS 4978 joist and plank structural light framing	GS, M50 No. 1, No. 2 No. 1, No. 2	SS, M75 select select
Western Whitewoods	USA	BS 4978 joist and plank structural light framing	SS select select	
Southern Pine	USA	BS 4978 joist and plank structural light framing light framing stud	GS No. 1, No. 2, No. 3 No. 1, No. 2, No. 3 Construction* Stud*	SS select select
Douglas Fir	UK	BS 4978	M50, SS	M75
Scots Pine	UK	BS 4978	GS, M50	SS, M75†
European Spruce	UK	BS 4978	M75	
Sitka Spruce	UK	BS 4978	M75	

Notes

[1] The common species/grade combinations given in this table are for particular use with the other tables in this Part and for the cross section sizes given in those tables.

Definitive and more comprehensive tables for assigning species/grade combinations to strength classes are given in BS 5268: Part 2: 1984.

[2] The grading rules for American and Canadian Lumber are those approved by the American Lumber Standards Board of Review and the Canadian Lumber Standards Accreditation Board respectively (*see* BS 5268: Part 2: 1984)

* Only 38mm × 89mm cross section.

† These species/grade combinations given under SC4 may qualify for SC5 but have been listed here for use with the table.

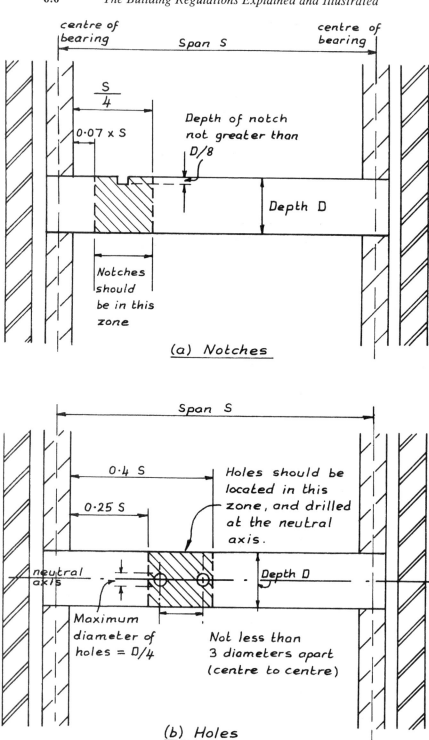

Fig. 6.1 Notches and holes in floor and roof joists.

(a)   Floor joists , small house.

Dead load not more than 0·25 kN/m².

Clear span 4 m , Centres 400 mm, Timber of strength Class SC3.

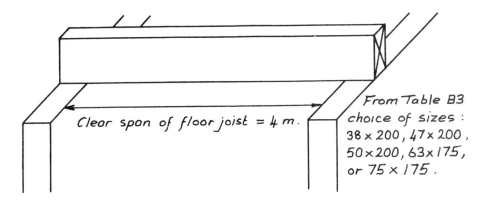

Clear span of floor joist = 4 m.

From Table B3 choice of sizes : 38 x 200, 47 x 200, 50 x 200, 63 x 175, or 75 x 175.

(b)   Rafter , small house.

Pitch 15° , Dead load not more than 0·50 kN/m²

Clear span 2·90 m , Centres 400 mm , Timber of strength Class SC3.

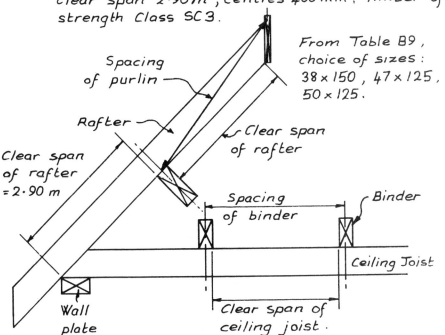

From Table B9 , choice of sizes : 38 x 150 , 47 x 125, 50 x 125.

Spacing of purlin

Rafter

Clear span of rafter

Clear span of rafter = 2·90 m

Spacing of binder

Binder

Ceiling Joist

Wall plate

Clear span of ceiling joist.

Fig. 6.2 Example of application of Tables B3 to B28.

AD A1/2

Table **B3**   **Floor joists**

Timber of strength class **SC3** *(see Table B1)*

Size of joist [mm × mm]	Not more than 0.25			More than 0.25 but not more than 0.50			More than 0.50 but not more than 1.25		
	400	**450**	**600**	**400**	**450**	**600**	**400**	**450**	**600**
	Maximum clear span of joist [m]								
38 × 75	1.22	1.09	0.83	1.14	1.03	0.79	0.98	0.89	0.70
38 × 89*	1.62	1.47	1.12	1.50	1.36	1.06	1.26	1.15	0.91
38 × 100	1.91	1.78	1.38	1.80	1.64	1.28	1.49	1.36	1.09
38 × 125	2.54	2.45	2.01	2.43	2.30	1.83	2.01	1.85	1.50
38 × 140*	2.85	2.74	2.40	2.72	2.59	2.17	2.33	2.15	1.76
38 × 150	3.05	2.93	2.56	2.91	2.76	2.40	2.50	2.35	1.93
38 × 175	3.55	3.40	2.96	3.37	3.19	2.77	2.89	2.73	2.36
38 × 184*	3.73	3.56	3.10	3.53	3.34	2.90	3.03	2.86	2.48
38 × 200	4.04	3.85	3.35	3.82	3.61	3.13	3.27	3.09	2.68
38 × 225	4.53	4.29	3.73	4.25	4.02	3.50	3.65	3.44	2.99
47 × 75	1.41	1.33	1.02	1.35	1.24	0.96	1.16	1.06	0.84
47 × 100	2.11	2.00	1.67	2.00	1.90	1.54	1.74	1.60	1.29
47 × 125	2.73	2.63	2.38	2.61	2.51	2.17	2.33	2.15	1.76
47 × 150	3.27	3.14	2.84	3.13	3.01	2.66	2.78	2.62	2.24
47 × 175	3.80	3.66	3.28	3.64	3.50	3.07	3.21	3.03	2.63
47 × 200	4.33	4.17	3.71	4.15	3.99	3.48	3.63	3.43	2.98
47 × 225	4.81	4.67	4.13	4.65	4.45	3.88	4.04	3.82	3.32
50 × 75	1.45	1.37	1.08	1.39	1.30	1.01	1.22	1.11	0.88
50 × 100	2.18	2.06	1.76	2.06	1.95	1.62	1.82	1.67	1.35
50 × 125	2.79	2.68	2.44	2.67	2.56	2.28	2.40	2.24	1.84
50 × 150	3.33	3.21	2.92	3.19	3.07	2.75	2.86	2.70	2.33
50 × 175	3.88	3.73	3.38	3.71	3.57	3.17	3.30	3.12	2.71
50 × 200	4.42	4.25	3.82	4.23	4.07	3.58	3.74	3.53	3.07
50 × 225	4.88	4.74	4.26	4.72	4.57	3.99	4.16	3.94	3.42
63 × 100	2.41	2.29	2.01	2.28	2.17	1.90	2.01	1.91	1.60
63 × 125	3.00	2.89	2.63	2.88	2.77	2.52	2.59	2.49	2.16
63 × 150	3.59	3.46	3.15	3.44	3.31	3.01	3.10	2.98	2.63
63 × 175	4.17	4.02	3.66	4.00	3.85	3.51	3.61	3.47	3.03
63 × 200	4.73	4.58	4.18	4.56	4.39	4.00	4.11	3.95	3.43
63 × 225	5.15	5.01	4.68	4.99	4.85	4.46	4.62	4.40	3.83
75 × 125	3.18	3.06	2.79	3.04	2.93	2.67	2.74	2.64	2.40
75 × 150	3.79	3.66	3.33	3.64	3.50	3.19	3.28	3.16	2.86
75 × 175	4.41	4.25	3.88	4.23	4.07	3.71	3.82	3.68	3.30
75 × 200	4.92	4.79	4.42	4.77	4.64	4.23	4.35	4.19	3.74
75 × 225	5.36	5.22	4.88	5.20	5.06	4.72	4.82	4.69	4.16

Notes

* North American surfaced size
† Dead load is the load supported by the joist, excluding the mass of the joist

Partition loads have not been allowed for in Tables B3 and B4

AD A1/2

Table **B4**　**Floor joists**

Timber of strength class **SC4** *(see Table B1)*

Size of joist [mm × mm]	Dead load† [kN/m²]								
	Not more than 0.25			More than 0.25 but not more than 0.50			More than 0.50 but not more than 1.25		
	Spacing of joists [mm]								
	400	450	600	400	450	600	400	450	600
	Maximum clear span of joist [m]								
38 × 75	1.34	1.26	1.09	1.29	1.22	1.05	1.17	1.11	0.93
38 × 89*	1.72	1.62	1.40	1.64	1.55	1.34	1.47	1.39	1.21
38 × 100	2.02	1.91	1.66	1.92	1.82	1.58	1.70	1.62	1.42
38 × 125	2.65	2.55	2.28	2.53	2.43	2.15	2.25	2.14	1.89
38 × 140*	2.96	2.85	2.59	2.83	2.72	2.47	2.54	2.44	2.18
38 × 150	3.17	3.05	2.77	3.03	2.91	2.65	2.72	2.62	2.37
38 × 175	3.69	3.55	3.22	3.53	3.39	3.08	3.17	3.05	2.76
38 × 184*	3.87	3.73	3.39	3.71	3.57	3.24	3.33	3.20	2.90
38 × 200	4.20	4.04	3.68	4.02	3.87	3.52	3.62	3.48	3.15
38 × 225	4.70	4.54	4.13	4.52	4.35	3.95	4.07	3.91	3.54
47 × 75	1.49	1.41	1.22	1.43	1.35	1.17	1.29	1.23	1.07
47 × 100	2.23	2.12	1.84	2.11	2.00	1.75	1.87	1.77	1.56
47 × 125	2.84	2.73	2.48	2.72	2.61	2.37	2.44	2.34	2.07
47 × 150	3.40	3.27	2.97	3.25	3.13	2.84	2.93	2.81	2.55
47 × 175	3.95	3.80	3.46	3.78	3.64	3.31	3.41	3.28	2.97
47 × 200	4.50	4.33	3.95	4.31	4.15	3.78	3.89	3.74	3.39
47 × 225	4.94	4.81	4.43	4.79	4.66	4.24	4.36	4.20	3.81
50 × 75	1.54	1.45	1.26	1.47	1.39	1.21	1.33	1.26	1.10
50 × 100	2.30	2.18	1.90	2.17	2.06	1.80	1.92	1.82	1.61
50 × 125	2.90	2.79	2.53	2.77	2.67	2.42	2.50	2.40	2.13
50 × 150	3.46	3.34	3.03	3.32	3.19	2.90	2.99	2.87	2.61
50 × 175	4.03	3.88	3.53	3.86	3.71	3.38	3.48	3.34	3.04
50 × 200	4.59	4.42	4.03	4.40	4.23	3.85	3.97	3.81	3.46
50 × 225	5.02	4.88	4.52	4.86	4.73	4.33	4.45	4.28	3.89
63 × 100	2.51	2.41	2.12	2.40	2.28	2.01	2.11	2.01	1.78
63 × 125	3.12	3.01	2.74	2.99	2.88	2.62	2.69	2.59	2.35
63 × 150	3.73	3.59	3.27	3.58	3.44	3.13	3.22	3.10	2.82
63 × 175	4.33	4.18	3.81	4.16	4.00	3.65	3.75	3.61	3.28
63 × 200	4.86	4.73	4.34	4.71	4.56	4.16	4.28	4.12	3.74
63 × 225	5.29	5.15	4.81	5.13	4.99	4.66	4.76	4.62	4.20
75 × 125	3.30	3.18	2.90	3.16	3.05	2.77	2.85	2.75	2.50
75 × 150	3.94	3.80	3.46	3.78	3.64	3.32	3.41	3.28	2.99
75 × 175	4.57	4.41	4.03	4.39	4.23	3.86	3.97	3.82	3.48
75 × 200	5.06	4.93	4.59	4.91	4.78	4.40	4.52	4.36	3.97
75 × 225	5.51	5.36	5.02	5.34	5.20	4.86	4.96	4.82	4.45

Notes
* North American surfaced size
† Dead load is the load supported by the joist, excluding the mass of the joist

Partition loads have not been allowed for in Tables B3 and B4

AD A1/2

Table **B5** **Ceiling joists**

Timber of strength class **SC3** *(see Table B1)*

Size of joist [mm × mm]	Dead load† [kN/m²]					
	Not more than 0.25			More than 0.25 but not more than 0.50		
	Spacing of joists [mm]					
	400	450	600	400	450	600
	Maximum clear span of joist [m]					
38 × 75	1.21	1.20	1.17	1.17	1.16	1.12
38 × 89*	1.54	1.53	1.48	1.48	1.46	1.41
38 × 100	1.81	1.79	1.74	1.74	1.71	1.64
38 × 125	2.45	2.41	2.32	2.32	2.28	2.18
38 × 140*	2.84	2.79	2.68	2.68	2.63	2.51
38 × 150	3.10	3.05	2.93	2.93	2.87	2.73
38 × 175	3.77	3.70	3.54	3.54	3.46	3.28
38 × 184*	4.01	3.94	3.76	3.76	3.68	3.48
38 × 200	4.44	4.36	4.15	4.15	4.06	3.83
38 × 225	5.11	5.02	4.77	4.77	4.66	4.39
47 × 75	1.35	1.33	1.30	1.30	1.28	1.24
47 × 100	2.00	1.98	1.91	1.91	1.88	1.80
47 × 125	2.69	2.65	2.55	2.55	2.50	2.38
47 × 150	3.39	3.34	3.19	3.19	3.13	2.97
47 × 175	4.10	4.03	3.85	3.85	3.77	3.56
47 × 200	4.82	4.73	4.50	4.50	4.41	4.16
47 × 225	5.54	5.43	5.16	5.16	5.04	4.75
50 × 75	1.39	1.38	1.34	1.34	1.32	1.28
50 × 100	2.06	2.03	1.96	1.96	1.93	1.85
50 × 125	2.76	2.72	2.61	2.61	2.57	2.45
50 × 150	3.48	3.42	3.28	3.28	3.21	3.05
50 × 175	4.21	4.13	3.94	3.94	3.86	3.65
50 × 200	4.94	4.85	4.61	4.61	4.51	4.25
50 × 225	5.66	5.56	5.28	5.28	5.16	4.86

Notes

* North American surfaced size
† Dead load is the load supported by the joist, excluding the mass of the joist

In calculating the ceiling joist sizes no account has been taken of trimming (e.g. around flues) or other loads (e.g. water tanks).

AD A1/2

Table **B6** **Binders** supporting ceiling joists

Timber of strength class **SC3** *(see Table B1)*

Size of binder [mm × mm]	Dead load† [kN/m²]											
	Not more than 0.25						More than 0.25 but not more than 0.50					
	Spacing of binders [mm]											
	1200	1500	1800	2100	2400	2700	1200	1500	1800	2100	2400	2700
	Maximum clear span of binder [m]											
38 × 89*	1.05	1.00	0.97	0.93	0.90	0.88	0.98	0.93	0.89	0.86	0.83	0.80
38 × 100	1.21	1.16	1.11	1.07	1.04	1.01	1.13	1.07	1.02	0.98	0.95	0.92
38 × 125	1.60	1.52	1.46	1.40	1.35	1.31	1.47	1.39	1.33	1.27	1.23	1.18
38 × 140*	1.83	1.74	1.66	1.60	1.54	1.49	1.68	1.59	1.51	1.45	1.39	1.34
38 × 150	1.99	1.88	1.80	1.73	1.67	1.61	1.82	1.72	1.64	1.56	1.50	1.45
38 × 175	2.38	2.25	2.15	2.06	1.98	1.91	2.18	2.05	1.94	1.86	1.78	1.72
38 × 184*	2.52	2.38	2.27	2.18	2.09	2.02	2.30	2.17	2.05	1.96	1.88	1.80
38 × 200	2.77	2.62	2.49	2.39	2.30	2.22	2.53	2.38	2.25	2.15	2.06	1.94
38 × 225	3.17	2.99	2.84	2.72	2.61	2.52	2.88	2.70	2.56	2.44	2.31	2.17
47 × 100	1.33	1.27	1.22	1.18	1.14	1.11	1.24	1.17	1.12	1.08	1.04	1.01
47 × 125	1.75	1.66	1.59	1.53	1.48	1.43	1.61	1.52	1.45	1.39	1.34	1.29
47 × 150	2.17	2.06	1.96	1.89	1.82	1.76	1.99	1.88	1.78	1.71	1.64	1.58
47 × 175	2.59	2.45	2.34	2.24	2.16	2.09	2.37	2.23	2.12	2.02	1.94	1.87
47 × 200	3.01	2.85	2.71	2.60	2.50	2.41	2.75	2.58	2.45	2.34	2.24	2.16
47 × 225	3.44	3.24	3.08	2.95	2.84	2.74	3.13	2.93	2.78	2.65	2.54	2.42
50 × 100	1.37	1.31	1.26	1.21	1.17	1.14	1.27	1.21	1.15	1.11	1.07	1.03
50 × 125	1.80	1.71	1.63	1.57	1.52	1.47	1.65	1.56	1.49	1.43	1.37	1.33
50 × 150	2.22	2.11	2.01	1.93	1.86	1.80	2.04	1.92	1.83	1.75	1.68	1.62
50 × 175	2.66	2.51	2.39	2.30	2.21	2.14	2.43	2.28	2.17	2.07	1.99	1.92
50 × 200	3.09	2.91	2.78	2.66	2.56	2.47	2.81	2.64	2.51	2.39	2.30	2.21
50 × 225	3.52	3.32	3.16	3.02	2.90	2.80	3.20	3.00	2.85	2.72	2.61	2.49
63 × 100	1.51	1.44	1.39	1.34	1.29	1.25	1.40	1.33	1.27	1.22	1.18	1.14
63 × 125	1.97	1.88	1.79	1.73	1.67	1.61	1.82	1.72	1.64	1.57	1.51	1.46
63 × 150	2.44	2.31	2.21	2.12	2.04	1.98	2.24	2.11	2.00	1.92	1.84	1.78
63 × 175	2.90	2.75	2.62	2.51	2.42	2.34	2.65	2.50	2.37	2.27	2.18	2.10
63 × 200	3.37	3.18	3.03	2.90	2.79	2.70	3.07	2.89	2.74	2.62	2.51	2.42
63 × 225	3.83	3.62	3.44	3.29	3.17	3.06	3.49	3.28	3.11	2.96	2.85	2.74
75 × 125	2.12	2.01	1.92	1.85	1.79	1.73	1.95	1.84	1.75	1.68	1.62	1.56
75 × 150	2.61	2.47	2.36	2.26	2.18	2.11	2.39	2.25	2.14	2.05	1.97	1.90
75 × 175	3.10	2.93	2.80	2.68	2.58	2.50	2.83	2.67	2.53	2.42	2.33	2.25
75 × 200	3.59	3.39	3.23	3.10	2.98	2.88	3.28	3.08	2.92	2.79	2.68	2.59
75 × 225	4.08	3.85	3.66	3.51	3.38	3.26	3.72	3.49	3.31	3.16	3.04	2.93

Notes

* North American surfaced size

† Dead load is the load supported by the joist, excluding the mass of the joist as calculated for the purpose of Table B5

In calculating the ceiling joist sizes no account has been taken of trimming (e.g. around flues) or other loads (e.g. water tanks)

l

AD A1/2

Table **B7**   **Ceiling joists**

Timber of strength class **SC4** *(see Table B1)*

Size of joist [mm × mm]	Dead load† [kN/m²]					
	Not more than 0.25			More than 0.25 but not more than 0.50		
	Spacing of joists [mm]					
	400	450	600	400	450	600
	Maximum clear span of joist [m]					
38 × 75	1.29	1.28	1.24	1.24	1.23	1.19
38 × 89*	1.63	1.62	1.57	1.57	1.55	1.49
38 × 100	1.92	1.89	1.83	1.83	1.80	1.73
38 × 125	2.58	2.54	2.45	2.45	2.40	2.29
38 × 140*	2.99	2.94	2.82	2.82	2.77	2.63
38 × 150	3.26	3.21	3.07	3.07	3.01	2.86
38 × 175	3.95	3.89	3.71	3.71	3.63	3.44
38 × 184*	4.21	4.13.	3.94	3.94	3.86	3.64
38 × 200	4.65	4.57	4.35	4.35	4.25	4.01
38 × 225	5.35	5.25	4.99	4.99	4.87	4.59
47 × 75	1.43	1.41	1.37	1.37	1.36	1.31
47 × 100	2.11	2.08	2.01	2.01	1.98	1.90
47 × 125	2.83	2.79	2.68	2.68	2.63	2.50
47 × 150	3.56	3.50	3.35	3.35	3.29	3.12
47 × 175	4.30	4.23	4.03	4.03	3.95	3.73
47 × 200	5.05	4.95	4.71	4.71	4.61	4.35
47 × 225	5.79	5.68	5.39	5.39	5.27	4.96
50 × 75	1.47	1.45	1.41	1.41	1.40	1.35
50 × 100	2.17	2.14	2.07	2.07	2.04	1.95
50 × 125	2.90	2.86	2.75	2.75	2.70	2.57
50 × 150	3.65	3.59	3.44	3.44	3.37	3.19
50 × 175	4.41	4.33	4.13	4.13	4.04	3.82
50 × 200	5.16	5.07	4.82	4.82	4.72	4.45
50 × 225	5.92	5.80	5.51	5.51	5.39	5.07

Notes

* North American surfaced size

† Dead load is the load supported by the joist, excluding the mass of the joist

In calculating the ceiling joist sizes no account has been taken of trimming (e.g. around flues) or other loads (e.g. water tanks)

AD A1/2

Table **B8** **Binders** supporting ceiling joists

Timber of strength class **SC4** *(see Table B1)*

	Dead load† [kN/m²]											
	Not more than 0.25						More than 0.25 but not more than 0.50					
	Spacing of binders [mm]											
	1200	1500	1800	2100	2400	2700	1200	1500	1800	2100	2400	2700
Size of binder [mm × mm]	Maximum clear span of binder [m]											
38 × 89*	1.11	1.06	1.02	0.99	0.95	0.93	1.03	0.98	0.94	0.90	0.87	0.85
38 × 100	1.28	1.22	1.18	1.13	1.10	1.06	1.19	1.13	1.08	1.04	1.00	0.97
38 × 125	1.68	1.60	1.53	1.47	1.42	1.38	1.55	1.47	1.40	1.34	1.29	1.25
38 × 140*	1.93	1.83	1.75	1.68	1.62	1.57	1.77	1.67	1.59	1.52	1.46	1.41
38 × 150	2.09	1.98	1.89	1.82	1.75	1.69	1.92	1.81	1.72	1.65	1.58	1.53
38 × 175	2.50	2.36	2.25	2.16	2.08	2.01	2.29	2.15	2.04	1.95	1.87	1.80
38 × 184*	2.65	2.50	2.38	2.28	2.20	2.12	2.42	2.27	2.16	2.06	1.98	1.91
38 × 200	2.91	2.75	2.61	2.50	2.41	2.32	2.65	2.49	2.36	2.26	2.16	2.08
38 × 225	3.32	3.13	2.97	2.85	2.74	2.64	3.02	2.83	2.68	2.56	2.46	2.36
47 × 100	1.41	1.34	1.29	1.24	1.20	1.17	1.31	1.24	1.18	1.14	1.10	1.06
47 × 125	1.84	1.75	1.67	1.61	1.55	1.50	1.70	1.60	1.53	1.46	1.41	1.36
47 × 150	2.28	2.16	2.06	1.98	1.91	1.84	2.09	1.97	1.87	1.79	1.72	1.66
47 × 175	2.72	2.57	2.45	2.35	2.26	2.18	2.49	2.34	2.22	2.12	2.04	1.96
47 × 200	3.16	2.98	2.84	2.72	2.61	2.52	2.88	2.71	2.57	2.45	2.35	2.27
47 × 225	3.60	3.39	3.23	3.09	2.97	2.86	3.28	3.07	2.91	2.78	2.67	2.57
50 × 100	1.44	1.38	1.32	1.28	1.23	1.20	1.34	1.27	1.21	1.17	1.12	1.09
50 × 125	1.89	1.79	1.72	1.65	1.59	1.54	1.74	1.64	1.57	1.50	1.44	1.40
50 × 150	2.34	2.21	2.11	2.03	1.95	1.89	2.14	2.02	1.92	1.84	1.77	1.70
50 × 175	2.78	2.63	2.51	2.40	2.32	2.24	2.55	2.40	2.27	2.17	2.09	2.01
50 × 200	3.23	3.05	2.90	2.78	2.68	2.59	2.95	2.77	2.63	2.51	2.41	2.32
50 × 225	3.68	3.47	3.30	3.16	3.04	2.93	3.35	3.15	2.98	2.85	2.73	2.63
63 × 100	1.59	1.52	1.46	1.40	1.36	1.32	1.48	1.40	1.34	1.28	1.24	1.20
63 × 125	2.07	1.97	1.88	1.81	1.75	1.69	1.91	1.80	1.72	1.65	1.58	1.53
63 × 150	2.56	2.42	2.31	2.22	2.14	2.07	2.34	2.21	2.10	2.01	1.93	1.87
63 × 175	3.04	2.87	2.74	2.63	2.53	2.44	2.78	2.62	2.48	2.37	2.28	2.20
63 × 200	3.52	3.33	3.17	3.03	2.92	2.82	3.22	3.02	2.87	2.74	2.63	2.53
63 × 225	4.01	3.78	3.59	3.44	3.31	3.20	3.65	3.43	3.25	3.10	2.98	2.87
75 × 125	2.22	2.11	2.02	1.94	1.87	1.81	2.04	1.93	1.84	1.76	1.70	1.64
75 × 150	2.73	2.59	2.47	2.37	2.28	2.21	2.51	2.36	2.25	2.15	2.07	1.99
75 × 175	3.24	3.07	2.92	2.80	2.70	2.61	2.97	2.79	2.65	2.54	2.44	2.35
75 × 200	3.75	3.54	3.38	3.23	3.11	3.01	3.43	3.22	3.06	2.92	2.81	2.71
75 × 225	4.26	4.02	3.83	3.66	3.52	3.40	3.88	3.65	3.46	3.31	3.17	3.06

Notes

* North American surfaced size

† Dead load is the load supported by the joist, excluding the mass of the joist as calculated for the purpose of Table B7

In calculating the ceiling joist sizes no account has been taken of trimming (e.g. around flues) or other loads (e.g. water tanks)

AD A1/2

Table **B9** **Common or jack rafters** for roofs having a pitch more than 10° but not more than 22½° with access only for purposes of maintenance or repair

Timber of strength class **SC3** *(see Table B1)*

Size of rafter [mm × mm]	Dead load† [kN/m²]								
	Not more than 0.50			More than 0.50 but not more than 0.75			More than 0.75 but not more than 1.00		
	Spacing of rafters [mm]								
	400	450	600	400	450	600	400	450	600
	Maximum clear span of rafter [m]								
38 × 89*	1.54	1.51	1.44	1.44	1.41	1.33	1.36	1.33	1.24
38 × 100	1.85	1.82	1.72	1.72	1.68	1.57	1.62	1.57	1.46
38 × 125	2.50	2.44	2.30	2.30	2.24	2.08	2.15	2.08	1.92
38 × 140*	2.87	2.80	2.62	2.63	2.55	2.37	2.44	2.37	2.18
38 × 150	3.10	3.03	2.76	2.84	2.76	2.53	2.64	2.55	2.34
47 × 100	2.19	2.15	2.03	2.03	1.98	1.85	1.90	1.85	1.71
47 × 125	2.91	2.84	2.66	2.67	2.59	2.40	2.48	2.40	2.21
47 × 150	3.56	3.47	3.05	3.25	3.15	2.80	3.01	2.91	2.60
50 × 100	2.30	2.25	2.13	2.13	2.07	1.93	1.99	1.93	1.78
50 × 125	3.03	2.96	2.74	2.78	2.70	2.50	2.58	2.50	2.30
50 × 150	3.70	3.56	3.13	3.37	3.27	2.88	3.13	3.03	2.68

Notes
* North American surfaced size
† Dead load is the load supported by the rafter, excluding the mass of the rafter

AD A1/2

Table **B10** **Purlins** supporting rafters to which Table B9 refers

Timber of strength class **SC3** (*see Table B1*)

Size of purlin [mm × mm]	Dead load† [kN/m²]																	
	Not more than 0.50						More than 0.50 but not more than 0.75						More than 0.75 but not more than 1.00					
	Spacing of purlins [mm]																	
	1500	1800	2100	2400	2700	3000	1500	1800	2100	2400	2700	3000	1500	1800	2100	2400	2700	3000
	Maximum clear span of purlin [m]																	
50 × 100	1.27	1.16	1.07	1.00	0.94	0.89	1.16	1.06	0.98	0.91	0.86	0.81	1.07	0.98	0.90	0.84	0.79	0.75
50 × 125	1.58	1.44	1.33	1.25	1.17	1.11	1.44	1.32	1.22	1.14	1.07	1.01	1.34	1.22	1.13	1.05	0.99	0.94
50 × 150	1.89	1.72	1.59	1.49	1.40	1.33	1.73	1.58	1.46	1.36	1.28	1.21	1.60	1.46	1.35	1.26	1.18	1.12
50 × 175	2.20	2.00	1.85	1.73	1.63	1.55	2.01	1.83	1.69	1.58	1.49	1.41	1.86	1.70	1.57	1.46	1.38	1.30
50 × 200	2.50	2.28	2.11	1.97	1.86	1.76	2.29	2.09	1.93	1.80	1.70	1.61	2.12	1.93	1.79	1.67	1.57	1.49
50 × 225	2.80	2.56	2.37	2.21	2.09	1.98	2.56	2.34	2.16	2.02	1.90	1.80	2.38	2.17	2.00	1.87	1.76	1.67
63 × 100	1.41	1.29	1.19	1.11	1.05	0.99	1.29	1.18	1.09	1.02	0.96	0.91	1.20	1.09	1.01	0.94	0.89	0.84
63 × 125	1.76	1.60	1.48	1.39	1.31	1.24	1.61	1.46	1.36	1.27	1.19	1.13	1.49	1.36	1.25	1.17	1.10	1.05
63 × 150	2.10	1.92	1.77	1.66	1.56	1.48	1.92	1.75	1.62	1.52	1.43	1.35	1.78	1.62	1.50	1.40	1.32	1.25
63 × 175	2.44	2.23	2.06	1.93	1.82	1.72	2.23	2.04	1.89	1.76	1.66	1.57	2.07	1.89	1.75	1.63	1.54	1.46
63 × 200	2.78	2.54	2.35	2.20	2.07	1.96	2.54	2.32	2.15	2.01	1.89	1.79	2.36	2.15	1.99	1.86	1.75	1.66
63 × 225	3.12	2.85	2.64	2.47	2.32	2.20	2.85	2.61	2.41	2.25	2.12	2.01	2.65	2.42	2.23	2.09	1.97	1.86
75 × 125	1.90	1.73	1.61	1.50	1.42	1.34	1.74	1.59	1.47	1.37	1.29	1.23	1.61	1.47	1.36	1.27	1.20	1.13
75 × 150	2.27	2.07	1.92	1.80	1.69	1.61	2.08	1.90	1.76	1.64	1.55	1.47	1.93	1.76	1.63	1.52	1.43	1.36
75 × 175	2.64	2.41	2.23	2.09	1.97	1.87	2.42	2.21	2.04	1.91	1.80	1.71	2.24	2.05	1.89	1.77	1.67	1.58
75 × 200	3.01	2.75	2.55	2.38	2.25	2.13	2.75	2.52	2.33	2.18	2.05	1.95	2.55	2.33	2.16	2.02	1.90	1.80
75 × 225	3.37	3.08	2.86	2.67	2.52	2.39	3.09	2.82	2.61	2.44	2.30	2.18	2.87	2.62	2.42	2.27	2.13	2.02

Note
† Dead load is the load supported by the rafter as calculated for the purposes of Table B9

AD A1/2

Table **B11**   **Common or jack rafters** for roofs having a pitch more than 10° but not more than 22½° with access only for purposes of maintenance or repair

Timber of strength class **SC4** *(see Table B1)*

Size of rafter [mm × mm]	Dead load† [kN/m²]								
	Not more than 0.50			More than 0.50 but not more than 0.75			More than 0.75 but not more than 1.00		
	Spacing of rafters [mm]								
	400	450	600	400	450	600	400	450	600
	Maximum clear span of rafter [m]								
38 × 89*	1.98	1.94	1.84	1.84	1.79	1.68	1.73	1.68	1.55
38 × 100	2.36	2.31	2.18	2.18	2.12	1.97	2.03	1.97	1.82
38 × 125	3.09	3.01	2.75	2.82	2.74	2.52	2.62	2.54	2.33
38 × 140*	3.49	3.40	2.99	3.18	3.09	2.75	2.95	2.85	2.55
38 × 150	3.74	3.57	3.14	3.40	3.29	2.89	3.15	3.05	2.69
47 × 100	2.76	2.70	2.53	2.53	2.46	2.29	2.36	2.29	2.10
47 × 125	3.54	3.45	3.04	3.23	3.14	2.79	3.00	2.90	2.59
47 × 150	4.11	3.91	3.45	3.80	3.61	3.18	3.56	3.38	2.97
50 × 100	2.88	2.82	2.64	2.64	2.57	2.38	2.46	2.38	2.19
50 × 125	3.68	3.55	3.12	3.36	3.26	2.87	3.11	3.01	2.67
50 × 150	4.22	4.01	3.55	3.90	3.71	3.27	3.65	3.47	3.05

Notes
* North American surfaced size
† Dead load is the load supported by the rafter, excluding the mass of the rafter

AD A1/2

Table **B12**   **Purlins** supporting rafters to which Table B11 refers

Timber of strength class **SC4** (*see Table B1*)

Size of purlin [mm × mm]	Dead load† [kN/m²]																	
	Not more than 0.50						More than 0.50 but not more than 0.75						More than 0.75 but not more than 1.00					
	Spacing of purlins [mm]																	
	1500	1800	2100	2400	2700	3000	1500	1800	2100	2400	2700	3000	1500	1800	2100	2400	2700	3000
	Maximum clear span of purlin [m]																	
50 × 100	1.50	1.37	1.27	1.19	1.12	1.06	1.38	1.25	1.16	1.08	1.02	0.97	1.28	1.16	1.07	1.00	0.93	0.84
50 × 125	1.87	1.71	1.58	1.48	1.39	1.32	1.71	1.56	1.45	1.35	1.27	1.20	1.59	1.45	1.34	1.25	1.16	1.04
50 × 150	2.24	2.04	1.89	1.77	1.67	1.58	2.05	1.87	1.73	1.62	1.52	1.44	1.90	1.73	1.60	1.50	1.39	1.25
50 × 175	2.60	2.38	2.20	2.06	1.94	1.84	2.38	2.17	2.01	1.88	1.77	1.68	2.21	2.01	1.86	1.74	1.62	1.46
50 × 200	2.96	2.71	2.51	2.34	2.21	2.09	2.71	2.48	2.29	2.14	2.02	1.91	2.52	2.30	2.12	1.98	1.85	1.67
50 × 225	3.32	3.03	2.81	2.63	2.47	2.35	3.04	2.78	2.57	2.40	2.26	2.14	2.82	2.57	2.38	2.22	2.08	1.87
63 × 100	1.67	1.53	1.41	1.32	1.24	1.18	1.53	1.40	1.29	1.21	1.14	1.08	1.42	1.29	1.20	1.12	1.05	1.00
63 × 125	2.08	1.90	1.76	1.64	1.55	1.47	1.90	1.74	1.61	1.50	1.42	1.34	1.77	1.61	1.49	1.39	1.31	1.24
63 × 150	2.49	2.27	2.10	1.97	1.85	1.76	2.28	2.08	1.92	1.80	1.69	1.61	2.11	1.93	1.78	1.67	1.57	1.49
63 × 175	2.89	2.64	2.45	2.29	2.16	2.04	2.65	2.42	2.24	2.09	1.97	1.87	2.46	2.24	2.08	1.94	1.83	1.73
63 × 200	3.29	3.01	2.79	2.61	2.46	2.33	3.02	2.76	2.55	2.39	2.25	2.13	2.80	2.56	2.37	2.21	2.08	1.97
63 × 225	3.69	3.37	3.13	2.93	2.76	2.62	3.38	3.09	2.86	2.68	2.52	2.39	3.14	2.87	2.65	2.48	2.34	2.21
75 × 125	2.25	2.06	1.90	1.78	1.68	1.59	2.06	1.88	1.74	1.63	1.54	1.46	1.91	1.75	1.62	1.51	1.42	1.35
75 × 150	2.69	2.46	2.28	2.13	2.01	1.90	2.46	2.25	2.08	1.95	1.84	1.74	2.29	2.09	1.93	1.81	1.70	1.61
75 × 175	3.13	2.86	2.65	2.48	2.34	2.22	2.87	2.62	2.42	2.27	2.14	2.03	2.66	2.43	2.25	2.10	1.98	1.88
75 × 200	3.56	3.26	3.02	2.82	2.66	2.53	3.26	2.98	2.76	2.58	2.44	2.31	3.03	2.77	2.56	2.40	2.26	2.14
75 × 225	3.99	3.65	3.38	3.17	2.99	2.83	3.66	3.35	3.10	2.90	2.73	2.59	3.40	3.11	2.88	2.69	2.53	2.40

Note
† Dead load is the load supported by the rafter as calculated for the purposes of Table B11

AD A1/2

Table **B13**   **Common or jack rafters** for roofs having a pitch more than 22½° but not more than 30° with access only for purposes of maintenance or repair

Timber of strength class **SC3** *(see Table B1)*

Size of rafter [mm × mm]	Dead load† [kN/m²]								
	Not more than 0.50			More than 0.50 but not more than 0.75			More than 0.75 but not more than 1.00		
	Spacing of rafters [mm]								
	400	450	600	400	450	600	400	450	600
	Maximum clear span of rafter [m]								
38 × 89*	1.77	1.74	1.66	1.66	1.62	1.52	1.56	1.52	1.42
38 × 100	2.13	2.08	1.97	1.97	1.92	1.80	1.85	1.80	1.67
38 × 125	2.89	2.82	2.65	2.65	2.58	2.39	2.47	2.39	2.20
38 × 140*	3.34	3.26	3.01	3.05	2.96	2.74	2.83	2.74	2.51
38 × 150	3.63	3.54	3.19	3.30	3.21	2.91	3.06	2.96	2.70
47 × 100	2.51	2.46	2.32	2.32	2.26	2.10	2.17	2.10	1.94
47 × 125	3.36	3.28	3.03	3.07	2.98	2.76	2.85	2.76	2.53
47 × 150	4.17	4.00	3.51	3.78	3.67	3.22	3.50	3.38	2.99
50 × 100	2.63	2.57	2.42	2.42	2.36	2.20	2.26	2.20	2.03
50 × 125	3.51	3.42	3.12	3.20	3.11	2.86	2.97	2.87	2.63
50 × 150	4.33	4.11	3.62	3.93	3.78	3.31	3.63	3.51	3.07

Notes
* North American surfaced size
† Dead load is the load supported by the rafter, excluding the mass of the rafter

AD A1/2

Table B14   Purlins supporting rafters to which Table B13 refers

Timber of strength class **SC3** (*see Table B1*)

Size of purlin [mm × mm]	Dead load† [kN/m²]																	
	Not more than 0.50						More than 0.50 but not more than 0.75						More than 0.75 but not more than 1.00					
	Spacing of purlins [mm]																	
	1500	1800	2100	2400	2700	3000	1500	1800	2100	2400	2700	3000	1500	1800	2100	2400	2700	3000
	Maximum clear span of purlin [m]																	
50 × 100	1.23	1.12	1.04	0.97	0.91	0.87	1.12	1.02	0.95	0.88	0.83	0.79	1.04	0.95	0.87	0.82	0.77	0.73
50 × 125	1.53	1.40	1.29	1.21	1.14	1.08	1.40	1.27	1.18	1.10	1.04	0.98	1.29	1.18	1.09	1.02	0.96	0.91
50 × 150	1.83	1.67	1.55	1.45	1.36	1.29	1.67	1.53	1.41	1.32	1.24	1.17	1.55	1.41	1.30	1.22	1.14	1.08
50 × 175	2.13	1.95	1.80	1.68	1.59	1.50	1.95	1.77	1.64	1.53	1.44	1.37	1.80	1.64	1.52	1.42	1.33	1.26
50 × 200	2.43	2.22	2.05	1.92	1.81	1.71	2.22	2.02	1.87	1.75	1.65	1.56	2.05	1.87	1.73	1.61	1.52	1.44
50 × 225	2.73	2.49	2.30	2.15	2.03	1.92	2.49	2.27	2.10	1.96	1.85	1.75	2.30	2.10	1.94	1.81	1.71	1.61
63 × 100	1.38	1.26	1.16	1.09	1.02	0.97	1.25	1.14	1.06	0.99	0.93	0.88	1.16	1.06	0.98	0.91	0.86	0.81
63 × 125	1.71	1.56	1.44	1.35	1.27	1.20	1.56	1.42	1.31	1.23	1.16	1.10	1.44	1.31	1.21	1.13	1.07	1.01
63 × 150	2.04	1.86	1.72	1.61	1.52	1.44	1.86	1.70	1.57	1.47	1.38	1.31	1.72	1.57	1.45	1.36	1.28	1.21
63 × 175	2.37	2.16	2.00	1.87	1.76	1.67	2.16	1.97	1.83	1.71	1.61	1.52	2.00	1.82	1.69	1.58	1.49	1.41
63 × 200	2.70	2.46	2.28	2.14	2.01	1.91	2.46	2.25	2.08	1.95	1.83	1.74	2.28	2.08	1.92	1.80	1.69	1.60
63 × 225	3.03	2.77	2.56	2.40	2.26	2.14	2.76	2.52	2.34	2.18	2.06	1.95	2.56	2.34	2.16	2.02	1.90	1.80
75 × 125	1.85	1.69	1.56	1.46	1.38	1.31	1.69	1.54	1.43	1.33	1.26	1.19	1.56	1.43	1.32	1.23	1.16	1.10
75 × 150	2.21	2.01	1.87	1.75	1.65	1.56	2.01	1.84	1.70	1.59	1.50	1.42	1.86	1.70	1.57	1.47	1.39	1.31
75 × 175	2.56	2.34	2.17	2.03	1.91	1.81	2.34	2.14	1.98	1.85	1.74	1.65	2.17	1.98	1.83	1.71	1.61	1.53
75 × 200	2.92	2.67	2.47	2.31	2.18	2.07	2.66	2.43	2.25	2.11	1.99	1.88	2.47	2.25	2.09	1.95	1.84	1.74
75 × 225	3.27	2.99	2.77	2.59	2.45	2.32	2.99	2.73	2.53	2.37	2.23	2.11	2.77	2.53	2.34	2.19	2.06	1.95

Note
† Dead load is the load supported by the rafter as calculated for the purposes of Table B13

AD A1/2

Table **B15**   **Common or jack rafters** for roofs having a pitch more than 22½° but not more than 30° with access only for purposes of maintenance or repair

Timber of strength class **SC4** *(see Table B1)*

Size of rafter [mm × mm]	Dead load† [kN/m²]								
	Not more than 0.50			More than 0.50 but not more than 0.75			More than 0.75 but not more than 1.00		
	Spacing of rafters [mm]								
	400	450	600	400	450	600	400	450	600
	Maximum clear span of rafter [m]								
38 × 89*	2.30	2.25	2.13	2.13	2.08	1.94	2.00	1.94	1.80
38 × 100	2.74	2.68	2.52	2.52	2.45	2.27	2.35	2.27	2.10
38 × 125	3.62	3.53	3.18	3.30	3.20	2.91	3.06	2.95	2.69
38 × 140*	4.12	3.96	3.48	3.74	3.62	3.18	3.46	3.34	2.95
38 × 150	4.40	4.17	3.67	4.02	3.83	3.36	3.71	3.57	3.12
47 × 100	3.19	3.12	2.92	2.92	2.84	2.63	2.71	2.63	2.41
47 × 125	4.16	4.00	3.51	3.78	3.66	3.21	3.49	3.37	2.98
47 × 150	4.82	4.58	4.04	4.44	4.22	3.71	4.14	3.93	3.45
50 × 100	3.34	3.25	3.02	3.05	2.96	2.74	2.83	2.74	2.51
50 × 125	4.33	4.11	3.61	3.92	3.77	3.31	3.62	3.50	3.07
50 × 150	4.95	4.70	4.15	4.56	4.33	3.81	4.25	4.04	3.54

Notes
* North American surfaced size
† Dead load is the load supported by the rafter, excluding the mass of the rafter

AD A1/2

Structural stability 6.21

Table **B16** Purlins supporting rafters to which Table B15 refers

Timber of strength class **SC4** (see Table B1)

Size of purlin [mm × mm]	Not more than 0.50						More than 0.50 but not more than 0.75						More than 0.75 but not more than 1.00					
	1500	1800	2100	2400	2700	3000	1500	1800	2100	2400	2700	3000	1500	1800	2100	2400	2700	3000
50 × 100	1.46	1.33	1.23	1.15	1.09	1.03	1.33	1.22	1.12	1.05	0.99	0.94	1.23	1.12	1.04	0.97	0.91	0.86
50 × 125	1.82	1.66	1.54	1.43	1.35	1.28	1.66	1.51	1.40	1.31	1.23	1.17	1.53	1.40	1.29	1.21	1.14	1.07
50 × 150	2.17	1.98	1.84	1.72	1.62	1.53	1.98	1.81	1.67	1.56	1.47	1.40	1.84	1.67	1.55	1.45	1.36	1.28
50 × 175	2.53	2.31	2.14	2.00	1.88	1.78	2.31	2.11	1.95	1.82	1.71	1.62	2.14	1.95	1.80	1.68	1.58	1.50
50 × 200	2.88	2.63	2.44	2.28	2.15	2.03	2.63	2.40	2.22	2.08	1.95	1.85	2.43	2.22	2.05	1.92	1.81	1.71
50 × 225	3.23	2.95	2.73	2.56	2.41	2.28	2.95	2.69	2.49	2.33	2.19	2.08	2.73	2.49	2.30	2.15	2.03	1.92
63 × 100	1.63	1.49	1.38	1.29	1.21	1.15	1.49	1.36	1.26	1.17	1.11	1.05	1.38	1.26	1.16	1.09	1.02	0.97
63 × 125	2.02	1.85	1.71	1.60	1.51	1.43	1.85	1.68	1.56	1.46	1.37	1.30	1.71	1.56	1.44	1.35	1.27	1.20
63 × 150	2.41	2.21	2.04	1.91	1.80	1.71	2.20	2.01	1.86	1.74	1.64	1.55	2.04	1.86	1.72	1.61	1.52	1.44
63 × 175	2.81	2.56	2.37	2.22	2.09	1.98	2.56	2.34	2.17	2.03	1.91	1.81	2.37	2.17	2.00	1.87	1.76	1.67
63 × 200	3.20	2.92	2.71	2.53	2.39	2.26	2.92	2.67	2.47	2.31	2.18	2.06	2.71	2.47	2.29	2.14	2.01	1.91
63 × 225	3.58	3.28	3.04	2.84	2.68	2.54	3.28	2.99	2.77	2.59	2.44	2.32	3.04	2.77	2.57	2.40	2.26	2.14
75 × 125	2.19	2.00	1.86	1.74	1.64	1.55	2.00	1.83	1.69	1.58	1.49	1.41	1.85	1.69	1.57	1.46	1.38	1.31
75 × 150	2.61	2.39	2.21	2.07	1.95	1.85	2.39	2.18	2.02	1.89	1.78	1.69	2.21	2.02	1.87	1.75	1.65	1.56
75 × 175	3.03	2.77	2.57	2.41	2.27	2.15	2.77	2.53	2.35	2.19	2.07	1.96	2.57	2.35	2.17	2.03	1.91	1.81
75 × 200	3.45	3.16	2.93	2.74	2.58	2.45	3.16	2.89	2.67	2.50	2.36	2.24	2.93	2.67	2.48	2.31	2.18	2.07
75 × 225	3.87	3.54	3.28	3.07	2.90	2.75	3.54	3.24	3.00	2.81	2.65	2.51	3.28	3.00	2.78	2.60	2.45	2.32

Dead load⁺ [kN/m²], Spacing of purlins [mm], Maximum clear span of purlin [m]

Note
⁺ Dead load is the load supported by the rafter as calculated for the purposes of Table B15

AD A1/2

Table **B17** **Common or jack rafters** for roofs having a pitch more than 30° but not more than 42½° with access only for purposes of maintenance or repair

Timber of strength class **SC3** *(see Table B1)*

Size of rafter [mm × mm]	Dead load† [kN/m²]								
	Not more than 0.50			More than 0.50 but not more than 0.75			More than 0.75 but not more than 1.00		
	Spacing of rafters [mm]								
	400	450	600	400	450	600	400	450	600
	Maximum clear span of rafter [m]								
38 × 89*	2.64	2.49	2.17	2.40	2.27	1.97	2.22	2.09	1.82
38 × 100	2.94	2.78	2.42	2.68	2.53	2.20	2.47	2.34	2.03
38 × 125	3.54	3.36	2.93	3.23	3.06	2.67	2.99	2.83	2.46
38 × 140*	3.89	3.68	3.22	3.55	3.36	2.94	3.29	3.11	2.71
38 × 150	4.10	3.89	3.41	3.75	3.56	3.11	3.48	3.29	2.87
47 × 100	3.25	3.08	2.68	2.96	2.80	2.44	2.74	2.59	2.25
47 × 125	3.91	3.70	3.24	3.57	3.38	2.95	3.31	3.13	2.73
47 × 150	4.51	4.28	3.76	4.13	3.92	3.43	3.84	3.64	3.18
50 × 100	3.34	3.17	2.76	3.05	2.89	2.51	2.82	2.67	2.32
50 × 125	4.02	3.81	3.34	3.67	3.48	3.04	3.40	3.22	2.81
50 × 150	4.63	4.40	3.87	4.25	4.03	3.53	3.95	3.74	3.27

Notes
* North American surfaced size
† Dead load is the load supported by the rafter, excluding the mass of the rafter

AD A1/2

Table B18 Purlins supporting rafters to which Table B17 refers

Timber of strength class SC3 (see Table B1)

Size of purlin [mm × mm]	Dead load† [kN/m²]																	
	Not more than 0.50						More than 0.50 but not more than 0.75						More than 0.75 but not more than 1.00					
	Spacing of purlins [mm]																	
	Maximum clear span of purlin [m]																	
	1500	1800	2100	2400	2700	3000	1500	1800	2100	2400	2700	3000	1500	1800	2100	2400	2700	3000
50 × 100	1.16	1.07	0.99	0.93	0.87	0.83	1.04	0.97	0.90	0.84	0.79	0.75	0.96	0.90	0.83	0.77	0.73	0.69
50 × 125	1.45	1.32	1.23	1.15	1.08	1.02	1.31	1.20	1.11	1.04	0.97	0.92	1.21	1.10	1.02	0.95	0.89	0.85
50 × 150	1.73	1.58	1.46	1.37	1.29	1.22	1.57	1.43	1.32	1.23	1.16	1.10	1.44	1.31	1.21	1.13	1.07	1.01
50 × 175	2.01	1.83	1.70	1.59	1.49	1.42	1.82	1.66	1.54	1.43	1.35	1.28	1.67	1.53	1.41	1.32	1.24	1.17
50 × 200	2.29	2.09	1.93	1.81	1.70	1.61	2.07	1.89	1.75	1.64	1.54	1.46	1.91	1.74	1.61	1.50	1.41	1.34
50 × 225	2.57	2.34	2.17	2.03	1.91	1.81	2.33	2.12	1.96	1.84	1.73	1.64	2.14	1.95	1.81	1.69	1.59	1.50
63 × 100	1.33	1.22	1.13	1.05	0.99	0.94	1.21	1.10	1.02	0.95	0.90	0.85	1.11	1.01	0.94	0.88	0.82	0.78
63 × 125	1.63	1.49	1.38	1.29	1.21	1.15	1.48	1.35	1.25	1.16	1.10	1.04	1.36	1.24	1.15	1.07	1.01	0.95
63 × 150	1.93	1.76	1.63	1.53	1.44	1.36	1.75	1.60	1.48	1.38	1.30	1.23	1.61	1.47	1.36	1.27	1.20	1.13
63 × 175	2.23	2.04	1.89	1.77	1.67	1.58	2.03	1.85	1.71	1.60	1.51	1.43	1.87	1.70	1.58	1.47	1.39	1.31
63 × 200	2.54	2.32	2.15	2.01	1.90	1.80	2.30	2.10	1.95	1.82	1.72	1.63	2.12	1.94	1.79	1.68	1.58	1.50
63 × 225	2.85	2.60	2.41	2.26	2.13	2.02	2.58	2.36	2.18	2.04	1.93	1.83	2.38	2.17	2.01	1.88	1.77	1.68
75 × 125	1.79	1.63	1.51	1.41	1.33	1.26	1.62	1.48	1.37	1.28	1.21	1.14	1.49	1.36	1.26	1.18	1.11	1.05
75 × 150	2.10	1.92	1.78	1.67	1.57	1.49	1.91	1.74	1.61	1.51	1.42	1.35	1.76	1.60	1.49	1.39	1.31	1.24
75 × 175	2.43	2.22	2.06	1.92	1.81	1.72	2.20	2.01	1.86	1.74	1.64	1.56	2.03	1.85	1.71	1.60	1.51	1.43
75 × 200	2.75	2.52	2.33	2.18	2.06	1.95	2.50	2.28	2.11	1.98	1.86	1.77	2.30	2.10	1.95	1.82	1.72	1.63
75 × 225	3.08	2.82	2.61	2.45	2.31	2.19	2.80	2.56	2.37	2.22	2.09	1.98	2.58	2.36	2.18	2.04	1.92	1.82

Note
† Dead load is the load supported by the rafter as calculated for the purposes of Table B17

AD A1/2

Table **B19** **Common or jack rafters** for roofs having a pitch more than 30° but not more than 42½° with access only for purposes of maintenance or repair

Timber of strength class **SC4** *(see Table B1)*

Size of rafter [mm × mm]	Dead load† [kN/m²]								
	Not more than 0.50			More than 0.50 but not more than 0.75			More than 0.75 but not more than 1.00		
	Spacing of rafters [mm]								
	400	450	600	400	450	600	400	450	600
	Maximum clear span of rafter [m]								
38 × 89*	3.07	2.91	2.54	2.80	2.65	2.31	2.59	2.45	2.13
38 × 100	3.43	3.24	2.83	3.13	2.96	2.57	2.89	2.73	2.38
38 × 125	4.10	3.89	3.41	3.75	3.55	3.10	3.48	3.29	2.87
38 × 140*	4.48	4.25	3.73	4.10	3.89	3.40	3.81	3.61	3.15
38 × 150	4.72	4.48	3.94	4.33	4.10	3.60	4.02	3.81	3.33
47 × 100	3.78	3.58	3.13	3.45	3.27	2.85	3.16	3.02	2.64
47 × 125	4.51	4.28	3.76	4.13	3.92	3.43	3.83	3.63	3.18
47 × 150	5.17	4.92	4.33	4.75	4.51	3.97	4.42	4.19	3.68
50 × 100	3.89	3.68	3.22	3.53	3.36	2.94	3.22	3.10	2.72
50 × 125	4.63	4.40	3.87	4.25	4.03	3.53	3.94	3.74	3.27
50 × 150	5.31	5.05	4.45	4.88	4.64	4.08	4.54	4.31	3.79

Notes

* North American surfaced size
† Dead load is the load supported by the rafter, excluding the mass of the rafter

AD A1/2

Table B20   **Purlins** supporting rafters to which Table B19 refers

Timber of strength class **SC4** (*see Table B1*)

Size of purlin [mm × mm]	Dead load† [kN/m²]																	
	Not more than 0.50						More than 0.50 but not more than 0.75						More than 0.75 but not more than 1.00					
	Spacing of purlins [mm]																	
	1500	1800	2100	2400	2700	3000	1500	1800	2100	2400	2700	3000	1500	1800	2100	2400	2700	3000
	Maximum clear span of purlin [m]																	
50 × 100	1.40	1.27	1.18	1.10	1.04	0.98	1.26	1.15	1.07	1.00	0.94	0.89	1.16	1.06	0.98	0.92	0.86	0.82
50 × 125	1.72	1.57	1.45	1.36	1.28	1.21	1.56	1.42	1.32	1.23	1.16	1.10	1.43	1.31	1.21	1.13	1.06	1.01
50 × 150	2.05	1.87	1.73	1.62	1.53	1.45	1.86	1.69	1.57	1.47	1.38	1.31	1.71	1.56	1.44	1.35	1.27	1.20
50 × 175	2.38	2.17	2.01	1.88	1.77	1.68	2.16	1.97	1.82	1.70	1.60	1.52	1.99	1.81	1.68	1.57	1.47	1.40
50 × 200	2.71	2.48	2.29	2.14	2.02	1.92	2.46	2.24	2.08	1.94	1.83	1.73	2.26	2.07	1.91	1.79	1.68	1.59
50 × 225	3.04	2.78	2.57	2.41	2.27	2.15	2.76	2.52	2.33	2.18	2.05	1.95	2.54	2.32	2.15	2.00	1.89	1.79
63 × 100	1.58	1.44	1.34	1.25	1.18	1.12	1.43	1.31	1.21	1.13	1.07	1.01	1.32	1.20	1.11	1.04	0.98	0.93
63 × 125	1.93	1.76	1.63	1.53	1.44	1.36	1.75	1.60	1.48	1.38	1.30	1.23	1.61	1.47	1.36	1.27	1.20	1.13
63 × 150	2.29	2.09	1.93	1.81	1.71	1.62	2.07	1.89	1.75	1.64	1.54	1.46	1.91	1.74	1.61	1.51	1.42	1.35
63 × 175	2.65	2.42	2.24	2.10	1.98	1.87	2.40	2.19	2.03	1.90	1.79	1.70	2.21	2.02	1.87	1.75	1.65	1.56
63 × 200	3.01	2.75	2.55	2.39	2.25	2.13	2.73	2.50	2.31	2.16	2.04	1.93	2.52	2.30	2.13	1.99	1.87	1.78
63 × 225	3.37	3.08	2.86	2.67	2.52	2.39	3.06	2.80	2.59	2.42	2.28	2.17	2.82	2.58	2.39	2.23	2.10	1.99
75 × 125	2.12	1.93	1.79	1.68	1.58	1.50	1.92	1.75	1.62	1.52	1.43	1.36	1.77	1.62	1.49	1.40	1.32	1.25
75 × 150	2.49	2.28	2.11	1.98	1.86	1.77	2.26	2.07	1.91	1.79	1.69	1.60	2.09	1.90	1.76	1.65	1.55	1.47
75 × 175	2.87	2.63	2.44	2.28	2.15	2.04	2.61	2.39	2.21	2.07	1.95	1.85	2.41	2.20	2.04	1.90	1.79	1.70
75 × 200	3.26	2.98	2.76	2.59	2.44	2.32	2.96	2.71	2.51	2.35	2.21	2.10	2.73	2.50	2.31	2.16	2.04	1.93
75 × 225	3.65	3.34	3.09	2.90	2.73	2.59	3.31	3.03	2.81	2.63	2.48	2.35	3.06	2.79	2.59	2.42	2.28	2.16

Note

† Dead load is the load supported by the rafter as calculated for the purposes of Table B19

AD A1/2

Table **B21**   **Joists** for flat roofs with access only for the purposes of maintenance or repair

Timber of strength class **SC3** *(see Table B1)*

Size of joist [mm × mm]	Dead load† [kN/m²]								
	Not more than 0.50			More than 0.50 but not more than 0.75			More than 0.75 but not more than 1.00		
	Spacing of joists [mm]								
	400	450	600	400	450	600	400	450	600
	Maximum clear span of joist [m]								
38 × 75	1.22	1.20	1.18	1.18	1.16	1.12	1.14	1.12	1.08
38 × 89*	1.54	1.53	1.49	1.49	1.47	1.41	1.43	1.41	1.35
38 × 100	1.81	1.79	1.74	1.74	1.71	1.64	1.67	1.64	1.57
38 × 125	2.45	2.41	2.32	2.32	2.28	2.18	2.22	2.18	2.07
38 × 140*	2.84	2.80	2.68	2.68	2.63	2.51	2.56	2.51	2.37
38 × 150	3.10	3.05	2.93	2.93	2.87	2.73	2.79	2.73	2.57
38 × 175	3.77	3.70	3.47	3.54	3.46	3.27	3.36	3.28	3.09
38 × 184*	4.01	3.94	3.64	3.76	3.68	3.43	3.56	3.48	3.26
38 × 200	4.44	4.34	3.96	4.15	4.06	3.73	3.93	3.83	3.54
38 × 225	5.06	4.87	4.44	4.77	4.60	4.18	4.50	4.37	3.97
47 × 75	1.35	1.34	1.30	1.30	1.28	1.24	1.26	1.24	1.19
47 × 100	2.00	1.98	1.91	1.91	1.88	1.80	1.84	1.80	1.72
47 × 125	2.69	2.65	2.55	2.55	2.50	2.38	2.43	2.38	2.26
47 × 150	3.39	3.34	3.19	3.19	3.13	2.97	3.04	2.97	2.80
47 × 175	4.10	4.03	3.72	3.85	3.77	3.50	3.65	3.56	3.33
47 × 200	4.82	4.65	4.24	4.50	4.38	4.00	4.26	4.16	3.80
47 × 225	5.40	5.21	4.76	5.10	4.92	4.48	4.86	4.68	4.26
50 × 75	1.39	1.38	1.34	1.34	1.32	1.28	1.30	1.28	1.23
50 × 100	2.06	2.03	1.96	1.96	1.93	1.85	1.89	1.85	1.77
50 × 125	2.76	2.72	2.61	2.61	2.57	2.45	2.50	2.45	2.32
50 × 150	3.48	3.42	3.26	3.28	3.21	3.05	3.12	3.05	2.87
50 × 175	4.21	4.13	3.79	3.94	3.86	3.58	3.74	3.65	3.40
50 × 200	4.91	4.74	4.32	4.61	4.47	4.08	4.36	4.26	3.88
50 × 225	5.50	5.31	4.85	5.20	5.02	4.58	4.96	4.78	4.35
63 × 100	2.28	2.25	2.17	2.17	2.14	2.05	2.08	2.05	1.95
63 × 125	3.04	3.00	2.88	2.88	2.82	2.69	2.74	2.69	2.54
63 × 150	3.82	3.75	3.51	3.59	3.52	3.31	3.41	3.34	3.14
63 × 175	4.60	4.47	4.09	4.31	4.21	3.85	4.08	3.98	3.67
63 × 200	5.27	5.09	4.65	4.99	4.81	4.39	4.75	4.58	4.18
63 × 225	5.90	5.70	5.22	5.59	5.39	4.93	5.33	5.14	4.69
75 × 125	3.27	3.22	3.09	3.09	3.03	2.88	2.94	2.88	2.72
75 × 150	4.08	4.02	3.71	3.84	3.76	3.51	3.65	3.56	3.34
75 × 175	4.88	4.71	4.32	4.59	4.46	4.08	4.35	4.25	3.88
75 × 200	5.55	5.36	4.91	5.26	5.07	4.64	5.02	4.84	4.42
75 × 225	6.21	6.00	5.50	5.89	5.68	5.20	5.62	5.42	4.96

Notes

* North American surfaced size
† Dead load is the load supported by the joist, excluding the mass of the joist

Access only for maintenance 0.75 kN/m² or a concentrated load of 0.9 kN

AD A1/2

Table **B22** **Joists** for flat roofs with access only for the purposes of maintenance or repair

Timber of strength class **SC4** *(see Table B1)*

Size of joist [mm × mm]	Dead load† [kN/m²]								
	Not more than 0.50			More than 0.50 but not more than 0.75			More than 0.75 but not more than 1.00		
	Spacing of joists [mm]								
	400	450	600	400	450	600	400	450	600
	Maximum clear span of joist [m]								
38 × 75	1.29	1.28	1.24	1.24	1.23	1.19	1.21	1.19	1.14
38 × 89*	1.63	1.62	1.57	1.57	1.55	1.49	1.51	1.49	1.43
38 × 100	1.92	1.89	1.83	1.83	1.80	1.73	1.76	1.73	1.65
38 × 125	2.58	2.54	2.45	2.45	2.40	2.29	2.34	2.29	2.17
38 × 140*	2.99	2.94	2.82	2.82	2.77	2.63	2.69	2.63	2.49
38 × 150	3.26	3.21	3.07	3.07	3.01	2.86	2.93	2.86	2.70
38 × 175	3.96	3.89	3.61	3.71	3.63	3.40	3.52	3.44	3.23
38 × 184*	4.21	4.13	3.79	3.94	3.86	3.57	3.73	3.64	3.39
38 × 200	4.65	4.51	4.11	4.35	4.25	3.87	4.11	4.01	3.68
38 × 225	5.25	5.06	4.62	4.96	4.78	4.35	4.71	4.54	4.13
47 × 75	1.43	1.41	1.37	1.37	1.36	1.31	1.33	1.31	1.26
47 × 100	2.11	2.08	2.01	2.01	1.98	1.90	1.93	1.90	1.81
47 × 125	2.83	2.79	2.68	2.68	2.63	2.50	2.56	2.50	2.37
47 × 150	3.56	3.50	3.32	3.35	3.29	3.12	3.19	3.12	2.94
47 × 175	4.30	4.23	3.87	4.03	3.95	3.64	3.82	3.73	3.46
47 × 200	5.00	4.82	4.40	4.71	4.56	4.15	4.46	4.34	3.95
47 × 225	5.60	5.41	4.94	5.30	5.11	4.66	5.05	4.87	4.43
50 × 75	1.47	1.45	1.41	1.41	1.40	1.35	1.37	1.35	1.29
50 × 100	2.17	2.14	2.07	2.07	2.04	1.95	1.99	1.95	1.86
50 × 125	2.90	2.86	2.75	2.75	2.70	2.57	2.62	2.57	2.43
50 × 150	3.65	3.59	3.39	3.44	3.37	3.19	3.27	3.19	3.01
50 × 175	4.41	4.32	3.94	4.13	4.04	3.72	3.91	3.82	3.53
50 × 200	5.10	4.92	4.49	4.82	4.64	4.24	4.56	4.42	4.03
50 × 225	5.71	5.51	5.04	5.40	5.21	4.76	5.15	4.96	4.52
63 × 100	2.40	2.37	2.29	2.29	2.25	2.15	2.19	2.15	2.04
63 × 125	3.20	3.15	3.02	3.02	2.96	2.82	2.88	2.82	2.66
63 × 150	4.00	3.93	3.65	3.76	3.68	3.44	3.57	3.49	3.28
63 × 175	4.81	4.64	4.24	4.50	4.39	4.01	4.27	4.16	3.81
63 × 200	5.46	5.28	4.83	5.17	4.99	4.56	4.94	4.76	4.34
63 × 225	6 11	5.91	5.41	5.79	5.59	5.12	5.53	5.33	4.87
75 × 125	3.43	3.37	3.23	3.24	3.17	3.02	3.08	3.02	2.85
75 × 150	4.27	4.20	3.86	4.02	3.93	3.64	3.81	3.73	3.47
75 × 175	5.06	4.89	4.48	4.79	4.63	4.23	4.54	4.41	4.03
75 × 200	5.75	5.56	5.10	5.45	5.26	4.82	5.21	5.02	4.59
75 × 225	6.43	6.22	5.71	6.10	5.89	5.40	5.83	5.63	5.15

Notes

* North American surfaced size

† Dead load is the load supported by the joist, excluding the mass of the joist

Access only for maintenance 0.75 kN/m² or a concentrated load of 0.9 kN

AD A1/2

Table **B23**   **Joists** for flat roofs with access not limited to the purposes of maintenance or repair

Timber of strength class **SC3** *(see Table B1)*

Size of joist [mm × mm]	Dead load† [kN/m²]								
	Not more than 0.50			More than 0.50 but not more than 0.75			More than 0.75 but not more than 1.00		
	Spacing of joists [mm]								
	400	450	600	400	450	600	400	450	600
	Maximum clear span of joist [m]								
38 × 75	0.76	0.76	0.75	0.75	0.74	0.73	0.74	0.73	0.71
38 × 89*	1.04	1.03	1.01	1.01	1.01	0.98	0.99	0.98	0.95
38 × 100	1.28	1.27	1.24	1.24	1.23	1.19	1.21	1.19	1.15
38 × 125	1.86	1.85	1.81	1.81	1.78	1.72	1.74	1.72	1.64
38 × 140*	2.19	2.18	2.13	2.13	2.10	2.04	2.07	2.04	1.94
38 × 150	2.42	2.40	2.34	2.34	2.31	2.24	2.27	2.24	2.16
38 × 175	3.00	2.97	2.88	2.88	2.85	2.75	2.79	2.75	2.63
38 × 184*	3.21	3.18	3.08	3.08	3.04	2.93	2.98	2.93	2.81
38 × 200	3.59	3.55	3.38	3.44	3.40	3.25	3.32	3.26	3.12
38 × 225	4.20	4.15	3.80	4.02	3.95	3.65	3.86	3.79	3.51
47 × 75	0.94	0.93	0.92	0.92	0.91	0.89	0.90	0.89	0.86
47 × 100	1.50	1.49	1.47	1.47	1.46	1.42	1.44	1.42	1.38
47 × 125	2.07	2.06	2.01	2.01	1.99	1.94	1.96	1.94	1.87
47 × 150	2.68	2.65	2.59	2.59	2.55	2.47	2.51	2.47	2.38
47 × 175	3.31	3.27	3.18	3.18	3.13	3.02	3.07	3.02	2.89
47 × 200	3.95	3.91	3.63	3.78	3.73	3.49	3.64	3.58	3.37
47 × 225	4.61	4.48	4.08	4.40	4.32	3.92	4.22	4.14	3.79
50 × 75	0.99	0.99	0.97	0.97	0.96	0.94	0.95	0.94	0.91
50 × 100	1.55	1.54	1.52	1.52	1.50	1.47	1.48	1.47	1.43
50 × 125	2.14	2.12	2.07	2.07	2.05	1.99	2.02	1.99	1.93
50 × 150	2.76	2.73	2.66	2.66	2.63	2.54	2.58	2.54	2.44
50 × 175	3.40	3.36	3.25	3.27	3.22	3.10	3.15	3.10	2.97
50 × 200	4.06	4.01	3.71	3.89	3.83	3.57	3.74	3.67	3.44
50 × 225	4.73	4.58	4.16	4.51	4.40	4.00	4.33	4.25	3.87
63 × 100	1.74	1.73	1.70	1.70	1.68	1.64	1.66	1.64	1.59
63 × 125	2.39	2.37	2.31	2.31	2.29	2.22	2.25	2.22	2.14
63 × 150	3.07	3.04	2.95	2.95	2.92	2.82	2.86	2.82	2.70
63 × 175	3.77	3.73	3.51	3.61	3.56	3.38	3.48	3.43	3.26
63 × 200	4.48	4.39	4.00	4.28	4.22	3.85	4.12	4.04	3.72
63 × 225	5.11	4.93	4.49	4.93	4.75	4.32	4.75	4.59	4.18
75 × 125	2.59	2.57	2.51	2.51	2.48	2.40	2.43	2.40	2.31
75 × 150	3.31	3.28	3.19	3.19	3.15	3.04	3.08	3.04	2.91
75 × 175	4.06	4.01	3.72	3.89	3.83	3.58	3.75	3.68	3.45
75 × 200	4.82	4.64	4.24	4.60	4.47	4.08	4.42	4.32	3.94
75 × 225	5.40	5.20	4.75	5.20	5.02	4.58	5.04	4.85	4.42

Notes

* North American surfaced size
† Dead load is the load supported by the joist, excluding the mass of the joist

Full access allowed 1.50 kN/m² or a concentrated load of 1.8 kN

AD A1/2

Table **B24** **Joists** for flat roofs with access not limited to the purposes of maintenance or repair

Timber of strength class **SC4** *(see Table B1)*

Size of joist [mm × mm]	Not more than 0.50			More than 0.50 but not more than 0.75			More than 0.75 but not more than 1.00		
	Spacing of joists [mm]								
	400	450	600	400	450	600	400	450	600
	Maximum clear span of joist [m]								
38 × 75	0.93	0.93	0.92	0.92	0.91	0.90	0.90	0.90	0.88
38 × 89*	1.21	1.20	1.18	1.18	1.17	1.15	1.16	1.15	1.12
38 × 100	1.43	1.42	1.40	1.40	1.39	1.36	1.37	1.36	1.32
38 × 125	1.98	1.96	1.92	1.92	1.90	1.85	1.87	1.85	1.79
38 × 140*	2.32	2.30	2.25	2.25	2.23	2.16	2.19	2.16	2.08
38 × 150	2.56	2.54	2.47	2.47	2.45	2.37	2.40	2.37	2.28
38 × 175	3.17	3.13	3.05	3.05	3.01	2.90	2.94	2.90	2.77
38 × 184*	3.39	3.35	3.24	3.26	3.21	3.09	3.14	3.09	2.96
38 × 200	3.79	3.75	3.52	3.63	3.58	3.38	3.50	3.44	3.26
38 × 225	4.43	4.35	3.95	4.23	4.16	3.80	4.06	3.98	3.67
47 × 75	1.05	1.04	1.03	1.03	1.02	1.00	1.01	1.00	0.98
47 × 100	1.60	1.59	1.56	1.56	1.55	1.51	1.52	1.51	1.46
47 × 125	2.20	2.18	2.13	2.13	2.11	2.05	2.07	2.05	1.98
47 × 150	2.83	2.80	2.73	2.73	2.70	2.61	2.65	2.61	2.50
47 × 175	3.49	3.45	3.31	3.35	3.30	3.18	3.23	3.18	3.04
47 × 200	4.16	4.12	3.78	3.98	3.92	3.63	3.83	3.76	3.51
47 × 225	4.84	4.66	4.24	4.62	4.49	4.08	4.43	4.33	3.94
50 × 75	1.08	1.08	1.06	1.06	1.05	1.04	1.04	1.04	1.01
50 × 100	1.65	1.64	1.61	1.61	1.59	1.55	1.57	1.55	1.51
50 × 125	2.26	2.24	2.19	2.19	2.17	2.11	2.13	2.11	2.03
50 × 150	2.91	2.88	2.81	2.81	2.77	2.68	2.72	2.68	2.57
50 × 175	3.59	3.55	3.38	3.44	3.39	3.25	3.32	3.27	3.12
50 × 200	4.28	4.23	3.86	4.09	4.03	3.71	3.93	3.86	3.58
50 × 225	4.94	4.76	4.33	4.74	4.58	4.17	4.55	4.42	4.02
63 × 100	1.85	1.83	1.80	1.80	1.78	1.74	1.76	1.74	1.68
63 × 125	2.52	2.50	2.44	2.44	2.41	2.34	2.37	2.34	2.25
63 × 150	3.23	3.20	3.11	3.11	3.07	2.96	3.01	2.96	2.84
63 × 175	3.97	3.92	3.65	3.80	3.75	3.51	3.66	3.60	3.39
63 × 200	4.71	4.56	4.16	4.50	4.39	4.00	4.32	4.24	3.87
63 × 225	5.31	5.12	4.67	5.12	4.93	4.49	4.95	4.77	4.34
75 × 125	2.73	2.71	2.64	2.64	2.61	2.53	2.56	2.53	2.43
75 × 150	3.49	3.46	3.32	3.36	3.31	3.19	3.24	3.19	3.06
75 × 175	4.27	4.22	3.86	4.09	4.03	3.72	3.93	3.87	3.59
75 × 200	5.00	4.82	4.40	4.82	4.64	4.24	4.63	4.49	4.10
75 × 225	5.60	5.40	4.94	5.40	5.21	4.76	5.23	5.04	4.60

Notes

* North American surfaced size

† Dead load is the load supported by the joist, excluding the mass of the joist

Full access allowed 1.50 kN/m² or a concentrated load of 1.8 kN

AD A1/2

Table B25   Purlins supporting sheeting or decking for roofs having a pitch of more than 10° but not more than 30°

Timber of strength class **SC3** *(see Table B1)*

Size of purlin [mm × mm]	Dead load† [kN/m²]																	
	Not more than 0.25						More than 0.25 but not more than 0.50						More than 0.50 but not more than 0.75					
	Spacing of purlins [mm]																	
	900	1200	1500	1800	2100	2400	900	1200	1500	1800	2100	2400	900	1200	1500	1800	2100	2400
	Maximum clear span of purlin [m]																	
50 × 100	1.91	1.80	1.62	1.48	1.37	1.28	1.67	1.56	1.43	1.31	1.21	1.13	1.51	1.40	1.30	1.18	1.09	1.02
50 × 125	2.58	2.24	2.01	1.83	1.70	1.59	2.29	1.99	1.78	1.62	1.50	1.41	2.06	1.80	1.61	1.47	1.36	1.27
50 × 150	3.07	2.68	2.40	2.19	2.03	1.90	2.73	2.37	2.13	1.94	1.80	1.68	2.48	2.15	1.93	1.76	1.63	1.52
50 × 175	3.57	3.11	2.79	2.55	2.36	2.21	3.17	2.76	2.47	2.26	2.09	1.96	2.88	2.50	2.24	2.05	1.90	1.77
50 × 200	4.05	3.54	3.17	2.90	2.69	2.52	3.61	3.14	2.82	2.57	2.38	2.23	3.28	2.85	2.55	2.33	2.16	2.02
50 × 225	4.54	3.96	3.56	3.25	3.02	2.83	4.04	3.52	3.16	2.89	2.67	2.50	3.68	3.20	2.86	2.62	2.42	2.27
63 × 100	2.27	2.01	1.80	1.65	1.52	1.43	1.96	1.78	1.59	1.46	1.35	1.26	1.77	1.62	1.45	1.32	1.22	1.14
63 × 125	2.85	2.48	2.23	2.04	1.89	1.77	2.54	2.20	1.98	1.81	1.67	1.56	2.30	2.00	1.79	1.64	1.52	1.42
63 × 150	3.40	2.96	2.66	2.43	2.25	2.11	3.02	2.63	2.36	2.16	2.00	1.87	2.75	2.39	2.14	1.96	1.81	1.69
63 × 175	3.94	3.44	3.09	2.83	2.62	2.45	3.51	3.05	2.74	2.51	2.32	2.17	3.19	2.78	2.49	2.27	2.11	1.97
63 × 200	4.47	3.91	3.51	3.22	2.98	2.80	3.99	3.48	3.12	2.85	2.65	2.48	3.63	3.16	2.83	2.59	2.40	2.25
63 × 225	5.00	4.37	3.94	3.61	3.35	3.14	4.46	3.89	3.50	3.20	2.97	2.78	4.07	3.54	3.18	2.91	2.69	2.52

Note
† Dead load is the load supported by the purlin, excluding the mass of the purlin

AD A1/2

Table B26 **Purlins** supporting sheeting or decking for roofs having a pitch of more than 10° but not more than 30°

Timber of strength class **SC4** *(see Table B1)*

Size of purlin [mm × mm]	Dead load† [kN/m²]																	
	Not more than 0.25						More than 0.25 but not more than 0.50						More than 0.50 but not more than 0.75					
	Spacing of purlins [mm]																	
	900	1200	1500	1800	2100	2400	900	1200	1500	1800	2100	2400	900	1200	1500	1800	2100	2400
	Maximum clear span of purlin [m]																	
50 × 100	2.47	2.14	1.92	1.76	1.63	1.52	2.16	1.90	1.70	1.55	1.44	1.34	1.94	1.72	1.54	1.41	1.30	1.22
50 × 125	3.06	2.66	2.39	2.18	2.02	1.89	2.72	2.36	2.11	1.93	1.79	1.67	2.47	2.14	1.92	1.75	1.62	1.51
50 × 150	3.65	3.18	2.85	2.61	2.42	2.26	3.24	2.82	2.53	2.31	2.14	2.00	2.95	2.56	2.29	2.09	1.94	1.81
50 × 175	4.23	3.69	3.31	3.03	2.81	2.63	3.77	3.28	2.94	2.69	2.49	2.33	3.42	2.98	2.67	2.44	2.25	2.11
50 × 200	4.81	4.20	3.77	3.45	3.20	3.00	4.28	3.73	3.35	3.06	2.83	2.65	3.90	3.39	3.04	2.78	2.57	2.40
50 × 225	5.38	4.70	4.22	3.87	3.59	3.36	4.80	4.18	3.75	3.43	3.18	2.98	4.37	3.80	3.41	3.11	2.88	2.70
63 × 100	2.74	2.39	2.14	1.96	1.81	1.70	2.44	2.12	1.90	1.73	1.60	1.50	2.21	1.92	1.72	1.57	1.45	1.36
63 × 125	3.39	2.95	2.65	2.42	2.25	2.10	3.01	2.62	2.35	2.15	1.99	1.86	2.74	2.38	2.13	1.95	1.80	1.69
63 × 150	4.03	3.52	3.16	2.89	2.68	2.51	3.59	3.12	2.80	2.56	2.38	2.22	3.26	2.84	2.54	2.33	2.15	2.01
63 × 175	4.67	4.08	3.67	3.36	3.11	2.92	4.16	3.63	3.26	2.98	2.76	2.58	3.79	3.30	2.96	2.70	2.50	2.34
63 × 200	5.30	4.64	4.17	3.82	3.55	3.32	4.73	4.13	3.71	3.39	3.15	2.94	4.31	3.75	3.37	3.08	2.85	2.67
63 × 225	5.93	5.19	4.67	4.28	3.98	3.73	5.29	4.62	4.15	3.80	3.53	3.30	4.83	4.21	3.78	3.45	3.20	3.00

Note
† Dead load is the load supported by the purlin, excluding the mass of the purlin

AD A1/2

Table B27 **Purlins** supporting sheeting or decking for roofs having a pitch of more than 30° but not more than 35°

Timber of strength class **SC3** (*see Table B1*)

Size of purlin [mm × mm]	Dead load† [kN/m²]																	
	Not more than 0.25						More than 0.25 but not more than 0.50						More than 0.50 but not more than 0.75					
	Spacing of purlins [mm]																	
	900	1200	1500	1800	2100	2400	900	1200	1500	1800	2100	2400	900	1200	1500	1800	2100	2400
	Maximum clear span of purlin [m]																	
50 × 100	1.80	1.72	1.59	1.46	1.35	1.26	1.59	1.48	1.40	1.28	1.19	1.11	1.44	1.33	1.25	1.16	1.07	1.00
50 × 125	2.54	2.20	1.98	1.81	1.67	1.57	2.19	1.95	1.74	1.59	1.47	1.38	1.96	1.76	1.58	1.44	1.33	1.24
50 × 150	3.02	2.63	2.36	2.16	2.00	1.87	2.67	2.32	2.08	1.90	1.76	1.65	2.42	2.10	1.88	1.72	1.59	1.49
50 × 175	3.50	3.05	2.74	2.51	2.32	2.17	3.10	2.70	2.42	2.21	2.05	1.92	2.81	2.44	2.19	2.00	1.85	1.73
50 × 200	3.98	3.47	3.12	2.86	2.65	2.48	3.53	3.07	2.76	2.52	2.33	2.18	3.20	2.78	2.49	2.28	2.11	1.97
50 × 225	4.46	3.89	3.50	3.20	2.97	2.78	3.96	3.45	3.09	2.83	2.62	2.45	3.59	3.12	2.80	2.56	2.37	2.21
63 × 100	2.16	1.99	1.78	1.63	1.51	1.41	1.88	1.75	1.57	1.44	1.33	1.24	1.70	1.56	1.42	1.30	1.20	1.12
63 × 125	2.81	2.45	2.20	2.01	1.86	1.74	2.49	2.17	1.94	1.77	1.64	1.54	2.26	1.96	1.76	1.60	1.48	1.39
63 × 150	3.34	2.91	2.62	2.39	2.22	2.08	2.96	2.58	2.31	2.11	1.96	1.83	2.69	2.34	2.09	1.91	1.77	1.66
63 × 175	3.87	3.38	3.04	2.78	2.58	2.41	3.43	2.99	2.68	2.45	2.27	2.13	3.12	2.71	2.43	2.22	2.06	1.92
63 × 200	4.39	3.84	3.45	3.16	2.93	2.75	3.90	3.40	3.05	2.79	2.59	2.42	3.54	3.08	2.77	2.53	2.34	2.19
63 × 225	4.91	4.30	3.87	3.54	3.29	3.08	4.37	3.81	3.42	3.13	2.91	2.72	3.97	3.46	3.10	2.84	2.63	2.46

Note

† Dead load is the load supported by the purlin, excluding the mass of the purlin

AD A1/2

Table B28 **Purlins** supporting sheeting or decking for roofs having a pitch of more than 30° but not more than 35°

Timber of strength class **SC4** (*see Table B1*)

Size of purlin [mm × mm]	Not more than 0.25						More than 0.25 but not more than 0.50						More than 0.50 but not more than 0.75					
	Spacing of purlins [mm]																	
	900	1200	1500	1800	2100	2400	900	1200	1500	1800	2100	2400	900	1200	1500	1800	2100	2400
	Maximum clear span of purlin [m]																	
50 × 100	2.39	2.11	1.90	1.73	1.60	1.50	2.06	1.87	1.67	1.53	1.41	1.32	1.85	1.69	1.51	1.38	1.28	1.19
50 × 125	3.01	2.62	2.35	2.15	1.99	1.86	2.66	2.31	2.07	1.89	1.75	1.64	2.41	2.09	1.87	1.71	1.58	1.48
50 × 150	3.59	3.12	2.80	2.56	2.38	2.22	3.18	2.76	2.47	2.26	2.09	1.96	2.88	2.50	2.24	2.04	1.89	1.77
50 × 175	4.16	3.63	3.26	2.98	2.76	2.59	3.69	3.21	2.88	2.63	2.44	2.28	3.34	2.91	2.60	2.38	2.20	2.06
50 × 200	4.73	4.13	3.71	3.39	3.15	2.95	4.19	3.65	3.28	3.00	2.78	2.60	3.80	3.31	2.97	2.71	2.51	2.35
50 × 225	5.29	4.62	4.15	3.80	3.53	3.30	4.69	4.09	3.67	3.36	3.11	2.91	4.26	3.71	3.33	3.04	2.82	2.63
63 × 100	2.72	2.36	2.12	1.94	1.80	1.68	2.40	2.09	1.87	1.71	1.58	1.48	2.16	1.89	1.69	1.55	1.43	1.34
63 × 125	3.34	2.91	2.61	2.39	2.22	2.07	2.96	2.57	2.31	2.11	1.95	1.83	2.68	2.33	2.09	1.91	1.77	1.65
63 × 150	3.97	3.46	3.11	2.85	2.64	2.47	3.52	3.06	2.75	2.51	2.33	2.18	3.19	2.78	2.49	2.27	2.11	1.97
63 × 175	4.59	4.01	3.60	3.30	3.06	2.87	4.07	3.55	3.19	2.92	2.70	2.53	3.70	3.22	2.89	2.64	2.45	2.29
63 × 200	5.21	4.56	4.10	3.76	3.49	3.27	4.63	4.04	3.63	3.32	3.08	2.88	4.21	3.66	3.29	3.01	2.79	2.61
63 × 225	5.82	5.10	4.59	4.21	3.91	3.66	5.18	4.52	4.07	3.72	3.45	3.23	4.71	4.11	3.69	3.37	3.13	2.93

Dead load† [kN/m²]

Note
† Dead load is the load supported by the purlin, excluding the mass of the purlin

Table 6.1 Softwood floorboards (tongued and grooved).

Finished thickness of board (mm)	Maximum span of board (centre to centre of joists) (mm)
16	450
19	600

Example applications of the tables are given in Fig. 6.2 above. It should be remembered that all *spans*, except for floorboards, are measured as the clear dimension between supports, and all *spacings* are the dimensions between longitudinal centres of members.

Structural work of bricks, blocks and plain concrete

If a wall of these materials comes within the scope of Part C of Section 1 of AD A1/2, it is not necessary to calculate loads or wall thicknesses, provided the wall is built with the thicknesses required by Part C and complies with the rules therein and in all other respects complies with BS 5628 *Code of practice for the structural use of masonry*. Part 1: 1978: *Unreinforced masonry* and Part 3: 1985: *Materials and components, design and workmanship.*

Part C may be applied to any wall which is:

AD A1/2
sec. 1
Part C
C1 & C2

(a) an external wall, compartment wall, internal load-bearing wall or separating wall of a residential building of not more than three storeys, and

(b) an external wall or internal load-bearing wall of a small single-storey non-residential building or small annexe to a residential building (such as a garage or outbuilding) *provided that*:

(i) the building design complies with the requirements of paragraphs C14 to C17 of Part C, *and*

AD A1/2
sec. 1
Part C
C4

(ii) the wall construction details comply with the requirements of paragraphs C18 to C40 of Part C.

Building design requirements (Part C paragraphs C14 to C17)

These are concerned with the design, wind speed, the imposed load, the building proportions and the plan area of each storey or sub-division.

DESIGN WIND SPEED (V_s).   When determined in accordance with CP3: Chapter V *Loading*, Part 2: 1972 *Wind loads*, this should not exceed 44 metres/second, where $V_s = V \times S_1 \times S_2 \times S_3$, and

V = basic wind speed for the building location (see wind map in Code of Practice)

S_1 = topography factor

S_2 = factor for ground roughness, building size and height above ground (Class B building size is to be assumed and an allowance made to increase the effective building height if close to a cliff or escarpment (see BRE Digest 119)).

S_3 = probability factor (not less than one)

AD A1/2
sec. 1
Part C
C17

IMPOSED LOADS. These should not exceed:

(i) on any upper floor, $2 \cdot 0$ kN/m^2 or $1 \cdot 8$ kN concentrated;
(ii) on any ceiling, $0 \cdot 25$ kN/m^2 distributed and $0 \cdot 9$ kN concentrated, or alternatively $0 \cdot 75$ kN/m^2 distributed; and
(iii) on any roof, $0 \cdot 75$ kN/m^2 distributed or $0 \cdot 9$ kN concentrated.

AD A1/2
sec. 1
Part C
C16

BUILDING PROPORTIONS.   For residential buildings of not more than three storeys:

(i) the height of any part of a wall or roof of the building should not exceed 15 m, as measured from the lowest finished surface of the ground adjoining the building;
(ii) the width of the building should not be less than at least half the height of the building;
(iii) any wing of the building which projects more than twice its own width from the remainder of the building should have a width at least equal to half its height. ('Height' is measured to the highest part of any roof or wall of the building or wing.)

For small single-storey non-residential buildings:

(i) the height of the building should not exceed 3 m.
(ii) the width of the building measured in the direction of the roof span should not exceed 9 m.

For annexes attached to residential buildings the height of any part should not exceed 3 m.

PLAN AREA OF STOREY.   The plan area of each storey which is completely bounded by structural walls on all sides should not be more than 70 m^2. However, if the storey is bounded in this way on all sides but one, the limiting area is 30 m^2.

These requirements are summarised in Figs. 6.3 and 6.4 below.

Wall construction requirements (Part C paragraphs C18 to C40)

These are concerned with height and length, materials, buttressing, loading conditions, openings and recesses, and lateral support.

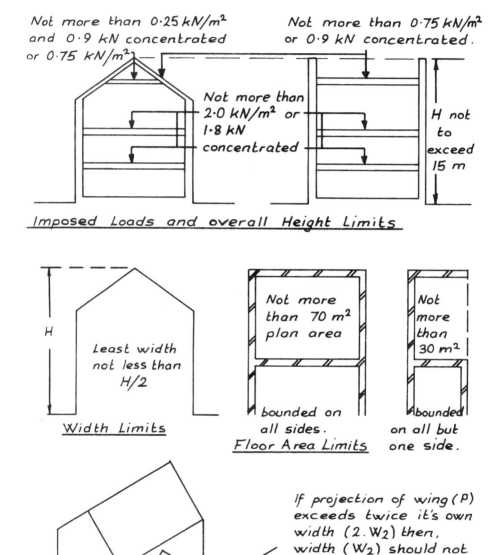

Fig. 6.3 Building design requirements for residential buildings not exceeding three storeys in height.

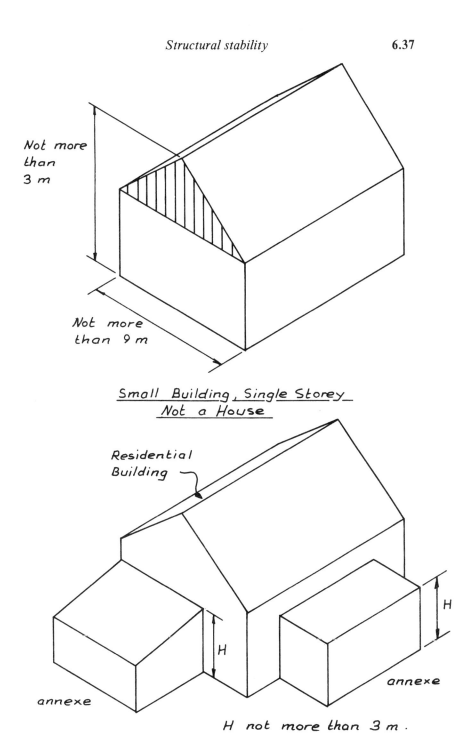

Not more
than
3 m

Not more
than 9 m

<u>Small Building, Single Storey</u>
<u>Not a House</u>

Residential
Building

H

H

annexe

annexe

H not more than 3 m .

<u>Annexe to a House</u>

Fig. 6.4 Building design requirements, small non-residential buildings and annexes.

Height and Length

The height or length of a wall should not be more than 12 m and together with storey heights should be measured in accordance with the following rules:

- The height of the ground storey of a building is measured from the base of the wall to the underside of the next floor above.
- The height of an upper storey is measured from the level of the underside of the floor of that storey, in each case to the level of the underside of the next floor above.
- For a top storey which comprises a gable wall, measure to a level midway between the gable base and the top of the roof lateral support along the line of the roof slope, but if there is also lateral support about ceiling level, to the level of that lateral support.
- Where a compartment or separating wall (as defined) comprises a gable, measure the height from its base to the base of the gable.
- Any other gable wall (except a compartment or separating wall) should be measured from its base to half the height of the gable.
- Any wall which is not a gable wall should be measured from its base to its highest part, excluding any parapet not exceeding 1·2 m in height.
- Walls are regarded as being divided into separate lengths by securely tied buttressing walls, piers or chimneys for the purposes of measuring their length. These separate lengths are measured centre to centre of the piers, etc. These special requirements are noted in Fig. 6.5.

AD A1/2
sec. 1
Part C
C18 & C19

Materials and workmanship

BRICKS AND BLOCKS.   The wall should be constructed of bricks or blocks, properly bonded and solidly put together with mortar. The materials should comply with the following standards:

- Clay bricks or blocks to BS 3921: 1974: or DD 34: 1974 (BS 1 Draft for Development 34).
- Calcium silicate bricks to BS 187: 1978 or DD 59: 1958 (BS 1 Draft for Development 59).
- Concrete bricks or blocks to BS 6073: Part 1: 1981.
- Square dressed natural stone to BS 5390: 1976 (1984).

Additionally, brick or blocks should have a compressive strength of not less than the following:

(a) when used in any part of a wall with storey heights not exceeding 2·7 m (*except* in the ground storey or the outer leaf of an upper storey external cavity wall of a three-storey building), 5 N/mm^2 for bricks and 2·8 N/mm^2 for blocks.

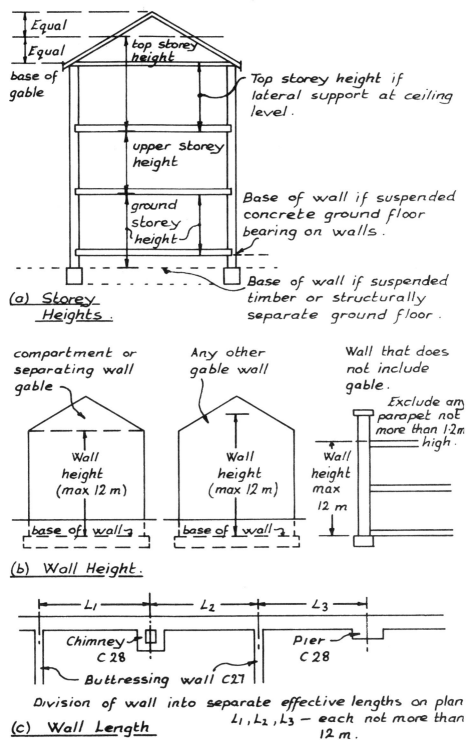

(a) Storey Heights.

top storey height

Top storey height if lateral support at ceiling level.

Equal
Equal
base of gable

upper storey height

ground storey height

Base of wall if suspended concrete ground floor bearing on walls.

Base of wall if suspended timber or structurally separate ground floor.

(b) Wall Height.

compartment or separating wall gable

Wall height (max 12 m)

base of wall

Any other gable wall

Wall height (max 12 m)

base of wall

Wall that does not include gable.

Exclude any parapet not more than 1·2m high.

Wall height max 12 m

(c) Wall Length

L_1
L_2
L_3

Chimney C 28

Pier C 28

Buttressing wall C27

Division of wall into separate effective lengths on plan L_1, L_2, L_3 — each not more than 12 m.

Fig. 6.5 Rules for measurement, C19.

(b) if used in any circumstances other than those described in (a), 7 N/mm^2.

AD A1/2
sec. 1
Part C
C21 & C22
It should be noted that in determining the ground storey height for the purposes of (a) above, the measurement is made from the upper surface of the ground floor and not from the base of the wall in this case.

AD A1/2
sec. 1
Part C
C23
MORTAR.   The mortar used in any wall to which Part C of section 1 of AD A1/2 applies should be at least equal in strength to a 1 : 1 : 6 Portland cement / lime / fine aggregate mortar measured by volume of dry materials, or to the proportions given in BS 5628 *Code of practice for the structural use of masonry*; Part 1: 1978 *Unreinforced masonry*, for mortar designation (iii).

AD A1/2
sec. 1
Part C
C20
WALL TIES.   These should comply with BS 1243: 1978 *Specification for metal ties for cavity wall construction* unless conditions of severe exposure occur. In that case austenitic stainless steel or suitable non-ferrous ties should be used.

Buttressing walls, piers and chimneys

Any load-bearing wall should be bonded or securely tied at each end to a buttressing wall, pier or chimney. (This does not apply to single leaf walls less than 2·5 m in height and length which form part of a small single storey non-residential building or annexe.) These supporting elements should be of such dimensions as to provide effective lateral support over the full wall height from its base to its top.

If, additionally, such supporting elements are bonded or securely tied to the supporting wall at intermediate points in the length of the wall, then the wall may be regarded as being divided into separate distinct lengths by these buttressing walls, piers or chimneys. Each of the distinct lengths may then be regarded as a supported wall, and the
AD A1/2
sec. 1
Part C
C26
length of any wall is the distance between adjacent supporting elements.

BUTTRESSING WALLS should have:
(a) one end bonded or securely tied to the supported wall;
(b) the other end bonded or securely tied to another buttressing wall, pier or chimney;
(c) no opening or recess greater than 0·6 m^2 in area within a horizontal distance of 550 mm from the junction with the supported wall, and openings and recesses generally disposed so as not to impair the supporting effect of the buttressing wall;
(d) a length of not less than one sixth of the height of the supported wall;
(e) the minimum thickness required by the appropriate rule, according to whether the buttressing wall is actually an external compart-

ment, separating or internal load-bearing wall or a wall of a small building or annexe; but if the wall is none of these, then a thickness, t, (see Fig. 6.6 below) of not less than the greater of

(i) half the thickness required of a solid external, compartment or separating wall of the same height and length as the buttressing wall, less 5 mm; *or*

(ii) if the buttressing wall is part of a house and the supported wall as a whole is not more than 6 m high and 10 m in length, 75 mm; *or*

(iii) in any other case, 90 mm (see Fig. 6.6).

ADA1/2
sec. 1
Part C
C27

PIERS may project on either or both sides of the supported wall and should:

(a) run from the base of the supported wall to the level of the roof lateral support, or to the top of the wall if there is no roof lateral support;

(b) have a thickness, measured at right angles to the length of the supported wall and including the thickness of that wall, of at least three times the thickness required of the supported wall; *and*

(c) measure at least 190 mm in width. (The measurement being parallel to the length of the supported wall.)

CHIMNEYS should have:

(a) a horizontal cross-section area, excluding any fireplace opening or flue, of not less than the area required of a pier in the same wall *and*

(b) a thickness overall of at least twice the thickness required of the supported wall.

It should be noted that requirements in respect of plan dimensions of piers do not apply to piers in walls of small buildings and annexes, for which there are special rules (see Fig. 6.7).

AD A1/2
sec. 1
Part C
C28

Loading conditions

FLOOR SPANS.   The wall should not support any floor members with a span of more than 6 m. (Span is measured centre to centre of bearings.)

LATERAL THRUST.   Where the levels of the ground or oversite concrete on either side of a wall differ, the thickness of the wall as measured at the higher level should not be less than one quarter of the difference in level.

In the case of a cavity wall, the thickness is taken as the sum of the leaf thicknesses. However, if the cavity is filled with fine concrete, the overall thickness may be taken.

The lateral thrust occasioned in these circumstances is the only one

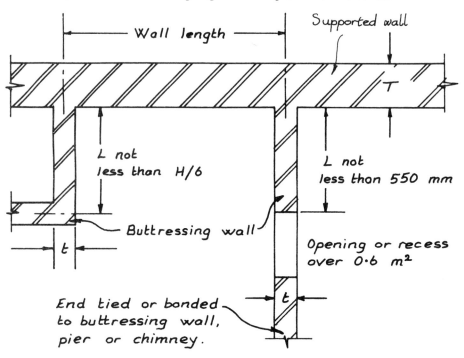

Wall length

Supported wall

T

L not less than H/6

L not less than 550 mm

Buttressing wall

Opening or recess over 0·6 m²

t

End tied or bonded to buttressing wall, pier or chimney.

t

t = thickness from C27 of Part C to section 1 of A.D.A 1/2 .

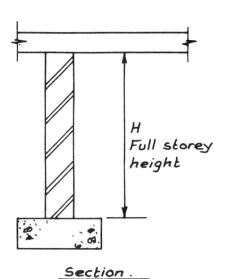

H Full storey height

Section.

Fig. 6.6 Buttressing walls.

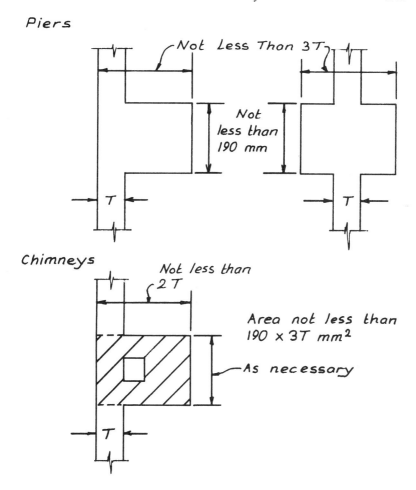

Fig. 6.7 Piers and chimneys.

which a wall must be expected to sustain, apart from that due to direct wind load and the transmission of wind load.

VERTICAL LOADING. The total dead and imposed load transmitted by a wall at its base should not exceed 70 kN/m. All vertical loads carried by a wall should be properly distributed. This may be assumed for precast concrete floors, concrete floor slabs and timber floors complying with Part B of section 1 of AD A1/2. Distributed loading may also be assumed for lintels with a bearing length of 150 mm or more. Where the clear span of the lintel is 1200 mm or less the bearing length may be reduced to 100 mm.

These requirements are summarised in Fig. 6.8.

AD A1/2
sec. 1
Part C
C24 & C25

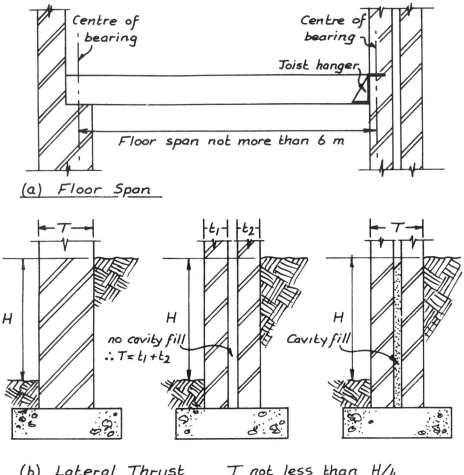

(a) Floor Span

(b) Lateral Thrust   T not less than H/4

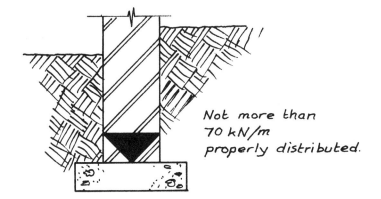

(c) Vertical Loading.

Fig. 6.8 Loading requirements.

Openings and Recesses

Openings or recesses in a wall should not be placed in such a manner as to impair the stability of any part of it. Adequate support for the super-structure should be provided over every opening and recess.

As a general rule, any opening or recess in a wall should be flanked on each side by a length of wall equal to at least one sixth of the width of the opening or recess, in order to provide the required stability. Accordingly, the minimum length of wall between two openings or recesses should not be less than one sixth of the *combined* width of the two openings or recesses.

However, where long span roofs or floors bear onto a wall containing openings or recesses it may be necessary to increase the width of the flanking portions of wall. Table C6 to Part C of section 1 of AD A1/2 contains factors that enable this to be done.

Where several openings and/or recesses are formed in a wall, their total width should, at any level, be not more than two thirds of the length of the wall at that level.

No opening or recess should exceed 3 m in length. These requirements are illustrated in Fig. 6.9 below.

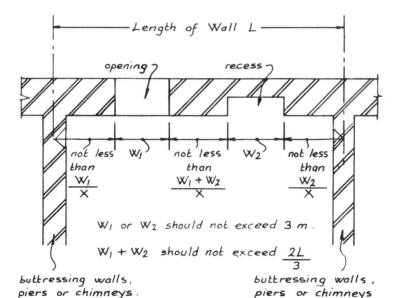

Fig. 6.9 Openings and recesses.

AD A1/2, Section 1
Part C

Table **C6**   **Value of factor 'X'**

Nature of roof span	Maximum roof span [m]	Minimum thickness of wall inner leaf [mm]	Span of floor is parallel to wall	Span of timber floor into wall		Span of concrete floor into wall	
				max 4.5m	max 6.0 m	max 4.5 m	max 6.0 m
				Value of factor 'X'			
roof spans parallel to wall	not applicable	100	6	6	6	6	6
		90	6	6	6	6	5
timber roof spans into wall	9	100	6	6	5	4	3
		90	6	4	4	3	3

Chases

The depth of vertical chases should not be more than one-third the thickness of the wall, or in a cavity wall, one-third the thickness of the leaf concerned. Depth of horizontal chases should be not more than one-sixth the thickness of the wall or leaf. Chases should not be placed in such a manner as to impair the stability of the wall, particularly where hollow blocks are used (see Fig. 6.10).

Overhanging

AD A1/2
sec. 1
Part C
C29 to C32

Where a wall overhangs a supporting structure beneath it, the amount of the overhang should not be such as to impair the stability of the wall. No limits are specified, but this would generally be interpreted as allowing an overhang of one-third the thickness of the wall (see Fig. 6.11).

Lateral support

AD A1/2
sec 1
Part C
C33 & C34

Floor or roof lateral support is horizontal support or stiffening, intended to stabilise or stiffen a wall by restraining its movement in a direction at right angles to the wall length. The restraint or support is provided by connecting a floor or roof to the wall in such a way that the

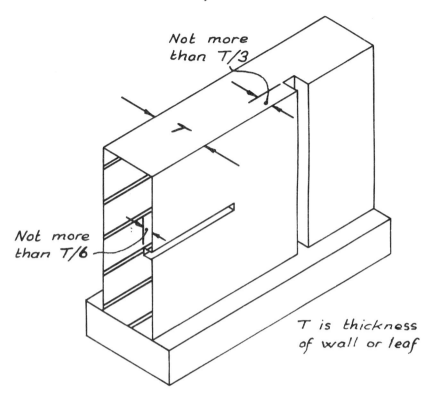

Fig. 6.10 Chases.

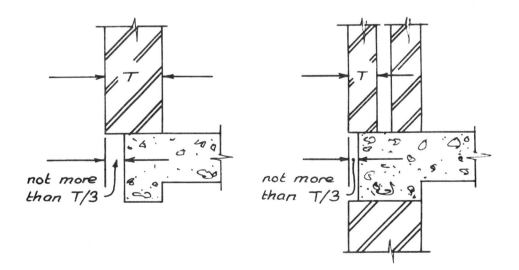

Fig. 6.11 Overhanging.

floor or roof acts as a stiffening frame or diaphragm, transferring the lateral forces to walls, buttressing walls, piers or chimneys.

ROOF LATERAL SUPPORT.   This should be provided for all external, compartment, separating and internal load-bearing walls irrespective of their length, at the point of junction between the roof and supported wall (i.e. at eaves level and along the verges).

Walls should be strapped to roofs at not exceeding 2 m centres using galvanised mild steel or other durable metal straps, with a minimum cross-section of 30 mm × 5 mm.

Eaves strapping need not be provided for a roof which:

(a) has a pitch of 15° or more;
(b) is tiled or slated;
(c) is of a type known by local experience as being resistant to damage by wind gusts;
(d) has main timber members spanning onto the supported wall at intervals of not more than 1·2 m; and,
(e) has a bearing by each timber member of not less than 90 mm (if no wallplate) or 75 mm (if onto a timber wallplate). Figure 6.12 below, shows methods of providing satisfactory lateral support at separating or gabled end wall positions.

AD A1/2
sec. 1
Part C
C37

FLOOR LATERAL SUPPORT.   This should be provided for any external, compartment or separating wall which exceeds 3 m in length.

It should also be provided for any internal wall (which is not a compartment or separating wall) at the top of each storey, irrespective of its length.

Wall should be strapped to floors above ground level at not exceeding 2 m centres using galvanised mild steel or other durable metal straps, with a minimum cross-section of 30 mm × 5 mm.

There are certain cases where, because of the nature of the floor construction, it is not necessary to provide restraint straps:

● where a floor forms part of a house having not more than two storeys and:
(a) has timber members spanning so as to penetrate into the supported wall at intervals of not more than 1·2 m with at least 90 mm bearing directly on the walls or 75 mm bearing onto a timber wall plate; or,
(b) the joists are carried on the supported wall by *restraint* type joist hangers, described in BS 5628: Part 1, at not more than 2 m centres.

● where a concrete floor has a bearing onto the supported wall of at least 90 mm.
● where two floors are at or about the same level on either side of a supported wall contact between floors and wall may be continuous

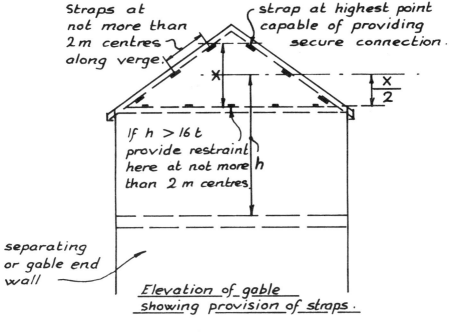

Straps at
not more than
2 m centres
along verge.

strap at highest point
capable of providing
secure connection.

$\dfrac{X}{2}$

If h > 16 t
provide restraint
here at not more h
than 2 m centres.

separating
or gable end
wall

Elevation of gable
showing provision of straps.

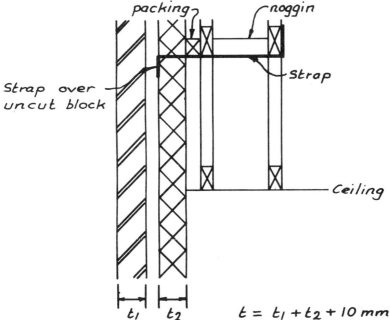

packing   noggin

Strap over
uncut block

Strap

Ceiling

t_1 t_2 $t = t_1 + t_2 + 10\ mm$

Section through gable at roof level
showing method of strapping.

Fig. 6.12 Lateral support for roofs.

AD A1/2
sec. 1
Part C
C36

or intermittent. If intermittent, the points of contact should be at or about the same positions on plan at intervals not exceeding 2 m. Figure 6.13 below summarises these provisions.

Interruption of lateral support

It is clear that in certain circumstances it may be necessary to interrupt the continuity of lateral support for a wall. This occurs chiefly where a stairway or similar structure adjoins a supported wall and necessitates the formation of an opening in a floor or roof.

This is permitted provided certain precautions are taken:

● The opening extends for a distance not exceeding 3 m measured parallel to the supported wall.
● If the connection between wall and floor or roof is provided by means of anchors, these should be spaced closer than 2 m on either side of the opening so as to result in the same number of anchors being used as if there were no opening.
● Other forms of connection should be provided throughout the length of each part of the wall on either side of the opening.

AD A1/2
sec. 1
Part C
C38

● There should be no other interruption of lateral support (see Figure 6.14).

Thickness of walls

Provided the building design and wall construction requirements discussed above are satisfied, it is permissible to determine the thickness of a wall without calculation.

The minimum thicknesses required depend upon the wall height and length, and the rules applying to walls of bricks or blocks are set out in Table C2 to Part C of section 1 of AD A1/2 (see below) and illustrated in Figure 6.15.

AD A1/2
sec. 1
Part C
C4 & C5

These thicknesses do not apply to parapet walls, for which there are special rules (see below) or to bays, and gables over bay windows above the level of the lowest window sill.

As a general rule, the thickness of any storey of a brick or block wall should not be less than one sixteenth of the height of that storey.

AD A1/2
sec. 1
Part C
C6 & C7

However, walls of stone, flints, clunches of bricks or other burnt or vitrified material should have a thickness of at least 1⅓ times the thickness required of brick or block walls.

AD A1/2
sec. 1
Part C
C9

Irrespective of the materials used in construction, no part of a wall should be thinner than any other part of the wall that it supports.

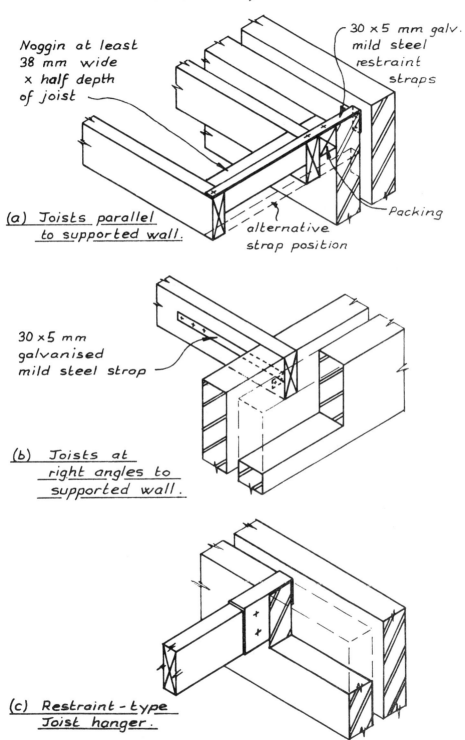

Noggin at least
38 mm wide
× half depth
of joist

30 × 5 mm galv.
mild steel
restraint
straps

Packing

(a) Joists parallel
to supported wall.

alternative
strap position

30 × 5 mm
galvanised
mild steel strap

(b) Joists at
right angles to
supported wall.

(c) Restraint-type
Joist hanger.

Fig. 6.13 Floor lateral support.

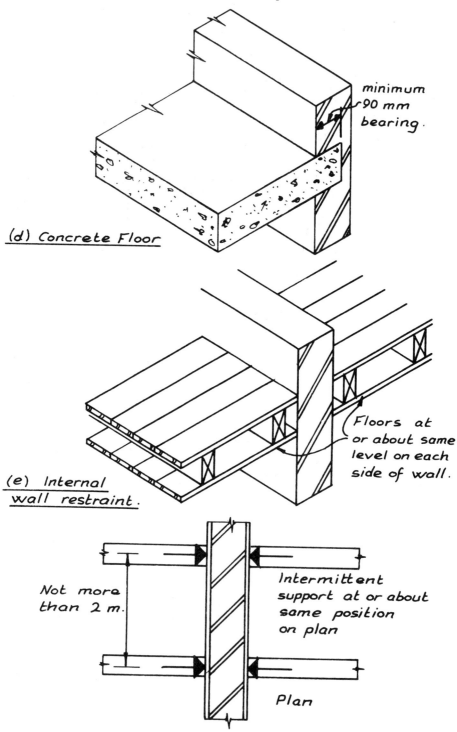

minimum 90 mm bearing.

(d) Concrete Floor

Floors at or about same level on each side of wall.

(e) Internal wall restraint.

Not more than 2 m.

Intermittent support at or about same position on plan

Plan

Fig. 6.13 (Contd.)

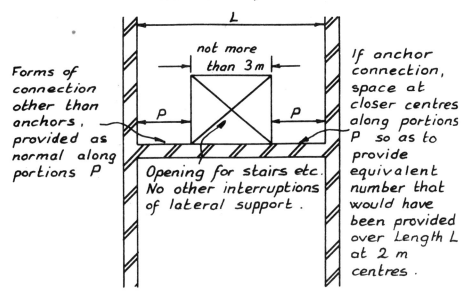

Fig. 6.14 Interruption of lateral support.

AD A1/2, Section 1
Part C

Table C2 *Minimum thickness of certain external walls, compartment walls and separating walls.*

(1)	(2)	(3)
Height of wall	Length of wall	Thickness of wall
Not exceeding 3·5 m . .	Not exceeding 12 m . .	190 mm for the whole of its height
Exceeding 3.5 m but not exceeding 9 m	Not exceeding 9 m . .	190 mm for the whole of its height
	Exceeding 9 m but not exceeding 12 m	290 mm from the base for the height of one storey, and 190 mm for the rest of its height
Exceeding 9 m but not exceeding 12 m	Not exceeding 9 m . .	290 mm from the base for the height of one storey, and 190 mm for the rest of its height
	Exceeding 9 m but not exceeding 12 m	290 mm from the base for the height of two storeys, and 190 mm for the rest of its height

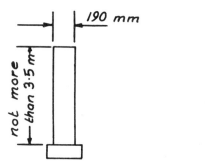

Length not more than 12 m

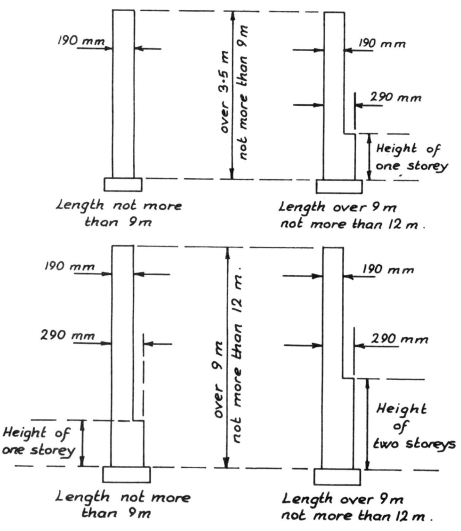

Fig. 6.15 Thickness of solid external, compartment and separating walls. (See Table C2.)

Solid internal load-bearing walls which are not compartment or separating walls

For these walls the sum of the wall thickness, plus 5 mm, should be equal to at least half the thickness that would be required by Table C2 for an external wall, compartment wall or separating wall of the same height and length.

Where a wall forms the lowest storey of a three-storey building, and it carries loading from both upper storeys, its thickness should not be less than the thickness calculated above or 140 mm, *whichever is greater.* Thus there is an absolute minimum thickness of 140 mm for such walls.

AD A1/2
sec. 1
Part C
C10

Cavity walls

Any external, compartment or separating wall which is built as a cavity wall should consist of two leaves, each leaf built of bricks or blocks.

The leaves of these walls should be properly tied together with wall ties to BS 1243: 1978, or other not less suitable ties. Ties should be placed at centres 900 mm horizontally and 450 mm vertically, and at any opening at least one tie should be provided for each 300 mm of height close to the opening unless the leaves are connected by a bonded jamb.

The cavity should be at least 50 mm, and not more than 75 mm, in width at any level. However, if vertical twist type ties are used, with horizontal spacing reduced to 750 mm, the cavity width may be up to 100 mm. Each leaf should be at least 90 mm thick at any level.

The sum of the thicknesses of the two leaves, plus 10 mm, should not be less than the thickness required for a solid wall by Table C2. (See also Figure 6.16 below.)

AD A1/2
sec. 1
Part C
C8

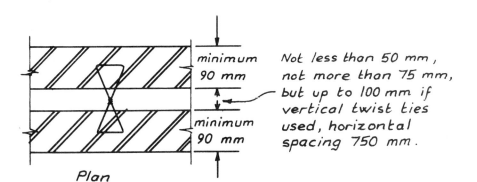

Fig. 6.16 Cavity walls.

Parapets

Referring to Figure 6.17(a), the minimum thickness, t, for a solid parapet wall should not be less than the greater of:

(a) H/4; or,
(b) 150 mm.

For a cavity parapet the minimum thickness, t, is related to the maximum parapet height as shown in Fig. 6.17(b).

Block and brick dimensions

The wall thicknesses specified in Part C relate to the *work size* of the materials used. This means the size specified in the relevant British Standard as the size to which the brick or block must conform, account being taken of any permissible deviations or tolerances specified in the British Standard.

Some walls may be constructed of bricks or blocks having modular dimensions derived from BS 4011: 1966 *Recommendations for the coordination of dimensions in buildings. Coordinating sizes for building components and assemblies* without the bricks or blocks themselves being covered by a British Standard.

AD A1/2
sec. 1
Part C
C13

In these cases, the thicknesses prescribed in Part C may be reduced by an amount not exceeding that allowed in a British Standard for the same material.

External walls of small buildings and annexes

The external walls of small buildings and annexes have to comply with special rules.

The external walls of such buildings may be not less than 90 mm thick if,

(a) the walls are bonded at each end and intermediately to piers or buttressing walls of not less than 190 mm square in horizontal section (including wall thickness), or larger as necessary for stability; and,

AD A1/2
sec. 1
Part C
C12, C39
& C40

(b) the piers, etc., are positioned so that they divide the wall into distinct lengths and each length is not more than 3 m. (This does not apply if the wall is less than 2·5 m high and long.)

The wall should be built as a solid wall of bricks and blocks and should carry only distributed loading from the roof of the building or annexe, and not be subjected to any lateral thrust from the roof (see Fig. 6.18 below).

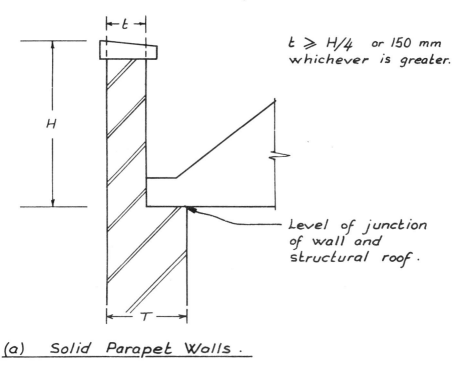

$t \geqslant H/4$ or 150 mm whichever is greater.

Level of junction of wall and structural roof.

(a) Solid Parapet Walls.

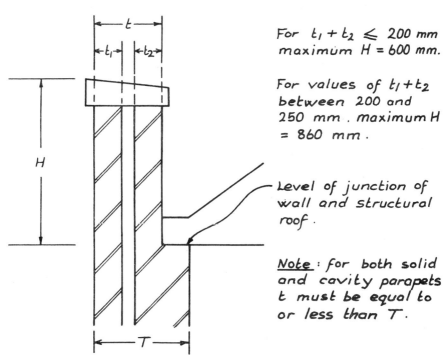

For $t_1 + t_2 \leqslant 200$ mm maximum $H = 600$ mm.

For values of $t_1 + t_2$ between 200 and 250 mm, maximum $H = 860$ mm.

Level of junction of wall and structural roof.

Note: for both solid and cavity parapets t must be equal to or less than T.

(b) Cavity Parapet walls

Fig. 6.17 Height of parapet walls.

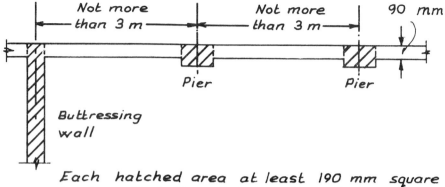

Each hatched area at least 190 mm square
(not applied if wall is less than 2·5 m high
and long ·) .

Fig. 6.18 Small buildings and annexes.

Dimensions of chimneys

The wholly external part of a chimney, constructed of masonry and not supported by adequate ties or otherwise stabilised will be deemed satisfactory if the width of the chimney, at the level of the highest point in the line of junction with the roof and at any higher level, is such that its height as measured from that level to the top of the external part of the chimney is not more than 4½ times that width. That height includes any pot or flue terminal on a chimney.

AD A1/2
sec. 1
Part D
D1
The width of chimney at any level is taken as the smallest width which can be shown on an elevation of the chimney from any direction. This is illustrated in Fig. 6.19.

Foundations and ground movement

In addition to the provisions of paragraph A1 of Schedule 1 to the Building Regulations 1985, that all the loads on a building must be sustained and transmitted safely to the ground (see page 6.1 above), there are requirements in paragraph A2 of Schedule 1 that the building shall be so constructed that movements of the subsoil caused by
Regs Sch 1
A2
swelling, shrinkage or freezing will not impair the stability of any part of the building.

Part E of section 1 of AD A1/2 provides rules for the construction of strip foundations of plain concrete. However, it does not specify the types of buildings for which the foundations are intended. It is assumed that since section 1 of AD A1/2 deals with structural elements for houses and other small buildings this includes residential buildings
AD A1/2
Part E
of not more than three storeys, small single-storey non-residential buildings and annexes as defined in Part C of section 1 of AD A1/2.

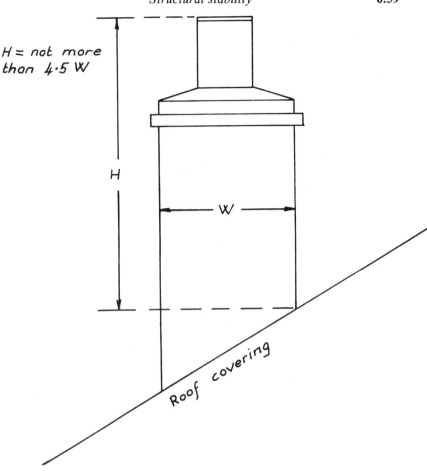

$H =$ not more than $4.5\ W$

H

W

Roof covering

Fig. 6.19 External part of chimneys, D1

Foundation requirements

Strip foundations of plain concrete placed centrally under the walls will be satisfactory if they comply with the following rules:

(a) No made ground or wide soil strength variation in the loaded area or weak soil patches likely to cause foundation failure;
(b) width of foundation strip is in accordance with the Table E1 to section 1 of AD A1/2 which is reproduced below.
(c) the concrete is composed of:

(i) cement to BS 12: 1978 *Specification for ordinary and rapid hardening Portland cement*; and,

Table E1 to Part E of section 1 of AD A1/2
(Minimum width of strip foundations)

(1) Type of subsoil	(2) Condition of subsoil	(3) Field test applicable	(4) Minimum width in millimetres for total load in kilonewtons per lineal metre of load-bearing walling of not more than					
			20 kN/m	30 kN/m	40 kN/m	50 kN/m	60 kN/m	70 kN/m
I Rock	Not inferior to sandstone, limestone or firm chalk	Requires at least a pneumatic or other mechanically operated pick for excavation	In each case equal to the width of wall					
II Gravel Sand	Compact Compact	Requires pick for excavation. Wooden peg 50 mm square in cross-section hard to drive beyond 150 mm	250	300	400	500	600	650
III Clay Sandy clay	Stiff Stiff	Cannot be moulded with the fingers and requires a pick or pneumatic or other mechanically operated spade for its removal	250	300	400	500	600	650
IV Clay Sandy clay	Firm Firm	Can be moulded by substantial pressure with the fingers and can be excavated with graft or spade	300	350	450	600	750	850
V Sand Silty sand Clayey sand	Loose Loose Loose	Can be excavated with a spade. Wooden peg 50 mm square in cross-section can be easily driven	400	600	Note: In relation to types V, VI and VII, foundations do not fall within the provisions of this Section if the total load exceeds 30 kN/m			
VI Silt Clay Sandy clay Silty clay	Soft Soft Soft Soft	Fairly easily moulded in the fingers and readily excavated	450	650				
VII Silt Clay Sandy clay Silty clay	Very soft Very soft Very soft Very soft	Natural sample in winter conditions exudes between fingers when squeezed in fist	600	850				

(ii) coarse and fine aggregate to BS 882: 1983 *Specification for aggregates from natural sources for concrete.*

(d) The concrete mix is:

(i) in the proportions 50 kg of cement: 0·1 m³ fine aggregate: 0.2 m³ coarse aggregate i.e. 1:3:6 or better; or,

(ii) Grade C15P concrete to BS 5328: 1981; or,

(iii) Grade 15 concrete to CP 110: 1972 *The structural use of concrete* (due to be superseded by BS 8110 *Structural use of concrete*).

(e) the concrete strip thickness is equal to or greater than the projection from the wall face, and never less than 150 mm;

(f) the upper level of a stepped foundation overlaps the lower level by twice the height of the step, by the thickness of the foundation, or 300 mm whichever is the greater.

(g) the height of a step is not greater than the thickness of the foundation.

(h) foundation strip projects beyond the faces of any pier, buttress or chimney forming part of a wall by at least as much as it projects beyond the face of the wall proper.

Table E1 to section 1 of AD A1/2 specifies seven sub-soil types, and the minimum strip widths to use vary according to the calculated load per metre run of the wall at foundation level. The table is reproduced above. AD A1/2 sec. 1 Part E E1 to E3

Where a wall load exceeds 70 kN per metre run the foundation will be outside the scope of Part E and must be properly designed on structural principles.

These requirements are illustrated in Fig. 6.20.

Design of structural members in buildings of all types

Section 1 of AD A1/2, which is discussed above, deals with a fairly restricted range of building types of traditional masonry construction. If the various parts of section 1 are complied with it is not necessary to provide design calculations.

Building types falling outside the scope of section 1 will need full structural calculations and design. Therefore, section 2 of AD A1/2 lists a series of British Standards and Codes of Practice that, if used appropriately, will satisfy the requirements of paragraphs A1 and A2 of Schedule 1 to the Building Regulations 1985.

Loading

Dead and imposed loads may be assessed by reference to BS 6399: *Design loading for buildings* Part 1: 1984 *Code of Practice for dead and imposed loads.*

Snow loads may vary due to an uneven depth of snow caused by sliding, wind, melting, etc.; therefore, the resulting load on the roof may be increased locally to take account of this. Guidance may be sought in BRE Digest 290 in these circumstances.

Wind loads may be assessed by reference to CP 3: Chapter V: Part 2: 1972 *Wind loads*. However, the S_3 factor should never be taken as less than 1.

If the actual load is greater than the design load from BS 6399: Part 1: 1984 the actual load should be used.

Foundations

Foundations should be designed in accordance with CP 2004: 1972 *Foundations*.

Structure above foundations

- Structural work of reinforced, prestressed or plain concrete should comply with:

(a) BS 8110 *The structural use of concrete* Part 1: 1985 *Code of Practice for design, materials and workmanship*, Part 2: 1985 *Recommendations for use in special circumstances* and Part 3: 1985 *Design charts for singly reinforced beams, doubly reinforced beams and rectangular columns*; or,

(b) CP 114: 1969 *Structural use of reinforced concrete in buildings* plus amendments.

- Structural work of composite steel and concrete construction should comply with CP 117 *Composite construction in structural steel and concrete* Part 1: 1965 *Simply supported beams in building*.
- Structural work of steel should comply with:

(a) BS 5950 *The structural use of steelwork in building*: Part 1: 1985 *Code of Practice for design in simple and continuous construction; hot rolled sections*, Part 2: 1985 *Specification for materials, fabrication and erection; hot rolled sections*, Part 4: 1982 *Code of Practice for design of floors with profiled steel sheeting*; or,

(b) BS 449 *The use of structural steel in building*, Part 2: 1969 *Metric units* and Addendum No. 1 (1975) to BS 449: Part 2: 1969 *The use of cold formed steel sections in building*. (The reference to BS 449 will be deleted in 1987.)

- Structural work of aluminium should comply with CP 118: 1969 *The structural use of aluminium*, using one of the alloys listed in Section 1.1 of the code. (Under section 5.3 of the code, the structure should be classified as a safe-life structure.)
- Structural work of masonry should comply with:

Examples : Cavity wall 60 kN/m run in different soil types, to rules of Table E1 .

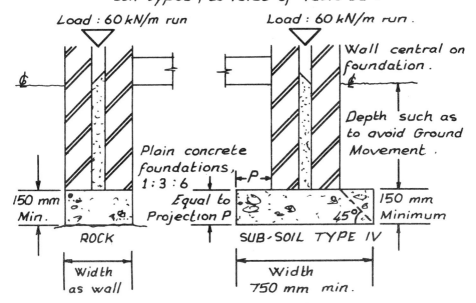

Load : 60 kN/m run

Load : 60 kN/m run .

Wall central on foundation .

Depth such as to avoid Ground Movement .

Plain concrete foundations, 1 : 3 : 6

Equal to Projection P

150 mm Min.

ROCK

150 mm Minimum

45°

SUB-SOIL TYPE IV

Width as wall

Width 750 mm min.

No made ground . No weak patches . No strength variation .

(a) *Plain Strip Foundation .*

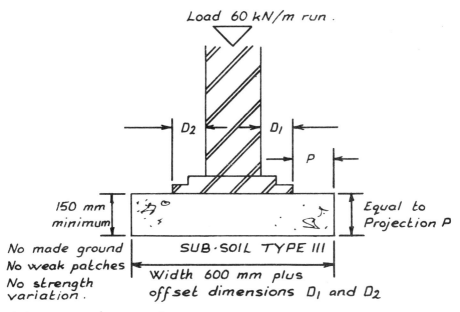

Load 60 kN/m run .

D_2 D_1

P

150 mm minimum

Equal to Projection P

No made ground No weak patches No strength variation .

SUB-SOIL TYPE III

Width 600 mm plus offset dimensions D_1 and D_2

(b) *Strip Foundation with Footing .*

Fig. 6.20 Strip foundations of plain concrete.

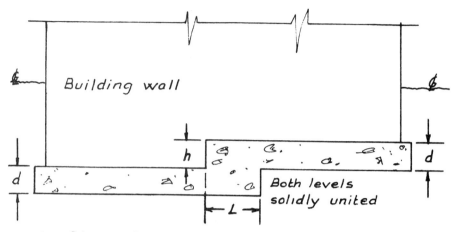

$L = 2h$ or d or 300 mm whichever is greater
h must not be greater than d.

(c) Steps in Foundations.

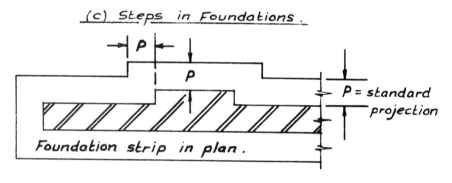

(d) Projections

Fig. 6.20 (Contd.)

BS 5628 *Code of Practice for the structural use of masonry*: Part 1: 1978 *Unreinforced masonry*, Part 3: 1985 *Materials and components, design and workmanship.*

AD A1/2 sec. 2

● Structural work of timber should comply with BS 5268 *Code of Practice for the structural use of timber*, Part 2: 1984 *Code of Practice for permissible stress design, materials and workmanship*, Part 3: 1985 *Code of Practice for trussed rafter roofs.*

Disproportionate collapse

Following on the Tribunal which held a public inquiry into the collapse of part of a block of flats known as Ronan Point, two new regulations were introduced in 1970.

These regulations applied only to buildings of five storeys or more (including basement storeys).

Paragraph A3 of Schedule 1 to the Building Regulations 1985 extends the scope of control to public buildings which incorporate a clear span exceeding nine metres between supports in addition to buildings of five storeys or more.

Such buildings must be constructed so that in the event of an accident the structure will not be damaged to an extent disproportionate to the cause of the damage.

Regs Sch. 1 A3

It is interesting to note that the term 'damage' has been used in paragraph A3, since all references to damage have been deliberately eliminated from paragraphs A1 and A2 of Schedule 1 (see introduction to this chapter page 6.1). The intention of paragraph A3 is surely to limit collapse, since damage to a building does not necessarily affect public health and safety.

AD A3 contains provisions designed to meet the requirements of paragraph A3 of Schedule 1. However, the provisions are only for buildings having five or more storeys. It is not clear whether this includes public buildings with spans in excess of 9 m which are also of five or more storeys, but it certainly excludes these buildings if they have less than five storeys.

Compliance with various British Standards and Codes of Practice will satisfy the requirement of paragraph A3 as follows:

- Structural work of reinforced, prestressed or plain concrete should comply with BS 8110 *The structural use of concrete*: Part 1: 1985 *Code of Practice for design, materials and workmanship*; Part 2: 1985 *Recommendations for use in special circumstances.*
- Structural work of steel should comply with BS 5950 *The structural use of steelwork in building*: Part 1: 1985, *Code of Practice for design in simple and continuous construction; hot rolled sections.*
- Structural work of masonry should comply with BS 5628 *Code of Practice for the structural use of masonry*: Part 1: 1978, *Unreinforced masonry.*

Apart from the references to British Standards and Codes of Practice listed above very little guidance is given in AD A3 as to the precautions that need to be taken to prevent or limit disproportionate collapse. This reflects the complexity of the problem. However, some additional information is provided which helps to shed light on the design principles to be adopted.

This uses the concept of the *protected key element*. This is a single structural element on which a large part of a structure relies, and is defined as supporting a floor or roof area of more than 70 m^2 or 15% of the area of a storey, whichever is less.

These elements are of utmost importance in the design, and the Codes and Standards listed above contain minimum loadings that protected key elements must withstand. For example, in BS 5950: Part 1: 1985 accident loadings are referred to in Clause 2.4.5.5. AD A3 requires that a protected key element be capable of withstanding a load of at least 34 kN/m^2 applied in any direction for steel structures covered by BS 5950.

If a member is not designed as a protected key element its failure should result only in localised failure of the structure as a whole. It should be limited, therefore, to the immediately adjacent storeys and should not exceed 70 m^2 or 15% of those storey areas, whichever is less.

AD A3

Chapter 7

Fire

Introduction

Part B of Schedule 1 to the Building Regulations 1985 is concerned with means of escape from buildings and fire spread within and between buildings. Since the regulations are made in the interests of public health and safety, they do not attempt to achieve non-combustible buildings, but rather to ensure the safety of the building, its occupants and the public.

Buildings must therefore be constructed so that, in the event of fire:

- the occupants are able to reach a place of safety.
- they will resist collapse for a sufficient period of time to allow evacuation of the occupants and prevent further rapid fire spread.
- the spread of fire within and between buildings is kept to a minimum.

The first requirement is met by providing an adequate number of exits and protected escape routes. The second is met by setting reasonable standards of fire resistance for the structural elements – the floors, roofs, load-bearing walls and frames. The third is met by:

(a) dividing large buildings into *compartments* and requiring higher standards of fire resistance of the walls and floors bounding a compartment,
(b) setting standards of non-combustibility and fire resistance for external walls,
(c) controlling the surface materials of walls and ceilings to inhibit flame spread,
(d) sealing and sub-dividing concealed spaces in the structure or fabric of a building to prevent the spread of unseen fire and smoke, and
(e) setting standards of resistance to fire penetration and flame spread for roof coverings.

Ideally, there should be no openings in any compartment wall or floor, but this is impractical. Openings are therefore permitted, provided they are suitably protected. Openings in compartment walls must be fitted with a self-closing fire-resistant door or shutter.

Compartment floors may be pierced by stairwells or lift shafts passing from one storey to another, and these could result in vertical spread of fire. This is prevented by enclosing stairwells or lift shafts within a fire-resisting structure termed a *protected shaft*. Any opening in a structure enclosing a protected shaft should be protected by fire-resisting doors or shutters.

Errata

Care should be taken when using AD B2/3/4 section 4 (Other residential) as a number of typographical errors appear in Tables 4.1 and 4.3.

In the headings to Table 4.1 (Minimum periods of fire resistance) the references in the table to notes 1 and 2 (which appear at the foot of the table) have been omitted. 1 should be placed after the heading 'Floor area of each storey' and 2 should be placed after the heading 'Cubic capacity of building'.

The cross (†) that appears next to the number 1 in the column 'Ground or upper storey', against the item '3 storey building or separated part (basements not counted) should be replaced with two asterisks (**).

In Table 4.3, Limitations on roof construction, the double asterisks next to the item 'no designation' in column 2 should be replaced by a single asterisk.

These corrections have been made in the text of this chapter.

Terminology

AD B2/3/4
Appendix L

Certain terms which apply generally throughout this chapter are defined here. Other terms are defined in the specific section to which they apply.

BASEMENT STOREY – a storey which has some part of the perimeter of its floor more than 1.2 m below the highest level of the ground adjoining that part of the floor. (See Fig. 7.1.)

BOUNDARY – when referring to any side of a building or compartment (including any external wall or part) means the usual legal boundary adjacent to that side, being taken up to the centre of any abutting railway, street, canal or river.

CEILING – includes any soffit, rooflight or other part of a building which encloses and is exposed overhead in a room, circulation space or protected shaft (but not including the surface of the frame of any rooflight).

CIRCULATION SPACE – a space used solely or predominantly as

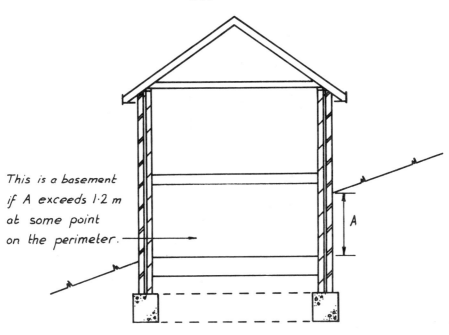

Fig. 7.1 Basement storey.

a means of access between a room and a protected shaft or between either a room or a protected shaft and an exit from the building or compartment.

COMPARTMENT – any part of a building separated from all other parts by one or more compartment walls and/or compartment floors. If any part of the top-storey of a building comes within a compartment, that compartment is taken to include any roof space above that part of the top-storey (see Fig. 7.2). See also 'separated part' below.

COMPARTMENT WALL/FLOOR – fire resisting construction provided to divide a building into compartments for the purposes of preventing fire spread.

CONCEALED SPACE (CAVITY) – a space which is concealed by the elements of a building (such as a roofspace or the space above a suspended ceiling) or contained within an element (such as the cavity in a wall). This definition does *not* include a room, cupboard, circulation space, protected shaft or space within a flue, chute, duct, pipe or conduit.

CONSERVATORY – a part of a single storey building in which the walls and roof are substantially glazed with translucent or transparent material.

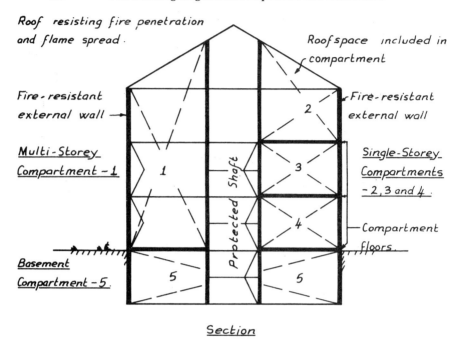

Roof resisting fire penetration and flame spread.

Roofspace included in compartment

Fire-resistant external wall →

Fire-resistant external wall

Multi-Storey Compartment – 1

Single-Storey Compartments – 2,3 and 4.

Compartment Floors.

Basement Compartment – 5.

Protected Shaft

Section

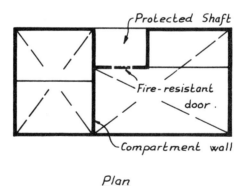

Protected Shaft

Fire-resistant door.

Compartment wall

Plan

Fig. 7.2 Division of buildings into compartments.

DOOR – includes any shutter, cover or other form of protection to an opening in any wall or floor of a building or in the structure surrounding a protected shaft. A door may have one or more leaves.

ELEMENT OF STRUCTURE
(a) Any member forming part of the structural frame of a building

or any other beam or column. (It does not include a member forming part of the roof structure only.)
(b) A floor (including a compartment floor) but not the lowest floor in a building or a platform floor.
(c) An external wall.
(d) A separating wall.
(e) A compartment wall.
(f) The structure enclosing a protected shaft.
(g) A load-bearing wall or load-bearing part of a wall.
(h) A gallery (see Fig. 7.3).

EXTERNAL CLADDING – means any material fixed to the external face of a wall for decoration or weather protection.

EXTERNAL WALL – includes a portion of a roof sloping at 70° or more to the horizontal if it adjoins a space within the building to which persons have access, other than for occasional maintenance and repair (see Fig. 7.4).

GALLERY – a floor (or raised storage area) which projects into another space but has less than half the floor area of that space.

NOTIONAL BOUNDARY – a boundary which is assumed to exist between two buildings on the same site where there is no actual boundary. The notional boundary line should be so placed that neither building contravenes any of the requirements of AD 2/3/4 relevant to the external walls facing each other (see Fig. 7.5).

PLATFORM FLOOR – a floor over a concealed space, which is supported by a structural floor.

PROTECTED SHAFT – a stairway, lift, escalator, duct, chute or other shaft which enables persons, things or air to pass between different compartments.

RELEVANT BOUNDARY – for a boundary to be considered relevant it should:

(a) be coincident with, or
(b) be parallel to, or
(c) not make an angle of more than 80° with the external wall (see Fig. 7.6.).

In certain circumstances a 'notional' boundary, as defined below, will be the relevant boundary. A wall may have more than one relevant boundary.

ROOFLIGHT – includes any domelight, lanternlight, skylight or other element which is intended to admit daylight.

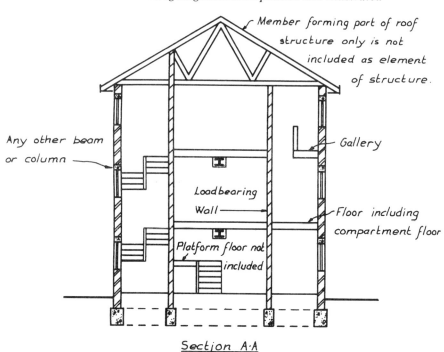

Member forming part of roof structure only is not included as element of structure.

Any other beam or column

Gallery

Loadbearing Wall

Floor including compartment floor

Platform floor not included

<u>Section A·A</u>

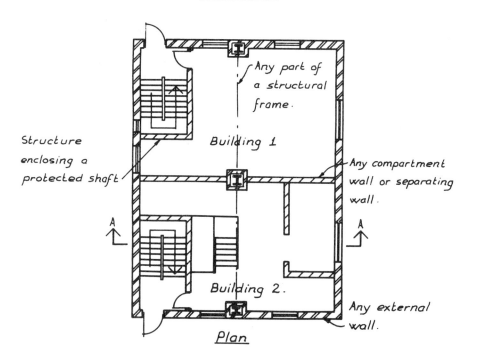

Any part of a structural frame.

Building 1

Structure enclosing a protected shaft

Any compartment wall or separating wall.

Building 2.

Any external wall.

<u>Plan</u>

Fig. 7.3 Elements of structure.

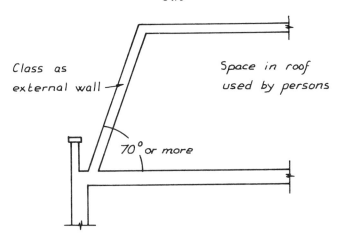

Fig. 7.4 Steeply pitched roofs.

ROOM – an enclosed space in a building, but not an enclosed circulation space or a protected shaft. (This term would also include cupboards that were not fittings and large rooms such as auditoria.)

SEPARATED PART (OF A BUILDING) – where a compartment wall completely divides a building from top to bottom and is in one plane the divided sections of the building are referred to as separated parts. The height of each separated part may then be treated individually (see Fig. 7.7 and rules for measurement below).

SEPARATING WALL – a wall or part of a wall which is common to adjoining buildings.

SINGLE STOREY BUILDING – a building which consists of a ground storey only. (A separated part consisting of a ground-storey only and with a roof which is accessible only for purposes of maintenance and repair may be treated as part of a single-storey building.)

UNPROTECTED AREA – in relation to an external wall or side of a building means:
(a) a window, door or other opening;
(b) any part of an external wall of fire resistance less than that required by B 2/3/4;
(c) any part of an external wall with external facing attached or applied, whether as cladding or not, the facing being of combustible material more than 1 mm thick. (Combustible in this context means any material which is not non-combustible or is not a material of limited combustibility) (see Fig. 7.8).

WALL SURFACE – does not include any unglazed portion of a door, any door frame, frame in which glazing is fitted, window frame, fireplace surround, mantleshelf, fitted furniture or trim but it *does* include the surface of any glazing and any part of a ceiling which slopes at an angle of 70° or more to the horizontal. (Trim includes any architrave, cover mould, picture rail, skirting or similar narrow member.)

AD B2/3/4
Appendix L

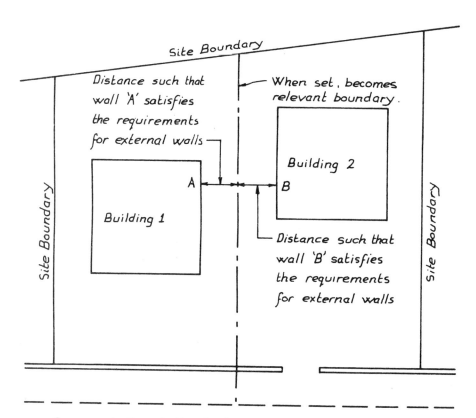

One .or both of the buildings new.
One or other of the buildings of residential or assembly use.
Existing building treated as identical new building but with existing unprotected area and fire resistance in external wall.

Fig. 7.5 Notional boundary.

Arrows connect walls with their
relevant boundaries.
An external wall may be on its
own relevant boundary — as woll 'A'

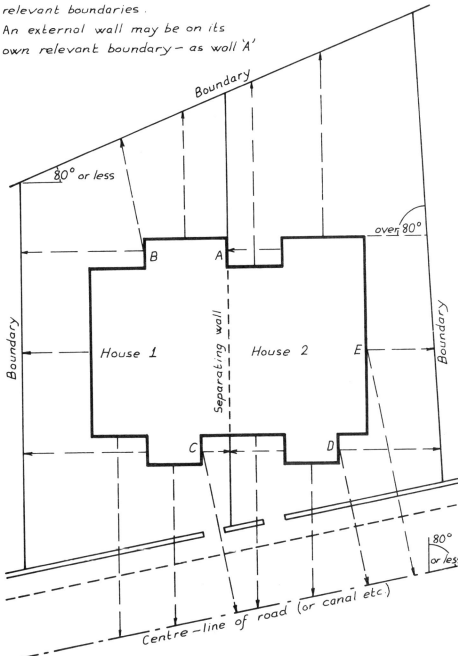

An external wall may have more than one Relevant Boundary,
as walls B, C, D and E.

Fig. 7.6 Relevant boundaries.

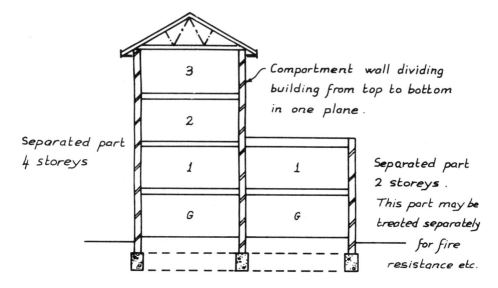

Fig. 7.7 Separated part.

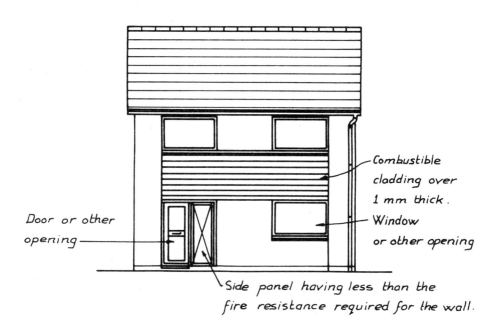

Fig. 7.8 Unprotected areas.

Purpose groups

The fire hazard presented by a building or compartment within a building depends upon both its size and the use to which it is put. AD B2/3/4 specifies nine purpose groups, according to the actual use of the building or compartment. Limits are set on the permitted size of any compartment according to its purpose group classification. Therefore the purpose group must be established before any further provisions can be considered.

AD B2/3/4 0.35

Where a building contains compartments or separated parts used for different purposes, each compartment or separated part should be classified separately.

AD B2/3/4 0.38

A building or compartment or separated part may be used for several different purposes. Only the main purpose is taken into account in deciding its purpose group classification. However, any ancillary uses may be treated as belonging to a purpose group in their own right in the following cases:

● where a flat or maisonette serves a part of the same building in another purpose group. (For example, a flat over a small shop occupied by the shop owner.)

● a storeroom in a shop if its area exceeds one-third of the total floor area of the shop.

● any ancillary use if its area exceeds one-fifth of the total floor area of the building, compartment or separated part. (There appears to be some confusion in the approved document here, since if one-fifth of the floor area is enough to denote *any* ancillary use then the reference to one-third in shops is superfluous. Presumably the intention here is for any *other* ancillary use.)

AD B/2/3/4 0.37

The purpose groups are set out in Table 0.1 to AD B2/3/4 which is reproduced on pp. 7.15–7.16. The nine purpose groups can be divided into two main sections:

● Residential – where there is sleeping accommodation (and therefore extra danger in the event of fire).
● Non-residential – where there is no sleeping accommodation.

AD B2/3/4 0.39

Some large buildings, such as shopping complexes, involve complicated mixes of purpose groups. In these cases special precautions may need to be taken to reduce any additional risks caused by the interaction of the different purpose groups (see section on *Varying the requirements* p. 7.122).

AD B2/3/4 0.40

Rules for measurement

AD B2/3/4
Appendix K

Many of the requirements concerning compartmentation and fire resistance, etc. in AD B2/3/4 are based on the height, area and cubic capacity of the building, compartment or separated part. For consistency, it is necessary to have a standard way of measuring these proportions. Appendix K of AD B2/3/4 indicates diagrammatically how the various forms of measurement should be made. These rules can be summarised as follows:

● HEIGHT – the height of the building or part is measured from the mean level of the ground adjoining the outside of the building's external walls to the level of half the vertical height of the roof, or to the top of the walls or parapet, whichever is the higher. This rule applies whether the roof has a monopitch, double pitch or is of a mansard type. The height to which a flat roof should be measured is

AD B2/3/4
Appendix K
K4

not clear from Appendix K. However, in the past it has been usual to measure to the underside of a flat roof (see Fig. 7.9(a)).

● AREA – the area of any storey of a building, compartment or separated part should be calculated as the total area in that storey within the finished inner surfaces of the enclosing walls. If there is no enclosing wall, the area is measured to the outermost edge of the floor on that side. The area should include any internal walls or partitions.

The area of a room, garage, conservatory or outbuilding is calculated by measuring to the inner surface of the enclosing walls.

The area of any part of a roof should be calculated as the actual

AD B2/3/4
Appendix K
K1

visible area of that part, as measured on a plane parallel to the roof slope (see Fig. 7.9(a)).

● CUBIC CAPACITY – the cubic capacity of a building, compartment or separated part should be calculated as the volume of the space between the finished surfaces of the enclosing walls, the upper surface of its lowest floor and the under surface of the roof or ceiling surface as appropriate. If there is no enclosing wall the measurement should be

AD B2/3/4
Appendix K
K2

taken to the outermost edge of the floor on that side. The cubic capacity should again include space occupied by other walls, shafts, ducts or structures within the measured space (see Fig. 7.9(b)).

● NUMBER OF STOREYS – the number of storeys in a building or separated part should be calculated at the position which gives the maximum number. Basement storeys are not counted. In most purpose group buildings galleries are also not counted as storeys. However, in assembly buildings, a gallery is included as a storey unless it is a fly gallery, loading gallery, stage grid, lighting bridge or other similar gallery, or is for maintenance and repair purposes. (The

AD B2/3/4
Appendix K
K3

common factor here is that these excluded galleries are not generally accessible to the public (see Fig. 7.9(b).)

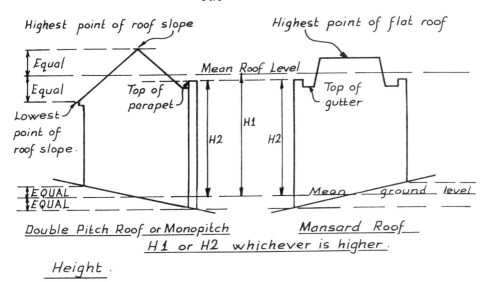

Highest point of roof slope

Highest point of flat roof

Equal

Equal

Mean Roof Level

Top of
parapet

Top of
gutter

Lowest
point of
roof slope.

H1

H2

H2

H2

EQUAL
EQUAL

Mean ground level

Double Pitch Roof or Monopitch

Mansard Roof

H1 or H2 whichever is higher.

Height .

Storey or compartment area

Room or garage area

Door or
window

If no wall, measure to
outermost edge of floorslab.

All measurements
to finished surfaces

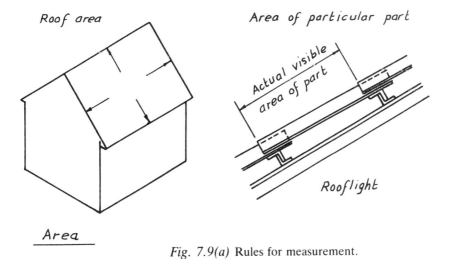

Roof area

Area of particular part

Actual visible
area of part

Rooflight

Area

Fig. 7.9(a) Rules for measurement.

Cubic capacity of compartment or building

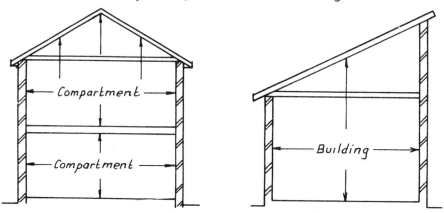

Cubic Capacity

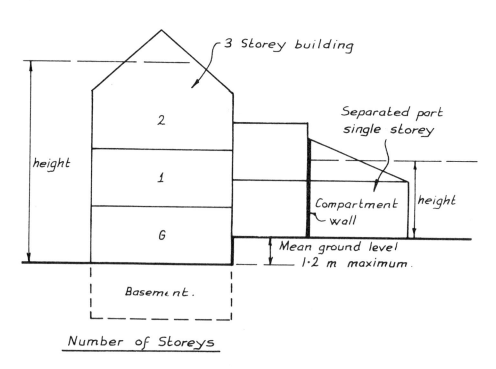

Number of Storeys

Fig. 7.9(b) Rules for measurement.

AD B/2/3/4

Table **0.1** **Designation of purpose groups**

Purpose for which building or a compartment of a building is intended to be used	Purpose group
Residential group private dwellinghouse which does not include a flat or a building containing flats	Dwellinghouse
a dwelling which is self-contained and is not a private dwellinghouse	Flat (includes a maisonette)
hospital, home, school or other similar establishment used as living accommodation for, or for the treatment care or maintenance of, persons suffering from disabilities due to illness or old age or other physical or mental disability, or under the age of five years, where such persons sleep in the premises	Institutional
hotel, boarding house, hostel and any other residential purpose not described above	Other Residential
Non-residential group public building[1] or a place of assembly of persons for social, recreational or business but not office, shop or industrial	Assembly
premises used for the purpose of administration, clerical work (including writing, book-keeping, sorting papers, filing, typing, duplicating, machine calculating, drawing and the editorial preparation of matter for publication), handling money or telephone and telegraph operating	Office
premises used for the carrying on of a retail trade or business (including the sale to members of the public of food or drink for immediate consumption, retail sales by auction, the business of lending books or periodicals for the purpose of gain and the business of a barber or hairdresser), and premises to which members of the public are invited to resort for the purpose of delivering their goods for repair or other treatment, or of themselves carrying out repairs to or other treatment of goods	Shop

AD B/2/3/4

Table **0.1**   **Designation of purpose groups** (*cont.*)

Purpose for which building or a compartment of a building is intended to be used	Purpose group
a factory within the meaning ascribed to that word by section 175 of the Factories Act 1961 (but not including slaughter houses and other premises referred to in paragraphs (d) and (c) of subsection (1) of that section)	Industrial
place for storage, deposit or parking of goods and materials (including vehicles) and any other non-residential purpose not described above[2]	Other non-residential

Notes
[1] Public building is defined in Building Regulation 2(2).
[2] A detached garage not more than 40 m² in area is included in the Dwellinghouse purpose group; as is a detached open carport of not more than 40 m², or a detached building which consists of a garage and open carport where neither the garage nor open carport exceeds 40 m² in area.

Means of escape in case of fire

Regs Sch. 1 B1   Certain buildings are required to be provided with means of escape in case of fire which is capable of being used safely and effectively at all material times. (No definition is given of material times.) The means of **B1(1)**   escape must be to a place of safety outside the building.

B1(2)   The above requirement can *only* be met by complying with the HMSO publication *The Building Regulations 1985 Mandatory Rules for Means of Escape in Case of Fire* (referred to as MOE B1 in this chapter). This is discussed below.

With the exception of loft conversions in certain domestic dwellings no specific guidance is given in MOE B1, reliance being placed instead on reference to British Standard Codes of Practice.

Application

Regulation B1 of Schedule 1 to the Building Regulations 1985 applies only to:

● A dwellinghouse of three or more storeys, whether it is being newly constructed, or altered and extended so as to provide a house with three or more storeys (by the addition of rooms in the roof, for example).

- A building of three or more storeys which is being materially changed in use so as to become a dwellinghouse.
- A building of three or more storeys which is being constructed and which will contain a flat on the third storey or above.
- A building which is or contains a shop.
- A building which is or contains an office.

In the case of a dwellinghouse or flat, means of escape need only be provided from the third storey or above. Similarly, in the case of a building containing a shop or office, means of escape need only be provided from the shop or office.

Regs Sch. 1
B1

Dwellinghouses

Means of escape need only be provided where a dwellinghouse of three or more storeys is being created. In order to satisfy the requirements the dwellinghouse must be constructed in accordance with the relevant clauses of BS 5588 *Fire precautions in the design and construction of buildings,* section 1.1: 1984 *Code of Practice for single family dwellinghouses.*

The Code of Practice deals with all aspects of fire precautions in dwellings. However, it is only those clauses that deal specifically with escape routes in dwellings of three storeys and above that are relevant. (See clauses 2, 4, 5, 6 and 7.3.)

MOE B1
1.1, 1.2, 1.3

Where an existing two-storey house is being extended by the addition of one or two rooms in the roofspace (thereby creating a three-storey dwelling), MOE B1 contains alternative provisions which may be substituted for those in BS 5588. These are contained in Appendix B to MOE B1 and are explained below.

MOE B1
1.4

Conversion to provide rooms in a roofspace

A number of terms have a special meaning in MOE B1:

HABITABLE ROOM – a room used for living purposes, including a kitchen but *not* a bathroom.

SELF-CLOSING – when applied to any door includes the use of rising butt hinges.

FIRE RESISTANCE – see page 7.39.

MOE B1
Appendix B
B2, B3, B4

The requirements for means of escape are illustrated in Figs. 7.10(a) and 7.10(b). The general principles being:

- Doors to habitable rooms should be self-closing to prevent the movement of smoke into the means of escape.
- The new stairway should be adequately protected by ½ hour fire resisting construction.
- Windows in the new third-storey should be large enough and suitably positioned to allow escape by means of a ladder to the ground.

MOE B1
Appendix B
B1

Flats

Any building of three or more storeys and which contains a flat on the third-storey or above must be constructed in accordance with the relevant clauses of BS Code of Practice CP3 *Code of basic data for the design of buildings*, Chapter IV *Precautions against fire*, Part 1: 1971 *Flats and maisonettes (in blocks over two-storeys)*.

The code of practice deals with all aspects of fire precautions in flats and maisonettes. However, it is only those clauses that deal with escape routes in flats and maisonettes of three-storeys and above that are relevant (see clauses 1.2, 3, 4.2, 4.3, 4.4, 5 *except* 5.6, 6 and Appendix A).

MOE B1
2.1, 2.2, 2.3

Shops

Any building which is or contains a shop must be constructed in accordance with the relevant sections of BS 5588 *Fire precautions in the design and construction of buildings*, Part 2: 1985 *Code of Practice for shops*.

The code of practice deals with all aspects of fire precautions in shops, however, it is only those sections that deal with escape routes that are relevant (see sections 1 (*except* clauses 1 and 3) 2, 3, 4 and 5 (*except* clauses 13.1, 14.1 to 14.4 and 23)).

MOE B1
3.1, 3.2, 3.3

Offices

Any building which is or contains an office must be constructed in accordance with the relevant sections of BS 5588 *Fire precautions in the design and construction of buildings*, Part 3: 1983 *Code of Practice for office buildings*.

The code of practice deals with all aspects of fire precautions in offices. However, it is only those sections that deal with escape routes that are relevant. (see sections 1 (*except* clauses 1 and 3), 2, 3, 4 and 5 (*except* clauses 12.1, 13.1 to 13.4 and 22)).

MOE B1
4.1, 4.2, 4.3

Other legislative requirements

It is often the case that the means of escape provisions contained in the

* Self-closing door

** Self-closing fire resisting door (minimum of 20 minutes in respect of integrity)

━━━ Full 1/2 hour fire resisting construction.

(A) Proposed Second Floor

Stairway rising in same staircase enclosure over existing stairway.

(A) Proposed First Floor

Note : doors marked * on ground floor also need to be fire resisting if more than one room is provided in roof space .

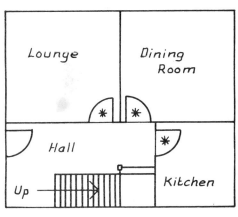

Existing Ground Floor

Fig. 7.10(a) Conversion to provide rooms in roof.

Window or rooflight

minimum 850 mm high
× 500 mm wide when
open and located so as
to be accessible from
ground by ladder.

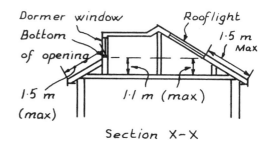

Section X-X

Doors provided at top or bottom
of stairway

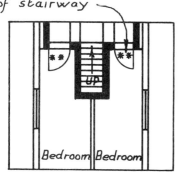

(B) Proposed Second
    Floor

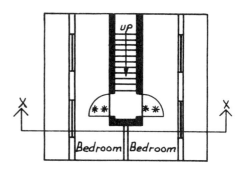

(C) Proposed Second
    Floor

Full ½ hour fire resisting construction including
underside of staircase if exposed in bedroom.

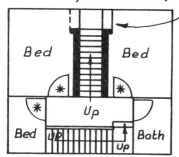

(B) Proposed First Floor
(Stairway rising from existing
  staircase enclosure through
  existing room)

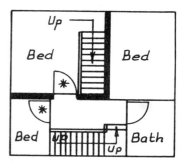

(C) Proposed First Floor
(Stairway rising from
  existing bedroom)

Fig. 7.10(b) Conversion to provide rooms in roof.

building regulations apply to buildings which are also covered by other legislation requiring means of escape.

● *The Fire Precautions Act 1971*
Under this Act a fire certificate is required for certain designated premises. These are:

Hotels and boarding houses, except those where sleeping accommodation is provided for not more than six people and none is provided above first floor or below ground floor.

Factories, offices, shops and railway premises where:
more than twenty people are employed or,
more than ten people are employed elsewhere than on the ground floor or,
explosive or highly flammable materials are stored or used. This applies to factories only.

This results from section 1 of the Act and the designation orders made under it. The fire certificate is granted by the fire authority on application in a prescribed form, and plans may be required. The fire authority must inspect the premises and must grant the fire certificate provided they are satisfied with the fire precautions generally, i.e. means of escape, fire-fighting equipment, fire alarms, etc. When the building regulations apply means of escape requirements to the building, the fire authority is not generally entitled to insist on alterations being made as a condition of granting a certificate. 1971 Act, sec. 5

1971 Act, sec. 13

There is a right to appeal to the magistrates' court against the fire authority's refusal to issue a fire certificate, etc. 1971 Act, sec. 9

Certain offices, shops and railway premises where people work must also be provided with appropriate means of escape in case of fire. This provision, as introduced in 1974, has been modified by the Fire Precautions (Modifications) Regulations 1976. 1971 Act, sec. 9A

The Fire Precautions Act 1971, as amended is set out as Appendix 2.

● *The Housing Act 1980*
Under this Act the local authority must require means of escape in certain houses in multiple occupation i.e., whose occupants do not form a single household. This applies where such a house has three or more storeys and with a combined floor area exceeding 500 m².

● *The Building Act 1984*
Section 72 of this Act empowers the local authority to require the provision of fire escapes in certain types of building of more than two storeys, and the means of escape is to be provided from any storey higher than twenty feet. The provision applies to buildings:

let in flats or tenement dwellings,
used as an inn, hotel, boarding house, hospital, boarding-school, children's home or similar institution,
used as a restaurant, shop, store, or warehouse which has on an

upper floor sleeping accommodation for people employed on the premises.

Where regulation B1 applies, section 72 has no application.

● *The Fire Certificates (Special Premises) Regulations 1976*
Under these regulations a fire certificate issued by the Health and Safety Executive is required in respect of certain manufacturing or storage premises used for hazardous processes and products causing special fire risk, e.g., certain chemical and petro-chemical plants.

Internal fire spread (surfaces)

Regs Sch. 1
B2

The spread of fire within a building may be inhibited by paying attention to the surfaces of materials used on walls and ceilings. These surfaces must:

(a) offer adequate resistance to spread of flame: and
(b) if ignited, have a rate of heat release which is reasonable in the circumstances.

AD B2/3/4
Appendix A
A4

In order to comply with (a) and (b) above, it is necessary for materials or products to meet certain levels of performance under surface spread of flame and/or fire propagation tests.

The surface spread of flame characteristics of a material may be determined by testing it in accordance with the method specified in BS 476: Part 7: 1971 *Surface spread of flame tests for materials.*

A strip of the material under test is placed with one end resting against a furnace and the rate at which flames spread along the material is measured.

Materials or products are thus placed in Classes 1, 2, 3 or 4, Class 1 representing a surface of very low flame spread. Class 4 (a surface of

AD B2/3/4
Appendix A
A5

rapid flame spread) is not acceptable under the provisions of the approved document.

In the event of a fire some materials release combustible gases at an earlier stage than others and are, therefore, more hazardous. The way in which combustible gases are released can be assessed by the method described in BS 476: Part 6: 1968 *Fire propagation tests for materials* and Part 6: 1981 *Method of test for fire propagation of products.*

The material or product is tested for a certain period of time in a furnace and is given two numerical indices related to its performance. The sub-index (i_1) is derived from the first three minutes of the test

AD B2/3/4
Appendix A
A6

whilst the overall test performance is denoted by the index of performance (I).

AD B2/3/4
Appendix A
A7

One further class of resistance is set out in the approved document – Class 0. This is not a British Standard classification, but is considered to impose a more strict control than Class 1.

Class 0 is defined as a material or the surface of a composite product which:

(a) is composed of materials of limited combustibility (see below) throughout; or

(b) has a surface material of Class 1 which has an index of performance (I) of not more than 12 and a sub-index (i_1) of not more than 6.

Certain materials consisting of a non-combustible core at least 8 mm thick and combustible facings not more than 0·5 mm thick on one or both sides may also be regarded as Class 0 but may need to comply with any surface flame spread ratings where these are specified.

AD B2/3/4
Appendix A
A8

The face of any thermoplastic material (see below) should only be regarded as a Class 0 surface if either,

(i) the material is bonded throughout to a non-thermoplastic substrate and the material and substrate together comply with (b) immediately above; or

(ii) the material complies with (b) above and is used as a lining to a non-thermoplastic Class 0 surface.

AD B2/3/4
Appendix A
A9

In Table A5 to Appendix A of AD B2/3/4 (which is reproduced below) the ratings of certain commonly used materials are given. Test results for proprietary materials may be obtained from manufacturers and trade associations. The Building Research Establishment and the Fire Protection Association also publish the results of fire tests on building products.

AD B2/3/4
Appendix A
A10

Table **A5**   **Typical ratings of some generic materials or products***

Classification	Material
Class 0 (this includes Class 1 materials)	1 any material of limited combustibility. Cored products listed in Table A7 must meet the test requirements given in paragraph A8(b). 2 brickwork, blockwork, concrete and ceramic tiles. 3 plasterboard (painted or not) with or without an air gap or fibrous or cellular insulating material behind 4 woodwool cement slabs. 5 mineral fibre tiles or sheets with cement or resin binding
Class 3**	6 timber or plywood with density more than 400 kg/m^3, painted or unpainted. 7 wood particle board or hardboard, either treated or painted

Notes

* Plastics materials are not included in this table because of their range of performance which is dependent on their formulation. Details of ratings to BS 476, Parts 6 and 7 are given in the documents referred to in A10.

** Timber products listed under Class 3 can be brought up to Class 1 with appropriate proprietary treatments.

Materials of limited combustibility

This term is new to building control legislation and is defined below. However, it also includes those materials which are defined as being non-combustible.

A non-combustible material is one which is either:

(a) totally inorganic, such as concrete, fired clay, masonry, etc., containing not more than 1% by weight or volume of organic material; or

(b) classified as such when tested in accordance with BS 476: Part 4: 1970 *Non-combustibility test for materials* or Part II: 1982 *Method of assessing the heat emission from building materials.*

AD B2/3/4
Appendix A
A13

Table A6 from AD 2/3/4 Appendix A is reproduced below and gives details of where non-combustible materials must be used.

Materials of limited combustibility are assessed by reference to the method specified in BS 476: Part II: 1982 and details of their uses is given in Table A7 of AD 2/3/4 Appendix A (see below).

AD B2/3/4 *Appendix A*

Table A6   Use of non-combustible materials

Use	Material
1 solid construction forming External walls, Separating walls, Compartment walls, Compartment floors and Protecting structure where there is provision in Section 1 to 6 for them to be constructed of materials of limited combustibility.	(a), (b)
	(c) or (d)
2 frames of hollow elements of structure referred to above.	
3 load-bearing elements of structure forming part of, or which carry, any element of structure referred to in 1 or 2 above.	
4 supports and fixings of any suspended ceiling meeting the provisions given in Table A2 (Types B, C and D).	
5 refuse chutes referred to in Appendix D, paragraph D6.	
6 flues meeting the requirements shown in Appendix F. Diagram F5 or F6.	

Notes

(a) Any material which when tested to BS 476: Part II does not flame and there is no rise in temperature on either the centre (specimen) or furnace thermocouples.

(b) Totally inorganic materials such as concrete, fired clay, ceramics, metals, plaster and masonry containing not more than 1 per cent by weight or volume of organic material. (Use in buildings of combustible metals such as magnesium/aluminium alloys should be assessed in each individual case.)

(c) Concrete bricks or blocks meeting BS 6073: Part 1: 1981.

(d) Products classified as non-combustible under BS 476: Part 4: 1970.

Table **A7**   **Use of materials of limited combustibility**

Use	Material
1 insulating linings to hollow elements of structure referred to under item 2 in Table A6.	(a), (b) or (c)
2 insulating linings to elements of structure referred to under item 3 in Table A6.	
3 class 0 materials meeting the provisions in paragraph A8(a).	
4 roof coverings meeting the provisions:	
(a) given in Note 1 of the tables for Limitations on roof construction in sections 1 to 6,	
(b) given in Appendix B, Table B1,	
(c) shown in Appendix C, diagram C2(c), or	
(d) shown in Appendix G, diagram G6.	
5 roof slabs meeting the provisions shown in Appendix C, diagram C2(b).	
6 cavity barriers meeting the provisions of Appendix G, paragraph G8(b)(vii).	
7 stairways where there is provision in sections 1 to 6 for them to be constructed of materials of limited combustibility.	
8 insulation used in the cavity of hollow elements of structure referred to in 1 above, or behind linings referred to in 2 above.	(a), (b), (c) or (d)
9 insulation above any suspended ceiling meeting the provisions given in Table A2 (Type D).	

Notes

(a) Any non-combustible material listed in Table A6.

(b) Any material of density 300 kg/m^3 or more, which when tested to BS 476: Part II, does not flame and the rise in temperature on the furnace thermocouple is not more than 20°C.

(c) Any material with a non-combustible core of 8 mm thick or more, having combustible facings (on one or both sides) not more than 0.5 mm thick. (Where a flame spread rating is specified, these materials must also meet the appropriate test requirements.)

(d) Any material of density less than 300 kg/m^3, which when tested to BS 476: Part II, does not flame for more than 10 seconds and the rise in temperature on the centre (specimen) thermocouple is not more than 35°C and the furnace thermocouple is not more than 25°C.

It is, of course, permissible to use non-combustible materials whenever a requirement for materials of limited combustibility is specified.

AD B2/3/4
Appendix A
A14

The use of plastics materials

It is often desirable to use certain plastics materials in windows, rooflights or suspended ceilings. However, due to their low softening temperatures some of these materials (referred to as thermoplastic materials) cannot be tested under BS 476: Part 7: 1971 for surface spread of flame characteristics.

Since these materials represent an increased fire risk their use is closely controlled in AD B2/3/4.

Table 7.1 Designation of Plastics Materials.

Type	Description of material	Method of test in accordance with BS 2782: 1970	Criteria (to be satisfied by each specimen used for test purposes unless otherwise prescribed)	Approved Document B2/3/4 Appendix references
(1)	(2)	(3)	(4)	(5)
1	Any plastics material	102C	The softening point of the material (expressed as the arithmetic mean of the softening points of the two specimens used) does not exceed 120°C; or	A11
		120A: 1976	145°C	
2	Any plastics material which satisfies both tests	102C	The softening point of the material (expressed as the arithmetic mean of the softening points of the two specimens used) does not exceed 120°C; or	A11
		120A: 1976	145°C	
		508A	When tested in a thickness of 3 mm, the rate of burning does not exceed 50 mm/min	B7

3	Polyvinyl chloride	508A	B5	(i) The flame does not reach the first mark; and (ii) the duration of flame or after-glow after the removal of the burner does not exceed 5 seconds
4	Polyvinyl chloride	508C 140D: 1980	B6 (a)	The distance of travel of the flame does not exceed 75 mm
5	Polyvinyl chloride	508D 140E: 1982	B6 (b)	(i) The specimen flames or glows for not more than 5 seconds; (ii) any material dropped from the specimen does not continue to burn after reaching the base of the test apparatus; (iii) charring or scorching does not extend over an area exceeding 20% of the area of the underside of the specimen; and (iv) the length of the charred or scorched edge of the underside of the specimen does not exceed 50 mm

AD B2/3/4 *Appendix B*

Table B1 Concessions for rooflights of plastic materials

Material, or minimum surface spread of frame on lower side	Space which rooflight serves	Limitations			For rooflight with external surface of		
		Maximum area of each rooflight [m²]	Rooflight area as percentage of floor area of space in which rooflight situated [%]	Separation of rooflight by material of limited combustibility [m]	Minimum distance from any point on the boundary [m]		
					Rigid pvc as paragraph B5	AD, BD, CA, CB, CC, CD, or no designation*	DA, DB, DC or DD
1 Rigid pvc as paragraph B5	any space (except a protected shaft)	no limit	no limit	no limit	6†	not applicable	not applicable
2 Class 3	(a) balcony, verandah, carport, covered way or loading bay which has at least one longer side wholly or permanently open, or detached swimming pool.	no limit	no limit	no limit	not applicable	6	22

(b) garage, conservatory or outbuilding with a maximum floor area of 40 m²	no limit	no limit	no limit	not applicable	6	22
(c) circulation space** (d) room in a** Residential Assembly, Office or Shop purpose group	5	no limit	2.8 minimum (if rooflight complies with limits in Diagram B1) 3.5 minimum (if not)	not applicable	6	22
(e) room in an** industrial or other non-residential purpose group.	5	20 per cent maximum (evenly distributed)	1.8 minimum	not applicable	6	22

Notes

* A material which cannot be designated because of its low softening temperature.

† No limit in the case of any space described in column (2), item 2(a) or (b)

** Single skin material only.

The various plastics materials are designated Types 1, 2, 3, 4 or 5 in Table 7.1 below. This designation does not appear in the approved document. The description, appropriate test mode by BS 2782: 1970 and the test criteria for each type are also set out in the table. It should be noted that polycarbonate materials are not classified as thermoplastics materials.

AD B2/3/4
Appendix B
B5, B6, B7

Windows

AD B2/3/4
Appendix B
B2

Any window to a room may be glazed with a single sheet of rigid pvc material Type 3.

Rooflights

The light-transmitting part of any rooflight may be constructed of plastics materials but any internal surface exposed between the light-transmitting part and the ceiling below should comply with the flame spread requirements for the ceiling (see Fig. 7.11).

Table B1 to Appendix B of AD B2/3/4 is illustrated below and gives details of the use of plastics materials in rooflights. The main requirements of the table are summarised below.

● Type 3 rigid pvc material may be used for a rooflight over any space except a protected shaft. It should be at least 6 m from any point on a boundary except for those buildings listed immediately below.
● *Rooflights serving*:
  (a) balconies, verandas, carports, covered ways or loading bays with one longer side permanently open, or detached swimming pools; or
  (b) garages, conservatories or outbuildings with a floor area not exceeding 40 m²;
  may consist of plastics materials with a lower surface of not less than Class 3 surface spread of flame. The rooflight should be 6 m from any point on the boundary if the external surface is designated AD, BD, CA, CB, CC, CD or cannot be designated. (For details of designatory letters see page 7.116). If the external surface is designated DA, DB, DC or DD the rooflight should be 22 m from any point on the boundary.
● The internal and external surface limits specified in (b) immediately above also apply to rooflights in all other types of buildings. However, there are additional limitations on the area and spacing of the rooflights.

● Individual rooflights serving circulation spaces or rooms in residential, assembly, office or shop purpose groups should not exceed 5 m² in area. They should be separated by materials of limited combustibility at least 2·8 m wide if the rooflight complies with the limits specified

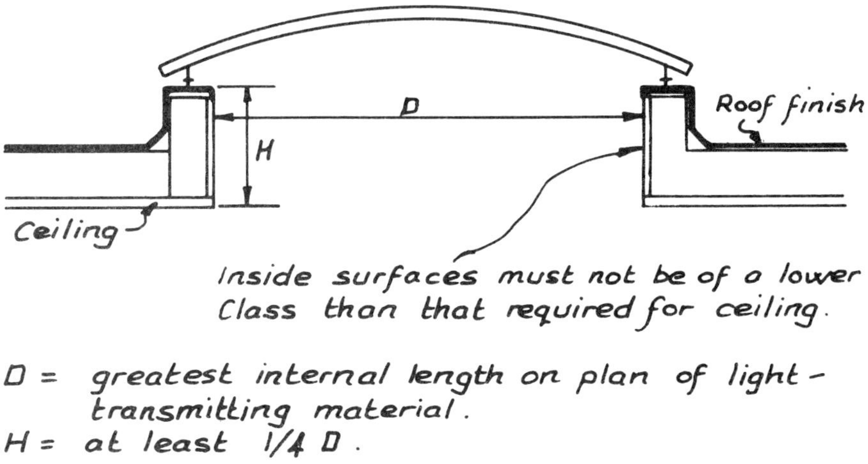

Inside surfaces must not be of a lower
Class than that required for ceiling.

D = greatest internal length on plan of light-
transmitting material.
H = at least 1/4 D.

Fig. 7.11 Limitations on the use of plastic materials in rooflights.

in Fig. 7.11 above or 3·5 m wide if this is not the case. The rooflight should consist of a single skin material.

- Individual rooflights serving rooms in industrial or other non-residential purpose groups should not exceed 5 m² in area and should be separated by materials of limited combustibility at least 1·8 m wide. They should be evenly distributed and should not exceed, in total, 20% of the floor area of the space in which they are situated. The rooflights should consist of single skin materials (see Fig. 7.12).

AD B2/3/4
Appendix B
B3

Suspended ceilings

Suspended ceilings in circulation spaces or rooms are permitted to contain one or more panels of Types 2, 4 or 5 provided they are not fire-protecting suspended ceilings. Table B2 to Appendix B of AD 2/3/4/ is reproduced below and gives details of the limitations on the use of plastics ceiling materials. The main points are:

- Surfaces within a ceiling void above a panel should comply with the surface flame spread requirements for the ceiling.
- Type 4 and Type 5 panels should not exceed 1 mm in thickness (or aggregate thickness where there are two or more sheets) and no panel should exceed 4 m² in area.
- Type 2 plastics ceiling panels are permitted providing:
- (a) they do not exceed 3 mm in thickness (or aggregate thickness where there are two or more sheets),
- (b) they have no side which exceeds 5 m in length,

$D = 6\,m$ if external surface of rooflight is AD, BD, CA, CB, CC, CD or cannot be designated. $D = 22\,m$ if external surface of rooflight is DA, DB, DC or DD.

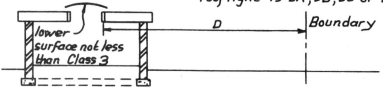

a) Balcony, verandah, carport, detached swimming pool, covered way or loading bay with one longer side permanently open.

Or: (b) Garage, Conservatory or outbuilding not exceeding 40 m² floor area.

Rooflight of single-skin material

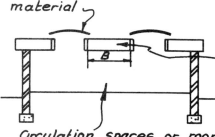

Material of limited combustibility separating rooflights
Area of each rooflight should not exceed 5 m².

Circulation spaces or rooms in Residential, Assembly, Office or Shop purpose groups

Distance D as above.

$B = 2.8\,m$ if rooflight complies with Fig 7.11 above.
$B = 3.5\,m$ in any other case.

Rooflight of single skin material

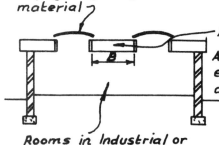

Material of limited combustibility
Area of each rooflight should not exceed 5 m². Rooflights evenly distributed and should not exceed 20% of floor area of space in which situated.

Rooms in Industrial or other non-residential purpose groups.

$B = 1.8\,m$ minimum.

Distance D as above.

Fig. 7.12 Plastics rooflights.

(c) in circulation spaces, individual panels should not exceed 2 m² in area with a total limit for all panels of 15% of the floor area of the space in which they are situated,

(d) in other rooms, individual panels should not exceed 4 m² in area. They should not exceed, in total, 30% of the floor area of the space in which they are situated for flats, institutional, other residential and assembly purpose groups or 50% in any other case.

(e) if individual panels are closer together than 575 mm they should be treated as a single panel for the purposes of the limitations on size and area specified above.

(f) each panel should be loosely mounted so that it will drop out of its mountings if softened by heat.

AD B2/3/4
Appendix B
B4

Specific requirements for internal surfaces

Table 7.2, which follows, is based on Tables 1.4, 2.4, 3.4, 4.5, 5.4 and 6.5 from AD B2/3/4 and gives the requirements of flame spread classification for the surfaces of walls and ceilings (including the exposed surfaces of rooflights) in any room, circulation space or protected shaft according to the type of building.

Different standards are set for 'small rooms', which are totally enclosed rooms of not more than 4 m² floor area in residential buildings or 30 m² in non-residential buildings, and for 'other rooms', 'circulation spaces and protected shafts'.

AD B2/3/4
secs. 1 to 6

The foregoing details on the use of plastics materials in windows, suspended ceilings and rooflights should also be taken into account. The fire spread ratings of some commonly used materials are given in Table A5 of Appendix A to AD B2/3/4 (see page 7.23).

Further requirements for ceilings

In buildings other than dwellinghouses, fire-protecting suspended ceilings may be used in order to contribute to the fire resistance of a floor. Different provisions with regard to surface spread of flame apply to these ceilings and these are considered below.

A ceiling in the top storey of a dwelling house with three or more storeys and any fire-resisting ceiling below a concealed space (cavity) in any building apart from a house with one or two storeys may also be required to comply with different provisions to those listed in Table 7.2. These ceilings are dealt with in the sections on *Concealed spaces* (p. 7.81) and *Compartmentation* (p. 7.47) below.

Internal fire spread (structure)

A number of factors need to be considered in order to reduce the effects of fire spread throughout the structure of a building as follows:

Regs Sch. 1
B3

AD **B2/3/4** *Appendix B*

Table **B2**   **Concessions for suspended ceilings of plastics materials**

Material	Limitations			Maximum area	
	Maximum length of side of panel [m]	Minimum distance between panels [mm]	Any one panel [m²]	Total area as percentage of floor area of space in which ceiling is situated	
1 pvc as paragraph B6 (total thickness 1 mm maximum)	no limit	no limit	4	no limit	
2 thermoplastic as paragraph B7* (total thickness 3 mm maximum)	5	575†	circulation spaces: 2	15%	
			rooms: 4	flats, institutional, other residential and assembly purpose groups: 30% elsewhere: 50%	

Notes

* Every panel should be loosely mounted so that it will fall out of its mountings when softened by heat.

† Panels may be closer if they are arranged as a group (or groups) which each meet the limitations on length, distance apart and area, as a single panel.

Table 7.2 Minimum requirements for surfaces of walls and ceilings.

(a) Residential buildings

Type of building	Small rooms (floor area not more than 4 m²)	Other rooms	Circulation spaces and protected shafts
1 or 2 storey house (basements not counted)	Class 3	walls: Class 1 ceilings: Class 3	walls: Class 1 ceilings: Class 3
Institutional	walls: Class 1 ceilings: Class 1	walls: Class 0 ceilings: Class 1 }	Class 0
All other residential buildings including houses over 2 storeys (basements not counted)	Class 3	walls: Class 1 ceilings: Class 1 }	Class 0

Note: It is permitted for part of the wall surface referred to above to be of a lower class (but not less than Class 3) provided the total lower classed area does not exceed half the floor area of the room and in any case 20 m².

(b) Non-residential buildings

Type of building	Small rooms (floor area not more than 30 m²)	Other rooms	Circulation spaces and protected shafts
Assembly, offices shops, industrial and other non-residential	Class 3	walls: Class 1 ceilings: Class 1 }	Class 0

Note: It is permitted for part of the wall surface referred to above to be of a lower class (but not less than Class 3) provided the total lower classed area does not exceed half the floor area of the room and in any case 60 m².

- The building must be so constructed that its stability will be maintained for a reasonable period during a fire, **B3(1)**
- The building, or the building as extended, must be sub-divided into compartments where this is necessary to inhibit the spread of fire, **B3(2)**
- Fire and smoke may spread unseen through concealed spaces in the structure or fabric of a building. These spaces must be sealed or sub-divided in a satisfactory manner, **B3(3)**
- Walls which are common to two or more buildings must offer adequate resistance to the spread of fire and smoke. Semi-detached and terraced houses are treated as separate buildings for the purposes of this requirement. **B3(4)** **B3(5)**

AD B2/3/4 *Appendix A*

Table A1   Specific provisions of test for fire resistance of elements of structure, etc.

Part of building	Minimum provisions when tested to BS 476: Part 8: 1972 [minutes]			Method of exposure
	Stability	Integrity	Insulation	
1 Structural frame, beam or column	*	no provision	no provision	exposed faces
2 Load-bearing wall which is not also an External wall, Separating wall, Compartment wall or Protecting structure (*see 4, 5, 6 or 7*)	*	no provision	no provision	each side separately
3 Floors				
(a) floor in upper storey of a 2-storey dwelling house (but not over a garage)	30	15	15	from underside (Note 1)
(b) any other floor (including a compartment floor)	*	*	*	from underside (Note 1)
4 External walls				
(a) any part less than 1 m from any point on relevant boundary	*	*	*	each side separately
(b) any part of the wall of a building used for Assembly purposes which is 1 m or more from the relevant boundary and is described in Note 2	* (max. 60)	* (max. 60)	15 * (max. 60)	from inside from outside

Item				Direction of exposure
(c) any part 1 m or more from the relevant boundary and is not a part described in (b) above	*	*	15	from inside
5 Separating wall	* (min. 60)	* (min. 60)	* (min. 60)	each side separately
6 Compartment wall	*	*	*	each side separately
7 Protecting structure (a) any glazing to a Protected Shaft described in Appendix E, Diagram E2	30	30	no provision	each side separately
(b) any other part between a Protected Shaft and a protected lobby/corridor described in Appendix E, Diagram E2	30	30	30	each side separately
(c) any part not described in (a) or (b) above	*	*	*	each side separately
8 Wall separating an attached or integral garage from a dwelling house	*	*	*	from garage side
9 Doors (a) in a Separating wall	no provision	† (min. 60)	no provision	each side separately when fitted in its frame
(b) in a Compartment wall if it separates a flat or maisonette from a space in common use	no provision	20	no provision	each side separately when fitted in its frame
(c) in a Compartment wall or Compartment floor not described in (b) above	no provision	†	no provision	each side separately when fitted in its frame

(continued on next page)

Table A1 *continued* **Specific provisions of test for fire resistance of elements of structure, etc.**

Part of building	Minimum provisions when tested to BS 476: Part 8: 1972 [minutes]			Method of exposure
	Stability	Integrity	Insulation	
(d) in a Protecting structure situated wholly or partly above the level of the adjoining ground in a building used for Flats, Other Residential, Assembly or Office purposes	no provision	30	no provision	each side separately when fitted in its frame
(e) in a Protecting structure not described in (d) above	no provision	** (min. 30)	no provision	each side separately when fitted in its frame
(f) any other door (including a door in a cavity barrier and a door between a dwelling house and garage)	no provision	20	no provision	each side separately when fitted in its frame
10 Casing around a drainage system described in Appendix F, Diagram F.2	30	30	30††	from outside
11 Cavity Barriers (a) cavity barrier 1 m × 1 m or larger	30	30	15	each side separately
(b) any other cavity barrier	30	30	no provision	each side separately
(c) ceiling described in Appendix G, Diagram G4	30	30	30	from underside

Modifications

†† No provision for insulation if the casing is more than 50 mm from any pipe in the enclosure (except a pipe passing through the casing).

** Half the period of fire resistance for the wall or floor in which the door is situated.

1 A suspended ceiling should only be relied on to contribute to the fire resistance of the floor if the ceiling meets the appropriate provisions given in Table A2.

2 Any part of the wall which is 7.5 m or less above the ground, or above a roof or any other part of the building to which people have access, if the building has 2 or more storeys.

Notes

* Period of fire resistance set out in Sections 1 to 6.

† Period of fire resistance for the wall or floor in which the door is situated.

Fire resistance and structural stability

If the structural elements of a building can be satisfactorily protected against the effects of fire for a reasonable period it will not only be possible for the safe evacuation of the occupants but also the spread of fire throughout the building will be kept to a minimum. In order to achieve this protection the elements of structure of a building are required by AD B2/3/4 to have specified minimum standards of fire resistance.

AD B2/3/4

AD B2/3/4
0.10

FIRE RESISTANCE of an element of a structure, a door, or other part of a building means the period of time for which a specimen construction (of the same specification as the particular element, door, etc.) would satisfy the requirements of the test by fire to the methods specified in BS 476: Part 8: 1972 *Test methods and criteria for fire resistance of elements of building construction.*

The requirements relate to the ability of an element of structure:

- to withstand a fire without collapse (stability),
- to resist fire penetration (integrity),
- to resist excessive heat penetration so that fire is not spread by radiation or conduction (insulation).

Clearly the criteria of resistance to fire and heat penetration are applicable only to fire separating elements such as walls and floors. The criterion of resistance to collapse is applicable to all load-bearing elements, such as columns and beams, in addition to floors and load-bearing walls.

AD B2/3/4
0.11

Table A1 to Appendix A of AD B2/3/4 (see below) shows the method of exposure for the various elements of structure, doors and other parts of a building, together with the BS 476 requirements each of which must satisfy in terms of stability, integrity and insulation. For some items, the table indicates the actual period of fire resistance demanded under each heading, but for others sections 1 to 6 of AD B2/3/4 give the detailed requirements in respect of fire resistance (see Tables 7.3 and 7.4 below).

AD B2/3/4
0.18

In addition to the elements of structure listed on page 7.4 there are requirements for some other elements of the building to be of fire resisting construction. Included in this category are some doors, pipe casings and cavity barriers. These are considered later under the actual element references.

AD B2/3/4
0.14

Minimum period of fire resistance

In order to establish the minimum period of fire resistance for the elements of structure of a building it is necessary, first, to determine the building's use or purpose group. The fire resistance period will then depend on the size of the building or compartment.

It will be seen that the requirements for basements are generally

Table 7.3 Minimum periods of fire resistance.
RESIDENTIAL BUILDINGS

| Type of building | Maximum dimensions | | | Minimum period [hours] for elements of structure in a | |
	Height of building or of separated part [m]	Floor area of each storey[1] [m²]	Cubic capacity of building[2] [m³]	Ground or upper storey	Basement storey (including floor over)
DWELLINGHOUSES single storey house or separated part (no basement)	no limit	no limit	no limit	½	not applicable
1, 2 or 3 storey house or separated part (basement not counted)	no limit	no limit	no limit	½	1†
4 storey house or separated part (basement not counted)	no limit	250	no limit	1*	1
house with any number of storeys	no limit	no limit	no limit	1	1½

					Z
FLATS					
single storey building or separated part (no basement)	no limit	3000	no limit	½	not applicable
1 or 2 storey building or separated part (basements not counted)	no limit	500	no limit	½	1
3 storey building or separated part (basement not counted)	no limit	250	no limit	1*	1
building with any number of storeys	28 no limit	3000 2000	8500 5500	1 1½	1½ 2
INSTITUTIONAL					
single storey building or separated part (no basement)	no limit	3000	no limit	½	not applicable
building, or	28	2000	no limit	1	1½
separated part, which is not single storey	over 28	2000	no limit	1½	2
OTHER RESIDENTIAL					
single storey building or separated part (no basement)	no limit	3000	no limit	½	not applicable

(continued on next page)

Table 7.3 Minimum periods of fire resistance.
RESIDENTIAL BUILDINGS (*continued*)

Type of building	Maximum dimensions			Minimum period [hours] for elements of structure in a		
	Height of building or of separated part [m]	Floor area of each storey[1] [m²]	Cubic capacity of building[2] [m³]	Ground or upper storey	Basement storey (including floor over)	X
OTHER RESIDENTIAL (contd.)						
1 or 2 storey building or separated part (basements not counted)	no limit	500	no limit	½	1	X
3 storey building or separated part (basements not counted)	no limit	250	no limit	1*	1	
building with any number of storeys	28 / no limit	3000 / 2000	8500 / 5500	1 / 1½	1½ / 2	

Notes

1. The floor area of each storey in the building or, if the building is divided into compartments, the floor area of each storey in the compartment of which the element of structure forms part.
2. The cubic capacity of the building or, if the building is divided into compartments, the cubic capacity of the compartment of which the element of structure forms part.
   X and Z – Buildings within these limits of size are referred to on pages 228 and 232.

Modifications

† Reduced to half hour if the area of the basement is 50 m² or less (but not for separating walls).

* Reduced to half hour for any floor (which is not also a compartment floor) but not for any part of the floor which contributes to the support of the building as a whole, and not for any beam which supports the floor.

Table 7.4 Minimum periods of fire resistance.
NON-RESIDENTIAL BUILDINGS

Type of building	Maximum dimensions			Minimum period [hours] for elements of structure in a		
	Height of building or of separated part [m]	Floor area¹ [m²]	Cubic capacity² [m³]	Ground or upper storey	Basement storey (including floor over)	
ASSEMBLY						
single storey building or separated part (no basement)	no limit	3000	no limit	½	not applicable	Z
	no limit	no limit	no limit	1	not applicable	
building or separated part which is not single storey	7.5	250	no limit	½	1†	X
	7.5	500	no limit	½	1	
	15	no limit	3500	1*	1	
	28	1000	7000	1	1½	
	no limit	no limit	7000	1½	2	
OFFICE						
single storey building or separated part (no basement)	no limit	3000	no limit	½	not applicable	Z
	no limit	no limit	no limit	1	not applicable	
building or separated part which is not single storey	7.5	250	no limit	½	1†	X
	7.5	500	no limit	½	1	
	15	no limit	3500	1*	1	
	28	5000	14000	1	1½	
	no limit	no limit	no limit	1½	2	

(continued on next page)

Table 7.4 Minimum periods of fire resistance.
NON-RESIDENTIAL BUILDINGS (*continued*)

Type of building	Maximum dimensions			Minimum period [hours] for elements of structure in a		
	Height of building or of separated part [m]	Floor area¹ [m²]	Cubic capacity² [m³]	Ground or upper storey	Basement storey (including floor over)	
SHOP						
single storey building or separated part (no basement)	no limit no limit no limit	2000 3000 no limit	no limit no limit no limit	½ 1 2	not applicable not applicable not applicable	Z
building or separated part which is not single storey (not sprinklered)	7.5 7.5 15 28 no limit	150 500 no limit 1000 2000	no limit no limit 3500 7000 7000	½ ½ 1* 1 2	1† 1 1 2 4	X
building or separated part which is not single storey (sprinklered)³	7.5 7.5 15 28 no limit	150 500 no limit 1000 4000	no limit no limit 3500 7000 14000	½ ½ 1* 1 2	1† 1 1 2 4	X
INDUSTRIAL						
single storey building or separated part (no basement)	no limit no limit no limit	2000 3000 no limit	no limit no limit no limit	½ 1 2	not applicable not applicable not applicable	Z

building or separated part which is not single storey					
7.5	250	no limit	½	1†	X
7.5	no limit	1700	½	1	
15	no limit	4250	1*	1	
28	no limit	8500	1	2	
28	no limit	28000	2	4	
over 28	2000	5500	2	4	

OTHER NON-RESIDENTIAL

single storey building or separated part (no basement)					
no limit	500	no limit	½	not applicable	Z
no limit	1000	no limit	1	not applicable	
no limit	3000	no limit	2	not applicable	
no limit	no limit	no limit	4	not applicable	

building or separated part which is not single storey					
7.5	150	no limit	½	1†	X
7.5	300	no limit	½	1	
15	no limit	1700	1*	1	
15	no limit	3500	1	2	
28	no limit	7000	2	4	
28	no limit	21000	4	4	
over 28	1000	no limit	4	4	

Modifications

† Reduced to half hour if the area of the basement is 50 m² or less (but not for separating walls).

* Reduced to half hour for any floor (which is not also a compartment floor) but not for any part of the floor which contributes to the support of the building as a whole, and not for any beam which supports the floor.

Notes

1 The floor area of each storey in the building or, where the building is divided into compartments, the floor area of each storey in the compartment of which the element of structure forms part.

2 The cubic capacity of the building or, where the building is divided into compartments, the cubic capacity of the compartment of which the structure forms a part.

3 Where the building is fitted throughout with an automatic sprinkler system meeting the relevant recommendations of BS 5306: Part 2: 1979.

X and Z – Buildings within these limits of size are referred to on pages 228 and 232.

more onerous than for the upper floors in the same building. This reflects the greater difficulty experienced in dealing with a basement fire. However, it is sometimes the case that, due to the slope of the ground, at least one side of a basement is accessible at ground level. This gives opportunities for smoke venting and fire fighting and in these circumstances it may be reasonable to adopt the less onerous fire resistance provisions of the upper elements of the construction for the elements of structure in the basement.

AD B2/3/4
0.16

The minimum periods of fire resistance required for the elements of structure of a building, compartment or separated part are given in Tables 7.3 and 7.4 above. These are based on Tables 1.1, 2.1, 3.1, 4.1, 5.1 and 6.1 from AD B2/3/4.

The following points should also be taken into account when using Tables 7.3 and 7.4:

- Any element of structure must have fire resistance at least equal to the fire resistance of any element which it carries or supports.
- If an element of structure forms part of more than one building or compartment, and is thus subject to two or more different fire resistances, it is the greater of these which applies.

AD B2/3/4
0.17

- A structural frame, beam, column or load-bearing wall of a *single storey building* (or which is part of the ground storey of a building which consists of a ground storey and one or more basement storeys) is generally not required to have fire resistance. (This reflects the view that, given satisfactory means of escape, and the restricted use of combustible materials as wall and ceiling linings, fire resistance in the elements of structure in the ground storey will contribute little to the safety of the occupants.) However, the above concession will only apply if the element of structure:

(a) is part of or supports an external wall and is sufficiently far from its relevant boundary to be regarded as a totally unprotected area;
(b) is not part of and does not support a separating wall, compartment wall or protecting structure;
(c) is not a wall between a house and an attached or integral garage; or

AD B2/3/4
sec. 1 to 6

(d) does not support a gallery.

- Further concessions relating to the fire resistance of external walls, separating walls and compartment walls are dealt with under the relevant sections below.

Table A3 of Appendix A gives notional periods of fire resistance for some common forms of construction. This table is based on a selection of constructions from the Building Research Establishment report *Guidelines for the construction of fire resisting structural elements* (HMSO 1982). The table is reproduced below and it will be seen that it covers only floor and wall constructions.

AD B2/3/4
Appendix A

The 1976 Building Regulations gave many more forms of construction than are provided by the current approved document. They also included fire protection to structural frameworks of beams and columns.

The publication referred to above contains much of this information, but in addition to this there are available various mineral based insulating boards which are capable of providing differing degrees of fire protection depending on their thickness and method of fixing.

A selection of examples from 'Cape Boards' *Fire Protection Handbook* is given on pp. 7.51–7.61. Full details may be obtained from the manufacturer (Cape Boards and Panels Ltd, Iver Lane, Uxbridge UB8 2JQ).

Compartmentation

In order to prevent the spread of fire within buildings AD B2/3/4 contains provisions for subdividing a building into compartments with restricted floor area or cubic capacity depending on the use of the building and sometimes its height.

The division is achieved by means of compartment walls and compartment floors which are elements of structure and therefore require fire resistance.

AD B2/3/4
0.19

Most multi-storey buildings are required to be compartmented because of the increased risk to life should a fire occur. However, this risk is obviously less in single-storey buildings and the provisions for compartmentation only apply to those with a significant sleeping risk (i.e. institutional buildings and other residential buildings). The maximum dimensions for buildings or compartments are given in Table 7.5 (p. 7.62).

AD B2/3/4
0.20 & 0.21
Tables 4.4
& 6.3

It can be seen that the fire resistance period for the elements of structure of a building or compartment tend to increase as the size of the building or compartment increases. It follows that it will frequently be advantageous to subdivide a building into compartments even if compartmentation is not required by AD B2/3/4 or, where compartmentation is required, to subdivide into smaller compartments than are required in order to reduce the fire resistance periods and achieve subsequent economies in construction.

AD B2/3/4
0.24

In addition to the above the following are also required to be constructed as compartment walls or floors.

- In buildings more than 28 m high, all floors more than 9 m above ground level, unless they are intermediate floors in maisonettes.

AD B2/3/4
2.23(a)

- All floors in an institutional building.

AD B2/3/4
3.23(a)

- Any wall or floor separating a flat or maisonette from any other part of the same building.

AD B2/3/4
2.23(b)

- Any wall or floor that separates a part of a building from another part that falls within a different purpose group.
- Any floor over a basement storey that exceeds 100 m^2 in area and is either in a dwellinghouse that has three or more storeys, or is in a

AD B2/3/4 *Appendix A*

Table **A3**   **Notional periods of fire resistance of some common constructions**

These constructions are a selection from the current edition of the BRE report *Guidelines for the construction of fire resisting structural elements.* (HMSO 1982)

A large number of constructions other than those shown are capable of providing the fire resistance looked for. For example, various mineral based insulating boards can be used. Because their performance varies and is dependent on their thickness, it is not possible to give specific thicknesses in this Table. However, manufacturers will normally be able to say what thickness would be needed to achieve the particular performance.

Floors: timber joist

Modified half hour (stability 30 minutes) (integrity 15 minutes) (insulation 15 minutes)	1	any structurally suitable flooring: floor joists at least 37 mm wide ceiling (a) 12.5 mm plasterboard* with joints taped and filled and backed by timber, or (b) 9.5 mm plasterboard* with 10 mm lightweight gypsum plaster finish
	2	at least 15 mm t&g boarding or sheets of plywood or wood chipboard, floor joists at least 37 mm wide ceiling (a) 12.5 mm plasterboard* with joints taped and filled, or (b) 9.5 mm plasterboard* with at least 5 mm neat gypsum plaster finish
Half hour	3	at least 15 mm t&g boarding or sheets of plywood or wood chipboard, floor joists at least 37 mm wide ceiling 12.5 mm plasterboard* with at least 5 mm neat gypsum plaster finish
	4	at least 21 mm t&g boarding or sheets of plywood or wood chipboard, floor joists at least 37 mm wide ceiling 12.5 mm plasterboard* with joints taped and filled

(*continued*)

| 1 hour | 5 | | at least 15 mm t&g plywood or wood chipboard, floor joists at least 50 mm wide |
| | | | ceiling not less than 30 mm plasterboard* with joints staggered and exposed joints taped and filled |

Floors: concrete

| 1 hour | 6 | | reinforced concrete floor not less than 95 mm thick, with not less than 20 mm cover on the lowest reinforcement |

Walls: internal

half hour load-bearing	7		framing members at least 44 mm wide† and spaced at not more than 600 mm apart, with lining (both sides) of 12.5 mm plasterboard* with all joints taped and filled
	8		100 mm reinforced concrete wall** with minimum cover to reinforcement of 25 mm
1 hour load-bearing	9		framing members at least 44 mm wide† and spaced at not more than 600 mm apart, with lining (both sides) at least 25 mm plasterboard* in 2 layers with joints staggered and exposed joints taped and filled
	10		solid masonry wall (with or without plaster finish) at least 90 mm thick (75 mm if non-load-bearing)
			Note: for masonry cavity walls, the fire resistance may be taken as that for a single wall of the same construction, whichever leaf is exposed to fire
	11		120 mm reinforced concrete wall** with at least 25 mm cover to the reinforcement

Table **A3** *continued* **Notional periods of fire resistance of some common constructions**

Walls: external

---

modified half hour (stability 30 minutes) (integrity 30 minutes) (insulation 15 minutes) load-bearing wall 1 m or more from relevant boundary	**12**	any external weathering system with at least 8 mm plywood sheathing, framing members at least 37 mm wide and spaced not more than 600 mm apart internal lining: 12.5 mm plasterboard* with at least 10 mm lightweight gypsum plaster finish
half hour load-bearing wall less than 1 m from the relevant boundary	**13**	100 mm brickwork or blockwork external face (with, or without, a plywood backing); framing members at least 37 mm wide and spaced not more than 600 mm apart internal lining: 12.5 mm plasterboard* with at least 10 mm lightweight gypsum plaster finish
1 hour load-bearing wall less than 1 m from the relevant boundary	**14**	solid masonry wall (with or without plaster finish) at least 90 mm thick (75 mm if non-load-bearing) **Note:** for masonry cavity walls, the fire resistance may be taken as that for a single wall of the same construction, whichever leaf is exposed to fire

---

Notes

* Whatever the lining material, it is important to use a method of fixing that the manufacturer says would be needed to achieve the particular performance. For example, if the lining is plasterboard the fixings should be at 150 mm centres as follows (where two layers are being used each should be fixed separately):
9.5 mm thickness   −30 mm galvanised nails
12.5 mm thickness   −40 mm galvanised nails
19 mm−25 mm thickness −60 mm galvanised nails

† Thinner framing members, such as 37 mm may be suitable depending on the loading conditions.

** A thinner wall may be suitable depending on the density of the concrete and the amount of reinforcement. (See *Guidelines for the construction of fire resisting structural elements* (HMSO 1982))

STRUCTURAL STEELWORK

THE BUILDING REGULATION REQUIREMENTS

GENERAL

The periods of fire resistance required for structural steelwork are given in Tables 7.3 and 7.4. In addition, any column or beam must have fire resistance of not less than the period required for any element which it carries and, if it forms part of more than one building or compartment, must comply with the maximum fire resistance specified for those buildings or compartments.

NON-COMBUSTIBILITY

A beam or column must be constructed wholly of non-combustible materials (including any protection) if it forms part of, or carries, any structure which itself is required to be constructed of non-combustible materials, (i.e. certain external walls, separating walls, compartment walls and floors and structure surrounding protected shafts).

Exceptions

Columns and beams are generally not required to have fire resistance in the following situations:
1. Beams which support only a roof structure. However, the rafters of portal frames may require fire protection where the columns form part of a wall requiring fire resistance, as the rafters and columns are structurally interdependent. Roof beams may also require fire protection where the roof is used as an escape route.
2. Columns or beams which form part of the ground storey in a single storey building or in a building consisting of a ground storey and one or more basement storeys.
However, any column or beam within or forming part of a wall, and any column which gives support to a wall or gallery, must have fire resistance of not less than that required for the wall or gallery.

THE PRODUCTS

Vermiculux, Monolux and Supalux can be used in the construction of fire protecting cladding to structural steelwork. All three products are non-combustible to BS 476: Part 4: 1970, and hence have Class O surfaces.
They are easy to work, dimensionally stable and unaffected by moisture which allows them to be fixed at any time during the building programme or in areas where high humidity or condensation may occur.
Vermiculux: a low density board, intended primarily for structural steel fire protection, which can be used to provide up to 4 hour fire resistance. It can be quickly and simply fixed by stapling or screwing adjacent boards together, and rebates on the short edges eliminate the need for cover strips at joints.
The finished casings can be plastered or decorated with paint, paper, vinyls etc. In areas liable to moderate damage, the corners can be protected with metal or plastic angle trims and in areas liable to impact damage, the casing can be protected with a galvanised metal facing.
Monolux: a robust board that can be used to provide up to 2 hour fire resistance. It can be finished in a wide range of veneers or laminates (including hard or soft plastics, sheet metals or natural timber) and can be edge screwed.
Supalux: a strong rigid board that can be used to provide up to 2 hour fire resistance when screwed to a light gauge steel framing.

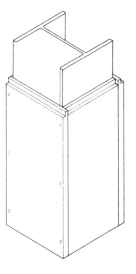

VERMICULUX

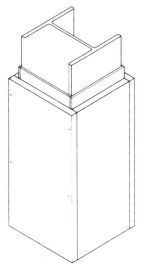

MONOLUX

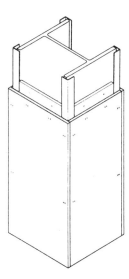

SUPALUX

HOW TO SPECIFY

1. Choose material to be used. In the majority of applications Vermiculux will most commonly be specified, as the more cost effective form of fire protection to structural steelwork. Monolux should be specified if, for example, a veneered finish or a more robust board is required. Supalux may be chosen, for example, in order to maintain a continuous appearance/ finish, where it has also been used in associated applications such as wall linings.

2. Establish period of fire protection required: see Tables 7.3 and 7.4.

3. Determine the Hp/A factor of the steel section, by calculation (see below), or by reference to tables 32 or 33.

4. Using the Hp/A factor together with the period of fire resistance required, determine the thickness of material and fixing by reference to pages 195 and 196 for Vermiculux, pages 197 and 198 for Monolux and pages 199 and 200 for Supalux.

Hp/A FACTORS

The period of fire protection to structural steel depends upon the Hp/A factor of the steel section. The Hp/A is a measure of the rate at which a section will heat up in a fire and the higher its value, the greater will be the thickness of fire protection material required.

The Hp/A is arrived at by dividing Hp, the rectangular perimeter of the exposed steelwork (using one of the formulae in table 30, related to the extent of exposure) in metres, by A, the cross sectional area of the steel member in square metres.

Table 32 (page 193) gives universal column and beam steel sections and their Hp/A values depending on how many sides need to be encased. Other symbols used for this factor include P/A, U/F, U/A, F/A, F/V, S/V. (For further details see ASFPCM publication).

Table 30: Hp for universal beams, universal columns and joists, (plain and castellated)					
Cased	4 sides	3 sides	3 sides	2 sides	1 side
	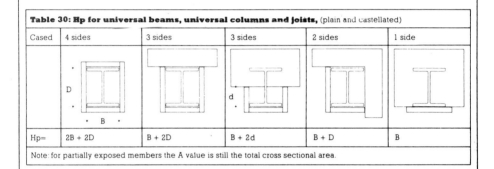				
Hp=	2B + 2D	B + 2D	B + 2d	B + D	B
Note: for partially exposed members the A value is still the total cross sectional area.					

Example: universal beam, serial size 457mm x 191mm x 98kg/m to be encased on three sides

Serial size = 457mm x 191mm
Actual size = 467.4mm (D) x 192.8mm (B)
Hp   = B + 2D (figure 2   table 30).
        = 192.8 + 467.4 + 467.4 = 1127.6mm = 1.1276m
A   = 125.3cm^2 = 0.01253m^2
Hp/A   = 1.1276/0.01253 = 89.99 = 90 m^{-1}

From this, the required thicknesses of the three products can be found for different periods of fire protection by using the charts on Vermiculux (page 48), Monolux (page 50), or Supalux (page 52).

Up to 1 hour fire protection at Hp/A 90m^{-1}, thickness required:- 20mm Vermiculux
                                                                    19mm Monolux
                                                                    9mm Supalux

2 hour fire protection at Hp/A 90m^{-1}, thickness required:-   20mm Vermiculux
                                                                  22mm Monolux

4 hour fire protection at Hp/A 90m^{-1}, thickness required:-   40mm Vermiculux

Hp/A for castellated sections

The temperature of protected castellated members increases at a slightly faster rate than conventional sections. To compensate for this the Hp/A values to be used are those of the original sections increased by 20%

Hp/A for wind and stability bracing

Bracing members are present in a building both to resist lateral (wind) forces and to provide overall stability to the structure.

They do not need the same level of protection as loadbearing members and as a result, some relaxation may be justified. It has therefore been recommended by the ASFPCM that:
a) no protection is generally necessary
b) where bracing is essential to the fire resistance of any structure, the protection may be based upon a value of Hp/A not greater than 200.

Table 31: Hp/A for structural tees, angles, channels and hollow sections.

There are a number of other steel sections, apart from universal beams and columns, that may need to be encased to provide a certain amount of fire protection. The Hp value can be calculated, once the width (B) and depth (D) of the section are known, by using the formulae below.

Steel section	cased	4 sides	3 sides	3 sides
Structural and rolled tees . B . D T				
	Hp=	2B + 2D	B + 2D	B + 2D
Angles . B . D ⌐				
	Hp=	2B + 2D	B + 2D	B + 2D
Channels . B . D [				
	Hp=	2B + 2D	2B + D	B + 2D
Hollow sections square or rectangular . B . D ▢				
	Hp=	2B + 2D	B + 2D	
Hollow sections circular D ◯			Note: the air space created in boxing a section improves the insulation. A value of Hp/A higher than that for profile protection would therefore be anomalous. Hence the circumference of the tube (and not 4D) is taken as the value for Hp.	
	Hp=	π D		

Table 32: Universal beams: Section factor Hp/A

Designation		Depth of section D	Width of section B	Area of section	Section factor Hp/A		
Serial size	Mass per metre				2 sided encasement	3 sided encasement	4 sided encasement
mm	kg	mm	mm	cm²	m⁻¹	m⁻¹	m⁻¹
914x419	388	920.5	420.5	494.5	25	45	55
	343	911.4	418.5	437.5	30	50	60
914x305	289	926.6	307.8	368.8	35	60	65
	253	918.5	305.5	322.8	40	65	75
	224	910.3	304.1	285.3	45	75	85
	201	903.0	303.4	256.4	45	80	95
838x292	226	850.9	293.8	288.7	40	70	80
	194	840.7	292.4	247.2	45	80	90
	176	834.9	291.6	224.1	50	90	100
762x267	197	769.6	268.0	250.8	40	70	85
	173	762.0	266.7	220.5	45	80	95
	147	753.9	265.3	188.1	55	95	110
686x254	170	692.9	255.8	216.6	45	75	90
	152	687.6	254.5	193.8	50	85	95
	140	683.5	253.7	178.6	50	90	105
	125	677.9	253.0	159.6	60	100	115
610x305	238	633.0	311.5	303.8	30	50	60
	179	617.5	307.0	227.9	40	70	80
	149	609.6	304.8	190.1	50	80	95
610x229	140	617.0	230.1	178.4	45	80	95
	125	611.9	229.0	159.6	55	90	105
	113	607.3	228.2	144.5	60	100	115
	101	602.2	227.6	129.2	65	110	130
533x210	122	544.6	211.9	155.8	50	85	95
	109	539.5	210.7	138.6	55	95	110
	101	536.7	210.1	129.3	60	100	115
	92	533.1	209.3	117.8	65	110	125
	82	528.3	208.7	104.4	70	120	140
457x191	98	467.4	192.8	125.3	55	90	105
	89	463.6	192.0	113.9	60	100	115
	82	460.2	191.3	104.5	60	105	125
	74	457.2	190.5	95.0	70	115	135
	67	453.6	189.9	85.4	75	130	150
457x152	82	465.1	153.5	104.5	60	105	120
	74	461.3	152.7	95.0	65	115	130
	67	457.2	151.9	85.4	70	125	145
	60	454.7	152.9	75.9	80	140	160
	52	449.8	152.4	66.5	90	160	180
406x178	74	412.8	179.7	95.0	60	105	125
	67	409.4	178.8	85.5	70	115	140
	60	406.4	177.8	76.0	75	130	155
	54	402.6	177.6	68.4	85	145	170
406x140	46	402.3	142.4	59.0	90	160	185
	39	397.3	141.8	49.4	110	190	220
356x171	67	364.0	173.2	85.4	65	105	125
	57	358.6	172.1	72.2	75	125	145
	51	355.6	171.5	64.6	80	135	165
	45	352.0	171.0	57.0	90	155	185
356x127	39	352.8	126.0	49.4	95	170	195
	33	348.5	125.4	41.8	115	195	225
305x165	54	310.9	166.8	68.4	70	115	140
	46	307.1	165.7	58.9	80	130	160
	40	303.8	165.1	51.5	90	150	180
305x127	48	310.4	125.2	60.8	70	125	145
	42	306.6	124.3	53.2	80	140	160
	37	303.8	123.5	47.5	90	155	180
305x102	33	312.7	102.4	41.8	100	175	200
	28	308.9	101.9	36.3	115	200	225
	25	304.8	101.6	31.4	130	225	260
254x146	43	259.6	147.3	55.1	75	120	150
	37	256.0	146.4	47.5	85	140	170
	31	251.5	146.1	40.0	100	160	200
254x102	28	260.4	102.1	36.2	100	170	200
	25	257.0	101.9	32.2	110	190	220
	22	254.0	101.6	28.4	125	215	250
203x133	30	206.8	133.8	38.0	90	145	180
	25	203.2	133.4	32.3	105	165	210

Table 33: Universal columns: Section factor Hp/A						
Designation		Depth of section D	Width of section B	Area of section	Section factor Hp/A		
Serial size	Mass per metre				2 sided encasement	3 sided encasement	4 sided encasement
mm	kg	mm	mm	cm²	m⁻¹	m⁻¹	m⁻¹
356x406	634	474.7	424.1	808.1	10	15	20
	551	455.7	418.5	701.8	10	20	25
	467	436.6	412.4	595.5	15	20	30
	393	419.1	407.0	500.9	15	25	35
	340	406.4	403.0	432.7	20	30	35
	287	393.7	399.0	366.0	20	30	45
	235	381.0	395.0	299.8	25	40	50
356x368	202	374.7	374.4	257.9	30	45	60
	177	368.3	372.1	225.7	35	50	65
	153	362.0	370.2	195.2	40	55	75
	129	355.6	368.3	164.9	45	65	90
305x305	283	365.3	321.8	360.4	20	30	40
	240	352.6	317.9	305.6	20	35	45
	198	339.9	314.1	252.3	25	40	50
	158	327.2	310.6	201.2	30	50	65
	137	320.5	308.7	174.6	35	55	70
	118	314.5	306.8	149.8	40	60	85
	97	307.8	304.8	123.3	50	75	100
254x254	167	289.1	264.5	212.4	25	40	50
	132	276.4	261.0	167.7	30	50	65
	107	266.7	258.3	136.6	40	60	75
	89	260.4	255.9	114.0	45	70	90
	73	254.0	254.0	92.9	55	80	110
203x203	86	222.3	208.8	110.1	40	60	80
	71	215.9	206.2	91.1	45	70	95
	60	209.6	205.2	75.8	55	80	110
	52	206.2	203.9	66.4	60	95	125
	46	203.2	203.2	58.8	70	105	140
152x152	37	161.8	154.4	47.4	65	100	135
	30	157.5	152.9	38.2	80	120	160
	23	152.4	152.4	29.8	100	155	205

Table 34: Vermiculux casings: fire performance

Fire performance: up to 4 hour fire resistance to BS476: Part 8: 1972 depending on the Hp/A factor of the steel section to be encased.

Authority: Fire Research Station letter dated 5 November 1980

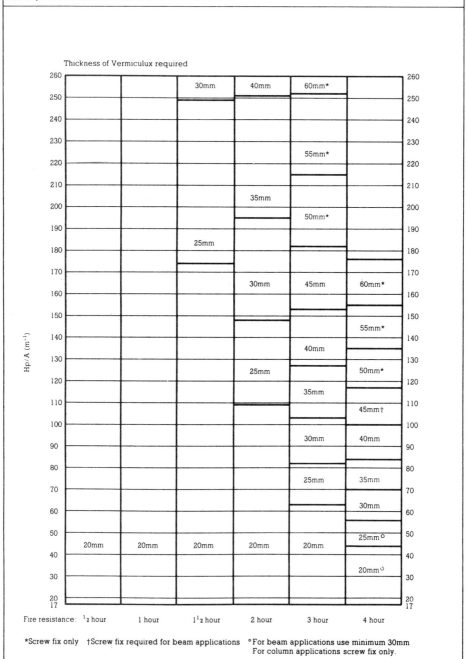

Thickness of Vermiculux required

*Screw fix only   †Screw fix required for beam applications   °For beam applications use minimum 30mm
For column applications screw fix only.

Table 35: Vermiculux casings: fixing details				
Construction:	to form box casing	abutting structural soffits or walls		
	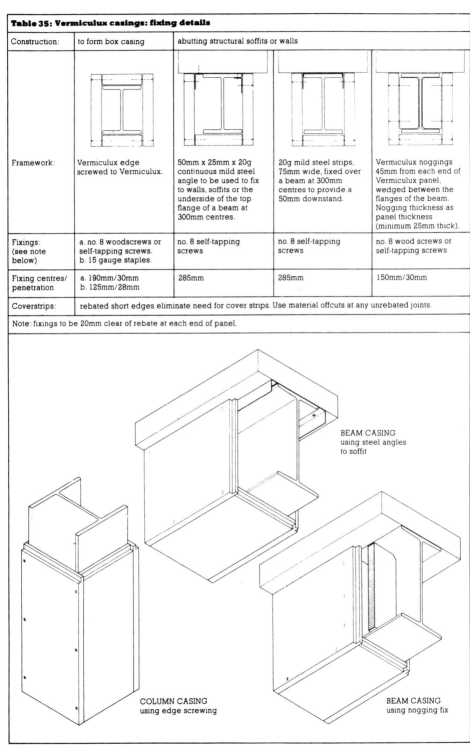			
Framework:	Vermiculux edge screwed to Vermiculux.	50mm x 25mm x 20g continuous mild steel angle to be used to fix to walls, soffits or the underside of the top flange of a beam at 300mm centres.	20g mild steel strips, 75mm wide, fixed over a beam at 300mm centres to provide a 50mm downstand.	Vermiculux noggings 45mm from each end of Vermiculux panel, wedged between the flanges of the beam. Nogging thickness as panel thickness (minimum 25mm thick).
Fixings: (see note below)	a. no. 8 woodscrews or self-tapping screws. b. 15 gauge staples.	no. 8 self-tapping screws	no. 8 self-tapping screws	no. 8 wood screws or self-tapping screws
Fixing centres/ penetration	a. 190mm/30mm b. 125mm/28mm	285mm	285mm	150mm/30mm
Coverstrips:	rebated short edges eliminate need for cover strips. Use material offcuts at any unrebated joints.			
Note: fixings to be 20mm clear of rebate at each end of panel.				

BEAM CASING
using steel angles
to soffit

COLUMN CASING
using edge screwing

BEAM CASING
using nogging fix

Table 36: Monolux casings: fire performance

Fire performance: up to 2 hour fire resistance to BS476: Part 8: 1972 depending on the Hp/A factor of the steel section to be encased.

Authority: Fire Research Station letter dated 5 November 1980

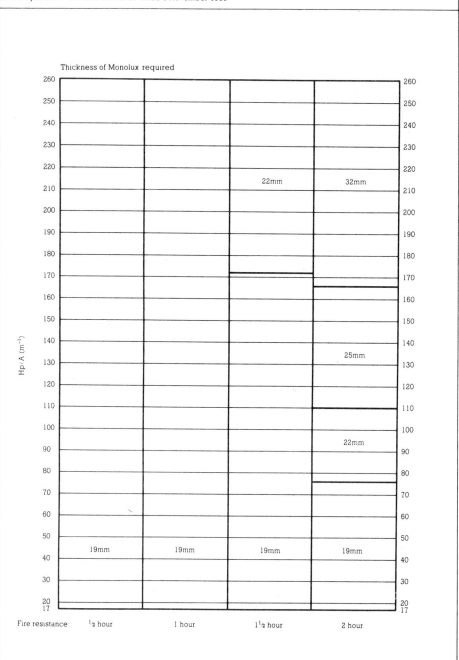

Table 37: Monolux casings: fixing details			
Construction:	to form box casing	abutting structural soffits or walls	
	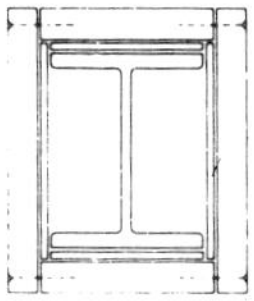	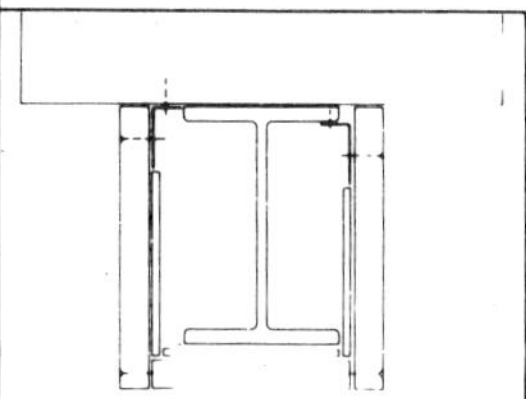	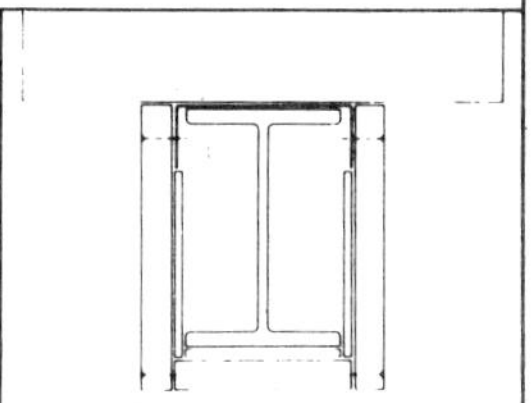
Framework:	Monolux to Monolux	50mm x 25mm x 20g continuous mild steel angle to be used to fix to walls, soffits or the underside of the top flange of beams at 300mm centres.	20g mild steel strips 75mm wide, fixed over a beam at maximum 490mm centres to provide 45mm downstand.
Fixings:	no. 8 woodscrews or self-tapping screws	no. 8 self-tapping screws	no. 8 self-tapping screws
Fixing centres/ penetration	230mm/30mm	490mm	490mm
Cover strips:	6mm Supalux, 75mm wide, fixed inside circumferential joints, to one side of joint at 160mm centres.		

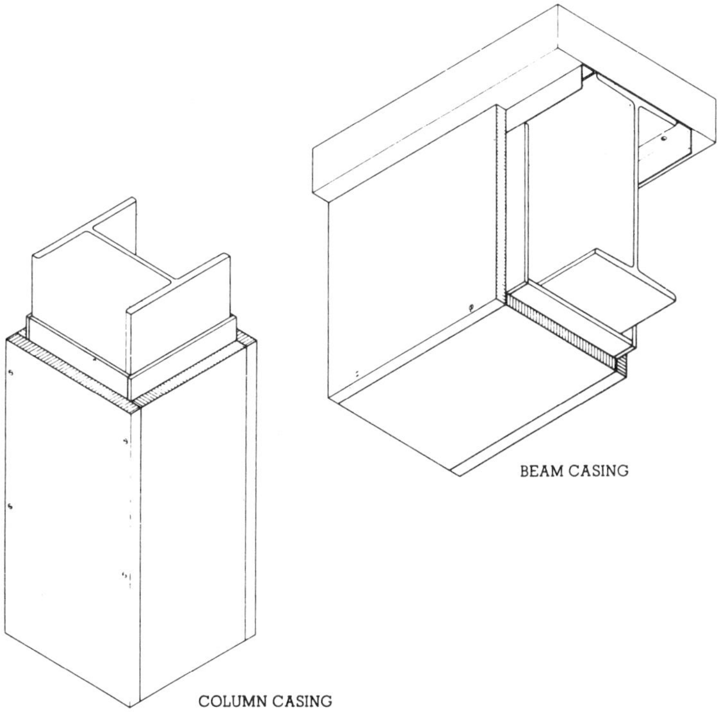

BEAM CASING

COLUMN CASING

Table 38: Supalux casings: fire performance

Fire performance: up to 2 hour fire resistance to BS476: Part 8: 1972 depending on the Hp/A factor of the steel section to be encased.

Authority: Fire Research Station letter dated 5 November 1980.

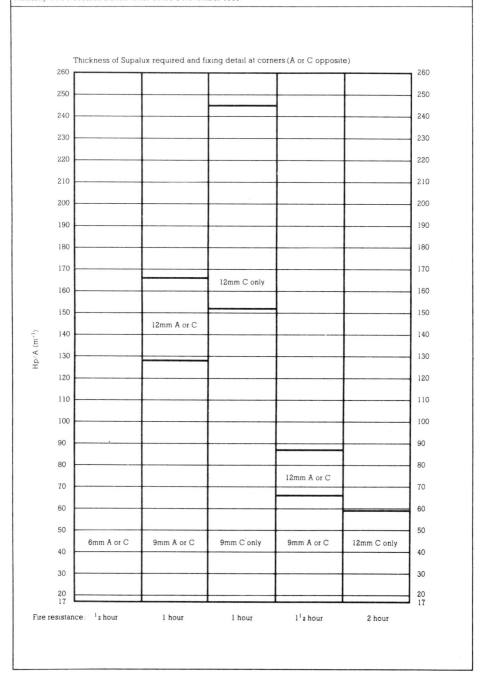

Thickness of Supalux required and fixing detail at corners (A or C opposite)

Table 39: Supalux casings: fixing details

Construction	to form box casing		abutting structural soffits or walls	
	Detail A	Detail C		
Framework:	25mm x 25mm x 18 to 22g mild steel angle for columns or at lower flange of beams.	40mm x 20mm x 18 to 22g channels to achieve 25mm air gap over flanges of columns or lower flanges of beams.	32mm x 19mm x 20g continuous mild steel angle for fixing to walls, soffits or the underside of the top flange of a beam at 300mm centres.	20g mild steel strips, 75mm wide, fixed over a beam at 270mm centres.
Fixings:	no. 8 self-tapping screws	no. 8 self-tapping screws	no. 8 self-tapping screws	no. 8 self-tapping screws
Fixing centres:	230mm	300mm	270mm	270mm
Cover strips:	Supalux, same thickness as casing, 75mm wide, fixed inside circumferential joints, to both sides of joint at 160mm centres.			

In the Detail C illustration the dimension **25mm** is labelled.

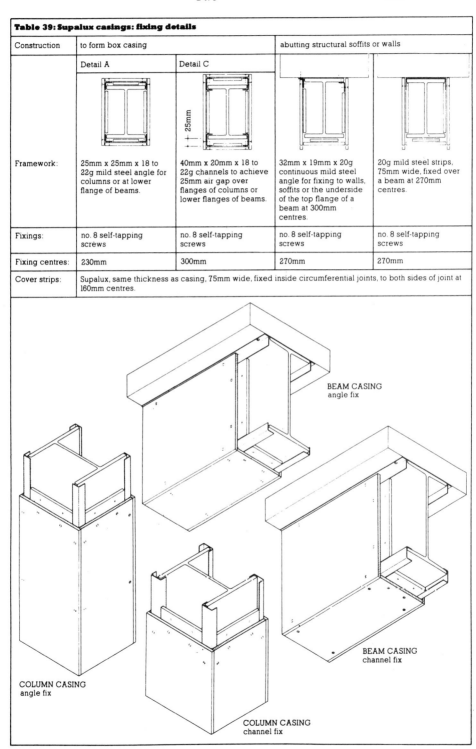

BEAM CASING
angle fix

BEAM CASING
channel fix

COLUMN CASING
angle fix

COLUMN CASING
channel fix

Table 7.5 Maximum dimensions of buildings or compartments.

Type of building	Height of building	Floor area of any storey in building or compartment (m^2)	Cubic capacity of building or compartment (m^3)
(a) Residential Buildings			
Institutional			
Single storey	Any	3000	Any
Multi-storey	Any	2000	Any
Other Residential			
Single storey	Any	3000	Any
Multi-storey	not over 28 m	3000	8500
Multi-storey	over 28 m**	2000	5500
(b) Non-residential Buildings			
Assembly			
Multi-storey	Any	Any	7000
Office			
Multi-storey	Any	Any	Any
Shop			
Multi-storey	Any	2000*	7000*
Industrial			
Multi-storey	not over 28 m	Any	28000
Multi-storey	over 28 m**	2000	5500
Other Non-residential			
Multi-storey	not over 28 m	Any	21000†
Multi-storey	over 28 m**	1000	Any

Notes

*   These limits may be doubled where the building is fitted throughout with an automatic sprinkler system which complies with BS 5306 *Code of Practice for fire extinguishing installations and equipment on premises*, Part 2: 1979 *Sprinkler systems*.

†   Table 6.4 of AD B2/3/4 gives this limit as 2100 m^3. This would appear to be a typographical error since all previous regulations give this value as 21000 m^3 as shown in table above.

** See also notes in text regarding compartment floors in buildings over 28 m high.

building or compartment in a shop or other residential building irrespective of the number of storeys.

AD B2/3/4 2.23(c)

● Any wall enclosing a refuse storage chamber in a flat or maisonette.

Specific requirements for compartment walls and floors

Compartment walls and floors divide buildings into compartments thereby restricting horizontal and vertical fire spread from one compartment to another.

Compartment walls and floors should have fire resistance as specified in Tables 7.3 and 7.4 above according to the purpose group and size of the building or compartment in question.

In addition to the periods of fire resistance given in the tables mentioned above, AD B2/3/4 specifies periods for certain compartment walls and floors which override those values as follows:

- Where a compartment wall or floor separates part of a flat, institutional building or other residential building from a part of the building used for non-residential purposes, then it should have at least one hour's fire resistance. **AD B2/3/4**
Tables 2.1,
3.1, 4.1
- A compartment wall which separates a flat or maisonette from any other part of the same building is not required to have fire resistance of more than one hour *unless*,

(a) it is load-bearing; or,
(b) it forms part of a protected shaft; or,
(c) it forms part of the boundary with a different purpose group and the minimum period of fire resistance required for any element of structure in that other part exceeds one hour. **AD B2/3/4**
Table 2.1

- Where a small garage is attached to or forms part of a house, any floor over the garage should have a fire resistance of at least half an hour. Any wall between house and garage should have at least half an hour's fire resistance. Any opening in that wall between house and garage should have a threshold at least 100 mm above the level of the garage floor and be fitted with a half hour fire resisting self-closing door (see Fig. 7.13). **AD B2/3/4**
sec. 1
1.29
- The upper floor of a two-storey dwelling is regarded as a special case. Such a floor, when tested for fire resistance from the underside is required only to provide,

(a) stability for half an hour; and,
(b) integrity for 15 minutes; and,
(c) insulation for 15 minutes.

This is termed 'modified half-hour' fire resistance (see Table A1, Appendix A item 3, 'Floors').

Non-combustibility requirements for compartment walls and floors

Where a compartment wall or floor is required to have fire resistance of one hour or more, it should be constructed of materials of limited combustibility except for the surfaces of walls or ceilings which comply with provisions for internal surfaces above, or combustible floor finishes, however, it should achieve its required fire resistance without assistance from the finishes.

Section

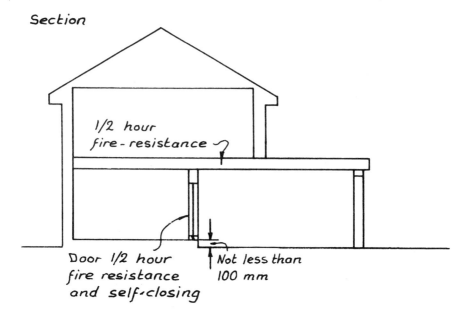

1/2 hour
fire-resistance

Door 1/2 hour
fire resistance
and self-closing

Not less than
100 mm

Plan

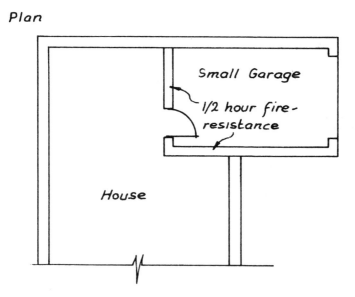

Small Garage

1/2 hour fire-
resistance

House

Fig. 7.13 Attached small garages.

This requirement for construction in materials of limited combustibility does not apply in the following cases:

- Where one hour's fire resistance is required for a compartment *wall* in a flat, institutional building or other residential building solely because it separates a part of the building from a non-residential part of the same building. AD B2/3/4 Tables 2.1, 3.1, 4.1
- Where one hour's fire resistance is required for a compartment *floor* in a flat or other residential building solely because it separates a part of the building from a non-residential part of the same building. AD B2/3/4 3.24 & Table 3.1
- Where the regulations apply to existing floors of a *non-residential* building solely because of a material alteration (see regulation 3(2)) and the building will not exceed 15 m in height. Requirements as to non-combustibility also apply to any beam or column forming part of a compartment wall or floor or any structure carrying it. AD B2/3/4 5.26 & 6.24

The following walls and floors should also be constructed of materials of limited combustibility:

- In a dwellinghouse of three or more storeys (basements not counted), the floor over a basement which exceeds 100 m^2 in area.
- In a block of flats exceeding four storeys (basements not counted), any compartment floor or wall.
- In a block of flats four storeys high (basements not counted), any compartment wall and the floor over any basement.
- In a block of flats not exceeding three storeys high (basements not counted), any floor over, or wall in, a basement. AD B2/3/4 1.24 & 2.24

Fire protecting suspended ceilings

Table A2 to Appendix A of AD B2/3/4, which is reproduced below, gives details of fire protecting suspended ceilings which can contribute to the fire resistance of a compartment floor. Apart from those listed in the table, suspended ceilings should not be assumed capable of providing fire resistance. AD B2/3/4 Appendix A Table A2

Junctions and openings in compartment walls and floors

Since the purpose of compartmentation is to prevent fire spreading throughout a building, it follows that any points of weakness in compartment walls and floors must be adequately protected. These points of weakness occur at junctions between compartment walls or floors and other compartment walls, external walls, separating walls and protecting structure.

Appendix D of AD B2/3/4 requires that the various structures be bonded together or the junction fire-stopped (see Fig. 7.14). AD B2/3/4 Appendix D D4

Where a compartment wall and a roof meet, the wall should be carried at least 375 mm above the roof covering surface, measured at

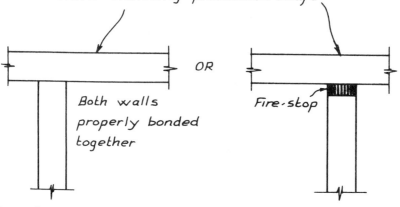

Fig. 7.14 Junction of compartment and other walls.

AD B2/3/4 *Appendix A*

Table **A2**   **Limitations on fire-protecting suspended ceilings**

Height of building or of separated part [m]	Type of floor	Provision for fire resistance of floor [hours]	Description of suspended ceiling
less than 15	not compartment	1 or less	Type A, B, C or D
	compartment	less than 1	
		1	Type B, C or D
15 or more	any	1 or less	Type C or D
no limit	any	more than 1	Type D

Notes

Ceiling type	Description
A	Surface of ceiling exposed to the cavity should be Class 0 or Class 1.
B	Surface of ceiling exposed to the cavity should be class 0. Supports and fixings should be non-combustible.
C	Surface of ceiling exposed to the cavity should be Class 0. Ceiling should be jointless (i.e. not contain access panels). Supports and fixings should be non-combustible.
D	Ceiling should be of a material of limited combustibility and be jointless (i.e. not contain access panels). Supports and fixings should be non-combustible. Any insulation above the ceiling should be of a material of limited combustibility.

right angles to the roof, unless the junction between the wall and roof is fire-stopped and the roof construction complies with the description given for separating wall junctions (see *Separating walls* p. 7.89 and Fig. 7.26).

AD B2/3/4
Appendix D
D3

Combustible materials should not be carried through, into or across the ends, or over the top, of a compartment wall in such a way as to reduce the effectiveness of the wall in resisting fire and the spread of fire. However, certain combustible roof materials may be carried over a compartment wall in the same way as described for separating walls (see *Separating walls* p. 7.89 and Fig. 7.26).

Combustible structural members, such as timber beams, joists, purlins and rafters may be built into or carried through compartment walls constructed of masonry or concrete provided the holes for them are kept as small as possible and fire-stopped. Trussed rafters may also bridge a compartment wall, but failure of a truss in one compartment due to fire must not result in failure of a truss in another compartment.

AD B2/3/4
Appendix D
D5

The only openings permitted in compartment walls or floors are one or more of the following:

- An opening fitted with a door which has the appropriate fire resistance given in Table A1 of Appendix A to AD B2/3/4 and is fitted in accordance with Appendix F of AD B2/3/4 (see *Fire doors* below).
- An opening for a protected shaft (see *Protected shafts* p. 207).
- An opening for a refuse chute for non-combustible construction.
- An opening for a pipe, ventilation duct, chimney, appliance, ventilation duct or duct encasing one or more flue pipes, provided it complies with the relevant parts of Appendix F of AD B2/3/4 (see *Pipes, Ventilating ducts* and *Flues* pp. 7.74 and 7.75).

Fire doors

All fire-resisting doors should be fitted with automatic self-closing devices capable of closing the door against any latch and from any angle. Rising butt hinges are not considered as automatic self-closing devices unless the door is:

AD B2/3/4
Appendix F
F3

- To a flat or maisonette.
- In a cavity barrier.
- Between a dwellinghouse and a garage.
- Any door in a loft conversion of a dwellinghouse which is required by Appendix B of the mandatory rules for means of escape in case of fire (see above), to be self-closing.

AD B2/3/4
Appendix L

As a general rule, no device should be provided to hold a door open. However, in some cases a self-closing device may be considered a hindrance to normal use. In such cases a fire-resisting door may be held open by:

- A fusible link device (but not if the door is fitted in an opening provided as a means of escape).
- A smoke-susceptible electro-magnetic or electro-mechanical device, provided the door can be readily opened manually. (This provision also applies to doors provided for means of escape.) In this context a 'smoke-susceptible device' is one which automatically closes a door in the event of each or any one of:

AD B2/3/4
Appendix F
F4 & F6

(a) smoke detection by appropriate apparatus;
(b) manual operation by a suitably located switch;
(c) failure of the electricity supply to the device, smoke detector, or switch;

AD B2/3/4
Appendix L

(d) operation of a fire alarm system, if fitted.

No fire-resisting door should be hung on hinges containing combustible material or a material with a melting point less than 800°C. However,

AD B2/3/4
Appendix F
F5

other types of hinges may be used if approved under the relevant test procedure.

All fire-resisting doors should have the appropriate fire resistance described in Table A1 to Appendix A of AD B2/3/4 (see page 7.36). However, it is permissible for two fire-resisting doors to be fitted in an opening if each door is self-closing and the required level of fire

AD B2/3/4
Appendix F
F2
AD B2/3/4
Appendix F
F7

resistance can be achieved by the two doors together. However, if these two doors are fitted in 'an opening provided for a means of escape, one of them may be held open by a fusible link if the other is easily openable by hand and has at least half an hour's fire resistance.

The general requirement for fire doors to be self-closing does *not* apply to a door in an opening in the enclosing structure to a protected shaft which contains only a lift or lifts if the opening is protected as follows:

- A door is provided which has fire resistance of not less than half an hour, and the opening contains another door which *is* fitted with an automatic self-closing device and is held open by a fusible link and that other door has fire resistance of not less than that required of the structure around the opening.
- A door is provided which has fire resistance of not less than that required for the structure around the opening. (This provision does

AD B2/3/4
Appendix F
F3

not apply if the opening is in a compartment wall and there is another similar door on the opposite side of the lift shaft at the same level.) (See Fig. 7.15.)

Protected shafts

Protected shafts should only be built:

(a) For the purposes set out in the definition in Appendix L (see above page 7.5); or,
(b) for the accommodation of pipes or ducts; or,
(c) for sanitary accommodation and/or washrooms;

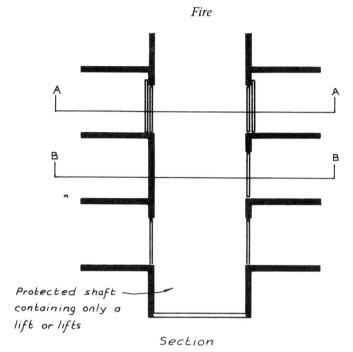

Protected shaft
containing only a
lift or lifts

Section

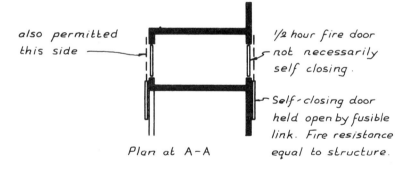

also permitted
this side

½ hour fire door
not necessarily
self closing.

Self-closing door
held open by fusible
link. Fire resistance
equal to structure.

Plan at A-A

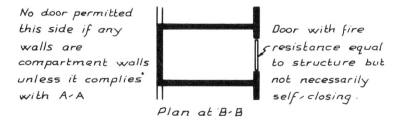

No door permitted
this side if any
walls are
compartment walls
unless it complies
with A-A

Door with fire
resistance equal
to structure but
not necessarily
self-closing.

Plan at B-B

Fig. 7.15 Doors to lift shafts.

AD B2/3/4
Appendix E
E4
and they should form a complete barrier between the parts of the building which they connect.

Protecting structure is defined as any wall, floor or other structure enclosing a protected shaft, but *not*:

(a) A wall which also forms part of an external wall, separating wall or compartment wall; or,
(b) a floor which is also a compartment floor or which is laid directly upon the ground; or,
(c) a roof.

The requirements for separating and compartment walls and compartment floors are sufficient to ensure safety of the shaft. External walls, the roof and the ground are exempt because they do not protect other compartments (see Fig. 7.16).

Any protecting structure as defined should have fire resistance as specified in AD B2/3/4 section 1 to 6 (see Tables 7.3 and 7.4 above), and must withstand tests from both sides separately.

Where a protecting structure is required to have fire resistance of one hour or more, that structure should be constructed of materials of limited combustibility, except for surface finishes which meet the
AD B2/3/4
Appendix E
E1
AD B2/3/4
2.31
requirements for internal surfaces discussed above. This requirement, however, does not apply to any protecting structure within the ground or upper storeys of flats or maisonettes if the building does not exceed three storeys (basements not counted).

AD B2/3/4
Appendix E
E1
These requirements as to the use of materials of limited combustibility also apply to any beam or column forming part of a protective structure or carrying it.

There should be no oil pipe or ventilating duct within any protected shaft which contains any stairway and/or lift. Where a protected shaft contains a pipe carrying natural gas the pipe should be of screwed steel
AD B2/3/4
Appendix E
E4 & E6
or of all welded steel construction in accordance with the Gas Safety Regulations S.I. 1972 No. 1178 and the shaft should be adequately ventilated to the external air (see Fig. 7.17).

A protecting structure should have no openings other than those specifically permitted below:

● Where a protected shaft contains one or more lifts:
(a) it should be ventilated to the external air by one or more
AD B2/3/4
Appendix E
E5
    permanent openings at the top of the shaft, of total unobstructed area at least $0 \cdot 1 \text{ m}^2$ per lift; and
(b) it may have an opening to allow lift cables to pass to the lift motor room. If the opening is formed at the bottom of the shaft it must be kept as small as possible (see Fig. 7.17).
● Where a protected shaft contains a ventilating duct, or is itself a ventilating duct any inlets to, outlets from and openings for the duct should comply with the provisions of AD B2/3/4 Appendix F, (see *Pipes, ventilation ducts and flues* p. 7.74).

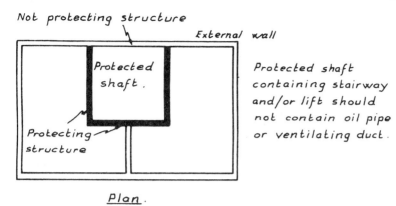

Not protecting structure

External wall

Protected shaft.

Protecting structure

Plan.

Protected shaft containing stairway and/or lift should not contain oil pipe or ventilating duct.

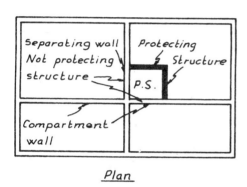

Separating wall Not protecting structure

Protecting Structure

P.S.

Compartment wall

Plan

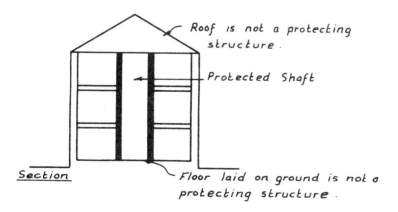

Roof is not a protecting structure.

Protected Shaft

Section

Floor laid on ground is not a protecting structure.

Fig. 7.16 Protecting structure.

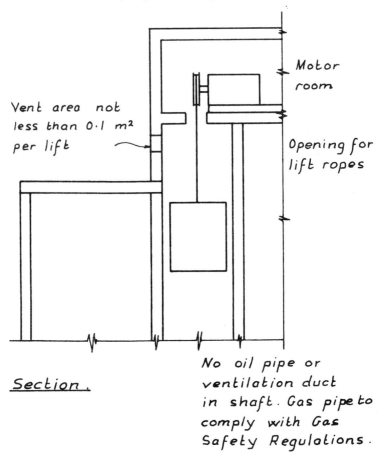

Vent area not
less than 0·1 m²
per lift

Motor
room

Opening for
lift ropes

Section.

No oil pipe or
ventilation duct
in shaft. Gas pipe to
comply with Gas
Safety Regulations.

Fig. 7.17 Protected shaft containing lifts.

● It is permissible to form an opening for pipes (other than those specifically forbidden above), provided the pipe complies with Appendix F.
● Any opening, other than those detailed above, should be fitted with a fire resisting door complying with Appendix F (see above).

The following special requirements apply to doors in protected shafts:

● Where a protected shaft is wholly or partly above ground level in a building used for flats, other residential, assembly or office purposes any door in the shaft must have fire resistance of at least half an hour.
● In any other case, any door must have fire resistance of at least half

that required for the protecting structure *or* half an hour, whichever is the greater.

Openings in an external wall, separating wall, compartment wall or compartment floor enclosing a protected shaft, are not required to comply with these rules. Such openings must accord with the appropriate rules for the element concerned.

AD B2/3/4
Appendix E
E7

A protected shaft containing a stairway is often approached by way of a corridor or lobby.It is sometimes desirable to glaze the wall between the shaft and the corridor or lobby in order to allow light and visibility in both directions.

This glazing is permitted provided it has at least half an hour's fire resistance in terms of stability and integrity and the following conditions are met:

(a) The protecting structure is not required to have more than one hour's fire resistance, and
(b) the corridor or lobby has at least half an hour's fire separation from the rest of the floor (openings included) (see Fig. 7.18).

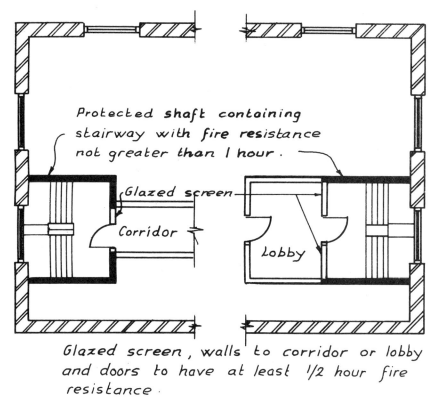

Glazed screen, walls to corridor or lobby and doors to have at least 1/2 hour fire resistance.

Fig. 7.18 Glazed screen separating protected shaft from lobby or corridor.

Pipes, ventilation ducts and flues

It is impossible to construct a building without passing *some* pipes or ducts through the walls and floors, and such penetration of the elements of structure is a source of flame and smoke spread. Appendix F of AD B2/3/4 therefore attempts to control the specifications of such pipes or ducts and of their associated enclosing structures.

Pipes

AD B2/3/4
Appendix L

For the purposes of Appendix F, the term 'pipe' includes a ventilating pipe for an above ground drainage system, but does not include any flue pipe or other form of ventilating pipe.

As is usual, the expression *pipe* here may be read as *pipe-line*, and should be taken to include all pipe fittings and accessories.

Requirements

Where a pipe as defined passes through an opening in:

    (i) a separating wall or protecting structure; or

    (ii) a compartment wall or compartment floor, (except an opening

AD B2/3/4
Appendix F
F8

       wholly enclosed within a protected shaft); or

(iii) a cavity barrier;

AD B2/3/4
Appendix F
F9

then either a proprietary sealing system should be used which will maintain the fire resistance of the floor, wall or cavity barrier (and has been shown by test to do so,) or, the nominal internal diameter of the pipe should not exceed the relevant dimension listed in Table F1 of Appendix F of AD B2/3/4, and the opening should be as small as practicable, and fire-stopped around the pipe.

AD B2/3/4
Appendix F
F12

The specification of a pipe may vary throughout its length. If this occurs, then the diameter of that portion of the pipe which actually penetrates a structure should accord with the tabular limit appropriate to the lowest specification of pipe connected in the pipe-line within a distance of 1 m (measured along the pipe) from the actual penetration point. (Specification (a) is deemed to be the 'highest', and specification (c) the 'lowest'.)

AD B2/3/4
Appendix F
F11

Where a pipe of specification (b) penetrates a structure it is permissible to pass it through or connect it to a pipe or sleeve of specification (a) provided the pipe or sleeve of specification (a) extends on both sides of the structure for a minimum distance of 1 m. The maximum internal diameter of sleeving material may then be substituted for the diameter of the pipe (see Fig. 7.19).

The following above ground drainage system pipes complying with specification (b) of Table F1 may be passed through openings in a separating wall between houses, or through openings in a compartment wall or compartment floor between flats and maisonettes:

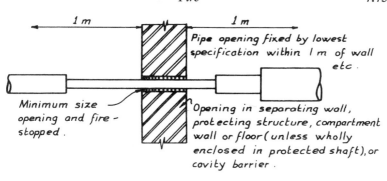

Pipe opening fixed by lowest specification within 1 m of wall etc.

1 m — 1 m

Minimum size opening and fire-stopped.

Opening in separating wall, protecting structure, compartment wall or floor (unless wholly enclosed in protected shaft), or cavity barrier.

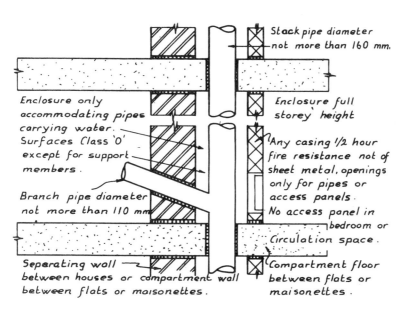

Stack pipe diameter not more than 160 mm.

Enclosure only accommodating pipes carrying water. Surfaces Class '0' except for support members.

Enclosure full storey height

Any casing 1/2 hour fire resistance not of sheet metal, openings only for pipes or access panels.

No access panel in bedroom or Circulation space.

Branch pipe diameter not more than 110 mm

Separating wall between houses or compartment wall between flats or maisonettes.

Compartment floor between flats or maisonettes.

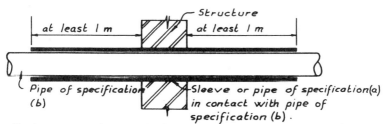

Structure

at least 1 m — at least 1 m

Pipe of specification (b)

Sleeve or pipe of specification(a) in contact with pipe of specification (b).

If above conditions satisfied then maximum nominal internal diameter of sleeving material (i.e. 160 mm) may be substituted for diameter of pipe (b).

Fig. 7.19 Penetration of elements of structure by pipes.

AD B2/3/4

Table **F1**   **Maximum nominal internal diameter of pipes**

Situation	Pipe material and maximum nominal internal diameter [mm]		
	Non-combustible material[1] (a)	**Lead, aluminium or aluminium alloy, asbestos-cement or upvc[2]** (b)	**Any other material** (c)
1 structure (but not a Separating Wall) enclosing a Protected Shaft which is not a stairway or lift shaft.	160	110	40
2 Separating Wall between dwelling houses, or Compartment Wall or Compartment Floor between flats.	160	160 (stack pipe)[3] 110 (branch pipe)[3]	40
3 any other situation	160	40	40

Notes

[1] A non-combustible material (such as cast iron or steel) which if exposed to a temperature of 800°C will not soften nor fracture to the extent that flame or hot gases will pass through the wall of the pipe.

[2] upvc pipes complying with BS 4514: 1983. uPVC pipe complying with BS 5255: 1976.

[3] Pipes forming part of an above ground drainage system and enclosed as shown in Diagram F2.

(a) a stack pipe of not more than 160 mm nominal internal diameter, provided it is contained within an enclosure in each storey; *and*

(b) a branch pipe of not more than 110 mm nominal internal diameter, provided it discharges into a stack pipe which is contained in an enclosure, the enclosure being partly formed by the wall penetrated by the branch pipe.

The enclosure referred to in both (a) and (b) immediately above should comply with the following requirements:

(a) In any storey, the enclosure should extend from floor to ceiling or from floor to floor if the ceiling is suspended.

(b) Each side of the enclosure should be formed by a separating wall, compartment wall, external wall or casing.

(c) The internal surface of the enclosure should meet the requirements of Class 0, except for any supporting members.

(d) No access panel to the enclosure is fitted in any bedroom or circulation space.

(e) The enclosure should not be used for any purpose except to accommodate drainage or water supply pipes.

The 'casing' referred to in Appendix F Diagram F2 and (b) immediately above, should provide at least half an hour's fire resistance, including any access panel, and it should not be formed of sheet metal. The only openings permitted in a casing are openings for the passage of a pipe, or openings fitted with an access panel. The pipe opening, whether it be in the structure or the casing, should be as small as is practicable and fire-stopped around the pipe (see Fig. 7.19 above).

AD B2/3/4
Appendix F
Diagram F2

Ventilating ducts

Ventilating ducts, normally forming part of an air-conditioning system, convey air to various parts of a building. It is, therefore, inevitable that they will need to pass through compartment walls and floors at some stage.

The form of fire protection required from Appendix F of AD B2/3/4 will depend on whether the duct:

(a) passes through a compartment wall or floor directly; or,

(b) is contained within or is itself a protected shaft.

AD B2/3/4
Appendix F
F14

Where the ventilating duct passes directly through a compartment wall or floor it should be fitted with an automatic fire shutter at the point of penetration and the opening for the duct should be kept as small as practicable and fire-stopped.

AD B2/3/4
Appendix F
F15

Where a protected shaft contains a ventilating duct or is itself a ventilating duct, the duct should:

(a) have automatic fire shutters fitted at inlets and outlets to reduce, as far as practicable, the risk of fire spread from one compartment to another (unless some other provision, such as a shunt duct, is made); and,

(b) not be built or lined with any material which might substantially increase the risk of such fire spread.

AD B2/3/4
Appendix F
F16

Where a protected shaft containing a ventilating duct is also used for other purposes, the duct should be enclosed to prevent fire spreading from the duct into the shaft, however no specific details are given as to the construction or fire resistance of the enclosure.

AD B2/3/4
Appendix F
F17

Where a ventilating duct forms part of an air recirculatory system (air-conditioning systems would be included here) there is a danger of smoke from a fire in one part of the building being circulated throughout the building. F18 of Appendix F requires that one or more optical smoke detectors be fitted in the ductwork. These detectors, which respond to the scattering or absorption of light by smoke particles in a light beam, should be capable of affecting the operation of the ventilating system so that contaminated air is diverted to the outside of the building if the smoke reaches an optical density of 0·5 dB/m (see Fig. 7.20).

Flues

Where any chimney, appliance ventilation duct or duct encasing one or more flue pipes, passes through a compartment wall or floor then,

(a) any flue in the chimney; or,
(b) the passage in the appliance ventilation duct; or,
(c) the space within the duct encasing flue pipes,

should be separated from the compartment wall or floor and from each compartment adjoining the wall or floor by non-combustible construction of fire resistance equal to at least half that required for the compartment wall or floor.

Similarly, where any chimney, appliance ventilation duct or duct encasing one or more flue pipes forms part of a compartment wall, the flue, passage or space described above should be separated from any compartment adjoining the wall by non-combustible construction having at any level at least half the fire resistance required for the wall at that level (see Fig. 7.21).

AD B2/3/4
Appendix F
F18 & F19

For the purposes of the above an *appliance ventilation duct* is a duct provided to convey combustion air to a gas appliance.

AD B2/3/4
Appendix L

Fire stops

A *fire stop* is defined in Appendix L to AD B2/3/4 as a seal provided to close any small gaps or imperfections of fit between elements, components or construction in a building, or any joint, and intended to restrict the penetration of smoke or flame through these gaps.

Therefore, fire stops should be provided where any pipes, ducts, conduits or cables pass through openings in cavity barriers (for definition see below), or elements of structure. (This requirement does *not* apply to elements which are required to have fire resistance only because they are load-bearing.)

AD B2/3/4
Appendix H
H1

The openings should be kept as small and as few in number as possible, and the fire-stopping should not restrict the thermal movement of pipes or ducts.

If non-rigid fire-stopping materials are used they should be reinforced or supported by materials of limited combustibility to prevent displacement, unless they have been shown by test to be satisfactory. Such reinforcement or support should always be provided if the unsupported span is more than 100 mm.

AD B2/3/4
Appendix H
H2

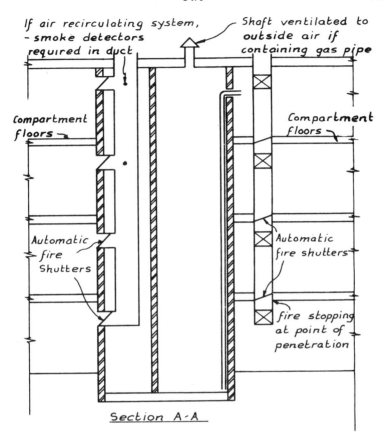

If air recirculating system, - smoke detectors required in duct

Shaft ventilated to outside air if containing gas pipe

Compartment floors

Compartment floors

Automatic fire Shutters

Automatic fire shutters

fire stopping at point of penetration

Section A-A

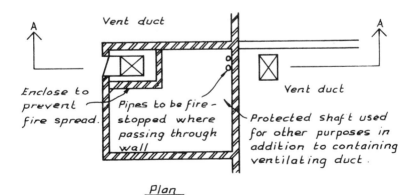

A

Vent duct

A

Enclose to prevent fire spread.

Pipes to be fire-stopped where passing through wall

Vent duct

Protected shaft used for other purposes in addition to containing ventilating duct.

Plan

Fig. 7.20 Protected shaft containing ventilating duct.

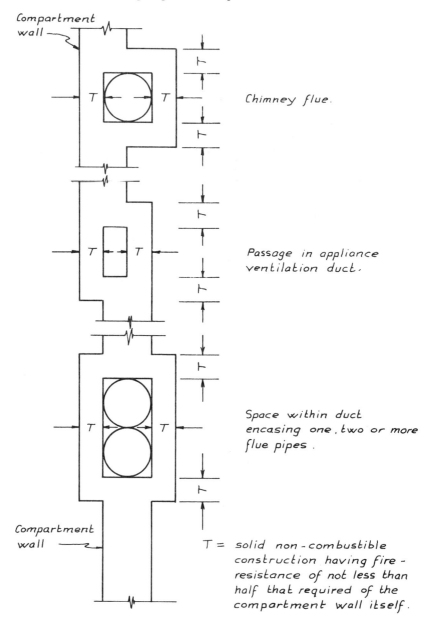

Fig. 7.21 Chimneys, etc., contained in a compartment wall.

Suitable fire-stopping materials include:

- Cement mortar,
- Gypsum based plaster,
- Cement gypsum based vermiculite/perlite mixes,
- Glass, crushed rock, blast furnace slag or ceramic based products (with or without resin binders),
- Intumescent mastics,
- Any proprietary sealing systems capable of maintaining the fire resistance of the element concerned. (Test results would be necessary to prove acceptability.)

AD B2/3/4
Appendix H
H3

Stairways

Stairways are not included in the definition of element of structure, and therefore they are not required to provide any period of fire resistance.

However, all stairways and their landings are required to be constructed of materials of limited combustibility, unless they are:

- In a maisonette,
- In a building or compartment for which the elements of structure require a fire resistance period of less than one hour,
- In a ground or upper storey (but not a basement) of a building consisting of flats or maisonettes having not more than three storeys,
- An external stairway between the ground and a floor or flat roof which is not more than 6 m above finished ground level,
- A stairway that is not within a protected shaft in a building or compartment that is occupied as a shop.

The limitations regarding incombustibility of materials do not extend to floor finishes.

AD B2/3/4
secs. 1 to 6

It should be noted that certain stairways may need to be enclosed and protected to meet certain sections of the document *Mandatory rules for means of escape in case of fire* (see above page 7.16).

Concealed spaces

Many buildings constructed today contain large hidden void spaces within floors, walls and roofs. This is particularly true of system-built housing, schools and other local authority buildings such as old people's homes.

These buildings may also contain combustible wall panels, frames and insulation thereby increasing the risk of unseen smoke and flame spread through these concealed spaces.

Therefore, despite compartmentation and the use of fire-resistant construction, many buildings have been destroyed as a result of fire spreading through cavities formed by, or in, constructional elements, and by-passing compartment walls/floors, etc.

Appendix G of AD B2/3/4 contains provisions designed to reduce the chance of hidden fire spread by making sure that cavities are:

- Closed around their edges to prevent fire from entering the concealed space,
- Interrupted if there is a chance that the cavity could form a route around a barrier to fire (such as a compartment wall or floor),
- Sub-divided if they are very large.

AD B2/3/4
Appendix G
G1

This closing, interruption or sub-division of concealed spaces is achieved by using *cavity barriers*. These are defined in Appendix L as any form of construction which is intended to close a cavity (concealed space) and prevent the penetration of smoke or flame, or is fitted inside a cavity (concealed space) in order to restrict the movement of smoke or flame within the cavity. Therefore, providing it meets the requirements for cavity barriers a form of construction designed for some other use (such as a compartment wall) may be acceptable as a cavity barrier.

AD B2/3/4
Appendix G
G2

Cavity closing

In order to prevent fire spread from one element to another (such as between a wall and a floor or suspended ceiling) a cavity barrier should be located around the perimeter of each element and particularly at the point where cavities meet.

Similarly, where there is an opening through an element (for a door, etc.) a cavity barrier should be placed around the entire perimeter of the opening so as to seal the cavity (see Fig. 7.22).

The above requirements do not apply to a cavity in a wall of masonry construction provided it is constructed as shown in Fig. 7.23 below.

AD B2/3/4
Appendix G
G3

Interruption of cavities

Where an element (such as a wall, floor, roof, ceiling or other structure, or a frame fitted with a fire resisting door) which is required to form a barrier to fire abuts another element containing a cavity there is a risk that smoke and flame could by-pass the fire barrier via the cavity. Cavity barriers should, therefore, be provided to interrupt the cavities at the point of contact between the fire barrier and the element containing the cavity (see Fig. 7.22).

Cavities in some elements are excluded from the above provisions regarding interruption, mainly on the grounds that they present little risk to unseen fire spread. These include any cavity:

AD B2/3/4
Appendix G
G4

(a) in an external wall of masonry construction (see Fig. 7.23),

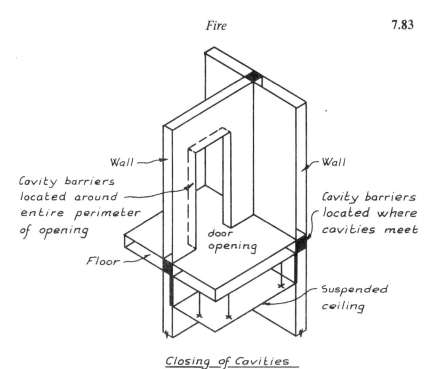

Wall

Cavity barriers located around entire perimeter of opening

Floor

Wall

Cavity barriers located where cavities meet

door opening

Suspended ceiling

<u>Closing of Cavities</u>

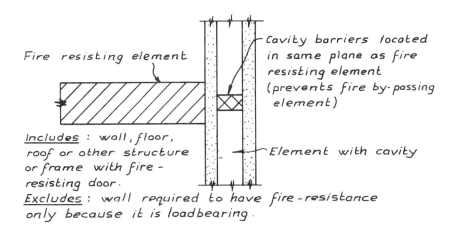

Fire resisting element

Cavity barriers located in same plane as fire resisting element (prevents fire by-passing element)

<u>Includes</u> : wall, floor, roof or other structure or frame with fire-resisting door.

Element with cavity

<u>Excludes</u> : wall required to have fire-resistance only because it is loadbearing.

<u>Interrupting Cavities</u>

Fig. 7.22 Cavity barriers.

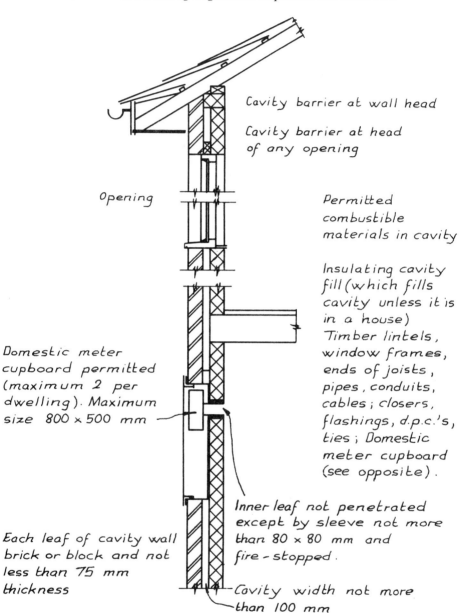

Cavity barrier at wall head

Cavity barrier at head of any opening

Opening

Permitted combustible materials in cavity

Insulating cavity fill (which fills cavity unless it is in a house)
Timber lintels, window frames, ends of joists, pipes, conduits, cables; closers, flashings, d.p.c.'s, ties; Domestic meter cupboard (see opposite).

Domestic meter cupboard permitted (maximum 2 per dwelling). Maximum size 800 × 500 mm

Inner leaf not penetrated except by sleeve not more than 80 × 80 mm and fire-stopped.

Each leaf of cavity wall brick or block and not less than 75 mm thickness

Cavity width not more than 100 mm

Fig. 7.23 Wall cavity exempt from AD B2/3/4 Appendix G, G3, G4, G6.

(b) under a floor next to the ground or oversite concrete,

(c) in a wall which requires fire-resistance only because it is load-bearing (therefore does not form a barrier to fire),

(d) in a roof space at the junction with an external wall if the provision of the cavity barrier would prevent free ventilation of the roofspace,

(e) within a floor or roof, or enclosed by a roof, provided the lower side of that cavity is enclosed by a ceiling which:

  (i) extends throughout the whole building or compartment;
  (ii) is not designed to be demountable;
  (iii) has at least half an hour's fire resistance;
  (iv) is imperforate except for any openings permitted in a cavity barrier (see below);
  (v) has an upper surface facing the cavity of at least Class 1 surface spread of flame;
  (vi) has a lower surface with an index of performance (I) not exceeding 12 and a sub-index (i_1) not exceeding 6; (see Fig. 7.24 below, detail A),

(f) within or enclosed by the roof of a one or two-storey dwellinghouse.

For houses with three or more storeys the stairway will normally be enclosed with fire-resisting construction. This should be carried up to the underside of the roof surface to form a cavity barrier unless a ceiling is provided as in (e) immediately above, (see Fig. 7.24). AD B2/3/4
Appendix G
G5

Cavity sub-division

Any cavity, including a roof space, should generally be sub-divided into separate sections by cavity barriers placed across the cavity at intervals not greater than the distances specified in Table G1 to Appendix G of AD B2/3/4 (see p. 7.88). These distances are measured along the members bounding the cavity and depend on the cavity location, the purpose group of the building or compartment, and the class of surface exposed in the cavity (see Fig. 7.25). AD B2/3/4
Appendix G
G6

Again, certain low-risk cavities are excluded from the above provisions as follows:

(a) a cavity in an external wall of masonry construction (see Fig. 7.23 above);

(b) under a floor next to the ground or oversite concrete, provided *either*

  (i) there is no access to the cavity for persons, *or*
  (ii) the height of the cavity is not more than 1 m; *or*

(c) between sheeting consisting of material of limited combustibility covering a roof, provided

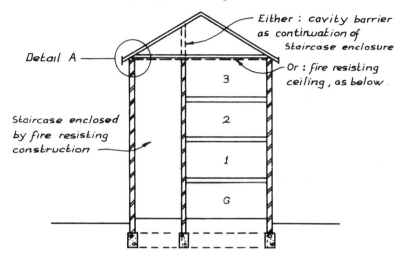

House with 3 or more storeys

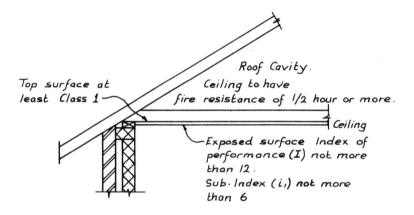

(i)   Ceiling should extend throughout building or compartment.
(ii) Ceiling should be imperforate except for openings allowed under G11
(iii) Ceiling should not be demountable

Detail A

Fig. 7.24 Fire resisting ceilings.

Subdivision of Cavities   G6

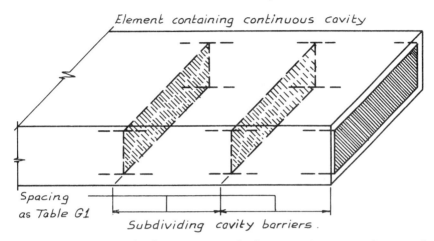

Element containing continuous cavity

Spacing
as Table G1

Subdividing cavity barriers.

This requirement does not apply to : certain cavity walls
in masonry construction.
Floors next to ground or oversite concrete if no access
or not more than 1 n high space, cavity between
non-combustible roof sheeting under certain conditions.

Fig. 7.25 Subdivision of cavities.

(i) if the sheets are flat, the cavity is filled with an insulating
      material having a surface of not lower than Class 1, *or*
(ii) if one sheet is flat and the other is corrugated, the sheets are
      separated by insulating material having a surface of not lower
      than Class 1, and that insulating material is in contact with   **AD B2/3/4**
      both sheets in line with each corrugation.   **Appendix G**
                                                                          G7

Construction of cavity barriers

Where a cavity barrier required by Appendix G has a surface of such
dimensions that its perimeter would enclose a square 1 m × 1 m, then
that cavity barrier should have at least half an hour's fire resistance.
   Smaller cavity barriers may be formed of:

● Asbestos-free board giving protection equivalent to that afforded by
   asbestos building board or insulating board (but not asbestos-

AD B2/3/4 *Appendix G*

Table **G1**   **Maximum dimensions of cavities**

Location of cavity	Purpose group of building or compartment	Class of surface exposed in cavity (excluding surface of any pipe cable or conduit, or insulation to any pipe)	Maximum dimension in any direction [m]
Between a roof and a ceiling	dwellinghouse, and flat	any	no limit
	institutional, and other residential	any	15 (with area limited to 100m^2)
	assembly, office, shop, industrial and other non-residential	any	20
Any other cavity	any	Class 0	20
		any other class	8

cement sheet) at least 9 mm thick.
- Plasterboard at least 12·5 mm thick,
- Steel at least 3 mm thick (steel lintels in cavity walls would comply with this),
- Timber at least 38 mm thick,
- Wire reinforced mineral wool blanket, at least 50 mm thick,
- Cement mortar, plaster or other material of limited combustibility at least 25 mm thick,
- Polythene sleeved mineral wool, or mineral wool slabs, in either case under compression when installed in the cavity,
- Any construction giving at least half an hour's fire resistance.

AD B2/3/4
Appendix G
G8 ·

Cavity barriers should be tightly fitted against rigid construction or, where they abut against slates, tiles, corrugated sheeting and similar non-rigid construction, have such junctions fire-stopped.

AD B2/3/4
Appendix G
G9

Cavity barriers should also be fixed in such a way that their performance is unlikely to be affected by:

(a) building movements due to subsidence, shrinkage or thermal change; *or*,
(b) failure of their fixings, or any material or construction which they abut, due to fire; *or*,
(c) collapse in a fire of any services that penetrate them.

AD B2/3/4
Appendix G
G10

Openings in cavity barriers

Cavity barriers should be imperforate except for one or more openings:

(a) for a pipe which complies with Appendix F; *or*
(b) for a cable, or for a conduit containing one or more cables; *or*
(c) fitted with an automatic fire shutter; *or*
(d) for a duct fitted with an automatic fire shutter where it passes through the barrier; *or*
(e) for a continuous duct formed in mild steel at least 0·7 mm thick; *or*
(f) fitted with a door which complies with Appendix F and having at least half an hour's fire resistance.

AD B2/3/4
Appendix G
G11

Separating walls

A separating wall is one which is common to two adjoining buildings and which restricts the spread of fire from one building to the other.

Apart from certain permitted openings (see below), a separating wall should be imperforate. It should provide a complete vertical barrier to fire between the buildings separated, including their roof spaces.

A separating wall should have fire resistance *either*,

(a) as specified in sections 1 to 6 of AD B2/3/4 according to its purpose group and size (see Tables 7.3 and 7.4 above); or,
(b) at least one hour,

whichever is the greater. It should withstand test from each side separately.

As a general rule any separating wall should be constructed wholly of materials of limited combustibility, apart from surface finishes complying with sections 1 to 6 and Appendices A and B of AD B2/3/4 (see Table 7.2, p. 7.35). The wall should provide its required fire resistance without assistance from such finishes. The permitted exceptions to this rule are,

AD B2/3/4
Appendix C
C1

● Dwellinghouses of not more than three storeys (basements not counted),
● Single storey institutional buildings with a floor area not exceeding 3000 m²,
● Single storey flats or maisonettes with a floor area not exceeding 3000 m² or flats and maisonettes of not more than two storeys with a floor area (per storey) not exceeding 500 m²,
● Any other single storey building which is permitted to be uncompartmented or is below the limits indicated by the letter Z in Tables 7.3 and 7.4, pp. 7.40–7.45,
● Any other multi-storey building which is permitted to be uncompart-

mented and is below the limits indicated by the letter X in Tables 7.3 and 7.4 above.

The above requirements as to construction in materials of limited combustibility apply also to any beam or column forming part of a separating wall and any structure carrying it.

It should be noted that in spite of the exceptions listed above, if either building adjoining the separating wall requires to be constructed of materials of limited combustibility then that is the controlling factor for the wall.

AD B2/3/4
sec. 1 to 6

Junction of separating wall with external wall and roof

AD B2/3/4
Appendix C
C3

Where an external wall carries across the end of a separating wall, the walls should be bonded together or the junction fire-stopped, so as to prevent fire spreading around the ends of the separating wall (see Fig. 7.26).

AD B2/3/4
Appendix C
C2

Where a separating wall and a roof meet, the wall should be carried at least 375 mm above the roof covering surface, measured at right angles to the roof slope, unless the roof and its covering have been designed to resist fire penetration and spread. Acceptable design solutions are illustrated in Fig. 7.26 for buildings in different purpose groups.

Combustible material should not be carried through, into or across the ends or over the top of a separating wall in such a way as to reduce the effectiveness of the wall in resisting fire and the spread of fire.

Some exceptions are permitted in the case of certain roof constructions. In the roofs shown at (b) and (c) in Fig. 7.26 the following combustible materials may be carried over the top of the separating wall:

(a) Roof boarding serving as a base for roof covering; *or*;
(b) woodwool slabs; *or*;
(c) timber slating or tiling battens.

AD B2/3/4
Appendix C
C4

In each case the materials should be solidly bedded in mortar or similar material and the space between the battens should be filled up solid with mortar to the underside of the roof covering (see Fig. 7.26).

Separating walls should be imperforate except for the following:

● An opening for a door which is needed as a means of escape in case of fire. The door should have the same fire resistance as the wall and should be fixed in accordance with the provisions of Appendix F (see above).

AD B2/3/4
Appendix C
C5

● An opening for a pipe complying with the provisions of Appendix F, (see above).

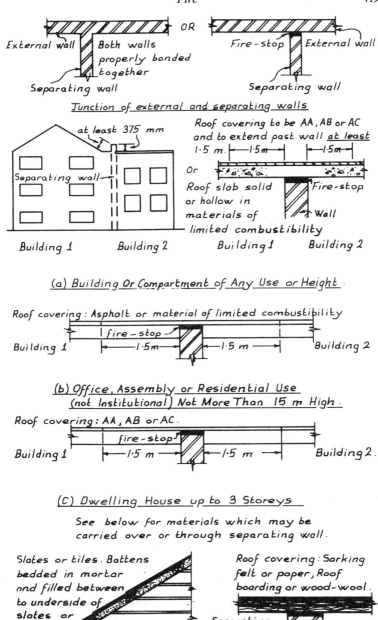

External wall Both walls properly bonded together

Separating wall

OR

Fire-stop **External wall**

Separating wall

Junction of external and separating walls

at least 375 mm

Separating wall

Building 1 Building 2

Roof covering to be AA, AB or AC and to extend past wall *at least* 1.5 m. |—1.5 m—| |—1.5 m—|

Or

Roof slab solid or hollow in materials of limited combustibility

Fire-stop
Wall

Building 1 Building 2

(a) Building Or Compartment of Any Use or Height.

Roof covering: Asphalt or material of limited combustibility

Building 1 | fire-stop | |—1.5 m—| |—1.5 m—| Building 2

(b) Office, Assembly or Residential Use (not Institutional) Not More Than 15 m High.

Roof covering: AA, AB or AC.

Building 1   fire-stop |—1.5 m—| |—1.5 m—| Building 2.

(C) Dwelling House up to 3 Storeys

See below for materials which may be carried over or through separating wall.

Slates or tiles. Battens bedded in mortar and filled between to underside of slates or tiles.

Separating wall

Roof covering: Sarking felt or paper, Roof boarding or wood-wool.

Separating wall

Combustible Materials Permitted over Separating Wall.

Fig. 7.26 Separating walls.

External fire spread

Regs Sch. 1
B4
The external walls of a building are required to resist the spread of fire over their surfaces and from one building to another. In assessing the adequacy of resistance to fire spread regard must be had to the height, B4(1) use and position of the building.

The roof of a building must also offer adequate resistance to the spread of fire across its surface and from one building to another B4(2) having regard to the use and position of the building.

External walls

External walls serve to restrict the outward spread of fire to the property boundary and also help resist fire from outside the building. Fire spread between buildings usually occurs by radiation through openings in external walls (termed unprotected areas), the risk of fire spread being related to:

● The severity of the fire,
● The fire resistance offered by the facing external walls,
● The number and disposition of the unprotected areas,
● The distance between the buildings.

In general, the severity of a fire will be related to the amount of combustible material contained within a building. Certain types of buildings, such as shops, industrial buildings and warehouses may contain large quantities of combustible materials and are usually AD B2/3/4
0.30 required to be sited further from their boundaries than other types of buildings.

External walls – general constructional requirements

External walls are *elements of structure* and therefore, they are required to have at least the period of fire resistance specified in AD B2/3/4 Parts 1 to 6 (see Tables 7.3 and 7.4 pp. 7.40–7.45). However, if an external wall is *either*,

(a) non-load-bearing; *or*,
(b) a wall of a single-storey building, or a ground storey wall of a building consisting of a ground storey and one or more basement storeys, and not supporting a gallery,

then, provided the wall is sufficiently far from its relevant boundary to be regarded as a totally unprotected area, it is not required to have fire resistance.

As a general rule, any external wall of a building or separated part exceeding 15 m in height should be constructed of materials of limited combustibility, whatever its distance from the relevant boundary. From the wording of AD B2/3/4 paragraph 2.7 it would appear that an exception is made to this rule regarding flats and maisonettes which are more than 1 m from the relevant boundary and do not exceed three storeys in height. (However a floor to ceiling height in excess of 5 m would certainly be unusual!)

AD B2/3/4
sec. 1 to 6

AD B2/3/4
2.7

Similarly, any external wall situated within 1 m of any point on the relevant boundary should also be constructed wholly of materials of limited combustibility. The permitted exceptions to this rule are:

- Dwellinghouses, flats or maisonettes of not more than three storeys,

AD B2/3/4
1.7(a) & 2.7

- Single-storey institutional buildings which are permitted to be uncompartmented or have a floor area not exceeding 3000 m²,

AD B2/3/4
3.7(b)

- Any other single-storey building which is permitted to be uncompartmented or is below the limits indicated by the letter Z in Tables 7.3 and 7.4 above,
- Any other multi-storey building which is below the limits indicated by the letter X in Tables 7.3 and 7.4, 7.40–7.45.

AD B2/3/4
4.7, 5.7 &
6.7

Where an external wall is required to be constructed of materials of limited combustibility, it is permissible to incorporate internal linings which comply with the requirements for surface flame spread, and external cladding complying with the provisions listed below. The wall should, however, provide its required fire resistance without assistance from such linings or claddings.

These requirements as to construction in materials of limited combustibility also apply to any beam or column forming part of an external wall and any structure carrying it.

External cladding is permitted to be combustible in certain circumstances. The limiting factors are the height of the building and the distance to the relevant boundary.

Table 7.6 below sets out the provisions controlling the use of external cladding. It is based on Tables 1.2, 2.2, 3.2, 4.2, 5.2 and 6.2 of AD B2/3/4. Since all these tables are identical, one typical example is reproduced.

It should be recalled that where a portion of a roof slopes at 70° or more to the horizontal and adjoins a space within a building to which persons have access, other than for occasional maintenance and repair, it is to be regarded as an external wall in applying any provisions in AD B2/3/4 (see Fig. 7.4 above).

This ensures that where habitable rooms, corridors, etc., are within steeply pitched roofs, the roof will satisfy the same fire resistance and non-combustibility requirements as the wall proper.

External walls – special constructional requirements

After the disastrous fire at the Summerland Leisure complex on the

AD B2/3/4 sec. 1 to 6

Table **7.6**   **Limitations on external cladding (All buildings)**

Maximum height of building [m]	Distance of cladding from any point on the relevant boundary*	
	Less than 1 m	**1 m or more**
15	Class 0	no provision
over 15	Class 0	any cladding less than 15 m above the ground → timber at least 9 mm thick; or any material with an index of performance (I) not more than 20
		any cladding 15 m or more above the ground → Class 0

Notes

For meaning of Class 0 and index of performance (I) *(see Appendix A)*

* The relevant boundary might be a notional boundary *(see Appendix J)*

Isle of Man, special requirements were introduced to prevent other assembly buildings from suffering a similar fate.

The Summerland centre was constructed largely of plastics materials which extended to ground level. A fire was deliberately started adjacent to the building which, because of its rapid surface spread of flame characteristics, quickly became engulfed in fire.

Therefore, any assembly building which has more than one storey (galleries counted, but not basements) should have only those unprotected areas indicated in Fig. 7.27 below.

This has the effect of eliminating combustible claddings from any part of the building below the dotted lines in Fig. 7.27 below. Above this level the external cladding should comply with the requirements listed in Table 7.6 above.

AD B2/3/4
5.11

External walls – permitted limits of unprotected areas

Permitted unprotected areas of external walls are exempt from the requirements as to fire resistance and construction in materials of limited combustibility. The general principle is that an external wall should prevent fire reaching the boundary and thus endangering adjoining property. The fire resistance to be provided by an external wall therefore depends both upon the fire hazard of the building itself and its distance from the boundary. The greater the distance of the wall from the boundary, the less fire protection need be provided by

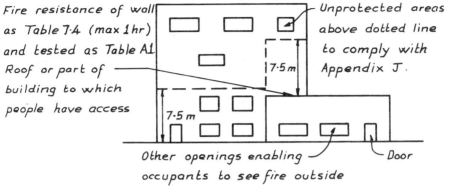

Assembly building of more than one storey.

Fire resistance of wall as Table 7.4 (max 1 hr) and tested as Table A1.
Roof or part of building to which people have access

7.5 m

7.5 m

Unprotected areas above dotted line to comply with Appendix J.

Other openings enabling occupants to see fire outside — Door

Part of building below dotted lines :—
Unprotected areas as shown above
Surfaces including glazed openings (but not door or any frame) :—
(a) Class O ·, if less than 1m to boundary.
(b) Index of performance (I) not more than 12, sub-Index (i₁) not more than 6, if more than 1 m to the boundary.

Fig. 7.27 External walls – special requirements for assembly buildings.

the wall. Indeed, if far enough away from the boundary the wall need provide no protection at all i.e. it may consist entirely of unprotected area. However, load-bearing parts of the wall should still provide fire resistance as required by AD B2/3/4 sections 1 to 6.

Appendix J of AD B2/3/4 therefore allows a certain area of an external wall to be unprotected. This permitted limit of unprotected area varies both with the purpose group classification and the distance from the relevant boundary.

Small openings

Certain openings, etc., in walls have little effect on fire protection. Accordingly, J5 of Appendix J provides that four areas are not to be taken into account in calculating the extent of unprotected areas:

- Any unprotected area of not more than 0.1 m^2 which is at least 1.5 m away from any other unprotected area in the same side of the building or compartment, except an area of external wall forming part of a protected shaft.
- One or more unprotected areas, with a total area of not more than 1 m^2, which are at least 4 m away from any other unprotected area in

the same side of the building or compartment, except a small area of not more than 0.1 m^2 as described above.

- Any unprotected area in an external wall forming part of a protected shaft.
- An unprotected area in the side of an uncompartmented building, if the area is at least 28 m above the ground adjoining the building.

AD B2/3/4
Appendix J
J5 &
Diagrams
J2 & J3

Where part of an external wall is regarded as unprotected area merely because of combustible cladding, the unprotected area presented by that cladding is to be calculated as only half the actual cladding area (see Fig. 7.28).

Therefore any wall which is situated within 1 m of the relevant boundary should contain only those unprotected areas listed above.

AD B2/3/4
Appendix J
J9

The rest of the wall will need to meet the fire resistance requirements contained in AD B2/3/4 sections 1 to 6.

Where a wall is situated 1 m or more from the relevant boundary, the permitted limit of unprotected areas may be determined by any one of three alternative methods which are given in Appendix J. An applicant may use whichever of these methods gives the most favourable result for his own building. Again, the rest of the wall will

AD B2/3/4
Appendix J
J10

need to meet the fire resistance requirements contained in AD B2/3/4 sections 1 to 6.

Method 1 – residential buildings

Method 1 applies only to dwellinghouses, flats, maisonettes or other residential buildings (*not* institutional buildings) which:

- are not less than 1 m from the relevant boundary,
- are not more than three storeys high (basements not counted),
- have no side which exceeds 24 m in length.

The permitted limit of unprotected area in an external wall of any of these buildings is given in Table J1 of Appendix J to AD B2/3/4 (see

AD B2/3/4
Appendix J
J11

below). It varies according to the size of the building and distance of the wall from the relevant boundary (see Fig. 7.29).

Where a building does not come within the scope of Method 1, then the rules of Methods 2 or 3 should be applied. It should be noted that even for buildings covered by Method 1, it may sometimes be advantageous to apply Method 2 or 3 instead.

Method 2 – enclosing rectangles

This method of calculating the permitted limit of unprotected areas is based on the smallest rectangle of a height and width taken from Table J2 to Appendix J of AD B2/3/4, which would totally enclose all the relevant unprotected areas in the side of a building or compartment.

Small openings to be discounted.

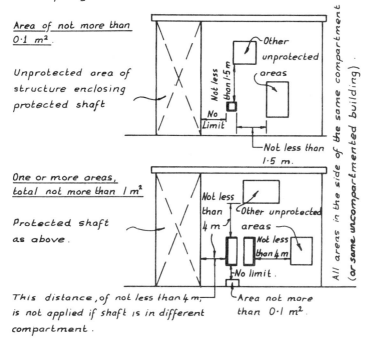

Area of not more than
0·1 m².

Unprotected area of
structure enclosing
protected shaft

One or more areas,
total not more than 1 m²

Protected shaft
as above.

This distance, of not less than 4 m,
is not applied if shaft is in different
compartment.

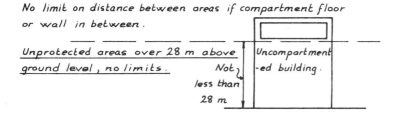

No limit on distance between areas if compartment floor
or wall in between.

Unprotected areas over 28 m above
ground level, no limits.

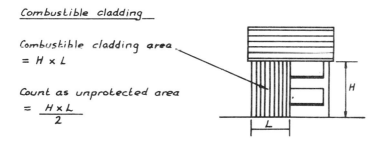

Combustible cladding

Combustible cladding area.
= H × L

Count as unprotected area
= $\frac{H \times L}{2}$

Fig. 7.28 Calculation of unprotected area limit, small openings and
combustible cladding.

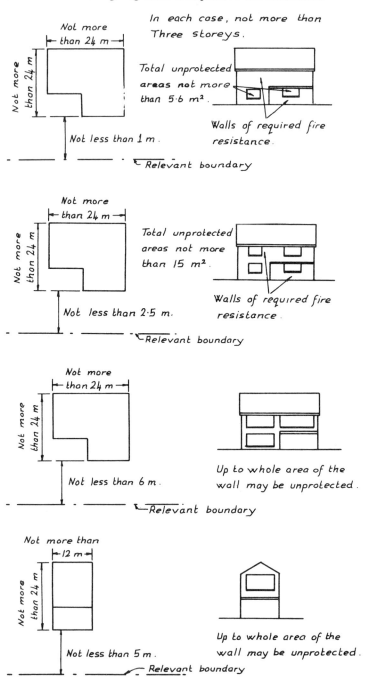

Fig. 7.29 Permitted limit of unprotected area – Method 1.

AD B2/3/4 *Appendix J*

Table **J1**   **Permitted unprotected areas in small residential buildings**

Minimum distance (A) between side of building and boundary [m]	Maximum length of side (B) [m]	Maximum total area of unprotected area [m²]
1.0	24	5.6
2.5	24	15
5.0	12	no limit
6.0	24	no limit

This is referred to as the *enclosing rectangle* and is usually larger than the actual rectangle that would enclose these areas (see Fig. 7.30).

The unprotected areas are projected at right angles onto a *plane of reference* and Table J2 then gives the distance that the relevant boundary must be from the plane of reference according to the *unprotected percentage*, the height and width of the enclosing rectangle and the purpose group of the building. The bold figures in Table J2 relate to shop, industrial or other non-residential buildings, whilst those in brackets relate to residential, office or assembly buildings.

The plane of reference is a vertical plane which touches some part of the outer surface of a building or compartment. It should not pass through any part of the building (except projections such as balconies or copings) and it should not cross the relevant boundary. It can be at any angle to the side of the building and in any position which is most favourable to the building designer, although it is usually best if roughly parallel to the relevant boundary. Method 2 can be used to determine the maximum permitted unprotected areas for a given boundary position (Fig. 7.31) *or* how close to the boundary a particular design of building may be (Fig. 7.32).

It is permissible to calculate the enclosing rectangle separately for each compartment in a building. Therefore the provision of compartment walls and floors in a building can effectively reduce the enclosing rectangle thereby decreasing the distance to the boundary without affecting the amount of unprotected areas provided. This technique is demonstrated in Fig. 7.33 which also shows how the enclosing rectangle method is applied in practice.

AD B2/3/4
Appendix J
J12

Method 2 is quick and easy to use in practice but in certain circumstances it may give an uneconomical result with regard to the permitted distance from the boundary and it may unduly restrict the designer's freedom in choice of window areas, etc. It takes no account of the true distance from the boundary of unprotected areas in deeply indented buildings since all unprotected areas must be projected onto

B2/3/4 *Appendix J*

Table J2 Permitted unprotected percentages in relation to enclosing rectangles

Width of enclosing rectangle [m]	Distance from relevant boundary for unprotected percentage not exceeding								
	20%	30%	40%	50%	60%	70%	80%	90%	100%
	Minimum boundary distance [m] Figures in brackets are for residential, office or assembly								
Enclosing rectangle 3m high									
3	1.0 (1.0)	1.5 (1.0)	2.0 (1.0)	2.0 (1.5)	2.5 (1.5)	2.5 (1.5)	2.5 (2.0)	3.0 (2.0)	3.0 (2.0)
6	1.5 (1.0)	2.0 (1.0)	2.5 (1.5)	3.0 (2.0)	3.0 (2.0)	3.5 (2.0)	3.5 (2.5)	4.0 (2.5)	4.0 (3.0)
9	1.5 (1.0)	2.5 (1.0)	3.0 (1.5)	3.5 (2.0)	4.0 (2.5)	4.0 (2.5)	4.5 (3.0)	5.0 (3.0)	5.0 (3.5)
12	2.0 (1.0)	2.5 (1.5)	3.0 (2.0)	3.5 (2.0)	4.0 (2.5)	4.5 (3.0)	5.0 (3.0)	5.5 (3.5)	5.5 (3.5)
15	2.0 (1.0)	2.5 (1.5)	3.5 (2.0)	4.0 (2.5)	4.5 (2.5)	5.0 (3.0)	5.5 (3.5)	6.0 (3.5)	6.0 (4.0)
18	2.0 (1.0)	2.5 (1.5)	3.5 (2.0)	4.0 (2.5)	5.0 (2.5)	5.0 (3.0)	6.0 (3.5)	6.5 (4.0)	6.5 (4.0)
21	2.0 (1.0)	3.0 (1.5)	3.5 (2.0)	4.5 (2.5)	5.0 (3.0)	5.5 (3.0)	6.0 (3.5)	6.5 (4.0)	7.0 (4.5)
24	2.0 (1.0)	3.0 (1.5)	3.5 (2.0)	4.5 (2.5)	5.0 (3.0)	5.5 (3.5)	6.0 (3.5)	7.0 (4.0)	7.5 (4.5)
27	2.0 (1.0)	3.0 (1.5)	4.0 (2.0)	4.5 (2.5)	5.5 (3.0)	6.0 (3.5)	6.5 (4.0)	7.0 (4.0)	7.5 (4.5)
30	2.0 (1.0)	3.0 (1.5)	4.0 (2.0)	4.5 (2.5)	5.5 (3.0)	6.0 (3.5)	6.5 (4.0)	7.5 (4.0)	8.0 (4.5)
40	2.0 (1.0)	3.0 (1.5)	4.0 (2.0)	5.0 (2.5)	5.5 (3.0)	6.5 (3.5)	7.0 (4.0)	8.0 (4.0)	8.5 (5.0)
50	2.0 (1.0)	3.0 (1.5)	4.0 (2.0)	5.0 (2.5)	6.0 (3.0)	6.5 (3.5)	7.5 (4.0)	8.0 (4.0)	9.0 (5.0)
60	2.0 (1.0)	3.0 (1.5)	4.0 (2.0)	5.0 (2.5)	6.0 (3.0)	7.0 (3.5)	7.5 (4.0)	8.5 (4.0)	9.5 (5.0)
80	2.0 (1.0)	3.0 (1.5)	4.0 (2.0)	5.0 (2.5)	6.0 (3.0)	7.0 (3.5)	8.0 (4.0)	9.0 (4.0)	9.5 (5.0)
no limit	2.0 (1.0)	3.0 (1.5)	4.0 (2.0)	5.0 (2.5)	6.0 (3.0)	7.0 (3.5)	8.0 (4.0)	9.0 (4.0)	10.0 (5.0)

Enclosing rectangle 6m high

3	1.5 (1.0)	2.0 (1.0)	2.5 (1.5)	3.0 (2.0)	3.0 (2.0)	3.5 (2.0)	3.5 (2.5)	4.0 (2.5)	4.0 (3.0)
6	2.0 (1.0)	3.0 (1.5)	3.5 (2.0)	4.0 (2.5)	4.5 (3.0)	5.0 (3.0)	5.5 (3.5)	5.5 (4.0)	6.0 (4.0)
9	2.5 (1.0)	3.5 (2.0)	4.5 (2.5)	5.0 (3.0)	5.5 (3.5)	6.0 (4.0)	6.0 (4.5)	7.0 (4.5)	7.0 (5.0)
12	3.0 (1.5)	4.0 (2.5)	5.0 (3.0)	5.5 (3.5)	6.5 (4.0)	7.0 (4.5)	7.5 (5.0)	8.0 (5.0)	8.5 (5.5)
15	3.0 (1.5)	4.5 (2.5)	5.5 (3.0)	6.0 (4.0)	7.0 (4.5)	7.5 (5.0)	8.0 (5.5)	9.0 (5.5)	9.0 (6.0)
18	3.5 (1.5)	4.5 (2.5)	5.5 (3.5)	6.5 (4.0)	7.5 (4.5)	8.0 (5.0)	9.0 (5.5)	9.5 (6.0)	10.0 (6.5)
21	3.5 (1.5)	5.0 (2.5)	6.0 (3.5)	7.0 (4.0)	8.0 (5.0)	9.0 (5.5)	9.5 (6.0)	10.0 (6.5)	10.5 (7.0)
24	3.5 (1.5)	5.0 (2.5)	6.0 (3.5)	7.0 (4.5)	8.5 (5.0)	9.5 (5.5)	10.0 (6.0)	10.5 (7.0)	11.0 (7.0)
27	3.5 (1.5)	5.0 (2.5)	6.5 (3.5)	7.5 (4.5)	8.5 (5.0)	9.5 (6.0)	10.5 (6.5)	11.0 (7.0)	12.0 (7.5)
30	3.5 (1.5)	5.0 (2.5)	6.5 (3.5)	8.0 (4.5)	9.0 (5.0)	10.0 (6.0)	11.0 (6.5)	12.0 (7.0)	12.5 (8.0)
40	3.5 (1.5)	5.5 (2.5)	7.0 (3.5)	8.5 (4.5)	10.0 (5.5)	11.0 (6.5)	12.0 (7.0)	13.0 (8.0)	14.0 (8.5)
50	3.5 (1.5)	5.5 (2.5)	7.5 (3.5)	9.0 (4.5)	10.5 (5.5)	11.5 (6.5)	13.0 (7.5)	14.0 (8.0)	15.0 (9.0)
60	3.5 (1.5)	5.5 (2.5)	7.5 (3.5)	9.5 (5.0)	11.0 (5.5)	12.0 (6.5)	13.5 (7.5)	15.0 (8.5)	16.0 (9.5)
80	3.5 (1.5)	6.0 (2.5)	7.5 (3.5)	9.5 (5.0)	11.5 (6.0)	13.0 (7.0)	14.5 (7.5)	16.0 (8.5)	17.5 (9.5)
100	3.5 (1.5)	6.0 (2.5)	8.0 (3.5)	10.0 (5.0)	12.0 (6.0)	13.5 (7.0)	15.0 (8.0)	16.5 (8.5)	18.0 (10.0)
120	3.5 (1.5)	6.0 (2.5)	8.0 (3.5)	10.0 (5.0)	12.0 (6.0)	14.0 (7.0)	15.5 (8.0)	17.0 (8.5)	19.0 (10.0)
no limit	3.5 (1.5)	6.0 (2.5)	8.0 (3.5)	10.0 (5.0)	12.0 (6.0)	14.0 (7.0)	16.0 (8.0)	18.0 (8.5)	19.0 (10.0)

Table J2 *(contd)* **Permitted unprotected percentages in relation to enclosing rectangles**

Width of enclosing rectangle [m]	Distance from relevant boundary for unprotected percentage not exceeding								
	20%	30%	40%	50%	60%	70%	80%	90%	100%
	Minimum boundary distance [m] Figures in brackets are for residential, office or assembly								
Enclosing rectangle 9m high									
3	1.5 (1.0)	2.5 (1.0)	3.0 (1.5)	3.5 (2.0)	4.0 (2.5)	4.0 (2.5)	4.5 (3.0)	5.0 (3.0)	5.0 (3.5)
6	2.5 (1.0)	3.5 (2.0)	4.5 (2.5)	5.0 (3.0)	5.5 (3.5)	6.0 (4.0)	6.5 (4.5)	7.0 (4.5)	7.0 (5.0)
9	3.5 (1.5)	4.5 (2.5)	5.5 (3.5)	6.0 (4.0)	6.5 (4.5)	7.5 (5.0)	8.0 (5.5)	8.5 (5.5)	9.0 (6.0)
12	3.5 (1.5)	5.0 (3.0)	6.0 (3.5)	7.0 (4.5)	7.5 (5.0)	8.5 (5.5)	9.0 (6.0)	9.5 (6.5)	10.5 (7.0)
15	4.0 (2.0)	5.5 (3.0)	6.5 (4.0)	7.5 (5.0)	8.5 (5.5)	9.5 (6.0)	10.0 (6.5)	11.0 (7.0)	11.5 (7.5)
18	4.5 (2.0)	6.0 (3.5)	7.0 (4.5)	8.5 (5.0)	9.5 (6.0)	10.0 (6.5)	11.0 (7.0)	12.0 (8.0)	12.5 (8.5)
21	4.5 (2.0)	6.5 (3.5)	7.5 (4.5)	9.0 (5.5)	10.0 (6.5)	11.0 (7.0)	12.0 (7.5)	13.0 (8.5)	13.5 (9.0)
24	5.0 (2.0)	6.5 (3.5)	8.0 (5.0)	9.5 (5.5)	11.0 (6.5)	12.0 (7.5)	13.0 (8.0)	13.5 (9.0)	14.5 (9.5)
27	5.0 (2.0)	7.0 (3.5)	8.5 (5.0)	10.0 (6.0)	11.5 (7.0)	12.5 (7.5)	13.5 (8.5)	14.5 (9.5)	15.0 (10.0)
30	5.0 (2.0)	7.0 (3.5)	9.0 (5.0)	10.5 (6.0)	12.0 (7.0)	13.0 (8.0)	14.0 (9.0)	15.0 (9.5)	16.0 (10.5)
40	5.5 (2.0)	7.5 (3.5)	9.5 (5.5)	11.5 (6.5)	13.0 (7.5)	14.5 (8.5)	15.5 (9.5)	17.0 (10.5)	17.5 (11.5)
50	5.5 (2.0)	8.0 (4.0)	10.0 (5.5)	12.5 (6.5)	14.0 (8.0)	15.5 (9.0)	17.0 (10.0)	18.5 (11.5)	19.5 (12.5)
60	5.5 (2.0)	8.0 (4.0)	11.0 (5.5)	13.0 (7.0)	15.0 (8.0)	16.5 (9.5)	18.0 (11.0)	19.5 (11.5)	21.0 (13.0)
80	5.5 (2.0)	8.5 (4.0)	11.5 (5.5)	13.5 (7.0)	16.0 (8.5)	17.5 (10.0)	19.5 (11.5)	21.5 (12.5)	23.0 (13.5)
100	5.5 (2.0)	8.5 (4.0)	11.5 (5.5)	14.5 (7.0)	16.5 (8.5)	18.5 (10.0)	21.0 (11.5)	22.5 (12.5)	24.5 (14.5)
120	5.5 (2.0)	8.5 (4.0)	11.5 (5.5)	14.5 (7.0)	17.0 (8.5)	19.5 (10.0)	21.5 (11.5)	23.5 (12.5)	26.0 (14.5)
no limit	5.5 (2.0)	8.5 (4.0)	11.5 (5.5)	15.0 (7.0)	17.5 (8.5)	20.0 (10.5)	22.5 (12.0)	24.5 (12.5)	27.0 (15.0)

Enclosing rectangle 12m high

3	2.0 (1.0)	2.5 (1.5)	3.0 (2.0)	3.5 (2.0)	4.0 (2.5)	4.5 (3.0)	5.0 (3.0)	5.5 (3.5)	5.5 (3.5)
6	3.0 (1.5)	4.0 (2.5)	5.0 (3.0)	5.5 (3.5)	6.5 (4.0)	7.0 (4.5)	7.5 (5.0)	8.0 (5.0)	8.5 (5.5)
9	3.5 (1.5)	5.0 (3.0)	6.0 (3.5)	7.0 (4.5)	7.5 (5.0)	8.5 (5.5)	9.0 (6.0)	9.5 (6.5)	10.5 (7.0)
12	4.5 (1.5)	6.0 (3.5)	7.0 (4.5)	8.0 (5.0)	9.0 (6.0)	9.5 (6.5)	11.0 (7.0)	11.5 (7.5)	12.0 (8.0)
15	5.0 (2.0)	6.5 (3.5)	8.0 (5.0)	9.0 (5.5)	10.0 (6.5)	11.0 (7.0)	12.0 (8.0)	13.0 (8.5)	13.5 (9.0)
18	5.0 (2.5)	7.0 (4.0)	8.5 (5.0)	10.0 (6.0)	11.0 (7.0)	12.0 (7.5)	13.0 (8.5)	14.0 (9.0)	14.5 (10.0)
21	5.5 (2.5)	7.5 (4.0)	9.0 (5.5)	10.5 (6.5)	12.0 (7.5)	13.0 (8.5)	14.0 (9.0)	15.0 (10.0)	16.0 (10.5)
24	6.0 (2.5)	8.0 (4.5)	9.5 (6.0)	11.5 (7.0)	12.5 (8.0)	14.0 (8.5)	15.0 (9.5)	16.0 (10.5)	16.5 (11.5)
27	6.0 (2.5)	8.0 (4.5)	10.5 (6.0)	12.0 (7.0)	13.5 (8.0)	14.5 (9.0)	16.0 (10.5)	17.0 (11.0)	17.5 (12.0)
30	6.5 (2.5)	8.5 (4.5)	10.5 (6.5)	12.5 (7.5)	14.0 (8.5)	15.0 (9.5)	16.5 (10.5)	17.5 (11.5)	18.5 (12.5)
40	6.5 (2.5)	9.5 (5.0)	12.0 (6.5)	14.0 (8.0)	15.5 (9.5)	17.5 (10.5)	18.5 (12.0)	20.0 (13.0)	21.0 (14.0)
50	7.0 (2.5)	10.0 (5.0)	13.0 (7.0)	15.0 (8.5)	17.0 (10.0)	19.0 (11.0)	20.5 (13.0)	23.0 (14.0)	23.0 (15.0)
60	7.0 (2.5)	10.5 (5.0)	13.5 (7.0)	16.0 (9.0)	18.0 (10.5)	20.0 (12.0)	21.5 (13.5)	23.5 (14.5)	25.0 (16.0)
80	7.0 (2.5)	11.0 (5.0)	14.5 (7.0)	17.0 (9.0)	19.5 (11.0)	21.5 (13.0)	23.5 (14.5)	26.0 (16.0)	27.5 (17.0)
100	7.5 (2.5)	11.5 (5.0)	15.0 (7.5)	18.0 (9.5)	21.0 (11.5)	23.0 (13.5)	25.5 (15.0)	28.0 (16.5)	30.0 (18.0)
120	7.5 (2.5)	11.5 (5.0)	15.0 (7.5)	18.5 (9.5)	22.0 (11.5)	24.0 (13.5)	27.0 (15.0)	29.5 (17.0)	31.5 (18.5)
no limit	7.5 (2.5)	12.0 (5.0)	15.5 (7.5)	19.0 (9.5)	22.5 (12.0)	25.0 (14.0)	28.0 (15.5)	30.5 (17.0)	34.0 (19.0)

Table J2 *(contd)*   **Permitted unprotected percentages in relation to enclosing rectangles**

Width of enclosing rectangle [m]	Distance from relevant boundary for unprotected percentage not exceeding								
	20%	30%	40%	50%	60%	70%	80%	90%	100%
	Minimum boundary distance [m] Figures in brackets are for residential, office or assembly								

Enclosing rectangle 15m high

Width of enclosing rectangle [m]	20%	30%	40%	50%	60%	70%	80%	90%	100%
3	2.0 (1.0)	2.5 (1.5)	3.5 (2.0)	4.0 (2.5)	4.5 (2.5)	5.0 (3.0)	5.5 (3.5)	6.0 (3.5)	6.0 (4.0)
6	3.0 (1.5)	4.5 (2.5)	5.5 (3.0)	6.0 (4.0)	7.0 (4.5)	7.5 (5.0)	8.0 (5.5)	9.0 (5.5)	9.0 (6.0)
9	4.0 (2.0)	5.5 (3.0)	6.5 (4.0)	7.5 (5.0)	8.5 (5.5)	9.5 (6.0)	10.0 (6.5)	11.0 (7.0)	11.5 (7.5)
12	5.0 (2.0)	6.5 (3.5)	8.0 (5.0)	9.0 (5.5)	10.0 (6.5)	11.0 (7.0)	12.0 (8.0)	13.0 (8.5)	13.5 (9.0)
15	5.5 (2.0)	7.0 (4.0)	9.0 (5.5)	10.0 (6.5)	11.5 (7.0)	12.5 (8.0)	13.5 (9.0)	14.5 (9.5)	15.0 (10.0)
18	6.0 (2.5)	8.0 (4.5)	9.5 (6.0)	11.0 (7.0)	12.5 (8.0)	13.5 (8.5)	14.5 (9.5)	15.5 (10.5)	16.5 (11.0)
21	6.5 (2.5)	8.5 (5.0)	10.5 (6.5)	12.0 (7.5)	13.5 (8.5)	14.5 (9.5)	16.0 (10.5)	16.5 (11.0)	17.5 (12.0)
24	6.5 (3.0)	9.0 (5.0)	11.0 (6.5)	13.0 (8.0)	14.5 (9.0)	15.5 (10.0)	17.0 (11.0)	18.0 (12.0)	19.0 (13.0)
27	7.0 (3.0)	9.5 (5.5)	11.5 (7.0)	13.5 (8.5)	15.0 (9.5)	16.5 (10.5)	18.0 (11.5)	19.0 (12.5)	20.0 (13.5)
30	7.5 (3.0)	10.0 (5.5)	12.0 (7.5)	14.0 (8.5)	16.0 (10.0)	17.0 (11.0)	18.5 (12.0)	20.0 (13.5)	21.0 (14.0)
40	8.0 (3.0)	11.0 (6.0)	13.5 (8.0)	16.0 (9.5)	18.0 (11.0)	19.5 (12.5)	21.0 (13.5)	22.5 (15.0)	23.5 (16.0)
50	8.5 (3.5)	12.0 (6.0)	15.0 (8.5)	17.5 (10.0)	19.5 (12.0)	21.5 (13.5)	23.0 (15.0)	25.0 (16.5)	26.0 (17.5)
60	8.5 (3.5)	12.5 (6.5)	15.5 (8.5)	18.0 (10.5)	21.0 (17.5)	23.5 (14.0)	25.0 (15.5)	27.0 (17.0)	28.0 (18.0)
80	9.0 (3.5)	13.5 (6.5)	17.0 (9.0)	20.0 (11.0)	23.0 (13.5)	25.5 (15.0)	28.0 (17.0)	30.0 (18.5)	31.5 (20.0)
100	9.0 (3.5)	14.0 (6.5)	18.0 (9.0)	21.5 (11.5)	24.5 (14.0)	27.5 (16.0)	30.0 (18.0)	32.5 (19.5)	34.5 (21.5)
120	9.0 (3.5)	14.0 (6.5)	18.5 (9.0)	22.5 (11.5)	25.5 (14.0)	28.5 (16.5)	31.5 (18.5)	34.5 (20.5)	37.0 (22.5)
no limit	9.0 (3.5)	14.5 (6.5)	19.0 (9.0)	23.0 (12.0)	27.0 (14.5)	30.0 (17.0)	34.0 (19.0)	36.0 (21.0)	39.0 (23.0)

Enclosing rectangle 18m high

3	2.0 (1.5)	2.5 (1.5)	3.5 (2.0)	4.0 (2.5)	5.0 (2.5)	5.0 (3.0)	6.0 (3.5)	6.5 (4.0)	6.5 (4.0)
6	3.5 (1.5)	4.5 (2.5)	5.5 (3.5)	6.5 (4.0)	7.5 (4.5)	8.0 (5.0)	9.0 (5.5)	9.5 (6.0)	10.0 (6.5)
9	4.5 (2.0)	6.0 (3.5)	7.0 (4.5)	8.5 (5.0)	9.5 (6.0)	10.0 (6.5)	11.0 (7.0)	12.0 (8.0)	12.5 (8.5)
12	5.0 (2.5)	7.0 (4.0)	8.5 (5.0)	10.0 (6.0)	11.0 (7.0)	12.0 (7.5)	13.0 (8.5)	14.0 (9.0)	14.5 (10.0)
15	6.0 (2.5)	8.0 (4.5)	9.5 (6.0)	11.0 (7.0)	12.5 (8.0)	13.5 (8.5)	14.5 (9.5)	15.5 (10.5)	16.5 (11.0)
18	6.5 (2.5)	8.5 (5.0)	11.0 (6.5)	12.0 (7.5)	13.5 (8.5)	14.5 (9.5)	16.0 (11.0)	17.0 (11.5)	18.0 (13.0)
21	7.0 (3.0)	9.5 (5.5)	11.5 (7.0)	13.0 (8.0)	14.5 (9.5)	16.0 (10.5)	17.0 (11.5)	18.0 (12.5)	19.5 (13.0)
24	7.5 (3.0)	10.0 (5.5)	12.0 (7.5)	14.0 (8.5)	15.5 (10.0)	16.5 (11.0)	18.5 (12.0)	19.5 (13.0)	20.5 (14.0)
27	8.0 (3.5)	10.5 (6.0)	12.5 (8.0)	14.5 (9.0)	16.5 (10.5)	17.5 (11.5)	19.5 (12.5)	20.5 (13.5)	21.5 (14.5)
30	8.0 (3.5)	11.0 (6.5)	13.5 (8.0)	15.5 (9.5)	17.0 (11.0)	18.5 (12.0)	20.5 (13.5)	21.5 (14.5)	22.5 (15.5)
40	9.0 (4.0)	12.0 (7.0)	15.0 (9.0)	17.5 (11.0)	19.5 (12.0)	21.5 (13.5)	23.5 (15.0)	25.0 (16.5)	26.0 (17.5)
50	9.5 (4.0)	13.0 (7.0)	16.5 (9.5)	19.0 (11.5)	21.5 (13.0)	23.5 (15.0)	26.0 (16.5)	27.5 (18.0)	29.0 (19.0)
60	10.0 (4.0)	14.0 (7.5)	17.5 (10.0)	20.5 (12.0)	23.0 (14.0)	26.0 (16.0)	27.5 (17.5)	29.5 (19.5)	31.0 (20.5)
80	10.0 (4.0)	15.0 (7.5)	19.0 (10.0)	22.5 (13.0)	26.0 (15.0)	28.5 (17.0)	31.0 (19.0)	33.5 (21.0)	35.0 (22.5)
100	10.0 (4.0)	16.0 (7.5)	20.5 (10.0)	24.0 (13.5)	28.0 (16.0)	31.0 (18.0)	33.5 (20.5)	36.0 (22.5)	38.5 (24.0)
120	10.0 (4.0)	16.5 (7.5)	21.0 (10.0)	25.5 (14.0)	29.5 (16.5)	32.5 (19.0)	35.5 (21.0)	39.0 (23.5)	41.5 (25.5)
no limit	10.0 (4.0)	17.0 (8.0)	22.0 (10.0)	26.5 (14.0)	30.5 (17.0)	34.0 (19.5)	37.0 (22.0)	41.0 (24.0)	43.5 (26.5)

Table J2 *(contd)*   Permitted unprotected percentages in relation to enclosing rectangles

Width of enclosing rectangle [m]	Distance from relevant boundary for unprotected percentage not exceeding								
	20%	30%	40%	50%	60%	70%	80%	90%	100%
	Minimum boundary distance [m] Figures in brackets are for residential, office or assembly								
Enclosing rectangle 21m high									
3	2.0 (1.0)	3.0 (1.5)	3.5 (2.0)	4.5 (2.5)	5.0 (3.0)	5.5 (3.0)	6.0 (3.5)	6.5 (4.0)	7.0 (4.5)
6	3.5 (1.5)	5.0 (2.5)	6.0 (3.5)	7.0 (4.0)	8.0 (5.0)	9.0 (5.5)	9.5 (6.0)	10.0 (6.5)	10.5 (7.0)
9	4.5 (2.0)	6.5 (3.5)	7.5 (4.5)	9.0 (5.5)	10.0 (6.5)	11.0 (7.0)	12.0 (7.5)	13.0 (8.5)	13.5 (9.0)
12	5.5 (2.5)	7.5 (4.0)	9.0 (5.5)	10.5 (6.5)	12.0 (7.5)	13.0 (8.5)	14.0 (9.0)	15.0 (10.0)	16.0 (10.5)
15	6.5 (2.5)	8.5 (5.0)	10.5 (6.5)	12.0 (7.5)	13.5 (8.5)	14.5 (9.5)	16.0 (10.5)	16.5 (11.0)	17.5 (12.0)
18	7.0 (3.0)	9.5 (5.5)	11.5 (7.0)	13.0 (8.0)	14.5 (9.5)	16.0 (10.5)	17.0 (11.5)	18.0 (12.5)	19.5 (13.0)
21	7.5 (3.0)	10.0 (6.0)	12.5 (7.5)	14.0 (9.0)	15.5 (10.0)	17.0 (11.0)	18.5 (12.5)	20.0 (13.5)	21.0 (14.0)
24	8.0 (3.5)	10.5 (6.0)	13.0 (8.0)	15.0 (9.5)	16.5 (10.5)	18.0 (12.0)	20.0 (13.0)	21.0 (14.0)	22.0 (15.0)
27	8.5 (3.5)	11.5 (6.5)	14.0 (8.5)	16.0 (10.0)	18.0 (11.5)	19.0 (13.0)	21.0 (14.0)	22.5 (15.0)	23.5 (16.0)
30	9.0 (4.0)	12.0 (7.0)	14.5 (9.0)	16.5 (10.5)	18.5 (12.0)	20.5 (13.0)	22.0 (14.5)	23.5 (16.0)	25.0 (16.5)
40	10.0 (4.5)	13.5 (7.5)	16.5 (10.0)	19.0 (12.0)	21.5 (13.5)	23.0 (15.0)	25.5 (16.5)	27.0 (18.0)	28.5 (19.0)
50	11.0 (4.5)	14.5 (8.0)	18.0 (11.0)	21.0 (13.0)	23.5 (14.5)	25.5 (16.5)	28.0 (18.0)	30.0 (20.0)	31.5 (21.0)
60	11.5 (4.5)	15.5 (8.5)	19.5 (11.5)	22.5 (13.5)	25.5 (15.5)	28.0 (17.5)	30.5 (19.5)	32.5 (21.0)	33.5 (22.5)
80	12.0 (4.5)	17.0 (8.5)	21.0 (12.0)	25.0 (14.5)	28.5 (17.0)	31.5 (19.0)	34.0 (21.0)	36.5 (23.5)	38.5 (25.0)
100	12.0 (4.5)	18.0 (9.0)	22.5 (12.0)	27.0 (15.5)	31.0 (18.0)	34.5 (20.5)	37.0 (22.5)	40.0 (25.0)	42.0 (27.0)
120	12.0 (4.5)	18.5 (9.0)	23.5 (12.0)	28.5 (16.0)	32.5 (18.5)	36.5 (21.5)	39.5 (23.5)	43.0 (26.5)	45.5 (28.5)
no limit	12.0 (4.5)	19.0 (9.0)	25.0 (12.0)	29.5 (16.0)	34.5 (19.0)	38.0 (22.0)	41.5 (25.0)	45.5 (26.5)	48.0 (29.5)

Enclosing rectangle 24m high

3	2.0 (1.0)	3.0 (1.5)	3.5 (2.0)	4.5 (2.5)	5.0 (3.0)	5.5 (3.5)	6.0 (3.5)	7.0 (4.0)	7.5 (4.5)
6	3.5 (1.5)	5.0 (2.5)	6.0 (3.5)	7.0 (4.5)	8.5 (5.0)	9.5 (5.5)	10.0 (6.0)	10.5 (7.0)	11.0 (7.0)
9	5.0 (2.0)	6.5 (3.5)	8.0 (5.0)	9.5 (5.5)	11.0 (6.5)	12.0 (7.5)	13.0 (8.0)	13.5 (9.0)	14.5 (9.5)
12	6.0 (2.5)	8.0 (4.5)	9.5 (6.0)	11.5 (7.0)	12.5 (8.0)	14.0 (8.5)	15.0 (9.5)	16.0 (10.5)	16.5 (11.5)
15	6.5 (3.0)	9.0 (5.0)	11.0 (6.5)	13.0 (8.0)	14.5 (9.0)	15.5 (10.0)	17.0 (11.0)	18.0 (12.0)	19.0 (13.0)
18	7.5 (3.0)	10.0 (5.5)	12.0 (7.5)	14.0 (8.5)	15.5 (10.0)	16.5 (11.0)	18.5 (12.0)	19.5 (13.0)	20.5 (14.0)
21	8.0 (3.5)	10.5 (6.0)	13.0 (8.0)	15.0 (9.5)	16.5 (10.5)	18.0 (12.0)	20.0 (13.0)	21.0 (14.0)	22.0 (15.0)
24	8.5 (3.5)	11.5 (6.5)	14.0 (8.5)	16.0 (10.0)	18.0 (11.5)	19.5 (12.5)	21.0 (14.0)	22.5 (15.0)	24.0 (16.0)
27	9.0 (4.0)	12.5 (7.0)	15.0 (9.0)	17.0 (11.0)	19.0 (12.5)	20.5 (13.5)	22.5 (15.0)	24.0 (16.0)	25.5 (17.0)
30	9.5 (4.0)	13.0 (7.5)	15.5 (9.5)	18.0 (11.5)	20.0 (13.0)	21.5 (14.0)	23.5 (15.5)	25.0 (17.0)	26.5 (18.0)
40	11.0 (4.5)	14.5 (8.5)	18.0 (11.0)	20.5 (13.0)	23.0 (14.5)	25.0 (16.0)	27.5 (18.0)	29.0 (19.0)	30.5 (20.5)
50	12.0 (5.0)	16.0 (9.0)	19.5 (12.0)	22.5 (14.0)	25.5 (16.0)	27.5 (17.5)	30.0 (19.5)	32.0 (21.0)	33.5 (22.5)
60	12.5 (5.0)	17.0 (9.5)	21.0 (12.5)	24.5 (15.0)	27.5 (17.0)	30.0 (19.0)	32.5 (21.0)	35.0 (23.0)	36.5 (24.5)
80	13.5 (5.0)	18.5 (10.0)	23.5 (13.5)	27.5 (16.5)	31.0 (18.5)	34.5 (21.0)	37.0 (23.5)	39.5 (25.5)	41.5 (27.5)
100	13.5 (5.0)	20.0 (10.0)	25.0 (13.5)	29.5 (17.0)	33.5 (20.0)	37.0 (22.5)	40.0 (25.0)	43.0 (27.5)	45.5 (29.5)
120	13.5 (5.5)	20.5 (10.0)	26.5 (13.5)	31.0 (17.5)	36.0 (20.5)	39.5 (23.5)	43.0 (26.5)	46.5 (29.0)	49.0 (31.0)
no limit	13.5 (5.5)	21.0 (10.0)	27.5 (13.5)	32.5 (18.0)	37.5 (21.0)	42.0 (24.0)	45.5 (27.5)	49.5 (30.0)	52.0 (32.5)

Table **J2** *(contd)*   Permitted unprotected percentages in relation to enclosing rectangles

Width of enclosing rectangle [m]	Distance from relevant boundary for unprotected percentage not exceeding								
	20%	30%	40%	50%	60%	70%	80%	90%	100%
	Minimum boundary distance [m] Figures in brackets are for residential, office or assembly								
Enclosing rectangle 27m high									
3	2.0 (1.0)	3.0 (1.5)	4.0 (2.0)	4.5 (2.5)	5.5 (3.0)	6.0 (3.5)	6.5 (4.0)	7.0 (4.0)	7.5 (4.5)
6	3.5 (1.5)	5.0 (2.5)	6.5 (3.5)	7.5 (4.5)	8.5 (5.0)	9.5 (6.0)	10.5 (6.5)	11.0 (7.0)	12.0 (7.5)
9	5.0 (2.0)	7.0 (3.5)	8.5 (5.0)	10.0 (6.0)	11.5 (7.0)	12.5 (7.5)	13.5 (8.5)	14.5 (9.5)	15.0 (10.0)
12	6.0 (2.5)	8.0 (4.5)	10.5 (6.0)	12.0 (7.0)	13.5 (8.0)	14.5 (9.0)	16.0 (10.5)	17.0 (11.0)	17.5 (12.0)
15	7.0 (3.0)	9.5 (5.5)	11.5 (7.0)	13.5 (8.5)	15.0 (9.5)	16.5 (10.5)	18.0 (11.5)	19.0 (12.5)	20.0 (13.5)
18	8.0 (3.5)	10.5 (6.0)	12.5 (8.0)	14.5 (9.0)	16.5 (10.5)	17.5 (11.5)	19.5 (12.5)	20.5 (13.5)	21.5 (14.5)
21	8.5 (3.5)	11.5 (6.5)	14.0 (8.5)	16.0 (10.0)	18.0 (11.5)	19.0 (13.0)	21.0 (14.0)	22.5 (15.0)	23.5 (16.0)
24	9.0 (3.5)	12.5 (7.0)	15.0 (9.0)	17.0 (11.0)	19.0 (12.5)	20.5 (13.5)	22.5 (15.0)	24.0 (16.0)	25.5 (17.0)
27	10.0 (4.0)	13.0 (7.5)	16.0 (10.0)	18.0 (11.5)	20.0 (13.0)	22.0 (14.0)	24.0 (16.0)	25.5 (17.0)	27.0 (18.0)
30	10.0 (4.0)	13.5 (8.0)	17.0 (10.0)	19.0 (12.0)	21.0 (13.5)	23.0 (15.0)	25.0 (17.0)	26.5 (18.0)	28.0 (19.0)
40	11.5 (5.0)	15.5 (9.0)	19.0 (11.5)	22.0 (14.0)	24.5 (15.5)	26.5 (17.5)	29.0 (19.0)	30.5 (20.5)	32.5 (22.0)
50	12.5 (5.5)	17.0 (9.5)	21.0 (12.5)	24.0 (15.0)	27.0 (17.0)	29.5 (19.0)	32.0 (21.0)	34.5 (22.5)	36.0 (24.0)
60	13.5 (5.5)	18.5 (10.5)	22.5 (13.5)	26.5 (16.0)	29.5 (18.5)	32.0 (20.5)	35.0 (22.5)	37.0 (24.5)	39.0 (26.5)
80	14.5 (6.0)	20.5 (11.0)	25.0 (14.5)	29.5 (17.5)	33.0 (20.5)	36.5 (22.5)	39.5 (25.0)	42.0 (27.5)	44.0 (29.5)
100	15.5 (6.0)	21.5 (11.0)	27.0 (15.5)	32.0 (19.0)	36.5 (21.5)	40.5 (24.5)	43.0 (27.0)	46.5 (30.0)	48.5 (32.0)
120	15.5 (6.0)	22.5 (11.5)	28.5 (15.5)	34.0 (19.5)	39.0 (22.5)	43.0 (26.0)	46.5 (28.5)	50.5 (32.0)	53.0 (34.0)
no limit	15.5 (6.0)	23.5 (11.5)	29.5 (15.5)	35.0 (20.0)	40.5 (23.5)	44.5 (27.0)	48.5 (29.5)	52.0 (33.0)	55.5 (35.0)

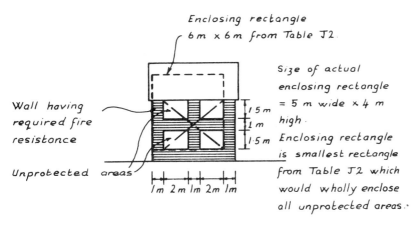

Enclosing rectangle
6 m × 6 m from Table J2.

Wall having
required fire
resistance

Unprotected areas

Size of actual
enclosing rectangle
= 5 m wide × 4 m
high.
Enclosing rectangle
is smallest rectangle
from Table J2 which
would wholly enclose
all unprotected areas.

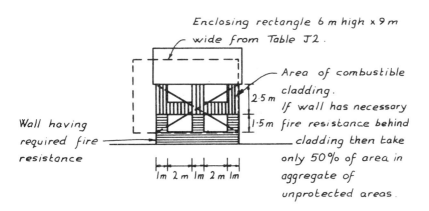

Enclosing rectangle 6 m high × 9 m
wide from Table J2.

Wall having
required fire
resistance

Area of combustible
cladding.
If wall has necessary
fire resistance behind
cladding then take
only 50% of area in
aggregate of
unprotected areas.

NOTE. Plane of reference
is taken to coincide
with surface of wall.

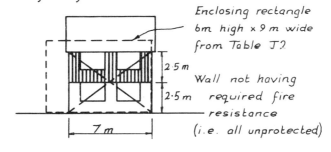

Enclosing rectangle
6m high × 9 m wide
from Table J2

Wall not having
required fire
resistance
(i.e. all unprotected)

Fig. 7.30 Enclosing rectangles.

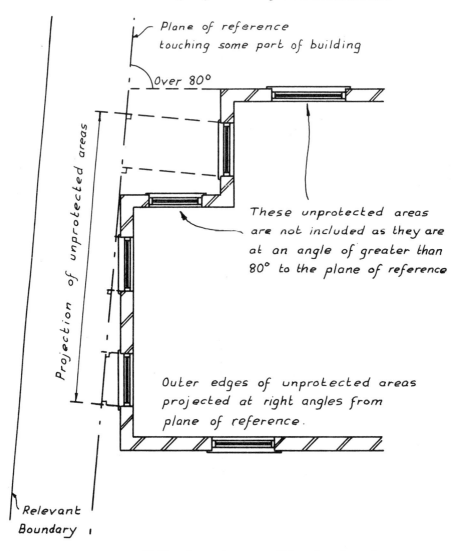

Plane of reference
touching some part of building

Over 80°

These unprotected areas
are not included as they are
at an angle of greater than
80° to the plane of reference

Projection of unprotected areas

Outer edges of unprotected areas
projected at right angles from
plane of reference.

Relevant
Boundary

If the boundary position is already
determined the distance between the
plane of reference and the relevant
boundary when related to the dimensions
of the enclosing rectangle will give the
maximum percentage of unprotected
area permitted.

Fig. 7.31 Determination of maximum unprotected areas for given boundary
position.

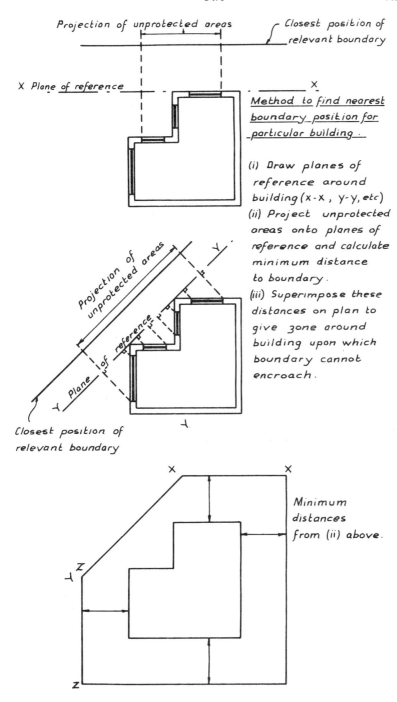

Projection of unprotected areas

Closest position of relevant boundary

X Plane of reference

X

Method to find nearest boundary position for particular building.

(i) Draw planes of reference around building (x-x , y-y, etc)

(ii) Project unprotected areas onto planes of reference and calculate minimum distance to boundary.

(iii) Superimpose these distances on plan to give zone around building upon which boundary cannot encroach.

Projection of unprotected areas

Plane of reference

Y

Closest position of relevant boundary

X   X

Minimum distances from (ii) above.

Z

Z

Fig. 7.32 Nearest position to boundary for given building design.

Residential, Office or Assembly Building

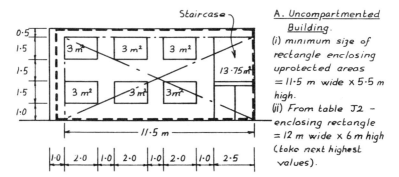

A. Uncompartmented Building.

(i) minimum size of rectangle enclosing uprotected areas = 11·5 m wide × 5·5 m high.

(ii) From table J2 – enclosing rectangle = 12 m wide × 6 m high (take next highest values).

(A). *uncompartmented building* (iii) Calculate aggregate of unprotected areas = 18 + 13·75 m² = 31·75 m².

(iv) Calculate uprotected percentage. (aggregate of unprotected areas as percentage of enclosing rectangle) = $\frac{31·75}{12 \times 6}$ × 100 = 44% ∴ use 50% column in table J2.

(v) Select distance from table (second part of table, fourth column, fourth row, figure in brackets) permitted distance to boundary = 3·5 m.

NOTES.

    (a) Minimum size of rectangle indicated by diagonal lines.

    (b) Enclosing rectangle indicated by dotted lines.

    (c) Relevant boundary is parallel with wall face, plane of reference coincides with wall face. This need not be the case.

The situation can be improved if the staircase is enclosed in a protecting structure and a compartment floor is provided:

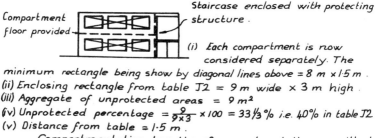

Staircase enclosed with protecting structure.

(i) Each compartment is now considered separately. The minimum rectangle being show by diagonal lines above = 8 m × 1·5 m.

(ii) Enclosing rectangle from table J2 = 9 m wide × 3 m high.

(iii) Aggregate of unprotected areas = 9 m²

(iv) Unprotected percentage = $\frac{9}{9 \times 3}$ × 100 = 33⅓% i.e. 40% in table J2

(v) Distance from table = 1·5 m.

    Compartmentation has therefore reduced the permitted distance to the boundary from 3·5 m to 1·5 m.

Fig. 7.33 Method 2 – effects of compartmentation.

a single plane of reference. It also assumes that the effects of a fire will be equally felt at all points on the boundary from all unprotected areas despite the fact that some windows, for example, may be shielded from certain parts of the boundary by fire resistant walls. For these reasons it may be preferable to use Method 3 – the aggregate notional areas technique – as this method is usually more accurate in practice.

Method 3 – aggregate notional areas

The basis of the method is to assess the effect of a building fire at a series of points 3 m apart on the relevant boundary.

A *vertical datum* of unlimited height is set at any position on the relevant boundary (see point P on Fig. 7.34). *A datum line* is drawn from this point to the nearest point on the building or compartment. A base line is then constructed at 90° to the datum line and an arc of 50 m radius is drawn centred on the vertical datum to meet the base line.

Using this method it is possible to exclude certain unprotected areas that would have to be considered under Method 2 (see Fig. 7.34). For those unprotected areas which remain (that is, those that cannot be excluded), it is necessary to measure the distance of each from the vertical datum. Table J3 to Appendix J of AD B2/3/4 contains a series of multiplication factors which are related to the distance from the vertical datum. The table is based on the fact that the amount of heat caused by a fire issuing from an unprotected area will decrease in proportion to its distance from the boundary (it does, in fact, correspond to an inverse square law of the type $y = 1/x^2$).

Therefore, each unprotected area is multiplied by its factor (which depends on its distance from the vertical datum) and these areas are then totalled to give the *aggregate notional area* for that particular vertical datum. The aggregate notional area thus achieved should not exceed:

Table **J3** **Multiplication factors for aggregate notional area**

Distance of Unprotected Area from vertical datum [m]		
Not less than	**Less than**	**Multiplication factor**
1.0	1.2	80.0
1.2	1.8	40.0
1.8	2.7	20.0
2.7	4.3	10.0
4.3	6.0	4.0
6.0	8.5	2.0
8.5	12.0	1.0
12.0	18.5	0.5
18.5	27.5	0.25
27.5	50.0	0.1
50.0	no limit	0.0

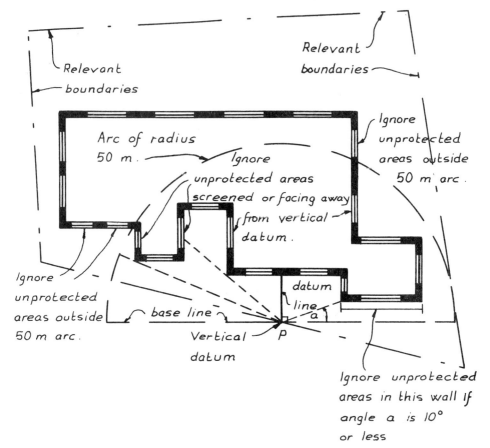

Exclude unprotected areas which :

- Are outside 50 m arc.

- Are screened or face away from the vertical datum.
- Make an angle of 10° or less with a line drawn from the vertical datum to the unprotected area.
- Are shown in Fig 7.28 (above).

Fig. 7.34 Aggregate notional areas.

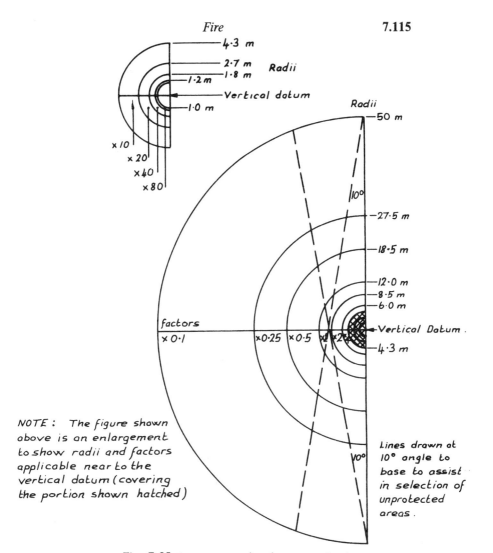

Fig. 7.35 Aggregate notional areas protractor.

- 210 m² for residential, assembly or office buildings; or,
- 90 m² for shop, industrial or other non-residential buildings.

In order to confirm that the unprotected areas in the building comply at other points on the boundary, it is necessary to repeat the above calculations at a series of points 3 m apart starting from the original vertical datum. In practice it is usually possible, by observation, to place the first vertical datum at the worst position thereby obviating the need for further calculations.

The series of measurements and calculations mentioned above may be simplified if a number of protractors are made corresponding to different scales (i.e. 1:50, 1:100 and 1:200). A typical example is illustrated in Fig. 7.35.

Roofs

Roofs are not required to provide fire resistance but should resist fire penetration from outside and spread of flame over their surfaces.

The type of construction permitted for a roof depends on the purpose group and size of the building and its distance from the boundary.

Types of construction are specified by the two letter designations from BS 476: Part 3: 1958 *External fire exposure roof tests.*

The first letter refers to flame penetration:

A – Not penetrated within one hour,
B – Penetrated in not less than half an hour,
C – Penetrated in less than half an hour,
D – Penetrated in preliminary flame test.

The second letter refers to the surface spread of flame test:

A – No spread of flame,
B – Not more than 21 inches (533·4 mm) spread,
C – More than 21 inches (533·4 mm) spread,
D – Those continuing to burn for five minutes after withdrawal of the test flame, or with a spread of more than 15 inches (381 mm) across the region of burning in the preliminary test.

AD B2/3/4
Appendix A
A3

Example
Roof surface classified AA. This means no fire penetration within one hour and no spread of flame.

Table A4 to Appendix A of AD B2/3/4 (see below) gives a series of roof constructions together with their two-letter notional designations.

In the example shown above a roof constructed in accordance with Part 1 of Table A4 would satisfy the AA rating if it was of natural slates, asbestos-cement slates, clay tiles or concrete tiles and it was supported as shown in the table.

Table 7.7 (below) is based on Tables 1.3, 2.3, 3.3, 4.3, 5.3, and 6.3 of AD B2/3/4 sections 1 to 6 and gives the notional two-letter designations for roofs in different buildings, according to their distance from the boundary. Once the notional two-letter designation has been established a form of construction may be chosen from Table A4. Where it is decided to use a different form of roof construction the

AD B2/3/4
secs. 1 to 6

manufacturer's details should be consulted to confirm that the necessary designation is achieved.

Special provisions apply to roofs passing over the top of separating walls or compartment walls (see *Separating Walls* above).

Where plastic rooflights form part of a roof structure they should comply with the provisions of Appendix B of AD B2/3/4 (see above page 7.30).

AD B2/3/4 Appendix A

Table A4 Notional designations of roof coverings

Part I: Pitched roofs covered with slates or tiles

Covering material	Supporting structure	Designation
1 Natural slates 2 Asbestos-cement slates 3 Clay tiles 4 Concrete tiles	1 timber rafters with or without underfelt, sarking, boarding, wood wool slabs, compressed straw slabs, plywood, wood or flax chipboard, or fibre insulating board	AA
5 Strip slates of bitumen felt Class 1 or 2	2 timber rafters and boarding, plywood, wood wool slabs, compressed straw slabs, wood or flax chipboard, or fibre insulating board	CC
6 Bitumen felt strip slates Type 2E, with underlayer of bitumen felt Type 2B	3 timber rafters and boarding, plywood, wood wool slabs, compressed straw slabs, wood or flax chipboard, or fibre insulating board	BB

Note
Any reference in this Table to bitumen felt of a specified type is
a reference to bitumen felt as so designated in BS 747: 1977.

(continued on next page)

Table A4   Notional designations of roof coverings (*cont.*)

Part II: Pitched roofs covered with preformed self-supporting sheets

Material	Details of covering		Supporting structure	Designation
	Construction			
Corrugated sheets of: (i) galvanised steel (ii) aluminium (iii) composite steel and asbestos (iv) asbestos cement or (v) pvc coated steel	1 single skin without underlay or with underlay of – (i) asbestos insulating board (ii) plasterboard (iii) fibre insulating board (iv) compressed straw slabs or (v) wood wool slab		structure of timber, steel or concrete	AA
Corrugated sheets of: (i) galvanised steel (ii) aluminium (iii) composite steel and asbestos (iv) asbestos cement or (v) pvc coated steel	2 double skin without interlayer or with inter-layer of – (i) resin-bonded glass fibre (ii) bitumen-bonded glass fibre (iii) mineral wool slab or blanket (iv) polystyrene, or (v) polyurethane		structure of timber, steel or concrete	AA

Part III: Pitched or flat roofs covered with fully supported material

Covering material	Supporting structure	Designation

1 aluminium sheet
2 copper sheet
3 zinc sheet
4 lead sheet
5 mastic asphalt
	1 timber joists and –
	  (i) tongued and grooved
	     boarding, or
	  (ii) plain edged boarding
		AA*

6 vitreous enamelled steel sheet	2 steel or timber joists with
	  deck of –
	  (i) wood wool slab
	  (ii) compressed straw slab
	  (iii) wood or flax chipboard
	  (iv) fibre insulating board, or
	  (v) 9.5 mm plywood
		AA

	3 concrete or clay pot slab (cast
	  in situ or precast), or non-
	  combustible deck of steel,
	  aluminium or asbestos-cement
	  (with or without insulation)
		AA

Note
* Lead sheet supported by timber joists and plain edged boarding shall be deemed to be of designation BA.

Part IV: Roofs covered with bitumen felt

Part IV(A): Flat roofs covered with bitumen felt

A flat roof comprising a covering of bitumen felt shall (irrespective of the felt specification) be deemed to be of designation AA if the felt is laid on a deck constructed of any of the materials prescribed in the Table in Part IV(B) and has a surface finish of
(a) bitumen bedded stone chippings covering the whole surface to a depth of not less than 12.5 mm,
(b) bitumen bedded tiles of a non-combustible material,
(c) sand and cement screed, or
(d) macadam.

(continued on next page)

Table A4 Notional designations of roof coverings (*cont.*)

Part IV(B): Pitched roofs covered with bitumen felt

Details of felt

Number of layers	Type of upper layer	Type of underlayer(s)	Deck of either of the following (having minimum thickness stated) plywood (6 mm), wood or flax chipboard (12·5 mm), T&G boarding (16 mm finished), or PE boarding (19 mm finished)	Deck of compressed straw slab	Deck of screeded wood wool slab	Asbestos-cement or steel single skin or cavity deck (without overlay or with overlay of fibre insulating board)	Aluminium single skin or cavity deck (without overlay or with overlay of fibre insulating board)	Concrete or clay pot slab (cast in situ or precast)
1 two or three layers built up in accordance with CP 144: Part 3: 1970	1 Type 1E	Type 1B (minimum mass 13 kg/10 m²)	CC	AC	AC	AC	AC	AB
	2 Type 2E	Type 1B (minimum mass 13 kg/10 m²)	BB	AB	AB	AB	AB	AB
	3 Type 2E	Type 2B	AB	AB	AB	AB	AB	AB
	4 Type 3E	Type 3B or 3G	BC	AC	AC	AB	AB	AB
2 single layer	Type 1E		CC	AC	AC	AC	CC	AC

Note
Any reference in this Table to bitumen felt of a specified type is a reference to bitumen felt as so designated in BS 747: 1977.

AD B2/3/4 Sections 1 to 6

Table 7.7   **Limitations on roof construction**

Description of building	Designation or covering of roof, or part of roof	Minimum distance from any point on a boundary			
		less than 6 m	at least 6 m	at least 12 m	at least 22 m
1 building with a cubic capacity of not more than 1500 m³ except terraced house (see below)	AA, AB or AC	●	●	●	●
	BA, BB or BC	○	●	●	●
	AD, BD,* CA, CB, CC or CD	○	●[1(a)]	●	●
	DA, DB, DC or DD*	○	○	○	●[1]
	thatch or wood shingles	○	●[1]	●	●
	glass or pvc[4]	●[2]	●	●	●
	no designation[5]*	○	●[1]	●[3]	●[3]
2 (i) building with a cubic capacity of more than 1500 m³; or, (ii) terraced house	AA, AB or AC	●	●	●	●
	BA, BB or BC	○	●	●	●
	AD*	○	●[1(a)]	●	●
	BA, CA, CB, CC, CD,† DA, DB, DC or DD	○	○	○	○
	thatch or wood shingles	○	○	○	○
	glass or pvc[4]	●[2]	●	●	●
	no designation[5]*	○	●[1]	●[3]	●[3]

● Acceptable
○ Not acceptable

Notes

* For rooflights having a lower surface of at least Class 3 surface spread of flame. *(see Appendix B, Table B1).*

† Rooflights with these designations, which have a lower surface of at least Class 3 surface spread of flame, are permitted subject to the limitations given in Appendix B, Table B1.

[1] The area of the part of the roof should not be greater than 3 m² and it should be at least 1·5 m from any similar part, with the roof between the parts covered with a Material of Limited Combustibility. *(see Appendix A, Table A7).*

[1(a)] As note 1 above but does not apply to dwellinghouses.

[2] Only for (a) a balcony, verandah, open carport, covered way or detached swimming pool, or (b) a garage, conservatory or outbuilding, with a floor area not greater than 40 m².

[3] Twice the height of the building if this gives a greater distance.

[4] Glass which cannot be designated; and rigid pvc as described in Appendix B, paragraph B5.

[5] A covering which cannot be designated because of its low softening temperature.

Glass if it can be designated is AA and does not need wire reinforcement.

Varying the requirements

Under the Building Regulations 1976 it often proved very difficult to achieve total compliance with every requirement. This was especially true when applying fire regulations to existing buildings that were being extended, altered or were the subject of a change of use.

Since the regulations were mandatory, the only course of action open to a designer was to apply for a relaxation of a requirement that was thought to be unduly onerous in the particular circumstances.

This system worked well and it was the policy of the Department of the Environment to issue to local authorities, from time to time, guidelines setting out the factors that they should take into account when deciding whether or not to approve a particular relaxation application.

These factors included:

- Whether the building was new or existing,
- The form of construction,
- The fire properties of the materials,
- The fire hazard (risk to life) and fire load (amount of combustible material stored within the building),
- The space separation from other buildings and the boundaries,
- The ease of access for fire fighting,
- The means of escape in case of fire,
- The provision of features such as sprinklers or automatic fire detection systems that would compensate for a reduction in standards.

Approved document B2/3/4 is not mandatory and therefore the relaxation procedure does not apply to it. (This is also true of the other approved documents.) Therefore, it is interesting to note that provisions for varying the requirements in AD B2/3/4 are now contained within each section of the document dealing with dwelling-houses, flats, institutional buildings, shops, industrial buildings and other non-residential buildings.

Presumably, the designer will need to negotiate with the local authority within the guidelines given by these variation sections, the factors mentioned above being taken into account by both parties in each particular case.

Varying the requirements – dwellinghouses

Under the Mandatory rules for means of escape in case of fire (MOE B1) certain special provisions apply where it is proposed to construct one or two rooms in the roofspace of a two-storey dwelling thereby creating a three-storey dwelling (see section on *Means of Escape* above).

Floors in an existing two-storey dwelling may only be capable of achieving a modified half hour fire resistance (see above page 7.63). However, AD B2/3/4 requires that floors in a dwelling of three or more storeys should have a minimum full half hour fire resistance.

It is considered reasonable to relax the requirement for the *existing* floor (thereby allowing the modified half hour standard) provided the following provisions are complied with by way of compensation:

- The means of escape provisions in MOE B1 Appendix B should be complied with.
- Any new floor provided should achieve the full half hour standard of fire resistance.
- The existing floor should only separate rooms.
- Where the new stairway to the top floor rises above a floor over a room, that part of the floor under the new stairway should achieve the full half hour standard of fire resistance.

It is sometimes the case that a floor is only capable of achieving a modified half hour standard of fire resistance because it is constructed with plain edged boarding on the upper surface. The addition of a 3·2 mm thickness of standard hardboard nailed to the floor boards can usually upgrade the floor to the full half hour standard, (see Fig. 7.36).

Other methods of upgrading existing timber floors can be found in BRE digest 208.

AD B2/3/4
sec. 1
1.47

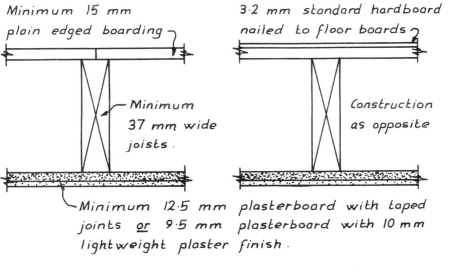

Fig. 7.36 Upgrading of existing floors in dwellings.

Varying the requirements – flats

If it is proposed to convert a building into flats, Part B of Schedule 1 of the Building Regulations will apply due to the material change of use.

It is often the case that the existing floors are of timber construction and have insufficient fire resistance for the proposed change of use. AD B2/3/4 may also require the floors to be constructed of materials of limited combustibility.

Clearly, without removing the floors completely, it may be difficult to meet the necessary requirements as to fire resistance and non-combustibility.

The provision of adequate, fully protected means of escape may enable the following variations in the provisions of AD B2/3/4:

● The required period of fire resistance of one hour for the elements of structure of a three-storey building may be reduced to half an hour.
● It may be possible when altering buildings of four or more storeys to require no more than a fire resistance of one hour for the elements of structure.
● Combustible floor construction may be acceptable for blocks of flats over four storeys high. (Paragraph 2.24 of section 2 of AD B2/3/4 normally requires these floors to be in materials of limited combustibility.)

AD B2/3/4
sec. 2
2.46 to
2.49

It should be stressed that the factors listed on page 7.122 above should be considered, in addition to the provision of an adequate, *fully* protected means of escape when considering a reduction in normal standards of fire resistance.

Varying the requirements – institutional buildings

Paragraph 3.24 of section 3 of AD B2/3/4 requires all upper floors in institutional buildings to be constructed in materials of limited combustibility.

In existing buildings which are being converted and have timber floors, this may be difficult and prohibitively expensive to achieve.

In new buildings it is often desirable to use timber construction to create a warmer and more homely atmosphere.

The use of combustible construction may be acceptable for the upper floors and the stairways in *existing* buildings provided the building does not exceed 15 m in height.

In *new* buildings combustible construction for upper floors and stairways may also be acceptable providing the following conditions are met:

● The building should not exceed two storeys in height (or three storeys if the top storey is used only for staff accommodation).
● The stairways should be fully enclosed and protected.

- A good standard of means of escape should be provided.
- A good standard of twenty-four hour supervision should be provided.

AD B2/3/4
sec. 3
3.44 to
3.47

Varying the requirements – shopping centres

Individual shops should generally be capable of complying with the provisions of AD B2/3/4. However, where a shop unit forms part of a covered shopping complex certain difficulties may arise. Clearly, it is not practical to compartment a shop from a mall serving it and maximum compartment sizes may thus be difficult to achieve. Certain other problems may arise concerning fire resistance, separating walls, surfaces of walls and ceilings and distances to boundaries.

In order to achieve a satisfactory standard of fire safety certain alternative arrangements and compensatory features may be acceptable:

- Unified ownership or management, thus ensuring future control.
- Continuing control of fire prevention measures.
- Adequate means of escape.
- Adequate smoke control provisions.
- Sprinkler protection to risk areas.
- Automatic fire detection system operating fire alarms.
- Adequate means of access for fire fighting.
- Construction in materials of limited combustibility (except for limited decorative features and materials in shop fascias).
- A general minimum standard of fire resistance of two hours (four hours in basements) for elements of structure, unless a low fire hazard is presented.
- Floors and walls between shop units generally constructed as compartment floors and walls.
- Large shop units over 3700 m² in area compartmented from a mall: compartmentation also provided between large opposing shop units (over 2000 m²) and a mall. Compartmentation could be provided by means of automatic fire shutters.

This list of measures is not comprehensive but does give a guide to the features to be considered. Further guidance may be found in the following publications:

- Fire prevention guide no. 1, *Fire precautions in town centre developments* HMSO 1972.
- *Smoke control methods in enclosed shopping complexes of one or more storeys. A design summary.* HMSO 1979.

AD B2/3/4
sec. 6
6.45 to
6.48

Varying the requirements – steel portal frames

Steel portal frames are commonly used in single storey industrial and commercial buildings.

Structurally, the portal frame acts as a single member. Therefore, where the column sections are built into the external walls collapse of the roof sections may result in destruction of the walls.

If the building is so situated that the external walls cannot be totally unprotected the provisions of AD B2/3/4 may require both rafter and column sections to be fire protected.

This would result in an uneconomic building which would defeat the object of using a portal frame.

It may be permissible to remove the requirement for fire protection to the rafter sections if the following provisions are met:

- Column sections should have the necessary fire resistance if they are built into or support a wall that cannot be totally unprotected.
- Column sections should be fixed rigidly to a base designed to prevent overturning.
- Brick, block or concrete protection should be provided to columns up to a protected ring beam designed to provide lateral support.
- Roof venting should be provided to give heat release in the early stages of a fire. (PVC rooflights evenly distributed covering 10% of the floor area would be acceptable) see Fig. 7.37.

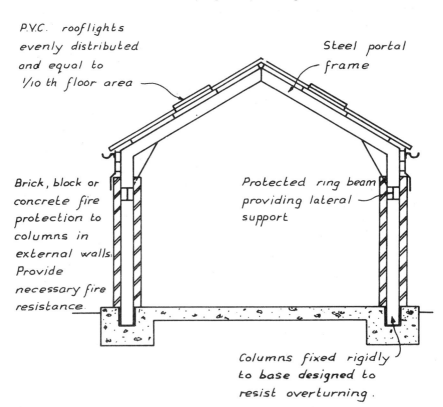

Fig. 7.37 Steel portal frames.

As an alternative to the above the method described in the publication, *The behaviour of steel portal frames in boundary conditions* (Constrado, NLA Tower, Addiscombe Road, Croydon, Surrey, 1980), may also be adopted.

AD B2/3/4
sec. 6
6.49 to
6.54

Varying the requirements – raised storage areas

The requirements regarding the fire resistance of elements of structure apply to raised storage areas. These are usually erected in single storey industrial buildings and may be supported by racking.

It may be possible to reduce the standard of fire resistance required or even allow unprotected steelwork if the following precautions are taken:

- The structure should be used for storage purposes only.
- The number of people using the floor at any one time should be limited.
- Members of the public should not be admitted.
- The layout and construction should be such as to warn persons using the floor of any outbreak of fire below.
- An adequate means of escape should be provided with discharge points near to exits from the building.
- If the storage area is extensive then sprinkler protection to the building as a whole may be advisable.

The ceiling surface under the raised storage area would also need to comply with surface spread of flame provisions. It may be possible to accept a lower standard if:

- The storage area is small,
- Persons escaping from fire do not have to pass under the storage area (see Fig. 7.38).

AD B2/3/4
sec. 6
6.56 to 6.60

Varying the requirements – multi-storey car parks

Multi-storey car parks tend to be large buildings, constructed of matcrials of limited combustibility and substantially open at the sides.

Difficulties may be encountered when applying the provisions of AD B2/3/4 since compartmentation is clearly impracticable and the large open sides would be treated as unprotected areas necessitating increased distances to boundaries, which might not be achievable. The height and cubic capacity of the car park could mean fire resistance periods in excess of two hours. This might be considered excessive due to the non-combustible nature of the construction and the limited fire hazard.

AD B2/3/4 therefore allows these requirements to be varied if ten conditions can be met:

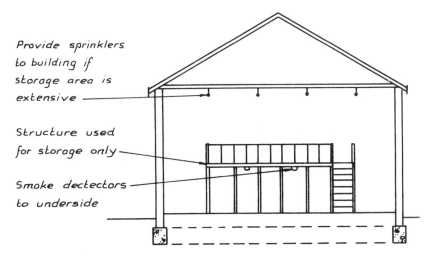

Provide sprinklers
to building if
storage area is
extensive ———

Structure used
for storage only —

Smoke dectectors —
to underside

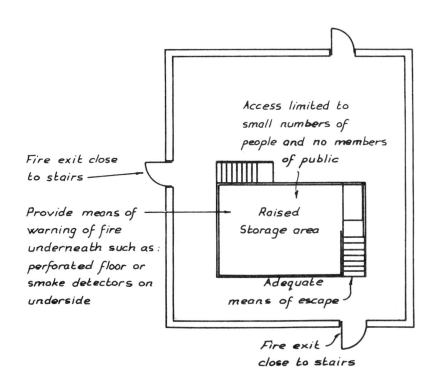

Fire exit close
to stairs ———

Provide means of ———
warning of fire
underneath such as :
perforated floor or
smoke detectors on
underside

Access limited to
small numbers of
people and no members
of public

Raised
Storage area

Adequate
means of escape

Fire exit
close to stairs

Fig. 7.38 Raised storage areas.

- The car park should only be used for cars and light vans.
- There should be no basement storey.
- Adjoining buildings should be separated from the car park by compartment or separating walls having the fire resistance required for the adjoining building.
- Elements of structure should be constructed of materials of limited combustibility.
- Openings in the sides of the car park should be provided at each level to give ½₀th of the floor area as free ventilation equally distributed on all sides.
- Adequate access for the fire brigade should be provided.
- Adequate alternative means of escape should be provided.
- The distance from any car space to an external exit or door to an escape stair should not exceed 45 m.
- Doors to escape stairs should have a minimum fire resistance of half an hour.
- Escape stairs should be enclosed in protecting structure with a fire resistance of at least one hour if the car park exceeds 15 m in height. (This is reduced to half an hour for car parks less than 15 m high.)

The extent of the variations is as follows:

- Compartmentation requirements for the car park itself may be omitted.
- A maximum period of fire resistance of one hour may be permitted where the car park exceeds 15 m in height. Below this height a lower standard may be acceptable.
- If at least a distance of 9 m may be achieved between the side of the car park and:

(i) its boundary; or,
(ii) the *opposite* side of an adjacent road; or
(iii) any other building on the same site which is not attached to the car park;

then the normal provisions for space separation may be omitted.

If this distance is less than 9 m then the provisions regarding space separation will still apply. This may create difficulties with ventilation. However, it is permissible to make up any deficiency with mechanical ventilation (see Fig. 7.39). AD B2/3/4 sec. 6 6.61 & 6.62

Varying the requirements – canopies over petrol pumps

Petrol pump canopies are covered by the building regulations unless they are totally detached and less than 30 m² in area (see Building Regulations 1985 Schedule 3, Class VI).

The only problem that arises is that associated with space separation since the open sides are, technically, unprotected areas.

Paragraph 6.65 of section 6 of AD B2/3/4 allows space separation

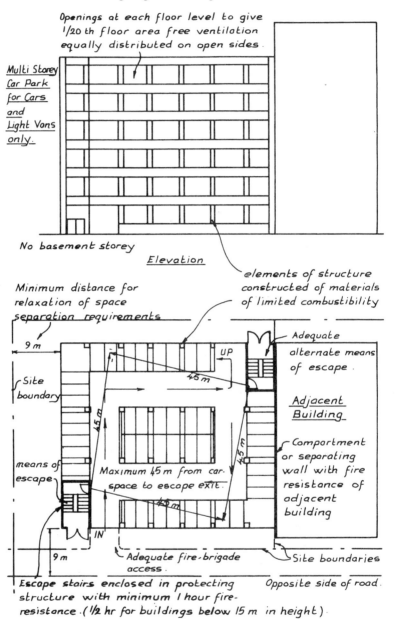

Fig. 7.39 Variation of requirements for fire resistance compartmentation and space separation in multi-storey car parks.

requirements to be disregarded for petrol pump canopies provided they are not immediately adjacent to a building on an adjoining site.

AD B2/3/4
sec. 6
6.63 to 6.65

Varying the requirements – sprinkler systems

Table 6.1 of AD B2/3/4 enables maximum compartment sizes in shops to be doubled if a sprinkler system is provided.

The provision of sprinkler systems may also be taken into account as a compensatory feature in the following cases:

- For increasing compartment sizes in other building types, such as industrial buildings.
- Where there is insufficient distance to boundaries in shops or industrial buildings, it may be appropriate to accept the less onerous separation distances relevant to residential, office or assembly uses.

AD B2/3/4
sec. 6
6.66 & 6.67

Chapter 8

Materials, workmanship, site preparation and moisture exclusion

Materials and workmanship

Introduction

Regulation 7 of the Building Regulations 1985 is concerned with the fitness and use of the materials necessary for carrying out building work. It is supported by its own approved document entitled, rather aptly, *Approved Document to support Regulation 7* (AD Reg. 7).

Apart from dealing generally with the standards of materials and workmanship needed for building work AD Regulation 7 is also concerned with:

- House Longhorn Beetle infestation,
- the use of high alumina cement,
- resistance to moisture and deleterious substances in subsoil,
- short-lived materials.

The use of materials which are unsuitable for permanent buildings, is covered by sections 19 and 20 of the Building Act 1984. Local authorities are enabled to reject plans for the construction of buildings of short-lived or otherwise unsuitable materials, or to impose a limit on their period of use. The Secretary of State may, by building regulations, prescribe materials which are considered unfit for particular purposes. Tables 1 and 2 of the 1976 regulations listed materials which were considered unfit if used as the weather-resisting part of any external wall or roof. Neither the 1985 regulations nor AD Regulation 7 prescribe any materials as unfit for particular purposes as yet.

Materials and workmanship generally

Reg. 7 Building work is required to be carried out with proper materials and in a workmanlike manner. This would be the case in any event under the general law.

Guidance on the choice and use of materials, and on ways of establishing the adequacy of workmanship is given in AD Regulation 7. However, the object is to ensure that materials comply with fundamental requirements as necessary to ensure public health and safety and to conserve energy. To this end, materials should be:

(a) Suitable in nature and quality in relation to the purposes for, and conditions in which, they are used; *and*
(b) adequately mixed and prepared;

Example: In concrete mixes the correct proportions must be used, there should be an appropriate water/cement ratio, mixing should be thorough, etc., *and*

(c) applied, used or fixed so as to adequately perform the functions for which they are designed.

Example: For reinforced concrete this would give control over the actual placing of the concrete, positioning of reinforcement, curing, etc.

The definition of *materials* is quite broad and covers products, components, fittings, items of equipment and materials used in the back-filling of excavations in connection with building work.

AD Reg. 7
0.1

It should be noted that the standards of materials and workmanship required by AD Regulation 7 will vary depending on the purpose of the part under consideration.

It follows, therefore, that the health and safety of the public is the most important consideration under Parts A to K of Schedule 1, whereas conservation of energy is the main criterion of Part L. Schedule 2, which deals with the provision of facilities for disabled people, is concerned with convenience. Accordingly, it is sufficient if the materials and workmanship are of such a standard that they serve their intended purpose.

AD Reg. 7
0.2 to 0.5

Fitness of materials

Guidance on the fitness of materials can be obtained from a number of sources:

● Past experience of a particular material actually in use,
● Materials covered by Agrément Certificates,
● Materials conforming to British Standards,
● Independent certification schemes, such as the kitemark scheme operated by the British Standards Institution,
● Materials covered by schemes which comply with BS 5750 *Quality systems*,

- Independent testing laboratories, calculations or other means, that show that a material is capable of performing its function,
- Local authority sampling and testing of materials under Regulation 16.

AD Reg. 7
sec. 1
1.1 & 1.2

However, in all cases the method of confirmation of fitness chosen must be appropriate to the purpose for and the conditions in which the material is to be used.

Short-lived materials

Only general guidance is given on the use of short-lived materials. These are materials which may be considered unsuitable due to their rapid deterioration when compared to the life of the building.
The main criteria to be considered are:

- Accessibility for inspection, maintenance and replacement.
- The effects of failure on public health and safety.

AD Reg. 7
sec. 1
1.3 to 1.5

Clearly, if a material or component is inaccessible and its failure would create a serious health risk it is unlikely that the material or component would be suitable.

Resistance to moisture and soil contaminants

Materials which are likely to suffer from the adverse effects of condensation, ground water or rain and snow may be satisfactory if:

(a) the construction of the building is such as to prevent moisture from reaching the materials; or,

AD Reg. 7
sec. 1
1.6

(b) the materials are suitably treated or otherwise protected from moisture.

AD Reg. 7
sec. 1
1.7

Similarly, materials which are in contact with the ground will only be satisfactory if they can adequately resist the effects of deleterious substances such as sulphates (see *Site preparation and moisture exclusion* page 8.5 below).

High alumina cement

AD Reg. 7
sec. 1
1.8

The deterioration of a number of high alumina cement concrete structures led, in 1975, to the exclusion of this material from all work except when used as a heat-resisting material. This exclusion still applies.

Special treatment against House Longhorn Beetle infestation

In specified areas in the south of England all softwood roof timbers, including ceiling joists, should be treated with a suitable preservative against the House Longhorn Beetle.

The specified areas are as follows:

The District of Bracknell

The Borough of Elmbridge

The Borough of Guildford other than the area of the former borough of Guildford

The District of Hart other than the area of the former urban district of Fleet

The District of Runnymede

The Borough of Spelthorne

The Borough of Surrey Heath

The Borough of Woking

In the Borough of Rushmoor, the area of the former urban district of Farnborough

The District of Waverley (other than the parishes of Godalming and Haslemere)

In the Royal Borough of Windsor and Maidenhead, the Parishes of Old Windsor, Sunningdale and Sunninghill.

No specific forms of treatment are given. However, the following methods applied under the 1976 regulations should still be satisfactory:

AD Reg. 7
sec. 1
1.9

(a) Treatment to BS 4072: 1974; or,
(b) treatment by sodium borate diffusion; or,
(c) treatment by complete immersion for at least 10 minutes in an organic-solvent type wood preservative containing at least 0·5% gamma HCH, dieldrin or other persistent organochlorine contact insecticide.

Adequacy of workmanship

It should be remembered that building regulations set different standards of workmanship to those imposed by, for example, a building specification. Building Regulations are not concerned with quality or value for money; they are concerned with public health and safety and the conservation of energy. Agrément certificates, British Standards and quality assurance schemes usually specify particular methods of working which can be used for assessing the adequacy of workmanship. The local authority is also empowered by Regulation 15 to test drains and sewers to check that they have been installed correctly (see Chapter 13 Drainage and waste disposal).

AD Reg. 7
sec. 2
2.1

Site preparation and moisture exclusion

Introduction

Part C of Schedule 1 to the Building Regulations 1985 is concerned with site preparation and resistance to moisture. In addition to moisture exclusion paragraph C2 contains provisions controlling sites containing dangerous or offensive substances. This replaces section 29 of the Building Act 1984 and also relates to chemical contaminants found in the ground to be covered by the building.

Certain provisions regarding the damp-proofing and weather resistance of floors and walls do not apply to buildings used solely for storage of plant or machinery in which the only persons habitually employed are storemen, etc. Other similar types of buildings where the air is so moisture-laden that any increase would not adversely affect the health of the occupants are also excluded. These buildings are referred to as 'excepted buildings' throughout this chapter.

Preparation of site

Regs. Sch. 1
C1

AD C1/2/3

The ground to be covered by the building is required to be reasonably free from vegetable matter.

Decaying vegetable matter could be a danger to health and it could also cause a building to become unstable if it occurred under foundations. AD C1/2/3, therefore, requires that the site should be cleared of all turf and vegetable matter at least to a depth to prevent future growth. This does not apply to excepted buildings.

AD C1/2/3
sec. 1
1.2

Where tree roots or readily compressible materials are present in the ground and these could affect the stability of the building special precautions may need to be taken. Useful guidance is contained in BRE Digest 63, 'Soils and Foundations: 1' (1965). Foundation failures have led to much litigation, e.g., *Low* v. *R. J. Haddock Ltd and Royal County of Berkshire* (1985) (see Chapter 6 Structural stability).

AD C1/2/3
sec. 1
1,3

Below ground services (such as foul or surface water drainage) should be designed to resist the effects of tree roots. This can be achieved by making services sufficiently robust or flexible and with joints that cannot be penetrated by roots.

AD C1/2/3
sec. 1
1.4

Dangerous and offensive substances

Regs. Sch. 1
C2

Precautions must be taken to prevent any substances found on or in the ground from causing a danger to health. This is, of course, the ground covered by the building and includes the area covered by the foundations.

AD C1/2/3

There is a special definition of *contaminant* for the purposes of AD C1/2/3 – any material (including faecal or animal matter) and any substance which is or could become toxic, corrosive, explosive, flammable or radioactive and therefore likely to be a danger to health or safety. This material must be in or on the ground to be covered by the building.

AD C1/2/3
0.2

Where a site is being redeveloped knowledge of its previous use, from planning or other local records, may indicate a possible source of contamination. Table 1 to AD C1/2/3 (see below) lists a number of site uses that are likely to contain contaminants.

Where the presence of contaminants has not been identified at an early stage, a later site survey may indicate possible contamination, Table 2 to AD C1/2/3 shows the signs to be looked for, indicates which materials may be responsible and suggests relevant actions that may be taken. The Environmental Health Officer should always be notified if contamination is suspected. He may then agree on the remedial measures necessary to make the site safe.

AD C1/2/3
sec. 2
2.1 & 2.2

AD C1/2/3

Table 1   Sites likely to contain contaminants

Asbestos works
Chemical works
Gas works, coal carbonisation plants and ancillary byproduct works
Industries making or using wood preservatives
Landfill and other waste disposal sites
Metal mines, smelters, foundries, steel works and metal finishing works
Munitions production and testing sites
Nuclear installations
Oil storage and distribution sites
Paper and printing works
Railway land, especially the larger sidings and depots
Scrap yards
Sewage works, sewage farms and sludge disposal sites
Tanneries

Where it may be necessary to remove large quantities of material, remedial measures may be possible but only with the benefit of expert advice. The appendix to AD C1/2/3 contains an introduction to the work of the expert adviser and is summarised below. It does not form part of the guidance given in section 2 and is for information only.

AD C1/2/3
sec. 2
2.4 & 2.5

Appendix to AD C1/2/3

Contaminants may occur separately or in combination with other materials with which they may react.

Some contaminants which:

AD C1/2/3

Table 2   **Possible contaminants and actions**

Signs of possible contamination	Possible contaminant	Relevant action
(a) Vegetation (absence, poor or unnatural growth)	metals, metal compounds	none
	organic compounds, gases	removal[1]
(b) Surface materials (unusual colours and contours may indicate wastes and residues)	metals, metal compounds	none
	oily and tarry wastes	removal, filling[2] or sealing
	asbestos (loose)	filling or sealing[4]
	other fibres	none
	organic compounds including phenols	removal or filling
	potentially combustible material including coal and coke dust	removal or inert filling[3]
	refuse and waste	removal
(c) Fumes and odours (may indicate organic chemicals at very low concentrations)	flammable, explosive and asphyxiating gases including methane and carbon dioxide	removal / the construction is to be free from unventilated voids
	corrosive liquids	*removal, filling or sealing
	faecal, animal and vegetable matter (biologically active)	removal or filling
(d) Drums and containers (whether full or empty)	various	*removal with all contaminated ground

Notes

Where removal is marked with an asterisk (*) the local authority may require the work to be done by a specialist.

Actions assume that ground will be covered with at least 100 mm in situ concrete.

[1] Removal   – the contaminant and any contaminated ground removed to depth of 1 m below lowest floor (or less if L.A. agrees) to place named by L.A.

[2] Filling   – Area of building covered to depth of 1 m (or less if L.A. agrees) with suitable material. Filling material and ground floor design considered together.

[3] Inert filling – wholly non-combustible and not easily changed by chemical reactions.

[4] Sealing   – imperforate barrier between contaminant and building sealed at joints, edges and service entries. Polythene may not always be suitable if contaminant is tarry waste or organic solvent.

- produce noxious fumes and vapours
- are combustible and may cause fire or explosion
- are radioactive

can pose a direct threat to occupants of a building.

Other contaminants may pose an indirect threat by attacking the fabric of the building.

There are four main stages in preparing proposals for remedial action:

- *Ground sampling* to define the vertical and horizontal distribution of each contaminant and to determine concentrations.
- *Sample analysis* to identify the most important contaminants.
- *Assessment of the hazards* that are associated with the various contaminants. The type of building to be erected will need to be considered as well as the effects of the hazards on the building and its occupants.
- *Remedial actions* may not always be necessary; it will depend on the hazard. However, if the risk to health is unacceptable remedial measures will need to be taken. Some commonly found contaminants are listed in the appendix together with the remedial measures that are appropriate. In most cases this involves partial or total removal, filling, sealing, ventilation of voids and construction in resistant or protective materials.

AD C1/2/3
sec. 2
Appendix

Subsoil drainage

Subsoil drainage must be provided *if* it is necessary to avoid:

Regs. Sch. 1
C3

(a) the passage of moisture from the ground to the inside of the building; or,
(b) damage to the fabric of the building.

There are no provisions in AD C1/2/3 concerning flooding of sites. It is assumed that appropriate steps will already have been taken to prevent this.

AD C1/2/3

AD C1/2/3
sec. 1
1.5

Ground water may also affect the stability of a building, requiring special precautions to be taken in foundations (see Chapter 6 Structural stability).

AD C1/2/3
sec. 1
1.6

Subsoil water may cause problems in the following cases:

- Where there is a high water table (i.e. within 0·25 m of the lowest floor in the building) (see Fig. 8.1).
- Where surface water may enter or damage the building fabric.
- Where an active subsoil drain is severed during excavations.

Where problems are anticipated it will usually be necessary either to

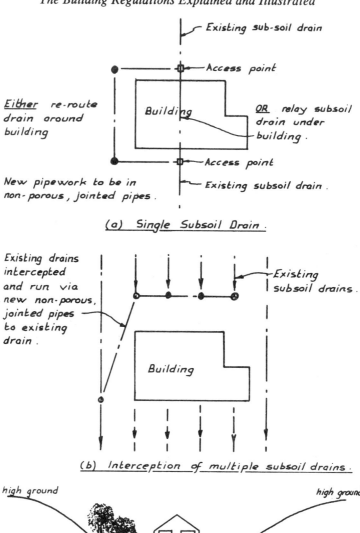

Existing sub-soil drain

Access point

Either re-route drain around building

Building

OR relay subsoil drain under building.

Access point

New pipework to be in non-porous, jointed pipes.

Existing subsoil drain.

(a)   Single Subsoil Drain.

Existing drains intercepted and run via new non-porous, jointed pipes to existing drain.

Existing subsoil drains.

Building

(b) Interception of multiple subsoil drains.

high ground

high ground

Willows and marsh plants etc

Surface of ground appears damp in dry weather.

(c) Indications of High Water Table

Fig. 8.1 Subsoil drainage.

drain the site of the building or to design and construct it to resist moisture penetration.

Severed subsoil drains should be intercepted and continued in such a way that moisture is not directed into the building. Figure 8.1 illustrates a number of possible solutions.

AD C1/2/3
sec. 1
1.7 to 1.10

Resistance to weather and ground moisture

The floors, walls and roof of a building are required to adequately resist the passage of moisture to the inside of the building.

Reg. Sch. 1
C 4

Protection of floors next to the ground

The term *floor* is taken to include any surface finish which is laid as part of the permanent construction. This would, presumably, exclude carpets, lino, tiles, etc., but would include screeds and granolithic finishes.

AD C4

AD C4
0.6

A ground floor should be constructed so that:

- Moisture is prevented from passing to the upper surface of the floor. (This does not apply to excepted buildings.)
- It will not be adversely affected by moisture from the ground.
- It will not transmit moisture to another part of the building that might be damaged (see Fig. 8.2).

AD C4
sec. 1
1.2

The term *moisture* is taken to include water vapour as well as liquid water. Damage caused by moisture is only significant if it would present an imminent danger to public health and safety or it would permanently reduce the performance of an insulating material.

AD C4
0.8

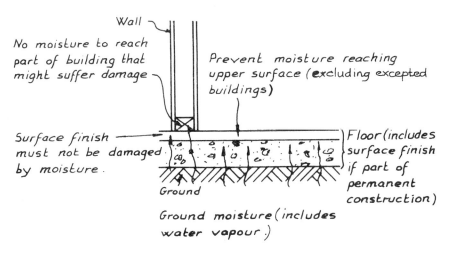

Fig. 8.2 Floors – functional requirements.

Floors supported directly by the ground

The requirements mentioned above can be met, for ground supported floors, by covering the ground with dense concrete incorporating a damp-proof membrane, laid on a hardcore bed.

This form of construction is illustrated in Fig. 8.3 below. However, the following points should also be considered.

- Hardcore laid under the floor next to the ground should not contain water-soluble sulphates or deleterious matter in such quantities as might cause damage to the floor.

  Broken brick or stone are the best hardcore materials. Clinker is dangerous unless it can be shown that the actual material proposed is free from sulphates, etc., and colliery shales should likewise be avoided. In any event, the builder might well be liable for breach of an implied common law warranty of fitness of materials: see *Hancock* v. *B. W. Brazier (Anerley), Ltd.*, [1966] 2 All E.R. 901, where builders were held liable for subsequent damage caused by the use of hardcore containing sulphates.
- Polythene membranes may be laid above or below the concrete floor slab, with joints sealed. If laid below the slab they should be supported by a layer of material that will not cause damage to the polythene.

  A three-coat layer of cold applied bitumen solution may also be applied to the top surface of a slab.

  Unless a surface membrane consists of pitchmastic or similar material it should be protected by a suitable floor finish or screed.
- AD C4 gives no guidance on the position of the floor relative to outside ground level. Since this type of floor is unsuitable if subjected to water pressure it is reasonable to assume that the top surface of the slab should not be below outside ground level unless special precautions are taken.

AD C4
sec. 1
1.4 to 1.6

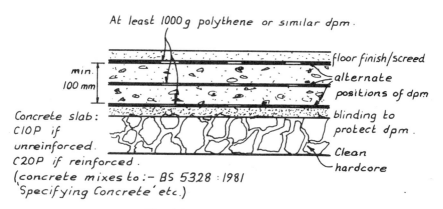

At least 1000 g polythene or similar dpm.

floor finish/screed
min. 100 mm
alternate positions of dpm
Concrete slab:
C10P if unreinforced.
C20P if reinforced.
(concrete mixes to:- BS 5328 : 1981
'Specifying Concrete' etc.)
blinding to protect dpm.
Clean hardcore

Fig. 8.3 Ground supported floor.

If it is proposed to lay a timber floor finish directly on the concrete slab it is permissible to bed the timber in a material that would also serve as a damp-proof membrane.

No guidance is given regarding suitable d.p.m. materials. However 12·5 mm of asphalt or pitchmastic will usually be satisfactory for most timber finishes and it may be possible to lay wood blocks in a suitable adhesive d.p.m. If a timber floor finish is fixed to wooden fillets embedded in the concrete, the fillets should be treated with a suitable preservative unless they are above the d.p.m. (see BS 1282: 1975 *Guide to the choice, use and application of wood preservatives* for suitable preservative treatments). AD C4
sec. 1
1.7

Clause 11 of CP 102: 1973 *Protection of buildings against water from the ground* may be used as an alternative to the above especially where ground water pressure is evident. AD C4
sec.1
1.8

Suspended timber floors

The performance requirements mentioned above may be met for suspended timber ground floors by:

- Covering the ground with suitable material to resist moisture and deter plant growth.
- Providing a ventilated space between the top surface of the ground covering and the timber.
- Isolating timber from moisture carrying materials by means of damp-proof courses. AD C4
sec. 1
1.9

A suitable form of construction is shown in Fig. 8.4 and is summarised below.

- The ground surface should be covered with at least 100 mm of concrete (mix C7·5P if there is no reinforcement in the slab) laid on clean broken brick or similar inert hardcore not containing harmful quantities of water-soluble sulphates or other materials which might damage the concrete. (The Building Research Station suggests that over 0·5% of water-soluble sulphates would be a harmful quantity.)

   Alternatively, the ground surface may be covered with at least 50 mm of concrete laid on 1000 g polythene membrane with the joints sealed. The membrane should be laid on a protective bed.
- The ground covering material should be laid so that *either* its top surface is not below the highest level of the ground adjoining the building *or* it falls to an outlet above the lowest level of the adjoining ground.
- There should be a space above the top of the concrete of at least 75 mm to any wall-plate and 125 mm to any suspended timber. There should be ventilation openings in all external walls allowing free ventilation to all parts of the floor. An actual ventilation area

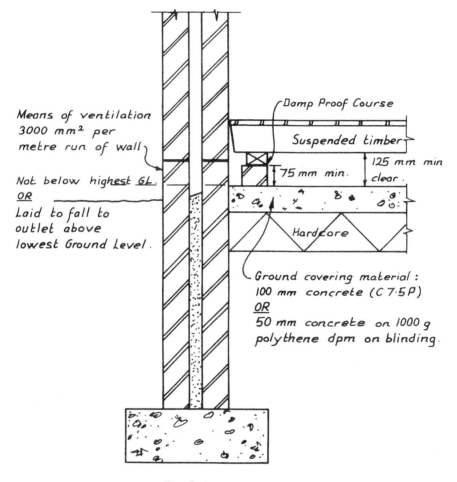

Fig. 8.4 Suspended timber floor.

equivalent to 3000 mm^2 per metre run of wall should be provided and any ducts needed to convey ventilating air should be at least 100 mm in diameter.

● Damp-proof courses of sheet materials, slates or engineering bricks bedded in cement mortar should be provided between timber members and supporting structures to prevent transmission of moisture from the ground.

AD C4
sec. 1
1.10 & 1.11

Again, the recommendations of Clause 11 of CP 102: 1973 may be used instead of the above.

Suspended concrete ground floors

This is the first time that suspended concrete ground floors have been mentioned in formal building control literature and this may reflect the increased use of this form of construction in recent years.

Moisture should be prevented from reaching the upper surface of the floor and the reinforcement should be protected against moisture if the construction is to be considered satisfactory. AD C4 sec. 1 1.12

Suspended concrete ground floors are either of pre-cast or in situ construction and may or may not incorporate a void space between the top of the ground and the underside of the floor. AD C4 does not require any space so formed to be ventilated, but, if it is not, then a damp-proof membrane must be provided as for ground supported floors (see Fig. 8.5 for details). AD C4 sec. 1 1.13

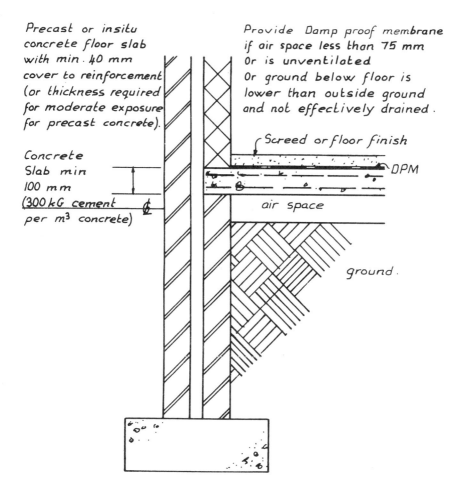

Precast or insitu concrete floor slab with min. 40 mm cover to reinforcement (or thickness required for moderate exposure for precast concrete).

Concrete Slab min 100 mm (300 kG cement per m³ concrete)

Provide Damp proof membrane if air space less than 75 mm Or is unventilated Or ground below floor is lower than outside ground and not effectively drained.

Screed or floor finish

DPM

air space

ground.

Fig. 8.5 Suspended concrete ground floors.

Protection of walls against moisture from the ground

The term *wall* is taken to include piers, columns and parapets and may include chimneys if they are attached to the building. Windows, doors and other openings are not included.

Walls should be constructed so that:

● Moisture from the ground is prevented from reaching the inside of the building, (this does not apply to excepted buildings),
● They will not be adversely affected by moisture from the ground,
● They will not transmit moisture from the ground to another part of the building that might be damaged.

The requirements mentioned above can be met for internal and external walls by providing a damp-proof course of suitable materials in the required position.

AD C4
sec. 2
2.1 & 2.2

Figure 8.6 illustrates the main provisions, which are summarised below:

● The damp-proof course may be of any material that will prevent moisture movement. This would include bituminous sheet materials, engineering bricks or slates laid in cement mortar, polythene or pitch polymer materials.
● The damp-proof course and any damp-proof membrane in the floor should be continuous.
● Unless an external wall is suitably protected by another part of the building, the damp-proof course should be at least 150 mm above outside ground level.
● Where a damp-proof course is inserted in an external cavity wall the cavity should extend at least 150 mm below the lowest level of the damp-proof course. However, where a cavity wall is built directly off a raft foundation, ground beam or similar supporting structure, it is impractical to continue the cavity down 150 mm. The supporting structure should therefore be regarded as bridging the cavity, and protection be provided by a flashing or damp-proof course as required (see Fig. 8.6).

AD C4
sec. 2
2.3 & 2.4

Alternatively Clause 10 of CP 102: 1973, *Protection of walls against water from the ground*, may be followed especially in the case of walls (including basement walls) subjected to ground water pressure.

AD C4
sec. 2
2.5

Weather resistance of external walls

In addition to resisting ground moisture external walls should:

● Resist the passage of rain or snow to the inside of the building (this does not apply to excepted buildings).
● Not be damaged by rain or snow.

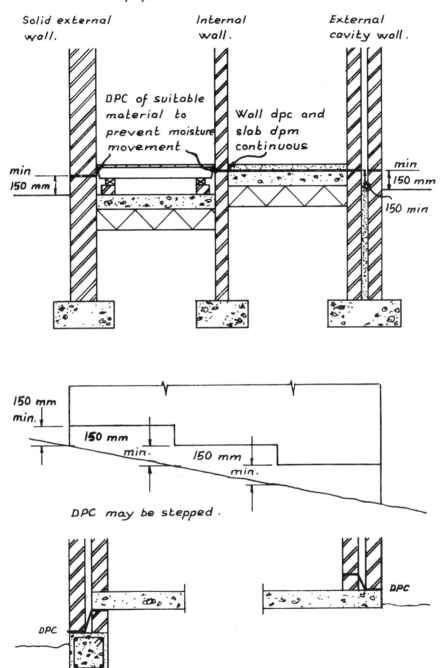

Solid external wall.

Internal wall.

External cavity wall.

DPC of suitable material to prevent moisture movement

Wall dpc and slab dpm continuous

min 150 mm

min 150 mm

150 min

150 mm min.

150 mm min.

150 mm min.

DPC may be stepped.

DPC

DPC

Cavity Wall on Ground Beam or Raft.

Fig. 8.6 Protection of walls against moisture from the ground.

● Not transmit moisture due to rain or snow to another part of the building that might be damaged.

There are a number of forms of wall construction which will satisfy the above requirements:

● A solid wall of sufficient thickness holds moisture during bad weather until it can be released in the next dry spell.
● An impervious cladding prevents moisture from penetrating the outside face of the wall.
● The outside leaf of a cavity wall holds moisture in a similar manner to a solid wall, the cavity preventing any penetration to the inside leaf.

These principles are illustrated in Fig. 8.7 below.

Solid external walls

The construction of a solid external wall will depend on the severity of exposure to wind-driven rain. This may be assessed for a building in a given area by using BSI Draft for Development DD 93: 1984.

In conditions of *very* severe exposure it may be necessary to use an impervious cladding. However, in conditions of severe exposure a solid wall may be constructed as shown in Fig. 8.8. The following points should also be considered:

● The brickwork or blockwork should be rendered or given an equivalent form of protection.
● Rendering should have a textured finish and be at least 20 mm thick in two coats. This permits easier evaporation of moisture from the wall.
● The bricks or blocks and mortar should be matched for strength to prevent cracking of joints or bricks and joints should be raked out to a depth of at least 10 mm in order to provide a key for the render.
● The render mix should not be too strong or cracking may occur. A mix of 1:1:6 cement:lime:sand is recommended for all walls except those constructed of dense concrete blocks where 1:½:4 should prove satisfactory.
● Rendering should be given protection for at least three days after application.
● Further details of a wide range of render mixes may be obtained from BS 5262: 1976 *External rendered finishes.*
● Where the top of a wall is unprotected by the building structure it should be provided with a coping and damp-proof course, unless the coping and joints form a complete barrier to moisture.

● Damp-proof courses should be provided to direct moisture towards the outside face of the wall (see Fig. 8.8).

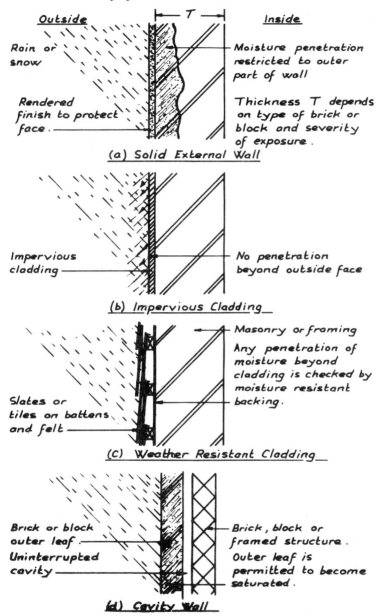

Outside   T   Inside

Rain or snow

Rendered finish to protect face.

(a) Solid External Wall

Moisture penetration restricted to outer part of wall

Thickness T depends on type of brick or block and severity of exposure.

Impervious cladding

(b) Impervious Cladding

No penetration beyond outside face

Slates or tiles on battens and felt

(c) Weather Resistant Cladding

Masonry or framing

Any penetration of moisture beyond cladding is checked by moisture resistant backing.

Brick or block outer leaf.
Uninterrupted cavity

(d) Cavity Wall

Brick, block or framed structure. Outer leaf is permitted to become saturated.

Fig. 8.7 Weather resistance of external walls – principles.

The performance requirements for solid and cavity external walls can also be met by complying with BS 5628 *Code of Practice for the structural use of masonry*: Part 3: 1985 *Materials and components, design and workmanship,* or BS 5390: 1976 *Code of Practice for stone masonry.*

AD C4
sec. 2
2.9

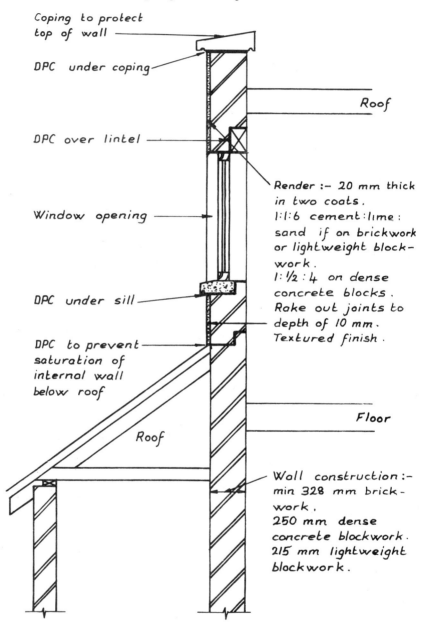

Fig. 8.8 Solid external walls – moisture exclusion.

External cavity walls

In order to satisfy the performance requirements an external cavity wall should consist of the following:

- An outside leaf of masonry (brick, block, natural or reconstructed stone).
- Minimum 50 mm uninterrupted cavity. Where a cavity is bridged (by a lintel, etc.) a damp-proof course or tray should be inserted in the wall so that the passage of moisture from the outer to the inner leaf is prevented. This is not necessary where the cavity is bridged by a wall tie, or where the bridging occurs, presumably, at the top of a wall and is then protected by the roof. Where an opening is formed in a cavity wall, the jambs should have a suitable vertical damp-proof course or the cavity should be closed so as to prevent the passage of moisture.
- An inside leaf of masonry or framing with suitable lining (see Fig. 8.9).

AD C4
sec. 2
2.11

Weather resistance and cavity insulation

Since the installation of cavity insulation effectively bridges the cavity of a cavity wall and could give rise to moisture penetration to the inner leaf it is most important that it be carried out correctly and efficiently. AD C4 lists a number of British Standards and Codes of Practice that cover the various materials that may be incorporated into a cavity wall:

- Rigid materials which are built in as the wall is constructed should be the subject of a current British Board of Agrément Certificate.
- Urea-formaldehyde foam inserted after the wall has been constructed should comply with BS 5617: 1985 *Specification for urea-formaldehyde (UF) foam systems, etc.* and should be installed in accordance with BS 5618: 1985 *Code of Practice for the thermal insulation of cavity walls, etc.*
- Other insulating materials inserted after the wall has been constructed should either comply with BS 232 *Thermal insulation of cavity walls by filling with blown man-made mineral fibre, etc.,* or be the subject of a current British Board of Agrément Certificate.
- Where materials are inserted into a cavity after the wall has been constructed, the suitability of the wall for filling should be assessed, before installation, in accordance with BS 8208 *Guide to the assessment of suitability of external cavity walls for filling with thermal insulants,* Part 1: 1985 *Existing traditional cavity construction.*

AD C4
sec. 2
2.13 & 2.14

Claddings for external walls

The principles of external claddings are illustrated in Fig. 8.7(b) and (c) above. Therefore, the cladding should be either:

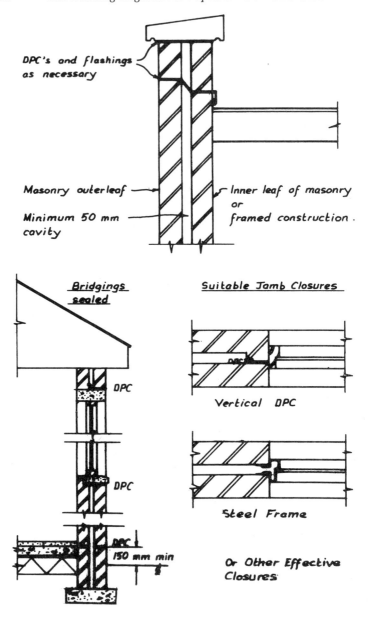

DPC's and flashings as necessary

Masonry outerleaf

Minimum 50 mm cavity

Inner leaf of masonry or framed construction.

Bridgings sealed

DPC

DPC

DPC

150 mm min

Suitable Jamb Closures

DPC

Vertical DPC

Steel Frame

Or Other Effective Closures

Fig. 8.9 Prevention of dampness in cavity walls.

(a) jointless (or have sealed joints) and be impervious to moisture (such as sheets of metal, glass, plastic or bituminous materials); or

(b) have overlapping dry joints and consist of impervious or weather resisting materials (such as natural stone or slate, cement based products, fired clay or wood).

Dry jointed claddings should be backed by a material (such as sarking felt) which will direct any penetrating moisture to the outside surface of the structure.

Moisture-resisting materials consisting of bituminous or plastic products lapped at the joints are permitted but they should be permeable to water vapour unless there is a ventilated space behind the cladding.

Materials that are jointless or have sealed joints should be designed to accommodate structural and thermal movement.

Dry joints between cladding units should be designed either to resist moisture penetration or to direct any moisture entering them to the outside face of the structure. The suitability of dry joints will depend on the design of the joint and cladding and the severity of exposure of the building.

All external claddings should be securely fixed.

AD C4
sec. 3
3.1 to 3.7

Weather resistance of roofs

The roof of a building should:

- Resist the passage of rain or snow to the inside of the building.
- Not be damaged by rain or snow.
- Not transmit moisture due to rain or snow to another part of the building that might be damaged.

The requirements for external wall claddings mentioned above apply equally to roof covering materials.

AD C4
sec. 3
3.1 to 3.7

The performance requirements for external wall and roof claddings can also be met by complying with:

- BS code of practice 143 *Sheet roof and wall coverings* (this includes recommendations for aluminium, zinc, galvanised corrugated steel, lead, copper and semi-rigid asbestos bitumen sheet).
- BS 5247 *Code of Practice for sheet wall and roof coverings* Part 14: 1975 *Corrugated asbestos cement.*
- BS 8200: 1985 *Code of Practice for the design of non-load-bearing external vertical enclosures of buildings.*

The following codes refer to walls only:

- BS code of practice 297: 1972 *Pre-cast concrete cladding (non-load-bearing).*
- BS code of practice 298: 1972 *Natural stone cladding (non-load-bearing).*

AD C4
sec. 3
3.8

Chapter 9

Toxic substances

Introduction

In recent years there has been evidence to suggest that fumes from urea-formaldehyde foam, when used as a cavity wall filling, can have an adverse effect on the health of people occupying the building. This is still a contentious issue, but has nevertheless become a subject for building control.

Cavity insulation

Regs Sch. 1 D1 Where insulating material is inserted into a cavity in a cavity wall reasonable precautions must be taken to prevent toxic fumes from penetrating occupied parts of the building.

AD D1 It should be noted that Approved Document D1 does not require total exclusion of formaldehyde fumes from buildings but merely that these should not increase to an irritant concentration.

AD D1 1.1
AD D1 1.2(a) The inner leaf of the cavity wall should provide a continuous barrier to the passage of fumes and for this purpose it should be of brick or block construction.

Before work is commenced the wall should be assessed for suitability in acordance with BS 8208 *Guide to assessment of suitability of external walls for filling with thermal insulants* Part 1: 1985 *Existing traditional cavity construction.*

AD D1 1.2(b) The work should be carried out by a person holding a current BSI Certificate of Registration of Assessed Capability for this particular type of work.

AD D1 1.2(c) The urea-formaldehyde foam should comply with the requirements of BS 5617: 1985 *Specification for urea-formaldehyde (UF) foam systems etc.* and the installation with BS 5618: 1985 *Code of practice for thermal insulation of cavity walls etc.*

AD D1 1.2(d)
AD D1 1.2(e)

Chapter 10

Sound insulation

Introduction

Sound insulation requirements are covered by Part E of Schedule 1 to the Building Regulations 1985. This Part applies only to certain separating walls and floors of dwellings. The purpose of the provisions is to control sound from adjoining parts of buildings. There is no control over sound entering a dwelling through external walls.

The accompanying Approved Document AD E1/2/3 gives much more detailed guidance over a wider range of wall and floor constructions than in any previous regulations. The basic requirements for *reasonable resistance* to airborne and/or impact sound, however, remain unchanged. This is interesting, since a wide body of opinion is in favour of removing sound insulation from building regulation control. The provision of sound insulation can only be justified if it can be shown that its omission would put at risk the health of the occupants of the building. Since sound levels that would cause actual physical damage are not usually encountered between dwellings the concern must be for mental rather than physical health.

Therefore, two questions arise:

(i) Are separate requirements for sound insulation in dwellings necessary in building regulations?

Fire resistance and structural stability provisions already require non-combustible, imperforate construction for both separating walls and floors. Since the external walls and roof of a dwelling are not required to be sound resisting a high sound level from traffic, etc. is unavoidable.

(ii) If separate sound insulation requirements are thought to be necessary how is it possible to judge a reasonable standard of resistance to airborne and/or impact sound?

In the past the standard for resistance to airborne sound for separating walls has been that achieved by a solid brick or block wall with an average mass of 415 kg/m^2 and 12·5 mm of plaster each side. It is interesting to note that this has been reduced to 375 kg/m^2 in AD E1/2/3. People vary in their response to unwanted sound and the standard mentioned above may prove totally inadequate for many people, especially those who are studying or who are unwell.

Walls

Regs Sch. 1
E1

A wall which,

(a) separates any dwelling from another dwelling or from another building; or,

(b) separates any habitable room in a dwelling from any other part of the same building which is not used exclusively with that dwelling;

must be so constructed as to provide reasonable resistance to the transmission of airborne sound.

With regard to (b) immediately above the following points should be noted:

- A *habitable room* means a room used for dwelling purposes but not a kitchen or scullery.
- Walls that separate habitable rooms in a dwelling from other places in the same building which are used only for inspection, maintenance or repair of the building, its services or fixed plant or machinery are not required to have sound insulation.

Regs Sch. 1
E1

Presumably, the intention here is to exclude places used *occasionally* for repair or maintenance but to require sound insulation between habitable rooms and corridors, stairwells, lift shafts, laundry rooms, machinery or tank rooms, etc., where sound is likely to be more constant (see Fig. 10.1).

The Building Regulations are concerned with two types of sound sources in buildings:

- Airborne sources such as musical instruments, speech or audio-equipment set up vibrations in the surrounding air which impinge on enclosing walls and floors. These are set into vibration and cause the air to vibrate beside them thereby transmitting the sound to an adjoining space on the other side of the wall or floor. Vibrations may also be transmitted via elements connected to the wall or floor.
- Impact sources such as footsteps or heavy machinery set up vibrations directly in the elements that they strike which then transmit the vibrations to adjacent spaces.

The Building Regulations require walls to provide adequate resistance only to the transmission of *airborne* sound. Floors must reduce *airborne* sound and also, if they are above a dwelling, *impact* sound.

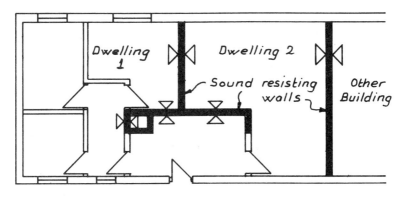

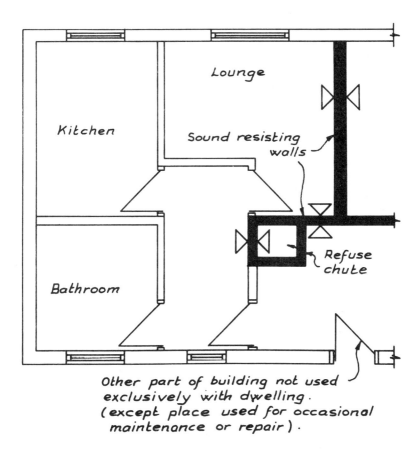

Fig. 10.1 Resistance to airborne sound of walls in dwellings.

Whatever the source of the sound it may be transmitted through an element in two ways:

- Direct transmission – sound is transmitted directly through the element from one side to the other. This may be reduced by using heavy materials which are not set into vibration easily or by forming a break in the construction such as a cavity in a wall.
- Flanking (indirect) transmission – sound is transmitted round the ends of elements via cavities in external walls or through ceilings and floors at junctions with walls. Adequate detailing of junctions is essential in order to reduce flanking transmission. The introduction of steps or staggers between buildings can also be of assistance in reducing flanking transmission.

AD E1/2/3
0.2 to 0.14

AD E1/2/3 provides two ways of satisfying the requirements of the Building Regulations for airborne sound insulation of walls:

AD E1/2/3
sec. 1
(i) A series of examples of widely used forms of construction is given which may be adopted by the building designer; or,

AD E1/2/3
0.1 & sec. 3
(ii) A form of construction may be repeated which has been used in a similar building and has been shown by tests to be acceptable.

Typical wall constructions

Four main types of wall construction are described in section 1 of AD E1/2/3 – solid masonry, cavity masonry, solid masonry core with freestanding lightweight panels and timber frame with absorbent cladding. Each wall construction is specified together with details of how to avoid flanking transmission at junctions between elements.

Solid masonry wall (Type 1) – direct transmission
This type of wall depends mainly on its own weight to resist airborne sound transmission. However, air paths through the wall due to poor workmanship (joints not filled properly and poor bonding at junctions with other elements) can reduce the effectiveness of the wall as a barrier to sound. Table 10.1 gives details of four commonly used solid wall constructions which will give adequate resistance to direct sound transmission.

Solid masonry wall (Type 1) – flanking transmission
It is most important to pay particular attention to detail at junctions between the sound resisting wall and other elements of the construction. Intermediate floor, ceiling, roof space and external wall junctions all provide weak points where flanking transmission may take place. Figures 10.2 and 10.3 illustrate the precautions that should be taken at these points of junction. The following should also be noted:

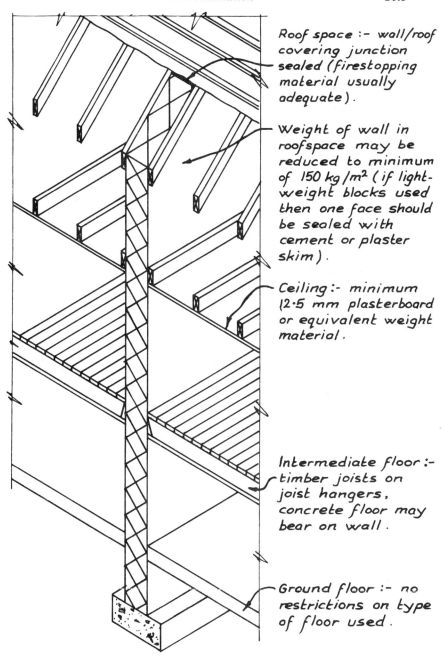

Roof space :- wall/roof covering junction sealed (firestopping material usually adequate).

Weight of wall in roofspace may be reduced to minimum of 150 kg/m² (if lightweight blocks used then one face should be sealed with cement or plaster skim).

Ceiling :- minimum 12·5 mm plasterboard or equivalent weight material.

Intermediate floor :- timber joists on joist hangers, concrete floor may bear on wall.

Ground floor :- no restrictions on type of floor used.

Fig. 10.2 Flanking transmission – wall and floor junctions (cavity and solid masonry party walls).

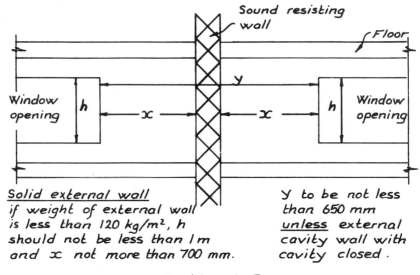

Sound resisting wall

Floor

Window opening

h

x

y

x

h

Window opening

Solid external wall
if weight of external wall
is less than 120 kg/m², h
should not be less than 1m
and x not more than 700 mm.

y to be not less
than 650 mm
unless external
cavity wall with
cavity closed.

Section A–B

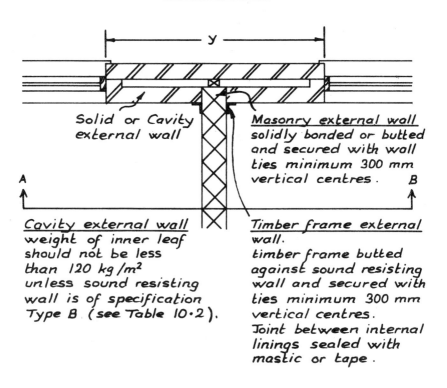

y

Solid or Cavity
external wall

Masonry external wall
solidly bonded or butted
and secured with wall
ties minimum 300 mm
vertical centres.

A

B

Cavity external wall
weight of inner leaf
should not be less
than 120 kg/m²
unless sound resisting
wall is of specification
Type B (see Table 10·2).

**Timber frame external
wall.**
timber frame butted
against sound resisting
wall and secured with
ties minimum 300 mm
vertical centres.
Joint between internal
linings sealed with
mastic or tape.

Fig. 10.3 Flanking transmission – external wall junction (cavity and solid
masonry party walls).

Table 10.1 Solid Masonry – Wall Type 1.

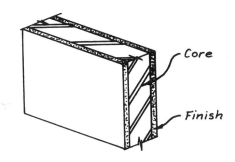

Wall specification	Core	Finish	Remarks
A	Brickwork of minimum weight 375 kg/m^2 (including plaster)	Plaster coat minimum 12·5 mm on each face.	Bricks laid frogs upwards and to include headers.
B	Brickwork of minimum weight (including plaster-board) 375 kg/m^2. Minimum weight of masonry alone 355 kg/m^2.	Plasterboard minimum thickness 12·5 mm on each face.	Bricks laid frogs upwards and to include headers. Brickwork should not be plastered.
C	Concrete blockwork of minimum weight 415 kg/m^2 (including plaster).	Plaster coat minimum thickness 12·5 mm on each face.	Blocks should extend full thickness of wall.
D	Dense concrete (in situ or large panels) of minimum weight 415 kg/m^2 (including plaster if used).	Plaster coat optional.	Joints between panels should be filled with mortar.

- Solid lightweight external masonry walls (i.e. less than 120 kg/m^2) should be divided up by windows or similar openings into small sections which do not vibrate freely.
- Where lightweight blocks are used to reduce weight in a roofspace these should be treated on one side with cement paint or a plaster skin coat to seal any possible air paths.
- There are no restrictions on the use of masonry as the outside leaf of an external cavity wall.
- No special precautions are necessary at the junction between a sound resisting wall and a ground floor.

AD E1/2/3
sec. 1
wall Type 1

Cavity masonry wall (Type 2) – direct transmission
This type of wall depends partly on its own weight and partly on the degree of isolation between the leaves in order to resist airborne sound transmission. Cavity walls do not generally behave better than solid walls of similar materials and weight.

In addition to maintaining properly filled mortar joints and bonding of junctions it is also important to space the leaves at least 50 mm apart and to ensure that this cavity does not become blocked. The leaves should be connected with butterfly pattern wall ties spaced at least 900 mm apart horizontally and 450 mm vertically. Care should be taken to see that cavity insulating material (other than loose fibres) inserted in the external cavity wall does not enter the cavity in the separating wall. Table 10.2 gives details of three commonly used cavity wall constructions which will give adequate resistance to direct sound transmission.

Table 10.2 Cavity Masonry – Wall Type 2.

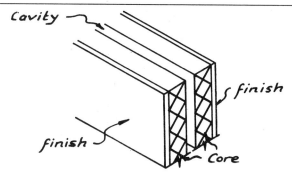

Wall specification	Core	Finish	Remarks
A	Brickwork in two leaves, of minimum weight 415 kg/m² (including plaster)*.	Plaster coat minimum 12·5 mm on each face.	Bricks laid frogs upwards. Minimum cavity width 50 mm.
B	Concrete blockwork in two leaves of minimum weight 415 kg/m² (including plaster).	Plaster coat minimum 12·5 mm on each face.	Minimum cavity width 50 mm.
C	Lightweight concrete blockwork of minimum weight 250 kg/m² (including plaster or dry lining).	Plaster coat minimum 12·5 mm on each face *or* dry lining to each face.	Minimum cavity width 75 mm. Face of blockwork should be sealed with cement paint where intermediate floor abuts.

Notes   * *reduced to minimum of 355 kg/m² where wall is stepped and/or staggered (Specification D).*

Cavity masonry wall (Type 2) – flanking transmission
The requirements listed above for solid masonry walls also apply, generally, to cavity masonry walls. The following should also be noted:

- Where a concrete intermediate floor construction is used it should be carried through to the cavity face of the wall leaf.
- The weight of the inner leaf of an external cavity wall should be at least 120 kg/m^2 unless the sound resisting wall is of Type B (see Table 10.2).
- At the junction between a cavity external wall and a cavity separating wall the air path in the cavity should be blocked to minimise the transmission of sound via the cavities.
- Where a party wall between dwellings is stepped or staggered the weight of the wall of specification Type A (i.e. two leaves of plastered brickwork) may be reduced to not less than 355 kg/m^2. This is referred to as specification D of wall Type 2 in AD E1/2/3 (see Figs 10.2 and 10.3 and Table 10.2 above).

AD E1/2/3
sec. 1
wall Type 2

Solid masonry core with freestanding lightweight panels (wall Type 3) – direct transmission
The resistance to airborne sound for this type of wall depends partly on the weight of the masonry core and partly on the isolation provided by the panels and air spaces.

Again, it is important to ensure that mortar joints in the masonry core are properly filled and that junctions with other elements are solidly bonded. The lightweight panels should be supported at floor and ceiling level only and not tied or fixed to the masonry core if adequate isolation is to be achieved. Table 10.3 gives details of four commonly used masonry core constructions and two types of lightweight panel.

Solid masonry core with freestanding lightweight panels (wall Type 3) – flanking transmission
The requirements listed above for solid masonry walls also apply, generally, to the solid masonry core in this form of construction. Additionally, extra precautions need to be taken at the junctions between the lightweight panels and adjacent elements. These precautions are summarised below and illustrated in Fig. 10.4:

- In the roofspace the gap between the ceiling and the masonry core should be sealed with a timber batten. The panel should also be sealed to the ceiling on the underside with mastic, tape or coving.
- At floor level lightweight panels should be fixed to a timber batten secured to the floor. Where timber joists are carried on joist hangers supported by the masonry core the spaces between the joists should be sealed with a timber batten. Again, the gap between ceiling and panel should be sealed with mastic, tape or coving.

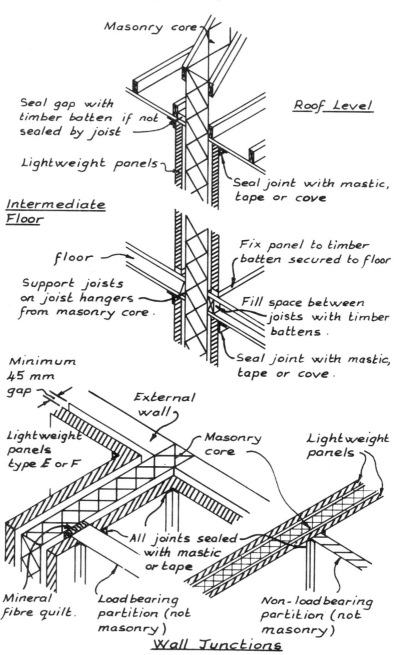

Masonry core

Roof Level

Seal gap with timber batten if not sealed by joist

Lightweight panels

Seal joint with mastic, tape or cove

Intermediate Floor

floor

Support joists on joist hangers from masonry core.

Fix panel to timber batten secured to floor

Fill space between joists with timber battens.

Seal joint with mastic, tape or cove.

Minimum 45 mm gap

External wall

Lightweight panels type E or F

Masonry core

Lightweight panels

All joints sealed with mastic or tape

Mineral fibre quilt.

Load bearing partition (not masonry)

Non-load bearing partition (not masonry)

Wall Junctions

Fig. 10.4 Flanking transmission – wall Type 3.

Table 10.3 Masonry Core with Lightweight Panels – Wall Type 3.

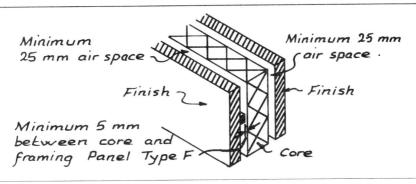

Wall specification	Core	Finish	Remarks
A and B	Brickwork or concrete blockwork of minimum weight 300 kg/m².	Panel type E or F*.	Minimum density of blocks 1500 kg/m³.
C	Concrete blockwork of minimum weight 200 kg/m²	Panel type E or F*.	Block density less than 1500 kg/m³.
D	Autoclaved aerated concrete blockwork of minimum weight 160 kg/m².	Panel type E or F*.	

Notes *Panel specifications	Construction	Notes
E	Two sheets plasterboard joined by cellular core of minimum weight 18 kg/m².	Panel joints taped. Panel spaced minimum 25 mm from masonry core.
F	Two sheets plasterboard with or without supporting framework. Each sheet at least 12·5 mm thick. Overall thickness at least 30 mm if no supporting framework.	Joints between sheets staggered. Sheets spaced minimum 25 mm from masonry core. Framing spaced minimum 5 mm from masonry core.

- Type 3 walls should only be used with a concrete ground floor construction in order to prevent air paths under the floor.
- At the junction with the external wall panels the joint should be sealed with mastic or tape. The external wall panel should be one of the specified types (see E and F, Table 10.3) and should not be fixed to the external wall.
- At the junction with a load-bearing partition the joint should be sealed with mastic or tape. The partition should be fixed to the

masonry core through a padding of mineral fibre quilt. It should *not* be of masonry construction.

AD E1/2/3
sec. 1
wall Type 3

● A non-load-bearing partition should be tightly butted against the lightweight panel and the joint should be filled with mastic or tape. Again, the partition should not be of masonry construction.

Timber frame (wall Type 4) – direct transmission
This form of construction relies mainly on the use of two isolated frames together with a degree of sound absorption in the air space in order to minimise the transmission of sound.

It is essential to isolate the frames from one another as far as possible. If it is necessary for structural reasons to connect the frames together this may be done using 14 to 16 gauge metal straps fixed below ceiling level and spaced a minimum horizontal distance of 1·2 m apart.

The detailing of services is important and the following rules should be observed:

● Avoid service penetrations where possible as these may create air paths.
● Electric power points may penetrate the wall cladding if they are backed by a similar thickness of cladding behind the socket box.
● Power points should not be placed back to back.

Fire stops are necessary in this form of construction (see Chapter 7, Fire). These should preferably be flexible but if rigid they should be fixed to only one frame.

Table 10.4 gives details of two basic forms of timber frame construction.

Timber frame (wall Type 4) – flanking transmission
Many of the principles already discussed for wall Type 2 also apply to timber frame walls. The main requirement is to seal the wall cavity from the rooms on each side at all junctions. Some alternative details are permitted as listed below and illustrated in Fig. 10.5:

● In the roofspace both frames may be carried through and the cladding finish reduced to a minimum of 25 mm. Alternatively, the cavity may be closed at ceiling level (but not with a rigid connection), and one frame may be continued through provided it has at least 25 mm of cladding on each side.
● At floor level the cladding may be carried through the floor thickness. Alternatively any detail may be used that will block the air paths between the rooms and the wall cavity.

AD E1/2/3
sec. 1
wall Type 4

● At the junction with an external cavity wall the air path in the cavity should be blocked to minimise transmission of sound via the cavity.

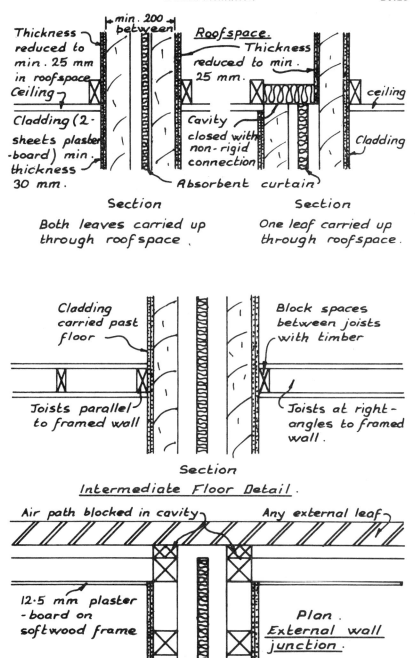

Thickness reduced to min. 25 mm in roofspace
Ceiling
Cladding (2-sheets plaster-board) min. thickness 30 mm.

min. 200 between

Roofspace.
Thickness reduced to min. 25 mm.

Cavity closed with non-rigid connection
Absorbent curtain

ceiling
Cladding

Section
Both leaves carried up through roofspace.

Section
One leaf carried up through roofspace.

Cladding carried past floor

Joists parallel to framed wall

Block spaces between joists with timber

Joists at right-angles to framed wall.

Section
Intermediate Floor Detail.

Air path blocked in cavity

Any external leaf

12.5 mm plaster-board on softwood frame

Plan.
External wall junction.

Fig. 10.5 Flanking transmission – wall Type 4.

Table 10.4 Timber Frame – Wall Type 4.

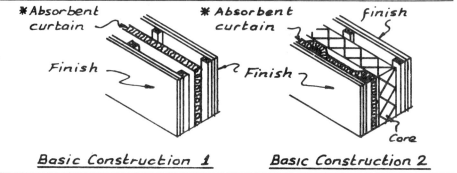

Wall specification	Core	Finish	Remarks
Basic construction 1	—	Minimum two sheets plasterboard (with or without plywood sheathing) at least 30 mm thickness.	Joints between sheets staggered to avoid air paths. *Mineral fibre quilt between frames (see below).
Basic construction 2	Brickwork or blockwork of any thickness.	As above.	As above.

Notes
* Absorbent curtain specification: Unfaced mineral fibre quilt (may be wire reinforced) of minimum density 12 kg/m³.
  Minimum thickness: 25mm if suspended in cavity between frames.
               50mm if fixed to one frame.

Refuse chutes

Special rules apply to walls separating refuse chutes from dwellings due to the excessive noise that may be generated.

A wall which separates any habitable room in a dwelling from any refuse chute in the same building should have an average mass (calculated over any portion of the wall measuring 1 metre square and including the mass of any plaster), of not less than 1320 kg/m².

A wall which separates any part of a dwelling other than a habitable room, from any refuse chute in the same building, should have an average mass (calculated over any portion of the wall measuring 1 metre square and including the mass of any plaster) of not less than 220 kg/m².

AD E1/2/3
sec. 1
1.4

Thus, if a refuse chute is placed next to a kitchen, scullery, etc., the wall between need only be a half brick wall (see Fig. 10.6).

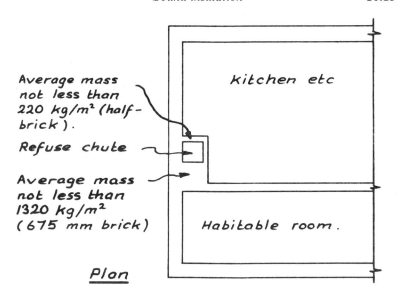

Average mass not less than 220 kg/m² (half-brick).

Refuse chute

Average mass not less than 1320 kg/m² (675 mm brick)

kitchen etc

Habitable room.

<u>Plan</u>

Fig. 10.6 Refuse chute separation.

Floors

Airborne sound

A floor which,

Regs Sch. 1
E2

(a) separates a dwelling from another dwelling; or,
(b) separates a dwelling from another part of the same building which is not used exclusively with that dwelling;

must be so constructed as to provide reasonable resistance to the transmission of *airborne* sound.

As with the requirements for walls, floors between dwellings and areas of a building that are used only for occasional repair or maintenance of the building, its services and its fixed plant or machinery are excluded from the requirements for sound insulation.

Regs Sch. 1
E2

Impact sound

A floor *above* a dwelling which,

Regs Sch. 1
E3

(a) separates it from another dwelling; or,
(b) separates it from another part of the same building which is not used exclusively with that dwelling;

must be so constructed as to provide reasonable resistance to the transmission of *impact* sound.

The exclusion mentioned above for airborne sound insulation also

Regs Sch. 1
E3
applies to impact sound. These requirements are illustrated in Fig. 10.7.

AD E1/2/3 again provides two ways of satisfying the requirements of the building regulations for airborne and impact sound insulation of floors:

AD E1/2/3
sec. 2
(i) A series of examples of commonly used forms of construction is given which may be adopted by the building designer; or,

AD E1/2/3
sec. 3
(ii) A form of construction may be repeated which has been used in a similar building and has been shown by tests to be acceptable.

Typical floor constructions

Three main types of floor construction are described in section 2 of AD E1/2/3 – concrete base with soft covering, concrete base with floating layer and timber base with floating layer. A selection of examples of each floor construction is given together with details of how to avoid flanking transmission at junctions between elements.

Concrete based floors (Types 1 and 2) – direct and flanking transmission
The weight of the concrete base (including any bonded screed, ceiling finish or floating layer), is the principal factor in determining resistance to airborne sound for these floor constructions. Impact sound is reduced by the soft covering or floating layer. Where airborne sound insulation alone is required the soft covering may be omitted from floor Type 1. Table 10.5 gives details of four common floor base constructions which will satisfy the requirements for adequate resistance to direct sound transmission.

The soft covering should consist of a resilient material (i.e. one that will return to its original thickness after being compressed) at least 4·5 mm thick. No guidance is given in AD E1/2/3 concerning the actual material to be used. However, rubber or sponge rubber underlay has proved satisfactory in the past. The floating layer should consist of a timber raft or screed on a layer of mineral fibre at least 13 mm thick (with a minimum density of 36 kg/m^2). A screeded finish may also rest on precompressed expanded polystyrene boarding provided this is of impact sound duty grade. Figure 10.8 shows typical details for floor Type 2. It should be noted that any of the concrete base specifications shown in Table 10.5 are suitable.

Flanking transmission may be avoided by paying attention to detail at the junctions between the sound resisting floor and external walls, internal walls and sound resisting separating walls. Pipe penetrations through floors are unavoidable and may create air paths unless properly detailed.

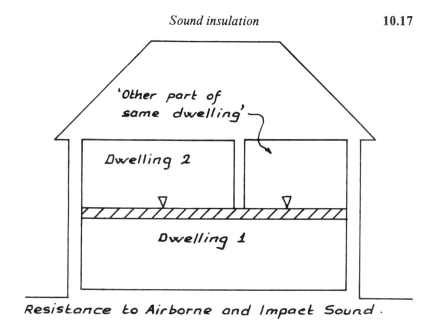

Resistance to Airborne and Impact Sound.

Resistance to Airborne Sound Only.

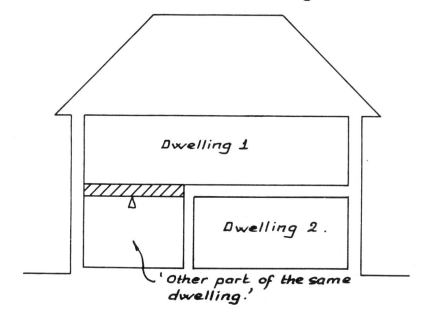

Fig. 10.7 Sound resistance of floors in dwellings.

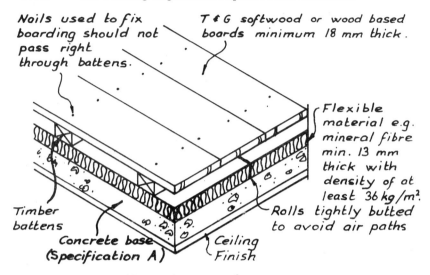

Noils used to fix boarding should not pass right through battens.

T & G softwood or wood based boards minimum 18 mm thick.

Flexible material e.g. mineral fibre min. 13 mm thick with density of at least 36 kg/m².

Rolls tightly butted to avoid air paths

Timber battens

Concrete base (Specification A)

Ceiling Finish

Floating Floor (Specification E) with Resilient Layer (Specification G)

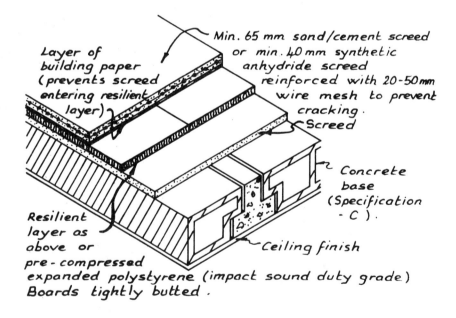

Layer of building paper (prevents screed entering resilient layer)

Min. 65 mm sand/cement screed or min. 40 mm synthetic anhydride screed reinforced with 20-50mm wire mesh to prevent cracking.

Screed

Concrete base (Specification - C).

Resilient layer as above or pre-compressed expanded polystyrene (impact sound duty grade) Boards tightly butted.

Ceiling finish

Floating Floor (Specification F) with Resilient Layer (Specification H).

Fig. 10.8 Sound insulation – floor Type 2.

Table 10.5. Concrete base – floor Types 1 and 2

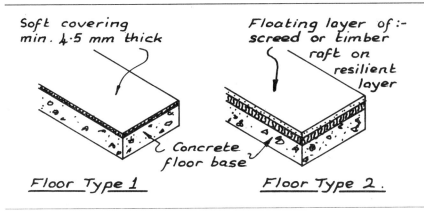

Floor base specification	Floor construction Type 1[1]	Floor construction Type 2[2]	Remarks
A	Solid concrete slab of minimum weight 365 kg/m².	Solid concrete slab of minimum weight 220 kg/m².	Weight of screed or bonded ceiling finish may be included.
B	Solid concrete slab with permanent shuttering of min. weight 365 kg/m².	Solid concrete slab with permanent shuttering of min. weight 220 kg/m².	Weight of concrete or metal shuttering, screed or bonded ceiling finish may be included.
C	Concrete beams with infilling blocks of minimum weight 365 kg/m².	Concrete beams with infilling blocks of minimum weight 220 kg/m².	Weight of clay or concrete blocks, screed or bonded ceiling finish may be included. Fill joints between beams and blocks.
D	Hollow concrete beams of minimum weight 365 kg/m².	Hollow concrete beams of minimum weight 220 kg/m².	Weight of screed or bonded ceiling finish may be included. Fill joints between beams.

Notes
[1] Full specification includes soft covering
[2] Full specification includes floating layer

Floor/wall junctions

As has already been mentioned, an external wall which is divided up by windows or similar openings will not vibrate freely and will, therefore, be less likely to allow flanking transmission. Accordingly, if the area of the openings is 20% or less of the area of the external wall the weight of the wall (or the inner leaf if it is a cavity wall) should not be less than 120 kg/m^2 (including plaster but *not* dry lining). For areas in excess of 20% there are no restrictions.

As a general rule the concrete floor base should pass through the wall (this does not apply to the screed which should be stopped off against the wall surface). If, however, the wall is a sound resisting or internal solid wall weighing 355 kg/m^2 or more the floor base *or* the wall may be passed through. In the latter case the floor base should be tied to the wall and the joint grouted.

If the floor base is of concrete beam construction (i.e. specification C or D) the first joint should be at least 300 mm from the outside face of the wall (or the outside face of the inner leaf of a cavity wall).

Special rules apply to floors with floating layers (Type 2) as follows:

- The wall finish may be plaster or dry lining.
- The resilient layer should be carried up against the wall to isolate the floating floor.
- A gap of at least 3 mm should be left between the floating floor and the skirting and this should be sealed with acrylic caulk or neoprene (this allows slight movement of the floating floor without air gaps being created).

Penetration of floors by pipes
Pipes usually penetrate floors adjacent to a wall. Whatever the weight of the wall the floor base should always be carried through the wall where pipes penetrate the floor.

The pipe should be run in a duct cased with a board material weighing at least 15 kg/m^2. The pipe and any branches within the duct should be wrapped in a minimum thickness of 25 mm of mineral fibre. The resilient layer should be carried up against the pipe wrapping to isolate the floating floor and a 3 mm gap should be left between floating floor and skirting and sealed as described above (see Figs 10.9 and 10.10).

AD E1/2/3
sec. 2
floor Types
1 & 2

Timber based floors (Type 3) – direct and flanking transmission
Since a timber floor radiates sound less efficiently than a concrete floor it may be constructed of lighter materials. The timber floor specifications described in AD E1/2/3 rely on the weights of the elements of the structural floor, pugging and the absorbent blanket to reduce airborne sound and the floating layer to reduce impact sound. They are similar in concept to floor Type 2 but consist entirely of timber.

The three floor specifications described in AD E1/2/3 are similar in form, the main differences being in the positioning of the resilient strip or layer (which reduces impact sound) and in the use of an absorbent blanket or pugging (to reduce airborne sound). Figure 10.11 gives full details of each floor specification.

Floor and wall junctions need careful detailing to avoid flanking transmission. Pipe penetrations can be dealt with as described above for Type 1 and 2 floors although it will be necessary to seal the joint between the duct casing and ceiling with, for example, tape or coving.

The main problem with Type 3 floors is the need to isolate the floating layer from the structural part of the floor (i.e. the floor joist) at the point of junction with a wall. The gap between the wall and the floating layer should be sealed with mineral fibre or a plastics foam strip glued to the wall. The junction between the ceiling and wall lining should also be sealed with tape. Figure 10.12 illustrates the main design principles that should be adopted at wall/floor junctions for Type 3 floors. Floor specification A has been used in the diagrams as an example, but any of the three specifications would be satisfactory.

AD E1/2/3
sec. 2
floor Type 3

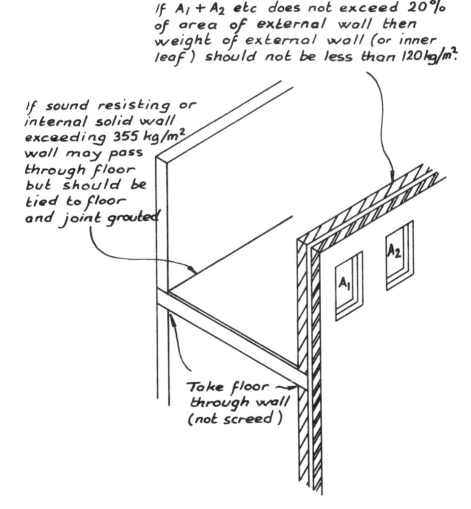

If A₁ + A₂ etc does not exceed 20% of area of external wall then weight of external wall (or inner leaf) should not be less than 120 kg/m².

If sound resisting or internal solid wall exceeding 355 kg/m² wall may pass through floor but should be tied to floor and joint grouted

Take floor through wall (not screed)

Fig. 10.9 Floor/wall junctions – general rules (Type 1 and 2 floors).

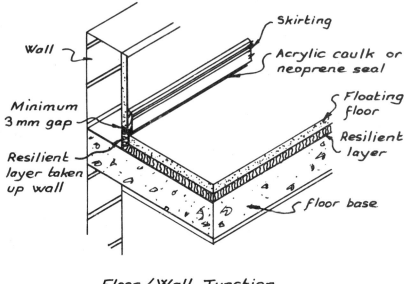

Skirting

Wall

Acrylic caulk or neoprene seal

Floating floor

Minimum 3 mm gap

Resilient layer

Resilient layer taken up wall

floor base

Floor / Wall Junction
Floor Type 2 .

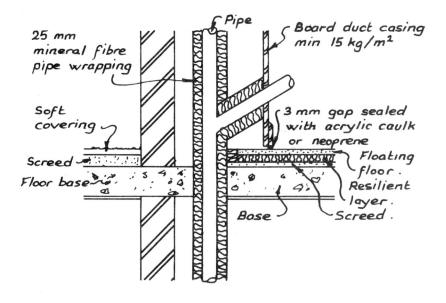

25 mm mineral fibre pipe wrapping

Pipe

Board duct casing min 15 kg/m²

Soft covering

3 mm gap sealed with acrylic caulk or neoprene

Screed

Floating floor .

Floor base

Resilient layer .

Base

Screed .

Penetration of Floor by Pipes .

Fig. 10.10 Floor/wall junctions – details (Type 1 and 2 floors).

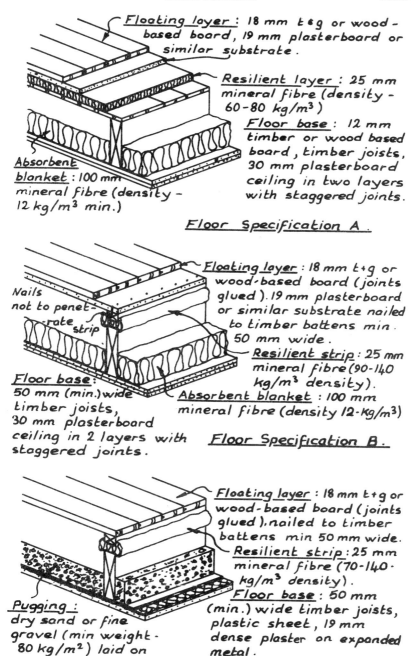

Floating layer : 18 mm t&g or wood-based board, 19 mm plasterboard or similar substrate.

Resilient layer : 25 mm mineral fibre (density - 60-80 kg/m³)

Floor base : 12 mm timber or wood based board, timber joists, 30 mm plasterboard ceiling in two layers with staggered joints.

Absorbent blanket : 100 mm mineral fibre (density - 12 kg/m³ min.)

Floor Specification A.

Floating layer : 18 mm t+g or wood-based board (joints glued). 19 mm plasterboard or similar substrate nailed to timber battens min. 50 mm wide.

Nails not to penet-rate strip

Resilient strip : 25 mm mineral fibre (90-140 kg/m³ density).

Floor base : 50 mm (min.) wide timber joists, 30 mm plasterboard ceiling in 2 layers with staggered joints.

Absorbent blanket : 100 mm mineral fibre (density 12·kg/m³)

Floor Specification B.

Floating layer : 18 mm t+g or wood-based board (joints glued), nailed to timber battens min 50 mm wide.

Resilient strip : 25 mm mineral fibre (70-140· kg/m³ density).

Floor base : 50 mm (min.) wide timber joists, plastic sheet, 19 mm dense plaster on expanded metal.

Pugging : dry sand or fine gravel (min weight - 80 kg/m²) laid on ceiling.

Floor Specification C.

Fig. 10.11 Timber base (with floating layer). Floor Type 3.

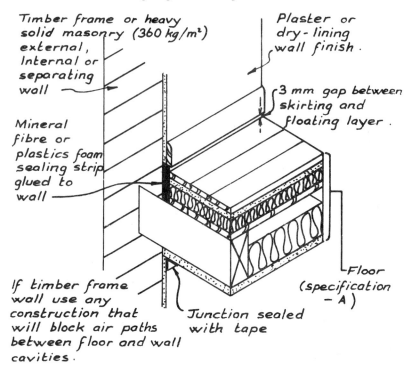

Timber frame or heavy solid masonry (360 kg/m²) external, Internal or separating wall

Plaster or dry-lining wall finish.

3 mm gap between skirting and floating layer.

Mineral fibre or plastics foam sealing strip glued to wall

If timber frame wall use any construction that will block air paths between floor and wall cavities.

Junction sealed with tape

Floor (specification - A)

Timber Frame or Heavy Solid Masonry Wall Junction

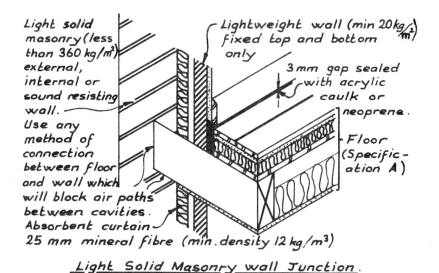

Light solid masonry (less than 360 kg/m²) external, internal or sound resisting wall.
Use any method of connection between floor and wall which will block air paths between cavities.
Absorbent curtain 25 mm mineral fibre (min. density 12 kg/m³)

Lightweight wall (min 20 kg/m²) fixed top and bottom only

3 mm gap sealed with acrylic caulk or neoprene.

Floor (Specification A)

Light Solid Masonry wall Junction.

Fig. 10.12 Wall/floor junctions – Type 3 floors.

Weights of masonry walls

Throughout section 1 and section 2 of AD E1/2/3 reference is made to minimum required weights for masonry components (including finishes where applicable).

These weights are expressed in kilograms per square metre (kg/m²) and therefore, no reference is made to the thickness of the walls specified.

In order that these weights can be translated into wall thicknesses, AD E1/2/3 contains two appendices with accompanying tables where various brick and block types are listed together with their respective weights and thicknesses. Appendix A deals with masonry separating walls and Appendix B with masonry walls abutting separating floors.

Homogeneous walls of either in situ concrete or large pre-cast concrete panels are not dealt with in the tables to Appendices A or B. However, the density of the concrete used should not be less than 2300 kg/m³ for natural aggregate concrete or 1760 kg/m³ for no-fines concrete. A moisture content of 3% by volume is assumed. Tables A and B from the Appendices to AD E1/2/3 are reproduced below.

AD E1/2/3
Appendix A
&
Appendix B

AD E1/2/3 *Appendix A*

Table A   Weights for blocks

Wall			Plaster finish		Average weight of brick to be used [kg]
Material and Dimensions [mm]	**Thickness**	**Specified weight at least [kg/m²]**	**Number of sides**	**Type**	
A Brickwork		300	—	—	1.84 (frog down)
brick size [mm] 65 × 102.5 × 215					1.47 (frog up)
		355	—	—	1.93 (frog up)
	215	375	2	lightweight	1.93 (frog up)
			2	gypsum	1.81 (frog up)
cavity wall	255	415	2	lightweight	2.42 (frog up)
			2	gypsum	2.31 (frog up)

Table **A**   **Weights for blocks** *(cont.)*

Wall			Plaster finish		Average weight of block to be used [kg]
Material and Dimensions [mm]	**Thickness**	**Specified weight at least [kg/m²]**	**Number of sides**	**Type**	
B Concrete blockwork block size [mm] 100 × 215 × 440 laid flat	215	160	—	—	5.8
		200	—	—	7.8
		300	—	—	14.2*
laid flat	215	415	2	lightweight	17.5
			2	gypsum	16.7
cavity wall	250	250	2	lightweight	10.45
			2	gypsum	9.74
		415	2	lightweight	18.9
			2	gypsum	18.1
block size [mm] 215 × 215 × 440	215	160	—	—	13.6
		200	—	—	17.7
		300	—	—	31.2*
	215	415	2	lightweight	37.4
			2	gypsum	36.0

Notes

* The weight is increased to achieve the minimum density.
 The average weight of the brick or concrete block to be used depends on achieving at least the following values for mortar and plaster:

(a) mortar – 1800 kg/m³ in joints 10 mm thick
(b) plaster – lightweight 10 kg/m²
                gypsum 17 kg/m².
Take the weight of concrete blocks at a moisture content of 3 per cent by volume.

AD E1/2/3 *Appendix B*

Table B Weights for bricks and blocks

Material and Dimensions [mm]	Orientation	Specified weight at least [kg/m²]	Number of sides	Type	Average weight of brick or block to be used [kg]
A Brickwork		355	—	—	1.93
brick size [mm] 65 × 102.5 × 215			1	lightweight	1.85
				gypsum	1.79
			2	lightweight	1.76
laid with frog up				gypsum	1.64
B Concrete blockwork		120	—	—	11.0
			1	lightweight	9.9
block size [mm] 100 × 215 × 440			1	gypsum	9.2
		355	—	—	15.4
			1	lightweight	15.0
				gypsum	14.6
			2	lightweight	14.5
blocks laid flat				gypsum	13.8
block size [mm] 215 × 215 × 440		355	—	—	33.4
			1	lightweight	32.4
				gypsum	31.7
			2	lightweight	31.4
				gypsum	29.9

The column headers span: **Wall** (Material and Dimensions, Orientation, Specified weight at least) and **Plaster finish** (Number of sides, Type).

Notes

The average weight of the brick or concrete block to be used depends on achieving at least the following values for mortar and plaster:

(a) mortar – 1800 kg/m³ in joints 10 mm thick
(b) plaster – lightweight 10 kg/m², gypsum 17 kg/m².

Take the weight of concrete blocks at a moisture content of 3 per cent by volume.

Repeated construction

Sections 1 and 2 of AD E1/2/3 are discussed above and deal with typical wall and floor construction details that may be adopted by a designer in order to satisfy Part E of Schedule 1 to the Building Regulations 1985.

Section 3 of AD E1/2/3 provides ways of meeting the regulation requirements by repeating an existing form of construction.

In order to do this two prerequisites must be met:

AD E1/2/3
sec. 3
3.1 & 3.2

(i) the existing wall or floor construction must be shown to be satisfactory; and,

(ii) the existing and proposed designs must be sufficiently similar.

Existing construction – assessment of performance

In order that the performance of an existing wall or floor may be assessed it is necessary to carry out tests in accordance with the method given in BS 2750 *Methods of measurement of sound insulation in buildings and of building elements*, Part 4: 1980 *Field measurements of airborne sound insulation between rooms* and Part 7: 1980 *Field measurements of impact sound insulation of floors.*

These tests allow the Standardised Level Differences D_nT for airborne sound insulation and the Standardised Impact Sound Pressure Levels L^1_nT for impact sound transmission to be determined.

From these values it is possible to calculate the Weighted Standardised Level Difference $D_nT_{,w}$ for airborne sound and the Weighted Standardised Sound Pressure Level $L^1_nT_{,w}$ for impact sound. These terms are defined in BS 5821: British Standard *Method for rating the sound insulation in buildings and of building elements*, Part 1: 1984 *Method for rating the airborne sound insulation in buildings and of building elements*, Part 2: 1984 *Method for rating the impact sound insulation.*

Table 1 to section 3 of AD E1/2/3 (see below) shows the values of $D_nT_{,w}$ and $L^1_nT_{,w}$ which should be achieved.

The test programme should be carried out in accordance with the following rules:

- Floors and walls should be tested between at least four pairs of rooms and there should be at least one habitable room in each pair.
- Only one set of measurements should be taken between each pair of rooms.
- The sound source should be placed in the larger room if both are habitable rooms.

AD E1/2/3
sec. 3
3.3 & 3.4

- If one room is a non-habitable room the sound source should be placed in that room.

AD E1/2/3 section 3

Table **1**   **Sound transmission values**

Type of performance	Mean values		
	Individual values	Test in at least 4 pairs of rooms	Test in at least 8 pairs of rooms
Airborne sound (minimum values)*	49 (walls) 48 (floors)	53 (walls) 52 (floors)	52 (walls) 51 (floors)
Impact sound (maximum values)**	65	61	62

Notes
*   Airborne sound – Weighted Standardised Level Difference ($D_nT_{,w}$)
** Impact sound – Weighted Standardised Sound Pressure Level (L_nT_w)

Existing constructions – degree of similarity

The degree of sound insulation provided by a certain form of construction depends not only on the wall or floor specification but also on other factors, such as size and shape of rooms and, for masonry buildings, the positions of the doors and windows.

Thus, in order that a satisfactory comparison may be made the following features of a proposed building should be similar to, but not necessarily identical with, an existing building:

● Specification of sound resisting walls and floors.
● The construction of walls and floors adjacent to the sound resisting walls and floors.
● The general arrangement of window and door openings where these are in an external wall with a masonry inner leaf and are adjacent to a sound resisting wall or floor.
● The general size and shape of the rooms on either side of sound resisting construction.
● The extent of any step or stagger in a sound resisting wall. It may be beneficial to provide a step or stagger in a proposed wall if one is not present in the existing building.

AD E1/2/3
sec. 3
3.5 to 3.7

AD E1/2/3 specifies certain allowable differences in details that have little effect on the performance of sound resisting elements. For example, the performance of sound resisting walls and floors is unlikely to be affected by the construction of a masonry cavity wall provided the inner leaf is of the same general type and its weight is not reduced.

In the case of sound resisting walls the following differences in construction are unlikely to reduce their performance:

- The material and thickness of the flooring of a Type 2 or Type 3 floor.
- A small reduction in the size of a step or stagger.

AD E1/2/3
sec. 3
3.8 & 3.9

- The type of timber floor provided, where it is not required to be sound resisting.

AD E1/2/3
sec. 3
3.10

It should be noted that whilst the test procedure and the values in Table 1 to AD E1/2/3 are provided to enable an *existing* construction to be assessed before new construction is undertaken the subsequent failure of the *new* construction to achieve the values in Table 1 is not of itself evidence of failure to comply with the requirements of the Building Regulations 1985.

Chapter 11

Ventilation

Introduction

The need to provide adequate ventilation to buildings has long been recognised in building control legislation. Formerly, however, it only applied to dwellings or buildings containing dwellings. The building regulations now extend this requirement to any building which contains bathrooms or rooms containing sanitary conveniences.

The regulations no longer contain any requirement for zones of open space outside the windows of habitable rooms, nor any control over ceiling heights. It is now permissible to ventilate one room via the windows in an adjoining room provided there is a permanent opening between the rooms of not less than $1/20$th of the combined floor area.

The latest changes have introduced the requirement for mechanical extract ventilation in kitchens, bathrooms and shower rooms. Also, in addition to normal ventilation through windows, etc., kitchens and habitable rooms in dwellings are required to have background ventilation. Minor changes have also been made in the regulations dealing with roof void ventilation. Significantly, some small roof areas have been excluded from the requirements.

Means of ventilation

In dwellings, common spaces in buildings containing two or more dwellings, bathrooms and rooms containing sanitary conveniences there must be adequate means of ventilation provided for people in the building.

Regs Sch. 1
F1

The provisions of Approved Document F1 are designed to ensure that suitable air quality is maintained in buildings.

AD F1

Without adequate ventilation, moisture (leading to mould growth) and pollutants (originating inside a building) may accumulate to such levels that they become a hazard to the health of users of the building.

The comfort and security of people in buildings must not be compromised by the means of ventilation if it is to be effectively used.

Interpretation

Special definitions apply to AD F1.

VENTILATION OPENING – includes any permanent or closeable means of ventilation which opens directly to external air as follows:

- opening lights in windows,
- louvres,
- airbricks,
- progressively openable ventilators,
- window trickle ventilators,
- doors.

Ventilation openings (especially in airbricks, trickle and progressively openable ventilators) should have a minimum dimension of at least 8 mm to prevent resistance to air flow. This would not of course apply to screens, baffles and vented fascias.

COMMON SPACE – a space associated with two or more dwellings.

HABITABLE ROOM – a room used for dwelling purposes but not including a kitchen.

BATHROOM – also means a shower room.

SANITARY ACCOMMODATION – a room which contains one or more closets or urinals. If sanitary accommodation contains one or more cubicles it is not necessary to provide separate ventilation to each if air is free to circulate throughout the space.

AD F1
0.2 to 0.6

General requirements

As a general rule ventilation may be provided by both natural and mechanical means. However, AD F1 *requires* that mechanical extract ventilation be provided in kitchens, bathrooms and shower rooms since in these rooms natural ventilation may be unable to cope with the quantities of moisture produced.

Natural ventilation

Kitchens and habitable rooms in dwellings should be provided with *background ventilation* which is controllable, secure and located to avoid draughts. This may be achieved by a ventilation opening with a total area of at least 4000 mm^2 (e.g. airbrick or trickle ventilator).

AD F1
0.7

The following rooms should have one or more ventilation openings

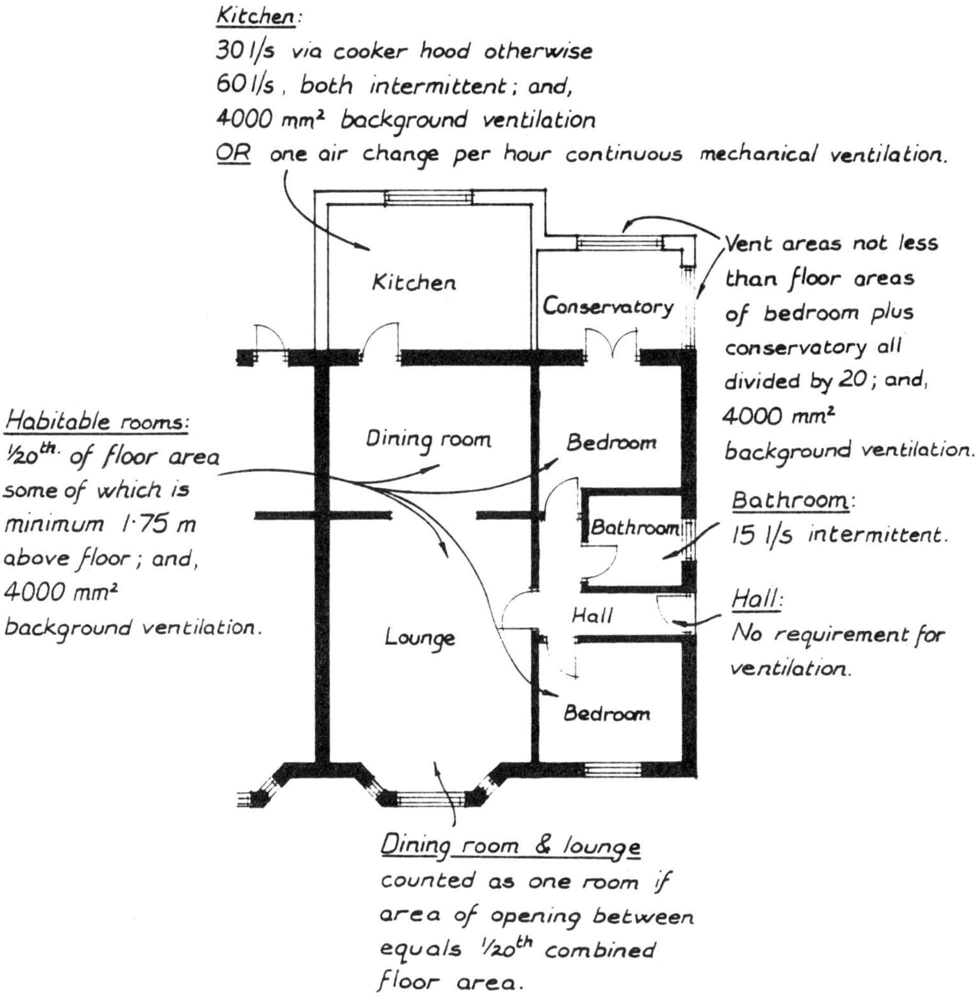

Kitchen:
30 l/s via cooker hood otherwise
60 l/s, both intermittent; and,
4000 mm² background ventilation
OR one air change per hour continuous mechanical ventilation.

Kitchen

Conservatory

Vent areas not less
than floor areas
of bedroom plus
conservatory all
divided by 20; and,
4000 mm²
background ventilation.

Habitable rooms:
1/20th of floor area
some of which is
minimum 1·75 m
above floor; and,
4000 mm²
background ventilation.

Dining room

Bedroom

Bathroom:
15 l/s intermittent.

Bathroom

Hall:
No requirement for
ventilation.

Hall

Lounge

Bedroom

Dining room & lounge
counted as one room if
area of opening between
equals 1/20th combined
floor area.

Fig. 11.1 Ventilation requirements in dwellings.

with an area of not less than $^1/_{20}$th of their floor area in order to provide *rapid ventilation*:

- habitable rooms in dwellings,
- sanitary accommodation in any building.

Additionally, some part of the required opening area should be at least 1.75 m above floor level.

Common spaces should have one or more ventilation openings with an area not less than $^1/_{50}$th of the floor area of the space (see Fig. 11.1).

Mechanical ventilation

For kitchens in dwellings, bathrooms in any building and where natural ventilation is not provided, AD F1 allows the use of mechanical ventilation. However, there seems to be some uncertainty in the Approved Document as to the best method of specifying air movement rates. This results in litres/sec (l/s) being quoted for kitchens and bathrooms whereas air changes per hour (ac/h) are quoted for common spaces and sanitary accommodation.

Ventilation to bathrooms and sanitary accommodation is permitted to be intermittent but in the latter case the fan must continue for a minimum of 15 minutes after the room has been left. This is usually achieved by connecting the extractor fan to the light switch, the fan continuing to operate for at least 15 minutes after the light is switched off.

The above requirements regarding natural and mechanical ventilation are summarised in Table 11.1 below.

AD F1
1.1 to 5.1

Alternative method

The requirements of Regulation F1 may also be satisfied by:

(a) providing mechanical ventilation capable of continuous operation throughout the dwelling; or,
(b) following clauses 2.3.2.1, 2.5.2.10, 2.5.2.11 and 3.1.1.1 of BS 5720: 1979 *Code of Practice for mechanical ventilation and air conditioning in buildings*; or,
(c) following clauses 9.8 and 9.9 of BS 5250: 1989 *Code of Practice: the control of condensation in buildings*.

Ventilation

Ventilating habitable rooms through adjoining rooms or spaces

AD F1
6.1

For ventilation purposes two habitable rooms or spaces may be treated as one if there is a permanent opening between them with an area equal to $\frac{1}{20}$th of their combined floor areas.

Table 11.1 Ventilation Requirements

	1 Room or space	2 Natural Ventilation (opening areas)	3 Mechanical Ventilation (extraction rates)
1	**In dwellings**		
(a)	Habitable rooms	Rapid ventilation: ventilation opening equal to at least $\frac{1}{20}$th room floor area. Some part at least 1.75 m above floor. Background ventilation: Ventilation opening equal to at least 4000 mm^2	*
(b)	Kitchens		Rapid ventilation: 60 litres/sec or 30 litres/ sec if in cooker hood. These rates may be intermittent (i.e. operated during cooking)
		Background Ventilation: *Either:* Ventilation opening equal to at least 4000 mm^2	*Or:* Continuous operation at one air change per hour
2	**In building containing dwellings**		
(a)	Common spaces	*Either:* Ventilation opening equal to at least $\frac{1}{50}$th floor area if common space or communicating common spaces	*Or:* One air change per hour if common space is wholly internal
3	**In any building**		
(a)	Sanitary accommodation	Rapid Ventilation: *Either:* Ventilation opening equal to $\frac{1}{20}$th room floor area. Some part at least 1.75 m above floor	*Or:* Three air changes per hour operated intermittently with 15 minute overrun
(b)	Bathrooms	No requirement specified in AD F1	15 litres/sec operated intermittently

Note. * No requirement specified in AD F1 but see BS 5720: 1979 *Code of practice for mechanical ventilation and air conditioning in buildings.*

A habitable room opening on to a conservatory or similar space, may be treated as one room with the conservatory for the purposes of ventilation. The opening between the room and conservatory (which may contain a door or window, for example) should comply with 6.1 above. The area of ventilation opening is required to be equal to $^1/_{20}$th of the combined floor area of room and conservatory, and again some part of it must be at least 1.75 m above floor level. Additionally, background ventilation must be provided to comply with Table 11.1 for both the conservatory and the enclosed room (see Fig. 11.1).

AD F1
6.2

Ventilation openings into courts

A ventilation opening serving a habitable room should not open into a totally enclosed court unless the distance from the vent opening to the opposite wall of the court is either:

(a) 15 m or more; or,
(b) at least half the vertical distance from the top of the vent opening to the top of the wall.

AD F1
6.3(a)

Where a court is unobstructed on one side, and its length from that side is more than twice its width, no vent opening should open on to it unless:

(a) the vent opening is in one of the longer sides, at a distance from the unobstructed side of less than twice the width of the court; or,
(b) the vent opening is in one of the longer sides and its distance from the opposite side is either:

    (i) 15 m or more, or
    (ii) at least half the vertical distance from the top of the vent opening to the top of the wall (see Fig. 11.2).

AD F1
6.3(b)

Condensation in roofs

In buildings, adequate provision must be made to prevent excessive condensation in roofs and roof voids over insulated ceilings.
When condensation occurs in roof spaces it can have two main effects:

Regs Sch. 1
F2

AD F2

(a) the thermal performance of the insulant materials may be reduced by the presence of the water; and,
(b) the structural performance of the roof may be affected due to increased risk of fungal attack.

Approved Document F2 requires that, under normal conditions, condensation in roofs and in spaces above insulated ceilings should be

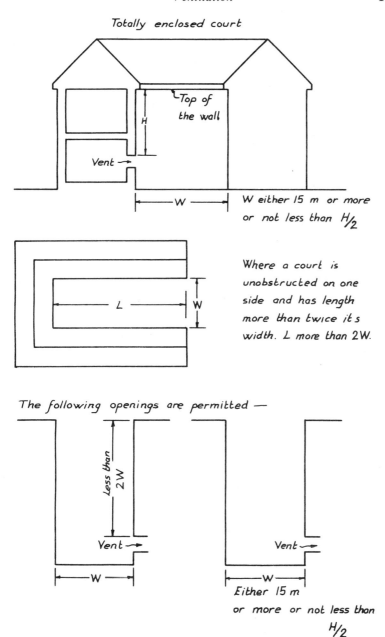

Fig. 11.2 Ventilation openings into courts.

limited such that the thermal and structural performance of the roof will not be substantially and permanently reduced.

AD F2 applies only to roofs where the insulation is placed at ceiling level (cold roofs) irrespective of whether the ceiling is flat or pitched. Warm roofs where the insulation is placed above the structural system and roof void do not present the same risks and, therefore, are not covered.

It should be noted that the provisions of AD F2 apply to roofs of any pitch even though a roof which exceeds 70° in pitch is required to be insulated as if it were a wall.

Small roofs over porches or bay windows, etc., may sometimes be excluded from the requirements of regulation F2 if there is no risk to health or safety.

AD F2
0.1 to 0.6

Roofs with a pitch of 15° or more

Pitched roofs should be cross-ventilated by permanent vents at eaves level on the two opposite sides of the roof, the vent areas being equivalent in area to a continuous gap along each side of 10 mm width.

AD F2
1.2

Mono-pitch or lean-to roofs should have ventilation at eaves level as above and also at high level either at the point of junction or through the roof covering at the highest practicable point. The high level ventilation should be equivalent in area to a continuous gap 5 mm wide (see Fig. 11.3).

AD F2
1.4

Roofs with a pitch of less than 15°

In low-pitched roofs the volume of air contained in the void is less and therefore the risk of saturation is greater.

This also applies to roofs with pitch greater than 15° where the ceiling follows the pitch of the roof. High level ventilation should be provided as in 1.4 above.

AD F2
2.1 & 2.5

Cross-ventilation should again be provided at eaves level but the ventilation gap should be increased to 25 mm width.

AD F2
2.2

Where the roof span exceeds 10 m or the roof plan is other than a simple rectangle, more ventilation, totalling 0.6% of the roof area, may be required.

AD F2
2.3

A free air space of at least 50 mm should be provided between the roof deck and the insulation. This may need to be formed using counter-battens if the joists run at right angles to the flow of air (see Fig. 11.4).

AD F2
2.4

Where it is not possible to provide proper cross-ventilation an alternative form of roof construction should be considered.

AD F2
2.6

It is possible to install vapour checks at ceiling level using polythene or foil-backed plasterboard, etc., to reduce the amount of moisture reaching the roof void. This is not acceptable as an alternative to ventilation unless a complete vapour barrier is installed.

AD F2
2.7

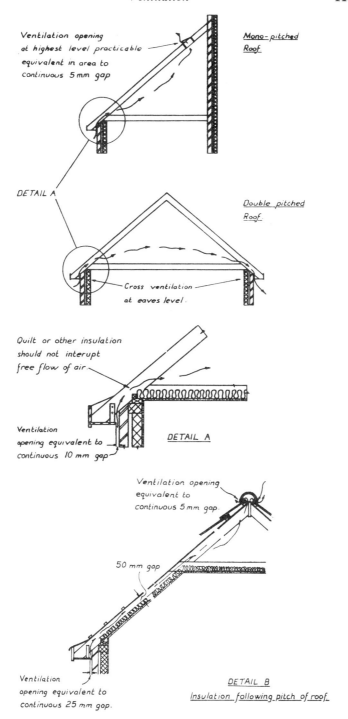

Fig. 11.3 Roof void ventilation – roofs pitched at 15° or more.

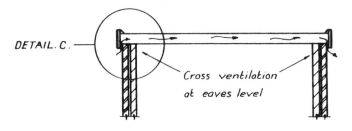

DETAIL. C.

Cross ventilation
at eaves level

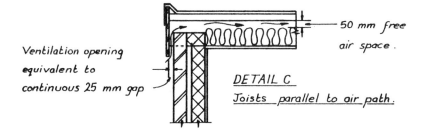

Ventilation opening
equivalent to
continuous 25 mm gap

50 mm free
air space.

DETAIL C
Joists parallel to air path.

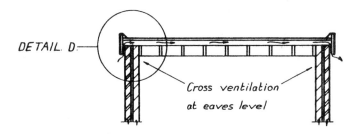

DETAIL. D.

Cross ventilation
at eaves level

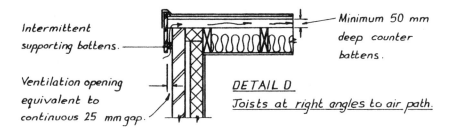

Intermittent
supporting battens.

Ventilation opening
equivalent to
continuous 25 mm gap.

Minimum 50 mm
deep counter
battens.

DETAIL D
Joists at right angles to air path.

Fig. 11.4 Roof void ventilation – roofs pitched at less than 15°.

The requirements can also be met for both flat and pitched roofs by following the relevant recommendations of BS 5250: 1989 *Code of Practice: the control of condensation in buildings*, Clauses 9.1 and 9.3.

AD F2
1.5 & 2.8

Chapter 12

Hygiene

Introduction

When first introduced, Part G of Schedule 1 to the Building Regulations 1985 consisted of four requirements grouped under the title 'Hygiene'.

The first of these requirements (G1 – Food Storage) required that dwellings be provided with adequate food storage accommodation. Since most people have refrigerators or deep freezers today this regulation has become outdated and food storage is no longer controlled by the building regulations.

Two other requirements (relating to bathrooms and the provision of sanitary conveniences) replace the equivalent sections in the Building Act 1984. Regulation G4 has been amended and now requires washing facilities to be provided in or adjacent to rooms containing water-closets.

The fourth requirement relates to unvented hot water storage systems and has been amended for the first time since its introduction in 1985.

Bathrooms

Regs Sch. 1
G2

Dwellings are required to be provided with a bathroom containing a fixed bath or shower. Hot and cold water must also be supplied to the bath or shower. This requirement replaces section 27 of the Building Act 1984.

AD G2

The above requirements apply to dwellings (i.e. houses, flats and maisonettes) and houses in multiple occupation (houses where the occupants are not part of a single household). In the latter case the facility should be available to all the occupants.

AD G2
1.1

AD G2
1.2

The hot and cold water supplies should be piped to the bath or shower and hot water may come from a central source such as a hot water cylinder or from a unit water heater.

The discharge from the bath or shower should be via a trap and waste pipe to a gulley, soil stack pipe or foul drain direct (see Approved

Document H1 and Chapter 13 for details of drainage).

In recent years a system of waste disposal has been developed in which the discharge from a waste appliance is fed into a macerator. The liquified contents are then pumped via a small bore pipe to the normal foul drainage system. AD G2 permits bath or shower wastes to be connected to such a system provided it is the subject of a current British Board of Agrément (BBA) Certificate.

AD G2
1.3

AD G2
1.4

Hot water storage

If a hot water storage system is not vented to the atmosphere adequate precautions must be taken to:

Regs Sch. 1
G3

(a) prevent the water temperature exceeding 100°C; and
(b) ensure that any hot water discharged from safety devices is conveyed safely to a disposal point where it is visible but will not be a danger to users of the building.

The above requirements do not apply to space heating systems, systems which heat or store water for industrial processes and systems which store 15 litres or less of water.

Approved Document G3 describes the provisions for an unvented hot water storage system. In such a system, the stored hot water is heated in a closed vessel. Without adequate safety devices an uncontrolled heat input would cause the water temperature to rise above the boiling point of water at atmospheric pressure (100°C). At the same time the pressure would increase until the vessel burst. This would result in an almost instantaneous conversion of water to steam with the large increase in volume producing a steam explosion.

Water for domestic use is required at temperatures below 100°C, therefore, an explosion cannot occur if the water is released at these temperatures, however great the pressure. Hence the precautions required by regulation G3 to prevent the water temperature exceeding 100°C.

Figure 12.1 illustrates the three independent levels of protection which should be provided for each source of energy supply to the stored water. These are:

● Thermostatic control (see Part L. Chapter 16).
● Non self-resetting thermal cut-outs to BS 3955: 1986 (electrical controls) or BS 4201: 1979 (for gas burning appliances).
● Temperature operated relief valves to BS 6283 *Safety devices for use in hot water systems* Part 2: 1982 or Part 3: 1982.

AD G3
Section 1
1.3

The protection devices are designed to work in sequence as the temperature rises. All three means of protection would have to fail for the water temperature to exceed 100°C.

AD G3 provides separate requirements for smaller (usually domes-

AD G3
Section 1

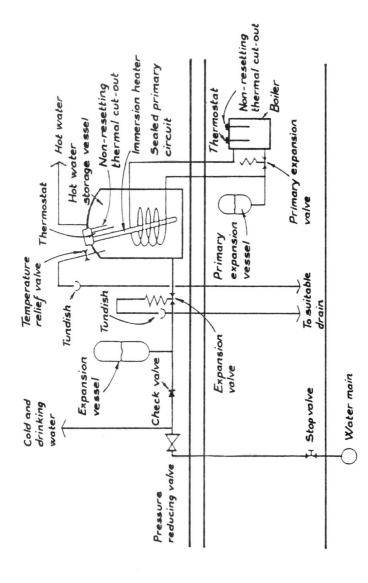

Fig. 12.1 Directly and indirectly heated unvented hot water storage system.

tic) systems (not exceeding 500 litres capacity with a heat input below 45 kW) in section 1. Systems which exceed 500 litres capacity or have a heat input in excess of 45 kW are dealt with in Section 2.

AD G3
Section 2

Section 1 hot water storage systems

A system covered by Section 1 of AD G3 should be in the form of a unit or package which is the subject of a current BBA Certificate. This means that the system should be factory made and supplied either as a *unit* (fitted with all the safety protection devices mentioned above and incorporating any other operating devices to stop primary flow, prevent backflow, control working pressure, relieve excess pressure and accommodate expansion fitted to the unit by the manufacturer) or as a *package* in which the safety devices are fitted by the manufacturer but the operating devices are supplied in kit form to be fitted by the installer.

AD G3
1.2

This approach ensures that the design and installation of the safety and operating devices are carried out by the manufacturer who is conversant with his own equipment and can control the training and supervision of his staff.

The BBA Certificate requirement ensures that the system is fit for its purpose and that information regarding installation, maintenance and use of the system is made available to all concerned.

Provision of non self-resetting thermal cut-outs

Storage systems may be heated directly or indirectly. (Figure 12.1 illustrates an indirect system.) In an indirect system the primary heater is usually a boiler and this heats a primary circuit which may be vented to atmosphere or unvented. Where the primary circuit is vented by a pipe of not less than 19 mm bore and has a water level not more than 2.5 m above the top of the primary heater coil it is termed a Low Head Vented (LHV) circuit and a thermal cut-out is not required in the primary circuit. In an unvented, indirectly heated system (see Fig. 12.1) the purpose of the non self-resetting thermal cut-out is to shut off the energy supply to the primary heater. It should also be wired up to a motorised valve or other BBA approved device to shut off the flow of water in the primary circuit.

Sometimes a unit system may incorporate a boiler. In this case the thermal cut-out may be located on the boiler.

In the case of a remotely sited boiler the thermal cut-out may also be located on the boiler providing it is installed by or under the supervision of a member of the Confederation of Registration of Gas Installers (CORGI).

Where a boiler is part of an unvented primary circuit it should be of a type recommended for use in unvented systems.

AD G3
1.4

In many cases an indirect system will also contain an alternative

AD G3
1.5

direct method of water heating (such as an immersion heater). This alternative heating source will also need to be fitted with a non self-resetting thermal cut-out.

AD G3
1.10

The non-resetting thermal cut-out should be connected to the heat source in accordance with the 15th edition of the Regulations for Electrical Installations of the Institution of Electrical Engineers.

Provision of temperature relief valves

Whether the unit or package is directly or indirectly heated the temperature relief valve should be situated on the storage vessel within the top 20% of the volume and preferably within 150 mm of the top.

BS 6283 requires that each valve is marked with a discharge rating (in kW). This rating should never be less than the maximum power input to the vessel which the valve protects. Valves should also comply with the following:

- They should not be disconnected except for replacement.
- They should not be relocated in any other position.
- The valve connecting boss should not be used to connect any other devices or fittings.
- They should discharge through a short length of pipe which is of at least the same bore as the valve's nominal outlet size.

AD G3
1.6

The discharge should either be direct or by way of a manifold which is large enough to take the total discharge of all the pipes connected to it. It should then continue via an air break to a tundish which is located vertically as near as possible to the valve.

AD G3
1.7

It may be possible to provide an equivalent degree of safety using other safety devices but these would need to be assessed by the British Board of Agrément.

Installation

AD G3
1.8

The installation of the system should be carried out by an approved installer as defined in the BBA Certificate. The Installation should also include the discharge pipe from the tundish (see below). It should also be verified that where a Low Head Vented (LHV) primary circuit is installed the vent pipe conditions required by paragraph 1.4. of AD G3 are met.

AD G3
1.9

A suitable metal discharge pipe which is at least one pipe size larger than the outlet pipe on the temperature relief valve should run from the tundish. It should terminate in a safe place where it is visible (e.g. a gulley) but cannot present a risk of contact to the users of the building. This is particularly important since any discharge will consist of scalding water and steam.

The discharge pipe should be laid to a fall and should not exceed 9 metres (or the equivalent in hydraulic resistance for a straight pipe) in length unless the bore is increased.

Further guidance on discharge pipes may be obtained from BBA guidance note Number 33.

Section 2 hot water storage systems

Systems within the scope of Section 2 exceed 500 litres in capacity or have a heat input of more than 45 kW. Generally they will be individual designs for specific projects and therefore, not systems appropriate for BBA Certification. Nevertheless, these systems should still conform to the same general safety requirements as in Section 1 including design by an appropriately qualified engineer and installation by an Approved Installer.

AD G3
2.1

The system should have safety devices conforming to BS 6700: 1987 *British Standard Specification for design, installation, testing and maintenance of services supplying water for domestic use within buildings and their curtilages.* (Section two Clause 7)

The system should also have an appropriate number of temperature relief valves which *either* comply with paragraph 1.3 of AD G3 (see above) giving a combined discharge rating at least equivalent to the heat input *or* are equally suitable and marked with the set temperature in °C and a discharge rating marked in kW. These markings should be at least equivalent to the heat input, measured in accordance with Appendix F of BS 6283 Part 2: 1982 or Appendix G of BS 6283 Part 3: 1982 and certified by BBA or another recognised testing body (e.g. the Associated Offices Technical Committee, AOTC).

AD G3
2.2

The temperature relief valves should be factory fitted to the storage vessel as described in paragraph 1.6 of AD G3.

AD G3
2.3

The non self-resetting thermal cut-outs should be installed in the system as described in Section 1 and the discharge pipes should also comply with that section.

AD G3
2.3 & 2.5

Sanitary conveniences and washing facilities

Adequate sanitary conveniences (i.e. closets and urinals) situated in purpose built accommodation or bathrooms, must be provided in buildings. This requirement replaces section 26 of the Building Act 1984.

Regs Sch. 1
G4

Additionally, adequate washbasins with suitable hot and cold water supplies must be provided in rooms containing water closets or in adjacent rooms or spaces.

These sanitary conveniences and washbasins must be separated from places where food is prepared and must be designed and installed so that they can be effectively cleaned.

It may be noted that section 66 of the 1984 Act enables the local authority to serve a notice on an occupier requiring him to replace any

1984 Act,
sec. 66

closet provided for his building which is not a water-closet. The notice can only be served where the building has a sufficient water supply and a sewer available. Where a notice requiring closet conversion is served, the local authority must bear half the cost of carrying out the work.

AD G4

A satisfactory level of performance will be achieved if:

● Sufficient numbers of the appropriate type of sanitary convenience are provided depending on the sex and age of the users of the building.
● Washbasins with hot and cold water supply are provided either in or adjacent to rooms containing water closets.

Both sanitary conveniences and washbasins should be sited, designed and installed so as not to be a health risk.

Provision of sanitary conveniences and washbasins

The following definitions apply in AD G4.

SANITARY CONVENIENCE – closets and urinals.

SANITARY ACCOMMODATION – a room containing closets or urinals. Other sanitary fittings may also be present. Sanitary accommodation containing more than one cubicle may be treated as a single room provided there is free air circulation throughout the room.

WATER-CLOSET – is defined by section 126 of the Building Act 1984 as a closet which has a separate fixed receptacle connected to a drainage system and separate provision for flushing from a supply of clean water, either by the operation of mechanism or by automatic action.

AD G4
1.1

AD G4 also permits the use of a chemical or other means of treatment where drains and water supply are not available. (It is not clear whether earth-closets would be permitted.)

AD G4
1.2

Houses, flats and maisonettes should have at least one closet. This also applies to houses in multiple occupation if the closet is available for the use of all the occupants.

In other types of buildings the scale of provision and the siting of appliances may be the subject of other legislation as follows:

● The Offices, Shops and Railway Premises Act 1963,
● The Factories Act 1961,
● The Food Hygiene (General) Regulations 1970,

AD G4
1.5

● Part M of Schedule 1 to the Building Regulations 1985 (Disabled People).

The requirement to provide satisfactory sanitary conveniences can also be met, subject to other legislation, by referring to the relevant clauses of BS 6465 *Sanitary Installations*, Part 1: 1984 which contains details of the scale of provision, selection and installation of sanitary appliances. AD G4 1.13

A room or space containing closets or urinals should be separated from any area in which food is prepared or washing up done. Closets, urinals and washbasins should have smooth, readily-cleaned, non-absorbent surfaces. AD G4 1.3 AD G4 1.6

Any flushing apparatus should be capable of cleansing the receptacle effectively. The receptacle should only be connected to a flush pipe or branch discharge pipe. AD G4 1.7

Any washbasins required by the provisions of regulation G4 should have a supply of hot water from a central source or unit water heater and a piped cold water supply. AD G4 1.8

Discharge from sanitary conveniences and washbasins

Water-closets should discharge via a trap and branch pipe to a soil stack pipe or foul drain. A closet is permitted to discharge to a soil stack pipe via a macerator system (see above) provided: AD G4 1.9

(a) a closet discharging directly to a gravity system is also available, AD G4 1.11
(b) the macerator system is the subject of a current BBA Certificate.

Urinals which are fitted with flushing apparatus should have an outlet fitted with an effective grating and trap and should discharge via a branch pipe to a soil stack pipe or foul drain (see Approved Document H1 and Chapter 13 for details of drainage). AD G4 1.10

Washbasins should discharge via a trap and branch discharge pipe to a soil stack. If on the ground floor, it is permissible to discharge the basin to a gulley or direct to a drain. AD G4 1.12

Chapter 13

Drainage and waste disposal

Introduction

This chapter describes Part H of Schedule 1 to the Building Regulations 1985 and the associated Approved Document H. Together, these documents cover:

- Foul water drainge (H1);
- Cesspools and tanks (H2);
- Rainwater drainage (H3); and,
- Solid waste storage (H4).

Formerly, the building regulations dealing with drainage were phrased in functional terms and considerable reliance had to be placed on British Standards and BRE Digests. Much of this information appears to have been included in Approved Document H and, except for very large installations, it would appear possible to design a satisfactory drainage system for a building without reference to other sources of information.

Some sections of the Building Act 1984 are concerned with sanitation and buildings, while others deal with drainage. A number of the relevant provisions of the 1984 Act will be referred to in this chapter.

At this stage three important provisions of the 1984 Act must be noted:

(i) Drainage of new buildings
Section 21 of the 1984 Act makes it unlawful to erect or extend any building unless satisfactory provision is made for the drainage of that building. The local authority *must* reject plans deposited under the regulations if no satisfactory provision for drainage is shown on them.

This provision must be read in light of the decision of the Divisional Court in *Chesterton R.D.C.* v. *Ralph Thompson Ltd.*, [1947] KB 300, holding that the local authority are not entitled to reject plans under section 37 on the ground that the sewerage system, into which the drains lead, is unsatisfactory. That is immaterial; the council must consider only the drainage of the particular building.

(ii) Drainage of buildings in combination
On housing estates buildings are invariably drained in combination, and section 22 of the 1984 Act enables the local authority to require the drainage of two or more buildings in combination by means of a private sewer. However, it should be noted that where plans have already been passed, this power can be exercised only by agreement with the owners.

(iii) Rainwater pipes must not be used to carry soil drainage or to provide ventilation for any system of soil drains
By section 60 of the 1984 Act a pipe for conveying rainwater from a roof may not be used for conveying soil or drainage from a sanitary convenience, or as a ventilating shaft to a foul drain. The practical effect of this provision is that all rainwater pipes must be trapped before entering a foul drain.

With regard to solid waste storage, all dwellings are now required to have satisfactory means of storing solid waste and the provisions of sections 23 (1) and (2) of the Building Act 1984 which required satisfactory means of access for removal of refuse have been replaced by paragraph H4 of Schedule 1 to the Building Regulations 1985.

This paragraph of the regulations must be read in light of other legislative provisions in respect of refuse disposal.

In particular, sections 72 to 82 of the Public Health Act 1936 should be referred to since those sections deal with the removal of refuse and allied matters. Thus, under section 72 of the 1936 Act a local authority may, and if required by the Minister must, undertake the removal of house refuse in either the whole or any part of their district, while sections 73 and 74 make provision for the removal of trade and other refuse. Section 23(3) of the Building Act 1984 requires the local authority's consent to close or obstruct the means of access by which refuse is removed from a house.

Sanitary pipework and drainage

Any system which carries foul water from appliances in a building to a sewer, cesspool, septic tank or settlement tank is required to be adequate.

Regs Sch. 1
H1(1)

FOUL WATER   is defined as waste water which comprises or includes:

● Waste from a sanitary convenience or other soil appliance.
● Water which has been used for cooking or washing.

Regs Sch. 1
H1(2)

Further guidance on the meaning of SANITARY CONVENIENCE is given in the explanatory notes to the *Manual to the Building Regulations 1985* where it is defined as a closet or urinal.

FOUL WATER OUTFALL   may be a foul or combined sewer, cesspool, septic tank or settlement tank. This term is not specifically defined in AD H1, however the term is inferred from the description of Performance on page 3.

The requirements of Paragraph H1 may be met by any foul water drainage system which:

- Conveys the flow of foul water to a suitable foul water outfall;
- Reduces to a minimum the risk of leakage or blockage;
- Prevents the entry of foul air from the drainage system to the building, under working conditions;
- Is ventilated; and,
- Is accessible for clearing blockages.

AD H1 sets out detailed provisions in two sections. Section 1 deals with sanitary pipework (i.e. above ground foul drainage) and section 2 with foul drainage (i.e. below ground foul drainage). There is also an appendix which purports to contain additional guidance for large buildings. It is somewhat surprising to discover, therefore, that it also contains details of special precautions relating to the drains of any building concerning settlement, surcharging, rodent control and ground loads.

Above ground foul drainage

A number of terms are used throughout AD H1. These are defined below and illustrated in Fig. 13.1. It should be noted that these definitions do *not* appear in the approved document.

DISCHARGE STACK – a ventilated vertical pipe which carries soil and waste water directly to a drain.

VENTILATING STACK – a ventilated vertical pipe which ventilates a drainage system either by connection to a drain or to a discharge stack or branch ventilating pipe.

BRANCH DISCHARGE PIPE (sometimes referred to as a BRANCH PIPE) – the section of pipework which connects an appliance to another branch pipe or a discharge stack if above the ground floor, or to a gully, drain or discharge stack if on the ground floor.

BRANCH VENTILATING PIPE – the section of pipework which allows a branch discharge pipe to be separately ventilated.

STUB STACK – an unventilated discharge stack.

A drainage system, whether above or below ground, should have

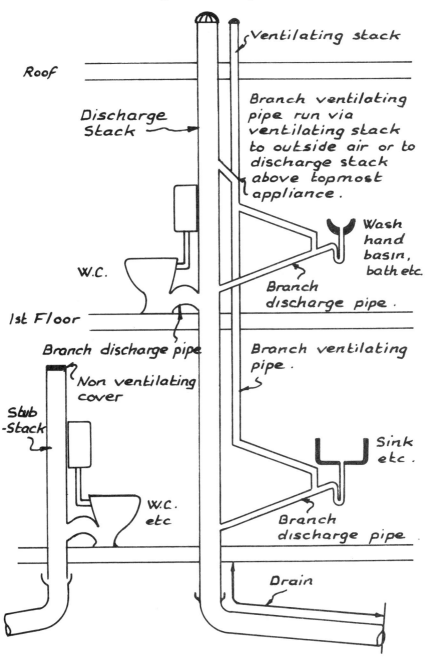

Fig. 13.1 Definitions.

sufficient *capacity* to carry the anticipated *flow* at any point. The *capacity* of the system, therefore, will depend on the size and gradient of the pipes whereas the *flow* will depend on the type, number and grouping of appliances. Table 13.1 below is based on information from BS 8301 and Table A1 of AD H1, and gives the expected flow rates for a range of appliances.

Since sanitary appliances are seldom used simultaneously the normal size of discharge stack or drain will be able to take the flow from quite a large number of appliances. Table 1 of AD H1 is reproduced below and is derived from BS 8301. It shows the approximate flow rates from dwellings and is based on an appliance grouping per household of 1 WC, 1 bath, 1 or 2 washbasins and 1 sink.

Pipe sizes

Since individual manufacturer's pipe sizes will vary, the sizes quoted in AD H1 are nominal and give a numerical designation in convenient round numbers. Similarly, equivalent pipe sizes for different pipe standards are contained in BS 5572 (Sanitary pipework) and BS 8301 (building drainage).

Table 13.1 Appliance flow rates.

Appliance	Flow rate (litres/sec.)
WC (9 litre washdown)	2.3
Washbasin	0.6
Sink	0.9
Bath	1.1
Shower	0.1
Washing machine	0.7
Urinal (per person unit)	0.15
Spray tap basin	0.06

Trap water seals

Trap water seals are provided in drainage systems to prevent foul air from the system entering the building. All discharge points into the system should be fitted with traps and these should retain a minimum seal of 25 mm under test and working conditions.

Traditionally the 'one pipe' and 'two pipe' systems of plumbing have required the provision of branch ventilating pipes and ventilating stacks unless special forms of trap are used. The 'single-stack' system of plumbing obviates the need for these ventilating pipes and is illustrated in Fig. 13.2. Table 13.2 below, which is based on Table 2 and

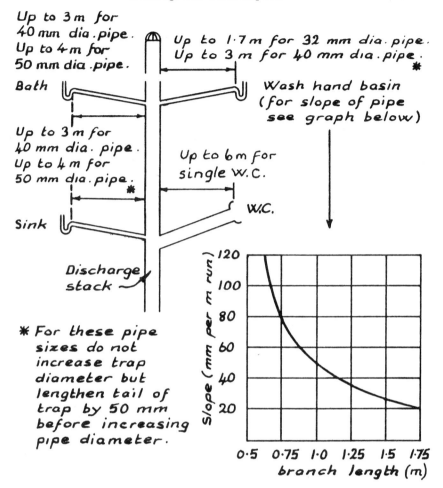

Up to 3 m for
40 mm dia. pipe.
Up to 4 m for
50 mm dia. pipe.

Bath

Up to 1.7 m for 32 mm dia. pipe.
Up to 3 m for 40 mm dia. pipe. ✳

Wash hand basin
(for slope of pipe
see graph below)

Up to 3 m for
40 mm dia. pipe.
Up to 4 m for
50 mm dia. pipe. ✳

Up to 6 m for
single W.C.

Sink

W.C.

Discharge
stack

✳ For these pipe
sizes do not
increase trap
diameter but
lengthen tail of
trap by 50 mm
before increasing
pipe diameter.

Slope (mm per m run)

120
100
80
60
40
20

0·5 0·75 1·0 1·25 1·5 1·75
branch length (m)

Appliance	Minimum diameter of pipe and trap (mm)	Depth of trap seal	Slope (mm/m)
Sink	40	75	18 – 90
Bath	40	75	18 – 90
W.C.	75 (min. dim)	50	9
Wash Basin.	32	75	See graph above.

Fig. 13.2 Single stack system – design limits.

AD H1, section 1

Table 1 Flow rates from dwellings.

Number of dwellings	Flow rate (litres/sec)
1	2.5
5	3.5
10	4.1
15	4.6
20	5.1
25	5.4
30	5.8

Table 13.2 Minimum dimensions of branch pipes and traps.

Appliance	Minimum diameter of pipe and trap (mm)	Depth of trap seal (mm)
Bidet	32	75
Shower Food waste disposal unit Urinal bowl Sanitary towel macerator	40	75
Industrial food waste disposal unit	50	75
Urinal (stall, 1 to 6 person positions)	65	50

Table A2 of AD H1, gives minimum dimensions of pipes and traps where it is proposed to use appliances other than those shown in Fig. 13.2. Additionally, it is permissible to reduce the depth of trap seal to 40 mm where sinks, baths or showers are installed on the ground floor and discharge to a gulley.

It should be stressed that the minimum pipe sizes given above relate to branch pipes serving a single appliance. Where a number of appliances are served by a single branch pipe which is unventilated, the diameter of the pipe should be at least the size given in Table 3 to section 1 of AD H1, which is reproduced below.

AD H1
sec. 1
1.12

AD H1, section 1

Table 3   **Common branch discharge pipes (unvented)**

Appliance	Max number to be connected	OR	Max length of branch [m]	Min size of pipe [mm]	Gradient limits (fall per metre)		
					min [mm]		max [mm]
wcs	8		15	100	9	to	90
urinals: bowls	5		*	50	18	to	90
stalls	6		*	65	18	to	90
washbasins	4		4 (no bends)	50	18	to	45

Note
* No limitation as regards venting but should be as short as possible.

If it is not possible to comply with the figures given in Table 13.1, Fig. 13.2 or Table 3 above, then the branch discharge pipe should be ventilated in order to prevent loss of trap seals. This is facilitated by means of a *branch ventilating pipe* which is connected to the discharge pipe within 300 mm of the appliance trap. The branch ventilating pipe may be run direct to outside air, where it should finish at least 900 mm above any opening into the building which is nearer than 3 m, or, it may be connected to the discharge stack above the 'spillover' level of the highest appliance served. In this case it should have a continuous incline from the branch discharge pipe to the point of connection with the discharge stack (see Fig. 13.3 below).

Where a branch ventilating pipe serves only one appliance it should have a minimum diameter of 25 mm. This should be increased to 32 mm diameter if the branch ventilating pipe is longer than 15 m or contains more than five bends.

AD H1 sec. 1 1.18 to 1.20

As appliance traps present an obstacle to the normal flow in a pipe they may be subject to periodic blockages. It is important, therefore, that they be fitted immediately after an appliance and either be removable or be fitted with a cleaning eye. Where a trap forms an integral part of an appliance (such as in a WC pan), the appliance should be removable.

AD H1 sec. 1 1.4

Branch discharge pipes – design requirements

In addition to size and gradient there are other design requirements for branch discharge pipes that should be adhered to in order to prevent loss of trap seals. In high buildings especially, back-pressure may build

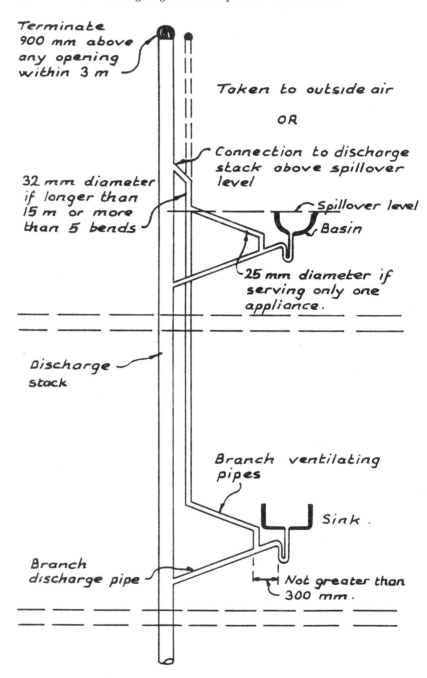

Terminate 900 mm above any opening within 3 m

Taken to outside air

OR

Connection to discharge stack above spillover level

32 mm diameter if longer than 15 m or more than 5 bends

Spillover level

Basin

25 mm diameter if serving only one appliance.

Discharge stack

Branch ventilating pipes

Sink.

Branch discharge pipe

Not greater than 300 mm.

Fig. 13.3 Branch ventilating pipes.

up at the foot of a discharge stack and may cause loss of trap seal in ground floor appliances. Therefore, the following requirements should be met:

- For multi-storey buildings up to five storeys high there should be a minimum distance of 750 mm between the point of junction of the lowest branch discharge pipe connection and the invert of the tail of the bend at the foot of the discharge stack. This is reduced to 450 mm for discharge stacks in single dwellings up to three storeys high (see Fig. 13.4). AD H1 sec. 1 1.8 & Appendix A3
- For appliances above ground floor level the branch pipe should only be run to a discharge stack or to another branch pipe. AD H1 1.5
- Ground floor appliances may be run to a separate drain, gully or stub stack. (A gully connection should be restricted to pipes carrying waste water only.) They may also be run to a discharge stack in the following circumstances:

(a) In buildings up to five storeys high – without restriction;
(b) In buildings with six to twenty storeys – to their own separate discharge stack; AD H1 sec. 1 1.6 & 1.7 Appendix A4
(c) In buildings over twenty storeys – ground and first floor appliances to their own separate discharge stack; (see Fig. 13.5).

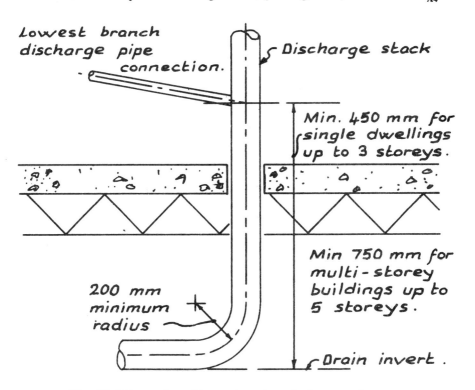

Fig. 13.4 Connection of lowest branch to discharge stack.

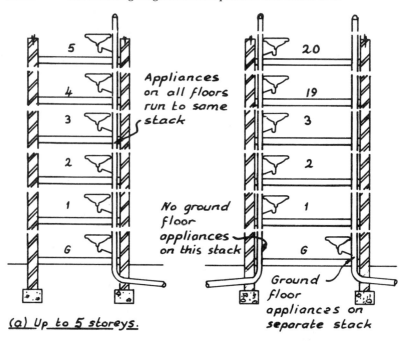

(a) Up to 5 storeys.

Appliances on all floors run to same stack

No ground floor appliances on this stack

Ground floor appliances on separate stack

(b) 6 to 20 storeys.

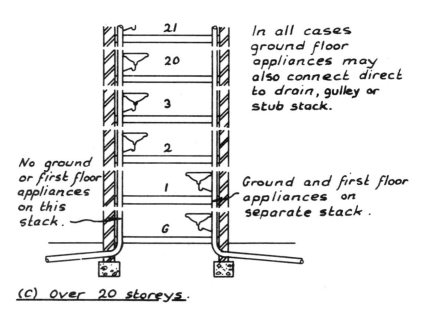

No ground or first floor appliances on this stack.

In all cases ground floor appliances may also connect direct to drain, gulley or stub stack.

Ground and first floor appliances on separate stack.

(c) Over 20 storeys.

Fig. 13.5 Provision of discharge stacks to ground floor appliances.

Back-pressure and blockages may occur where branches are connected so as to be almost opposite one another. This is most likely to occur where bath and wc branch connections are at or about the same level. Figure 13.6 illustrates ways in which possible cross flows may be avoided.

AD H1
sec. 1
1.7

Additionally, a long vertical drop from a ground floor water closet to a drain may cause self-syphonage of the WC trap. To prevent this the drop should not exceed 1·5 m from crown of trap to invert of drain (see Fig. 13.7).

AD H1
sec. 1
1.9

Similarly, there is a chance of syphonage where a branch discharge pipe connects with a gully. This can be avoided by terminating the branch pipe above the water level but below the gully grating or sealing plate (see Fig. 13.7).

AD H1
sec. 1
1.11

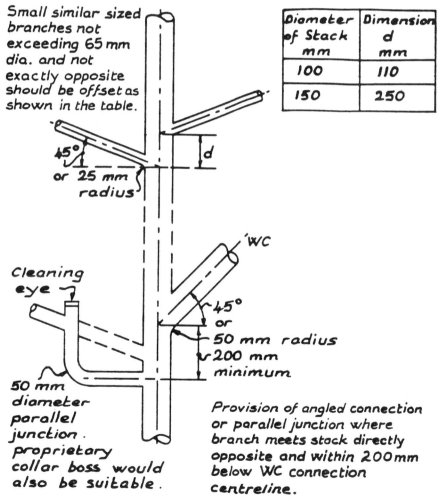

Small similar sized branches not exceeding 65 mm dia. and not exactly opposite should be offset as shown in the table.

Diameter of Stack mm	Dimension d mm
100	110
150	250

45° or 25 mm radius

d

'WC

45° or 50 mm radius 200 mm minimum

Cleaning eye

50 mm diameter parallel junction. proprietary collar boss would also be suitable.

Provision of angled connection or parallel junction where branch meets stack directly opposite and within 200 mm below WC connection centreline.

Fig. 13.6 Avoidance of cross flows in discharge stacks.

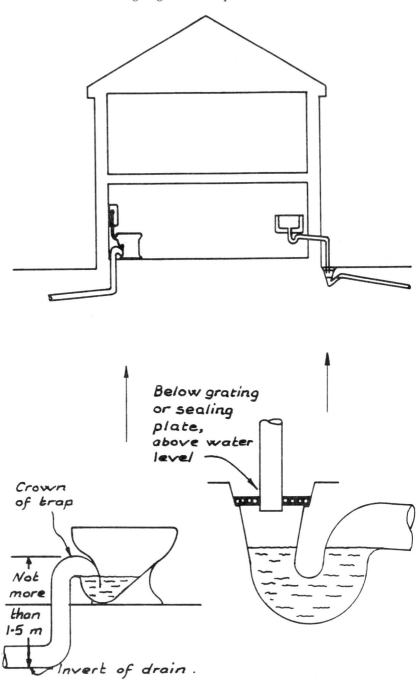

Fig. 13.7 Ground floor connections for water closets and gullies.

Self-syphonage can also be prevented by ensuring that bends in branch discharge pipes are kept to a minimum. Where bends are unavoidable they should be made with as large a radius as possible. This means that pipes with a diameter of up to 65 mm should have a minimum centre line radius of 75 mm. Junctions on branches should be swept in the direction of flow with a minimum radius of 25 mm or should make an angle of 45° with the discharge stack. Where a branch diameter is 75 mm or more the sweep radius should be increased to 50 mm (see Fig. 13.6).

AD H1
sec. 1
1.13

AD H1
sec. 1
1.14

Branch discharge pipes should be fully accessible for clearing blockages. Additionally rodding points should be provided so that access may be gained to any part of a branch discharge pipe which cannot be reached by removing a trap.

AD H1
sec. 1
1.21

Discharge stacks – design requirements

The satisfactory performance of a discharge stack will be ensured if it complies with the following rules:

- The foot of the stack should only connect with a drain and should have as large a radius as possible (at least 200 mm at the centre line);
- Ideally, there should be no offsets in the wet part of a stack (i.e. below the highest branch connection);
- If offsets are unavoidable then:
  (a) buildings over three storeys require a separate ventilation stack connected above and below the offset; and,
  (b) buildings up to three storeys should have no branch connection within 750 mm of the offset;
- The stack should be placed inside a building, unless the building has not more than three storeys. This rule is intended to prevent frost damage to discharge stacks and branch pipes;
- The stack should comply with the minimum diameters given in Table 4 to section 1 of AD H1 (see below). Additionally the minimum internal diameter permitted for a discharge stack serving urinals is 50 mm, or 75 mm for a water closet:

AD H1 section 1

Table 4 **Maximum capacities for discharge stacks**

Stack size {mm]	Max capacity [litres/sec]
50 *	1.2
65 *	2.1
75 †	3.4
90	5.3
100	7.2

Note
* No wcs.
† Not more than 1 syphonic wc with 75mm outlet.

- The diameter of a discharge stack should not reduce in the direction of flow;

- Adequate access points for clearing blockages should be provided and all pipes should be reasonably accessible for repairs.

Discharge stacks – ventilation requirements

In order to prevent the loss of trap seals it is essential that the air pressure in a discharge stack remains reasonably constant. Therefore, the stack should be ventilated to outside air. For this purpose it should be carried up to such a height that its open end will not cause danger to health or a nuisance. AD H1 recommends that the pipe should finish at least 900 mm above the top of any opening into the building within 3 m. The open end should be fitted with a durable ventilating cover (see Fig. 13.8).

The dry part of a discharge stack above the topmost branch, which serves only for ventilation, may be reduced in size in one and two storey houses to 75 mm diameter.

It is permissible to terminate a discharge stack inside a building if it is fitted with an air admittance valve. This valve allows air to enter the pipe but does not allow foul air to escape. It must be the subject of a current BBA Certificate and should not adversely affect the operation

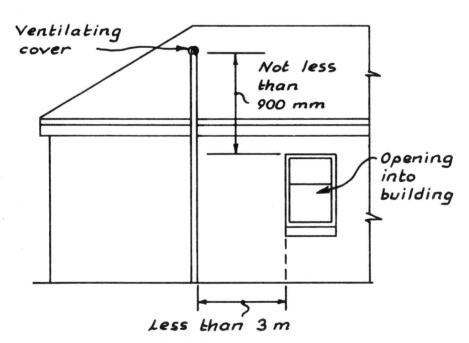

Fig. 13.8 Termination of discharge stacks.

of the underground drainage system which normally relies on ventilation from the open stacks of the sanitary pipework.

Some underground drains are subject to surcharging. Where this is the case the discharge stack should be ventilated by a pipe of not less than 50 mm diameter connected at the base of the stack above the expected flood level. This would also apply where a discharge pipe is connected to a drain near an intercepting trap although no minimum dimensions are specified in AD H1.

Stub stacks

There is one exception to the general rule that discharge stacks should be ventilated. This involves the use of an unvented stack (or *stub stack*). A stub stack should connect to a ventilated discharge stack or a drain which is not subject to surcharging and should comply with the dimensions given in Fig. 13.9. It is permissible for more than one ground floor appliance to connect to a stub stack.

AD H1
sec. 1
1.25 to 1.29
& 1.10

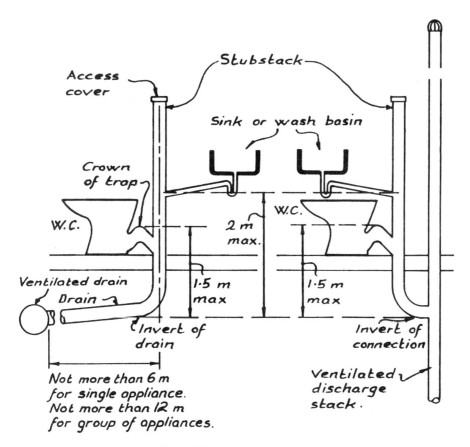

Fig. 13.9 Stub stacks.

Dry ventilating stacks

Where an installation requires a large number of branch ventilating pipes and the distance to a discharge stack is also large it may be necessary to use a dry ventilating stack.

It is normal to connect the lower end of a ventilating stack to a ventilated discharge stack below the lowest branch discharge pipe. It may also be connected directly to a bend as for discharge stacks (see page 13.10 above).

The upper end of a ventilating stack should either connect back into a ventilated discharge stack above the spill-over level of the highest appliance or it should terminate in the outside air as described for discharge stacks above.

Ventilating stacks should be at least 32 mm in diameter if serving a building containing dwellings not more than ten storeys high. For all other buildings reference should be made to BS 8301: 1985 *Code of practice for building drainage.*

**AD H1
Appendix
A5 to A8**

Materials for above ground drainage systems

Table 5 to section 1 of AD H1, which is reproduced below, gives details of the materials that may be used for pipes, fittings and joints in above ground drainage systems.

To prevent electrolytic corrosion, pipes of different metals should

AD H1 section 1

Table 5 Materials for sanitary pipework

Material	British Standard
Pipes	
cast iron	BS 416
copper	BS 864, BS 2871
galvanised steel	BS 3868
uPVC	BS 4514
polypropylene	BS 5254
plastics	BS 5255
ABS	
MUPVC	
polyethylene	
polypropylene	
Traps	
copper	BS 1184
plastics	BS 3943

**AD H1
sec. 1
1.31**

Note: Some of these materials may not be suitable for conveying trade effluent.

always be separated by non-metalic material. Additionally, pipes should be adequately supported without restricting thermal movement.

Care should be taken where pipes pass through fire separating elements (see Part B of Schedule 1 to the Building Regulations 1985 and Approved Document B).

Test for airtightness

In order to ensure that a completed installation is airtight it should be subjected to a pressure test of air or smoke of at least 38 mm water gauge for a maximum of three minutes. A satisfactory installation will maintain a 25 mm water seal in every trap during this period of time. uPVC pipes should not be smoke tested.

AD H1
sec. 1
1.32

Alternative method of design

The requirements of the Building Regulations 1985 for above ground drainage can also be met by following clauses 3, 4, and 7 to 12 of BS 5572: 1978 *Code of practice for sanitary pipework.*

AD H1
sec. 1
1.33

Below ground foul drainage

In most modern systems of underground drainage foul water and rainwater are carried separately. Section 2 of AD H1 deals specifically with below ground foul drainage. However, some public sewers are on the combined system taking both foul and rainwater in the same pipe. The provisions of AD H1 will apply equally to combined systems although pipe gradients and sizes may have to be adjusted to take the increased flows. Combined systems should never discharge to a cesspool or septic tank.

Where a sewer is above the level of the underground drainage system, sewage pumping equipment will be necessary. Information on these installations can be obtained from BS 8301 *Code of practice for building drainage.*

AD H1
sec. 2
2.1 & 2.2

The performance of a below ground foul drainage system depends on the drainage layout, the pipe cover and bedding, the pipe sizes and gradients, the materials used and the provisions for clearing blockages.

DRAINAGE LAYOUT   The drainage layout should be kept as simple as possible with pipes laid in straight lines and to even gradients. The number of access points provided should be limited to those essential for clearing blockages. If possible, changes of gradient and direction should be combined with access points, inspection chambers or manholes. Junctions between drains or sewers should be made obliquely or in the direction of flow.

A slight curve in a length of otherwise straight pipework is permissible provided the line can still be adequately rodded.

Bends should only be used in or close to inspection chambers and manholes, or at the foot of discharge or ventilating stacks. The radius of any bend should be as large as practicable.

It is important to ventilate an underground foul drainage system with a flow of air. Ventilated discharge pipes may be used for this purpose and should be positioned at the head of each main run and:

**AD H1
sec. 2
2.3 to 2.6**

● On any branch exceeding 6 m serving a single appliance.
● On any branch exceeding 12 m serving a group of appliances.
● On any drain fitted with an interceptor (especially on a sealed system).

PIPE COVER AND BEDDING   The degree of pipe cover to be provided will usually depend on:

**AD H1
sec. 2
2.8 & 2.9**

● The invert level of the connections to the drainage system.
● The slope and level of the ground.
● The necessary pipe gradients.
● The necessity for protection to pipes.

**AD H2
sec. 2
2.15**

In order to protect pipes from damage it is essential that they are bedded and backfilled correctly. The choice of materials for this purpose will depend mainly on the depth, size and strength of the pipes used.

Pipes used for underground drainage may be classed as rigid or flexible. Flexible pipes will be subject to deformation under load and will therefore need more support than rigid pipes so that the deformation may be limited to 5% of the pipe diameter.

AD H1 section 2

Table **8**   **Limits of cover for standard strength rigid pipes in any width of trench**

Pipe bore	Bedding class	Fields and gardens		Light traffic roads		Heavy traffic roads	
		Min	Max	Min	Max	Min	Max
100	D or N	0.4	4.2	0.7	4.1	0.7	3.7
	F	0.3	5.8	0.5	5.8	0.5	5.5
	B	0.3	7.4	0.4	7.4	0.4	7.2
150	D or N	0.6	2.7	1.1	2.5	—	—
	F	0.6	3.9	0.7	3.8	0.7	3.3
	B	0.6	5.0	0.6	5.0	0.6	4.6

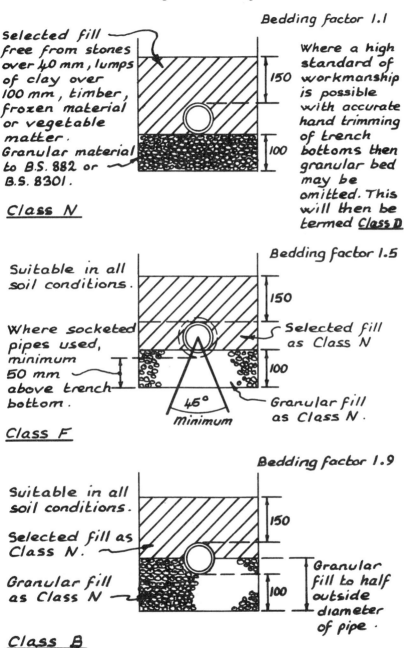

Bedding factor 1.1

Selected fill free from stones over 40 mm, lumps of clay over 100 mm, timber, frozen material or vegetable matter. Granular material to B.S. 882 or B.S. 8301.

Where a high standard of workmanship is possible with accurate hand trimming of trench bottoms then granular bed may be omitted. This will then be termed <u>Class D</u>

150

100

<u>Class N</u>

Bedding factor 1.5

Suitable in all soil conditions.

Where socketed pipes used, minimum 50 mm above trench bottom.

150

100

Selected fill as Class N

Granular fill as Class N.

45°
Minimum

<u>Class F</u>

Bedding factor 1.9

Suitable in all soil conditions.

Selected fill as Class N.

Granular fill as Class N

150

100

Granular fill to half outside diameter of pipe.

<u>Class B</u>

Fig. 13.10 Bedding classes for rigid pipes.

Rigid pipes

Table 8 of AD H1 is set out above and contains details of the limits of cover that need to be provided for standard strength rigid pipes in any width of trench. For details of the bedding classes referred to in the table, see Fig. 13.10.

The backfilling materials should comply with the following:

- Granular material should conform to BS 882: 1983 *Specification for aggregates from natural sources for concrete*; Table 4 or BS 8301: 1985 *Code of practice for building drainage*; Appendix D.
- Selected fill should be free from stones larger than 40 mm, lumps of clay over 100 mm, timber, frozen material or vegetable matter. It is possible that ground water may flow in trenches with granular bedding. Provisions may be required to prevent this.

AD H2
sec. 2
2.16

Flexible pipes

Flexible pipes should be provided with a minimum depth of cover of 900 mm under any road. This may be reduced to 600 mm in fields and gardens. The maximum permissible depth of cover is 10 m.

Figure 13.11 shows typical bedding and backfilling details for flexible pipes. Where it is necessary to construct a V-shaped trench due to the nature of the subsoil, care should be taken to ensure that the granular bedding material is properly contained.

AD H1
sec. 2
2.17

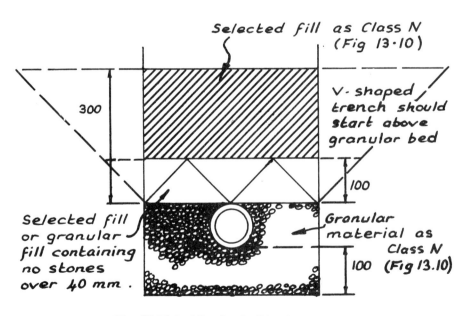

Fig. 13.11 Bedding for flexible pipes.

Special protection to pipes

Where rigid pipes have less cover than is specified above (see Table 8 above), the pipes should be surrounded in concrete to a thickness of at least 100 mm. Expansion joints should also be provided at each socket or sleeve joint face.

Flexible pipes under fields or gardens with less than 600 mm of cover should be bridged by pre-cast concrete paving slabs resting on at

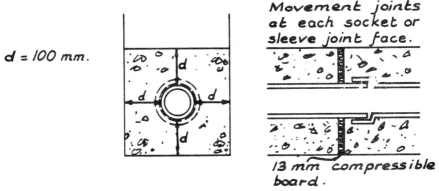

d = 100 mm.

Movement joints at each socket or sleeve joint face.

13 mm compressible board.

Concrete Encasement for Rigid or Flexible Pipes.

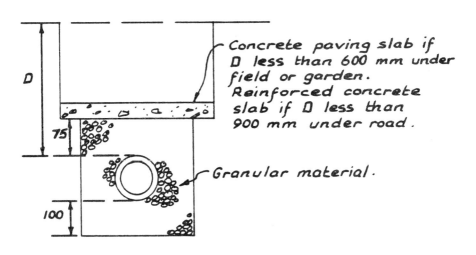

Concrete paving slab if D less than 600 mm under field or garden.
Reinforced concrete slab if D less than 900 mm under road.

Granular material.

Protection for Flexible Pipes.

Fig. 13.12 Special protection to pipes.

AD H1 section 2

Table 6   Recommended minimum gradients for foul drains

Peak flow [litres/sec]	Pipe size [mm]	Minimum gradient [1:...]	Maximum capacity [litres/sec]
<1	75	1:40	4.1
	100	1:40	9.2
>1	75	1:80	2.8
	100	1:80*	6.3
	150	1:150†	15.0

Notes
* Minimum of 1 wc.
† Minimum of 5 wcs.

AD H1
Appendix
A15 to A17

least 75 mm of granular fill. The concrete paving slab should be replaced with reinforced concrete surround or bridging for flexible pipes under roads with less than 900 mm of cover (see Fig. 13.12).

PIPE SIZES AND GRADIENTS.   Drains should be laid to falls and should be large enough to carry the expected flow. The rate of flow will depend on the appliances that are connected to the drain (see Table 1 and Table 13.1, page 13.5). The capacity will depend on the diameter and gradient of the pipes.

Table 6 to section 2 of AD H1 gives recommended minimum gradients for different sized foul drains and shows the maximum capacities they are capable of carrying. The table is set out below.

As a further design guide Diagram 7 from AD H1 is reproduced

AD H1 section 2

Table 7   Materials for below ground gravity drainage

Material	British Standard
Rigid pipes	
asbestos	BS 3656
vitrified clay	BS 65
concrete	BS 5911
grey iron	BS 437
Flexible pipes	
uPVC	BS 4660
	BS 5481

Note
Some of these materials may not be suitable for conveying trade effluent.

below. This gives discharge capacities for foul drains running at 0.75 proportional depth.

AD H1
sec. 2
2.10 to 2.12

Where foul and rainwater drainage systems are combined, the capacity of the system should be large enough to take the combined peak flow (see Rainwater drainage below).

AD H1
sec. 2
2.13

MATERIALS.   Table 7 to section 2 of AD H1, which is reproduced above, gives details of the materials that may be used for pipes, fittings and joints in below ground foul drainage systems.

Joints should remain watertight under working and test conditions and nothing in the joints, pipes or fittings should form an obstruction inside the pipeline. To avoid damage by differential settlement pipes should have flexible joints appropriate to the material of the pipes.

To prevent electrolytic corrosion, pipes of different metals should always be separated by non-metallic material.

AD H1
sec. 2
2.14

AD H1, section 2

Diagram 7   **Discharge capacities of foul drains running 0·75 proportional depth**

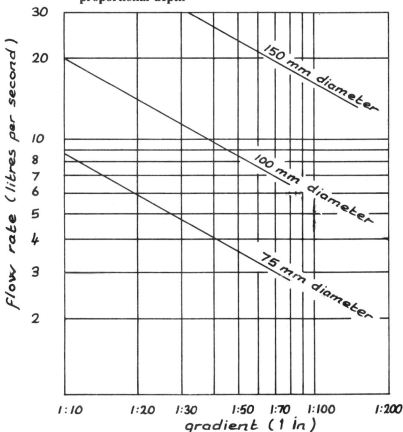

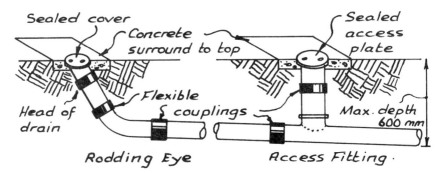

Sealed cover
Concrete surround to top
Sealed access plate
Flexible couplings
Head of drain
Max. depth 600 mm

Rodding Eye   **Access Fitting.**

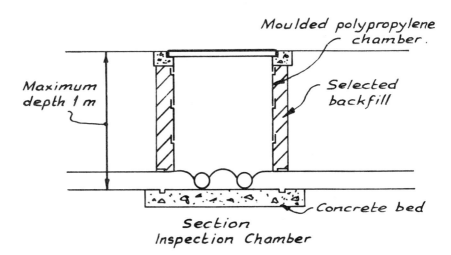

Moulded polypropylene chamber.

Maximum depth 1 m

Selected backfill

Concrete bed

Section
Inspection Chamber

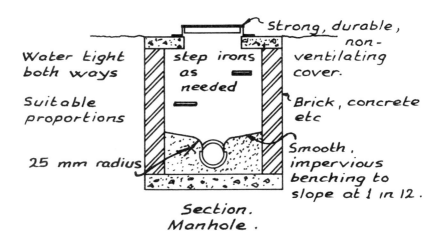

Strong, durable, non-ventilating cover.

Water tight both ways

step irons as needed

Suitable proportions

Brick, concrete etc

25 mm radius

Smooth, impervious benching to slope at 1 in 12.

Section.
Manhole.

Fig. 13.13 Access points.

PROVISIONS FOR CLEARING BLOCKAGES. Every part
of a drainage system should be accessible for clearing blockages. The
type of access point chosen and its siting and spacing will depend on
the layout of the drainage system and the depth and size of the drain
runs.

A drainage system designed in accordance with the provisions of
AD H1 should be capable of being rodded by normal means (i.e. *not*
by mechanical methods).

AD H1
sec. 2
2.18 & 2.19

Access points

Four types of access points are described in AD H1:

- Rodding eyes (or points). These are extensions of the drainage
  system to ground level where the open end of the pipe is capped with
  a sealing plate.
- Access fittings. Small chambers situated at the invert level of a pipe
  and without any real area of open channel.
- Inspection chambers. Chambers having working space at ground
  level.
- Manholes. Chambers large enough to admit persons to work at
  drain level.

Some typical access point details are illustrated in Fig. 13.13.

Whatever form of access point is used it should be of sufficient size
to enable the drain run to be adequately rodded. Table 9 to section 2 of
AD H1 sets out the maximum depths and minimum internal
dimensions for each type of access point. Where a large number of
branches enter an inspection chamber or manhole the sizes given in
Table 9 may need to be increased. It is usual to allow 300 mm for each
branch connection (thus a 1200 mm long manhole could cater for up to
four branch connections on each side).

AD H1
sec. 2
2.20

Access points – siting and spacing

Access points should be provided:

- At or near the head of any drain run.
- At any change of direction or gradient.
- At a junction, unless each drain run can be rodded separately from
  another access point.
- At a change of pipe size, unless this occurs at a junction where each
  drain run can be rodded separately from another access point.
- At regular intervals on long drain runs.

The spacing of access points will depend on the type of access used,
Table 10 to section 2 of AD H1 gives details of the maximum distances

AD H1, section 2

Table **9**   **Minimum dimensions for access fittings and chambers**

Type	Depth to (m)	Internal sizes		Cover sizes	
		Length × width (mm × mm)	Circular (mm)	Length × width (mm × mm)	Circular (mm)
Rodding eye		As drain but min 100			
Access fitting small large	0.6 or less	150 × 100 225 × 100	150 —	150 × 100 225 × 100	150 —
Inspection chamber	0.6 or less 1.0 or less	— 450 × 450	190* 450	— 450 × 450	190* 450†
Manhole	1.5 or less over 1.5 over 2.7	1200 × 750 1200 × 750 1200 × 840	1050 1200 1200	600 × 600 600 × 600 600 × 600	600 600 600
Shaft	over 2.7	900 × 840	900	600 × 600	600

Notes
* Drains up to 150 mm.
† For clayware or plastics may be reduced to 430 mm in order to provide support for cover and frame.

AD H1, section 2

Table **10**   **Maximum spacing of access points in metres**

From	To	Access Fitting		Junction	Inspection chamber	Manhole
		Small	Large			
Start of external drain*		12	12	—	22	45
Rodding eye		22	22	22	45	45
Access fitting small 150 diam 150 × 100 large 225 × 100		— —	— —	12 22	22 45	22 45
Inspection chamber		22	45	22	45	45
Manhole		22	45	45	45	90

Note
* See paragraphs 1.9 and 1.26.

that should be allowed for drains up to 300 mm in diameter and is set out below.

Access points – construction

Generally, access points should:

- Be constructed of suitable and durable materials.
- Exclude subsoil or rainwater.
- Be watertight under working and test conditions.

Table 11 to section 2 of AD H1 is shown below and lists materials which are suitable for the construction of access points.

Inspection chambers and manholes should:

- Have smooth impervious surface benching up to at least the top of the outgoing pipe to all channels and branches. The purpose of benching is to direct the flow into the main channel and to provide a safe foothold. For this reason the benching should fall towards the channel at a slope of 1 in 12 and should be rounded at the channel with a minimum radius of 25 mm (see Fig. 13.13).
- Be constructed so that branches discharge into the main channel at or above the horizontal diameter where half-round open channels are used. Branches which make an angle of more than 45° with the channel should be formed using a threequarter section branch bend.
- Have strong, removable, non-ventilating covers of suitable durable material (e.g. cast iron, cast or pressed steel or pre-cast concrete or uPVC).

AD H1, section 2

Table **11**   **Materials for access points**

Material	British Standard
1 Inspection chambers and manholes	
Clay	
bricks and blocks	BS 3921
vitrified	BS 65
Concrete	
precast	BS 5911
in situ	CP 110
Plastics	BBA Certificates
2 Rodding eyes and access fittings (excluding frames and covers)	as pipes see Table 7 BBA Certificates

● Be fitted with step irons, ladders, etc., if over 1.0 m deep.

A manhole or inspection chamber which is situated *within* a building should have an air-tight cover that is mechanically fixed (e.g. screwed down with corrosion resistant bolts). This requirement does not apply if the inspection chamber or manhole gives access to part of a drain which itself has inspection fittings and these are provided with watertight covers.

AD H1
sec. 2
2.23 to 2.25

Test for watertightness

After laying and backfilling, gravity below ground drains and private sewers not exceeding 300 mm in diameter should be pressure tested using air or water. For the air test, a head loss of up to 25 mm at 100 mm water gauge (or 12 mm at 50 mm water gauge) is permitted in a period of five minutes.

Water tested drains using a standpipe which is the same diameter as the drain should be subjected to a pressure of 1·5 m head of water. This should be measured above the invert at the top of the drain run. The section of drain to be tested should be filled up and left to stand for two hours and then topped up. Over the next 30 minutes the leakage should not exceed 0·05 litres per metre run for a 100 mm drain (equivalent to a drop of 6·4 mm per metre) or 0·08 litres per metre run for a 150 mm drain (equivalent to a drop of 4·5 mm per metre).

A drain may be damaged if a head of more than 4 m is applied to the lower end of the run. This may necessitate testing a long drain run in several sections.

AD H1
sec. 2
2.26 to 2.28

Special protection for drains adjacent to or under buildings

Where drains pass under buildings or through foundations and walls there is a risk that settlement of the building may cause pipes to fracture, with consequential blockages and leakage. In the past it was common practice to require pipes (which were rigid jointed) to be encased in concrete. Since the development of flexible pipe systems it has become essential to maintain this flexibility in order that any slight settlement of the building will not cause pipe fracture.

Therefore, drain runs under buildings should be surrounded with at least 100 mm of granular or other flexible filling. On some sites unusual ground conditions may lead to excessive subsidence. To protect drain runs from fracture it may be necessary to have additional flexible joints or use other solutions such as suspended drainage. Shallow drain runs under concrete floor slabs should be concrete encased with the slab where the crown of the pipe is less than 300 mm from the underside of the slab.

Where a drain passes through a wall or foundation the following solutions are possible:

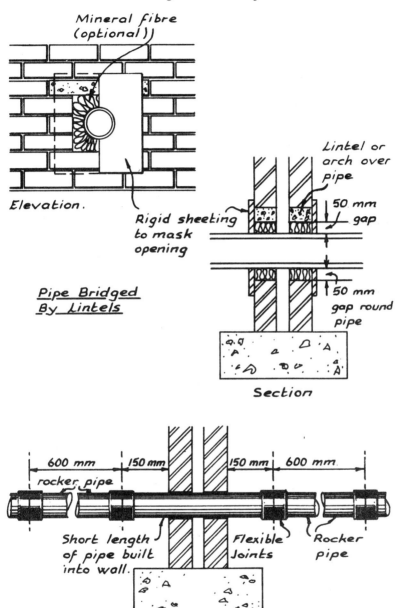

Mineral fibre
(optional)

Elevation.

Rigid sheeting
to mask
opening

Pipe Bridged
By Lintels

Lintel or
arch over
pipe

50 mm
gap

50 mm
gap round
pipe

Section

600 mm   150 mm   150 mm   600 mm

rocker pipe

Short length
of pipe built
into wall.

Flexible
Joints

Rocker
pipe

Pipe Built Into Wall

Fig. 13.14 Drains passing through foundations.

- The wall may be supported on lintels over the pipe. A clearance of 50 mm should be provided round the pipe perimeter and this gap should either be filled with a flexible material such as mineral fibre quilt or it should be masked on both sides of the wall with rigid sheet material to prevent the ingress of fill or vermin.
- A length of pipe may be built in to the wall with its joints not more than 150 mm from each face. Rocker pipes not exceeding 600 mm in length should then be connected to each end of the pipe using flexible joints (see Fig. 13.14).

AD H1
Appendix
A9 & A10

Where a drain or private sewer is laid close to a load-bearing part of a building, precautions should be taken to ensure that the drain or sewer trench does not impair the stability of the building.

Where any drain or sewer trench is within 1 m of the foundation of a wall, and the bottom of the trench is lower than the wall foundation, the trench should be filled with concrete up to the level of the underside of the foundation.

AD H1
Appendix
A11

Where a drain or sewer trench is 1 m or more from a wall foundation, and the trench bottom is lower than the foundation, the trench should be filled with concrete to within a vertical distance below the underside of the foundation of not more than the horizontal distance from the foundation to the trench less 150 mm (see Fig. 13.15).

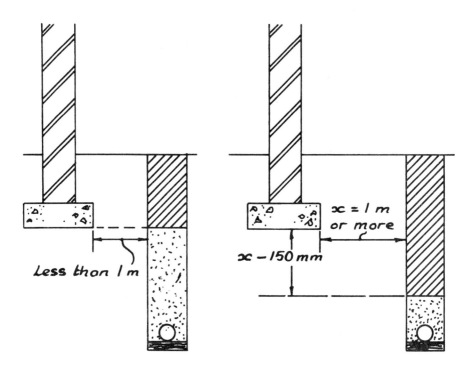

Fig. 13.15 Drain trenches.

The advice of the local authority should be sought regarding sites where unstable ground is present or there is a risk of drain surcharging or a high water table. They should also be consulted if it is intended to lay pipes on piles or beams or in a common trench.

AD H1
A12

Special protection – drain surcharging

Under certain weather conditions drains may be unable to cope with the increased flow and may back up (or become surcharged) creating the need to protect the building from flooding. Some parts of the drainage system may be unaffected by surcharging. These parts should by-pass any protective measures and should discharge into a surcharge free part of the system unless this is unavoidable. Typical protective measures may be obtained from BS 8301. If an anti-flood device is used extra ventilation should be provided to the system to prevent the loss of trap seals.

AD H1
A13

Special protection – rodent control

Generally, rodent infestation (especially by rats) is on the increase. Since rats use drains and sewers as effective communication routes some degree of control may be achieved by providing inspection chambers with screwed access covers on the pipework instead of open channels. Intercepting traps may also be provided as in the past, although they do increase the incidence of blockages unless adequately maintained. The local authority may be able to provide guidance regarding areas where rodent infestation is a problem.

AD H1
A14

Alternative method of design

Additional information on the design and construction of building drainage which meets the requirements of the Building Regulations 1985 is contained in BS 8301: 1985 *Code of practice for building drainage*. The Code also describes the discharge unit method of calculating pipe sizes.

AD H1
sec. 2
2.29

Cesspools, septic tanks and settlement tanks

Cesspools, septic tanks and settlement tanks should be:

- Ventilated.
- Of adequate capacity.
- Constructed to be impermeable to liquids.

They should also be sited and constructed so that:

- They are accessible for emptying.
- They are not prejudicial to health.
- They will not contaminate any underground water or water supply.

Capacity

The minimum permitted size for cesspools (18 m³) is a large capacity tank, and will tend to discourage their use and encourage the use of septic and settlement tanks, which may be much smaller (2·7 m³).

The septic tank is, of course, the better answer to the problem of sewage disposal for an isolated building. The cesspool was the mediaeval solution.

Minimum capacities are set for cesspools, septic tanks and settlement tanks in order to reduce danger of overflowing and malfunctioning. Septic tanks should only be considered if the subsoil is suitable for disposal of the effluent. Under the Control of Pollution Act 1974 a water authority may require further treatment of effluent discharged from a settlement or septic tank.

Siting and construction

Cesspools and tanks must be periodically desludged. This is usually carried out mechanically using a tanker. Because of the length of piping involved it is necessary that the cesspool or tank be sited within
30 m of a vehicular access. Emptying and cleaning should not involve the contents being taken through a dwelling or place of work, although it is permissible for access to be through an open covered space.

Cesspools and tanks should also be constructed of materials which are impervious to the contents and to ground water. This would include engineering brickwork in 1:3 cement mortar at least 220 mm thick, concrete at least 150 mm thick and glass reinforced concrete.

Prefabricated cesspools and tanks are available made of glass reinforced plastic, polyethylene or steel. These should comply with a BBA Certificate and should be installed strictly in accordance with the manufacturer's instructions. Care should be exercised over the stability of these tanks.

Additionally, cesspools should:

- Be covered and ventilated.
- Have no openings except for the inlet from the drain and the access for emptying. The access should have no dimension smaller than 600 mm and the inlet should be provided with access for inspection (see Fig. 13.16).

Septic or settlement tanks should:

- Contain at least two chambers operating in series.

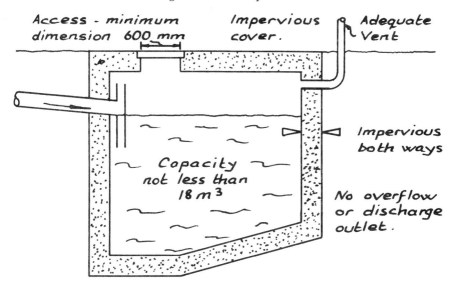

Access - minimum
dimension 600 mm

Impervious
cover.

Adequate
Vent

Impervious
both ways

Capacity
not less than
18 m³

No overflow
or discharge
outlet.

<u>Cesspools</u>

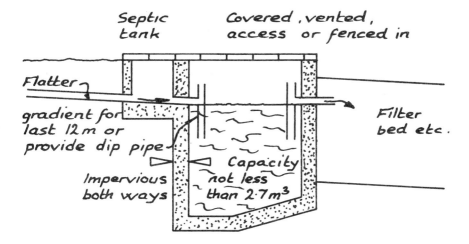

Septic
tank

Covered, vented,
access or fenced in

Flatter
gradient for
last 12 m or
provide dip pipe

Filter
bed etc.

Impervious
both ways

Capacity
not less
than 2·7 m³

<u>Septic or Settlement tanks.</u>

Fig. 13.16 Cesspools, septic tanks and settlement tanks.

● Be covered with heavy concrete covers or fenced. (If covered they should also be ventilated and provided with access for emptying as for cesspools.)
● Have inlets and outlets provided with access for inspection.

In order to avoid excessive disturbance to the contents of the tank the velocity of flow into the tank should be limited. This may be achieved by laying the last 12 m of the incoming drain at a gradient of 1 in 50 or flatter for all pipes up to 150 mm in diameter. Alternatively, a dip pipe may be provided (see Fig. 13.16) where the tank width does not exceed 1200 mm.

AD H2
1.4 to 1.10

Alternatively, the performance required may also be met by complying with the relevant clauses of BS 6297: 1983 *Code of practice for design and installation of small sewage treatment works and cesspools.*

AD H2
1.11

Rainwater drainage

Any system carrying rainwater from the roof of a building to a sewer, soakaway, watercourse or other suitable outfall is required to be adequate.

Regs Sch. 1
H3

The requirements of paragraph H3 may be met by any rainwater drainage system which:

AD H3

● Conveys the flow of rainwater to a suitable outfall (surface water or combined sewer, soakaway or watercourse).
● Reduces to a minimum the risk of leakage or blockage.
● Is accessible for clearing blockages.

AD H3
page 20

AD H3 contains no provisions for the drainage of areas such as small roofs and balconies less than 6 m^2 in area unless these areas receive additional flows of water from rainwater pipes or adjacent hard surfaces.

AD H3
0.1

Rainwater or surface water should never be discharged to a cesspool or septic tank.

AD H3
0.5

Gutters and rainwater pipes

A rainwater drainage system should be capable of carrying the anticipated flow at any point in the system. The flow will depend on the area of roofs to be drained and on the intensity of the rainfall. A maximum intensity of 75 mm in any one hour should be assumed in design calculations.

The ultimate capacity of gutters and rainwater pipes depends on their length, shape, size and gradient and on the number, disposition and design of outlets. AD H3 contains design data for half-round gutters up to 150 mm in diameter. They are assumed to be laid level

AD H3
0.2 & 0.3

AD H3, section 1

Table **2**   **Gutter sizes and outlet sizes**

Max roof area [m^2]	Gutter size [mm dia]	Outlet size [mm dia]	Flow capacity [litres/sec]
6.0	—	—	—
18.0	75	50	0.38
37.0	100	63	0.78
53.0	115	63	1.11
65.0	125	75	1.37
103.0	150	89	2.16

Note
Refers to nominal half round eaves gutters laid level with outlet at one end sharp edged. Round edged outlets allow smaller downpipe sizes.

and to have a sharp-edged outlet at one end only. Table 2 to section 1 of AD H3 is reproduced above and gives gutter and outlet sizes for different roof areas for lengths of gutter up to 50 times the water depth. The gutter capacity should be reduced for greater lengths.

AD H3 sec. 1 1.2

The maximum roof areas given in Table 2 are the largest effective areas which should be drained into the gutters given in the Table. The effective area of a roof will depend on whether the surface is flat or pitched. Table 1 to section 1 of AD H3 shows how the effective area may be calculated for different roof pitches. The factors given in the Table for roof pitches between 30° and 60° appear to be derived by dividing the plan area by the cosine of the angle of pitch, for example, $1/\text{Cos }30 = 1\cdot1547$, and $1/\text{Cos }45 = 1\cdot4142$. It would seem reasonable, therefore, to use this relationship for roofs of intermediate pitch. However, no guidance on this is given in the approved document.

AD H3 sec. 1 1.1

Gutters should also be fitted so that any overflow caused by abnormal rainfall will be discharged clear of the building.

AD H3, section 1

Table **1**   **Calculation of area drained**

Type of surface	Design area [m^2]
1 flat roof	plan area of relevant portion
2 pitched roof at 30° pitched roof at 45° pitched roof at 60°	plan area of portion × 1.15 plan area of portion × 1.40 plan area of portion × 2.00
3 pitched roof over 70° or any wall	elevational area × 0.5

Where it is not possible to comply with the conditions assumed in Table 2, further guidance is given in AD H3:

● Where an end outlet is not practicable the gutter should be sized to take the larger of the roof areas draining into it. If two end outlets are provided they may be 100 times the depth of flow apart.
● It may be possible to reduce pipe and gutter sizes if:

(a) the gutter is laid to fall towards the nearest outlet; or,
(b) a different shaped gutter is used with a larger capacity than the half round gutter; or,
(c) a rounded outlet is used.

AD H3
sec. 1
1.3 & 1.4

In these cases reference should be made to BS 6367: 1983 *Code of practice for roofs and paved areas*. Rainwater pipes should comply with the following rules:

● Discharge should be to a drain, gully, other gutter or surface which is drained.
● Any discharge into a combined system of drainage should be through a trap (e.g. into a trapped gully).
● Rainwater pipes should not be smaller than the size of the gutter outlet.
● Where more than one gutter serves a rainwater pipe the pipe should have an area at least as large as the combined areas of the gutter outlets.

AD H3
sec. 1
1.5 & 1.6

Materials

Materials used should be adequately strong and durable. Additionally:

● Gutters should have watertight joints.
● Downpipes placed inside a building should be capable of withstanding the test for airtightness described on page 13.18 above.
● Gutters and rainwater pipes should be adequately supported with no restraint on thermal movement.
● Pipes and gutters of different metals should be separated by non-metallic material to prevent electrolytic corrosion.

AD H3
sec. 1
1.7

If followed, the relevant clauses of BS 6367: 1983 *Code of practice for drainage of roofs and paved areas* will also satisfy the performance requirements for above ground rainwater drainage.

AD H3
sec. 1
1.8

Rainwater drainage below ground

Section 2 of AD H3 deals specifically with drainage systems carrying only rainwater. Combined systems (those carrying both foul and rainwater) are permitted by some drainage authorities where allow-

AD H3, section 2

Diagram **1**   **Discharge capacities of rainwater drains running full**

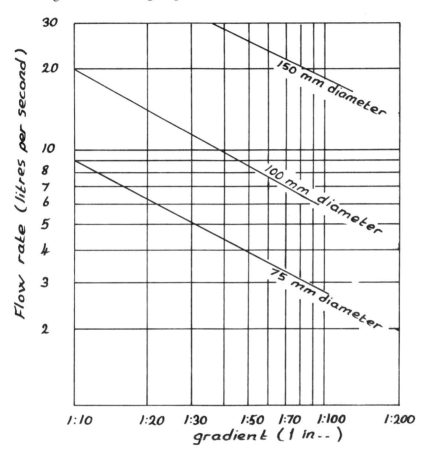

ance is made for the additional capacity. Where a combined system does not have sufficient capacity, rainwater will need to be taken via a separate system to its own outfall. Pumped systems of surface water drainage may be needed where there is a tendency to surcharging or gravity connections are impracticable. Reference should be made to BS 8301 in these cases.

With the exception of pipe gradients and sizes, the recommendations given above for below ground foul drainage (see pages 13.18 to 13.32) apply equally to rainwater drainage below ground.

Pipe sizes and gradients

Drains should be laid to falls and should be large enough to carry the expected flow. The rate of flow will depend on the area of the surfaces (including paved or other hard surfaces) being drained. The capacity will depend on the diameter and gradient of the pipes.

The minimum permitted diameter of any rainwater drain is 75 mm. For paved or other hard surfaces a rainfall intensity of 50 mm per hour should be assumed. Diagram 1 to section 2 of AD H3 is reproduced above and gives discharge capacities for rainwater drains running full. As an alternative to section 2 of AD H3 the relevant recommendations of BS 8301: 1985, *Code of practice for building drainage*, may be followed.

AD H3
sec. 2
2.6 & 2.7

AD H3
sec. 2
2.12

Solid waste storage

Buildings are required to have:

(a) Adequate means of storing solid waste;
(b) Adequate means of access for the users of the building to a place of storage; and,
(c) Adequate means of access from the place of storage to a street.

Regs Sch. 1
H4

The requirements of paragraph H4 may be met by providing solid waste storage facilities which are:

● Large enough, bearing in mind the quantity of refuse generated and the frequency of removal.
● Designed and sited so as not to present a health risk.
● Sited so as to be accessible for filling and emptying.

AD H4
0.1

Therefore the efficacy of the refuse storage system is dependent on its capacity and ease of collection by the relevant authorities.

Domestic buildings

Storage capacity

Assuming weekly collection, dwellinghouses, flats and maisonettes up to four storeys high should have, or have access to, a movable container with a minimum capacity of 0.12 m^3 or a communal container with a capacity between 0.75 m^3 and 1 m^3. These recommended capacities are based on a refuse output of 0.09 m^3 per dwelling per week. If weekly collections are not provided by the refuse collection authority then larger capacity containers or more individual containers will need to be provided. Dwellings in buildings over four storeys high should share a container fed by a chute unless this is impracticable. In the latter case suitable management arrangements should be provided for conveying the refuse to the place of storage.

AD H4
1.1 & 1.2

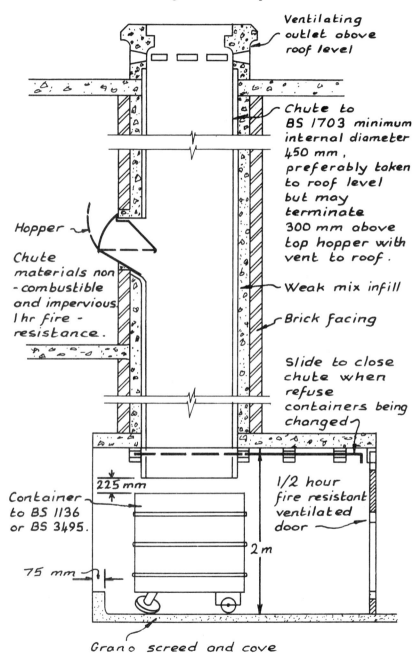

Ventilating
outlet above
roof level

Chute to
BS 1703 minimum
internal diameter
450 mm,
preferably taken
to roof level
but may
terminate
300 mm above
top hopper with
vent to roof.

Weak mix infill

Brick facing

Slide to close
chute when
refuse
containers being
changed

1/2 hour
fire resistant
ventilated
door

2 m

Hopper

Chute
materials non
-combustible
and impervious.
1 hr fire-
resistance.

Container
to BS 1136
or BS 3495.

225 mm

75 mm

Grano screed and cove

Fig. 13.17 Refuse chutes.

Design and siting

Simple dustbin-type containers should have close fitting lids.

In comparison with Part J of the Building Regulations 1976, AD H4 contains very little information on refuse chutes. This is compensated for by referring the reader to BS 5906: 1980 *Code of practice for storage and on site treatment of solid waste from buildings*, where full details of refuse chute systems may be obtained.

The provisions of AD H4 require that refuse chutes should be constructed with:

- Smooth, non-absorbent inner surfaces.
- Close fitting access hoppers at each storey containing a dwelling.
- Ventilation at top and bottom.

Containers need not be enclosed, but, if they are, sufficient space should be allowed for filling and emptying. A clear space of 150 mm should be provided between and around containers. The space enclosing communal containers should have a clear headroom of 2 m and be permanently ventilated at top and bottom. Figure 13.17 is based on the recommendations of BS 5906: 1980 and illustrates a typical refuse chute installation.

AD H4
1.3 to 1.5

Refuse containers should comply with the following rules with regard to siting:

- For new buildings it should be possible to collect a container without taking it through a building. (It is permissible to pass through a garage, car port or other covered space.)
- Containers should not be sited more than 25 m from the building which they serve or from any vehicle access.
- Householders should not be required to carry refuse more than 30 m to a container or chute.

AD H4
1.6 & 1.7

Non domestic buildings

In the development of non domestic buildings special problems may arise. It is therefore essential to consult the refuse collection authority for their requirements with regard to the following:

- The storage capacity required for the volume and nature of the waste produced. (The collection authority will be able to give guidance as to the size and type of container they will accept and the frequency of collection.)
- Storage method. (This may include details of any proposed on-site treatment and should be related to the future layout of the development and the building density.)
- Location of storage and treatment areas including access for vehicles and operatives.

- Measures to ensure adequate hygiene in storage and treatment areas.
- Measures to prevent fire risks.

AD H4
1.8

BS 5906: 1980 should, again, be consulted with regard to the above especially clauses 3 to 10, 12 to 15 and Appendix A.

AD H4
1.9

Chapter 14

Heat producing appliances

Introduction

Part J of Schedule 1 to the Building Regulations 1985 is concerned with the safe installation of heat producing appliances in buildings.

It is limited to fixed appliances burning solid fuel, oil or gas and to incinerators. (It is assumed that this means incinerators which burn solid fuel, oil or gas since no further guidance is given.) This excludes all electric heating appliances and small portable heaters such as paraffin stoves.

In order that it may function safely a heat producing appliance needs an adequate supply of combustion air and it must be capable of discharging the products of combustion to outside air. This must be achieved without allowing noxious fumes to enter the building and without causing damage by heat or fire to the fabric of the building.

In the accompanying Approved Document J, there has been an attempt at considerable simplification. This is to be warmly welcomed since the former regulations (which occupied Parts L and M of the Building Regulations 1976) were confusing and repetitive.

The Clean Air Acts 1956–1968

As a result of the Report of the Committee on Air Pollution (Cmnd. 9322, November 1954) the Clean Air Act 1956 was passed to give effect to some of the Committee's recommendations. It applies to England, Wales and Scotland and came into force on 31 December 1956. Its main provisions may be summarised briefly, and should be borne in mind in considering the effect of Part J of Schedule 1 to the Building Regulations 1985.

1956 Act secs 1 & 2 The Act makes it an offence to allow the emission of *dark smoke* from a chimney, but certain special defences are allowed, e.g., unavoidable failure of a furnace. DARK SMOKE is defined as smoke which appears to be as dark as, or darker than, shade 2 on the Ringelmann Chart. Regulations made under the Act amplify its provisions in relation to industrial and other buildings, and it should be noted that the prohibition on dark smoke applies to all buildings, railway engines and ships. However, its chief effect is on industrial and commercial premises.

House chimneys rarely emit dark smoke, but local authorities may, by order confirmed by the Secretary of State for the Environment, declare *smoke control areas*. In a smoke control area the emission of smoke from chimneys constitutes an offence, although it is a defence to prove that the emission of smoke was not caused by the use of any fuel other than an authorised fuel. Regulations prescribe the following authorised fuels: anthracite; briquetted fuels carbonised in the process of manufacture; coke; electricity; low temperature carbonisation fuels; low volatile steam coals; and fluidised char binderless briquettes. **1956 Act** secs 11–15

The 1956 Act, as amended, provides for the payment of grants by local authorities, and Exchequer contributions, towards the cost of any necessary adaptation or conversion of fireplaces to smokeless forms of heating in private dwellings in smoke control areas.

Heating appliances

Approved Document J is concerned only with heating appliances which produce smoke or gases, and these are divided into the following classes:

(1) Solid fuel and oil-burning appliances with a rated output up to 45 kW (referred to as 'Type 1' appliances in this chapter); and,
(2) Gas burning appliances with a rated input up to 60 kW (referred to as 'Type 2' appliances in this chapter).

There are no specific references to incinerators or to the installation of appliances with a higher rating than those given above. Since these will almost invariably be installed under the supervision of a heating engineer it may be considered that sufficient safeguards already exist. However, this does appear to be an area where further guidance could have been given.

Smaller appliances may not receive the attention of a qualified engineer. Accordingly, the requirements for Type 1 and 2 appliances are set out in detail in the Approved Document.

Solid fuel and oil-burning appliances may produce smoke and soot and considerable flue temperatures. The requirements for Type 1 appliances are therefore more stringent than for Type 2 (gas) appliances, because the design, manufacture and installation of the latter are more exactly controlled.

Minimum thickness of 100 mm or 200 mm of non-combustible material are required at many points by the Approved Document. This is intended to ensure that if brickwork is used, standard ½ brick or 1 brick thicknesses should be provided in these positions.

Interpretation

Only one definition appears in AD J1/2/3:

AD J1/2/3
sec. 1
1.1

NON-COMBUSTIBLE means capable of being classed as non-combustible when subjected to the non-combustibility test of BS 476, Part 4: 1970 (1984) *Non-combustibility test for materials* (see also Chapter 7 Fire, page 7.1).

A number of other terms are used in AD J1/2/3 and these are defined below. However, it must be stressed that these definitions do *not* appear in the Approved Document.

FACTORY-MADE INSULATED CHIMNEY means a chimney comprising a flue lining, non-combustible thermal insulation and outer casing.

FLUE means a passage conveying appliance discharge to the external air.

FLUE PIPE means a pipe forming a flue. It does not include a pipe built in as a lining to a chimney.

CHIMNEY includes any part of the structure of a building forming any part of a flue other than a flue pipe.

BALANCED-FLUED or ROOM-SEALED APPLIANCE means a gas appliance which draws its combustion air from a point immediately adjacent to the point where it discharges its combustion products, and is so designed that inlet, outlet and combustion chamber of the installed appliance are isolated from the room or internal space in which the appliance is situated, except for a door for igniting the appliance.

CONSTRUCTIONAL HEARTH means a hearth forming part of the structure of a building. It is usually a concrete slab.

For ease of reference the following terms have been used throughout this chapter. These terms do *not* appear in AD J1/2/3.

TYPE 1 APPLIANCE means a solid fuel or oil-burning appliance of output rating not more than 45 kW.

TYPE 2 APPLIANCE means a gas appliance with a rated input up to 60 kW.

Air supply

Heat producing appliances are required to be provided with an adequate supply of air for combustion of the fuel and for efficient operation of the chimney or flue.

Regs Sch. 1
J1

Air supply to Type 1 appliances

In order to satisfy the requirements of Paragraph J1 the appliance should either be room-sealed or should be situated in a room which has adequate ventilation. The area of ventilation that should be provided is shown in Table 14.1 which is derived from sections 2 and 4 of AD J1/2/3.

Where combustion air is drawn through a permanent air entry opening from an adjacent room or space, outside air should be admitted to that adjacent room or space as required by Table 14.1.

AD J1/2/3
sec. 1
1.2

Table 14.1 Supply of air for combustion – Type 1 (solid fuel and oil burning) appliances.

Type of appliance	Type of ventilation
1 solid fuel burning open appliance	a permanent air entry opening or openings with a total free area of at least 50 per cent of the appliance throat opening. (See BS 8303: 1986.)
2 other solid fuel appliance	a permanent air entry opening or openings with a total free area of at least 550 mm^2 per kW of rated output over 5 kW *(see also Note)*.
3 oil burning appliance	a permanent air entry opening with a total free area of at least 550 mm^2/ kW of appliance rated output over 5 kW.

Note
If the appliance is fitted with a draught stabilizer, then an additional permanent air entry opening (or openings) should be provided with a total free area of at least 300 mm^2/kW of appliance rated output.

AD J1/2/3
sec. 1, 2.1
and sec. 4
4.1

Air supply to Type 2 appliances

It is possible to install a wide range of gas burning appliances in buildings, some of which discharge the products of combustion into the room in which they are installed (e.g. gas cookers). Other appliances such as boilers and convector heaters may discharge into a conventional open flue or they may be room-sealed.

The performance requirements for air supply will be met if either the appliance is balanced-flued or it is situated in a room which has adequate ventilation.

AD J1/2/3
sec. 2
Part A
2.3

Table 14.2 below summarises the requirements for supply of combustion air and shows the areas of ventilation which should be provided.

Table 14.2   Air supply to Type 2 (gas burning) appliances.

Type of appliance	Area of permanent ventilation to outside air	Remarks
1 Gas cooker[1]	5000 mm^2	For rooms less than 10 m^3 in volume.
2 Balanced-flued appliance	—	Any appliance situated in a bathroom, shower room or private garage must be balanced-flued[2]
3 Open-flued appliance:	450 mm^2	per kW of rated input over 7 kW

Notes

[1] Gas cookers should be installed in a room containing an openable window or other opening to outside air. The area of permanent ventilation listed above should also be included if the room volume is less than 10 m^3.

[2] Gas Safety (Installation and Use) Regulations 1984.

AD J1/2/3
sec. 3
3.2, 3.3, 3.4

Discharge of products of combustion

Regs Sch. 1
J2

Heat producing appliances are required to have adequate provision for the discharge of the products of combustion to the outside air.

The requirements of this paragraph may be met by ensuring that flues, flue pipes and chimneys:

● Are of sufficient size.
● Contain only those openings necessary for inspection, cleaning or efficient working of the appliance.
● Are constructed of or lined with suitable materials.
● Are constructed at roof level so as to discharge in a safe manner.

Where an appliance is connected to a chimney built before 1 February 1966 (the date on which the first building regulations became operable) it will not be necessary to comply with certain provisions (see text below) relating to chimneys and flues. If applied, these requirements would make it virtually impossible to install an appliance without totally rebuilding the chimney..

AD J1/2/3
sec. 1
1.7

This provision assumes, of course, that the chimney is performing satisfactorily.

Discharge of products of combustion – Type 1 appliances

Type 1 appliances are permitted to discharge into balanced or low level flues, chimneys, factory-made insulated chimneys or flue pipes which discharge to external air.

AD J1/2/3
sec. 1
1.4

Oil burning balanced flued and low level discharge appliances

These appliances should be installed so that:

- The products of combustion may be dispersed externally.
- For a balanced flue, the inlet is situated externally to permit the free intake of air.

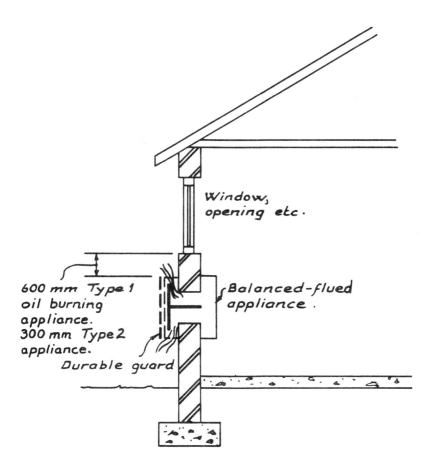

Fig. 14.1 Room sealed appliance.

- No part of the terminal is within 600 mm of any opening (openable windows, ventilator, etc.) into the building.

AD J1/2/3
sec. 4
4.4
- The terminal is protected by a durable guard where it could come into contact with people near the building. This is to prevent danger to the public and damage to the terminal (see Fig. 14.1).
- The entry of any matter which might restrict the flue is prevented.

Flues – general requirements

Whether in chimneys or flue pipes, flues should comply with the following rules:

- SIZE.   The size of the flue should be at least that given in Table 2 to AD J1/2/3 (solid fuel) or Table 14.3 (oil) as shown below and never less than the outlet on the appliance.

AD J1/2/3
sec. 2; 2.2
sec. 4; 4.2
- OPENINGS INTO FLUES.   Only the following openings into a flue, chimney or flue pipe are permitted:

AD J1/2/3
sec. 1
1.5
(a) An opening for inspection or cleaning, fitted with a non-combustible, rigid, double cased gas tight cover; and

(b) An opening in the same room or internal space as the appliance, fitted with a draught diverter, draught stabiliser or explosion door of non-combustible material.

- COMMUNICATIONS WITH FLUES.   No flue should communicate with more than one room or internal space in a building. This requirement does not, however, prohibit the provision of an inspection or cleaning opening allowing access to a flue from a room or space other than the one in which the appliance is

AD J1/2/3
sec. 1
1.6
installed (see Fig. 14.4 below). A flue may also serve more than one appliance in the same room.

- OUTLETS OF FLUES.   The outlet of any flue in a chimney, or any flue pipe, should be at least:

(a) 1 m above the highest point of contact between the chimney or flue pipe and the roof, for roofs pitched at less than 10°; and,

(b) 2·3 m measured horizontally from the roof surface for roofs pitched at 10° or more; and,

(c) 1 m above the top of any openable part of a window or skylight, or any ventilator or similar opening which is in a roof or external wall and is not more than 2·3 m horizontally from the top of the chimney or flue pipe; and,

AD J1/2/3
sec. 2;
2.3
(d) 600 mm above the top of any part of an adjoining building which is not more than 2·3 m horizontally from the top of the chimney or flue pipe.

AD J1/2/3
sec. 4;
4.5
The outlet from a flue serving an oil-fired pressure jet appliance may terminate anywhere above the roof line.

AD J1/2/3, Section 2

Table 2   Size of flues (solid fuel appliances)

Installation	Minimum flue size
Fireplace recess with an opening up to 500 mm × 550 mm	200 mm diameter or square section of equivalent area
Inglenook recess appliances	a free area of 15% of the area of the recess opening
Open fire	200 mm diameter or square section of equivalent area
Closed appliance up to 20 kW rated output burning bituminous coal	150 mm diameter or square section of equivalent area
Closed appliance up to 20 kW rated output	125 mm diameter or square section of equivalent area
Closed appliance above 20 kW and up to 30 kW rated output	150 mm diameter or square section of equivalent area
Closed appliance above 30 kW and up to 45 kW rated output	175 mm diameter or square section of equivalent area

Note
Should an offset be necessary in a flue run then the flue size should be increased by 25 mm on each dimension (diameter or each side of square flue).

Table **14.3**   Size of flues (oil burning appliances)

Installation	Minimum size of flue
(a) flue in a chimney for an appliance with an output rating up to 20 kW	100 mm diameter
(b) flue in a chimney with an output rating between 20 kW and 32 kW	125 mm diameter
(c) flue in a chimney with an output rating between 32 kW and 45 kW	150 mm diameter
(d) flue in flue pipe	at least the size of the outlet from the appliance

Note
For square flues cross-sectional area should be as for equivalent circular flue.

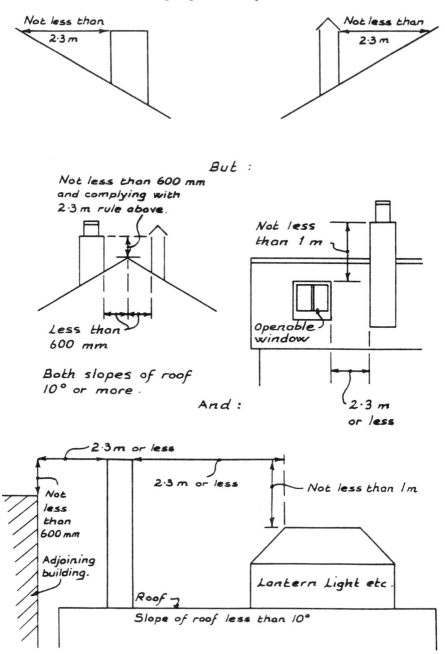

Fig. 14.2 Flue outlets Type 1 appliances.

Additionally, if the chimney or flue pipe passes through the roof within 2·3 m of the ridge and both slopes are at 10° or more to the horizontal, the top of the chimney or flue pipe may be not less than 600 mm above the ridge (see Fig. 14.2).

- HORIZONTAL FLUE RUNS. Ideally, these should be avoided except in the case of balanced or low level flues for oil burning appliances and back outlet solid fuel appliances. In the latter case the horizontal section of flue should not exceed 150 mm.

AD J1/2/3
sec. 2; 2.4
sec. 4; 4.3

- BENDS IN FLUES. If possible flues should be vertical. However, if it is necessary to form a bend in a flue it should not be greater than 45° to the vertical for oil burning appliances and 30° to the vertical for solid fuel appliances (see Fig. 14.3).

AD J1/2/3
sec. 2; 2.5
sec. 4; 4.3

- ACCESS FOR INSPECTION AND CLEANING. This should be provided for any appliance and its chimney and flue pipe. If a flue in a chimney is not directly over an appliance then a debris collecting space should be provided which has an access for inspection and cleaning, fitted with a sealed double-cased door (see Fig. 14.4).

AD J1/2/3
sec. 2;
1.5, 2.11

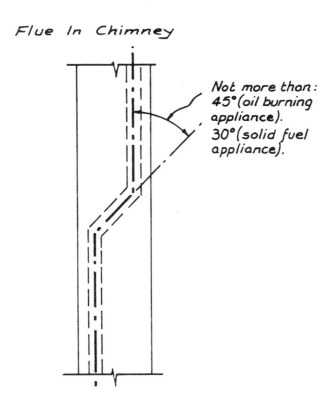

Fig. 14.3 Bend in flues – Type 1 appliances.

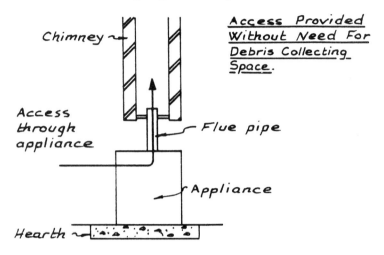

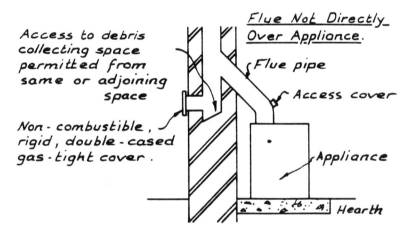

Fig. 14.4 Access for inspection and cleaning.

Flues – linings to chimneys

There is a general requirement that chimneys should be factory-made insulated chimneys or should be constructed of masonry. Masonry chimneys serving Type 1 appliances may be built of refractory material without a lining or may be lined with one of the following:

- Clay flue linings with rebated or socketed joints to BS 1181: 1971 (1977) *Clay flue linings and flue terminals.*
- Clay pipes and fittings to BS 65: 1981 *Specification for vitrified clay pipes, fittings and joints*, socketed, imperforate and acid resistant.

• Flue linings made from kiln-burnt aggregate and high alumina cement with rebated or socketed joints or steel collars around the joint.

The linings should be jointed and pointed with fire-proof mortar and built into the chimney with sockets uppermost. This prevents condensate from running out of the joints where it might adversely affect any caulking material. The space between the linings and the masonry should be filled with weak mortar or insulating concrete. For oil burning appliances, if the temperature of the flue gases is unlikely to exceed 260°C (under the worst operating conditions) then the provisions for gas burning appliances (see below) may be followed instead of the above.

AD J1/2/3 sec. 2; 2.12, 2.13 sec. 4; 4.7

AD J1/2/3 sec. 4; 4.7(b)

Factory-made insulated chimneys

These chimneys are prefabricated in a factory and are erected on site in sections.

For an appliance burning solid fuel the chimney should be constructed and tested to BS 4543 *Factory-made insulated chimneys*, Part 1: 1976 *Methods of test for factory-made insulated chimneys* and Part 2: 1976 *Specification for chimneys for solid fuel fired appliances*. For oil-fired appliances the chimney should comply with BS 4543 *Factory-made insulated chimneys*, Part 1: 1976 *Methods of test for factory-made insulated chimneys* and Part 3: 1976 *Specification for chimneys for oil-fired appliances*.

The chimney should also be installed in accordance with BS 6461: *Installation of chimneys and flues for domestic appliances burning solid fuel (including wood and peat)*: Part 2: 1984: *Code of practice for factory-made insulated chimneys for internal applications*; or to manufacturers' instructions.

AD J1/2/3 sec. 2; 2.16 sec. 4; 4.8

Flue pipes

Flue pipes serving Type 1 appliances should not pass through any roof space, and should only be used to connect an appliance to a chimney. Whether or not the space between the roof covering and the ceiling finish in a flat roof constitutes a roofspace is open to conjecture. The obvious intention is that flue pipes should be as short as possible and should only be used to connect an appliance to a proper chimney.

A horizontal connection is permitted to connect a back outlet appliance to a chimney but this should not exceed 150 mm in length (see Fig. 14.5).

AD J1/2/3 sec. 2 2.6

Flue pipes should be constructed of:

• Cast iron, in accordance with BS 41: 1973 (1981) *Cast iron spigot and socket flue or smoke pipes and fittings*.

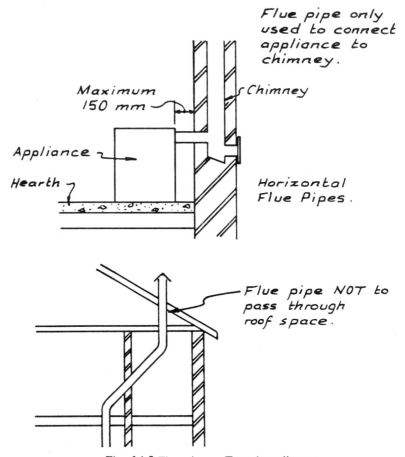

Fig. 14.5 Flue pipes – Type 1 appliances.

- Mild steel at least 3 mm thick.
- Stainless steel at least 1 mm thick as described in BS 1449: *Steel plate, sheet and strip*, Part 2: 1983 *Specification for stainless and heat resisting steel plate, sheet and strip*, for Grade 316 S11, 316 S13, 316 S16, 316 S31, 316 S33 or equivalent Euronorm 88–71 designation.
- Vitreous enamelled steel complying with BS 6999: 1989: *Specification for vitreous enamelled low carbon steel flue pipes, other components and accessories for solid fuel burning appliances with a maximum rated output of 45 kW.*

AD J1/2/3
sec. 2; 2.7,
2.8
sec. 4; 4.7

Where spigot and socket flue pipes are used the sockets should be placed uppermost.

It should be noted that where the flue gas temperature of a Type 1 oil-burning appliance does not exceed 260° C then it is permissible to connect the appliance to a flue pipe or chimney as described below for Type 2 appliances.

Discharge of products of combustion – Type 2 appliances

Section 3 of AD J1/2/3 deals specifically with gas burning appliances with a rated input up to 60 kW as follows:

- Cooking appliances (ovens, hotplates, grills, etc.).
- Balanced-flued appliances (boilers, convector heaters, water heaters, etc.).
- Decorative log and solid fuel fire effect appliances.
- Individual, natural draught, open-flued appliances (boilers, back boilers, etc.).

AD J1/2/3
sec. 3

Fuel effect fires are a special case since ceramic fuel is heated by a live flame. Where these have been tested by an approved authority they may be installed in accordance with the manufacturers' instructions. If this is not the case, they should either comply with BS 6714: 1986 or Section 2 of AD J1/2/3 (i.e. solid fuel burning appliances).

AD J1/2/3
sec. 3; 3.1

Apart from gas cooking appliances (which discharge their products of combustion into the air of the room in which they are situated), Type 2 appliances should discharge into balanced flues, flue linings in masonry chimneys, chimneys constructed of refractory materials without a lining (chimney walls), factory-made insulated chimneys, flue pipes or flexible flue liners.

Balanced flues

The requirements listed above (see page 14.6) for Type 1 appliances also apply to Type 2 appliances with one exception:

- Where an appliance terminal is wholly or partly beneath an opening (openable window, ventilator, etc.) no part of the terminal should be within 300 mm vertically of the bottom of the opening.

AD J1/2/3
sec. 3; 3.7

Additionally any appliance situated in a bathroom, shower room or private garage should be a balanced-flued appliance.

AD J1/2/3
sec. 3; 3.2

Flues – general requirements

Flues should comply with the following rules:

- SIZE.   The requirements for the cross-sectional measurements and areas of flues to Type 2 appliances are:

(a) The cross-sectional area of a flue serving a gas fire should be at least 12 000 mm^2 for round flues and 16 500 mm^2 for rectangular flues. Additionally, the flues should have a minimum dimension of 90 mm.

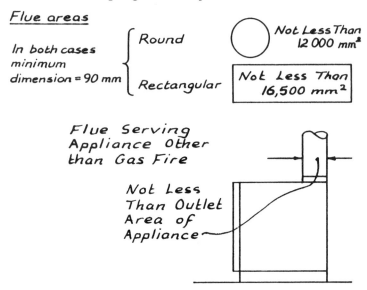

Fig. 14.6 Flue sizes – Type 2 appliances.

(b) The cross-sectional area of a flue serving any other appliance should not be less than the area of the appliance outlet (see Fig. 14.6).

AD J1/2/3
sec. 3; 3.5

These rules do not apply to balanced flued or solid fuel effect appliances.

● OPENINGS INTO FLUES.   The only openings permitted into a flue serving a Type 2 appliance are:

(a) An opening for inspection or cleaning, fitted with a gas-tight cover of non-combustible material; or,

AD J1/2/3
sec. 1; 1.5

(b) a draught diverter, draught stabiliser or explosion door.

● COMMUNICATIONS WITH FLUES.   No flue should communicate with more than one room or internal space in a building. However, an opening for cleaning or inspection is permitted as for Type 1 appliances (see above page 14.7).

AD J1/2/3
sec. 1; 1.6

● OUTLETS OF FLUES.   Any flue outlet should be:

(a) fitted with a flue terminal if any dimension measured across the axis of the flue outlet is less than 175 mm; and,
(b) placed so that an air current may freely pass over it at all times; and,

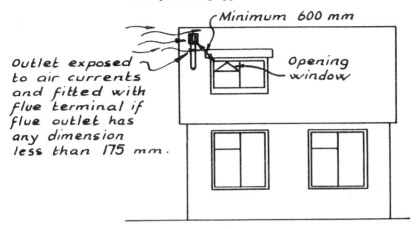

Minimum 600 mm

Outlet exposed
to air currents
and fitted with
flue terminal if
flue outlet has
any dimension
less than 175 mm.

Opening
window

Fig. 14.7 Flue outlets – Type 2 appliances.

(c) placed so that no part of the outlet is within 600 mm of any opening into the building (see Fig. 14.7).

AD J1/2/3
sec. 3; 3.8

● BENDS IN FLUES.   If possible flues should be vertical. However, if it is necessary to form a bend in a flue it should not be greater than 45° to the vertical.

AD J1/2/3
sec. 3; 3.6

Flues – linings to chimneys

There is a general requirement that chimneys should either be assembled from factory-made insulated components or they should be constructed of masonry.

AD J1/2/3
sec. 2
Part B
2.12

Masonry chimneys serving Type 2 appliances should be:

● Lined with any of the materials specified for Type 1 appliances (see page 14.11 above). The linings should be jointed and pointed with cement mortar and built into the chimney with sockets or rebates uppermost. The space between the linings and the masonry should be filled with weak mortar or insulating concrete; *or,*
● Constructed of flue blocks without a lining. Flue blocks should comply with BS 1289: *Flue blocks and masonry terminals for gas appliances:* Part 1: 1986 *Specification for precast concrete flue blocks and terminals* and Part 2: 1989 *Specification for clay flue blocks and terminals.*

AD J1/2/3
sec. 3; 3.11,
3.12

It is also permissible to line a chimney with a flexible flue liner if:

● The liner complies with BS 715: 1986 *Specification for metal flue pipes, fittings, terminals and accessories for gas-fired appliances with a rated input not exceeding 60 kW.*

- The chimneys was built before 1 February 1966; or,

AD J1/2/3
sec. 3; 3.13

- The chimney is already lined or is constructed of flue blocks as described above.

Where an appliance is connected to a chimney that is not lined or constructed of flue blocks as described in AD J1/2/3 (see above) then the chimney should be connected with a debris collection space with cleaning access. The collection space should extend at least 250 mm below the lowest point of entry of the appliance flue into the chimney and should have a minimum volume of 0·012 m³.

AD J1/2/3
sec. 3; 3.14

Factory-made insulated chimneys

AD J1/2/3
sec. 3; 3.16

Any of the factory-made insulated chimneys described above (see page 14.12) for Type 1 appliances may be used.

Flue pipes

AD J1/2/3
sec. 3; 3.9

Flue pipes for Type 2 appliances should be constructed of:

- Any of the materials specified for Type 1 appliances (see page 14.12 above).
- Asbestos cement as described in BS 567: 1973 (1984) *Specification for asbestos-cement flue pipes and fittings, light quality*, or BS 835: 1973 (1984) *Specification for asbestos-cement flue pipes and fittings, heavy quality.*
- Sheet metal to BS 715: 1970 *Sheet metal flue pipes and accessories for gas fired appliances.*
- Any other material which is suitable for its intended purpose.

Flue pipes should be fitted with the sockets uppermost.

Protection of building against fire and heat

The construction of fireplaces and chimneys and the installation of heat producing appliances and flue-pipes must be carried out so as to reduce to a reasonable level the risk of the building catching fire in consequence of their use.

Regs Sch. 1
J3

The requirements of this paragraph may be met by ensuring that hearths, fireplaces, chimneys and flue pipes:

- Are of sufficient size.
- Are constructed of suitable materials.
- Are suitably isolated from any adjacent combustible materials.

Protection of building against fire and heat – Type 1 appliances

Hearths for Type 1 appliances
Constructional hearths should be provided where a Type 1 appliance is to be installed. They should be constructed of solid non-combustible material at least 125 mm thick (including the thickness of any non-combustible floor under the hearth).

Constructional hearths built in connection with a fireplace recess should:

(a) Extend within the recess to the back and jambs of the recess; *and,*
(b) project at least 500 mm in front of the jamb; *and,*
(c) extend outside the recess to at least 150 mm beyond each side of the opening.

If not built in connection with a fireplace recess, the plan dimensions of the hearth should be such as to accommodate a square of at least 840 mm.

The requirement that the hearth should project 500 mm in front of the jambs for a fireplace recess is to reduce the danger of fire from cinders, etc.

Combustible material should not be placed under a constructional hearth for a Type 1 appliance within a vertical distance of 250 mm from the upper surface of the hearth, unless there is an air space of at least 50 mm between the combustible material and the underside of the hearth. Timber fillets supporting a hearth where it adjoins the floor are exempted from this rule (see Fig. 14.8).

AD J1/2/3
sec. 2; 2.18,
2.19

AD J1/2/3
sec. 1
Part C
1.24 & 1.25

Fireplace recesses

Fireplace recesses should be constructed of solid non-combustible material and should have a jamb on each side at least 200 mm thick, a solid back wall at least 200 mm thick, or a cavity wall back with each leaf at least 100 mm thick. These thicknesses are to run the full height of the recess. However, if a fireplace recess is in an external wall the back may be a solid wall of not less than 100 mm thickness. Similarly, if part of a wall acts as the back of two recesses on opposite sides of the wall, it may be a solid wall not less than 100 mm thick. It is assumed that this latter exemption does not apply to a wall separating buildings or dwellings within a building since the requirements for chimney walls (see below) specify a minimum thickness of 200 mm in these circumstances (see Fig. 14.9).

AD J1/2/3
sec. 2; 2.20

Walls adjoining Type 1 appliances

Where a constructional hearth for an appliance is not situated in a fireplace recess, any wall or partition within a distance of 150 mm from the edge of the hearth must be constructed of solid non-combustible

AD J1/2/3
sec. 2; 2.21

Minimum Plan Dimensions :

With Fireplace Recess.

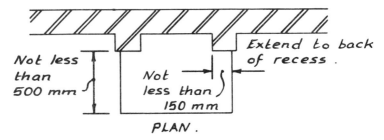

Not less
than
500 mm

Not
less than
150 mm

Extend to back
of recess.

PLAN.

Without Fireplace Recess

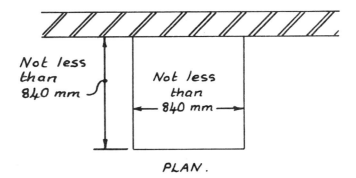

Not less
than
840 mm

Not less
than
840 mm

PLAN.

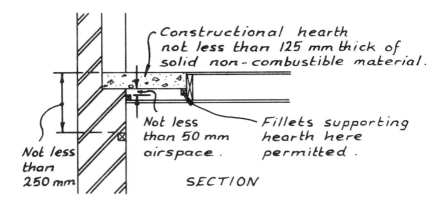

Constructional hearth
not less than 125 mm thick of
solid non-combustible material.

Not less
than 50 mm
airspace.

Fillets supporting
hearth here
permitted.

Not less
than
250 mm

SECTION

Position of Timber Fillets.

Fig. 14.8 Hearths for Type 1 appliances.

Recesses Built in Masonry

Fireplace recesses generally

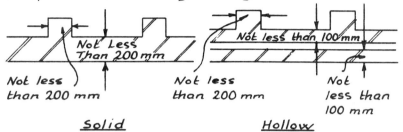

Solid   Hollow

Recesses in External Wall.

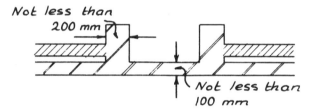

Back - to - Back Recesses

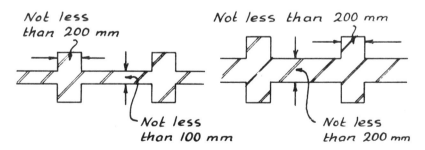

Within a Building.   On a Separating or Compartment Wall.

Fig. 14.9 Fireplace recess – Type 1 appliances.

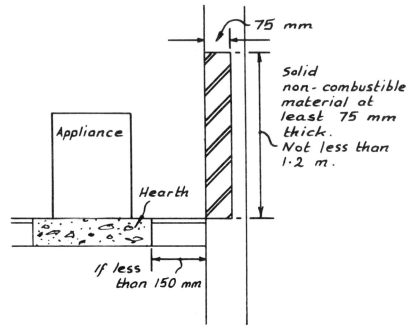

Fig. 14.10 Walls adjoining Type 1 appliances.

material at least 75 mm thick to a height of at least 1·2 m above the upper surface of the hearth (see Fig. 14.10).

Chimneys for Type 1 appliances – general requirements

Generally, if a chimney is built of masonry and is lined as described above any flue in that chimney should be:

- Surrounded and separated from any other flue in that chimney by at least 100 mm thickness of solid masonry material, excluding the thickness of any flue lining material.
- Separated by at least 200 mm of solid masonry material from another compartment of the same building, another building or another dwelling. (It is not clear how a cavity separating or compartment wall would be regarded, however.)
- Separated by at least 100 mm of solid masonry material from the outside air or from another part of the same building (but not a part which is a dwelling or a separate compartment). (See Fig. 14.11.)

AD J1/2/3
sec. 2; 2.14

Chimneys for solid fuel appliances should be designed to withstand a temperature of at least 1100° C without suffering structural changes which would impair the performance or stability of the chimney.

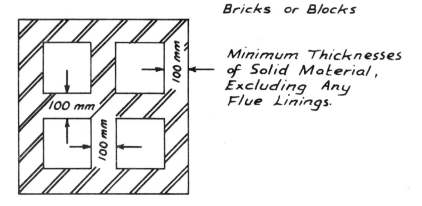

Bricks or Blocks

Minimum Thicknesses
of Solid Material,
Excluding Any
Flue Linings.

Chimney in Separating
or Compartment Wall.

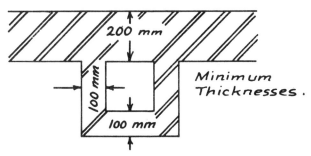

Minimum
Thicknesses.

Chimney in External Wall
or Internal Partition Wall.

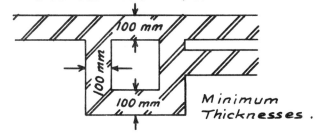

Minimum
Thicknesses.

Fig. 14.11 Chimneys – Type 1 appliances.

Chimneys for Type 1 appliances – proximity of combustible material

Combustible materials should not be placed nearer to a flue than 200 mm. Where the thickness of solid non-combustible material surrounding a flue in a chimney is less than 200 mm, no combustible material other than a floor board, skirting board, dado rail, picture rail, mantle-

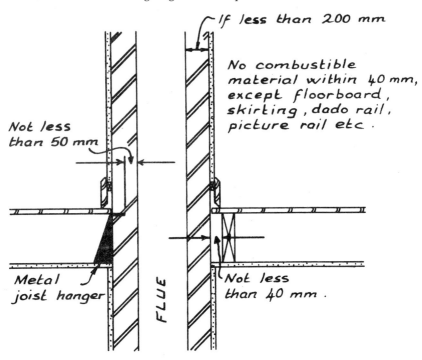

Fig. 14.12 Proximity of combustible material – Type 1 appliances.

shelf or architrave, should be placed within 40 mm of the outer surface of the chimney or fireplace recess.

AD J1/2/3
sec. 2; 2.15

No metal fastening in contact with combustible material should be placed within 50 mm of the flue (see Fig. 14.12).

Chimneys for Type 1 appliances – factory-made insulated chimneys

A chimney serving a Type 1 appliance may consist of a factory-made insulated chimney having:

- No part of the chimney passing through or attached to a part of the building forming a separate compartment, unless it is surrounded in non-combustible material having at least half the fire resistance required for the compartment wall or floor (see Chapter 7, Fire).
- No combustible material nearer to the outer surface of the chimney than the distance (X) used for the test procedures specified in BS 4543 *Factory-made insulated chimneys,* Part 1: 1976 *Methods of test for factory-made insulated chimneys.*
- A removable casing of suitable imperforate material enclosing any part of the chimney within a cupboard, storage space or roof space with no combustible material enclosed within the casing, and the

AD J1/2/3
sec. 2; 2.17
sec. 4; 4.9

distance between the inside of the casing and the outside of the chimney not less than the distance (X) specified above.

Placing and shielding of flue pipes for Type 1 appliances

A flue pipe adjacent to a wall or partition should be set at a minimum distance from any combustible material forming part of the wall or partition of at least:

(a) 3 times its external diameter; *or,*
(b) 1½ times its external diameter if the combustible material is protected by a shield of non-combustible material which is placed so that there is an airspace of at least 12·5 mm between the shield and the combustible material. The non-combustible shield should have a width equal to at least 3 times the external diameter of the flue pipe (see Fig. 14.13).

AD J1/2/3
sec. 2; 2.9

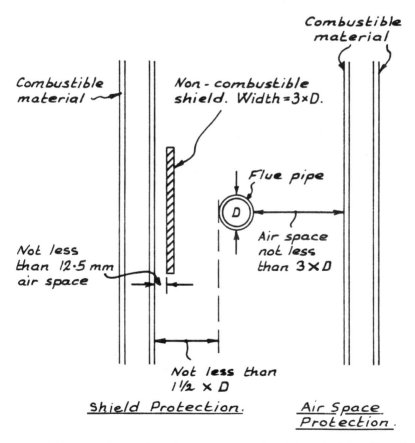

Fig. 14.13 Protection of flue pipes next to combustible materials – Type 1 appliances.

Positioning of Type 1 appliances

Where a Type 1 appliance is installed directly upon or over a constructional hearth, combustible material should not be laid closer to the base of the appliance than:

(a) *At the front*, 300 mm if the appliance is an open fire or stove which can, when opened, be operated as an open fire, or 225 mm in any other case;

(b) *at the back and sides*, 150 mm or as necessary to satisfy paragraph 2.22(b) AD J1/2/3 which relates to distance from hearth to walls (see below).

The distances fixed by this provision depend on the likelihood of danger from falling cinders or radiation. Where combustible material is not laid upon or over the constructional hearth, then the above distances should be the minimum distances from appliance base to edges of hearth.

Additionally, if any part of the back or sides of the appliance lies within 150 mm horizontally of the wall, then the wall should be of solid non-combustible construction at least 75 mm thick from floor level to a level of 300 mm above the top of the appliance.

If, however, any part of the back or sides of the appliance lies within 50 mm of the wall, then the wall should be of solid non-combustible AD J1/2/3 construction at least 200 mm thick from floor level to a level of sec. 2; 2.22 300 mm above the top of the appliance (see Fig. 14.14).

Special provisions relating to Type 1 appliances

Some oil-burning appliances are allowed to comply with lesser requirements due to their low operating temperatures.

The exceptions permitted are as follows:

- A Type 1 appliance which has a hearth temperature of not more than 100° C and is placed on an imperforate rigid seating of non-combustible material is not required to comply with the general rules regarding the construction of hearths for Type 1 appliances (see paragraphs 2.18 and 2.19 of AD J1/2/3 and pages 14.18 and 14.19 above).

- A Type 1 appliance which is constructed in such a manner that the surface temperature of the appliance's side and back panels does not exceed 100° C is not required to comply with the general rules regarding the construction of walls and partitions adjoining Type 1 AD J1/2/3 appliances (see paragraph 2.21 of AD J1/2/3 and pages 14.18 to sec. 4; 4.10; 14.21 above).
4.11

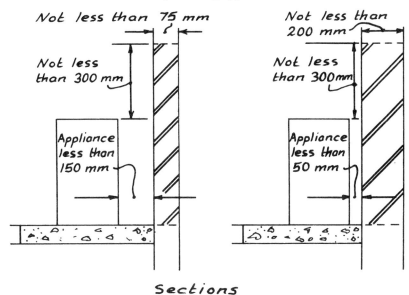

Not less than 75 mm

Not less than 300 mm

Appliance less than 150 mm

Not less than 200 mm

Not less than 300mm

Appliance less than 50 mm

Sections

Not less than 150 mm
(but see above)

Not less than 300 mm for open fire or stove but not less than 225 mm for any other appliance.

Appliance

Constructional hearth.

Plan.

Fig. 14.14 Positioning of Type 1 appliances.

Protection of building against fire and heat – Type 2 appliances

AD J1/2/3
sec. 3; 3.1

The provisions described below apply to all Type 2 gas burning appliances with a rated input up to 60 kW except decorative log or solid fuel fire-effect appliances. These should comply with section 2 of AD J1/2/3.

Hearths for Type 2 appliances

With the exception of a gas-fired back boiler a Type 2 appliance should be placed over a solid non-combustible hearth, at least 12 mm thick, which,

● extends at least 150 mm beyond the back and sides of the appliance.
● Extends forward at least 225 mm horizontally from any flame or incandescent material within the appliance.

Such a hearth is not required:

● If the appliance is installed so that no part of any flame or incandescent material is less than 225 mm above the floor.
● Where the appliance satisfies the requirements of the appropriate parts of BS 5258 *Safety of domestic gas appliances*, or BS 5386 *Specification for gas burning appliances* for installation without a hearth.

For a back boiler, the hearth should be constructed of solid non-combustible material:

● At least 125 mm thick; or,
● At least 25 mm thick on 25 mm non-combustible supports.

AD J1/2/3
sec. 3; 3.17,
3.18, 3.19

It should extend at least 150 mm beyond the back and sides of the appliance and extend forward at least 225 mm beyond the front of the appliance.

These requirements for gas appliance hearths are much less rigorous than those for solid fuel or oil-burning appliances, since there is no danger from falling fuel (see Fig. 14.15).

Shielding of structure adjoining Type 2 appliances

The back, top and sides of the appliance (including any associated draught diverter), should be separated from any combustible part of the building, by *either*,

(a) a shield of non-combustible material at least 25 mm thick, *or*,
(b) at least 75 mm air space.

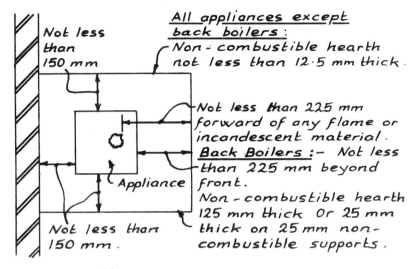

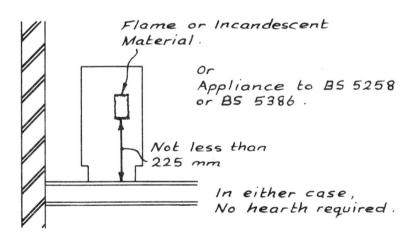

Fig. 14.15 Hearths for Type 2 appliances.

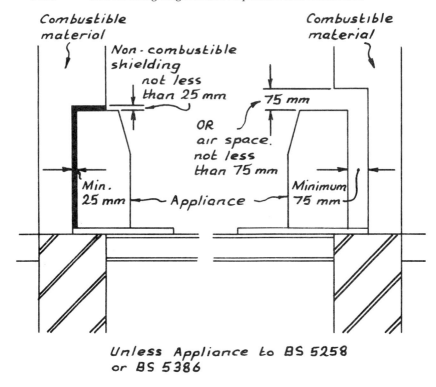

Fig. 14.16 Shielding of structure adjacent to Type 2 appliances.

AD J1/2/3
sec. 3
3.20

This requirement again need not be fulfilled if the appliance complies with the relevant recommendations of the appropriate parts of BS 5258 *Safety of domestic gas appliances* or BS 5386 *Specifications for gas burning appliances* (see Fig. 14.16).

Chimneys for Type 2 appliances

Any chimney wall which separates a flue from:
- another compartment of the same building; or,
- another building; or,
- another dwelling;

should have at least the fire resistance required for the compartment or separating wall.

In addition, there should be at least 25 mm of solid non-combustible material between:

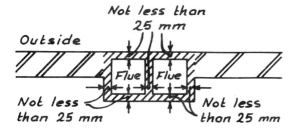

Not less than
25 mm

Outside

Flue · Flue

Not less than 25 mm

Not less than 25 mm

Another part of same building
(but not separate compartment)

<u>Chimney In External Wall</u>.

Another compartment, another building
or another dwelling.

Flue · Flue

Not less than 25 mm.

Not less than 25 mm.

At least fire-
resistance
required for
compartment
or
separating wall.

Another part of same building
(but not separate compartment)

<u>Chimney On Separating Or Compartment
Wall</u>.

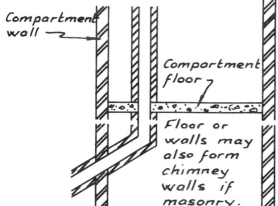

Compartment wall

Compartment floor

Chimney walls to
have at least
half fire
resistance
required of
compartment wall
or compartment
floor.

Floor or
walls may
also form
chimney
walls if
masonry.

<u>Chimney
Penetrating
Compartment
Wall or Floor</u>.

Fig. 14.17 Chimneys for Type 2 appliances.

- a flue and the outside; or,
- a flue and any part of the same building; or,
- flues in the same chimney.

It is permissible to pass a chimney serving a Type 2 appliance through a compartment wall or compartment floor providing the chimney walls have at least *half* the fire resistance required for the compartment wall or floor. Where the compartment wall or floor is constructed of masonry material it is also permitted to form the chimney wall (see Fig. 14.17). For more information see Chapter 7, Fire.

AD J1/2/3
sec. 3; 3.15

Placing and shielding of flue pipes for Type 2 appliances

Flue pipes serving Type 2 appliances should be placed so that:

- Every part of the flue pipe is at least 25 mm distant from any combustible material.
- Where the flue pipe passes through a roof, floor or wall formed of combustible materials, it is enclosed in a sleeve of non-combustible material and there is at least 25 mm air space between the flue and the sleeve.
- Where the flue pipe passes through a compartment wall or compartment floor it is cased with non-combustible material having at least half the fire resistance required for the compartment wall or floor.

AD J1/2/3
sec. 3; 3.10

Where a double-walled flue pipe is used the 25 mm air space should be measured from the outside of the inner pipe (see Fig. 14.18).

The requirements contained in AD J1/2/3 may also be met by complying with the relevant recommendations of the British Standards and Codes of Practice listed in Appendix 5 (see pages A5.1 to A5.11).

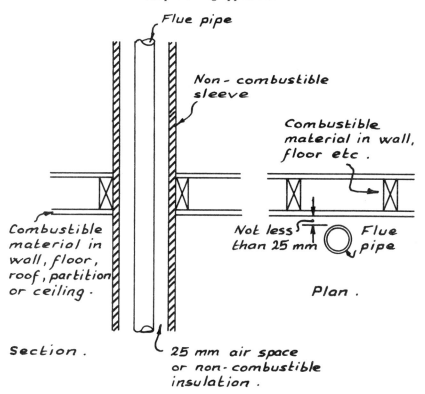

Flue pipe

Non - combustible sleeve

Combustible material in wall, floor etc .

Combustible material in wall, floor, roof, partition or ceiling .

Not less than 25 mm

Flue pipe

Plan .

Section .

25 mm air space or non-combustible insulation .

Pipe passing through wall or floor

Fig. 14.18 Placing and shielding of flue pipes – Type 2 appliances.

Chapter 15

Stairways, ramps and guards

Introduction

The control of stairways has always formed an important part of building regulations since stairways represent, in many cases, the only way out of a building in the event of fire. Also, the need to make buildings accessible to disabled people has resulted in ramps coming under the scope of control to a greater extent. Additionally, provisions are necessary for the safeguarding of stairways and ramps by means of balustrades, and for the protection of exposed areas such as landings, balconies and roofs or vehicle parks to which people have access.

Approved document K represents an attempt to reorganise and simplify Part H of the Building Regulations 1976. Most of the restrictions on the number of steps in a flight have been lifted (although only sixteen risers are permitted in a single flight where a stairway serves an area used for shop or assembly purposes), and new provisions which require balustrades to be designed so that they cannot be climbed by children, have been introduced.

Stairways and ramps

Regs Sch. 1
K1

Stairways and ramps which form part of the structure of a building are required to provide safe passage for users.

This requirement can be satisfied by reference to approved document K1 which is described below. However, reference may also be made to BS 5395 *Stairs, ladders and walkways* Part 1: 1977 *Code of practice for stairs* and Part 2: 1984 *Code of practice for the design of helical and spiral stairs* where additional information is given regarding the setting out of stairways.

Application

AD K1

Outside stairways and ramps are covered by the regulations if they form part of the structure of a building but ladders are not. (A ladder

AD K1
0.2

includes a flight if steeper than 55°, whether fixed or not.) It should be

noted that the regulations do not require buildings to contain stairways
and ramps but if they do then compliance is necessary.

AD K1
0.1

The provisions contained in AD K1 regarding stairways only apply if
the stairway forms part of a means of escape or rises more than 600
mm or has a drop at the side of more than 600 mm.

AD K1
sec. 1
1.2

Interpretation

A number of definitions are given which apply specially to stairways:

STAIRWAY – flights and landings are included in this term.

PRIVATE STAIRWAY – stairways in or serving only one dwelling.

COMMON STAIRWAY – stairways which serve two or more
dwellings.

GOING – the distance measured in plan across the tread less any
overlap with the next tread above or below.

RISE – the vertical distance between the top surfaces of two
consecutive treads (see Fig. 15.1).

AD K1
sec. 1
1.3

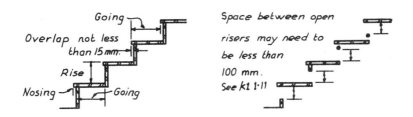

Fig. 15.1 Rise and going.

PITCH AND PITCH LINE – these terms are illustrated in AD K1
but are not defined; *however,*

PITCH LINE – may be defined as a notional line connecting the
nosings of all treads in a flight, including the nosing of the landing or
ramp at the top of the flight. The line is taken so as to form the greatest
possible angle with the horizontal, subject to the special requirements
for tapered treads (see below).

PITCH – may be defined as the angle between the pitch line and the
horizontal (see Fig. 15.2).

AD K1
sec. 1
1.4

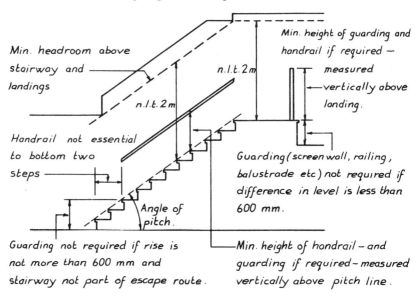

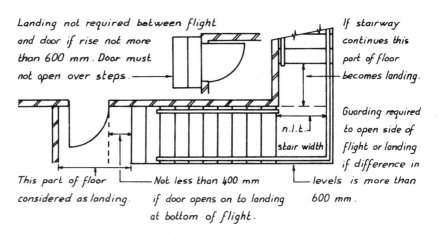

Fig. 15.2 General requirements.

General requirements for stairways, ramps and stepped ramps

Landings

AD K1
sec. 1
1.21

AD K1
sec. 1
1.22

As a general rule a landing should be provided at the top and bottom of every flight or ramp. Where a stairway or ramp is continuous, part of the floor of the building may count as a landing. The going of the landing should not be less than the width of the flight or ramp.

Landings should be level and free from permanent obstructions. (This would allow, for example, the placing of a temporary barrier such as a child's safety gate between a landing and a flight.) A door is permitted to swing across a landing at the bottom of a flight or ramp but only if it leaves an area 400 mm wide across the full width of the flight or ramp.

AD K1 sec. 1 1.21

AD K1 sec. 1 1.23

An exception to this general requirement to provide a landing between a door and a flight or ramp occurs when the total rise is less than 600 mm and the door slides or opens away from the flight or ramp. Furthermore, a landing of firm ground or paving at the top or bottom of an external flight or ramp may slope at a gradient of not more than 1 in 12 (see Fig. 15.2).

AD K1 sec. 1 1.24

AD K1 sec. 1 1.25 & 2.6

Handrails

Unless it is a means of escape route a rise of less than 600 mm does not require a handrail. However, any flight or ramp which has a total rise of more than 600 mm should have a handrail on at least one side and where the flight or ramp is 1 m or more wide a handrail should be fixed on both sides. In the case of a stairway, however, the handrail need not extend beside the bottom two steps.

AD K1 sec. 1 1.19 & 2.50

Handrails should provide firm support and be fixed at a height of between 840 mm and 1 m vertically above the pitch line (see Fig. 15.2).

AD K1 sec. 1 1.20 & 2.50

Headroom

Clear headroom of 2 m should be provided over the whole width of any stairway, ramp, stepped ramp or associated landing. Headroom is measured vertically from the pitch line, or, where there is no pitch line, from the top surface of any ramp or landing (see Fig. 15.2).

AD K1 1.9 & sec. 2 2.2

Stairway requirements

The particular requirements in respect of stairways are covered by Table 1 and Table 2 of AD K1, which are reproduced below.

These tables list specific rules for

(a) Private stairs
(b) Common stairs
(c) Stairways in:

    (i) an institutional building, other than a stairway used solely by staff;

    (ii) an assembly building and serving a part used for assembly purposes more than 100 m^2 in area;

    (iii) any other building and serving an area where more than fifty people may be occupied

(d) Stairways in buildings other than (a), (b) or (c) above.

AD K1

Table 1   Rise and going

		Rise (max)	Going (min)
1	private stair	220 mm	220 mm
2	common stair	190 mm	240 mm
3	stairway in:		
(a)	an institutional building (unless it will only be used by staff)	180 mm	280 mm
(b)	an assembly building and serving an area used for assembly purposes unless the area is less than 100 m²		
4	stairway not described in 1, 2 and 3 above	190 mm	250 mm

Notes
1 Diagram 2 shows how to measure rise and going
2 Stairways with any of the goings and rises within the ranges given below will meet the limitation on pitch (where it applies) and lie within the limits of $(2R + G)$:

Private stair –
● any rise between 155 and 220 mm used with any going between 245 and 260 mm
● any rise between 165 and 200 mm used with any going between 220 mm and 305 mm.

Common stair –
● any rise between 155 and 190 mm used with any going between 240 and 320 mm.

Rules applying to all stairways

AD K1
sec. 1
1.15

● In any stairway there should not be more than thirty-six rises in consecutive flights, unless there is a change in the direction of travel of at least 30° (see Fig. 15.3).

AD K1
sec. 1
1.7

● For any step the sum of twice its rise plus its going $(2R + G)$ should not be more than 700 mm nor less than 550 mm. This rule is subject to variation at tapered steps, for which there are special rules.

AD K1
sec. 1
1.5

● The rise of any step should generally be constant throughout its length and all steps in a flight should have the same rise and going. However, where a step adjoins ground or paving outside a building, that ground or paving may be at a slope (see page 15.4 above). In this

AD K1

Table **2** **Widths of stairways**

	Unobstructed width (min)
1 private stair providing access only to one room (not being a kitchen or living room), or to a bathroom, a closet, or both	600 mm
2 private stair other than 1 above	800 mm
3 common stair	900 mm
4 stairway in: (a) an institutional building (unless it will only be used by staff) (b) an assembly building and serving an area used for assembly purposes (unless the area is less than 100 m²) (c) any other building and serving an area which can be occupied by more than 50 people	1000 mm
5 any stairway not described in 1, 2, 3 or 4 above	800 mm

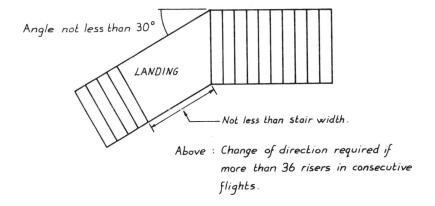

Fig. 15.3 Length of flights.

case the rise of the step should be measured at the centre of the width of the flight.
- Open risers are permitted in a stairway but for safety the treads should overlap each other by at least 15 mm.

- Each tread in a stairway should be level.

Tapered treads should comply with the following rules:

- The minimum going at any part of a tread within the width of a stairway should not be less than 50 mm.
- The going should be measured:

   (i) if the stairway is less than 1 m wide, at the centre point of the length or deemed length of a tread and

   (ii) if the stairway is 1 m or more wide, at points 270 mm from each

end of the length or deemed length of a tread. (When referring to a set of consecutive tapered treads of different lengths, the term 'deemed length' means the length of the shortest tread. This term is not used in AD K1.) (See Fig. 15.4.)

- All consecutive tapered treads in a flight should have the same taper.

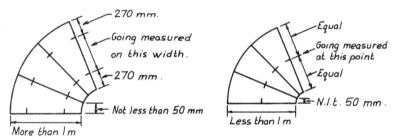

Tapered Treads of Equal Width.

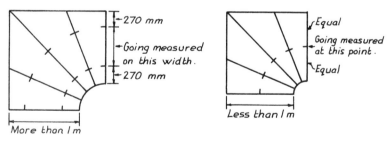

Tapered Treads of Unequal Width.

Fig. 15.4 Tapered treads.

Rules applying to private stairways

● The width of any stairway should generally not be less than 800 mm. However, if a stairway gives access only to either:

(a) a single room which is not a kitchen or living room, or
(b) a bathroom and/or watercloset, then the width of the stairway should not be less than 600 mm.

The width referred to above is the unobstructed clear width between handrails or other projections. However, minor intrusions such as strings, skirtings or newels may be ignored (see Fig. 15.5).

AD K1
sec. 1
1.12

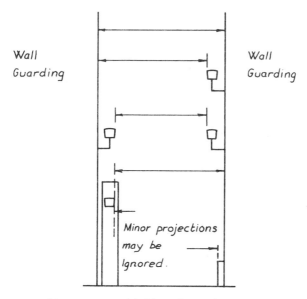

Wall
Guarding

Wall
Guarding

Minor projections
may be
Ignored.

Measuring Width of Flights, Landings
and Ramps.

Fig. 15.5 Widths of stairways.

● The height of any rise should not be more than 220 mm.
● The going of any step should generally not be less than 220 mm (but see the rules relating to tapered treads above).
● The pitch should not be more than 42°. This means that it is not possible to combine a maximum rise with a minimum going (see Fig. 15.6 and Table 1 for the practical limits for rise and going).

AD K1
sec. 1
1.8
AD K1
sec. 1
1.4
AD K1
sec. 1
1.8

In order to prevent small children from becoming trapped between the treads of open riser staircases there should be no opening in a riser

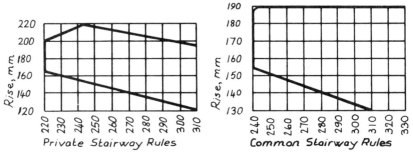

Permitted Combinations of Rise and Going, Within Heavy Lined Area.

Fig. 15.6 Practical limits for rise and going.

of such a size as to allow the passage of a sphere of 100 mm diameter. This rule also applies to common stairways, stairways in institutional buildings where children under five are likely to be present and stairways in any other residential buildings (see Fig. 15.1 above).

AD K1
sec. 1
1.11

Rules applying to common stairways

AD K1
sec. 1
1.12

● The unobstructed width of any stairway should not be less than 900 mm.
● The height of any rise should not be more than 190 mm.

AD K1
sec. 1
1.8

● The going of any step should generally not be less than 240 mm (but see the rules relating to tapered treads above).

AD K1
sec. 1
1.4

● The pitch should not be more than 38°. (Again, it is not possible to combine a maximum rise with a minimum going, see Fig. 15.6.)

Rules applying to institutional buildings

Institutional buildings are usually occupied by young children, old people or people with physical or mental disabilities. It is necessary, therefore, that staircases should be wider and of a slacker pitch than in other types of buildings.

AD K1
sec. 1
1.12

The width of any stairway should be not less than 1 m, the height of any rise not more than 180 mm and the going of any step not less than 280 mm (subject to the rules governing tapered treads).

AD K1
sec. 1
1.8

These rules also apply to assembly buildings where the stairway serves an area which exceeds 100 m² and is used for assembly purposes. Here again large numbers of people may be present including young, old and disabled.

However, if a stairway is used by staff only in an institutional building it need only comply with the requirements for other buildings listed below.

Rules applying to stairways in all other buildings

For stairways in buildings other than dwellings, institutional buildings or assembly buildings:

- The width of any stairway should be not less than 800 mm, the height of any rise not more than 190 mm and the going of any step not less than 250 mm (subject to the rules governing tapered treads).

AD K1 sec. 1 1.12
AD K1 sec. 1 1.8

The only exception to this is if the building contains a staircase serving an area capable of being occupied by more than fifty people. In this case the width should be increased to a minimum of 1 m.

AD K1 sec. 1 1.12

- The width of any stairway should not exceed 1800 mm. Stairways wider than this should be sub-divided with handrails, the sub-divisions complying with the minimum widths specified above. Stairways in institutional buildings are also covered by this requirement but not private or common stairs.

AD K1 sec. 1 1.13

- There should not be more than sixteen risers in a single flight where a stairway serves an area used for shop or assembly purposes.

AD K1 sec. 1 1.14

Ramp requirements

The particular requirements in respect of ramps are covered by section 2 of AD K1:

- The width of any ramp should not be less than that required of the same class of stairway (see above).

AD K1 sec. 2 2.3

- The slope of any ramp should not be more than 1 in 12.

AD K1 sec. 2 2.1

- The length of any ramp in a stepped ramp should be between 1 m and 2 m and the surface of any intermediate steps should be level.

AD K1 sec. 2 2.7

- There should be no permanent obstructions placed across any ramp.

AD K1 sec. 2 2.4

Guarding of stairways, ramps, stepped ramps and landings

Guarding should generally be provided at the sides of every flight, ramp or landing. However, guarding need not be provided beside the bottom two steps of a stairway nor beside any such stairway, ramp or landing where the drop is less than 600 mm provided it is not a means of escape route.

Suitable forms of guarding could be, for example, balustrades, railings, walls or screens.

AD K1 sec. 1 1.26

The rules that apply to prevent small children from being trapped in open riser staircases (see page 15.8 above) also apply to guarding; that is, there should be no opening of such a size as to allow the passage of a sphere of 100 mm diameter. This relates to private or common stairways, stairways in any residential buildings or stairways in institutional buildings used by children under five. Guarding should also be designed so that it cannot easily be climbed by small children. (This might preclude the use of horizontal 'ranch style' balustrading in the types of buildings referred to above.)

Certain minimum heights for guarding to flights, ramps and landings are given in AD K1 Table 3 which is reproduced below.

AD K1, section 1

Table **3**   **Height of guarding**

			Height (min)
1	private stairways	flights	840 mm
		landings	900 mm
2	common stairways	flights	900 mm
		landings	1000 mm
3	other stairways	flights	900 mm
		landings	1100 mm

It is possible for handrails to form the top of the guarding if the heights can be matched appropriately (see Fig. 15.2 above).

At the heights given above the guarding should be able to resist a horizontal force of 0·36 kN per metre of length for private or common stairways or 0·74 kN per metre for any other stairway. These requirements also apply to the guarding to ramps.

If the guarding contains any glazing this should be of laminated safety glass, toughened glass or glass blocks but not wired glass (see Fig. 15.7).

Related requirements

In addition to the requirements listed above the design and construction of stairways and ramps may be affected by the requirements of other regulations as follows:

B1 Means of Escape (see Chapter 7), Schedule 1 to the Building Regulations – Disabled People (Chapter 17).

Protection from falling

Stairways, ramps, floors and balconies, and any roof to which people

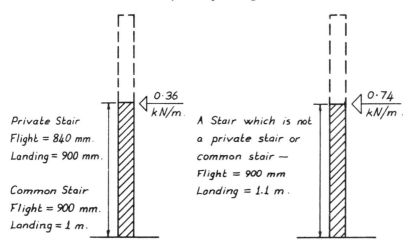

Private Stair
Flight = 840 mm.
Landing = 900 mm.

Common Stair
Flight = 900 mm.
Landing = 1 m.

0·36 kN/m.

A Stair which is not
a private stair or
common stair —
Flight = 900 mm
Landing = 1.1 m.

0·74 kN/m.

<u>*GUARD DESIGN*</u>

Fig. 15.7 Guarding to stairways and ramps.

normally have access are required to have barriers to protect users from the risk of falling.

Approved document K2/3 extends the provisions for guarding in AD K1 to cover any part of: **AD K2/3**

- A balcony, gallery, raised floor, roof (and round any rooflights or other openings) or other place to which people have access, unless that access is only for maintenance and repair purposes;
- Any light well, basement or sunken area next to a building;
- A vehicle park (but not, of course, on any vehicle access ramps); guarding is not needed where the drop is less than 600 mm or where it would obstruct normal use (for example, at the edge of loading bays). **AD K2/3 1.1**

Guarding requirements

Where guarding is provided to meet the requirements above, then that guarding should:

- Have a minimum height of 900 mm if it guards a floor in any part of a building serving only one dwelling; (see Fig. 15.7).
- Have a minimum height of 1100 mm if it guards a balcony or roof in a dwelling or any part of any other building. (This is reduced to 790 mm for balconies in assembly buildings where the guarding is in front of fixed seating); (see Fig. 15.8).
- Be capable of resisting a horizontal force of 0·36 kN per metre

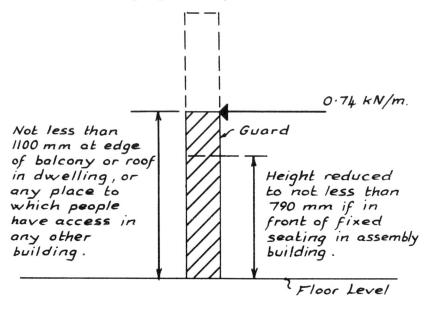

Fig. 15.8 Guarding to balconies, roofs, etc.

where protecting a floor in a single dwelling (see Fig. 15.7) or 0·74 kN per metre in any other case;

- Have any glazed part formed by glass blocks, toughened glass or laminated safety glass; (but not wired glass); and

AD K2/3
1.2

- Have no opening of such a size as to permit the passage of a sphere of 100 mm diameter if it is in a dwelling, an institutional building where children under five are likely to be present, or any other residential building. Guarding can consist of a wall, balustrade, parapet or similar barrier but should be designed so that it cannot easily be climbed by small children if in one of the buildings mentioned above.

AD K2/3
1.3

AD K2/3
1.2

AD K2/3
1.3

Vehicle barriers

Regs Sch. 1
K3

Vehicle ramps, and any floor and roof to which vehicles have access are required to have barriers in order to protect people in or about the building.

AD K2/3

Approved document K2/3 also provides guidance on the siting and design of vehicle barriers. It is concerned with vehicle parks which are expected to be used by vehicles of less than 2·5 tonnes (that is, cars and light vans). For these types of vehicles, barriers should be designed to resist a force of 150 kN per metre at a height of 375 mm at floor or roof edges or 610 mm at ramp edges (see Fig. 15.9).

AD K2/3
1.6

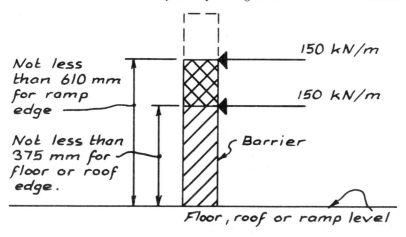

Fig. 15.9 Vehicle barriers.

The requirement to provide vehicle barriers can also be satisfied by following the relevant recommendations of BS 6180: 1982 *Code of practice for protective barriers in and about buildings.* This code also includes provisions for the design of barriers in vehicle parks used by vehicles weighing more than 2·5 tonnes or moving at speeds greater than 16 km/h (which are not covered by AD K2/3).

AD K2/3
1.7

Barriers can be formed by walls, parapets, balustrading or similar obstructions and should be at least the heights mentioned above (see page 15.13).

AD K2/3
1.5

Where the perimeter of any roof, ramp or floor to which vehicles have access is level with or above any adjacent floor, ground or vehicular route, barriers should be sited to protect the perimeter.

AD K2/3
1.4

Chapter 16

Conservation of fuel and power

Introduction

Part L of Schedule 1 to the Building Regulations 1985 is concerned with the conservation of fuel and power. This is supported by Approved Document L which covers the following topics:

AD L
Sections 1,
2 & 3

- Resistance to the passage of heat,
- Heating system controls,
- Insulation of heating services.

The 1990 revision to Part L has simplified the mandatory requirements of Schedule 1; one functional requirement replacing the five former paragraphs. Since two of these were phrased in terms of performance standards (L2 and L3) they were subject to relaxation in appropriate circumstances. This is no longer the case with the new paragraph L1 (see page 2.19 above).

Interpretation

The introduction to Approved Document L contains special definitions which apply throughout AD L.

AD L
0.14

- EXPOSED ELEMENT   means an element of a building which is exposed to the outside air.
- SEMI-EXPOSED ELEMENT   means an element which separates a heated part of the building from an unheated part which is exposed to the outside air and which does not comply with the recommendations for limitation of heat loss required by AD L (see Fig. 16.1). It should be noted that the term ELEMENT is not defined in AD L. However, from the context of the document it can be assumed to mean a wall, floor or roof.
- U VALUE   means the thermal transmittance coefficient, which is the rate of heat transfer in watts through one square metre of a structure when the combined radiant and air temperatures on each

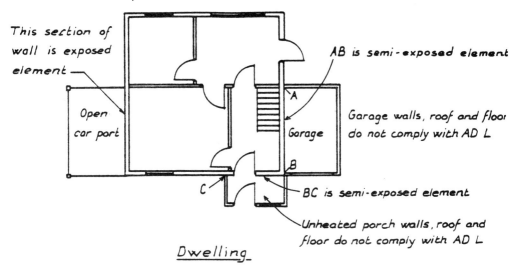

All external walls apart from AB and BC are exposed elements

This section of wall is exposed element —

AB is semi-exposed element

Open car port

Garage walls, roof and floor do not comply with AD L

Garage

BC is semi-exposed element

Unheated porch walls, roof and floor do not comply with AD L

Dwelling

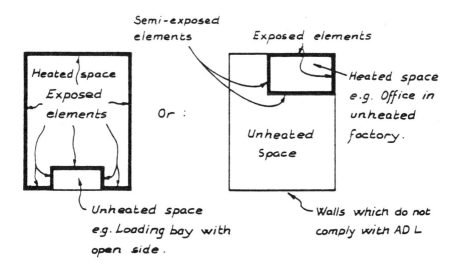

Semi-exposed elements

Exposed elements

Heated space
Exposed elements

Heated space e.g. Office in unheated factory.

Or :

Unheated Space

Unheated space e.g. Loading bay with open side .

Walls which do not comply with AD L

Other Building

Fig. 16.1 Exposed and semi-exposed elements.

side of the structure differ by 1 kelvin (i.e. 1°C). This is stated in watts per square metre of fabric per kelvin (W/m²K). An accuracy of two decimal places is acceptable in calculations and it should be noted that minor reductions in U valves due to the presence of cavity wall ties, built in joists and anchors, etc., may be ignored in calculations.

AD L
0.9, 0.10

- THERMAL CONDUCTIVITY – this is not specifically defined in AD L but is the amount of heat per unit area, conducted per unit time through a slab of material of unit thickness, per degree of temperature difference. It is expressed in watts per metre of thickness of material per degree kelvin (W/mK).

Values of thermal conductivities for particular products should be obtained from individual manufacturers. If this is inconvenient, values may be obtained from the CIBSE Guide (Chartered Institute of Building Services Engineers Guide, Section A3 *thermal properties of building structures* 1981). Part of this guide is reproduced in Table 3 of Appendix A of AD L (see below). These values give a general indication of the thermal conductivities which may be expected but certified test data for particular products should always be used in preference.

AD L
0.11

General Considerations

Windows and rooflights

Certain assumptions may be made when considering the areas of openings for windows and rooflights.

- A door containing 1 m² or more of glass should be treated as a window.
- A roof pitched at 70° or more to the horizontal should be treated as a wall.
- Any opening in a wall (including a meter cupboard recess) other than a window opening, may be treated as part of the wall area.
- At the option of the person carrying out the work lintels, jambs and sills may be counted as part of the window or roof-light area, but the U value of any of these elements should not exceed 1.2 W/m²K.

AD L
0.12

Rules for measurement of areas

- Areas of walls, floors and roofs should be measured between internal finished surfaces of the building. For roofs, this should be in the plane of the insulation.
- When calculating permitted window areas the exposed wall area used should include all openings.

AD L
0.12, 0.13

Large complex buildings

It is permissible to consider the different parts of large complex buildings separately when applying the measures for conservation of fuel and power contained in AD L.

AD L
0.15

Buildings with low level heating requirements

Those buildings which are not normally heated to any great extent (and would therefore have minimal heat losses) are not required to be insulated. A low level of heating is defined by reference to the output of the building's space heating system. This should not exceed:

- 50 watts per square metre of floor area for industrial and storage buildings.
- 25 watts per square metre of floor area for other non-domestic buildings.

    Sometimes, speculative industrial and commercial developments are constructed where the final use of the building is not known. In these circumstances full insulation would be required.

AD L
0.3, 0.4

Dwellinghouse extensions

Small extensions to dwellinghouses (i.e. not exceeding 10 m² floor area) are considered to have adequate resistance to the passage of heat if they are constructed in a similar manner to the existing dwelling.

AD L
0.2

Problems associated with increased thermal insulation

It has been known for a number of years that higher insulation levels have increased the risk of interstitial condensation occurring in the building fabric. Also, greater thermal stresses have been placed on exposed materials such as bituminous roofing felts causing these to fail well before the completion of their normal design life.

    By correct design and specification in addition to good workmanship and site supervision most of these problems may be overcome. To this end the Building Research Establishment has produced a guidance document entitled *Thermal Insulation: avoiding risks*, which contains practical guidance. Reference should also be made to Approved Document F: Ventilation (see Chapter 11 above) especially F2: Condensation in roofs.

AD L
0.5 to 0.8

Conservation of fuel and power

Paragraph L1 of Schedule 1 requires that reasonable provision should be made for the conservation of fuel and power in buildings. It applies to dwellings and any other building which has a floor area greater than 30 m².

Regs Sch. 1
L1

Section 1 of Approved Document L provides the following methods by which the limitation of heat loss through the building fabric may be demonstrated:

- Elemental approach.
- Calculation procedure.

Elemental approach

In this method AD L specifies certain maximum U values and window/rooflight areas which should not be exceeded, for different types of buildings.

Buildings other than dwellings

Table 16.1 shows the maximum U values and window/rooflight areas for buildings other than dwellings.

Table 16.1   Permitted U values, rooflight and window areas – buildings other than dwellings.

Building type	Max. single glazed window area (% exposed wall area) %	Max. single glazed rooflight area (% roof area) %	Max. U value of exposed elements W/m²K	Max. U value of semi-exposed walls and floors W/m²K
Other Residential	25	20	0.45	0.6
Shop, Office Assembly	35	20	0.45	0.6
Industrial Storage and other buildings	15	20	0.45	0.6

The maximum window and rooflight areas referred to in Table 16.1 are for single glazing. They may be doubled for double glazing and trebled where triple glazing or double glazing with a low emissivity coating (emissivity not exceeding 0.2) is used.

Shop display windows may be ignored when calculating permitted single glazed window areas. These values are illustrated in Fig. 16.2.

Dwellings

For dwellings, the U values are the same as for other buildings with the

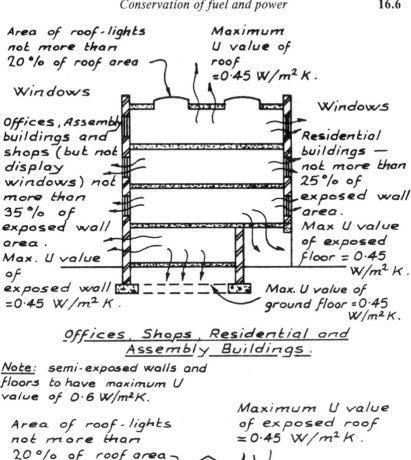

Area of roof-lights
not more than
20% of roof area

Maximum
U value of
roof
= 0.45 W/m² K.

Windows

Windows

Offices, Assembly
buildings and
shops (but not
display
windows) not
more than
35% of
exposed wall
area.
Max. U value
of
exposed wall
= 0.45 W/m² K.

Residential
buildings —
not more than
25% of
exposed wall
area.
Max U value
of exposed
floor = 0.45
W/m² K.

Max. U value of
ground floor = 0.45
W/m² K.

Offices, Shops, Residential and
Assembly Buildings.

Note: semi-exposed walls and
floors to have maximum U
value of 0.6 W/m²K.

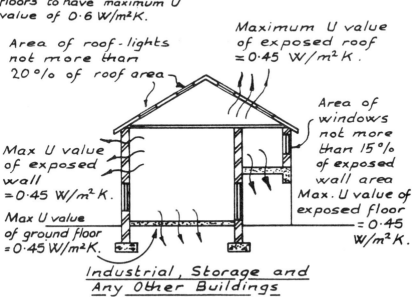

Maximum U value
of exposed roof
= 0.45 W/m² K.

Area of roof-lights
not more than
20% of roof area

Area of
windows
not more
than 15%
of exposed
wall area

Max U value
of exposed
wall
= 0.45 W/m² K.

Max. U value of
exposed floor
= 0.45
W/m² K.

Max U value
of ground floor
= 0.45 W/m²K.

Industrial, Storage and
Any Other Buildings

Fig. 16.2 Permitted U values, roof-light and window areas – buildings other
than dwellings.

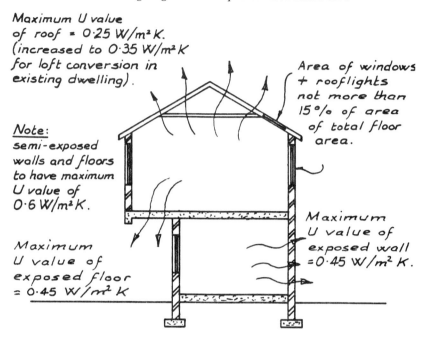

Fig. 16.3 Permitted U values, rooflight and window areas – dwellings.

exception of the roof. This should not exceed 0.25 W/m²K although the U value may be increased to 0.35 W/m²K for the roof of a loft conversion in an existing dwelling. Window and rooflight areas should be combined for calculation purposes and should not exceed 15% of the *total floor area* of the dwelling (i.e. add together all the floor areas and take 15% of this total). The rules concerning double and triple glazing stated above (under Table 16.1) also apply to dwellings. (The permitted values for dwellings are illustrated in Fig. 16.3 above.)

AD L
sec. 1
1.2, 1.8

Simply adhering to the maximum U values and window/rooflight areas given above gives a rather inflexible approach which does not take full account of the benefits of double or triple glazing. Accordingly, AD L permits a number of simple variations if improved glazing is provided.

- The U value of the walls may be increased to 0.6 W/m²K if half the total window area is double glazed.
- With all the windows double glazed the U value of the walls may be increased to 0.6 W/m²K, the roof to 0.35 W/m²K and the floor may be uninsulated (i.e. the pre-April 1990 insulation levels).

AD L
sec. 1
1.3

However, it should be noted that it is not permissible to use the increased U values listed above as well as the larger window areas allowed by double or triple glazing. (See page 16.5 above).

Additionally a small trade-off is permitted between the floor and roof whereby *decreasing* the ground floor U value to 0.35 W/m²K allows an *increased* roof U value of 0.35 W/m²K.

AD L
sec. 1
1.5

Insulation of ground floors

If a ground floor is sufficiently large it is possible to achieve the required U value of 0.45 W/m²K without adding insulation material. Diagram 2 from Section 1 of AD L is reproduced below and gives the range of floor dimensions for which insulation is required.

AD L
sec. 1
1.6

AD L, section 1

Diagram 2   Floor dimensions for which insulation is required

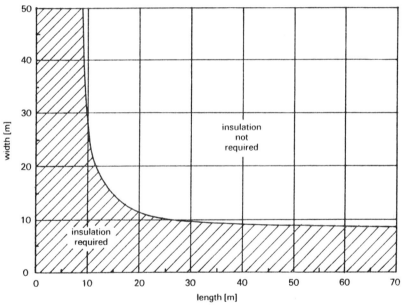

Note

For detached buildings the dimensions relate directly to the building. In the use of semi-detached and terraced buildings and blocks of flats the dimensions relate to the floor area under the whole building.

Elemental approach – specified insulation thickness

In order to achieve the U values specified above, a method is provided in Appendix B of AD L for choosing the required thickness of the principal insulating material in particular forms of construction.

This method is based on the fact that in most wall, floor and roof constructions the total insulation value largely depends on one part of the construction (e.g. the cavity fill material in an external cavity wall). This is because all good insulating materials have low thermal conductivity (i.e. a measure of the rate at which heat will pass through a material). Therefore, the thermal conductivity of a material may be used to assess its insulation value and the thermal conductivities of all the materials in a wall, floor or roof may be used to assess the insulation value of the total construction.

AD L
Appendix B

Using Tables 4 to 8 of Appendix B of AD L (which are reproduced below) it is possible to select the minimum thickness of insulation required in a number of wall, roof or floor constructions and also to make allowances for the contribution of the rest of the construction towards the overall insulation value.

Exposed walls – example calculation

Referring to Table 4 and Fig. 16.4:

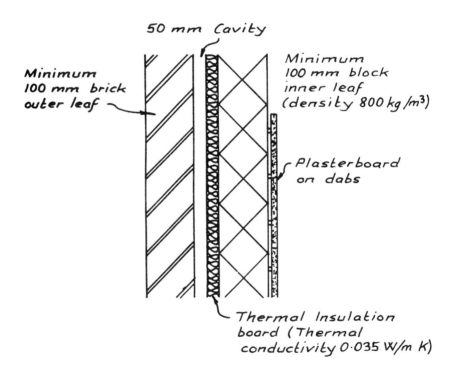

Fig. 16.4 Example wall calculation – dwelling.

AD L Appendix B

Table 4 Walls: Insulation thicknesses to achieve 0.45 W/m²K and 0.6 W/m²K

Part 1	Part 2		Allowable reduction in basic thickness [mm] for —								
Thermal conductivity of insulation material [W/mK]	Basic insulation thickness [mm] for U value [W/m²K]		Cavity	Brick leaf at least 100 mm thick	100 mm concrete block leaf of thermal conductivity [W/mK] of not more than					Plasterboard or lightweight plaster of thickness at least 13 mm
	0.45	0.6			0.1	0.2	0.3	0.4	0.5	
(1)	(2)	(3)	(4)	(5)	(6)	(7)	(8)	(9)	(10)	(11)
0.025	51	37	4	3	25	13	8	6	5	2
0.03	61	45	5	4	30	15	10	8	6	2
0.035	71	52	6	4	35	18	12	9	7	3
0.04	82	60	7	5	40	20	13	10	8	3
0.045	92	67	8	5	45	23	15	11	9	4
0.05	102	74	9	6	50	25	17	13	10	4

Notes

Where the thermal conductivity of the insulation material to be used does not coincide with a value listed in the Table, then interpolation between values on either side of the material value may be used.

Where the thermal conductivity of concrete blocks to be used does not coincide with the value listed in the Table, then interpolation between values on either side may be used.

Where the thickness of the block to be used exceeds 100 mm, then extrapolation may be used to obtain the appropriate reduction in insulation material.

Calculation data

Outside plus inside surface resistance of wall	$= 0.18$ m²K/W
Resistance of cavity	$= 0.18$ m²K/W
Thermal conductivity of brickwork	$= 0.84$ W/mK
Thermal conductivity of plasterboard and plaster	$= 0.16$ W/mK

- The thermal conductivity of the insulating material (0.035 W/mK) is chosen in column 1.
- Move horizontally to column 2 and read off the insulation base level thickness of 71 mm.

This thickness of insulation may be used in the wall or it may be more economical to take account of the remaining parts of the wall construction and thereby reduce the insulation thickness as follows:

- Assess each of the other parts of the construction that appear in part 2 of the table and total the reductions:

(i) Cavity (column 4)	6 mm
(ii) 100 mm brick outer leaf (column 5)	4 mm
(iii) 100 mm block inner leaf (column 7)	
(thermal conductivity not exceeding 0.2 W/mK)	18 mm
(iv) Plasterboard (column 11)	3 mm
Total reduction	31 mm

- Final insulation thickness = 71 – 31
                              = 40 mm

Where a thermal conductivity for the insulation material or blocks lies between the figures stated in the table an intermediate value may be obtained by linear interpolation. It is also permissible to increase the allowable reductions in base level thickness where thicker blocks or bricks are used. For example, in the calculation given above, if a 150 mm block inner leaf is used the reduction in base level thickness may be increased by a factor of $^{150}/_{100}$, therefore,

(i) 150 mm block inner leaf = $^{150}/_{100} \times 18$	
(thermal conductivity not exceeding 0·2 W/mK)	= 27 mm
(ii) Reductions for outer leaf, cavity and plasterboard	= 13 mm
Total reduction	= 40 mm
Final insulation thickness = 71–40	= 31 mm

Exposed roofs – example calculation for office building

Referring to Table 5 and Fig. 16.5 below:

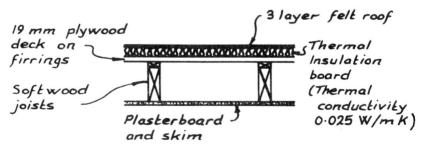

Fig. 16.5 Example roof calculation – office building.

AD L Appendix B

Table 5   Roofs: Insulation thicknesses to achieve 0.25 W/m²K and 0.45 W/m²K

Part 1			Part 2	
Thermal conductivity of insulation material [W/mK]	Basic insulation thickness [mm] for U value [W/m²K]		Allowable reduction in basic thickness [mm] for	
	0.25	0.45	Roof space	13 mm thick plasterboard ceiling
(1)	(2)	(3)	(4)	(5)
0.025	97	52	4	2
0.03	116	62	5	2
0.035	135	73	6	3
0.04	154	83	7	3
0.045	174	94	8	4
0.05	193	104	9	4

Calculation data

Outside plus inside surface resistance	= 0.14 m²K/W
Resistance of roof space	= 0.18 m²K/W
Thermal conductivity of plasterboard	= 0.16 W/mK

Notes

Where the thermal conductivity of the insulation material to be used does not coincide with a value listed in the Table, then interpolation between values on either side of the material value may be used.

Where the estimated thickness of insulation does not coincide with an available thickness, the next greater thickness should be used.

- The thermal conductivity of the insulating material (0.025 W/mK) is chosen in column 1.
- Move horizontally to column 3 (U value 0.45) and read off the insulation base level thickness of 52 mm.

This thickness of insulation may be used in the roof or it may be more economical to take account of the remaining parts of the roof construction and thereby reduce the insulation thickness as follows:

- Assess each of the other parts of the construction that appear in Part 2 of the table and total the reductions:

    (i) Roof space (column 4)   4 mm
    (ii) Plasterboard (column 5)   2 mm
                                                        Total reduction   6 mm

- Final insulation thickness = 52 – 6 = 46 mm

This example clearly illustrates the weakness of this method in that it is not possible to take account of all the materials used in the roof construction (i.e. the plywood deck and the felt roofing system). The method is restricted to those materials which appear in the table.

Exposed and semi-exposed floors

Table 8 of AD L (see below) may be used for exposed and semi-exposed floors in a similar manner to the tables used above for walls and roofs.

Ground floors

Tables 6 and 7 of AD L deal with solid ground-bearing floors and suspended ground floors respectively. As has been explained above, the larger the floor area of the building the lower will be the need to provide insulation, indeed in many cases insulation will not need to be provided at all.

As an example, take a detached building which has dimensions of 7 m by 8 m. Assuming a solid ground-bearing floor and insulation with thermal conductivity of 0.03 W/mK.

- The thermal conductivity of the insulating material (0.03 W/mK) is chosen in column 1 of the detached building section of Table 6.
- Move horizontally to column 2 (greater dimension up to 10, lesser dimension up to 10) and read off the insulation thickness of 38 mm.

    This is the thickness required and there are no reductions possible as in the other tables mentioned above.

    A curious lack of logic is apparent in column 6 of the detached building part of Tables 6 and 7. This column indicates in Table 6

AD L Appendix B

Table 8 Exposed and semi-exposed floors: Insulation thicknesses to achieve **0.45 W/m²K and 0.6 W/m²K**

Part 1 **Part 2**

Thermal conductivity of insulation material [W/mK] (1)	Basic insulation thickness [mm] for U value [W/m²K]		Allowable reduction in basic thickness [mm] for		
	0.45 (2)	0.60 (3)	At least 150 mm concrete slab (4)	At least 75 mm screed (5)	At least 10 mm wood block floor finish (6)
0.025	51	38	3	5	2
0.03	61	45	4	6	2
0.035	72	52	5	7	3
0.04	82	60	5	7	3
0.045	92	67	6	8	3
0.05	102	75	7	9	4

Calculation data

Outside plus inside surface resistance $= 0.18$ m²K/W
Thermal conductivity of concrete $= 1.13$ W/mK
Thermal conductivity of screed $= 0.41$ W/mK
Thermal conductivity of wood blocks $= 0.14$ W/mK

Notes
Where the estimated thickness of insulation does not coincide with
an available thickness, the next greater thickness should be used.

Where the thermal conductivity of the insulation material to be used
does not coincide with a value listed in the Table, then interpolation
between values on either side of the material value may be used.

AD L Appendix B

Table 6   Solid floors in contact with ground: Insulation thicknesses to achieve 0.45 W/m²K

Detached building

Thermal conductivity of insulation material [W/mK]	Greater dimension of floor [m]							
	Up to 10	10–15		15–20			Above 20	
	Lesser dimension of floor [m]							
	Up to 10	Up to 10	10–15	Up to 10	10–15	15–20	Up to 10	Above 10
(1)	(2)	(3)	(4)	(5)	(6)	(7)	(8)	(9)
0.025	31	25	15	22	•	•	21	•
0.03	38	30	18	26	•	•	25	•
0.035	44	35	21	31	11	•	29	•
0.04	50	39	24	35	13	•	33	•
0.045	57	44	27	40	14	•	37	•
0.05	63	49	30	44	16	•	41	•

Semi-detached and end terrace buildings

Thermal conductivity of insulation material [W/mK]	Greater dimension of floor [m]						
	Up to 10	10–15		15–20		Above 20	
				Lesser dimension of floor [m]			
	Up to 10	Up to 10	10–15	Up to 10	10–20	Up to 10	Above 10
(1)	(2)	(3)	(4)	(5)	(6)	(7)	(8)
0.025	25	21	•	19	•	18	•
0.03	30	25	•	23	•	22	•
0.035	35	29	•	27	•	26	•
0.04	39	33	•	30	•	29	•
0.045	44	37	•	34	•	33	•
0.05	49	41	•	38	•	37	•

Table 6   Solid floors in contact with ground: Insulation thicknesses to achieve 0.45 W/m²K (*cont.*)

Mid-terrace buildings

Thermal conductivity of insulation material [W/mK]	Distance between exposed edges of floor [m] (front to back dimension)	
(1)	Up to 10	Above 10
	(2)	(3)
0.025	16	• • • • • • •
0.03	19	
0.035	22	
0.04	25	
0.045	29	
0.05	32	

Key
• No insulation need be provided.

Notes
Where the estimated thickness of insulation does not coincide with an available thickness, the next greater thickness should be used.

Where the thermal conductivity of the insulation material to be used does not coincide with a value listed in the Table, then interpolation between values on either side of the material value may be used.

AD L Appendix B

Table 7   Suspended ground floors: Insulation thicknesses to achieve 0.45 W/m²K

Detached building

Thermal conductivity of insulation material [W/mK]	Greater dimension of floor [m]							
	Up to 10	10–15		15–20			Above 20	
	Lesser dimension of floor [m]							
	Up to 10	Up to 10	10–15	Up to 10	10–15	15–20	Up to 10	Above 10
(1)	(2)	(3)	(4)	(5)	(6)	(7)	(8)	(9)
0.025	26	22	12	20	•	•	19	•
0.03	31	26	14	24	•	•	23	•
0.035	36	30	17	28	•	•	27	•
0.04	42	34	19	32	11	•	30	•
0.045	47	39	21	36	12	•	34	•
0.05	52	43	24	40	13	•	38	•

Table 7 Suspended ground floors: Insulation thicknesses to achieve 0.45 W/m²K *(cont.)*

Semi-detached and end terrace buildings

Thermal conductivity of insulation material [W/mK]	Greater dimension of floor [m]						
	Up to 10	10–15		15–20		Above 20	
				Lesser dimension of floor [m]			
	Up to 10	Up to 10	10–15	Up to 10	10–20	Up to 10	Above 10
(1)	(2)	(3)	(4)	(5)	(6)	(7)	(8)
0.025	22	19	•	18	•	18	•
0.03	26	23	•	22	•	21	•
0.035	30	27	•	25	•	25	•
0.04	34	30	•	29	•	28	•
0.045	39	34	•	33	•	32	•
0.05	43	38	•	36	•	35	•

Mid-terrace buildings

Thermal conductivity of insulation material [W/mK]	Distance between exposed edges of floor [m]	
(1)	Up to 10 (2)	Above 10 (3)
0.025	16	•
0.03	20	•
0.035	23	•
0.04	26	•
0.045	29	•
0.05	33	•

Key
• No insulation need be provided.

Notes
Where the estimated thickness of insulation does not coincide with an available thickness, the next greater thickness should be used.

Where the thermal conductivity of the insulation material to be used does not coincide with a value listed in the Table, then interpolation between values on either side of the material value may be used.

that for thermal conductivities of 0.025 and 0.03 no insulation is required. However, for the remaining thermal conductivities (0.035, 0.04, 0.045 and 0.05) then certain thicknesses of insulation will be required (i.e. 11, 13, 14 and 16 mm respectively).

This would seem to be nonsense, since if no insulation is required then that is all that needs to be said and the thermal conductivity value is irrelevant.

Elemental approach – calcultion of insulation thickness

As was shown in the example roof calculation above, the use of Tables 4, 5 and 8 does not necessarily take into account all the features of a particular form of construction. This can only be achieved by carrying out a U value calculation and this is described in Appendix A of AD L.

Just as the thermal conductivity of a material determines the rate at which heat will pass through it, the U value or thermal transmittance coefficient of a particular form of construction is a measure of the rate of heat transfer through one square metre of the structure when the combined radiant and air temperatures at each side differ by 1 kelvin. A full description of the method of calculating U values is also given in the CIBSE Guide referred to above. However, the following brief notes may be of assistance in reminding readers of the basic procedure:

- U value $\quad = \dfrac{1}{\text{total thermal resistance of structure}}$

  $\quad = \dfrac{1}{R_{si} + R_1 + R_2 + R_3 \ldots R_n + R_{so}}$

- R_{si} $\quad$ = inside surface resistance
- $R_1, R_2, \ldots R_n$ = thermal resistances of each part of the structure
- R_{so} $\quad$ = outside surface resistance
- $R_{si} + R_{so}$ = 0.18 usual value for walls)
- The thermal resistance of a particular material is obtained by dividing the thickness of the material in metres by its thermal conductivity.

The thermal conductivity of a particular material may be obtained from the supplier or manufacturer or the CIBSE Guide mentioned above.

Average values of thermal conductivity for some commonly used building materials are given in Table 3 of Appendix A of AD L (see below). Paragraph A2 (b) of the same Appendix also lists some standard values for thermal resistance.

AD L Appendix A

Table 3   **Thermal conductivity of some common building materials**

Material	Density [kg/m²]	Thermal Conductivity [W/mK]
WALLS (External and Internal		
Asbestos cement sheet	700	0.35
Asbestos cement decking	1500	0.36
Brickwork (outer leaf)	1700	0.84
Brickwork (inner leaf)	1700	0.62
Cast concrete (dense)	2100	1.40
Cast concrete (lightweight)	1200	0.38
Concrete block (heavyweight)	2300	1.63
Concrete block (mediumweight)	1400	0.51
Concrete block (lightweight)	600	0.19
Fibreboard	300	0.06
Plasterboard	950	0.16
Tile hanging	1900	0.84
SURFACE FINISHES		
External rendering	1300	0.50
Plaster (dense)	1300	0.50
Plaster (lightweight)	600	0.16
ROOFS		
Aerated concrete slab	500	0.16
Asphalt	1700	0.50
Felt bitumen layers	1700	0.50
Screed	1200	0.41
Stone chippings	1800	0.96
Tile	1900	0.84
Wood woolslab	500	0.10
FLOORS		
Cast concrete	2000	1.13
Metal tray	7800	50.00
Screed	1200	0.41
Timber flooring	650	0.14
Wood blocks	650	0.14
INSULATION		
Expanded polystyrene (EPS) slab	25	0.035
Glass fibre quilt	12	0.040
Glass fibre slab	25	0.035
Mineral fibre slab	30	0.035
Phenolic foam	30	0.040
Polyurethane Board	30	0.025
Urea formaldehyde (UF) foam	10	0.040

Notes
Where the claimed thermal conductivity of a masonry material is lower than stated in the above Table, the claim should be supported by test certificates as required in Appendix 4 of the CIBSE Guide, 1980.

Reproduced from Section A3, CIBSE Guide, by permission of the Chartered Institution of Building Services Engineers.

AD L Appendix A (A2(b))

Standard values for thermal resistance

Exposed walls	outside surface	= 0.06 m²K/W
	inside surface	= 0.12 m²K/W
	air space (cavity)	= 0.18 m²K/W
Roofs	outside surface	= 0.04 m²K/W
	inside surface	= 0.10 m²K/W
	roof space (pitched)	= 0.18 m²K/W
	roof space (flat)	= 0.16 m²K/W
Exposed floors	outside surface	= 0.04 m²K/W
	inside surface	= 0.14 m²K/W

Example calculation of insulation thickness for exposed wall

Referring to Fig. 16.4 above the calculation is carried out as follows:

- Required thermal resistance for wall
  = $\frac{1}{u}$ $\frac{1}{0.45}$ = 2.22 m²K/W
- Thermal resistance of wall without insulation:

Part	Thickness (t) (m)	Thermal conductivity (K) (W/mK)	Thermal resistance ($\frac{t}{k}$) m²K/W)	
Outside surface	—	—	0.06	R_{so}
100 mm brick outer leaf	0.100	0.84	0.12	R_1
Cavity	—	—	0.18	R_2
100 mm block inner leaf	0.100	0.20	0.5	R_3
13 mm plasterboard on dabs	0.013	0.16	0.08	R_4
Inside surface	—	—	0.12	R_{si}
		Total Thermal Resistance =	1.06	

- Extra resistance to be supplied by insulation
  = 2.22 – 1.06 = 1.16 m²K/W
- Minimum thickness of insulation required
  = 1.16 × 0.035 × 1000
  = 41 mm

This value corresponds closely with that chosen from Table 4 (see page 16.11 above).

Calculation procedure

When using the elemental approach above it is necessary to comply with the maximum window and roof-light areas given in Table 16.1 and illustrated in Figs. 16.2 and 16.3. Since the purpose of Part L of Schedule 1 to the Building Regulations is the conservation of fuel and power, it should be possible to satisfy the requirements without rigid adherence to specified areas or U values providing the proposed building is not less efficient thermally than a building that was constructed using the specified areas and U values.

Calculation procedures 1 and 2 of AD L provide methods by which this may be achieved. The following conditions apply to procedures 1 and 2:

AD L
sec. 1
1.11

- The windows and rooflights of the building should be assumed to have the following U values:

  (i) single glazing: 5.7 W/m²K
  (ii) double glazing: 2.8 W/m²K
  (iii) triple glazing (or double glazing with low emissivity coating not exceeding 0.2): 2.0 W/m²K.

- U values higher than those shown in Table 16.1 or illustrated in Figs. 16.2 and 16.3 are allowable when using calculation procedures 1 and 2. This could result in surface condensation forming in certain circumstances. For this reason it may be desirable to limit the U values as follows:

  (i) For dwellings
    — exposed wall U value not exceeding 0.6 W/m²K
    — exposed roof U value not exceeding 0.35 W/m²K.
  (ii) For all other buildings – exposed wall or roof not exceeding 0.6 W/m²K.

AD L
sec. 1
1.19, 1.20

Calculation procedure 1

This procedure applies to all building types and allows greater flexibility between window/rooflight areas and/or insulation levels of the exposed and semi-exposed elements of the building envelope.

The essential feature of the calculation procedure is that the rate of heat loss from the proposed building must be shown by calculation to be no greater than that from a standard building of similar size and shape which is designed to comply with the elemental approach.

Interestingly, if the proposed building has smaller glazed areas than the maximum permitted under the elemental approach these smaller areas may be assumed in the standard building when comparing heat losses.

AD L
sec. 1
1.12 to 1.15

Example calculations to demonstrate the use of calculation procedure 1 are shown below:

Window/U value trade-off for dwelling – example calculation

A proposed two-storey semi-detached house is to have a frontage of 6 m internally, a depth of 7 m internally and a floor to ceiling height of 2.3 m. It is proposed to insulate the exposed walls and ground floor to a U value of 0.6 W/m²K and the roof to a U value of 0.35 W/m²K. Calculate the area of double-glazed windows that would be allowed in order to satisfy the requirements of paragraph L1 of Schedule 1. No roof-lights are required.

Referring to Fig. 16.6 below:

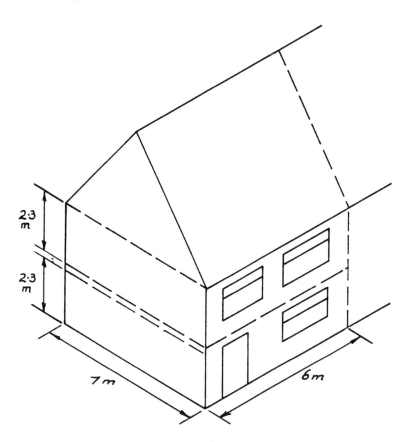

Fig. 16.6 Window/U value trade-off for dwelling – example calculation.

For standard house:

- Area of exposed walls (including windows) = $(6 + 6 + 7) \times 4.6$
    = 87.4 m^2
- Total floor area = $7 \times 6 \times 2$ floors
    = 84 m^2

- Area of single-glazed windows allowed $= 15\% \times 84$
                                               $= 12.6 \text{ m}^2$
- Area of exposed walls at U value of 0.45 $= 87.4 - 12.6$
                                               $= 74.8 \text{ m}^2$
- Area of roof and ground floor $= 6 \times 7$ $= 42.0 \text{ m}^2$
- Rate of heat loss through the exposed elements is calculated in the table below:

Element	Area (m²)	U value (W/m²K)	Rate of heat loss (W/K)
Exposed walls	74.8	0.45	33.66
Windows	12.6	5.70	71.82
Roof	42.0	0.25	10.50
Ground floor	42.0	0.45	18.90
Total rate of heat loss			134.88

For proposed house:
Let X = area of double glazed windows allowed

- Area of exposed walls at U value of $0.6 = (87.4 - X) \text{ m}^2$
- Area of roof and ground floor $= 6 \times 7 = 42 \text{ m}^2$
- Rate of heat loss through the exposed elements is calculated in the table below:

Element	Area (m²)	U value (W/m²K)	Rate of heat loss (W/K)
Exposed walls	$(87.4 - X)$	0.6	$0.6 (87.4 - X)$
Windows	X	2.8	2.8X
Roof	42	0.35	14.7
Ground floor	42	0.6	25.2
Total rate of heat loss			$2.2X + 92.34$

This rate of heat loss must not be greater than the rate of heat loss from the standard house above
(i.e.: 134.88 W/K)
Therefore
     $2.2 X + 92.34 = 134.88$
     therefore $X = \dfrac{134.88 - 92.34}{2.2} = 19\frac{1}{3} \text{ m}^2$

- Area of double glazed windows allowed $= 19\frac{1}{3} \text{ m}^2$
  This represents 23% of the total floor area of the dwelling.

Window/U value trade-off for office – example calculation

A three-storey detached office building has internal dimensions of 40 m × 10 m × 9 m. It is proposed to insulate the exposed floor, walls and roof to a U value of 0.6 W/m²K. 80% double glazed window areas and 20% double glazed rooflights are required. Confirm that the proposed building complies with the requirements of Part L.

Referring to Fig. 16.7 below:

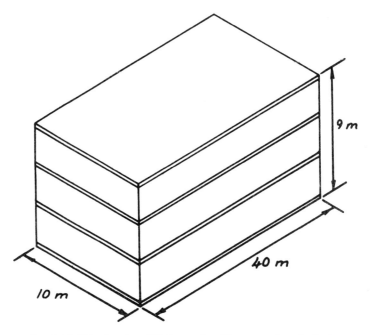

Fig. 16.7 Window/roof-light trade-off – example calculation.

For Proposed Building:

- Area of exposed walls (including windows) = (40 + 40 + 10 + 10) × 9
  = 900 m²
- Area of windows = 80% × 900 = 720 m²
- Area of exposed walls at U value 0·6 = 900 – 720
  = 180 m²

- Area of roof and ground floor = 40 × 10 = 400 m²
- Area of rooflights = 20% × 400 = 80 m²
- Area of roof at U value 0·6 = 400 – 80
  = 320 m²

- Rate of heat loss through the exposed elements is calculated in the table below:

Element	Area (m²)	U value (W/m²K)	Rate of heat loss (W/K)
Exposed walls	180	0·6	108
Windows	720	2·8	2016
Roof	320	0·6	192
Rooflights	80	2·8	224
Groundfloor	400	0·6	240
Total rate of heat loss			2780

For standard building:

- Area of exposed walls (including windows) $\quad = (40 + 40 + 10 + 10) \times 9$
  $= 900 \text{ m}^2$
- Area of windows $= 35\% \times 900 \qquad = 315 \text{ m}^2$
- Area of exposed walls at U value 0.45 $\quad = 900 - 315$
  $= 585 \text{ m}^2$

- Area of roof and ground floor =
  $40 \times 10 \qquad = 400 \text{ m}^2$
- Area of rooflights $= 20\% \times 400 \qquad = 80 \text{ m}^2$
- Area of roof at U value 0.45 $\qquad = 400 - 80$
  $= 320 \text{ m}^2$
- Rate of heat loss through the exposed elements is calculated in the table below:

Element	Area (m²)	U value (W/m²K)	Rate of heat loss (W/K)
Exposed walls	585	0.45	263.25
Windows	315	5.7	1795.5
Roof	320	0.45	144.0
Rooflights	80	5.7	456.0
Groundfloor	400	0.45	180.0
Total rate of heat loss			2838.75

The total rate of heat loss from the proposed building is less than that from the standard building, therefore the proposal complies with the requirements of Part L.

Calculation procedure 2

This procedure is applicable to all buildings and allows complete freedom of design. Any valid energy conservation measure may be used thus permitting full account to be taken of useful heat gains from solar radiation through the fabric, industrial processes, artificial lighting and any other forms of heat gain to which the building is subject.

An energy target calculation should be carried out to show that the annual energy use of the proposed building (after taking account of useful heat gains) is no greater than the calculated energy use of a similar building designed in accordance with the Elemental Approach described above.

Acceptable methods for calculating annual energy consumption would be:

- For dwellings – by the use of BREDEM WORKSHEET (see BRE Report BR 150: 1989 Building Regulations: Conservation of fuel and power – the 'energy target' method of compliance for dwellings).

AD L
sec. 1
1.16 to 1.18

- For all other buildings – compliance with the space and heating requirements section of CIBSE Energy Code 1981, Part 2a (worksheets 1a–1e).

Certification of calculations

Section 16(9) of the Building Act 1984 (see page 4.12 above) provides for the certification of energy consumption calculations by a suitably qualified approved person who must be registered under a recognised scheme approved by the Secretary of State. Since no such scheme exists at present there are no approved persons. Paragraph 1.21 of AD L recognises that a suitably qualified person (i.e. CIBSE) may still certify that calculations have been correctly carried out and local authorities and approved inspectors may accept these certificates in support of calculations. It is, however, prudent to settle any questions of competency with the local building control authority before certified calculations are submitted.

AD L
sec. 1
1.21

Heating and hot water supply system controls

Energy savings can also be made if heating and hot water storage systems are fitted with controls which adjust the energy input to the system to suit the normal usage of the building.

Under the terms of Section 2 of AD L this means providing space heating or hot water systems in buildings with automatic controls capable of controlling the operation and output of the space heating system and the temperature of the stored water.

Application

AD L covers control systems in all types of buildings the only exception being for those systems which control commercial or industrial processes.

AD L
sec. 2
2.1

Heating controls in dwellings

Dwellings are now required to have some form of sensing device which is capable of controlling the output from the heating system. This could be for example a room thermostat or individual thermostatic radiator valves.

AD L
sec. 2
2.2

Heating controls in buildings other than dwellings

AD L describes three types of heating system control which apply to buildings other than dwelllings:

- Room temperature control;
- Intermittent heat control; and,
- Boiler control.

Room temperature control

This may be effected by using individual room thermostats or thermostatic radiator valves or any other form of temperature sensing

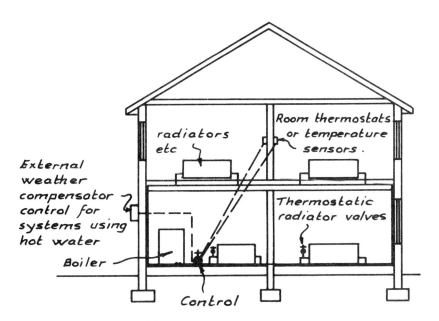

Fig. 16.8 Control of room temperatures.

devices on each part of the space heating system that is designed to be individually controlled. The placing of these will depend on the heating system provided, the orientation of the building and the presence of glazed areas, etc.

Space heating systems which use hot water are also required to be provided with a temperature sensing device placed outside the building to compensate for changes in the weather by regulating the temperature of the water flowing in the heating circuit. (However, it is debatable whether both compensating and thermostatic control are necessary; these should be alternatives.) See Fig. 16.8.

AD L
sec. 2
2.3(a) & (b)

Intermittent heat control

For buildings which are used intermittently such as offices, shops and factories where shift working is not carried out, controls are necessary to shut down the heating system at certain times (at night or weekends) and to switch it on again prior to recommencement of normal use.

The system of control used will depend on the size and type of the building and the output of the heating system as follows:

- For space heating systems with an output of not more than 100 kW a clock control, which can be set manually to give start and stop times, may be used.
- For space heating systems with an output in excess of 100 kW a more complex system of control is required which will take into account the rate at which the building will react when the heating is shut off and re-started. This control arrangement (known as 'optimum start control') allows variable start times for the heating system. However there is doubt about the effectiveness of many optimum start control installations and at the lower end of the size range such installations may not be financially viable.

If heating systems are completely shut off during periods when a building is unoccupied, frost, excessive humidity or condensation may cause damage to the structure, services or contents of the building. Therefore, controls may be provided which will allow certain minimum temperatures to be maintained.

AD L
sec. 2
2.3(c)

Boiler control

Since boilers run most efficiently when they are at, or near, full output, controls become essential when two or more gas or oil-fired boilers are required to supply the same heat demands, if this exceeds 100 kW.

The form of control provided (sequence control) should be able to detect variations in heat demands and so start, stop or modulate the boilers as required. In order to ensure stable control, care should be taken in the hydraulic design.

AD L
sec. 2
2.3(d)

Control of hot water storage

This requirement applies to all buildings including dwellings. The temperature of stored hot water needs careful control to avoid waste of energy and to ensure that the water is delivered at the correct temperature for the users of the building.
Two controls are required:

- All hot water storage vessels should be fitted with a thermostat to keep the water at the required temperature.
- A hot water storage vessel in excess of 150 litres and not heated by off-peak electricity should also be fitted with a time switch to shut off the heat when there is no hot water demand, in order to save energy.

See also details of unvented hot water storage system controls in Chapter 12.

AD L
sec. 2
2.4

Insulation of heating services

Hot water pipes and warm air ducts are required to have adequate thermal insulation unless they are intended to contribute to the useful heating of a room or space.
Hot water storage vessels are also required to have adequate thermal insulation. These requirements do not apply to storage and piping systems for the purpose of an industrial or commercial process.
AD L describes the provisions necessary to meet the requirements of paragraph L1 of Schedule 1 under two main headings:

AD L
sec. 3
3.1

- Insulation of pipes and ducts.
- Insulation of hot water storage vessels.

Pipes should be insulated with a material which:

- Has a thermal conductivity not exceeding 0.045 W/mK and a thickness at least equal to the outside diameter of the pipe up to a maximum of 40 mm; or,
- Satisfies the requirements of BS 5422: 1977 *Specification for the use of thermal insulating materials.*

For warm air ducts the insulation material should meet the recommendations of BS 5422: 1977 as defined for pipes above.

AD L
sec. 3
3.3

Hot water storage vessels

These should be insulated with a material which:

- Limits the heat loss in use to 90 W/m² of the surface area of the vessel; or,
- Satisfies the requirements of:

    (i) BS 5615: 1985 *Specification for insulating jackets for domestic hot water storage cylinders*; or,

    (ii) BS 699: 1984 *Specification for copper direct cylinders for domestic purposes*; or

    (iii) BS 1566 *Copper indirect cylinders for domestic purposes* Part 1: 1984 *Double feed indirect cylinders* and Part 2: 1984 *Specification for single feed indirect cylinders*; or,

    (iv) BS 3198: 1981 *Specification for copper hot water storage combination units for domestic purposes.*

AD L
sec. 3
3.2

If a segmental insulating jacket is used the segments may separate and allow heat to escape. They should, therefore, be taped together to prevent this from happening.

Chapter 17

Access for disabled people

Introduction

The law concerning access for disabled people to buildings has a relatively short history. The first provisions were contained in the Chronically Sick and Disabled Persons Act 1970. These provisions were mostly advisory and were only applied if it was reasonably practicable to do so. There were no enforcement powers contained in the Act and it proved to be rather ineffective. It was clear that some form of legislation with 'teeth' was required.

Therefore, it was considered that the Building Regulations were the most suitable medium for any future legislation. This resulted in the fourth amendment to the 1976 Regulations which introduced Part T – 'Facilities for Disabled People' in August 1985. When the recast Building Regulations were issued in November 1985 it was intended that Part T should also be recast in functional form, supported by an Approved Document which would explain the practical details.

However, it was becoming clear that Part T was too restrictive in application (applying mostly to single storey buildings) and that insufficient time was available for full consultation with all interested bodies in order to include a recast version in the 1985 Regulations. It was therefore reprinted unaltered, as Schedule 2 of the Building Regulations.

Since then the disabled lobby has been very active and after a considerable degree of consultation new regulations were presented to Parliament on 20 August 1987. These came into force as the Building (Disabled People) Regulations 1987 on 14 December 1987 and introduced a new Part M – 'Disabled People' to Schedule 1 of the 1985 Building Regulations. At about the same time Approved Document M – 'Access for Disabled People' was published and contains practical guidance on the application of the regulations.

Interpretation

DISABLED PEOPLE – this is a narrowly defined term which applies

Regs Sch. 1
M1

to those people with a physical impairment which limits their ability to walk or makes them dependent on a wheelchair for mobility.

RELEVANT PREMISES – are those premises to which Part M applies and include:

- New offices and shops containing any number of storeys.
- Those parts of new factories, educational establishments or public buildings which are on the storey containing the principal entrance to the building. (These buildings could, therefore, also contain any number of storeys.)

Regs Sch. 1
M1

Application

Part M of Schedule 1 to the Building Regulations 1985 applies to:

- Relevant premises in newly erected buildings.
- Alterations and extensions to existing buildings to the extent that any existing facilities for disabled people are maintained.

Regs Sch. 1
M1

For example, an extension over the principal entrance to an existing building would have to contain an entrance suitable for disabled people, unless one was provided elsewhere in the building. Additionally, Part M is specifically mentioned in Regulation 3(2)(a) as being one of the requirements contained in the definition of material alteration (see p. 2.12 above).

AD
M2/3/4
1.1, 1.2, 1.3
and 1985
Regs Reg.
3(2)

Under this provision the mere removal of a disabled person's sanitary convenience might constitute a material alteration of a building because the building would then be adversely affected by the work of removal.

The main provisions

It is interesting to note that Part M of Schedule 1 to the Building Regulations 1985 is entitled 'Disabled People' whilst Approved Document M is headed 'Access for disabled people'.

The former title is the more accurate since the regulations cover far more than just access.

The following are the facilities which need to be provided in relevant premises:

Regs Sch.
1, M2

- Suitable means of access into the building from outside.

Regs Sch.
1, M2

- Suitable means of access within the building to those parts which it is reasonable to provide access.

Regs Sch.
1, M3

- A reasonable number of sanitary conveniences suitable for disabled people.

Regs Sch.
1, M4

- A reasonable number of wheelchair spaces, where the building contains audience or spectator seating.

It should be noted that Part M applies only to those features outside a building which are needed to provide access to a suitable entrance. Also excluded from the need to comply are those parts of a building which are used for the inspection, repair or maintenance of the building, its services or machinery.

Finally, it is the intention of Part M that the means of access and the facilities provided should be for the benefit of occasional visitors to a building as well as those who work there.

AD
M2/3/4
2.2, 2.4, 2.5

Approved Document M

As with all the approved documents, AD M contains practical guidance on meeting the requirements of Part M of Schedule 1. It is not a mandatory document and designers are free to use other sources of design guidance providing they can satisfy the functional requirements.

Advice may be sought from the following organisations:

- The Access Committee for England, 35 Great Smith Street, London SW1.
- The Centre on Environment for the Handicapped, 35 Great Smith Street, London SW1
- The Wales Council for the Disabled, Caerbragdy Industrial Estate, Bedwas Road, Caerphilly, Mid Glamorgan.

The Access Committee have published a highly regarded document entitled 'Design Guidance Notes for Developers'.

Where work is to be carried out in schools or other educational establishments the DES publication Design Note 18, 1984 'Access for Disabled Persons to Educational Buildings' will satisfy the requirements of paragraphs M2 and M3 of Part M.

AD
M2/3/4
2.6

Approved Document M recognises that there may be circumstances when full provision of the requirements of Part M may not be reasonable. However, the hope is expressed (perhaps over-optimistically) that designers and developers will, wherever possible, go beyond the minimum level of provision demanded by Part M.

Means of access

In addition to the terms defined in Part M (see Interpretation, above) AD M2/3/4 also includes a number of words and phrases which require definition in the context of this approved document.

ACCESS – approach or entry to relevant premises which is convenient for the disabled.

AD
M2/3/4
0.2

ACCESSIBLE – relevant premises and the facilities provided in them,

AD
M2/3/4
0.3

which are suitably designed so that disabled people may reach and use them.

AD
M2/3/4
0.4

SUITABLE – means of access and facilities which are designed for the use of disabled people.

PRINCIPAL ENTRANCE STOREY – the storey of a building which contains the main entrance or entrances.

AD
M2/3/4
0.6

Sometimes it may be necessary to provide an alternative, accessible entrance into the building. (See below.) In this case the storey containing the alternative entrance would be the principal entrance storey.

Access to the building

In general, buildings should be designed so that the principal entrance is suitable for disabled people.

If it is necessary to provide separate entrances for visitors or customers and staff, each entrance should be suitable and accessible.

In certain cases it may not be possible to make the main entrance accessible due to space restriction and congestion or sloping ground. Sometimes, car parking spaces are provided in areas where access to the principal entrance is not possible. In these cases an additional accessible entrance may be provided, but this should also be for general use.

AD
M2
3.1 to 3.3

The requirements for the approach to the building are contained in Appendix A of AD M 2/3/4. These are illustrated in Fig. 17.1 and may be summarised as follows.

Ramps should:

- Ideally, be not steeper than 1 in 20 with an absolute maximum of 1 in 12.
- Have a landing at top and bottom as wide as the ramp and at least 1200 mm long, clear of any door swing.
- Have a maximum length of 10 metres between landings.
- Have intermediate landings as wide as the ramp and at least 1500 mm long, clear of any door swing.
- Have any open side protected by guard rails to comply with AD K and a raised kerb at least 100 mm high.
- Have a clear width of at least 1200 mm if with associated steps or 1010 mm clear width if without associated steps.
- Have a maximum width of 1800 mm.
- Have a handrail on at least one side or on both sides if steeper than 1 in 15 and more than 3 metres long.

Associated steps should:

- Not rise more than 1200 mm between landings.

- Have intermediate landings equal in length and width to the width of the flight.
- Have landings at top and bottom of the flight.
- Have uniform rises no greater than 150 mm high and uniform goings at least 280 mm long.

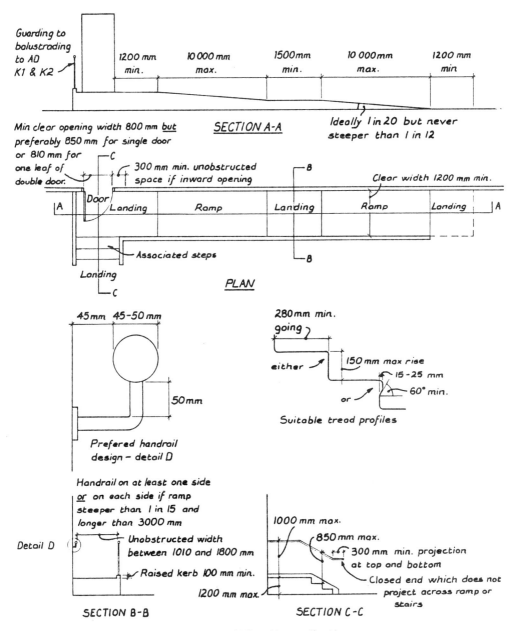

Fig. 17.1 Access to the building (Appendix A).

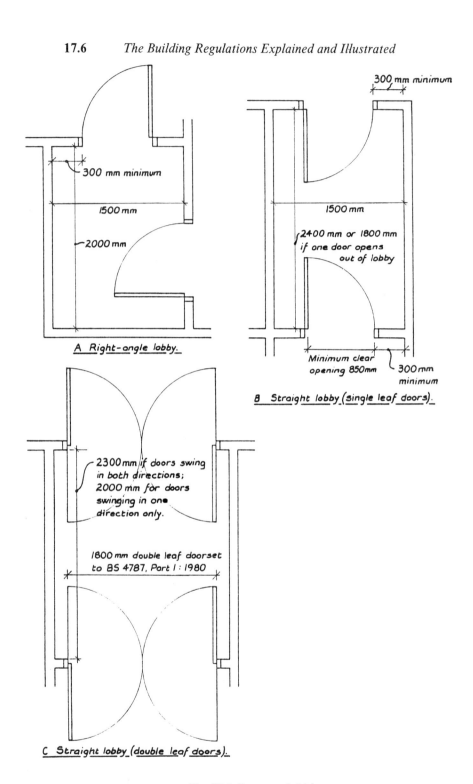

Fig. 17.2 Entrance lobbies.

- Have a clear width of at least 1010 mm up to a maximum of 1800 mm.
- Have a suitable handrail on each side and a suitable tread profile as illustrated in Fig. 17.1.

AD
M2/3/4
Appendix A,
A1, A2, A3
and A4

Entrance doors and lobbies

To enable the passage of a wheelchair-bound person, entrance doors and lobbies also need to comply with certain minimum dimensions. The exact dimensions will vary with the design of the doors and lobby.

Figure 17.2 shows the design principles which should be followed.

Entrance doors should have an absolute minimum clear width of 800 mm. Ideally, the minimum clear width should be that provided by a 1000 mm single leaf external doorset or by one leaf of an 1800 mm double leaf doorset (i.e. 850 mm clear or 810 mm clear – see Table 2, BS4787, Part 1: 1980).

Revolving doors are not negotiable by wheelchair-bound people and should always be accompanied by a conventional, accessible entrance door.

AD
M2/3/4
Appendix A,
A5, A7

AD
M2/3/4
Appendix A,
A5

AD
M2/3/4
Appendix A,
A6

Access within the principal entrance storey

Once inside the principal entrance of a building a disabled person must be able to reach the facilities which are required by Part M.

Access is also required to all relevant premises in the storey and to any lifts, ramps or stairways which need to be provided to reach relevant premises on other levels. This is particularly important since the principal entrance storey may be on split levels in which case it would be considered as a single storey requiring access to all parts.

Corridors, passageways, internal doors and internal lobbies can present problems for disabled people unless care is taken in their design and adequate space is provided to enable a wheelchair to be manoeuvred.

Corridors and passageways should have a clear width of at least 1200 mm. With internal doors the important factor is the minimum clear opening width. AD M2/3/4 allows an absolute minimum size of 750 mm but *recommends* the use of 900 mm single leaf internal doorsets or 1800 mm double leaf internal doorsets complying with Table 1 of BS 4787 (the minimum clear opening sizes are 770 mm for the single leaf doorset and 820 mm for one leaf of the double doorset).

Whichever type of door is used it is important to allow sufficient room for the door to be opened by a person in a wheelchair. Therefore, the space into which the door opens should be unobstructed on the door handle side for at least 300 mm.

It should be noted that BS 4787 does not permit a fire resisting single leaf doorset to exceed 900 mm in overall width.

Internal lobbies should comply with the minimum dimensions shown in Fig. 17.3.

AD
M2/3/4
2.3, 3.5

AD
M2/3/4
Appendix 3,
B1, B2, B3

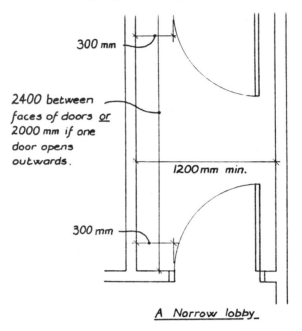

300 mm

2400 between faces of doors or 2000 mm if one door opens outwards.

1200 mm min.

300 mm

A   Narrow   lobby

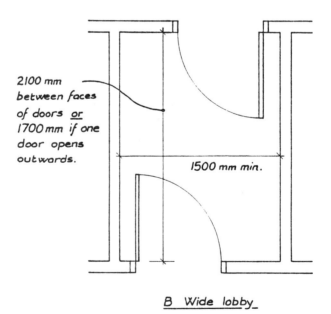

2100 mm between faces of doors or 1700 mm if one door opens outwards.

1500 mm min.

B   Wide   lobby

Fig. 17.3 Internal lobbies.

Access in multi-storey buildings

It should be remembered that if offices and shops contain relevant premises on more than one level then a suitable means of access should be provided to those other levels. This should be by means of a suitable lift or ramp and is only required to be provided to the storey above or below the principal entrance storey.

AD M2/3/4 effectively exempts small offices and shops from the need to install internal lifts or ramps by applying minimum floor area limits. Vertical circulation is only required if these limits are exceeded.

The actual limits set are, of course, a compromise and were the cause of much discussion during the drafting of the Approved Document. Opinion was divided between having defined floor area limits or leaving it flexible.

Apart from the problem of setting limits the fear was that buildings below the specified figures would never have suitable vertical circulation. On the other hand, if no limits are specified and the definition of 'small office or shop' is left to local authority interpretation then variations in application of the regulations are inevitable. In the event, the Secretary of State opted for the following minimum floor areas:

- Two storey buildings (i.e. only two floors to access) – 280 m² of relevant premises.
- Buildings exceeding two storeys (i.e. a maximum of three floors to access) – 200 m² of relevant premises.

The figures are derived by adding together the areas of all the relevant premises in a storey which use the same entrance from the street, even if they are in different parts of the same storey or are used for different relevant purposes. Thus the figures given are for each storey above or below the principal entrance storey. In calculating the figures given above it is permissible to exclude the area of the vertical circulation, sanitary accommodation or maintenance areas which are used in conjunction with the relevant premises. If lifts are not provided, then, it is necessary to provide a suitable stairway. It is, of course, essential to provide means of access from the lift, ramp or stairway to all relevant premises in the storey served.

AD
M2/3/4
3.9, 3.10,
3.11, 3.12

Lifts

A suitable lift design is shown in Fig. 17.4. Its main features are:

- An unobstructed, accessible landing space at least 1500 mm square in front of the lift doors.
- A door or doors with a clear opening width of 800 mm.
- A car with minimum dimensions of 1100 mm wide by 1400 mm deep.
- Landing and car controls between 1000 mm and 1400 mm from landing or car floor levels.

AD
M2/3/4
Appendix B,
B5

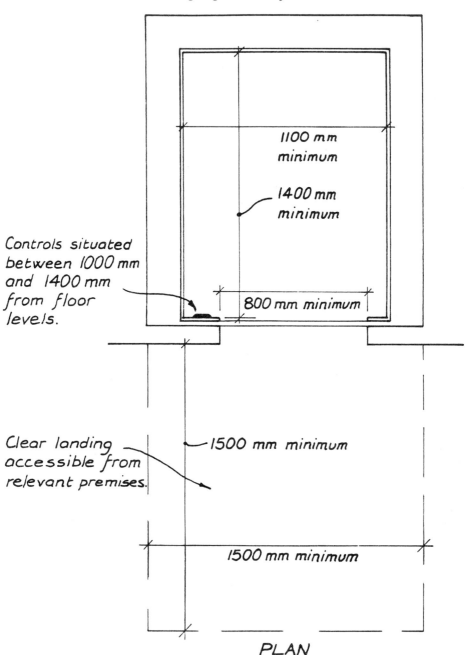

Fig. 17.4 Lift (suitable for disabled people).

Internal stairways

With certain exceptions, the stairway design shown in Fig. 17.1 is also suitable for internal stairways. The principal variations permitted are:

- Uniform risers should not exceed 170 mm in height.
- Uniform goings should not be less than 250 mm in length.
- The maximum rise of a flight between landings should not exceed 1800 mm.

This last figure is somewhat flexible since it depends to a large extent on site constraints such as landing levels or storey heights.

AD
M2/3/4
Appendix B,
B6

Internal ramps

AD
M2/3/4
Appendix B,
B7

Internal ramps should comply with the requirements which are specified for external ramps (see page 17.4 above and Fig. 17.1).

Access to restaurant and bar facilities

It may come as a surprise to find recommendations regarding means of access to restaurant and bar facilities in Approved Document M. It should be realised that by virtue of Regulation 2(1) a restaurant or bar is considered to be a shop and Regulation M2 requires access to be provided to those parts of relevant premises to which it is reasonable to provide access. Therefore, the full range of services offered should be accessible, including self-service counters and at least half the area where seating is provided. Sometimes, the nature of the service provided in a restaurant varies. For example, some areas may be self-service and some may be waitress service. In these cases at least half the area of each should be accessible.

AD
M2/3/4
3.6

Access to hotel and motel guest bedrooms

It is difficult to see how hotels or motels can be regarded as falling under the provisions of Part M. They do not come under the definition of 'shop' in Regulation 2(1) and so they must be assumed to be 'premises to which the public is admitted whether on payment or otherwise'. This is *not* the same as the definition of 'public building' contained in Regulation 2(2).

If this interpretation is correct then access is required to guest bedrooms in the principal entrance storey only.

The following main provisions apply:

- Each guest bedroom entrance door should be accessible.
- One guest bedroom out of every 20 should be suitable in terms of

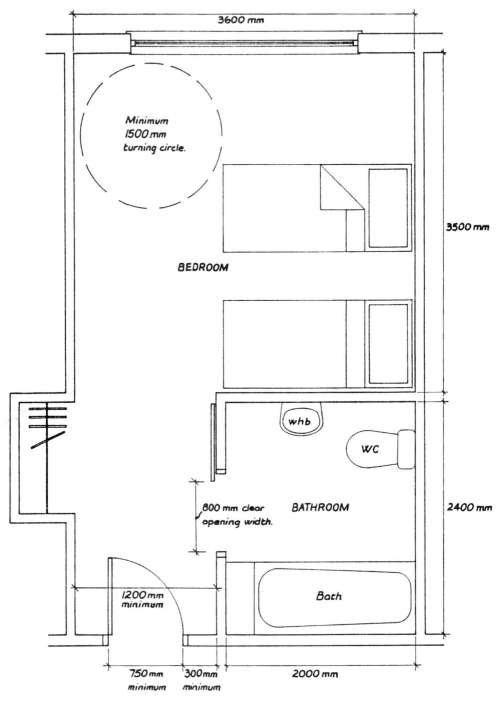

Fig. 17.5 Guest bedroom (hotels and motels).

layout and dimensions for a wheelchair bound person (i.e. if 21 guest bedrooms were provided in the principal entrance storey then 2 of them would have to be suitable for disabled people). See Fig. 17.5 for details.

AD
M2/3/4
3.7 and
Appendix B,
B4

Sanitary conveniences

Paragraphs 4.1 to 4.5 of AD M2/3/4 set out the requirements for the provision of sanitary conveniences suitable for disabled people in relevant premises.

The wording is somewhat vague and no clear indication is given as to whether separate male and female sanitary accommodation is preferred to unisex facilities.

The intention appears to be that *if* separate sanitary conveniences are provided in office, shop, factory or public premises for the use of visitors, customers or staff, then these should be designed to be accessible and suitable for disabled people, and at least unisex facilities should be provided. In general the sanitary convenience should be situated in the principal entrance storey, however, each office or shop premises in a building should have at least one unisex convenience unless there is no access by lift or ramp to the storeys containing the facilities. Larger shop or office premises should have additional unisex facilities although no guidance is given on the scale of provision *or* on what constitutes 'larger' premises.

The rules above also apply to the general provision of unisex sanitary conveniences in hotels and motels. Additionally, if the normal arrangement is to have guest bedrooms with en-suite facilities then this should also be the arrangement for guest bedrooms suitable for disabled people.

A suitable design for a unisex sanitary convenience is illustrated in Fig. 17.6.

AD
M2/3/4
4.1 to 4.5,
Appendix
C, C1 to C3

Audience or spectator seating

Where relevant premises contain fixed audience or spectator seating, then it is essential to make provision for disabled people by providing a sufficient number of wheelchair spaces which are accessible and provide a clear view of the event.

The spaces may be kept clear at all times or may contain seating which can be removed easily for each occasion.

Wheelchair spaces should be:

- At least 900 mm wide.
- At least 1400 mm deep.
- Dispersed throughout the theatre or stadium (and not grouped all together).

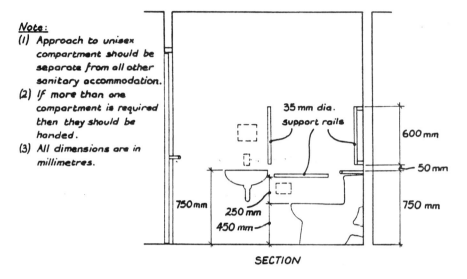

<u>Note:</u>
(1) Approach to unisex compartment should be separate from all other sanitary accommodation.
(2) If more than one compartment is required then they should be handed.
(3) All dimensions are in millimetres.

35 mm dia. support rails

600 mm

50 mm

750 mm

750 mm

250 mm

450 mm

SECTION

PLAN

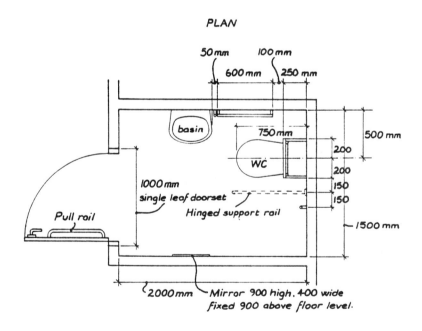

50 mm   100 mm

600 mm   250 mm

basin

750 mm   500 mm

WC   200

1000 mm   200
single leaf doorset   150
Hinged support rail   150

Pull rail   1500 mm

2000 mm   Mirror 900 high, 400 wide fixed 900 above floor level.

Fig. 17.6 Sanitary accommodation.

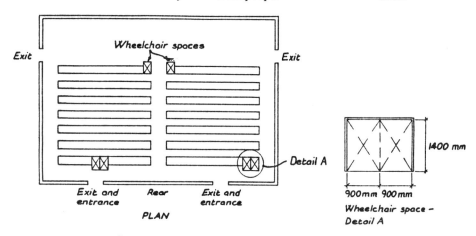

A Theatre - notional disposition of wheelchair spaces.

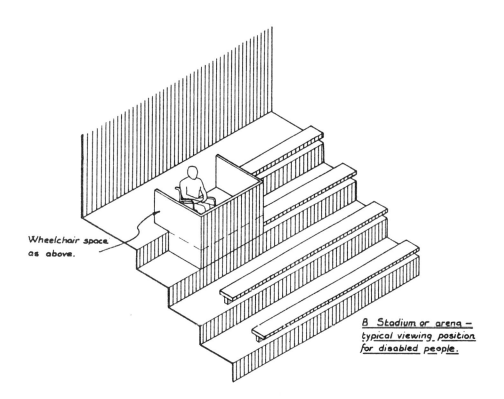

Fig. 17.7 Audience or spectator seating.

AD
M2/3/4
5.1 to 5.3,
Appendix
D, D1
There should be provided at least 6 spaces or one for every 100 public seats whichever figure is the greater.

Figure 17.7 shows a typical layout for audience or spectator seating.

III
Appendices

Appendix 1

The Building Act 1984 – selected provisions

Part I

BUILDING REGULATIONS

Power to make building regulations

1. – (1) The Secretary of State may, for any of the purposes of:

(*a*) securing the health, safety, welfare and convenience of persons in or about buildings and of others who may be affected by buildings or matters connected with buildings,

(*b*) furthering the conservation of fuel and power, and

(*c*) preventing waste, undue consumption, misuse or contamination of water,

make regulations with respect .to the design and construction of buildings and the provision of services, fittings and equipment in or in connection with buildings.

Power to make building regulations.

(2) Regulations made under subsection (1) above are known as building regulations.

(3) Schedule 1 to this Act has effect with respect to the matters as to which building regulations may provide.

(4) The power to make building regulations is exercisable by statutory instrument, which is subject to annulment in pursuance of a resolution of either House of Parliament.

2. – (1) Building regulations may impose on owners and occupiers of buildings to which building regulations are applicable such continuing requirements as the Secretary of State considers appropriate for securing, with respect to any provision of building regulations designated in the regulations as a provision to which those requirements relate that the purposes of that provision are not frustrated; but a continuing requirement imposed by virtue of this subsection does not apply in relation to a building unless a provision of building regulations so designated as one to which the requirement relates applies to that building.

Continuing requirements

(2) Building regulations may impose on owners and occupiers of buildings of a prescribed class (whenever erected, and whether or not any building regulations were applicable to them at the time of their erection) continuing requirements with respect to all or any of the following matters:

> (*a*) the conditions subject to which any services, fittings or equipment provided in or in connection with a building of that class may be used,
>
> (*b*) the inspection and maintenance of any services, fittings or equipment so provided,
>
> (*c*) the making of reports to a prescribed authority on the condition of any services, fittings or equipment so provided,

and so much of paragraph 8 of Schedule 1 to this Act as restricts the application of building regulations does not apply to regulations made by virtue of this subsection.

(3) If a person contravenes a continuing requirement imposed by virtue of this section, the local authority, without prejudice to their right to take proceedings for a fine in respect of the contravention, may:

> (*a*) execute any work or take any other action required to remedy the contravention, and
>
> (*b*) recover from that person the expenses reasonably incurred by them in so doing.

(4) Where a local authority have power under subsection (3) above to execute any work or take any other action, they may, instead of exercising that power, by notice require the owner or the occupier of the building to which the contravention referred to in that subsection relates to execute that work or take that action.

(5) Sections 99 and 102 below apply in relation to a notice given under subsection (4) above, subject to the modification that references in those sections to the execution of works are references to the execution of works or the taking of other action, and references to works shall be construed accordingly.

(6) Sections 8, 9, 10 and 39 below have effect in relation to continuing requirements imposed by virtue of this section subject to the modification that a direction under the said sections 8 and 9 below shall, if it so provides, cease to have effect at the end of such period as may be specified in the direction.

Exemption from building regulations

3. – (1) Building regulations may exempt a prescribed class of buildings, services, fittings or equipment from all or any of the provisions of building regulations.

(2) The Secretary of State may by direction exempt from all or any of the provisions of building regulations:

(*a*) a particular building, or

(*b*) buildings of a particular class at a particular location,

either unconditionally or subject to compliance with any conditions specified in the direction.

(3) A person who contravenes a condition specified in a direction given under subsection (2) above, or permits such a condition to be contravened, is liable on summary conviction to a fine not exceeding level 5 on the standard scale, and to a further fine not exceeding £50 for each day on which the offence continues after he is convicted.

4. – (1) Nothing in this Part of this Act with respect to building regulations, and nothing in any building regulations, applies in relation to:

(*a*) a building required for the purposes of a school or other educational establishment erected or to be erected according to plans that have been approved by the Secretary of State for Education and Science or the Secretary of State for Wales, or according to particulars submitted to and approved by the Secretary of State under section 14 of the Education Act 1980 or under regulations made under section 27(4) of that Act, or

(*b*) a building belonging to statutory undertakers, the United Kingdom Atomic Energy Authority, the British Airports Authority or the Civil Aviation Authority and held or used by them for the purposes of their undertaking, unless it is:

(i) a house, or in the case of the British Airports Authority a house or a hotel, or

(ii) a building used as offices or showrooms, and not forming part of a railway station or in the case of the British Airports Authority or the Civil Aviation Authority not being on an aerodrome owned by the Authority in question.

(2) The words 'the United Kingdom Atomic Energy Authority,' in subsection (1)(*b*) above (together with paragraph 4 of Schedule 6 to this Act) cease to have effect upon the coming into force of the repeal of section 5(5) of the Atomic Energy Authority Act 1954 contained in Schedule 7 to this Act.

5. – (1) Building regulations may exempt:

(*a*) a local authority,

(*b*) a county council, or

Marginal notes:
Exemption of particular classes of buildings, etc.

Exemption of educational buildings and buildings of statutory undertakers.

Exemption of public bodies from procedural requirements of building regulations.

(*c*) any other body that acts under an enactment for public purposes and not for its own profit and is prescribed for the purposes of this section,

from compliance with any requirements of those regulations that are not substantive requirements.

(2) A local authority, county council or other body that is exempted as mentioned in subsection (1) above is in subsection (3) below referred to as an 'exempt body'.

(3) Without prejudice to the obligation of an exempt body to comply with substantive requirements of building regulations, the function of enforcing building regulations that is conferred on local authorities by section 91(2) below is not exercisable in relation to work carried out by an exempt body, and accordingly:

(*a*) nothing in section 36(1) to (5) below applies in relation to work so carried out, and
(*b*) a local authority may not institute proceedings under section 35 below for a contravention of building regulations by an exempt body.

(4) In subsection (3) above, the reference to the carrying out of work includes a reference to the making of a material change of use as defined by and for the purposes of building regulations.

Approved documents

Approval of documents for purposes of building regulations. **6.** – (1) For the purpose of providing practical guidance with respect to the requirements of any provision of building regulations, the Secretary of State or a body designated by him for the purposes of this section may:

(*a*) approve and issue any document (whether or not prepared by him or by the body concerned), or
(*b*) approve any document issued or proposed to be issued otherwise than by him or by the body concerned,

if in the opinion of the Secretary of State or, as the case may be, the body concerned the document is suitable for that purpose.

(2) References in this section and section 7 below to a document include references to a part of a document; and accordingly, in relation to a document of which part only is approved, a reference in the following provisions of this section or in section 7 below to the approved document is a reference only to the part of it that is approved.

(3) An approval given under subsection (1) above takes effect in

accordance with a notice that is issued by the Secretary of State or, as the case may be, the body giving the approval and that:

(*a*) identifies the approved document in question,
(*b*) states the date on which the approval of it is to take effect, and
(*c*) specifies the provisions of building regulations for the purposes of which the document is approved.

(4) The Secretary of State or, as the case may be, the body that gave the approval may:

(*a*) from time to time approve and issue a revision of the whole or any part of an approved document issued by him or it for the purposes of this section, and
(*b*) approve any revision or proposed revision of the whole or any part of an approved document,

and subsection (3) above, with the necessary modifications, applies in relation to an approval that is given under this subsection to a revision as it applies in relation to an approval that is given under subsection (1) above to a document.

(5) The Secretary of State or, as the case may be, the body that gave the approval may withdraw his or its approval of a document under this section; and such a withdrawal of approval takes effect in accordance with a notice that is issued by the Secretary of State or body concerned and that:

(*a*) identifies the approved document in question, and
(*b*) states the date on which the approval of it is to cease to have effect.

(6) References in subsections (4) and (5) above and in section 7 below to an approved document are references to that document as it has effect for the time being, regard being had to any revision of the whole or any part of it that has been approved under subsection (4) above.

(7) Where a body ceases to be a body designated by the Secretary of State for the purposes of this section, subsections (4) and (5) above have effect as if any approval given by that body had been given by the Secretary of State.

(8) The power to designate a body for the purposes of this section is exercisable by order made by statutory instrument, which is subject to annulment in pursuance of a resolution of either House of Parliament.

7. – (1) A failure on the part of a person to comply with an approved document does not of itself render him liable to any civil or criminal proceedings; but if, in any proceedings whether civil or criminal, it is

Compliance or non-compliance with approved documents.

alleged that a person has at any time contravened a provision of building regulations:

(*a*) a failure to comply with a document that at that time was approved for the purposes of that provision may be relied upon as tending to establish liability, and

(*b*) proof of compliance with such a document may be relied on as tending to negative liability.

(2) In any proceedings, whether civil or criminal:

(*a*) a document purporting to be a notice issued as mentioned in section 6(3) above shall be taken to be such a notice unless the contrary is provided, and

(*b*) a document that appears to the court to be the approved document to which such a notice refers shall be taken to be that approved document unless the contrary is proved.

Relaxation of building regulations

Relaxation of building regulations. **8.** – (1) Subject to this section, the Secretary of State, if on an application for a direction under this section he considers that the operation of a requirement in building regulations would be unreasonable in relation to the particular case to which the application relates, may, after consultation with the local authority, give a direction dispensing with or relaxing that requirement.

(2) If building regulations so provide as regards a requirement contained in the regulations, the power to dispense with or relax that requirement under subsection (1) above is exercisable by the local authority (instead of by the Secretary of State after consultation with the local authority).

(3) Building regulations made by virtue of subsection (2) above may except applications of any description.

(4) If:

(*a*) building regulations so provide as regards any requirement contained in the regulations, and

(*b*) a public body considers that the operation of any such requirement would be unreasonable in relation to any particular work carried out or proposed to be carried out by or on behalf of the public body,

the public body may give a direction dispensing with or relaxing that requirement.

(5) In subsection (4) above, 'public body' means:

(*a*) a local authority,

(*b*) a county council, or
(*c*) any other body that is prescribed for the purposes of section 5 above.

(6) Building regulations may provide as regards a requirement contained in the regulations that subsections (1) to (5) above do not apply.

9. – (1) An application under section 8(1) or (2) above shall be in such form and shall contain such particulars as may be prescribed.

Application for relaxation.

(2) The application shall be made to the local authority, and, except where the power of giving the direction is exercisable by the local authority, the local authority shall at once transmit the application to the Secretary of State and give notice to the applicant that it has been so transmitted.

(3) An application by a local authority in connection with a building or proposed building in the area of that authority shall be made to the Secretary of State, except where the power of giving the direction is exercisable by that authority.

(4) Schedule 2 to this Act has effect as regards an application for a direction that will affect the application of building regulations to work that has been carried out before the making of the application.

10. – (1) Not less than 21 days before giving a direction under section 8(1), (2) or (4) above in respect of any particular work, the Secretary of State, the local authority or the public body, as the case may be, shall publish in a local newspaper circulating in the area where the site of the work is situated a notice:

Advertisement of proposal for relaxation of building regulations.

(*a*) indicating the situation and nature of the work and the requirement to be dispensed with or relaxed, and
(*b*) stating that representations with regard to the effect that the direction may have on public health or safety may be made by a date specified in the notice, being a date not less than 21 days from the date of the notice,

and, where the direction is proposed to be made on an application, the Secretary of State or the local authority may, as a condition of entertaining the application, require the applicant to pay or undertake to pay the cost of publication.

(2) No notice need be published under subsection (1) above where it appears to the Secretary of State, the local authority or the public body, as the case may be, that any effect that the direction may have on public health or safety will be limited to premises adjoining the site of the work, but in that case he, they or it shall give such notice to the owner and occupier of those premises.

(3) No notice need be published or given under subsection (1) or (2) above where the work affects only an internal part of a building.

(4) The Secretary of State may, instead of himself publishing or giving a notice under subsection (1) or (2) above, require the local authority to give or publish the notice.

(5) Before giving the direction, the Secretary of State, the local authority or the public body shall consider any representations duly made in pursuance of a notice published or given under subsection (1) or (2) above.

(6) If, after a local authority have received representations under this section, they refuse the application to which the representations relate and an appeal is brought against their refusal, the local authority shall transmit to the Secretary of State copies of those representations.

Type relaxation of building regulations.

11. – (1) If the Secretary of State considers that the operation of a requirement of building regulations would be unreasonable in relation to a particular type of building matter, he may, either on an application made to him or of his own accord, give a direction dispensing with or relaxing that requirement generally in relation to that type of building matter, either:

(*a*) unconditionally, or

(*b*) subject to compliance with any conditions specified in the direction, being conditions with respect to matters directly connected with the dispensation or relaxation.

(2) A direction under subsection (1) above:

(*a*) if it so provides, ceases to have effect at the end of such period as may be specified in the direction,

(*b*) may be varied or revoked by a subsequent direction of the Secretary of State.

(3) Building regulations may require a person making an application under subsection (1) above to pay the Secretary of State the prescribed fee, and:

(*a*) without prejudice to paragraph 10 of Schedule 1 to this Act, regulations made by virtue of this subsection may prescribe different fees for different cases, and

(*b*) the Secretary of State may in a particular case remit the whole or part of a fee payable by virtue of this subsection.

(4) Before giving a direction under subsection (1) above, the Secretary of State shall consult such bodies as appear to him to be representative of the interests concerned.

(5) Where the Secretary of State gives a direction under subsection (1) above, he shall publish notice of that fact in such manner as he thinks fit.

(6) A person who contravenes a condition specified in a direction given under subsection (1) above, or permits such a condition to be contravened, is liable on summary conviction to a fine not exceeding level 5 on the standard scale and to a further fine not exceeding £50 for each day on which the offence continues after he is convicted.

(7) If at any time a direction under subsection (1) above dispensing with or relaxing a requirement of building regulations ceases to have effect by virtue of subsection (2)(*a*) above, or is varied or revoked under subsection (2)(*b*) above, that fact does not affect the continued operation of the direction (with any conditions specified in it) in a case in which before that time:

(*a*) plans of the proposed work were, in accordance with building regulations, deposited with a local authority, or

(*b*) a building notice was served on the district surveyor in pursuance of section 83 of the London Building Acts (Amendment) Act 1939.

(8) In this section, 'building matter' means any building or other matter whatsoever to which building regulations are in any circumstances applicable.

Type approval of building matter

12. – (1) This section has effect with a view to enabling the Secretary of State, either on an application made to him or of his own accord, to approve a particular type of building matter as complying, either generally or in a class of case, with particular requirements of building regulations.

Power of Secretary of State to approve type of building matter.

(2) An application for the approval under subsection (1) above of a type of building matter shall comply with any requirements of building regulations as to the form of such applications and the particulars to be included in them.

(3) Where under subsection (1) above the Secretary of State approves a type of building matter as complying with particular requirements of building regulations either generally or in a class of case, he may issue a certificate to that effect specifying:

(*a*) the type of building matter to which the certificate relates,

(*b*) the requirements of building regulations to which the certificate relates, and

(*c*) where applicable, the class or classes of case to which the certificate applies.

(4) A certificate under subsection (3) above, if it so provides, ceases to have effect at the end of such period as may be specified in the certificate.

(5) If, while a certificate under subsection (3) above is in force, it is found, in a particular case involving building matter of the type to which the certificate relates, that:

(*a*) the building matter in question is of that type, and
(*b*) the case is one to which the certificate applies,

that building matter shall in that particular case be deemed to comply with the requirements of building regulations to which the certificate relates.

(6) The Secretary of State may vary a certificate under subsection (3) above, either on an application made to him or of his own accord; but, in the case of a certificate issued on an application made by a person under subsection (1) above, the Secretary of State, except where he varies it on the application of that person, shall before varying it give that person reasonable notice that he proposes to do so.

(7) Building regulations may require a person making an application under subsection (1) or (6) above to pay the Secretary of State the prescribed fee, and:

(*a*) without prejudice to paragraph 10 of Schedule 1 to this Act, regulations made by virtue of this subsection may prescribe different fees for different cases, and
(*b*) the Secretary of State may in a particular case remit the whole or part of a fee payable by virtue of this subsection.

(8) The Secretary of State may revoke a certificate issued under subsection (3) above, but, before doing so in the case of a certificate issued on an application under subsection (1) above, he shall give the person on whose application the certificate was issued reasonable notice that he proposes to do so.

(9) Where the Secretary of State issues a certificate under subsection (3) above or varies or revokes a certificate so issued, he shall publish notice of that fact in such manner as he thinks fit.

(10) If at any time a certificate under subsection (3) above ceases to have effect by virtue of subsection (4) above, or is varied or revoked under subsection (6) or (8) above, that fact does not affect the continued operation of subsection (5) above by virtue of that certificate in a case in which before that time:

(*a*) plans of the proposed work were, in accordance with building regulations, deposited with a local authority, or
(*b*) a building notice was served on the district surveyor in

pursuance of section 83 of the London Building Acts (Amendment) Act 1939.

(11) For the purposes of subsection (3) above, or of any variation of a certificate under subsection (6) above, a class of case may be framed in any way that the Secretary of State thinks fit.

(12) In this section, 'building matter' has the same meaning as in section 11 above.

13. – (1) The Secretary of State may by building regulations delegate to a person or body, to such extent and subject to such conditions as the Secretary of State may think fit, the powers of approval conferred on him by section 12 above.

(2) So far as those powers are for the time being so delegated to a person or body, section 12 above, except subsection (7) as far as the end of paragraph (*a*), and any building regulations made by virtue of subsection (7) shall (subject to any prescribed conditions) have effect in relation to that person or body with the substitution of references to that person or body for references to the Secretary of State.

Delegation of power to approve.

Consultation

14. – (1) The Secretary of State for the time being charged with the exercise of the power to make building regulations and the Secretary of State for Wales acting jointly shall appoint a committee, to be known as the Building Regulations Advisory Committee, for the purpose of advising the Secretary of State on the exercise of his power to make building regulations, and on other subjects connected with building regulations.

Consultation with Building Regulations Advisory Committee and other bodies.

(2) The Secretary of State may pay such expenses incurred by members of the Building Regulations Advisory Committee as he may, with the approval of the Treasury, determine.

(3) Before making any building regulations containing substantive requirements, the Secretary of State shall consult the Building Regulations Advisory Committee and such other bodies as appear to him to be representative of the interests concerned.

15. – (1) Where, in the case of a requirement as to:

(*a*) structural fire precautions,
(*b*) the provision of means of escape from buildings in case of fire, or
(*c*) the provision of means for securing that such means of escape can be safely and effectively used at all material times,

contained in building regulations, the power to dispense with or relax that requirement conferred by section 8(1) above is by virtue of section

Consultation with fire authority.

8(2) above exercisable by a local authority, or a public body proposes to exercise the power conferred on it by section 8(4) above, the local authority or public body, if they are not the fire authority, shall before exercising the power in relation to any premises or proposed premises consult the fire authority.

(2) In subsection (1) above, 'public body' has the meaning given by section 8(5) above.

Passing of plans

Passing or rejection of plans.

16. – (1) Where plans of any proposed work are, in accordance with building regulations, deposited with a local authority, it is the duty of the local authority, subject to any other section of this Act that expressly requires or authorises them in certain cases to reject plans, to pass the plans unless:

(*a*) they are defective, or
(*b*) they show that the proposed work would contravene any of the building regulations.

(2) If the plans:

(*a*) are defective, or
(*b*) show that the proposed work would contravene any of the building regulations,

the local authority may:

(i) reject the plans, or
(ii) subject to subsection (4) below, pass them subject to either or both of the conditions set out in subsection (3) below.

(3) The conditions mentioned in subsection (2) above are:

(*a*) that such modifications as the local authority may specify shall be made in the deposited plans, and
(*b*) that such further plans as they may specify shall be deposited.

(4) A local authority may only pass plans subject to a condition such as is specified in subsection (3) above if the person by whom or on whose behalf they were deposited:

(*a*) has requested them to do so, or
(*b*) has consented to their doing so.

(5) A request or consent under subsection (4) above shall be in writing.

(6) The authority shall within the relevant period from the deposit of the plans give notice to the person by whom or on whose behalf they were deposited whether they have been passed or rejected.

(7) A notice that plans have been rejected shall specify the defects on account of which, or the regulation or section of this Act for non-conformity with which, or under the authority of which, they have been rejected.

(8) A notice that plans have been passed shall:

(*a*) specify any condition subject to which they have been passed, and

(*b*) state that the passing of the plans operates as an approval of them only for the purposes of the requirements of:

    (i) the building regulations, and
    (ii) any section of this Act (other than this section) that expressly requires or authorises the local authority in certain cases to reject plans.

(9) Where the deposited plans are accompanied by:

(*a*) a certificate given by a person approved for the purposes of this subsection to the effect that the proposed work, if carried out in accordance with the deposited plans, will comply with such provisions of the regulations prescribed for the purposes of this subsection as may be specified in the certificate, and

(*b*) such evidence as may be prescribed that an approved scheme applies, or the prescribed insurance cover has been or will be provided, in relation to the certificate,

the local authority may not, except in prescribed circumstances, reject the plans on the ground that:

    (i) they are defective with respect to any provisions of the building regulations that are so specified, or
    (ii) they show that the proposed work would contravene any of those provisions.

(10) In any case where a question arises under this section between a local authority and a person who proposes to carry out any work:

(*a*) whether plans of the proposed work are in conformity with building regulations, or

(*b*) whether the local authority are prohibited from rejecting plans of the proposed work by virtue of subsection (9) above,

that person may refer the question to the Secretary of State for his determination; and in application for a reference under this subsection shall be accompanied by such fee as may be prescribed.

(11) Where:

(*a*) deposited plans accompanied by such a certificate and such evidence as are mentioned in subsection (9) above are passed by the local authority, or (*b*) notice of the rejection of deposited plans so accompanied is not given within the relevant period from the deposit of the plans,

the authority may not institute proceedings under section 35 below for a contravention of building regulations that:

(i) arises out of the carrying out of the proposed work in accordance with the plans, and
(ii) is a contravention of any of the provisions of the regulations specified in the certificate.

(12) For the purposes of this Part of this Act, 'the relevant period', in relation to the passing or rejection of plans, means five weeks or such extended period (expiring not later than two months from the deposit of the plans) as may before the expiration of the five weeks be agreed in writing between the person depositing the plans and the local authority.

(13) Until such day as the Secretary of State may by order appoint, subsection (10) above has effect as follows:

(10) Any question arising under this section between a local authority and the person by whom or on whose behalf plans are deposited as to whether the plans are defective, or whether the proposed work would contravene any of the regulations, may on the application of that person be determined by a magistrates' court, but no such application shall be entertained unless it is made before the proposed work has been substantially commenced.'

Approval of persons to give certificates etc.

17. – (1) Building regulations may make provision for the approval of persons for the purposes of section 16(9) above:

(*a*) by the Secretary of State, or
(*b*) by a body (corporate or unincorporated) that, in accordance with the regulations, is designated by the Secretary of State for the purpose,

and any such approval may limit the description of work, or the provisions of the regulations, in relation to which the person concerned is so approved.

(2) Any such designation as is referred to in paragraph (*b*) of subsection (1) above may limit the cases in which and the terms on which the body designated may approve a person and, in particular, may provide that any approval given by the body shall be limited as mentioned in that subsection.

(3) There shall be paid on an application for any such approval as is referred to in subsection (1) above:

(*a*) where the application is made to the Secretary of State, such fee as may be prescribed, (*b*) where the application is made to a body designated by him as mentioned in that subsection, such fee as that body may determine.

(4) The Secretary of State may approve for the purposes of section 16(9) above any scheme that appears to him to secure the provision of adequate insurance cover in relation to any certificate that is given under paragraph (*a*) of that subsection and is a certificate to which the scheme applies.

(5) Building regulations may prescribe for the purposes of section 16(9) above the insurance cover that is to be provided in relation to any certificate that is given under paragraph (*a*) of that subsection and is not a certificate to which an approved scheme applies and may, in particular, prescribe the form and content of policies of insurance.

(6) Building regulations may:

(*a*) contain provision prescribing the period for which, subject to any provision made by virtue of paragraph (*b*) or (*c*) below, any such approval as is referred to in subsection (1) above continues in force,

(*b*) contain provision precluding the giving of, or requiring the withdrawal of, any such approval as is referred to in subsection (1) above in such circumstances as may be prescribed,

(*c*) contain provision authorising the withdrawal of any such approval or designation as is referred to in subsection (1) above,

(*d*) provide for the maintenance by the Secretary of State of a list of bodies that are for the time being designated by him as mentioned in subsection (1) above and for the maintenance by the Secretary of State and by each designated body of a list of persons for the time being approved by him or them as mentioned in that subsection,

(*e*) make provision for the supply to local authorities of copies of any list of approved persons maintained by virtue of paragraph (*d*) above and for such copy lists to be made available for inspection, and

(*f*) make provision for the supply, on payment of a prescribed fee, of a certified copy of any entry in a list maintained by virtue of paragraph (*d*) above or in a copy list held by a local authority by virtue of paragraph (*e*) above.

(7) Unless the contrary is proved, in any proceedings (whether civil or criminal) a document that appears to the court to be a certified copy of an entry either in a list maintained as mentioned in subsection (6)(*d*) above or in a copy of such a list supplied as mentioned in subsection (6) (*e*) above:

(*a*) is presumed to be a true copy of an entry in the current list so maintained, and

(*b*) is evidence of the matters stated in it.

18. – (1) Where:

    (*a*) plans of a building or of an extension of a building are, in accordance with building regulations, deposited with a local authority, and

    (*b*) it is proposed to erect the building or extension, as the case may be, over a sewer or drain that is shown on the relative map of sewers,

the authority shall reject the plans unless they are satisfied that in the circumstances of the particular case they may properly consent to the erection of the proposed building or extension, either unconditionally or subject to compliance with any requirements specified in their consent.

    (2) Where:

    (*a*) plans of a building or of an extension of a building are, in accordance with building regulations, deposited with the council of a district or outer London borough, or a building notice in respect of a building or of an extension of a building is served in pursuance of section 83 of the London Building Acts (Amendment) Act 1939, and

    (*b*) it is proposed to erect the building or extension, as the case may be, over a water authority's sewer that is shown on the relative map of sewers,

the council of the district or borough, shall notify the water authority of the proposal.

    (3) A water authority may give directions to the council of a district or outer London borough as to the manner in which the council are to exercise their functions under subsection (1) above.

    (4) Any question arising under subsection (1) above between a local authority and the person by whom or on whose behalf plans are deposited as to:

    (*a*) whether the site on which it is proposed to erect a building or an extension of a building is over such a sewer or drain as is mentioned in that subsection, or

    (*b*) whether, and if so upon what conditions, a consent ought to be given by the local authority,

may on the application of that person be determined by a magistrates' court.

    (5) In this section:

'drain' includes a pipe (including associated works) provided in pursuance of section 12(6), 14(5), 21(4) or 26 of the Control of Pollution Act 1974;

'map of sewers' means:

(*a*) the map of sewers and drains kept by an authority under section 32(1) of the Public Health Act 1936, or

(*b*) a map of pipes kept by an authority under section 28(1) of the Control of Pollution Act 1974.

19. – (1) Where plans of a building are, in accordance with building regulations, deposited with a local authority, and the plans show that it is proposed to construct a building of materials to which this section applies, or to place or assemble on the site a building constructed of such materials, the authority may, notwithstanding that the plans conform with the regulations:

Use of short-lived materials.

(*a*) reject the plans, or

(*b*) in passing the plans:

(i) fix a period on the expiration of which the building must be removed, and

(ii) impose with respect to the use of the building such reasonable conditions, if any, as having regard to the nature of the materials used in its construction they deem appropriate,

but no condition shall be imposed that conflicts with any condition imposed on the grant of planning permission for that building under Part III of the Town and Country Planning Act 1971.

(2) If a building in respect of which plans ought under the building regulations to have been deposited, but have not been deposited, appears to the authority to be constructed of such materials as aforesaid, the authority, without prejudice to their right to take proceedings in respect of any contravention of the regulations, may:

(*a*) fix a period on the expiration of which the building must be removed, and

(*b*) if they think fit, impose such conditions with respect to the use of the building as might have been imposed under subsection (1) above upon the passing of plans for the building,

and where they fix such a period they shall forthwith give notice thereof, and of any conditions imposed, to the owner of the building.

(3) A local authority may from time to time extend any period fixed, or vary any conditions imposed, under this section; but, unless an application in that behalf is made of them by the owner of the building in question, they shall not exercise their power of varying conditions except when granting an extension, or further extension, of the period fixed with respect to the building.

(4) A person aggrieved by the action of a local authority under this section in rejecting plans, or in fixing or refusing to extend any period, or in imposing or refusing to vary any conditions, may appeal to a magistrates' court.

(5) The owner of a building in respect of which a period has been fixed under this section shall, on the expiration of that period, or, as the case may be, of that period as extended, remove the building, and, if he fails to do so:

(*a*) the local authority shall remove it and may recover from him the expenses reasonably incurred by them in so doing, and

(*b*) without prejudice to the right of the authority to exercise that power, he is liable on summary conviction to a fine not exceeding level 1 on the standard scale and to a further fine not exceeding £5 for each day during which the building is allowed to remain after he is convicted.

(6) A person who uses a building in contravention of a condition imposed under this section, or who permits a building to be so used, is liable on summary conviction to a fine not exceeding level 1 on the standard scale and to a further fine not exceeding £5 for each day on which the offence continues after he is convicted.

(7) Building regulations may provide that this section applies to any materials specified in the regulations as being materials that are, in the absence of special care, liable to rapid deterioration, or are otherwise unsuitable for use in the construction of permanent buildings.

(8) This section applies in relation to an extension of an existing building as it applies in relation to a new building.

(9) This section ceases to have effect upon the coming into force of section 20 below (which supersedes it).

Use of materials unsuitable for permanent building.

20. – (1) Where plans of any proposed work are, in accordance with building regulations, deposited with a local authority, and the plans show that the proposed work would include or consist of work to which this section applies, the authority may, notwithstanding that the plans conform with the regulations:

(*a*) reject the plans, or

(*b*) in passing the plans:

(i) fix a period on the expiration of which the work to which this section applies or the relevant building (as the authority may in passing the plans direct) must be removed, and

(ii) if they think fit, impose with respect to the use of the relevant building or with respect to the work to which this section applies such reasonable conditions, if any, as they consider appropriate,

but no condition as to the use of the relevant building shall be imposed that conflicts with any condition imposed or having effect as if imposed under Part III or IV of the Town and Country Planning Act 1971.

(2) If, in the case of any work in respect of which plans ought by virtue of building regulations to have been deposited with a local

authority but have not been so deposited, the work appears to the authority to include or consist of work to which this section applies, the authority, without prejudice to their right to take proceedings in respect of any contravention of the regulations, may:

(a) fix a period on the expiration of which the work to which this section applies or the relevant building (as the authority may in fixing the period direct) must be removed, and

(b) if they think fit, impose any conditions that might have been imposed under subsection (1) above in passing plans for the first-mentioned work,

and where they fix such a period they shall forthwith give notice thereof, and of any conditions imposed, to the owner of the relevant building.

(3) If, in the case of any work appearing to the local authority to fall within subsection (9)(b) below, plans of the work were not required by building regulations to be deposited with the authority, and were not so deposited, the authority may at any time within 12 months from the date of completion of the work:

(a) fix a period on the expiration of which the work must be removed, and

(b) if they think fit, impose any conditions that, if plans of the work had been required to be, and had been, so deposited, might have been imposed under subsection (1) above in passing the plans,

and where they fix such a period they shall forthwith give notice thereof, and of any conditions imposed, to the owner of the relevant building.

(4) A local authority may from time to time extend any period fixed, or vary any conditions imposed, under this section, but, unless an application in that behalf is made to them by the owner of the relevant building, they shall not exercise their power of varying conditions so imposed except when granting an extension or further extension of the period fixed with respect to the work or building, as the case may be.

(5) A person aggrieved by the action of a local authority under this section:

(a) in rejecting plans,

(b) in fixing or refusing to extend any period, or

(c) in imposing or refusing to vary any conditions,

may appeal to the Secretary of State within the prescribed time and in the prescribed manner.

(6) Where a period has been fixed under this section with respect to any work to which this section applies or with respect to the relevant building:

(*a*) the owner of that building shall on the expiration of that period, or, as the case may be, of that period as extended, remove the work or building with respect to which the period was fixed, and

(*b*) if he fails to do so, the local authority may remove that work or building, as the case may be, and may recover from him the expenses reasonably incurred by them in doing so.

(7) A person who:

(*a*) contravenes a condition imposed under this section or permits such a condition to be contravened, or

(*b*) contravenes subsection (6) above,

is liable on summary conviction to a fine not exceeding level 5 on the standard scale and to a further fine not exceeding £50 for each day on which the offence continues or, as the case may be, on which the work or building is allowed to remain after he is convicted; but this subsection does not prejudice a local authority's rights under subsection (6) above.

(8) In this section, 'the relevant building' means, in any particular case, the building mentioned in paragraph (*a*) or, as the case may be, paragraph (*b*) of subsection (9) below.

(9) This section applies to:

(*a*) any work consisting of a part of a building, being a part in the construction of which there is used any material or component of a type that, in relation to a part of that description, is prescribed for the purposes of this paragraph under subsection (10) below, and

(*b*) any work provided in or in connection with a building, being work consisting of a service, fitting or item of equipment of a type so prescribed for the purposes of this paragraph.

(10) The Secretary of State may by building regulations:

(*a*) prescribe a type of material or component for the purposes of subsection (9)(*a*) above if in his opinion materials or components of that type are likely to be unsuitable for use in the construction of a particular part of a permanent building in the absence of conditions with respect to the use of the building or with respect to any material or component of that type used in the construction of a part of that description,

(*b*) prescribe a type of service, fitting or equipment for the purposes of subsection (9)(*b*) above if in his opinion services, fittings or equipment of that type are likely to be unsuitable for provision in or in connection with a permanent building in the absence of conditions with respect to the use of the building or with respect to a service, fitting or equipment of that type so provided.

(11) Upon section 19 above ceasing to have effect:

(*a*) any building regulations made, period fixed, condition imposed or other thing done by virtue of the said section 19 shall be deemed to have been made, fixed, imposed or done by virtue of this section, and

(*b*) anything begun under the said section 19 may be continued under this Act as if begun under this section, but any appeal under section 19(4) that is pending at the time when the said section 19 ceases to have effect, and any proceedings arising out of such an appeal, shall proceed as if that section were still in force.

21. – (1) Where plans of a building or of an extension of a building are, in accordance with building regulations, deposited with a local authority, the authority shall reject the plans unless:

Provision of drainage.

(*a*) the plans show that satisfactory provision will be made for the drainage of the building or of the extension, as the case may be, or

(*b*) the authority are satisfied that in the case of the particular building or extension they may properly dispense with any provision for drainage,

(2) In subsection (1) above, 'drainage' includes the conveyance, by means of a sink and other necessary appliance, of refuse water and the conveyance of rain-water from roofs.

(3) Any question arising under subsection (1) above between a local authority and the person by whom, or on whose behalf, plans are deposited as to:

(*a*) whether provision for drainage may properly be dispensed with, or

(*b*) whether any provision for drainage proposed to be made ought to be accepted by the authority as satisfactory,

may on the application of that person be determined by a magistrates' court.

(4) A proposed drain shall not be deemed a satisfactory drain for the purposes of this section unless it is proposed to be made, as the local authority, or on appeal a magistrates' court, may require, either to connect with a sewer, or to discharge into a cesspool or some other place; but a drain shall not be required to be made to connect with a sewer unless:

(*a*) that sewer is within one hundred feet of the site of the building or, in the case of an extension, the site either of the extension or of the original building, and is at a level that makes it reasonably practicable to construct a drain to communicate with it, and, if it is not a public sewer, is a sewer that the person constructing the drain is entitled to use, and

(*b*) the intervening land is land through which that person is entitled to construct a drain.

(5) Notwithstanding paragraph (*a*) of subsection (4) above, a drain may be required to be made to connect with a sewer that is not within the distance mentioned in that paragraph, but is otherwise such a sewer as is therein mentioned, if the authority undertake to bear so much of the expenses reasonably incurred in constructing, and in maintaining and repairing, the drain as may be attributable to the fact that the distance of the sewer exceeds the distance so mentioned.

(6) If any question arises as to the amount of a payment to be made to a person under subsection (5) above, that question may on his application be determined by a magistrates' court, or he may require it to be referred to arbitration.

Drainage of buildings in combination.   **22.** – (1) Where:

(*a*) a local authority might under section 21 above require each of two or more buildings to be drained separately into an existing sewer, but

(*b*) it appears to the authority that those buildings may be drained more economically or advantageously in combination,

the authority may, when the drains of the buildings are first laid, require that the buildings be drained in combination into the existing sewer by means of a private sewer to be constructed either by the owners of the buildings in such manner as the authority may direct or, if the authority so elect, by the authority on behalf of the owners.

(2) A local authority shall not, except by agreement with the owners concerned, exercise the power conferred by subsection (1) above in respect of any building for whose drainage plans have been previously passed by them.

(3) A local authority who make such a requirement as aforesaid shall fix:

(*a*) the proportions in which the expenses of constructing, and of maintaining and repairing, the private sewer are to be borne by the owners concerned, or

(*b*) in a case in which the distance of the existing sewer from the site of any of the buildings in question is or exceeds one hundred feet, the proportions in which those expenses are to be borne by the owners concerned and the local authority,

and shall forthwith give notice of their decision to each owner affected.

(4) An owner aggrieved by the decision of a local authority under subsection (3) above may appeal to a magistrates' court.

(5) Subject to any such appeal:

(*a*) any expenses reasonably incurred in constructing, or in maintaining or repairing, the private sewer shall be borne in the proportions so fixed, and

(*b*) those expenses, or, as the case may be, contributions to them, may be recovered accordingly by the persons, whether the local authority or the owners, by whom they were incurred in the first instance.

(6) A sewer constructed by a local authority under this section is not deemed a public sewer by reason of the fact that the expenses of its construction are in the first instance defrayed by the authority, or that some part of those expenses is borne by them.

23. (3) It is unlawful for any person except with the consent of the local authority to close or obstruct the means of access by which refuse or faecal matter is removed from a building, and the local authority in giving their consent may impose such conditions as they think fit with respect to the improvement of an alternative means of access or the substitution of other means of access.

Provision of facilities for refuse.

(4) A person who contravenes subsection (3) above is liable on summary conviction to a fine not exceeding level 4 on the standard scale.

Note: Subsections (1) and (2) are repealed.

24. – (1) Where:

Provision of exits etc.

(*a*) plans of a building or an extension of a building are, in accordance with building regulations, deposited with a local authority, and

(*b*) the building or, as the case may be, the building as extended will be a building to which this section applies,

the authority shall reject the plans unless they show that the building, or, as the case may be, the building as extended, will be provided with such means of ingress and egress and passages or gangways as the authority, after consultation with the fire authority, deem satisfactory, regard being had to the purposes for which the building is intended to be, or is, used and the number of persons likely to resort to it at any one time.

(2) Any question arising under subsection (1) above between a local authority and the person by whom, or on whose behalf, plans are deposited as to whether the means of ingress or egress or passages or gangways already existing, or proposed to be provided, ought to be accepted by the authority as satisfactory may on the application of that person be determined by a magistrates' court.

(3) Where building regulations imposing requirements as to the

provision of means of escape in case of fire are applicable to a proposed building or proposed extension of a building, or would be so applicable but for a direction under section 8 above dispensing with such requirements:

(*a*) this section, and
(*b*) any provision of a local Act that has effect in place of this section,

does not apply in relation to the proposed building or extension.

(4) Subject to subsection (3) above, this section applies to:

(*a*) a theatre, and a hall or other building that is used as a place of public resort,
(*b*) a restaurant, shop, store or warehouse to which members of the public are admitted and in which more than twenty persons are employed,
(*c*) a club required to be registered under the Licensing Act 1964,
(*d*) a school not exempted from the operation of building regulations, and
(*e*) a church, chapel or other place of public worship,

but not:

(i) a private house to which members of the public are admitted occasionally or exceptionally,

(ii) a building that was used as a church, chapel or other place of public worship immediately before the date on which section 36 of the Public Health Acts Amendment Act 1890, or a corresponding provision in a local Act, came into operation in the district or rating district, or

(iii) a building that was so used immediately before the 1st October 1937 (the date of commencement of the Public Health Act 1936) in a district or rating district where neither the said section 36 nor such a corresponding provision ever came into operation.

Provision of water supply.   **25.** – (1) Where plans of a house are, in accordance with building regulations, deposited with a local authority, the authority shall reject the plans unless a proposal is put before them that appears to them to be satisfactory for providing the occupants of the house with a supply of wholesome water sufficient for their domestic purposes:

(*a*) by connecting the house to a supply of water in pipes provided by statutory water undertakers,
(*b*) if in all the circumstances it is not reasonable to require the house to be connected as aforesaid, by otherwise taking water into the house by means of a pipe, or
(*c*) if in all the circumstances neither of the preceding alternatives can reasonably be required, by providing a supply of water within a reasonable distance of the house,

and the authority are satisfied that the proposal can and will be carried into effect.

(2) Any question arising under subsection (1) above between a liocal authority and the person by whom, or on whose behalf, plans are deposited as to whether the local authority ought to pass the plans may on the application of that person be determined by a magistrates' court.

(3) If, after any such plans as aforesaid have been passed, it appears to the local authority that the proposal for providing a supply of water:

(*a*) has not been carried into effect, or
(*b*) has not resulted in a supply of wholesome water sufficient for the domestic purposes of the occupants,

the authority shall give notice to the owner of the house prohibiting him from occupying it, or permitting it to be occupied, until the authority, being satisfied that such a supply has been provided, have granted him a certificate to that effect.

(4) Until a certificate is granted under subsection (3) above, the owner shall not occupy the house or permit it to be occupied.

(5) A person aggrieved by the refusal of the authority to grant such a certificate may apply to a magistrates' court for an order authorising the occupation of the house, and, if the court is of opinion that a certificate ought to have been granted, the court may make an order authorising the occupation of the house, and such an order shall have the like effect as a certificate of the local authority.

(6) A person who contravenes subsection (4) above is liable on summary conviction to a fine not exceeding level 1 on the standard scale and to a further fine not exceeding £2 for each day on which the offence continues after he is convicted.

Note: Sections 26 to 29 are repealed.

Determination of questions

30. – (1) If any question arises between a local authority and a person who has executed, or proposes to execute, any work:

Determination of questions.

(*a*) as to the application to that work of any building regulations,
(*b*) whether the plans of the work are in conformity with building regulations, or
(*c*) whether the work has been executed in accordance with the plans as passed by the authority,

the question may, on an application made jointly by him and the local authority, be referred to the Secretary of State for determination, and his decision is final.

(2) The Secretary of State may at any stage of the proceedings on the reference, and shall if so directed by the High Court, state in the form of a special case for the opinion of the High Court any question of law arising in those proceedings.

(3) The Secretary of State may by order repeal the words ', and his decision is final' in subsection (1) above.

(4) The Secretary of State may by order repeal this section, but such a repeal does not affect applications referred to him before the date on which the repeal takes effect.

Proposed departure from plans

Proposed departure from plans.

31. – (1) Where plans of any proposed work have been passed under section 16 above by a local authority, the person by or on whose behalf the plans were in accordance with building regulations deposited with the authority may, and in such cases as may be prescribed shall, for the purpose of obtaining the approval of the authority to any proposed departure or deviation from the plans as passed, deposit plans of the departure or deviation.

(2) Section 16 above applies in relation to plans deposited under subsection (1) above as it applies in relation to the plans originally deposited.

Lapse of deposit of plans

Lapse of deposit of plans.

32. – (1) Where plans of any proposed work have, in accordance with building regulations, been deposited with a local authority, and:

(*a*) the plans have been passed by the authority, or
(*b*) notice of rejection of the plans has not been given within the relevant period from their deposit,

and the work to which the plans relate has not been commenced within three years from the deposit of the plans, the local authority may, at any time before the work is commenced, by notice to the person by whom or on whose behalf the plans were deposited, or other the owner for the time being of the land to which the plans relate, declare that the deposit of the plans is of no effect.

(2) Where a notice has been given under subsection (1) above, this Act and the building regulations shall, as respects the proposed work, have effect as if no plans had been deposited.

Tests for conformity with building regulations

33. – (1) The following subsection has effect for the purpose of enabling a local authority to ascertain, as regards any work or proposed work to which building regulations for the enforcement of which they are responsible are applicable, whether any provision of building regulations is or would be contravened by, or by anything done or proposed to be done in connection with, that work.

(2) The local authority have power for that purpose:

(*a*) to require a person by whom or on whose behalf the work was, is being or is proposed to be done to carry out such reasonable tests of or in connection with the work as may be specified in the requirement, or

(*b*) themselves to carry out any reasonable tests of or in connection with the work, and to take any samples necessary to enable them to carry out such a test.

(3) Without prejudice to the generality of subsection (2) above, the matters with respect to which tests may be required or carried out under that subsection include:

(*a*) tests of the soil or subsoil of the site of a building,

(*b*) tests of any material, component or combination of components that has been, is being or is proposed to be used in the construction of a building, and tests of any service, fitting or equipment that has been, is being or is proposed to be provided in or in connection with a building.

(4) A local authority have power, for the purpose of ascertaining whether there is or has been, in the case of a building, a contravention of a continuing requirement that applies in relation to that building:

(*a*) to require the owner or occupier of the building to carry out such reasonable tests as may be specified in the requirement under this paragraph, or

(*b*) themselves to carry out any tests that they have power to require under paragraph (*a*) above, and to take any samples necessary to enable them to carry out such a test;

and in this subsection 'continuing requirement' means a continuing requirement imposed by building regulations made by virtue of section 2(1) or (2) above.

(5) The expense of carrying out any tests that a person is required to carry out under this section shall be met by that person, except that the local authority, on an application made to them, may, if they think it reasonable to do so, direct that the expense of carrying out any such tests, or such part of that expense as may be specified in the direction, shall be met by the local authority.

(6) Any question arising under this section between a local authority and a person as to the reasonableness of:

    (*a*) a test specified in a requirement imposed on him by the authority under this section,

    (*b*) a refusal by the authority to give a direction under subsection (5) above on an application made by him, or

    (*c*) a direction under that subsection given on such an application,

may on the application of that person be determined by a magistrates' court; and in a case falling within paragraph (*b*) or (*c*) above the court may order the expense to which the application relates to be met by the local authority to such extent as the court thinks just.

Classification of buildings

Classification of buildings.

34. For the purposes of building regulations and of a direction given or instrument made with reference to building regulations, buildings may be classified by reference to size, description, design, purpose, location or any other characteristic whatsoever.

Breach of building regulations

Penalty for contravening building regulations.

35. If a person contravenes any provision contained in building regulations, other than a provision designated in the regulations as one to which this section does not apply, he is liable on summary conviction to a fine not exceeding level 5 on the standard scale and to a further fine not exceeding £50 for each day on which the default continues after he is convicted.

Removal or alteration of offending work.

36. – (1) If any work to which building regulations are applicable contravenes any of those regulations, the local authority, without prejudice to their right to take proceedings for a fine in respect of the contravention, may by notice require the owner:

    (*a*) to pull down or remove the work, oʀ

    (*b*) if he so elects, to effect such alterations in it as may be necessary to make it comply with the regulations.

(2) If, in a case where the local authority are, by any section of this Part of this Act other than section 16, expressly required or authorised to reject plans, any work to which building regulations are applicable is executed:

    (*a*) without plans having been deposited,

    (*b*) notwithstanding the rejection of the plans, or

    (*c*) otherwise than in accordance with any requirements subject to which the authority passed the plans, the authority may by notice to the owner:

> (i) require him to pull down or remove the work, or
>
> (ii) require him either to pull down or remove the work or, if he so elects, to comply with any other requirements specified in the notice, being requirements that they might have made under the section in question as a condition of passing plans.

(3) If a person to whom a notice has been given under subsection (1) or (2) above fails to comply with the notice before the expiration of 28 days, or such longer period as a magistrates' court may on his application allow, the local authority may:

(*a*) pull down or remove the work in question, or

(*b*) effect shall alterations in it as they deem necessary,

and may recover from him the expenses reasonably incurred by them in doing so.

(4) A notice under subsection (1) or (2) above (called a 'section 36 notice') shall not be given after the expiration of 12 months from the date of the completion of the work in question.

(5) A section 36 notice shall not be given, in a case where plans were deposited and the work was shown on them, on the ground that the work contravenes any building regulations or, as the case may be, does not comply with the authority's requirements under any section of this Part of this Act other than section 16, if:

(*a*) the plans were passed by the authority, or

(*b*) notice of their rejection was not given within the relevant period from their deposit,

and if the work has been executed in accordance with the plans and of any requirement made by the local authority as a condition of passing the plans.

(6) This section does not affect the right of a local authority, the Attorney General or any other person to apply for an injunction for the removal or alteration of any work on the ground that it contravenes any regulation or any provision of this Act; but if:

(*a*) the work is one in respect of which plans were deposited,

(*b*) the plans were passed by the local authority, or notice of their rejection was not given within the relevant period from their deposit, and

(*c*) the work has been executed in accordance with the plans,

the court on granting an injunction has power to order the local authority to pay to the owner of the work such compensation as the court thinks just, but before making any such order the court shall in accordance with rules of court cause the local authority, if not a party to the proceedings, to be joined as a party to them.

Obtaining of report where section 36 notice given.

37. – (1) In a case where:

(*a*) a person to whom a section 36 notice has been given gives to the local authority by whom the notice was given notice of his intention to obtain from a suitably qualified person a written report concerning work to which the section 36 notice relates, and

(*b*) such a report is obtained and submitted to the local authority and, as a result of their consideration of it, the local authority withdraw the section 36 notice,

the local authority may pay to the person to whom the section 36 notice was given such amount as appears to them to represent the expenses reasonably incurred by him in consequence of their having given him that notice including, in particular, his expenses in obtaining the report.

(2) Subject to subsection (3) below, if a person to whom a section 36 notice has been given gives notice under subsection (1)(*a*) above, then, so far as regards the matters to which the section 36 notice relates, the reference to 28 days in section 36(3) above shall be construed as a reference to 70 days.

(3) Notice under subsection (1)(*a*) above shall be given before the expiry of the period of 28 days referred to in section 36(3) above, or, as the case may be, within such longer period as a court allows under section 36(3); and, where such a longer period has been so allowed before notice is given under subsection (1)(*a*) above, subsection (2) above does not apply.

Civil liability.

38. – (1) Subject to this section:

(*a*) breach of a duty imposed by building regulations, so far as it causes damage, is actionable, except in so far as the regulations provide otherwise, and

(*b*) as regards such a duty, building regulations may provide for a prescribed defence to be available in an action for breach of that duty brought by virtue of this subsection.

(2) Subsection (1) above, and any defence provided for in regulations made by virtue of it, do not apply in the case of a breach of such a duty in connection with a building erected before the date on which that subsection comes into force unless the regulations imposing the duty apply to or in connection with the building by virtue of section 2(2) above or paragraph 8 of Schedule 1 to this Act.

(3) This section does not affect the extent (if any) to which breach of:

(*a*) a duty imposed by or arising in connection with this Part of this Act or any other enactment relating to building regulations, or

(*b*) a duty imposed by building regulations in a case to which subsection (1) above does not apply,

is actionable, or prejudice a right of action that exists apart from the enactments relating to building regulations.

(4) In this section, 'damage' includes the death of, or injury to, any person (including any disease and any impairment of a person's physical or mental condition).

Appeals in certain cases

39. – (1) If a local authority refuse an application to dispense with or relax a requirement in building regulations that they have power to dispense with or relax, the applicant may by notice in writing appeal to the Secretary of State within one month from the date on which the local authority notify the applicant of their refusal.

(2) If, within:

(*a*) a period of two months beginning with the date of an application, or

(*b*) such extended period as may at any time be agreed in writing between the applicant and the local authority,

the local authority do not notify the applicant of their decision on the application, subsection (1) above applies in relation to the application as if the local authority had refused the application and notified the applicant of their decision at the end of the said period.

(3) The notice of appeal shall set out the grounds of appeal, and a copy of the notice of appeal shall be sent to the local authority.

(4) The local authority, on receiving a copy of the notice of appeal, shall at once transmit to the Secretary of State a copy of the application and a copy of all the documents furnished by the applicant for the purposes of his application.

(5) The local authority shall at the same time give to the Secretary of State in writing any representations that they desire to make as regards the appeal, and shall send a copy to the appellant.

(6) If the Secretary of State allows the appeal, he shall give such directions for dispensing with or relaxing building regulations as may be appropriate.

40. – (1) A person aggrieved by the giving of a section 36 notice may appeal to a magistrates' court acting for the petty sessions area in which is situated land on which there has been carried out any work to which the notice relates.

(2) Subject to subsection (3) below, on an appeal under this section the court shall:

(*a*) if it determines that the local authority were entitled to give the notice, confirm the notice, and
(*b*) in any other case, give the local authority a direction to withdraw the notice.

(3) If, in a case where the appeal is against a notice under section 36(2) above, the court is satisfied that:

(*a*) the local authority were entitled to give the notice, but
(*b*) in all the circumstances of the case the purpose for which was enacted the section of this Act by virtue of which the notice was given has been substantially achieved,

the court may give a direction under subsection (2)(*b*) above.

(4) An appeal under this section shall be brought:

(*a*) within 28 days of the giving of the section 36 notice, or
(*b*) in a case where the person to whom the section 36 notice was given gives notice under section 37(1)(*a*) above, within 70 days of the giving of the section 36 notice.

(5) Where an appeal is brought under this section:

(*a*) the section 36 notice is of no effect pending the final determination or withdrawal of the appeal, and
(*b*) section 36(3) above has effect in relation to that notice as if after the words '28 days' there were inserted the words '(beginning, in a case where an appeal is brought under section 40 below, on the date when the appeal is finally determined or, as the case may be, withdrawn)'.

(6) If, on an appeal under this section, there is produced to the court a report that has been submitted to the local authority under section 37(1) above, the court, in making an order as to costs, may treat the expenses incurred in obtaining the report as expenses incurred for the purposes of the appeal.

Appeal to Crown Court. **41.** – (1) Where a person:

(*a*) is aggrieved by an order, determination or other decision of a magistrates' court under this Part of this Act, or under Part IV of this Act as it applies in relation to this Part, and
(*b*) is not by any other enactment authorised to appeal to the Crown Court

he may appeal to the Crown Court.

(2) Subsection (1) above does not confer a right of appeal in a case in which each of the parties concerned might under this Act have required that the dispute should be determined by arbitration instead of by a magistrates' court.

42. – (1) Where the Secretary of State gives a decision in proceedings:

(*a*) on an appeal under section 20 or 39 above,

(*b*) on a reference under section 16 above or 50 below, or

(*c*) on an application for a direction under section 8 above where the power of giving the direction is not exercisable by the local authority,

the relevant person or the local authority or, as the case may be, the approved inspector may appeal to the High Court against the decision on a point of law.

(2) In subsection (1) above, 'the relevant person' means:

(*a*) as regards an appeal under the said section 20 or 39, the appellant,

(*b*) as regards a reference under the said section 16 or 50, the person on whose application the reference was made,

(*c*) as regards such an application as is mentioned in subsection (1)(*c*) above, the applicant.

(3) At any stage of the proceedings on such an appeal, reference or application as is mentioned in subsection (1) above:

(*a*) the Secretary of State may state a question of law arising in the course of the proceedings in the form of a special case for the decision of the High Court, and

(*b*) a decision of the High Court on a case so stated is deemed to be a judgement of the court within the meaning of section 16 of the Supreme Court Act 1981 (appeals from the High Court to the Court of Appeal).

(4) In relation to proceedings in the High Court or the Court of Appeal brought by virtue of this section, the power to make rules of court includes power to make rules:

(*a*) prescribing the powers of the High Court or the Court of Appeal with respect to the remitting of the matter with the opinion or direction of the court for re-hearing and determination by the Secretary of State, and

(*b*) providing for the Secretary of State, either generally or in such circumstances as may be prescribed by the rules, to be treated as a party to any such proceedings and to be entitled to appear and to be heard accordingly.

[margin note: Appeal and statement of case to High Court in certain cases.]

(5) No appeal to the Court of Appeal shall be brought by virtue of this section except with the leave of the High Court or the Court of Appeal.

(6) In this section, 'decision' includes a direction, and references to the giving of a decision shall be construed accordingly.

(7) Until such day as the Secretary of State may by order appoint, subsections (1) and (2) above have effect as if:

(*a*) in subsection (1)(*b*), for 'section 16 above or 50 below' there were substituted 'section 30 above',

(*b*) in subsection (1), the words 'or, as the case may be, the approved inspector' were omitted, and

(*c*) in subsection (2)(*b*), for 'section 16 or 50' there were substituted 'section 30' and the words '(jointly with the local authority)' were inserted after 'application'.

Procedure on appeal to Secretary of State on certain matters. **43.** – (1) On an appeal to the Secretary of State under section 20 or 39 above, the Secretary of State may at his discretion afford to the appellant and the local authority an opportunity of appearing before, and being heard by, a person appointed by the Secretary of State for the purpose.

(2) On determining such an appeal, the Secretary of State shall give such directions, if any, as he considers appropriate for giving effect to his determination.

(3) Without prejudice to paragraph 10(*c*) of Schedule 1 to this Act, building regulations may, in connection with such an appeal, include such supplementary provisions with respect to procedure as the Secretary of State thinks fit.

Application of building regulations to Crown etc.

Application to Crown. **44.** – (1) Except in so far as building regulations provide otherwise, the substantive requirements of building regulations:

(*a*) apply in relation to work carried out or proposed to be carried out by or on behalf of a Crown authority (whether or not in relation to a Crown building) as they would apply if the person by or on behalf of whom the work was or is to be carried out were not a Crown authority, and

(*b*) so far as they consist of continuing requirements, apply to Crown authorities (whether or not in relation to Crown buildings) as they apply to persons who are not Crown authorities.

(2) In so far as building regulations so provide as regards any of the

substantive requirements of building regulations, those requirements:

(*a*) apply in relation to work carried out or proposed to be carried out as mentioned in subsection (1)(*a*) above in inner London, and

(*b*) so far as they consist of continuing requirements, apply to Crown authorities there as mentioned in subsection (1)(*b*) above,

even if those requirements do not apply there in the case of work carried out or proposed to be carried out otherwise than by or on behalf of a Crown authority or, in the case of continuing requirements, do not apply there to persons other than Crown authorities.

(3) Except in so far as building regulations provide otherwise, building regulations and the enactments relating to building regulations:

(*a*) apply in relation to work carried out or proposed to be carried out in relation to a Crown building otherwise than by or on behalf of a Crown authority, and, in the case of section 2 above and building regulations made by virtue of it, apply in relation to a Crown building to persons other than Crown authorities, as they would apply if the building were not a Crown building, and

(*b*) apply in relation to work carried out or proposed to be carried out by or on behalf of a government department acting for a person other than a Crown authority as they would apply if the work had been or were to be carried out by that person.

(4) Section 38 above and any building regulations made by virtue of subsection (1) of that section apply in relation to duties imposed by building regulations in their application in accordance with subsections (1) to (3) above.

(5) Where:

(*a*) work is carried out or proposed to be carried out by or on behalf of a Crown authority, or

(*b*) a Crown authority is or (apart from any dispensation or relaxation) will be subject to continuing requirements,

that authority may exercise the like powers of dispensing with or relaxing the substantive requirements of building regulations or, as the case may be, the continuing requirements in question as are conferred on the Secretary of State and local authorities by virtue of section 8 above (other than a power that by virtue of paragraph 6 of Schedule 1 to this Act is exercisable otherwise than by a local authority), subject to:

(i) the like requirements as to consultation (if any) as apply by virtue of paragraph 3 of Schedule 1 to this Act, in the case of a local authority (but not the requirements of the said section 8 as to consultation with the local authority), and

(ii) the like requirements as in the case of the Secretary of State apply by virtue of section 10 above,

and no application is necessary for the exercise of any such powers by virtue of this subsection.

(6) In relation to continuing requirements, references in subsection (5) above to section 8 above are references to it as modified by section 2(6) above.

(7) For the purposes of subsection (5) above, work carried out or proposed to be carried out by or on behalf of a government department acting for another Crown authority shall be treated as carried out or proposed to be carried out by or on behalf of that department (and not by or on behalf of the other Crown authority).

(8) In this section:

'continuing requirement' means a continuing requirement of building regulations imposed by virtue of section 2(1) or (2)(*a*) or (*b*) above;

'Crown authority' means the Crown Estate Commissioners, a Minister of the Crown, a government department, any other person or body whose functions are performed on behalf of the Crown (not being a person or body whose functions are performed on behalf of Her Majesty in her private capacity), or a person acting in right of the Duchy of Lancaster or the Duchy of Cornwall;

'Crown building' means a building in which there is a Crown interest or a Duchy interest;

'Crown interest' means an interest belonging to her Majesty in right of the Crown, or belonging to a government department, or held in trust for Her Majesty for the purposes of a government department;

'Duchy interest' means an interest belonging to Her Majesty in right of the Duchy of Lancaster, or belonging to the Duchy of Cornwall.

(9) If any question arises under this section as to which Crown authority is entitled to exercise any such powers as are mentioned in subsection (5) above, that question shall be referred to the Treasury, whose decision is final.

(10) This section, with any necessary modifications, applies in relation to the making of a material change in the use of a building within the meaning of building regulations made for the purposes of paragraph 8(1)(*e*) of Schedule 1 to this Act as it applies in relation to the carrying out of work.

Application to United Kingdom Atomic Energy Authority.

45. – (1) The provisions of section 44(1) and (4) to (10) above apply in relation to the United Kingdom Atomic Energy Authority (in this section referred to as 'the Authority') as if:

(*a*) the Authority were a Crown authority,

(*b*) a building belonging to or occupied by the Authority were a Crown building, and

(*c*) the references in subsection (1) to not being a Crown authority were references to being neither a Crown authority nor the Authority,

but the said provisions do not by virtue of this subsection apply in relation to dwelling-houses or offices belonging to or occupied by the Authority.

(2) Subject to the said provisions as applied by subsection (1) above, building regulations and the enactments relating to building regulations do not apply in relation to buildings belonging to or occupied by the Authority, except dwellinghouses and offices.

Part II

SUPERVISION OF BUILDING WORK ETC. OTHERWISE THAN BY LOCAL AUTHORITIES

Supervision of plans and work by approved inspectors

47. – (1) If:

(*a*) a notice in the prescribed form (called an 'initial notice') is given jointly to a local authority by a person intending to carry out work and a person who is an approved inspector in relation to that work,

(*b*) the initial notice is accompanied by such plans of the work as may be prescribed,

(*c*) the initial notice is accompanied by such evidence as may be prescribed that an approval scheme applies, or the prescribed insurance cover has been or will be provided, in relation to the work, and

(*d*) the initial notice is accepted by the local authority,

then, so long as the initial notice continues in force, the approved inspector by whom the notice was given shall undertake such functions as may be prescribed with respect to the inspection of plans of the work specified in the notice, the supervision of that work and the giving of certificates and other notices.

(2) A local authority to whom an initial notice is given:

(*a*) may not reject the notice except on prescribed grounds, and

(*b*) shall reject the notice if any of the prescribed grounds exists,

Giving and acceptance of initial notice.

and, in a case where the work to which an initial notice relates is work of such a description that, if plans of it had been deposited with the local authority, the authority could, under any enactment, have imposed requirements as a condition of passing the plans, the local authority may impose the like requirements as a condition of accepting the initial notice.

(3) Unless, within the prescribed period, the local authority to whom an initial notice is given give notice of rejection, specifying the ground or grounds in question, to each of the persons by whom the initial notice was given, the authority is conclusively presumed to have accepted the initial notice and to have done so without imposing any such requirements as are referred to in subsection (2) above.

(4) An initial notice:

(a) comes into force when it is accepted by the local authority, either by notice given within the prescribed period to each of the persons by whom it was given or by virtue of subsection (3) above, and

(b) subject to section 51(3) below, continues in force until:

(i) it is cancelled by a notice under section 52 below, or
(ii) the occurrence of, or the expiry of a prescribed period of time beginning on the date of, such event as may be prescribed;

and building regulations may empower a local authority to extend (whether before or after its expiry) any such period of time as is referred to in paragraph (ii) above.

(5) The form prescribed for an initial notice may be such as to require:

(a) either or both of the persons by whom the notice is to be given to furnish information relevant for the purposes of this Act, Part II or IV of the Public Health Act 1936 or any provision of building regulations, and

(b) the approved inspector by whom the notice is to be given to enter into undertakings with respect to his performance of any of the functions referred to in subsection (1) above.

(6) The Secretary of State may approve for the purposes of this section any scheme that appears to him to secure the provision of adequate insurance cover in relation to any work that is specified in an initial notice and is work to which the scheme applies.

(7) Building regulations may prescribe for the purposes of this section the insurance cover that is to be provided in relation to any work that is specified in an initial notice and is not work to which an approved scheme applies and may, in particular, prescribe the form and content of policies of insurance.

48. – (1) So long as an initial notice continues in force, the function of enforcing building regulations that is conferred on a local authority by section 91(2) below is not exercisable in relation to the work specified in the notice, and accordingly:

(*a*) a local authority may not give a notice under section 36(1) above in relation to the work so specified, and

(*b*) a local authority may not institute proceedings under section 35 above for a contravention of building regulations that arises out of the carrying out of the work so specified.

(2) For the purposes of the enactments specified in subsection (3) below:

(*a*) the giving of an initial notice accompanied by such plans as are referred to in section 47(1)(*b*) above shall be treated as the deposit of plans,

(*b*) the plans accompanying an initial notice shall be treated as the deposited plans,

(*c*) the acceptance or rejection of an initial notice shall be treated as the passing or, as the case may be, the rejection of plans, and

(*d*) the cancellation of an initial notice under section 52(5) below shall be treated as a declaration under section 32 above that the deposit of plans is of no effect.

(3) The enactments referred to in subsection (2) above are:

(*a*) section 36(2) above,

(*b*) section 36(5) above, in so far as it relates to a notice under section 36(2) above and to non-compliance with any such requirement as is referred to in that subsection,

(*c*) section 36(6) above, in so far as it relates to a contravention of this Act,

(*d*) section 18(2) above, and

(*e*) sections 219 to 225 of the Highways Act 1980 (the advance payments code).

(4) For the purposes of section 13 of the Fire Precautions Act 1971 (exercise of fire authority's powers where provisions of building regulations as to means of escape apply):

(*a*) the acceptance by a local authority of an initial notice relating to any work shall be treated as the deposit of plans of the work with the authority in accordance with building regulations, and

(*b*) the references in subsections (1)(ii) and (3)(*b*) of that section to matters or circumstances of which particulars are not or were not required by or under the building regulations to be supplied to the local authority in connection with the deposit of plans shall be construed as a reference to matters or circumstances of which particulars would not be or, as the case may be, would not have been required to be so supplied if plans were to be or had been deposited with the authority in accordance with building regulations.

49. – (1) In this Act, 'approved inspector' means a person who, in accordance with building regulations, is approved for the purposes of this Part of this Act:

(*a*) by the Secreary of State, or

(*b*) by a body (corporate or unincorporated) that, in accordance with the regulations, is designated by the Secretary of State for the purpose.

(2) Any such approval as is referred to in subsection (1) above may limit the description of work in relation to which the person concerned is an approved inspector.

(3) Any such designation as is referred to in subsection (1)(*b*) above may limit the cases in which and the terms on which the body designated may approve a person and, in particular, may provide that any approval given by the body shall be limited as mentioned in subsection (2) above.

(4) There shall be paid on an application for any such approval as is referred to in subsection (1) above:

(*a*) where the application is made to the Secretary of State, such fee as may be prescribed,

(*b*) where the application is made to a body designated by him as mentioned in that subsection, such fee as that body may determine.

(5) Building regulations may:

(*a*) contain provision prescribing the period for which, subject to any provision made by virtue of paragraph (*b*) or (*c*) below, any such approval as is referred to in subsection (1) above continues in force,

(*b*) contain provision precluding the giving of, or requiring the withdrawal of, any such approval as is referred to in subsection (1) above in such circumstances as may be prescribed,

(*c*) contain provision authorising the withdrawal of any such approval or designation as is referred to in subsection (1) above,

(*d*) provide for the maintenance:

(i) by the Secretary of State of a list of bodies that are for the time being designated by him as mentioned in subsection (1) above, and

(ii) by the Secretary of State and by each designated body of a list of persons for the time being approved by him or them as mentioned in that subsection,

(*e*) make provision for the supply to local authorities of copies of any list of approved inspectors maintained by virtue of paragraph (*d*) above and for such copy lists to be made available for inspection, and

(*f*) make provision for the supply, on payment of a prescribed fee, of a certified copy of any entry in a list maintained by virtue of paragraph (*d*) above or in a copy list held by a local authority by virtue of paragraph (*e*) above.

(6) Unless the contrary is proved, in any proceedings (whether civil or criminal) a document that appears to the court to be a certified copy of an entry either in a list maintained as mentioned in subsection (5)(*d*) above or in a copy of such a list supplied as mentioned in subsection (5)(*e*) above:

(*a*) is presumed to be a true copy of an entry in the current list so maintained, and

(*b*) is evidence of the matters stated in it.

(7) An approved inspector may make such charges in respect of the carrying out of the functions referred to in section 47(1) above as may in any particular case be agreed between him and the person who intends to carry out the work in question or, as the case may be, by whom that work is being or has been carried out.

(8) Nothing in this Part of this Act prevents an approved inspector from arranging for plans or work to be inspected on his behalf by another person; but such a delegation:

(*a*) shall not extend to the giving of a certificate under section 50 or 51 below, and

(*b*) shall not affect any liability, whether civil or criminal, of the approved inspector which arises out of functions conferred on him by this Part of this Act or by building regulations,

and, without prejudice to the generality of paragraph (*b*) above, an approved inspector is liable for negligence on the part of a person carrying out an inspection on his behalf in like manner as if it were negligence by a servant of his acting in the course of his employment.

50. – (1) Where an approved inspector:

Plans certificates.

(*a*) has inspected plans of the work specified in an initial notice given by him,

(*b*) is satisfied that the plans neither are defective nor show that work carried out in accordance with them would contravene any provision of building regulations, and

(*c*) has complied with any prescribed requirements as to consultation or otherwise,

he shall, if requested to do so by the person intending to carry out the work, give a certificate in the prescribed form (called a 'plans certificate') to the local authority and to that person.

(2) If any question arises under subsection (1) above between an

approved inspector and a person who proposes to carry out any work whether plans of the work are in conformity with building regulations, that person may refer the question to the Secretary of State for his determination.

(3) An application for a reference under subsection (2) above shall be accompanied by such fee as may be prescribed.

(4) Building regulations may authorise the giving of an initial notice combined with a certificate under subsection (1) above, and may prescribe a single form for such a combined notice and certificate; and where such a prescribed form is used:

- (a) a reference in this Part of this Act to an initial notice or to a plans certificate includes a reference to that form, but
- (b) should the form cease to be in force as an initial notice by virtue of section 47(4) above, nothing in that subsection affects the continuing validity of the form as a plans certificate.

(5) A plans certificate:
- (a) may relate either to the whole or to part only of the work specified in the initial notice concerned, and
- (b) does not have effect unless it is accepted by the local authority to whom it is given.

(6) A local authority to whom a plans certificate is given:

- (a) may not reject the certificate except on prescribed grounds, and
- (b) shall reject the certificate if any of the prescribed grounds exists.

(7) Unless, within the prescribed period, the local authority to whom a plans certificate is given give notice of rejection, specifying the ground or grounds in question, to:

- (a) the approved inspector by whom the certificate was given, and
- (b) the other person to whom the approved inspector gave the certificate,

the authority shall be conclusively presumed to have accepted the certificate.

(8) If it appears to a local authority by whom a plans certificate has been accepted that the work to which the certificate relates has not been commenced within the period of three years beginning on the date on which the certificate was accepted, the authority may rescind their acceptance of the certificate by notice, specifying the ground or grounds in question, given:

- (a) to the approved inspector by whom the certificate was given, and
- (b) to the person shown in the initial notice concerned as the person intending to carry out the work.

51. – (1) Where an approved inspector is satisfied that any work specified in an initial notice given by him has been completed, he shall give:

(*a*) to the local authority by whom the initial notice was accepted, and

(*b*) to the person by whom the work was carried out,

such certificate with respect to the completion of the work and the discharge of his functions as may be prescribed (called a 'final certificate').

(2) Section 50(5) to (7) above has effect in relation to a final certificate as if any reference in those subsections to a plans certificate were a reference to a final certificate,

(3) Where a final certificate:

(*a*) has been given with respect to any of the work specified in an initial notice, and

(*b*) has been accepted by the local authority concerned,

the initial notice ceases to apply to that work, but section 48(1) above continues to apply, by virtue of this subsection, in relation to that work as if the initial notice continued in force in relation to it.

52. – (1) If, at a time when an initial notice is in force:

(*a*) the approved inspector becomes or expects to become unable to carry out (or to continue to carry out) his functions with respect to any of the work specified in the initial notice,

(*b*) the approved inspector is of the opinion that any of the work is being so carried out that he is unable adequately to carry out his functions with respect to it, or

(*c*) the approved inspector is of the opinion that there is a contravention of any provision of building regulations with respect to any of that work and the circumstances are as mentioned in subsection (2) below,

the approved inspector shall cancel the initial notice by notice in the prescribed form given to the local authority concerned and to the person carrying out or intending to carry out the work.

(2) The circumstances referred to in subsection (1)(*c*) above are:

(*a*) that the approved inspector has, in accordance with building regulations, given notice of the contravention to the person carrying out the work, and

(*b*) that, within the prescribed period, that person has neither pulled down nor removed the work nor effected such alterations in it as may be necessary to make it comply with building regulations.

(3) If, at a time when an initial notice is in force, it appears to the person carrying out or intending to carry out the work specified in the notice that the approved inspector is no longer willing or able to carry out his functions with respect to any of that work, he shall cancel the initial notice by notice in the prescribed form given to the local authority concerned and, if it is practicable to do so, to the approved inspector.

(4) If a person fails without reasonable excuse to give to a local authority a notice that he is required to give by subsection (3) above, he is liable on summary conviction to a fine not exceeding level 5 on the standard scale.

(5) If, at a time when an initial notice is in force, it appears to the local authority by whom the initial notice was accepted that the work to which the initial notice relates has not been commenced within the period of three years beginning on the date on which the initial notice was accepted, the authority may cancel the initial notice by notice in the prescribed form given:

(*a*) to the approved inspector by whom the initial notice was given, and
(*b*) to the person shown in the initial notice as the person intending to carry out the work.

(6) A notice under subsection (1), (3) or (5) above has the effect of cancelling the initial notice to which it relates with effect from the day on which the notice is given.

Effect of initial notice ceasing to be in force.

53. – (1) This section applies where an initial notice ceases to be in force by virtue of section 47(4)(*b*)(i) or (ii) above.

(2) Building regulations may provide that, if:
(*a*) a plans certificate was given before the day on which the initial notice ceased to be in force,
(*b*) that certificate was accepted by the local authority (before, on or after that day), and
(*c*) before that day, that acceptance was not rescinded by a notice under section 50(8) above,

then, with respect to the work specified in the certificate, such of the functions of a local authority referred to in section 48(1) above as may be prescribed for the purposes of this subsection either are not exercisable or are exercisable only in prescribed circumstances.

(3) If, before the day on which the initial notice ceased to be in force, a final certificate:
(*a*) was given in respect of part of the work specified in the initial notice, and

(b) was accepted by the local authority (before, on or after that day),

the fact that the initial notice has ceased to be in force does not affect the continuing operation of section 51(3) above in relation to that part of the work.

(4) Notwithstanding anything in subsections (2) and (3) above, for the purpose of enabling the local authority to perform the functions referred to in section 48(1) above in relation to any part of the work not specified in a plans certificate or final certificate, as the case may be, building regulations may require the local authority to be provided with plans that relate not only to that part but also to the part to which the certificate in question relates.

(5) In any case where this section applies, the reference in subsection (4) of section 36 above to the date of the completion of the work in question has effect, in relation to a notice under subsection (1) of that section, as if it were a reference to the date on which the initial notice ceased to be in force.

(6) Subject to any provision of building regulations made by virtue of subsection (2) above, if, before the initial notice ceased to be in force, an offence under section 35 above was committed with respect to any of the work specified in that notice, proceedings for that offence may be commenced by the local authority at any time within six months beginning with the day on which the function of the local authority referred to in section 48(1) above became exercisable with respect to the provision of building regulations to which the offence relates.

(7) The fact that an initial notice has ceased to be in force does not affect the right to give a new initial notice relating to any of the work that was specified in the original notice and in respect of which no final certificate has been given and accepted; but where:

(a) a plans certificate has been given in respect of any of that work,
(b) the conditions in paragraphs (a) to (c) of subsection (2) above are fulfilled with respect to that certificate, and
(c) such a new initial notice is given and accepted,

section 50(1) above does not apply in relation to so much of the work to which the new initial notice relates as is work specified in the plans certificate.

Supervision of their own work by public bodies

54. – (1) This section applies where a body (corporate or unincorporated) that acts under an enactment for public purposes and not for   Giving, acceptance its own profit and is, or is of a description that is, approved by the Secretary of State in accordance with building regulations (in this Part of this Act referred to as a 'public body'):

(*a*) intends to carry out in relation to a building belonging to it work to which the substantive requirements of building regulations apply,

(*b*) considers that the work can be adequately supervised by its own servants or agents, and

(*c*) gives to the local authority in whose district the work is to be carried out notice in the prescribed form (called a 'public body's notice') together with such plans of the work as may be prescribed.

(2) A public body's notice is of no effect unless it is accepted by the local authority to whom it is given; and that local authority:

(*a*) may not reject the notice except on prescribed grounds, and
(*b*) shall reject the notice if any of the prescribed grounds exists,

and, in a case where the work to which the public body's notice relates is work of such a description that, if plans of it had been deposited with the local authority, the authority could, under an enactment, have imposed requirements as a condition of passing the plans, the local authority may impose the like requirements as a condition of accepting the public body's notice.

(3) Unless, within the prescribed period, the local authority to whom a public body's notice is given give notice of rejection, specifying the ground or grounds in question, the authority is conclusively presumed to have accepted the public body's notice and to have done so without imposing any such requirements as are referred to in subsection (2) above.

(4) Section 48 above has effect for the purposes of this section:

(*a*) with the substitution of a reference to a public body's notice for any reference to an initial notice, and
(*b*) with the substitution, in subsection (2)(*a*), of a reference to subsection (1)(*c*) of this section for the reference to section 47(1)(*b*).

(5) The form prescribed for a public body's notice may be such as to require the public body by whom it is to be given:

(*a*) to furnish information relevant for the purposes of this Act, Part II or IV of the Public Health Act 1936 or any provision of building regulations, and
(*b*) to enter into undertakings with respect to consultation and other matters.

(6) Where a public body's notice is given and accepted by the local authority to whom it is given, the provisions of Schedule 4 to this Act have effect, being provisions that correspond, as nearly as may be, to those made by the preceding provisions of this Part of this Act for the case where an initial notice is given and accepted.

Supplementary

55. – (1) A person aggrieved by the local authority's rejection of: **Appeals.**

(*a*) an initial notice or a public body's notice, or

(*b*) a plans certificate, a final certificate, a public body's plans certificate or a public body's final certificate,

may appeal to a magistrates' court acting for the petty sessions area in which is situated land on which there will be, or there has been, carried out any work to which the notice or certificate relates.

(2) On an appeal under subsection (1) above, the court shall:

(*a*) if it determines that the notice or certificate was properly rejected, confirm the rejection, and

(*b*) in any other case, give a direction to the local authority to accept the notice or certificate.

(3) Where a person is aggrieved by a determination, confirmation, direction or other decision of a magistrates' court under this section, he may appeal to the Crown Court.

57. – (1) If a person: **Offences.**

(*a*) gives a notice or certificate that:

(i) purports to comply with the requirements of this Part of this Act or, as the case may be, of section 16(9) above, and

(ii) contains a statement that he knows to be false or misleading in a material particular, or

(*b*) recklessly gives a notice or certificate that:

(i) purports to comply with those requirements, and

(ii) contains a statement that is false or misleading in a material particular,

he is guilty of an offence.

(2) A person guilty of an offence under subsection (1) above is liable:

(*a*) on summary conviction, to a fine not exceeding the statutory maximum or imprisonment for a term not exceeding six months or both, and

(*b*) on conviction on indictment, to a fine or imprisonment for a term not exceeding two years or both.

(3) Where an approved inspector or person approved for the purposes of section 16(9) above is convicted of an offence under this section, the court by or before which he is convicted shall, within one month of the date of conviction, forward a certificate of the conviction to the person by whom the approval was given.

Means of escape from fire

72. – (1) If it appears to a local authority, after consultation with the fire authority, that –

(*a*) a building to which this section applies is not provided, or
(*b*) a proposed building that will be a building to which this section applies will not be provided,

with such means of escape in case of fire as the local authority, after such consultation, deem necessary from each storey whose floor is more than twenty feet above the surface of the street or ground on any side of the building, the authority shall by notice require the owner of the building, or, as the case may be, the person proposing to erect the building, to execute such work or make such other provision in regard to the matters aforesaid as may be necessary.

(2) Sections 99 and 102 below apply in relation to a notice given under subsection (1) above in so far as it requires a person to execute works.

(3) In so far as such a notice requires a person to make provision otherwise than by the execution of works, he is, if he fails to comply with the notice, liable on summary conviction to a fine not exceeding level 4 on the standard scale and to a further fine not exceeding £2 for each day on which the offence continues after he is convicted.

(4) In proceedings under subsection (3) above, it is open to the defendant to question the reasonableness of the authority's requirements.

(5) Where building regulations imposing requirements as to the provision of means of escape in case of fire are applicable to a proposed building or proposed extension of a building, or would be so applicable but for a direction under section 8 above dispensing with such requirements –

(*a*) this section, and
(*b*) any provision of a local Act that has effect in place of this section, does not apply in relation to the proposed building or extension.

(6) This section applies to a building that exceeds two storeys in height and in which the floor of any upper storey is more than twenty

feet above the surface of the street or ground on any side of the building and that –

(*a*) is let in flats or tenement dwellings,

(*b*) is used as an inn, hotel, boarding-house, hospital, nursing home, boarding-school, children's home or similar institution, or

(*c*) is used as a restaurant, shop, store or warehouse and has on an upper floor sleeping accommodation for persons employed on the premises.

(7) This section has effect subject to section 30(3) of the Fire Precautions Act 1971.

Defective premises

76. – (1) If it appears to a local authority that –

(*a*) any premises are in such a state (in this section referred to as a 'defective state') as to be prejudicial to health or a nuisance, and

(*b*) unreasonable delay in remedying the defective state would be occasioned by following the procedure prescribed by sections 93 to 96 of the Public Health Act 1936,

the local authority may serve on the person on whom it would have been appropriate to serve an abatement notice under the said section 93 (if the local authority had proceeded under that section) a notice stating that the local authority intend to remedy the defective state and specifying the defects that they intend to remedy.

(2) Subject to subsection (3) below, the local authority may, after the expiration of nine days after service of a notice under subsection (1) above, execute such works as may be necessary to remedy the defective state, and recover the expenses reasonably incurred in so doing from the person on whom the notice was served.

(3) If, within seven days after service of a notice under subsection (1) above, the person on whom the notice was served serves a counter-notice that he intends to remedy the defects specified in the first-mentioned notice, the local authority shall take no action in pursuance of the first-mentioned notice unless the person who served the counter-notice –

(*a*) fails within what seems to the local authority a reasonable time to begin to execute works to remedy the said defects, or

(*b*) having begun to execute such works fails to make such progress towards their completion as seems to the local authority reasonable.

(4) In proceedings to recover expenses under subsection (2) above, the court –

(*a*) shall inquire whether the local authority were justified in concluding that the premises were in a defective state, or that unreasonable delay in remedying the defective state would have been occasioned by following the procedure prescribed by sections 93 to 96 of the Public Health Act 1936, and

(*b*) if the defendant proves that he served a counter-notice under subsection (3) above, shall inquire whether the defendant failed to begin the works to remedy the defects within a reasonable time, or failed to make reasonable progress towards their completion,

and if the court determines that –

(i) the local authority were not justified in either of the conclusions mentioned in paragraph (*a*) of this subsection, or

(ii) there was no failure under paragraph (*b*) of this subsection,

the local authority shall not recover the expenses or any part of them.

(5) Subject to subsection (4) above, in proceedings to recover expenses under subsection (2) above, the court may –

(*a*) inquire whether the said expenses ought to be borne wholly or in part by some person other than the defendant in the proceedings, and

(*b*) make such order concerning the expenses or their apportionment as appears to the court to be just,

but the court shall not order the expenses or any part of them to be borne by a person other than the defendant in the proceedings unless the court is satisfied that that other person has had due notice of the proceedings and an opportunity of being heard.

(6) A local authority shall not serve a notice under subsection (1) above, or proceed with the execution of works in accordance with a notice so served, if the execution of the works would, to their knowledge, be in contravention of a building preservation order under section 29 of the Town and Country Planning Act 1947.

(7) The power conferred on a local authority by subsection (1) above may be exercised notwithstanding that the local authority might instead have proceeded under Part VI of the Housing Act 1985 (repair notices).

Dangerous building

77. – (1) If it appears to a local authority that a building or structure, or part of a building or structure, is in such a condition, or is used to carry such loads, as to be dangerous, the authority may apply to a magistrates' court, and the court may –

(*a*) where danger arises from the condition of the building or structure, make an order requiring the owner thereof –

> (i) to execute such work as may be necessary to obviate the danger, or
> (ii) if he so elects, to demolish the building or structure, or any dangerous part of it, and remove any rubbish resulting from the demolition, or

(*b*) where danger arises from overloading of the building or structure, make an order restricting its use until a magistrates' court, being satisfied that any necessary works have been executed, withdraws or modifies the restriction.

(2) If the person on whom an order is made under subsection (1)(*a*) above fails to comply with the order within the time specified, the local authority may –

(*a*) execute the order in such manner as they think fit, and
(*b*) recover the expenses reasonably incurred by them in doing so from the person in default,

and, without prejudice to the right of the authority to exercise those powers, the person is liable on summary conviction to a fine not exceeding level 1 on the standard scale.

(3) This section has effect subject to the provisions of the Town and Country Planning Act 1971 relating to listed buildings, buildings subject to building preservation orders and buildings in conservation areas.

Dangerous building – emergency measures

78. – (1) If it appears to a local authority that –

(*a*) a building or structure, or part of a building or structure, is in such a state, or is used to carry such loads, as to be dangerous, and
(*b*) immediate action should be taken to remove the danger, they may take such steps as may be necessary for that purpose.

(2) Before exercising their powers under this section, the local authority shall, if it is reasonably practicable to do so, give notice of their intention to the owner and occupier of the building, or of the premises on which the structure is situated.

(3) Subject to this section, the local authority may recover from the owner the expenses reasonably incurred by them under this section.

(4) So far as expenses incurred by the local authority under this section consist of expenses of fencing off the building or structure, or arranging for it to be watched, the expenses shall not be recoverable in respect of any period –

(*a*) after the danger has been removed by other steps under this section, or

(*b*) after an order made under section 77(1) above for the purpose of its removal has been complied with or has been executed as mentioned in subsection (2) of that section.

(5) In proceedings to recover expenses under this section, the court shall inquire whether the local authority might reasonably have proceeded instead under section 77(1) above, and, if the court determines that the local authority might reasonably have proceeded instead under the subsection, the local authority shall not recover the expenses or any part of them.

(6) Subject to subsection (5) above, in proceedings to recover expenses under this section, the court may –

(*a*) inquire whether the expenses ought to be borne wholly or in part by some person other than the defendant in the proceedings, and

(*b*) make such order concerning the expenses or their apportionment as appears to the court to be just.

but the court shall not order the expenses or any part of them to be borne by any person other than the defendant in the proceedings unless it is satisfied that that other person has had due notice of the proceedings and an opportunity of being heard.

(7) Where in consequence of the exercise of the powers conferred by this section the owner or occupier of any premises sustains damage, but section 106(1) below does not apply because the owner or occupier has been in default –

(*a*) the owner or occupier may apply to a magistrates' court to determine whether the local authority were justified in exercising their powers under this section so as to occasion the damage sustained, and

(*b*) if the court determines that the local authority were not so justified, the owner or occupier is entitled to compensation, and section 106(2) and (3) below applies in relation to any dispute as regards compensation arising under this subsection.

(8) The proper officer of a local authority may, as an officer of the local authority, exercise the powers conferred on the local authority by subsection (1) above.

(9) This section does not apply to premises forming part of a mine or quarry within the meaning of the Mines and Quarries Act 1954.

Ruinous and dilapidated buildings and neglected sites

79. – (1) If it appears to a local authority that a building or structure is by reason of its ruinous or dilapidated condition seriously detrimental to the amenities of the neighbourhood, the local authority may by notice require the owner thereof –

(*a*) to execute such works of repair or restoration, or
(*b*) if he so elects, to take such steps for demolishing the building or structure, or any part thereof, and removing any rubbish or other material resulting from or exposed by the demolition,

as may be necessary in the interests of amenity.

(2) If it appears to a local authority that –

(*a*) rubbish or other material resulting from, or exposed by, the demolition or collapse of a building or structure is lying on the site or on any adjoining land, and
(*b*) by reason thereof the site or land is in such a condition as to be seriously detrimental to the amenities of the neighbourhood,

the local authority may by notice require the owner of the site or land to take such steps for removing the rubbish or material as may be necessary in the interests of amenity.

(3) Sections 99 and 102 below apply in relation to a notice given under subsection (1) or (2) above, subject to the following modifications –

(*a*) section 99(1) requires the notice to indicate the nature of the works of repair or restoration and that of the works of demolition and removal of rubbish or material, and
(*b*) section 99(2) authorises the local authority to execute, subject to that subsection, at their election either the works of repair or restoration or the works of demolition and removal of rubbish or material.

(4) This section does not apply to an advertisement as defined in section 290(1) of the Town and Country Planning Act 1971.

(5) This section has effect subject to the provisions of the Town and Country Planning Act 1971 relating to listed buildings, buildings subject to building preservation order and buildings in conservation areas.

Notice to local authority of intended demolition

80. – (1) This section applies to any demolition of the whole or part of a building except –

(*a*) a demolition in pursuance of a demolition order made under Part IX of the Housing Act 1985, and
(*b*) a demolition –

(i) of an internal part of a building, where the building is occupied and it is intended that it should continue to be occupied,

(ii) of a building that has a cubic content (as ascertained by external measurement) of not more than 1750 cubic feet, or, where a greenhouse, conservatory, shed or prefabricated garage forms part of a larger building, of that greenhouse, conservatory, shed or prefabricated garage, or

(iii) without prejudice to sub-paragraph (ii) above, of an agricultural building (as defined in section 26 of the General Rate Act 1967), unless it is contiguous to another building that is not itself an agricultural building or a building of a kind mentioned in that sub-paragraph.

(2) No person shall begin a demolition to which this section applies unless –

(*a*) he has given the local authority notice of his intention to do so, and

(*b*) either –

(i) the local authority have given a notice to him under section 81 below, or

(ii) the relevant period (as defined in that section) has expired.

(3) A notice under subsection (2) above shall specify the building to which it relates and the works of demolition intended to be carried out, and it is the duty of a person giving such a notice to a local authority to send or give a copy of it to –

(*a*) the occupier of any building adjacent to the building.

[(*b*) any public gas supplier (as defined in Part I of the Gas Act 1986) in whose authorised area (as so defined) the building is situated], and

(*c*) the Area Electricity Board in whose area the building is situated.

(4) A person who contravenes subsection (2) above is liable on summary conviction to a fine not exceeding level 4 on the standard scale.

Local authority's power to serve notice about demolition

81. – (1) A local authority may give a notice under this section to –

(*a*) a person on whom a demolition order has been served under [Part IX of the Housing Act 1985,]

(*b*) a person who appears to them not to be intending to comply with an order made under section 77 above or a notice given under section 79 above, and

(*c*) a person who appears to them to have begun or to be intending to begin a demolition to which section 80 above otherwise applies.

(2) Nothing contained in a notice under this section prejudices or affects the operation of any of the relevant statutory provisions, as defined in section 53(1) of the Health and Safety at Work etc. Act 1974; and accordingly, if a requirement of such a notice is inconsistent with a requirement imposed by or under the said Act of 1974, the latter requirement prevails.

(3) Where –

(*a*) a person has given a notice under section 80 above, or
(*b*) the local authority have served a demolition order on a person under [Part IX of the Housing Act 1985,]

a notice under this section may only be given to the person in question within the relevant period.

(4) In this section and section 80 above, 'the relevant period' means –

(*a*) in a case such as is mentioned in subsection (3)(*a*) above, six weeks from the giving of the notice under section 80 above, or such longer period as the person who gave that notice may in writing allow, and
(*b*) in a case such as is mentioned in subsection (3)(*b*) above, seven days after the local authority served a copy of the demolition order in accordance with [Part IX of the Housing Act 1985,] or such longer period as the person on whom the copy was served may in writing allow.

(5) It is the duty of the local authority to send or give a copy of a notice under this section to the owner and occupier of any building adjacent to the building to which the notice relates.

(6) It is also the duty of the local authority to send or give a copy of a notice under this section –

(*a*) if it contains such a requirement as is specified in section 82(1)(*h*) below, to the statutory undertakers concerned, and
(*b*) if it contains such a requirement as is specified in section 82(1)(*i*) below –

(i) to the fire authority, if they are not themselves the fire authority, and
(ii) to the Health and Safety Executive, if the premises are special premises.

(7) In this section and section 82 below, 'special premises' means premises for which a fire certificate is required by virtue of regulations under the Health and Safety at Work etc. Act 1974.

Notices under section 81

82. – 1(1) A notice under section 81(1) above may require the person to whom it is given –

   (*a*) to shore up any building adjacent to the building to which the notice relates,
   (*b*) to weatherproof any surfaces of an adjacent building that are exposed by the demolition,
   (*c*) to repair and make good any damage to an adjacent building caused by the demolition or by the negligent act or omission of any person engaged in it,
   (*d*) to remove material or rubbish resulting from the demolition and clearance of the site,
   (*e*) to disconnect and seal, at such points as the local authority may reasonably require, any sewer or drain in or under the building,
   (*f*) to remove any such sewer or drain, and seal any sewer or drain with which the sewer or drain to be removed is connected.
   (*g*) to make good to the satisfaction of the local authority the surface of the ground disturbed by anything done under paragraph (*e*) or (*f*) above,
   (*h*) to make arrangements with the relevant statutory undertakers for the disconnection of the supply of gas, electricity and water to the building,
   (*i*) to make such arrangements with regard to the burning of structures or materials on the site as may be reasonably required –

   (i) if the building is or forms part of special premises, by the Health and Safety Executive and the fire authority, and
   (ii) in any other case, by the fire authority, and

   (*j*) to take such steps relating to the conditions subject to which the demolition is to be undertaken, and the condition in which the site is to be left on completion of the demolition, as the local authority may consider reasonably necessary for the protection of the public and the preservation of public amenity.

(2) No one shall be required under paragraph (*c*), (*e*) or (*f*) of subsection (1) above to carry out any work in land outside the premises on which the works of demolition are being carried out if he has no right to carry out that work, but, subject to section 101 below, the person undertaking the demolition, or the local authority acting in his default, may break open any street for the purpose of complying with any such requirement.

(3) Before a person complies with a requirement under paragraph (*e*), (*f*) or (*g*) of subsection (1) above, he shall give to the local authority –

   (*a*) at least 48 hours' notice in the case of a requirement under paragraph (*e*) or (*f*), or (*b*) at least 24 hours' notice, in the case of a requirement under paragraph (*g*),

and a person who fails to comply with this subsection is liable on summary conviction to a fine not exceeding level 2 on the standard scale.

(4) This section does not authorise interference with apparatus or works of statutory undertakers authorised by an enactment to carry on an undertaking for the supply of electricity, gas or water.

(5) Without prejudice to the generality of subsection (4) above, this section does not exempt a person from –

(*a*) the obligation to obtain any consent required under section 67 of Schedule 3 to the Water Act 1945 (interference with valves and other apparatus) or section 68 of that Schedule (alterations to supply pipes and other apparatus),
(*b*) criminal liability under any enactment relating to the supply of gas or electricity or
(*c*) the requirements of regulations under section 31 of the Gas Act 1972 (public safety).

(6) Section 99 below applies in relation to a notice given under section 81(1) above.

Appeal against notice under s. 81

83. – (1) Section 102 below applies in relation to a notice given under section 81 above.

(2) among the grounds on which an appeal may be brought under section 102 below against such a notice are –

(*a*) in the case of a notice requiring an adjacent building to be shored up, that the owner of the building is not entitled to the support of that building by the building that is being demolished, and ought to pay, or contribute towards, the expenses of shoring it up,
(*b*) in the case of a notice requiring any surfaces of an adjacent building to be weatherproofed, that the owner of the adjacent building ought to pay, or contribute towards, the expenses of weatherproofing those surfaces.

(3) Where the grounds on which an appeal under section 102 below is brought include a ground specified in subsection (2) above –

(*a*) the appellant shall serve a copy of his notice of appeal on the person or persons referred to in that ground of appeal, and
(*b*) on the hearing of the appeal the court may make such orders as it thinks fit –

(i) in respect of the payment of, or contribution towards, the cost of the works of any such person, or

(ii) as to how any expenses that may be recoverable by the local authority are to be borne between the appellant and any such person.

SCHEDULE 1

Building Regulations

1. Building regulations may:

(*a*) provide for particular requirements of the regulations to be deemed to be complied with where prescribed methods of construction, prescribed types of materials or other prescribed means are used in or in connection with buildings.

(*b*) be framed to any extent by reference to a document published by or on behalf of the Secretary of State or another person or a body, or by reference to the approval or satisfaction of a prescribed person or body.

2. Building regulations may include provision as to:

(*a*) the giving of notices,

(*b*) the deposit of plans of proposed work or work already executed (including provision as to the number of copies to be deposited),

(*c*) the retention by local authorities of copies of plans deposited with them in accordance with the regulations,

(*d*) the inspection and testing of work,

(*e*) the taking of samples.

3. Building regulations may provide for requiring local authorities and approved inspectors in prescribed circumstances to consult a prescribed person before taking a prescribed step in connection with any work or other matter to which building regulations are applicable.

4. Building regulations may:

(*a*) authorise local authorities to accept, as evidence that the requirements of building regulations as to matters of a prescribed description are or would be satisfied, certificates to that effect by persons of a class or description prescribed in relation to those matters or by a person nominated in writing by the Secretary of State in a particular case,

(*b*) provide for the issue by local authorities of certificates to the effect that, so far as the authority concerned have been able to ascertain after taking all reasonable steps in that behalf, the requirements of building regulations as to matters of a prescribed description are satisfied in a particular case, and for such certificates to be evidence (but not conclusive evidence) of compliance with the regulations, (*c*) make provision:

    (i) for prohibiting, in prescribed circumstances, the carrying out of proposed work of a prescribed class involving matters of a prescribed description unless there has been deposited with the prescribed authority as regards those matters a certificate such as is mentioned in sub-paragraph (*a*) above,

    (ii) for enabling, in cases where such a certificate is required by virtue of paragraph (i) above, a dispute as to whether a certificate ought to be issued to be referred to the Secretary of State,

    (iii) for enabling the Secretary of State, on such a reference, to give such directions as he thinks fit.

5. – (1) Building regulations may authorise local authorities to charge prescribed fees for or in connection with the performance of prescribed functions of theirs relating to building regulations.

(2) The Secretary of State may by order repeal this paragraph.

6. Building regulations may make a prescribed person or class of persons responsible (instead of local authorities) for performing prescribed functions of local authorities under or in connection with building regulations, and for that purpose may provide for a prescribed enactment relating to building regulations and a prescribed provision of such regulations to apply (with any prescribed modifications) in relation to a prescribed person or a person of a prescribed class as that enactment or provision applies in relation to a local authority.

7. Without prejudice to the generality of section 1(1) of this Act, building regulations may:

(*a*) for any of the purposes mentioned in section 1(1) of this Act, make provision with respect to any of the following matters:

    (i) preparation of sites,

    (ii) suitability, durability and use of materials and components (including surface finishes),

    (iii) structural strength and stability, including:

        (*a*) precautions against overloading, impact and explosion,

        (*b*) measures to safeguard adjacent buildings and services,

        (*c*) underpinning,

    (iv) fire precautions, including:

        (*a*) structural measures to resist the outbreak and spread of fire and to mitigate its effects,

        (*b*) services, fittings and equipment designed to mitigate the effects of fire or to facilitate fire-fighting,

        (*c*) means of escape in case of fire and means for securing that such means of escape can be safely and effectively used at all material times,

    (v) resistance to moisture and decay,

    (vi) measures affecting the transmission of heat,

    (vii) measures affecting the transmission of sound,

    (viii) measures to prevent infestation,

    (ix) measures affecting the emission of smoke, gases, fumes, grit or dust or other noxious or offensive substances,

    (x) drainage (including waste disposal units),

    (xi) cesspools and other means for the reception, treatment or disposal of foul matter,

    (xii) storage, treatment and removal of waste,

    (xiii) installations utilising solid fuel, oil, gas, electricity or any other fuel or power (including appliances, storage tanks, heat exchangers, ducts, fans and other equipment),

    (xiv) water services (including wells and bore-holes for the supply of water) and fittings and fixed equipment associated therewith,

    (xv) telecommunications services (including telephones and radio and television wiring installations),

    (xvi) lifts, escalators, hoists, conveyors and moving footways,

    (xvii) plant providing air under pressure,

    (xviii) standards of heating, artificial lighting, mechanical ventilation and air-conditioning and provision of power outlets,

    (xix) open space about buildings and the natural lighting and ventilation of buildings,

    (xx) accommodation for specific purposes in or in connection with buildings, and the dimensions of rooms and other spaces within buildings,

    (xxi) means of access to and egress from buildings and parts of buildings,

    (xxii) prevention of danger and obstruction to persons in and about buildings (including passers-by),

    (xxiii) matters connected with or ancillary to any of the foregoing matters,

(b) require things to be provided or done in connection with buildings (as well as regulating the provision or doing of things in or in connection with buildings),

(c) prescribe the manner in which work is to be carried out.

8. – (1) Building regulations may be made with respect to:

(a) alterations and extensions of buildings and of services, fittings and equipment in or in connection with buildings,

(b) new services, fittings or equipment provided in or in connection with buildings,

(c) buildings and services, fittings and equipment in or in connection with buildings, so far as affected by:

    (i) alterations or extensions of buildings, or

    (ii) new, altered or extended services, fittings or equipment in or in connection with buildings, (*d*) the whole of a building, together with any services, fittings or equipment provided in or in connection with it, in respect of which there are or are proposed to be carried out any operations that by virtue of section 123(1) of this Act constitute the construction of a building for the purposes of this paragraph,

(*e*) buildings or parts of buildings, together with any services, fittings or equipment provided in or in connection with them, in cases where the purposes for which or the manner or circumstances in which a building or part of a building is used change or changes in a way that constitutes a material change of use of the building or part within the meaning of the expression 'material change of use' as defined for the purposes of this paragraph by building regulations.

(2) So far as they relate to matters mentioned in sub-paragraph (1) above, building regulations may be made to apply to or in connection with buildings erected before the date on which the regulations came into force but, except as aforesaid (and subject to section 2(2) of this Act), shall not apply to buildings erected before that date.

9. Building regulations may authorise local authorities, subject to and in accordance with the regulations, to fix by means of schemes and to recover such charges for or in connection with the performance of functions of theirs relating to building regulations as they may determine in accordance with principles by the regulations.

10. Building regulations may:

(*a*) provide for a provision thereof to apply generally, or in a particular area,

(*b*) make different provision for different areas and generally different provision for different circumstances or cases,

(*c*) include such supplemental and incidental provisions as appear to the Secretary of State expedient.

11. – (1) Building regulations may repeal or modify:

(*a*) any of the following provisions of this Act: sections 15, 18, 19, 21 to 29, 41, 59 to 87, 91 to 119, 123(2) and 126 (except as to the definitions of 'contravention', 'local authority' paragraph (*a*), 'modifications', 'plans', 'prescribed' and 'substantive require-ments'), and paragraphs 1 and 5 to 14 of Schedule 3, or

(*b*) any provision of an Act passed before the 20th September 1974,

if it appears to the Secretary of State that it is inconsistent with, or is unnecessary or requires alteration in consequence of, any provision contained in or made under any enactment relating to building regulations.

(2) Building regulations may:

(*a*) repeal or alter section 12(1) of the Local Government (Miscellaneous Provisions) Act 1976 (byelaws as to supply of heat) or any provision of byelaws in force by virtue of it, and

(*b*) make any modification of section 12(2) of that Act that the Secretary of State considers is appropriate in consequence of the repeal or alteration.

SCHEDULE 2

Relaxation of Building Regulations for Existing Work

Application of Schedule

1. This Schedule applies to a direction under section 8 of this Act that will affect the application of building regulations to work that has been carried out before the giving of the direction.

Cases where no direction may be given

2. Neither the Secretary of State nor a local authority shall give a direction to which this Schedule applies:

(*a*) if the local authority have, before the making of the application for the direction, become entitled under section 36(3) of this Act to pull down, remove or alter the work to which the application relates, or

(*b*) if, when the application is made, there is in force an injunction or other direction given by a court that requires the work to be pulled down, removed or altered.

Suspension of certain provisions while application pending

3. – (1) Subject to the following provisions of this Schedule, after the making of an application for a direction to which this Schedule applies, and until the application is withdrawn or finally disposed of, no section 36 notices shall be given as regards the work to which the application relates on the ground that it contravenes the requirement to which the application relates.

(2) If an application for a direction to which this Schedule applies is made less than 12 months after the completion of the work to which the application relates, section 36(4) of this Act does not prevent the giving of a notice as regards that work at any time within a period of 3 months from the date on which the application is withdrawn or finally disposed of.

(3) If an application for a direction to which this Schedule applies is

made after a section 36 notice has been given on the ground that the work to which the application relates contravenes the requirement to which the application relates (not being an application prohibited by paragraph 2 of this Schedule), section 36(3) of this Act has effect in relation to that work as if for the reference to the period there mentioned there were substituted a reference to a period expiring 28 days after the application is withdrawn or finally disposed of, or such longer period as a magistrates' court may allow.

(4) Subject to the following provisions of this Schedule, if an application for a direction to which this Schedule applies is made after any person has, in consequence of the carrying out of the work to which the application relates in contravention of building regulations, become liable to a penalty continuing from day to day, the daily penalty is not recoverable in respect of any day after the making of the application and before it is withdrawn or finally disposed of.

(5) In a case where an application is withdrawn or is finally disposed of without any direction being given, the Secretary of State or, as the case may be, the local authority may order that the daily penalty is not recoverable in respect of any day during such further period not exceeding 28 days as may be specified in the order.

4. Paragraphs 3(1), (3) and (4) above do not apply to an application that is a repetition, or substantially a repetition, of a previous application under section 8 of this Act.

Saving for criminal liability incurred before making of application

5. The giving of a direction to which this Schedule applies does not affect the liability of a person for an offence committed before the giving of the direction, except so far as that liability depends on the continuation of the offence after the giving of the direction.

Termination of proceedings under section 36 on giving of direction

6. If, before the giving of a direction to which this Schedule applies, a section 36 notice has been given, and the contravention of building regulations by virtue of which the notice was given comes to an end when the direction is given, the local authority is not, after the giving of the direction, entitled to proceed under section 36(3) of this Act by virtue of that notice.

Appendix 2

Fire Precautions Act 1971 – as amended

Premises for which fire certificates are required

Use of premises for which fire certificate is compulsory

1. – (1) A certificate issued under this Act by the fire authority (in this Act referred to as a 'fire certificate') shall, subject to any exemption conferred by or under this Act, be required in respect of any premises which are put to a use for the time being designated under this section (in this Act referred to as a 'designated use').

(2) For the purposes of this section the Secretary of State may by order designate particular uses of premises, but shall not so designate any particular use unless it falls within at least one of the following classes of use, that is to say, –

    (*a*) use as, or for any purpose involving the provision of, sleeping accommodation;

    (*b*) use as, or as part of, an institution providing treatment or care;

    (*c*) use for purposes of entertainment, recreation or instruction or for purposes of any club, society or association;

    (*d*) use for purposes of teaching, training or research;

    (*e*) use for any purpose involving access to the premises by members of the public, whether on payment or otherwise.

    (*f*) use as place of work.

(3) An order under this section may provide that a fire certificate shall not by virtue of this section be required for premises of any description specified in the order, notwithstanding that they are or form part of premises which are put to a designated use.

(4) For the purposes of any provision made in an order under this section by virtue of subsection (3) above a description of premises may be framed by reference to the purpose for which premises are used or the frequency of their use for any purpose or by reference to any other circumstances whatsoever; and different provision may be made in pursuance of that subsection in relation to different designated uses.

(5) An order under this section may include such supplementary

and incidental provisions as appear to the Secretary of State to be necessary or expedient for the purposes of the order.

(6) An order under this section may be varied or revoked by a subsequent order thereunder.

(7) The power to make orders under this section shall be exercisable by statutory instrument, which shall be subject to annulment in pursuance of a resolution of either House or Parliament.

(8) Without prejudice to any exemption conferred by or under this Act, where premises consisting of a part of a building are put to a designated use, any other part of the building which is occupied together with those premises in connection with that use of them shall for the purposes of this Act be treated as forming part of the premises put to that use.

2. No fire certificate shall by virtue of section 1 of this Act be required in respect of premises of any of the following descriptions, that is to say, – *Premises exempt from section 1*

> (*d*) any premises appropriated to, and used solely or mainly for, public religious worship;
>
> (*e*) any premises consisting of or comprised in a house which is occupied as a single private dwelling.

Fire certificates

5. – (1) An application for a fire certificate with respect to any premises must be made to the fire authority in the prescribed form and, – *Application for, and issue of, fire certificate*

> (*a*) must specify the particular use or uses of the premises which it is desired to have covered by the certificate; and
>
> (*b*) must give such information as may be prescribed about the premises and any prescribed matter connected with them; and
>
> (*c*) if the premises consist of part of a building, must, in so far as it is available to the applicant, give such information as may be prescribed about the rest of the building and any prescribed matter connected with it.

(2) On receipt of an application for a fire certificate with respect to any premises the fire authority may require the applicant within such time as they may specify –

> (*a*) to furnish them with such plans of the premises as they may specify; and
>
> (*b*) if the premises consist of part of a building, to furnish them, in so far as it is possible for him to do so, with such plans of such other part or parts of the building as they may specify;

and if the applicant fails to furnish the required plans within that time or such further time as the authority may allow, the application shall be deemed to have been withdrawn at the end of that time or further time, as the case may be.

(3) Where an application for a fire certificate with respect to any premises has been duly made and all such plans (if any) as are required to be furnished under subsection (2) above in connection with it have been duly furnished, it shall be the duty of the fire authority to cause to be carried out an inspection of the relevant building (including any part of it which consists of premises to which any exemption conferred by or under this Act applies), and if the fire authority are satisfied as regards any use of the premises which is specified in the application that, –

    (*a*) the means of escape in case of fire with which the premises are provided; and

    (*b*) the means (other than means for fighting fire) with which the relevant building is provided for securing that the means of escape with which the premises are provided can be safely and effectively used at all material times; and

    (*c*) the means of fighting fire (whether in the premises or affecting the means of escape) with which the relevant building is provided for use in case of fire by persons in the building; and

    (*d*) the means with which the relevant building is provided for giving to persons in the premises warning in case of fire,

are such as may reasonably be required in the circumstances of the case in connection with that use of the premises, the authority shall issue a certificate covering that use.

(4) Where the fire authority, after causing to be carried out under subsection (3) above an inspection of the relevant building, are, as regards any use of the premises specified in the application, not satisfied that the means mentioned in that subsection are such as may reasonably be required in the circumstances of the case in connection with that use, they shall by notice served on the applicant, –

    (*a*) inform him of that fact and of the steps which would have to be taken (whether by way of making alterations to any part of the relevant building or of otherwise providing that building or, as the case may be, the premises with any of those means) to satisfy them as aforesaid as regards that use; and

    (*b*) notify him that they will not issue a fire certificate covering that use unless those steps are taken (whether by the applicant or otherwise) within a specified time;

and if at the end of that time or such further time as may be allowed by the authority or by any order made by a court on, or in proceedings arising out of, an appeal under section 9 of this Act against the notice, a certificate covering that use has not been issued, it shall be deemed to have been refused.

6. – (1) Every fire certificate issued with respect to any premises shall specify, –

   (*a*) the particular use or uses of the premises which the certificate covers; and

   (*b*) the means of escape in case of fire with which the premises are provided; and

   (*c*) the means (other than means for fighting fire) with which the relevant building is provided for securing that the means of escape with which the premises are provided can be safely and effectively used at all material times; and

   (*d*) the type, number and location of the means for fighting fire (whether in the premises or affecting the means of escape) with which the relevant building is provided for use in case of fire by persons in the building; and

   (*e*) the type, number and location of the means with which the relevant building is provided for giving to persons in the premises warning in case of fire,

and may, where appropriate, do so by means of or by reference to a plan.

(2) A fire certificate issued with respect to any premises may impose such requirements as the fire authority consider appropriate in the circumstances, –

   (*a*) for securing that the means of escape in case of fire with which the premises are provided are properly maintained and kept free from obstruction;

   (*b*) for securing that the means with which the relevant building is provided as mentioned in subsection (1)(*c*) to (*e*) above are properly maintained;

   (*c*) for securing that persons employed to work in the premises receive appropriate instruction or training in what to do in case of fire, and that records are kept of instruction or training given for that purpose;

   (*d*) for limiting the number of persons who may be in the premises at any one time; and

   (*e*) as to other precautions to be observed in the relevant building in relation to the risk, in case of fire, to persons in the premises.

(3) Any requirements imposed by virtue of subsection (2) above by a fire certificate issued with respect to any premises –

   (*a*) may, in so far as they apply to the premises, be framed either so as to apply to the whole of the premises or so as to apply to one or more parts of them; and

   (*b*) where the premises do not constitute the whole of the relevant building, may (where appropriate) be framed either so as to apply to the whole of the rest of that building or so as to apply to one or more parts of the rest of it, and different requirements may, in either case, be imposed in relation to different parts; and a fire certificate covering more than one use of the premises to which it relates may by virtue of subsection (2) above impose different requirements in relation to different uses of the premises or of any part of the premises.

(4) For the purposes of this Act a fire certificate issued with respect to any premises shall be treated as requiring every matter specified in the certificate in accordance with subsection (1)(*b*), (*c*), (*d*) or (*e*) above to be kept in accordance with its specification in the certificate; and references in this Act to requirements imposed by a fire certificate shall be construed accordingly.

(5) In so far as requirement imposed by a fire certificate issued with respect to any premises requires everything to be done or not to be done to or in relation to any part of the relevant building, the person responsible for any contravention thereof shall (subject to any provision included in the certificate in pursuance of this subsection) be the occupier of that part; but if as regards any such requirement, in so far as it requires anything to be done or not to be done to or in relation to any part of the relevant building, the fire authority consider it appropriate in the circumstances to provide that some other person or persons shall be responsible for any contravention thereof instead of, or in addition to, the occupier of that part, they may so provide in the certificate and, if the certificate covers more than one use of the premises, may in pursuance of this subsection make different provision therein in relation to different uses of the premises.

(6) Subject to subsection (7) below, a fire authority –

(*a*) shall not issue a fire certificate which would have the effect of making a person responsible under or by virtue of subsection (5) above for contraventions of a requirement imposed by the certificate, or make in a fire certificate any amendment which would have that effect, unless (in either case) they have previously consulted the person in question about his proposed responsibility for contraventions of the requirement; and

(*b*) shall not amend a fire certificate so as to vary any requirement imposed by it, in a case where any person already responsible under or by virtue of subsection (5) above for contraventions of that requirement is to continue to be so responsible when the variation takes effect, unless they have previously consulted that person about the proposed variation;

but, without prejudice to any right of appeal conferred by section 9 of this Act, a fire certificate shall not be invalidated by any failure of the fire authority by whom it is issued to comply with the requirements of this subsection.

(7) Where a fire authority propose to issue a new fire certificate with

respect to any premises as an alternative to amending an existing fire certificate, and the new certificate would have the effect of reimposing without variation a requirement imposed by the existing certificate and of making any person who is responsible under or by virtue of subsection (5) above for contraventions of the existing requirement continue to be so responsible for contraventions of it as reimposed, the authority shall not be required under subsection (6) above to consult that person by reason only of that fact.

(8) A fire certificate issued with respect to any premises other than premises in relation to which a notice under section 3 of this Act is in force shall be sent to the occupier of the premises and shall be kept in the premises so long as it is in force.

(9) A fire certificate issued with respect to any premises in relation to which a notice under section 3 of this Act is in force shall be sent to the notified person and, if that person is not the occupier of the premises, a copy of the certificate shall be sent to the occupier of the premises; and so long as the certificate is in force –

(a) the certificate shall be kept in the relevant building; and
(b) where a copy of the certificate is by this subsection required to be sent to the occupier of the premises, the copy shall be kept in the premises.

9. – (1) A person who is aggrieved –

Right of appeal as regards matters arising out of ss.5 to 8

(a) by anything mentioned in a notice served under section 5(4) of this Act as a step which would have to be taken as a condition of the issue of a fire certificate with respect to any premises, or by the period allowed by such a notice for the taking of any steps mentioned in it; or
(b) by the refusal of the fire authority to issue a fire certificate with respect to any premises; or
(c) by the inclusion of anything in, or the omission of anything from, a fire certificate issued with respect to any premises by the fire authority; or
(d) by the refusal of the fire authority to cancel or to amend a fire certificate issued with respect to any premises; or
(e) by any direction given in pursuance of section 8(4)(b) of this Act; or
(f) by anything mentioned in a notice served under section 8(5) of this Act with respect to any premises as a step which must be taken if the fire authority are not to become entitled to cancel the fire certificate relating to the premises, or by the period allowed by such a notice for the taking of any steps mentioned in it; or
(g) by the amendment or cancellation in pursuance of section 8(6), (7) or (9) of this Act of a fire certificate issued with respect to any premises,

may, within twenty-one days from the relevant date, appeal to the court, and on any such appeal the court may make such order as it thinks fit.

(2) In this section 'the relevant date' means –

(*a*) in relation to a person aggrieved by any such refusal, direction, cancellation or amendment as is mentioned in subsection (1) above or by any matter mentioned in paragraph (*a*) or (*f*) of that subsection, the date on which he was first served by the fire authority with notice of the refusal, direction, cancellation, amendment or matter in question;

(*b*) in relation to a person aggrieved by the inclusion of anything in, or the omission of anything from, a fire certificate issued with respect to any premises, the date on which the inclusion or omission was first made known to him;

and for the purposes of paragraph (*b*) above a person who is served with a fire certificate or a copy of, or any part of, a fire certificate shall be taken to have had what the certificate or that part of it does and does not contain made known to him at the time of the service on him of the certificate or copy.

(3) Where an appeal is brought under this section against the refusal of the fire authority to issue a fire certificate with respect to any premises or the cancellation or amendment in pursuance of section 8(7) or (9) of this Act of a fire certificate issued with respect to any premises, a person shall not be guilty of an offence under section 7(1) or (2) of this Act by reason of the premises in question being put to a designated use or used as a dwelling at a time between the relevant date and the final determination of the appeal.

(4) Where an appeal is brought under this section against the inclusion in a fire certificate of anything which has the effect of making the certificate impose a requirement, a person shall not be guilty of an offence under section 7(4) of this Act by reason of a contravention of that requirement which occurs at a time between the relevant date and the final determination of the appeal.

(5) Where an appeal is brought under this section against –

(*a*) the inclusion in a fire certificate, in pursuance of subsection (5) of section 6 of this Act, of a provision making any person responsible for contraventions of any requirement imposed by the certificate; or

(*b*) the omission from a fire certificate of a provision which, if included in pursuance of that subsection, would prevent any person from being, as the occupier of any premises, responsible under that subsection for contraventions of any requirement imposed by the certificate, that person shall not be guilty of an offence under section 7(4) of this Act by reason of a contravention of that requirement which occurs at a time between the relevant date and the final determination of the appeal.

9A. – (1) All premises to which this section applies shall be provided with such means of escape in case of fire for the persons employed to work therein as may reasonably be required in the circumstances of the case.

Duty to provide certain premises with means of escape in case of fire

(2) The premises to which this section applies are –

(*a*) office premises, shop premises and railway premises to which the Offices, Shops and Railway Premises Act 1963 applies; and
(*b*) premises which are deemed to be such premises for the purposes of the Act;

being (in each case) premises in which persons are employed to work.

(3) In determining, for the purposes of this section, what means of escape may reasonably be required in the case of any premises, regard shall be had (amongst other things) not only to the number of persons who may be expected to be working in the premises at any time but also to the number of persons (other than those employed to work therein) who may reasonably be expected to be resorting to the premises at that time.

(4) In the event of a contravention of subsection (1) above the occupier of the premises shall be guilty of an offence and liable on summary conviction to a fine not exceeding level 5 on the standard scale.

13. – (1) Where an application is made for a fire certificate with respect to any premises and –

Exercise of certain powers of fire authority in England or Wales where building regulations as to means of escape apply

(*a*) the relevant building is a building to which at the time of its erection building regulations imposing requirements as to means of escape in case of fire applied; and
(*b*) in connection with the erection of that building plans were, in accordance with building regulations, deposited with a local authority,

the fire authority shall not in pursuance of section 5(4) of this Act make the issue of a certificate conditional on the making to the building of structural or other alterations relating to escape from the premises unless –

(i) there are in force under section 12 of this Act regulations applying to the premises in relation to any use of the premises specified in the application, being regulations which impose requirements as to means of escape in case of fire or means for securing that any means of escape can be safely and effectively used at all material times, and the fire authority are satisfied that alterations to the relevant building are necessary to bring the premises into compliance with the regulations in respect of those requirements; or

(ii) the fire authority are satisfied that the means of escape in case of fire with which the premises are provided or the means of the sort mentioned in section 5(3)(*b*) of this Act with which the relevant building is provided are inadequate in relation to any use of the premises so specified by reason of matters or circumstances of which particulars were not required by or under the building regulations to be supplied to the local authority in connection with the deposit of plans.

(2) Where an application is made for a fire certificate with respect to any premises in the circumstances described in subsection (1)(*a*) and (*b*) above and since the erection of the building plans have, in accordance with building regulations, been deposited with a local authority in connection with any proposals relating to the building, subsection (1) above shall have effect in relation to that application as if in paragraph (ii) the reference to the deposit of plans included a reference to the deposit of plans in connection with those proposals.

(3) Where, while a fire certificate is in force with respect to any premises, the fire authority receive notice under subsection (2) of section 8 of this Act of any proposals falling within that subsection to which building regulations imposing requirements as to means of escape in case of fire apply, and in connection with those proposals plans have, in accordance with building regulations, been deposited with a local authority, the fire authority shall not in pursuance of subsection (4) of that section make the carrying out of those proposals conditional on the making to the relevant building of structural or other alterations relating to escape from the premises unless –

(*a*) there are in force under section 12 of this Act regulations applying to the premises in relation to any use of the premises covered by the certificate, being regulations which impose requirements such as are mentioned in subsection (1)(i) above, and the fire authority are satisfied that the carrying out of the proposals in compliance with the requirements of the building regulations will not of itself ensure that, when the proposals have been carried out, the premises will comply with the regulations under section 12 in respect of the requirements such as are mentioned in subsection (1)(i) above which the regulations under section 12 impose; or

(*b*) the fire authority are satisfied that, by reason of matters or circumstances of which particulars are not required by or under the building regulations to be supplied to the local authority in connection with the deposit of plans, the carrying out of the proposals in compliance with the requirements of the building regulations will not of itself ensure that, when the proposals have been carried out, the means of escape in case of fire with which the premises will then be provided and the means of the sort mentioned in section 5(3)(*b*) of this Act with which the relevant building will then be provided will be adequate in relation to every use of the premises covered by the certificate.

(4) In this section 'structural or other alterations relating to escape from the premises', in relation to any such premises as are mentioned in this section, means structural or other alterations directly connected with the provision of the premises with adequate means of escape in case of fire or the provision of the relevant building with adequate means of the sort mentioned in section 5(3)(*b*) of this Act.

(6) This section does not extend to Scotland.

16. – (1) Where it is proposed to erect a building or to make any extension of or structural alteration to a building and, in connection with the proposals, plans are, in accordance with building regulations, deposited with a local authority, then, if it appears to the local authority likely –

> (*a*) that the first use to which any premises constituting or comprised in the building or, as the case may be, the building as extended will be put after the proposals are carried out will be a use which at the time of the deposit of the plans was a designated use; or
>
> (*b*) that the first use to which any such premises will be put after the proposals are carried out will be use as a dwelling, and that one or more of the conditions set out in section 3(1)(*a*) and (*b*) of this Act will then be fulfilled as regards those premises,

the local authority, if they are not the fire authority, shall consult the fire authority before passing the plans.

Duty of local authority to consult fire authority in certain cases before passing plans

(2) Where it is proposed to change the use to which a building or part of building is put and, in connection with that proposal, plans are, in accordance with building regulations, deposited with a local authority, then, if it appears to the local authority likely –

> (*a*) that the first use to which any premises constituting or comprised in the building will be put after the time when that change of use occurs will be a use which at the time of the deposit of the plans was a designated use; or
>
> (*b*) that the first use to which any such premises will be put after the time when that change of use occurs will be use as a dwelling, and that one or more of the conditions set out in section 3(1)(*a*) and (*b*) of this Act will then be fulfilled as regards those premises,

the local authority, if they are not the fire authority, shall consult the fire authority before passing the plans.

(3) This section does not extend to Scotland.

Duty of fire authorities to consult other authorities before requiring alterations to building

17. – (1) Before a fire authority –

(a) serve on the applicant for a fire certificate with respect to any premises a notice under section 5(4) of this Act informing him that they will not issue a certificate unless alterations are made to the relevant building; or

(b) serve in respect of any premises a notice under section 8(4) or (5) or section 12(8)(b) of this Act mentioning as a step which would have to be taken anything involving the making of alterations to the relevant building.

the authority shall –

(i) if the premises are situated in England and Wales (elsewhere than in Greater London) or in an outer London borough and the fire authority are not the local authority for the area in which the premises are situated, consult that local authority;

(ii) if the premises are situated in Scotland, consult the buildings authority (within the meaning of section 1 of the Building (Scotland) Act 1959) for the area in which the premises are situated, and

(iii) if the premises are used as a place of work and are within the field of responsibility of one or more enforcing authorities within the meaning of Part I of the Health and Safety at Work etc. Act 1974, consult that authority or each of those authorities.

(2) For the avoidance of doubt it is hereby declared that a local authority buildings authority or other authority who have in accordance with this section been consulted by a fire authority proposing to serve any such notice as is mentioned in subsection (1) above may be a person aggrieved within the meaning of section 9 of this Act.

(3) Section 18(7) of the Health and Safety at Work etc. Act 1974 (meaning in Part I of that Act of 'enforcing authority' and of such an authority's 'field of responsibility') shall apply for the purposes of this section as it applies for the purposes of that Part.

Appendix 3

Private certification and public bodies' forms

The following are the forms prescribed for use under the Building Regulations (Approved Inspectors, etc.) 1985, and are based on those printed in Schedule 2 of those regulations.

FORM 1 – INITIAL NOTICE

Section 47 of the Building Act 1984 ('the Act')

The Building (Approved Inspectors etc.) Regulations 1985 ('the 1985 regulations')

INITIAL NOTICE

To: **(1)**

1. This notice relates to the following work: **(2)**

2. The approved inspector in relation to the work is: **(3)**

3. The person intending to carry out the work is: **(4)**

4. With this notice are the following documents, which are those relevant to the work described in this notice **(4)**:

   [(a) in the case of a notice signed by an inspector approved by a designated body in accordance with regulation 3(2) of the 1985 regulations, a copy of the notice of his approval,]

(b) a declaration signed by the insurer that a named scheme of insurance approved by the Secretary of State applies in relation to the work described in the notice,

[(c) in the case of the erection or extension of a building, a plan to a scale of not less than 1:1250 showing the boundaries and location of the site and a statement—

  (i) as to the approximate location of any proposed connection to be made to a sewer, or

  (ii) if no connection is to be made to a sewer, as to the proposals for the discharge of any proposed drain, including the location of any cesspool, or

  (iii) if no provision is to be made for drainage, of the reasons why none is necessary,]

[(d) where it is proposed to erect a building or extension over a sewer or drain shown on the relative map of sewers, a statement as to the location of the building or extension and the precautions to be taken in building over the sewer or drain,]

[(e) a statement of any local enactment relevant to the work, and of the steps to be taken to comply with it.]

5. The work [is]/[is not] **(5)** minor work **(6)**.

[6. I **(7)** declare that I do not, and will not while this notice is in force, have any financial or professional interest **(8)** in the work described.] **(9)**

7. The approved inspector [will]/[will not] **(10)** be obliged to consult the fire authority by regulation 11 of the 1985 regulations.

[8. I **(7)** undertake to consult the fire authority before giving a plans certificate in accordance with section 50 of the Act or a final certificate in accordance with section 51 of the Act in respect of any of the work described above.] **(9)**

9. I **(7)** am aware of the obligations laid upon me by Part II of the Act by regulation 10 of the 1985 regulations.

Signed   Signed

Approved Inspector.   Person intending to
                                    carry out the work.

Date   Date

NOTES

(1) Name and address of local authority.

(2) Location and description of the work, including the use of any building to which the work relates.

(3) Name and address.

(4) The local authority may reject this notice only on prescribed grounds. These are set out in Schedule 3 to the 1985 regulations. They include failure to provide relevant documents. The documents listed in paragraph 4 of the notice relevant to the work described above should therefore be sent with this notice. Any sub-paragraph which does not apply should be deleted.

(5) Delete whichever does not apply.

(6) 'Minor work' is defined in regulation 9(5) of the 1985 regulations. If the work is not minor work, the declaration in paragraph 6 must be made.

(7) Name of the approved inspector.

(8) 'Professional or financial interest' is defined in regulation 9 of the 1985 regulations.

(9) Delete this statement if it does not apply.

(10) Delete whichever does not apply. If the inspector is obliged to consult the fire authority, the declaration in paragraph 8 must be made.

Form 2 – **PLANS CERTIFICATE**

Section 50 of the Building Act 1984 ('the Act')

The Building (Approved Inspectors etc.) Regulations 1985 ('the 1985 regulations')

PLANS CERTIFICATE

1. This certificate relates to the following work: **(1)**

2. I am an approved inspector for the purposes of Part II of the Act and the above work is [the whole]/[part] **(2)** of the work described in an initial notice given by me and dated **(3)**.

3. With this certificate is the declaration, signed by the insurer, that a named scheme of insurance approved by the Secretary of State applies in relation to the work to which the certificate relates.

4. Plans of the work specified above have been submitted to me and I am satisfied that the plans neither are defective nor show that work carried out in accordance with them would contravene any provision of building regulations.

5. The work [is]/[is not] **(2)** minor work. **(4)**

[6. I declare that I have had no financial or professional interest **(5)** in the work described since giving the initial notice described in paragraph 2.] **(6)**

[7. I have consulted the fire authority in accordance with regulation 11.] **(6)**

8. The plans to which this certificate relates bear the following date and reference number: **(7)**

| | Signed |
| Date | Approved Inspector |

Notes

(1) Location and description of the work, including the use of any building to which the work relates.
(2) Delete whichever does not apply.
(3) Date.
(4) 'Minor work' is defined in regulation 9(5) of the 1985 regulations.

If the work is not minor work, the declaration in paragraph 6 must be made.

(5) 'Professional or financial interest' is defined in regulation 9 of the 1985 regulations.

(6) Delete this statement if it does not apply.

(7) Date and reference number.

FORM 3 – COMBINED INITIAL NOTICE AND
PLANS CERTIFICATE

Sections 47 and 50 of the Building Act 1984 ('the Act')

The Building (Approved Inspectors etc.) Regulations 1985 ('the 1985 regulations')

COMBINED INITIAL NOTICE AND PLANS CERTIFICATE

To: **(1)**

1. This notice relates to the following work: **(2)**

2. The approved inspector in relation to the work is: **(3)**

3. The person intending to carry out the work is: **(3)**

4. With this notice are the following documents, which are those relevant to the work described in this notice **(4)**:

[(a) in the case of a notice signed by an inspector approved by a designated body in accordance with regulation 3(2) of the 1985 regulations, a copy of the notice of his approval,]
(b) a declaration signed by the insurer that a named scheme of insurance approved by the Secretary of State applies in relation to the work described in the notice,
[(c) in the case of the erection or extension of a building, a plan to a scale of not less than 1:1250 showing the boundaries and location of the site and a statement—
    (i) as to the approximate location of any proposed connection to be made to a sewer, or
   (ii) if no connection is to be made to a sewer, as to the proposals for the discharge of any proposed drain, including the location of any cesspool, or
  (iii) if no provision is to be made for drainage, of the reasons why none is necessary,]
[(d) where it is proposed to erect a building or extension over a sewer or drain shown on the relative map of sewers, a statement as to the location of the building or extension and the precautions to be taken in building over the sewer or drain,]
[(e) a statement of any local enactment relevant to the work, and of the steps to be taken to comply with it.]

5. The work [is]/[is not] **(5)** minor work **(6)**

[6. I **(7)**   declare that I do not, and will not while this notice is in force, have any financial or professional interest **(8)** in the work described.] **(9)**

7. I **(7)** am satisfied that plans relating to the work described above have been submitted to me, and that they neither are defective nor show work which, if carried out in accordance with them, would contravene any provision of building regulations.

8. The approved inspector [is]/[is not] **(10)** obliged to consult the fire authority by regulation 11 of the 1985 regulations.

[9. I **(7)** have consulted the fire authority in accordance with regulation 11.] **(9)**

[10. I **(7)** undertake to consult the fire authority before giving a final certificate in accordance with section 51 of the Act in respect of any work described above.] **(9)**

11. The plans to which this certificate relates bear the following date and reference number: **(11)**

12. I **(7)** am aware of the obligations laid upon me by Part II of the Act and by regulation 10 of the 1985 regulations.

Signed   Signed

Approved Inspector.   Person intending to
                                                 carry out the work.

Date   Date

NOTES

    (1) Local authority's name and address.
    (2) Location and description of the work, including the use of any building to which the work relates.
    (3) Name and address.
    (4) The local authority may reject this notice only on prescribed grounds. These are set out in Schedules 3 and 4 to the 1985 regulations. They include failure to provide relevant documents. The documents listed in paragraph 4 of the notice relevant to the work described above should therefore be sent with this notice. Any sub-paragraph which does not apply should be deleted.
    (5) Delete whichever does not apply.
    (6) 'Minor work' is defined in regulation 9(5) of the 1985 regulations. If the work is not minor work, the declaration in paragraph 6 must be made.
    (7) Approved inspector's name.

(8) 'Professional or financial interest' is defined in regulation 9 of the 1985 regulations.

(9) Delete this statement if it does not apply.

(10) Delete whichever does not apply. If the inspector is obliged to consult the fire authority, the declarations in paragraphs 9 and 10 must be made.

(11) Date and reference number.

FORM 4 – FINAL CERTIFICATE

Section 51 of the Building Act 1984

The Building (Approved Inspectors etc.) Regulations 1985 ('the 1985 regulations')

FINAL CERTIFICATE

1. This certificate relates to the following work: **(1)**

2. I am an approved inspector and the work described above was [the whole]/[part] **(2)** of the work described in an initial notice given by me and dated **(3)**.

3. Subject to what is said in paragraph 4 below, the work described above has been completed and I have performed the functions assigned to me by regulation 10 of the 1985 regulations.

[4. The work described above involves the insertion of insulating material into a cavity wall and this [has]/[has not] **(2)** been carried out.] **(4)**

5. The work described above does not include, so far as I am aware, the erection of any building or extension over a sewer shown on the relative map of sewers, except—

   (*a*) work about which information was given with the initial notice, or

   (*b*) work about which I notified the local authority on **(3)** in accordance with my obligation under regulation 10 of the 1985 regulations.

[6. Final certificates have now been issued in respect of all the work described in the initial notice referred to in paragraph 2 above.] **(4)**

7. With this certificate is a declaration signed by the insurer that a named scheme of insurance approved by the Secretary of State applies in relation to the work to which the certificate relates.

8. The work [is]/[is not] **(2)** minor work **(5)**.

[9. I have had no professional or financial interest in the work described above since giving the initial notice described in paragraph 2 above.] **(4)**

[10. I have consulted the fire authority in accordance with regulation 11 of the 1985 regulations.] **(4)**

Signed

Date   Approved Inspector.

Notes

(1) Location and description of the work, including the use of any building to which the work relates.
(2) Delete whichever does not apply.
(3) Date.
(4) Delete this statement if it does not apply.
(5) 'Minor work' is defined in regulation 9(5) of the 1985 regulations. If the work is not minor work, the declaration in paragraph 9 must be made.

FORM 5 – NOTICE OF CANCELLATION BY APPROVED INSPECTOR

Section 52(1) of the Building Act 1984

The Building (Approved Inspectors etc.) Regulations 1985 ('the 1985 regulations')

NOTICE OF CANCELLATION BY APPROVED INSPECTOR

To: **(1)**

1. This notice relates to the following work: **(2)**

2. An initial notice dated **(3)** has been given and the above work was described in it.

3. I am the approved inspector in relation to that work.

4. I hereby cancel the initial notice.

[5. I gave notice to the person carrying out the work in accordance with regulation 17 of the 1985 regulations and he failed to remedy the contravention within the prescribed period. The contravention is **(4)**

.]

Signature and date.

NOTES

(1) Name and address of the person to whom the notice is given. It must be given to the local authority and the person carrying out or intending to carry out the work.
(2) Location and description of the work, including the use of any building to which the work relates.
(3) Date.
(4) Delete this statement if it does not apply. If it applies, specify the provision of building regulations (including the specific requirement) which is contravened.

FORM 6 – NOTICE OF CANCELLATION BY PERSON CARRYING OUT WORK

Section 52(3) of the Building Act 1984

The Building (Approved Inspectors etc.) Regulations 1985

NOTICE OF CANCELLATION BY PERSON CARRYING OUT WORK

To: **(1)**

1. This notice relates to the following work: **(2)**

2. An initial notice dated **(3)** has been given and the above work was specified in it.

3. I am [the person carrying out the work]/[intending to carry out the work]. **(4)**

4. I hereby cancel the initial notice.

Signature and date.

NOTES

(1) Name and address of the person to whom the notice is given. It must be given to the local authority and, if practicable, to the approved inspector.
(2) Location and description of the work, including the use of any building to which the work relates.
(3) Date.
(4) Delete whichever does not apply.

FORM 7 – NOTICE OF CANCELLATION BY LOCAL AUTHORITY

Section 52(5) of the Building Act 1984

The Building (Approved Inspectors etc.) Regulations 1985

NOTICE OF CANCELLATION BY LOCAL AUTHORITY

To: **(1)**

1. This notice relates to the following work: **(2)**

2. I am authorised to sign this notice by the following local authority: **(3)**

3. The authority accepted an initial notice on **(4)** and the above work was described in it.

4. It appears to the local authority that the work to which the initial notice relates has not been commenced within the period of three years beginning on the date on which the initial notice was accepted, and the local authority hereby cancel the initial notice.

Signature and date.

NOTES

(1) Name and address of the person to whom the notice is given. This notice must be given to the approved inspector and the person shown in the initial notice as the person intending to carry out the work.
(2) Location and description of the work, including the use of any building to which the work relates.
(3) Local authority's name and address.
(4) Date.

FORM 8 – PUBLIC BODY'S NOTICE

Section 54 of the Building Act 1984 ('the Act')

The Building (Approved Inspectors etc.) Regulations 1985 ('the 1985 regulations')

PUBLIC BODY'S NOTICE

To: **(1)**

   1. This notice relates to the following work: **(2)**

   2. **(3)**

is approved under Part II of the Act and intends to carry out in relation to a building belonging to it the work described above which can be adequately supervised by its own servants or agents.

   3. With this notice are the following documents, which are those relevant to the work described in this notice **(4)** :

     [(a) in the case of the erection or extension of a building, a plan to a scale of not less than 1:1250 showing the boundaries and location of the site and a statement—
        (i) as to the approximate location of any proposed connection to be made to a sewer, or
        (ii) if no connection is to be made to a sewer, as to the proposals for the discharge of any proposed drain, including the location of any cesspool, or
        (iii) if no provision is to be made for drainage, of the reasons why none is necessary,]
     [(b) where it is proposed to erect a building or extension over a sewer or drain shown on the relative map of sewers, a statement as to the location of the building or extension and the precautions to be taken in building over the sewer or drain,]
     [(c) a statement of any local enactment relevant to the work, and of the steps to be taken to comply with it.]

   4. The public body [will]/[will not] **(5)** be obliged to consult the fire authority by regulation 21 of the 1985 regulations.

   [5. **(3)**
undertakes to consult the fire authority before giving a public body's plans certificate in accordance with paragraph 2 of Schedule 4 to the Act or a public body's final certificate in accordance with paragraph 3

of Schedule 4 to the Act in respect of any of the work described above.] **(6)**

Signature and date.

NOTES

(1) Local authority's name and address.
(2) Location and description of the work, including the use of any building to which the work relates.
(3) Name and address of public body.
(4) The local authority may reject this notice only on prescribed grounds. These are set out in Schedule 6 to the 1985 regulations. They include failure to provide relevant documents. The documents listed in paragraph 3 relevant to the work described above should therefore be sent with this notice. Any sub-paragraph which does not apply should be deleted.
(5) Delete whichever does not apply. If the inspector is obliged to consult the fire authority, the declaration in paragraph 5 must be made.
(6) Delete this statement if it does not apply.

FORM 9 – PUBLIC BODY'S PLANS CERTIFICATE

Paragraph 2 of Schedule 4 to the Building Act 1984 ('the Act')

The Building (Approved Inspectors etc.) Regulations 1985 ('the 1985 regulations')

PUBLIC BODY'S PLANS CERTIFICATE

1. This certificate relates to the following work: **(1)**

2. **(2)**

is an approved public body under Part II of the Act and the above work is [the whole]/[part] **(3)** of work described in a public body's notice given by the body and dated **(4)**.

3. Plans of the work described above have been inspected by a servant or agent of the public body who is competent to assess the plans and he is satisfied that the plans neither are defective nor show work which, if carried out in accordance with them, would contravene any provision of building regulations.

[4. The fire authority has been consulted in accordance with regulation 21.] **(5)**

5. The plans inspected bear the following date and reference number: **(6)**

Signature and date.

NOTES

(1) Location and description of the work, including the use of any building to which the work relates.
(2) Name and address of public body.
(3) Delete whichever does not apply.
(4) Date.
(5) Delete this statement if it does not apply.
(6) Date and reference number.

FORM 10 – COMBINED PUBLIC BODY'S NOTICE AND PLANS CERTIFICATE

Paragraph 2(2) of Schedule 4 to the Building Act 1984 ('the Act')

The Building (Approved Inspectors etc.) Regulations 1985 ('the 1985 regulations')

COMBINED PUBLIC BODY'S NOTICE AND
PLANS CERTIFICATE

To: **(1)**

  1. This certificate relates to the following work: **(2)**

  2. **(3)**

is an approved public body under Part II of the Act.

  3. With this notice are the following documents, which are those relevant to the work described in this notice **(4)**:

    [(a) in the case of the erection or extension of a building, a plan to a scale of not less than 1:1250 showing the boundaries and location of the site and a statement—
      (i) as to the approximate location of any proposed connection to be made to a sewer, or
      (ii) if no connection is to be made to a sewer, as to the proposals for the discharge of any proposed drain, including the location of any cesspool, or
      (iii) if no provision is to be made for drainage, of the reasons why none is necessary,]
    [(b) where it is proposed to erect a building or extension over a sewer or drain shown on the relative map of sewers, a statement as to the location of the building or extension and the precautions to be taken in building over the sewer or drain,]
    [(c) a statement of any local enactment relevant to the work, and of the steps to be taken to comply with it.]

  4. Plans of the work described above have been inspected by a servant or agent of the public body who is competent to assess the plans and he is satisfied that the plans neither are defective nor show work which, if carried out in accordance with them, would contravene any provision of building regulations.

  [5. The fire authority has been consulted in accordance with regulation 21 of the 1985 regulations.] **(5)**

[6. The body undertakes to consult the fire authority before giving a final certificate in accordance with paragraph 3 of Schedule 4 to the Act in respect of the work described above.] **(5)**

7. The plans inspected bear the following date and reference number: **(6)**

Signature and date.

NOTES

(1) Local authority's name and address.
(2) Location and description of the work, including the use of any building to which the work relates.
(3) Name and address of public body.
(4) The local authority may reject this notice only on prescribed grounds. These are set out in Schedules 6 and 7 of the 1985 regulations. They include failure to provide relevant documents. The documents listed in paragraph 3 relevant to the work described above should therefore be sent with this notice. Any sub-paragraph which does not apply should be deleted.
(5) Delete this statement if it does not apply.
(6) Insert the date and reference number.

FORM 11 – PUBLIC BODY'S FINAL CERTIFICATE

Paragraph 3 of Schedule 4 to the Building Act 1984

The Building (Approved Inspectors etc.) Regulations 1985 ('the 1985 regulations')

PUBLIC BODY'S FINAL CERTIFICATE

1. This certificate relates to the following work: **(1)**

2. The work described above is [the whole]/[part] **(2)** of the work described in a public body's notice given by   **(3)**   on   **(4)**   . Subject to what is said in paragraph 3 below, the work has been supervised by the servant or agent of   **(3)**   to ensure compliance with those substantive requirements of building regulations which apply to it.

[3. The work to which this certificate relates involves the insertion of insulating material into a cavity wall and this [has]/[has not] **(2)** been carried out.] **(5)**

[4. A public body's final certificate has now been issued in respect of all the work specified in the public body's notice referred to in paragraph 2.] **(5)**

[5. The fire authority has been consulted in accordance with regulation 21.] **(5)**

Signature and date.

NOTES

   (1) Location and description of the work, including the use of any building to which the work relates.
   (2) Delete whichever does not apply.
   (3) Public body's name.
   (4) Date.
   (5) Delete this statement if it does not apply.

Appendix 4

The NHBC system of building control

NHBC Building Control Services Ltd – a corporate body which is a subsidiary of the National House-Building Council (NHBC) – is the only Approved Inspector to date. It is approved to carry out building control work for low rise dwellings, i.e., up to and including four storeys, or three storeys plus a basement, together with any buildings ancillary to their use. Building control functions are not undertaken for conversions, extensions or non-residential work. The fees payable to the NHBC for its building control service are comparable to those charged by local authorities and the larger builder building in excess of ten dwellings on a site has an increased cost advantage.

In order to obtain approval for its subsidiary to act as an Approved Inspector, the NHBC had to provide two different types of insurance policy:

● *Ten year no fault insurance* against breaches of the building regulations relating to site preparation and resistance to moisture, structure, fire, drainage, heat producing appliances. The limit on cover is related to the original cost of the work allowing for inflation during the ten year period up to a maximum of 12% per annum compound.

● *Insurance against the approved inspector's liabilities in negligence* for fifteen years from the issue of the Final Certificate for each dwelling. The limit of cover is twice the cost of the building work (unless there is also a simultaneous claim made under the no fault policy), together with cover against claims for personal injury (which is normally £100,000 a dwelling). This is also proof against inflation up to 12% compound per annum and is subject to a minimum of £1 million a site.

A builder wishing to use the NHBC as an approved inspector must follow the procedure set out in Part II of the Building Act 1984 and the Building (Approved Inspectors) Regulations 1985, as discussed in

Chapter 4. Full details of the scheme can be obtained from NHBC (58 Portland Place, London W1N 4BU) and the specimen documentation in this Appendix is reproduced by permission from the NHBC handbook *At your service*.

NHBC also offers a plans approval service which is of especial help to larger builders who work in different local authority areas. Both *site approvals* and *house type approvals* are possible. Site approvals, including foundations, superstructure, site layout and drainage, is a matter for agreement between the builder and NHBC operating through its regional offices. There are no special forms. Houses likely to be repeated on a number of sites are appropriate for house type approval, which is normally given for three years. It covers superstructure and ground floor construction and can include alternatives and variations. Once approval is given, the house type can be built anywhere in England and Wales, subject only to possible restrictions imposed by the design itself, e.g., in areas of high exposure, and to the obtaining of site approval for foundations, drainage and site layout.

Type approval applies to:

- Dwellings up to and including four storeys.
- Garages and annexes attached to such dwellings.

Once type approval is granted, the procedure for volume house builders is straightforward:

- The builder sends the initial notice to the NHBC Regional Office, together with a plan to a scale of 1:1250 showing location and site boundaries: see Figs A4.1 and A4.2.

NOTE: This must be done at the same time as the builder submits the detailed planning application to the local authority.

- NHBC forward the initial notice to the local authority.
- NHBC inspectors then assume building control functions.
- Building control fees are payable direct to the NHBC.

Individual house types

In this case, the builder must submit to NHBC Regional Office site layout plans showing the drainage together with foundation details not later than 21 days before building is to commence. Site layout plans must be to a scale of not less than 1:500. Proof of type approval, or plans for individual house types, normally to a scale of not less than 1:100, must be submitted at the same time.

In both cases, once the dwelling is complete, the NHBC will issue its usual Notice of Insurance Cover in the normal way. However, buyers receive some additional cover – relating to building control matters – during a ten year period and the NHBC accepts liability in negligence for fifteen years. The approved inspector's final certificate is combined with the Notice of Insurance Cover (see Fig. A4.3).

There are three main advantages to the developer using the NHBC services:

- For the volume or national builder, national type plans approval means that the construction work can be carried out anywhere in the country to the same approved plan.
- There is only one inspecting agency for building control.
- The purchaser obtains additional insurance cover where the NHBC acts as approved inspector.

*This form should be filled in by the Vendor and sent to
NHBC Regional Office covering the area where the site is located, at the same date
as he submits his detailed Planning Application.*

NHBC BUILDING CONTROL SERVICES LTD.

("The Approved Inspector")

*Please read carefully
notes below and
overleaf.*

INITIAL NOTICE

Insert Name of Local
Authority in whose
area work is to
take place.

1. To:

2. This Notice relates to work at the following site address:

No. of dwellings to be built	
Site at	
Estate & Road	
Name of Town or Village	
County	Postal Code if known

Insert No. of dwellings
and site address
exactly as in
planning application.

To be completed by
the Vendor registering
the dwellings with
NHBC not by the
builder unless also
the Vendor.

3. The person intending to carry out the work is:

Name		NHBC Reg. No.
Address		
County	Postal Code	Telephone Number

4. The ... ration of Insurance is set out below and a description of the documents enclosed with this Notice is overleaf.

5. The work is not minor work.

For the
attention of
NHBC
Regional
Office

6. The Approved Inspector declares it does not, and will not while this Notice is in force, have any financial or professional interest in the work described.

7. The Approved Inspector will/will not be obliged to consult the fire authority by Regulation 11 of the 1985 Approved Inspector Regulations.

8. The Approved Inspector is not obliged to consult the fire authority before giving a Plans Certificate in accordance with Section 50 of the Act or a Final Certificate in accordance with Section 51 of the Act in respect of any of the work described above.

9. The Approved Inspector is aware of the obligations laid upon it by Part 11 of the Building Act 1984 and by Regulation 10 of the 1985 Regulations.

Signed _____   Dated _____   Signed _____   Dated _____

Approved Inspector   *Vendor*

PLEASE TURN OVER.

**For NHBC Building
Control Services Ltd.
use only.**

Declaration of Insurance
We declare that the NHBC Building Control Scheme of Insurance approved by the Secretary of State applies in relation to the work specified in this Notice.
Director General — NHBC
Secretary — NHBC

N.H.B.C. REGIONAL OFFICE STAMP

Fig. A4.1

The documents, see page 10, which must be enclosed with this Notice which are relevant to the work are:

Important Note:

VENDOR MUST DELETE ANY SUB-PARAGRAPH WHICH IS NOT RELEVANT.

(a) A plan to a scale of not less than 1:1250 showing the boundaries and location of the site and

  (i) the approximate location of any proposed connection to be made to a sewer, or

  (ii) if no connection is to be made to a sewer, details of the proposals for the discharge of any proposed drain, including the location of any cesspool.

(b) A statement as to the location of any building to be erected over a sewer or drain shown on the relative map of sewers and the precautions to be taken in building over the sewer or drain.

(c) A statement of any local enactment relevant to the work and of the steps to be taken to comply with it (see below for details).

LOCAL ENACTMENTS

Complete this section if applicable

ACCESS FOR FIRE BRIGADE

Vendor: Please sign statement below if the work is located in: Berkshire, Bournemouth, Cheshire, Clwyd, Cumbria, Derbyshire, East Sussex, Essex, Greater Manchester, Hampshire, Humberside, Isle of Wight, Kent, Lancashire, Leicestershire, Merseyside, Poole, South Yorkshire, Staffordshire, Surrey, Tyne & Wear or West Midlands:

If the planning consent so requires we shall comply with the local enactment relating to access for the fire brigade in the manner prescribed by the local authority.

Signed ______________________ Vendor ______________________

DRAINAGE (SEPARATE SOIL AND SURFACE WATER)

Vendor: Please sign the statement below if the work is located in Lancashire, South Yorkshire, Staffordshire, West Glamorgan or West Yorkshire:

We confirm that each building will be provided with a separate system of drainage.

Signed ______________________ Vendor ______________________

Note: Underground Parking and Subsidence. See Page 11 for details of the very few cases where an undertaking similar to that above must be given.

NHBC Building Control Services Limited, 58 Portland Place, London, W1N 4BU
National House-Building Council, 58 Portland Place, London, W1N 4BU

Fig. A4.1 (cont.)

Examples of documents to be enclosed by vendor with initial notice

1. Enclose site location plan and show approximate location(s) of connection(s) with existing public sewer(s).

Example

Site Address

Blackacre Field
Roseheath
Norton Wallop
Gloucester

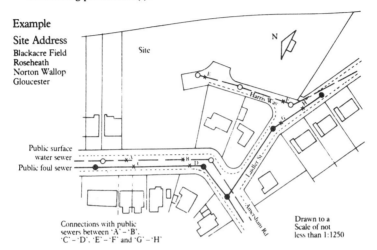

Public surface water sewer
Public foul sewer

Connections with public
sewers between 'A' – 'B',
'C' – 'D', 'E' – 'F' and 'G' – 'H'

Drawn to a
Scale of not
less than 1:1250

2. Enclose this only if building is to be constructed over a sewer shown on the map of sewers held by the local authority.

Example

Proposed site
of 6 houses
off Old London Road.

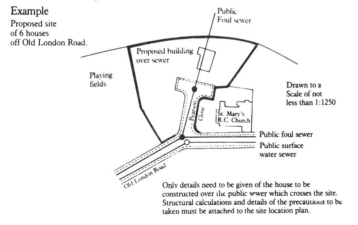

Drawn to a
Scale of not
less than 1:1250

Public foul sewer
Public surface
water sewer

Only details need to be given of the house to be
constructed over the public sewer which crosses the site.
Structural calculations and details of the precautions to be
taken must be attached to the site location plan.

Fig. A4.2

HB6BC (1985)   NATIONAL HOUSE-BUILDING COUNCIL

STANDARD NOTICE OF INSURANCE COVER
(and Final Certificate)
(see page 5)

The Dwelling has been subject to the system of spot check inspections operated by NHBC and appears to have been designed and constructed substantially in accordance with the Council's Requirements.

This Notice is therefore issued and brings into operation Sections II and III of the NHBC House Purchaser's Insurance Policy which has already been issued. Section IV is brought into operation by the Final Certificate below.

Please note that NHBC does not always inspect the finishings before issuing this Notice as these can be inspected by the Purchaser.

.... *Director-General*   .... *Secretary*
NATIONAL HOUSE-BUILDING COUNCIL

FINAL CERTIFICATE

Issued by NHBC Building Control Services Limited ("the Approved Inspector") pursuant to Section 51 of the Building Act 1984 and the Building (Approved Inspectors etc) Regulations 1985 ("the 1985 Regulations").

1. This Certificate relates to the Dwelling identified above.

2. The Dwelling was part of the work described in the Initial Notice given by the Approved Inspector and dated

3. Subject to what is said in paragraph 4 below, the Dwelling has been completed and the Approved Inspector has performed the functions assigned to it by Regulation 10 of the 1985 Regulations.

4. The insertion of insulating material into a cavity wall of the Dwelling is required and this has/has not been carried out. (Note: there are sound technical reasons why it is often wise to defer the insertion of the insulating material until after completion).

5. Final Certificates have now been issued in respect of all the work described in the Initial Notice referred to in paragraph 2 above.

6. The Approved Inspector has consulted the fire authority in accordance with Regulation 11 of the 1985 Regulations.

Fig. A4.3

7. As far as the Approved Inspector is aware, the Dwelling was not erected over a sewer shown on the relative map of sewers unless:
   (a) information to that effect was given with the Initial Notice, *or*
   (b) the Approved Inspector notified the Local Authority in accordance with its obligation under Regulation 10 of the 1985 Regulations on

8. The Declaration of Insurance is set out below.

9. The Dwelling is not minor work.

10. The Approved Inspector has had no professional or financial interest in the Dwelling since giving the Initial Notice referred to in Paragraph 2.

Director – NHBC Building Control Services Limited

G.C.Mills

Secretary – NHBC Building Control Services Limited

Declaration of Insurance

We declare that the NHBC Building Control scheme of insurance approved by the Secretary of State applies in relation to the Dwelling.

Director General – NHBC

Secretary – NHBC

The following details to be completed on behalf of First Purchaser

First Purchaser: ....

Address ....

....

....

Purchase Price: ....

Date of Completion of First Purchase: ....

SPECIMEN

NHBC Building Control Services Limited, 58 Portland Place, London, W1N 4BU.
National House-Building Council, 58 Portland Place, London, W1N 4BU.

Fig. A4.3 (cont.)

Appendix 5

British Standards and Codes of Practice

Chapter 2 – The Building Regulations and Approved Documents.
The Building Regulations 1985, Schedule 2
BS 5810: 1979 *Access for the disabled to buildings.*

Chapter 6 – Structural stability
The Building Regulations 1985, Schedule 1
A1/2
BS 12: 1978 *Specification for ordinary and rapid-hardening Portland cement*
Amendment slip number 1: AMD 4259.
BS 187: 1978 *Specification for calcium silicate (sandlime and flintlime) bricks*
BS 449 *The use of structural steel in building,* Part 2: 1969 *Metric units*
Amendment slip number 1: AMD 416
2: AMD 523
3: AMD 661
4: AMD 1135
5: AMD 1787
6: AMD 4576.
Addendum No. 1 (1975) to BS 449: Part 2: 1969 *The use of cold formed steel sections in building*
Amendment slip number 1: AMD 1765
2: AMD 1929.
BS 882: 1983 *Specification for aggregates from natural sources for concrete*
BS 1243: 1978 *Specification for metal ties for cavity wall construction*
Amendment slip number 1: AMD 3651
2: AMD 4024
BS 1297: 1970 *Grading and sizing of softwood flooring*
BS 3921: 1974 *Clay bricks and blocks*
BS 4011: 1966 *Recommendations for the co-ordination of dimensions in buildings*
Co-ordinating sizes for building components and assemblies
Amendment slip number 1: AMD 1775.
BS 4471 *Specification for dimensions for softwood,* Part 1: 1978 *Sizes of sawn and planed timber.*
BS 4978: 1975 *Timber grades for structural use.*
Amendment slip number 1: AMD 1869
2: AMD 2508
3: AMD 2730

4: AMD 2935

5: AMD 4567.

BS 5268 *Code of practice for the structural use of timber*, Part 2: 1984 *Code of practice for permissible stress design, materials and workmanship*

Amendment slip number 1: AMD 4723

Part 3: 1985 *Code of practice for trussed rafter roofs*

BS 5328: 1981 *Methods for specifying concrete, including ready-mixed concrete*

BS 5390: 1976 *Code of practice for stone masonry*

Amendment slip number 1: AMD 4272.

BS 5628 *Code of practice for the structural use of masonry*, Part 1: 1978 *Unreinforced masonry*

Amendment slip number 1: AMD 2747

2: AMD 3445

3: AMD 4800.

Part 3: 1985 *Materials and components, design and workmanship.*

BS 5950 *The structural use of steelwork in building*, Part 1: *Code of practice for design in simple and continuous construction; hot rolled sections,*

Part 2: *Specification for materials, fabrication and erection; hot rolled sections,*

Part 4: 1982 *Code of practice for design of floors with profiled steel sheeting*

BS 6073 *Precast concrete masonry units*, Part 1: 1981 *Specification for precast concrete masonry units*

Amendment slip number 1: AMD 3944

2: AMD 4462.

BS 6399 *Design loading for buildings*, Part 1: 1984 *Code of practice for dead and imposed loads*

BS 8110 *The structural use of concrete*, Part 1: *Code of practice for design, materials and workmanship,*

Part 2: *Recommendations for use in special circumstances,*

Part 3: *Design charts for singly reinforced beams, doubly reinforced beams and rectangular columns.*

CP 3: Chapter V *Loading*, Part 2: 1972 *Wind loads.*

CP 110 *The structural use of concrete*, Part 1: 1972 *Design, materials and workmanship*

Amendment slip number 1: AMD 2289

2: AMD 3451.

Part 2: 1972 *Design charts for singly reinforced beams, doubly reinforced beams and rectangular columns,*

Part 3: 1972 *Design charts for circular columns and prestressed beams.*

CP 111: 1970 *Structural recommendations for load bearing walls*

Amendment slip number 1: AMD 744

2: AMD 2031.

CP 114: 1969 *Structural use of reinforced concrete in buildings*

Amendment slip number 1: AMD 1241

2: AMD 1552

3: AMD 1923

4: AMD 2304

*5: AMD 4780.

* Applicable to reprint issues from 1977

CP 117 *Composite construction is structural steel and concrete,* Part 1: 1965 *Simply supported beams in building.*
CP 118: 1969 *The structural use of aluminium*
   Amendment slip number 1: AMD 1129.
CP 2004: 1972 *Foundations*
   Amendment slip number 1: AMD 1755.

DD 34: 1974 *Clay bricks with modular dimensions.*
DD 59: 1978 *Calcium silicate bricks with modular dimensions.*

A3
BS 5628 *Code of practice for the structural use of masonry,* Part 1: 1978 *Unreinforced masonry*
   Amendment slip number 1: AMD 2747
                       2: AMD 3445
                       3: AMD 4800.

BS 5950 *The structural use of steelwork in building,* Part 1: *Code of practice for design in simple and continuous construction; hot rolled sections.*

BS 8110 *Structural use of concrete,* Part 1: *Code of practice for design, materials and workmanship,*
   Part 2: *Recommendations for use in special circumstances.*

CP 110 *The structural use of concrete,* Part 1: 1972 *Design, materials and workmanship*
   Amendment slip number 1: AMD 2289
                       2: AMD 3451.

Chapter 7 – Fire

The Building Regulations 1985, Schedule 1
B1
BS 5588 *Fire precautions in the design and construction of buildings,* Section 1.1: 1984 *Code of practice for single family dwellinghouses.*

CP3 *Code of basic data for the design of buildings,* Chapter IV *Precautions against fire,* Part 1: 1971 *Flats and maisonettes (in blocks over two storeys).*
   Amendment slip number 1: 1972 (AMD 851)
   Amendment slip number 2: 1973 (AMD 1077)
   Amendment slip number 3: 1976 (AMD 1889)
   Amendment slip number 4: 1978 (AMD 2708)
BS 5588 *Fire precautions in the design and construction of buildings,* Part 2: 1985 *Code of practice for shops.*
BS 5588 *Fire precautions in the design and construction of buildings,* Part 3: 1983 *Code of practice for office buildings.*

B2/3/4
BS 476 *Fire tests on building materials and structures,* Part 3: 1958 *External fire exposure roof tests,*
   Part 4: 1970 *Non-combustibility test for materials*
   Amendment slip number 1: AMD 2483
                       2: AMD 4390.
   Part 6: 1968 *Fire propagation test for materials,*

Part 6: 1981 *Method of test for fire propagation for products*
   Amendment slip number 1: AMD 4329,
Part 7: 1971 *Surface spread of flame tests for materials,*
Part 8: 1972 *Test methods and criteria for the fire resistance of elements of building construction*
   Amendment slip number 1: AMD 1873
                         2: AMD 3816,
Part 11: 1982 *Method for assessing the heat emission from building materials.*
BS 747: 1977 *Specification for roofing felts*
   Amendment slip number 1: AMD 3775.
BS 2782: 1970 *Method of testing plastics*
   Amendment slip number 1: AMD 936
                         2: AMD 999
                         3: AMD 1524
                         4: AMD 2222
                         5: AMD 3177
                         6: AMD 3899.
BS 2782 *Methods of testing plastics,*
Part 1 *Thermal properties*
Method 102C: 1970 Softening point of thermoplastic moulding material,
Methods 120A to 120E: 1976 Determination of the Vicat softening temperature of thermoplastics,
Method 140D: 1980 Flammability of a test piece 550mm × 35mm of thin polyvinyl chloride sheeting (laboratory method),
Method 140E: 1982 Flammability of a small, inclined, test piece exposed to an ethanol flame (laboratory method),
Method 508C: 1970 Degree of flammability of thin polyvinyl chloride sheeting,
Method 508D: 1970 Flammability (alcohol cup test).
BS 4514: 1983 *Specification for unplasticized PVC soil and ventilating pipes, fittings and accessories*
   Amendment slip number 1: AMD 4517.
BS 5306 *Code of practice for fire extinguishing installations and equipment on premises,*
Part 2: 1979 *Sprinkler systems*
   Amendment slip number 1: AMD 3586
                         2: AMD 4219.
BS 6073 *Precast concrete masonry units,* Part 1: 1981 *Specification for precast concrete masonry units*
   Amendment slip number 1: AMD 3944
                         2: AMD 4462.

CP 144 *Roof coverings,*
Part 3: 1970 *Built-up bitumen felt*
   Amendment slip number 1: AMD 2527.

Chapter 8 – Materials, workmanship, site preparation and moisture exclusion

The Building Regulations 1985, Regulation 7.
BS 5750 *Quality systems.*
The Building Regulations 1985, Schedule 1

C4

BS 1282: 1975 *Guide to the choice, use and application of wood preservatives.*

BS 5262: 1976 *Code of practice for external rendered finishes*
    Amendment slip number 1: AMD 2103.

BS 5328: 1981 *Specifying concrete, including ready-mixed concrete.*

BS 5390: 1976 *Code of practice for stone masonry*
    Amendment slip number 1: AMD 4272.

BS 5617: 1985 *Specification for urea-formaldehyde (UF) foam systems suitable for thermal insulation of cavity walls with masonry or concrete inner and outer leaves.*

BS 5618: 1985 *Code of practice for the thermal insulation of cavity walls (with masonry or concrete inner and outer leaves) by filling with urea-formaldehyde (UF) foam systems.*

BS 5628 *Code of practice for the structural use of masonry,*
    Part 3: 1985 *Materials and components, design and workmanship.*

BS 6232 *Thermal insulation of cavity walls by filling with blown man-made mineral fibre,*
    Part 1: 1982 *Specification for the performance of installation systems,*
    Part 2: 1982 *Code of practice for installation of blown man-made mineral fibre in cavity walls with masonry and/or concrete leaves.*

BS 8200: 1985 *Code of practice for design of non-loadbearing external vertical enclosures of buildings.*

BS 8208: *Guide to assessment of suitability of external cavity walls for filling with thermal insulants,*
    Part 1: 1985 *Existing traditional cavity construction.*

CP 102: 1973 *Protection of buildings against water from the ground.*

CP 143 *Sheet roof and wall coverings,*
    Part 1: 1958 *Aluminium, corrugated and troughed*
    Amendment slip number 1: AMD 4346,
    Part 5: 1964 *Zinc*
    Part 10: 1973 *Galvanised corrugated steel*
    Part 11: 1970 *Lead*
    Part 12: 1970 *Copper*
    Amendment slip number 1: AMD 863,
    Part 15: 1973 *Aluminium*
    Amendment slip number 1: AMD 4473,
    Part 16: 1974 *Semi-rigid asbestos bitumen sheet.*

CP 297: 1972 *Precast concrete cladding (non-loadbearing).*

CP 298: 1972 *Natural stone cladding (non-loadbearing).*

DD 93: 1984 *Methods for assessing exposure to wind-driven rain.*

Chapter 9 – Toxic substances

The Building Regulations 1985, Schedule 1
D1

BS 5617: 1985 *Specification for urea-formaldehyde (UF) foam systems suitable for thermal insulation of cavity walls with masonry or concrete inner and outer leaves.*

BS 5618: 1985 *Code of practice for thermal insulation of cavity walls (with masonry or concrete inner and outer leaves) by filling with urea-formaldehyde (UF) foam systems.*

BS 8208: *Guide to assessment of suitability of external cavity walls for filling with thermal insulants,*

Part 1: 1985 *Existing traditional cavity construction.*

Chapter 10 – Sound insulation

The Building Regulations 1985, **Schedule 1**
E1/2/3
BS 2750 *Methods of measurement of sound insulation in buildings and of building elements,*

Part 4: 1980 *Field measurements of airborne sound insulation between rooms,*

Part 7: 1980 *Field measurements of impact sound insulation of floors.*

BS 5821 *British Standard method for rating the sound insulation in buildings and building elements,*

Part 1: 1984 *Method for rating the airborne sound insulation in building and of internal building elements,*

Part 2: 1984 *Method for rating the impact sound insulation.*

Chapter 11 – Ventilation

The Building Regulations 1985, Schedule 1
F1 and F2
BS 5250: 1989 *Code of practice: the control of condensation in buildings.*

BS 5270: 1979 *Code of practice for mechanical ventilation and air conditioning in buildings.*

Chapter 12 – Hygiene

The Building Regulations 1985, Schedule 1
G3
BS 3955: 1986 *Specification for electrical controls for household and similar general purposes.*

BS 4201: 1979 (1984) *Specification for thermostats for gas burning appliances*
Amendment slip number 1: AMD 4531.

BS 6283 *Safety devices for use in hot water systems,*

Part 2: 1982 *Specification for temperature relief valves for use at pressures up to and including 10 bar,*

Part 3: 1982 *Specification for combined temperature and pressure relief valves for pressures up to and including 10 bar.*

BS 6700: 1987 *Specification for design, installation, testing and maintenance of services supplying water for domestic use within buildings and their curtilages.*

G4
BS 6465 *Sanitary installations.*

Part 1: 1984 *Code of practice for scale of provision, selection and installation of sanitary appliances.*

Chapter 13 – Drainage and waste disposal

The Building Regulations 1985, Schedule 1
H1
BS 65: 1981 *Specification for vitrified clay pipes, fittings and joints*
    Amendment slip number   1: AMD 4328
                            2: AMD 4394.
BS 416: 1973 *Cast iron spigot and socket soil, waste and ventilating pipes (sand cast and spun) and fittings*
    Amendment slip number   1: AMD 3113.
BS 437: 1978 *Specification for cast iron spigot and socket drain pipes and fittings.*
BS 864 *Capillary and compression tube fittings of copper and copper alloy,*
Part 2: 1983 *Specification for capillary and compression fittings for copper tubes*
    Amendment slip number   1: AMD 5097
                            2: AMD 5651.
BS 882: 1983 *Specification for aggregates from natural sources for concrete*
    Amendment slip number   1: AMD 5150.
BS 2871 *Copper and copper alloys. Tubes,*
Part 1: 1971 *Copper tubes for water, gas and sanitation.*
    Amendment slip number   1: AMD 1422
                            2: AMD 2203.
BS 3656: 1981 *Specification for asbestos-cement pipes, joints and fittings for sewerage and drainage.*
BS 3868: 1973 *Prefabricated drainage stack units: galvanized steel.*
BS 3921: 1985 *Specification for clay bricks.*
BS 3943: 1979 *Specification for plastics waste traps*
    Amendment slip number   1: AMD 3206
                            2: AMD 4191
                            3: AMD 4692.
BS 4514: 1983 *Specification for unplasticized PVC soil and ventilating pipes, fittings and accessories*
    Amendment slip number   1: AMD 4517.
BS 4660: 1973 *Unplasticized PVC underground drain pipe and fittings*
    Amendment slip number   1: AMD 2514
                            2: AMD 3708
                            3: AMD 4006
                            4: AMD 4081
                            5: AMD 4441.
BS 5254: 1976 *Polypropylene waste pipe and fittings (external diameter 34.6mm, 41.0mm and 54.1mm)*
    Amendment slip number   1: AMD 3588
                            2: AMD 4438.
BS 5255: 1976 *Specification for plastics waste pipe and fittings*
    Amendment slip number   1: AMD 3565
                            2: AMD 3854
                            3: AMD 4472.
BS 5481: 1977 *Specification for unplasticized PVC pipe and fittings for gravity sewers*
    Amendment slip number   1: AMD 3631
                            2: AMD 4436.

BS 5572: 1978 *Code of practice for sanitary pipework*
 Amendment slip number 1: AMD 3613
          2: AMD 4202.
BS 5911 *Precast concrete pipes and fittings for drainage and sewerage,*
Part 1: 1981 *Specification for concrete cylindrical pipes, bends, junctions and manholes, unreinforced or reinforced with steel cages or hoops,*
 Amendment slip number 1: AMD 4035,
Part 2: 1982 *Specification for inspection chambers and street gullies*
 Amendment slip number 1: AMD 5146.
BS 8110 *Structural use of concrete,*
Part 1: 1985 *Code of practice for design and construction.*
BS 8301: 1985 *Code of practice for building drainage,*
 Amendment slip number 1: AMD 5904.

H2
BS 5328: 1981 *Methods for specifying concrete including ready mixed concrete*
 Amendment slip number 1: AMD 4862
          2: AMD 4970.
BS 6297: 1983 *Code of practice for design and installation of small sewage treatment works and cesspools.*

H3
BS 6367: 1983 *Code of practice for drainage of roofs and paved areas*
 Amendment slip number 1: AMD 4444.
BS 8301: 1985 *Code of practice for building drainage*
 Amendment slip number 1: AMD 5904.

H4
BS 5906: 1980 (1987) *Code of practice for the storage and on-site treatment of solid waste from buildings.*

Chapter 14 – Heat producing appliances

The Building Regulations 1985, Schedule 1
J1/2/3
BS 41: 1973 (1981) *Cast iron spigot and socket flue or smoke pipes and fittings.*
BS 65: 1981 *Specification for vitrified clay pipes, fittings and joints,*
 Amendment slip number 1: AMD 4328
          2: AMD 4394.
BS 476 *Fire tests on building materials and structures,*
Part 4: 1970 (1984) *Non-combustibility tests for materials,*
 Amendment slip number 1: AMD 2483
          2: AMD 4390
BS 567: 1973 (1984) *Specification for asbestos-cement flue pipes and fittings, light quality.*
BS 715: 1986 *Specification for metal flue pipes, fittings, terminals and accessories for gas-fired appliances with a rated input not exceeding 60 kW.*
BS 835: 1973 (1984) *Specification for asbestos-cement flue pipes and fittings, heavy quality.*
BS 1181: 1971 (1977) *Specification for clay flue linings and flue terminals.*
BS 1289 *Flue blocks and masonry terminals for gas appliances,*

Part 1: 1986 *Specification for precast concrete flue blocks and terminals,*
Part 2: 1989 *Specification for clay flue blocks and terminals.*
BS 1449 *Steel plate, sheet and strip,*
Part 2: 1983 *Specification for stainless and heat resisting steel plate, sheet and strip,*
    Amendment slip number   1: AMD 4807.
BS 4543 *Factory-made insulated chimneys,*
Part 1: 1976 *Methods of test for factory-made insulated chimneys,*
Part 2: 1976 *Specification for chimneys for solid fuel fired appliances,*
    Amendment slip number   1: AMD 2794
                                2: AMD 3475
                                3: AMD 3878,
Part 3: 1976 *Specification for chimneys for oil fired appliances,*
    Amendment slip number   1: AMD 2981
                                2: AMD 3476
BS 5258 *Safety of domestic gas appliances,*
Part 1: 1986 *Specification for central heating boilers and circulators,*
Part 4: 1987 *Specification for fanned-circulation ducted-air heaters,*
Part 5: 1975 *Gas fires,*
    Amendment slip number   1: AMD 4076
                                2: AMD 4745,
Part 7: 1977 *Storage water heaters,*
Part 8: 1980 *Combined appliances: gas fire/back boiler,*
Part 12: 1980 *Decorative gas log and other fuel effect appliances (2nd and 3rd family gases),*
    Amendment slip number   1: AMD 5434,
Part 13: 1986 *Specification for convector heaters.*
BS 5386 *Specification for gas burning appliances,*
Part 1: 1976 *Gas burning appliances for instantaneous production of hot water for domestic use,*
    Amendment slip number   1: AMD 2990,
Part 2: 1981 (1986) *Mini water heaters (2nd and 3rd family gases),*
Part 3: 1980 *Domestic cooking appliances burning gas,*
    Amendment slip number   1: AMD 4162
                                2: AMD 4405
                                3: AMD 4878
                                4: AMD 5220,
Part 4: 1983 *Built-in domestic cooking appliances.*
BS 5410 *Code of practice for oil firing,*
Part 1: 1977 *Installations up to 44 kW output capacity for space heating and hot water supply purposes,*
    Amendment slip number   1: AMD 3637.
BS 5546: 1979 *Code of practice for installation of gas hot water supplies for domestic purposes (2nd family gases).*
BS 5864: 1980 *Code of practice for installation of gas-fired ducted air heaters of rated output not exceeding 60 kW (2nd family gases),*
    Amendment slip number   1: AMD 3972.
BS 5871: 1980 (1983) *Code of practice for installation of gas fires, convectors and fire/back boilers (2nd family gases),*

Amendment slip number 1: AMD 3973
                       2: AMD 4638

BS 6172: 1982 *Code of practice for installation of domestic gas cooking appliances (2nd family gases).*

BS 6173: 1982 *Code of practice for installation of gas catering appliances (2nd family gases).*

BS 6461 *Installation of chimneys and flues for domestic appliances burning solid fuel (including wood and peat),*

Part 2: 1984 *Code of practice for factory-made insulated chimneys for internal applications.*

BS 6714: 1986 *Specification for installation of decorative log and other fuel effect appliances (1st, 2nd and 3rd family gases).*

BS 6798: 1987 *Specification for installation of gas-fired hot water boilers of rated input not exceeding 60 kW.*

BS 6999: 1989 *Specification for vitreous enamelled low carbon steel flue pipes, other components and accessories for solid fuel burning appliances with a maximum rated output of 45 kW.*

BS 8303: 1986 *Code of practice for installation of domestic heating and cooking appliances burning solid mineral fuels,*

Amendment slip number 1: AMD 5723.

Chapter 15 – Stairways, ramps and guards

The Building Regulations 1985, Schedule 1
K1
BS 5395 *Stairs, ladders and walkways.*
Part 1: 1977 *Code of practice for stairs*
Amendment slip number 1: AMD 3355
                       2: AMD 4450,
Part 2: 1984 *Code of practice for the design of helical and spiral stairs.*

K2/3
BS 6180: 1982 *Code of practice for protective barriers in and about buildings.*

Chapter 16 – Conservation of fuel and power

The Building Regulations 1985, Schedule 1
L1
BS 699: 1984 *Specification for copper direct cylinders for domestic purposes.*
Amendment slip number 1: AMD 5792
BS 1566 *Copper indirect cylinders for domestic purposes,*
Part 1: 1984 *Double feed indirect cylinders,*
Amendment slip number 1: AMD 5790
Part 2: 1984 *Specification for single feed indirect cylinders,*
Amendment slip number 1: AMD 5791.
BS 3198: 1981 *Specification for copper hot water storage combination units for domestic purposes,*
Amendment slip number 1: AMD 4372.
BS 5422: 1977 *Specification for the use of thermal insulating materials,*
Amendment slip number 1: AMD 2599
                       2: AMD 5744.

BS 5615: 1985 *Specification for insulating jackets for domestic hot water storage cylinders.*

Chapter 17 – Access for Disabled People

The Building Regulations 1985, Schedule 1
M2
BS 4787: *Internal and external door sets, door leaves and frames,*
Part 1: 1980 *Specification for dimensional requirements,*
   Amendment slip number   1: AMD 4737.

Table of cases

Note – The following abbreviations of Reports are used:
  AC – Law Reports Appeal Case series
  All ER – All England Law Reports
  BLR – Building Law Reports
  CILL – Construction Industry Law Letter
  CLD – Construction Law Digest
  ConLR – Construction Law Reports
  CBNS – Common Bench Reports, New Series
  KB, Law Reports – King's Bench Division series
  QB, Law Reports – Queen's Bench Division series
  WLR – Weekly Law Reports

Index